GEN

The Picnic

LESLEY
McDOWELL

THE PICNIC

BLACK & WHITE PUBLISHING

First published 2007
by Black & White Publishing Ltd
99 Giles Street, Edinburgh, EH6 6BZ

1 3 5 7 9 10 8 6 4 2 07 08 09 10 11

ISBN 13: 978 1 84502 129 0
ISBN 10: 1 84502 129 0

A CIP catalogue record for this book is available from The British Library.

Typeset by RefineCatch Ltd, Bungay, Suffolk

Printed and bound by MPG Books Ltd. Bodmin, Cornwall

For Angus McDowell
1940–2007

Acknowledgements

I would like to thank Angus McDowell, Douglas McDowell and Robin McDowell for their wonderful reminiscences and anecdotes, without which this book would not have been possible; Irene McDowell and Elisabeth Mahoney for their support and encouragement from the very beginning; Gillian Mackay for taking this story on in the first place; Ewan Morrison for pushing the pen and paper across the kitchen table at me; and Dexter Petley for his much-valued wisdom and experience. I would also like to thank the team at Black & White, especially Janne Møller and my editor, Patricia Marshall.

PART ONE

1995

Smell the salt in the air.

Sadie likes it because she's not used to living by the sea. Every evening after she picks her way over wet cobbles and struggles against the east-coast wind, she smells it on her hair and her coat and it reminds her of some pleasurable thing that might be a memory or a dream of day trips to the seaside when she was little.

So she likes standing here, just like this, across the road from the old entrance walls of the university, which might have been a memory or a dream too, only she knew, on the day she came for her interview, what they would look like. She knew what was going to appear on the approach road, with its fields high on one side and its sand slipping down to the sea on the other, because she had been on that road once before. A day trip many years ago that included a visit to a ruined castle and an anxious choice between two teashops, Pepita's or Juanita's, that her mother, Lily, was too thrawn to make. The tearooms are gone so it might have been a dream but the ruined castle is still here and so it is a memory.

And as Sadie stands here, deliberating between memories and dreams partly because it's still early in the morning and she's feeling dozy, the wind picks up and pulls her briefcase, light with only a few essays and a notebook inside, right up behind her. Her thin grey coat is fine for a west-coast winter but it's no use here. It isn't keeping her warm but she can't afford to replace it. She's at the bottom of the lecturer's pay scale and there's little left after she's paid for rent and food. So she scowls at the morning in spite of the pleasure of the salty air.

> Why didn't, I just go to bed? That stupid fucking essay. Oh and thank you very much – just splash me, why don't you? Why the hell do students need bloody cars when there's only about three streets?

And the cold wind is making her shiver and feel bad-tempered even before the day has properly started.

> That second tutorial – haven't enough . . . have I enough?

And she curses the cobbles that hamper her progress across the street and darken her mood even more.

> Just the same old thing, just exactly what it was before – think they can talk to you any way they bloody well like just because they've been here forever. Bet he doesn't even think he's done anything wrong. 'Yes there will be a permanent post but you won't get it – this is more of a teaching post than a research post which is why you got it.' It was that Oxbridge fucker he wanted – couldn't have taught a cat to drink milk but then he *was* researching the English Channel in

> Victorian poetry and we all know how important that is, don't we?

The memory of the day before will not go away. Sadie has been here, in her first proper academic post, for exactly a day over four months. Yesterday, a senior member of the department, a professor, had asked to meet with her, as the department's latest appointee. He was anxious to tell her, in a polite tone of voice, that he had not selected her for the post. Others had done that. He had preferred someone else. And he wanted to tell her too that, if she worked hard and made friends, she would get a good reference when she left.

> I've been through all this before – I'm not going through this again.

And now it moves suddenly, the anger from yesterday that she hasn't quite got over yet, and lights instead upon something else, something that is much less important but that matters to her all the same. Sadie bends her head in towards the wind but it is no use. She will have to give up trying to keep her head down in the hope that the wind will not ruin her hair. It is a lately acquired thing, her vanity. She never paid much attention to her appearance, not until the end of her teens anyway, and, although she can't really recall what made it so important, all of a sudden, Sadie knows now, at twenty-six, that she has a fine but fragile sense of how she wants to appear in front of the world. So the wind wins easily and her defeat has a more serious impact than it should have. It angers her even more than the memory of ill-judged remarks by some obsolete professor the day before.

But she has no more time for thoughts like these, not now – not when she's lifting the latch on the gate and letting herself in by the back door of the departmental building, creaking open that old, white wooden door. Sadie has a full day ahead of her. She needs time to prepare. And then, when she peers in, as gloomy as the basement corridor is, she can just make out the awkward, shifting shape of a student who is standing at the other end of it, right outside her office door. He is waiting for her. He doesn't know how busy her day is going to be – that she will need time by herself. He believes he can see her at any time and so he is waiting, expecting and wanting her attention, before she has even had time to remove her coat or sort out her hair.

As her feet carry her too soon, too soon, to her office door Sadie will have to stifle that impulse to tell him to go away – to tell him to go now, straightaway, that he can come back during office hours when she is ready and calmed and knows what to say, to make him disappear.

'Dr Mathieson.'

'Benedict, isn't it?'

Sadie's key is in her briefcase and she has to set it down on the floor to open it without everything tumbling out and the student doesn't move out of her way but lets her bend down in front of him, which riles her more and compromises her too because, if she were not Dr Sadie Mathieson but the Obsolete Professor of the day before, she knows the student would have stepped back in a deferential manner and given her room.

'Yeah, it's about the essay . . .'

'I haven't really got time to talk about it right now.'

The key is in the lock and the door is open and she can escape the dark, stuffy hallway into a big, bright room with its high-up windows that look out to the sea. Sadie puts her briefcase on her desk with what she hopes is authority and turns away from him as she starts to unbutton her coat.

'I just wanted to ask about an extension – I've had some family stuff going on at home, you know? So I haven't really had the time . . .'

She turns back and he scratches his head as he tells what is probably a lie.

> Scratching your head, not looking you straight in the eye, playing with your hair – all signs of evasion or lying. Seen it on TV somewhere – one of those daytime programmes. Can it be that fucking obvious?

But Sadie doesn't care. She just wants rid of him. She wants to have the room to herself so whatever it takes to get him to leave is what she will say.

'That's fine – take an extra day. Any more than that and you lose five per cent but I'll let you have one more day.'

'Oh, that's great, Dr Mathieson – thanks, thanks a lot!'

It works and now he's gone – off to tell the others in the class that the way to a penalty-free essay extension from Dr Sadie Mathieson is to turn up first thing in the morning when she's too tired to argue. And her need to be alone will be taken for weakness or inexperience or both and, yes, she may regret it later but, for now, she has the room to herself. And so she picks up the kettle and fills it at the sink in the corner of the room, as she does every morning as soon as she arrives, puts a teabag in a mug and opens up a can of Marvel.

> Oh for a 'do not disturb' sign!

Now that Sadie has been disturbed so early, she is tense, expecting the next knock at the door. And she has too much to do. There is a tutorial, then a booked appointment with a student, then another tutorial and another one. And suddenly she feels tired, the way she does just before she gives a lecture – that stage-struck feeling that should energise her with 'I'm too scared to' but instead deadens her nerves with 'I haven't the energy to'. And Sadie thinks how preferable it would be to go to the library, where no one can find her, and read for a while.

> Why can't they stick to fucking office hours if they have to come in here with their bloody problems? That's what they're for.

But she knows she may be the only one who sees it this way. She can't be too sure of that, though. She hasn't been here long enough yet to find out how her colleagues

> What a word – what a fucking false word 'colleagues'. Who the hell am I kidding?

view it all, put up with it, sort it to suit themselves. There is so much she has yet to find out but she knows that she will have to find a way to keep her distance, preserve her space, if she is going to make a success of this post. She cannot leave it open for just anybody to walk right in, uninvited, unarranged, no, no, that would not do. That would not do.

And it is just then, as the kettle clicks off and Sadie sighs and pours the hot water over the tea bag, idly watching the brown deepen inside one of the cheap mugs she purchased at the last minute in the supermarket the day after she arrived, that she is intruded upon for a second time. The phone on the desk rings and Sadie turns round to stare at it. She doesn't want to answer it. She is still in a bad mood, she hasn't even taken a sip of her tea yet and she wants to be alone but maybe she should answer it, just in case. And so she crosses the room, puts her mug on the desk and lifts the receiver.

And, as soon as she does, she hears that bright, sharp voice, 'Sadie!'

Only her mother would call her at work at this time in the morning. And when Sadie hears Lily's familiar tone, she knows she must forgive herself. She must forgive herself quickly, right now, because Lily is as welcome to her at this moment as the student was and that is not a good way to think about your own mother.

'Oh, Mum?' No, it is not good and Sadie is not pleased to hear her voice. She can't forgive it or herself. She can't hide her displeasure.

Her mother hears it straightaway and offers an apology that isn't anything of the sort. 'Well, I'm very sorry to get you at work. But Something's Happened.'

Lily has every justification for calling her at work so early in the day – Sadie can see those capital letters as her mother emphasises her last words. This is Important and there is so little of Importance in her mother's life – but that is an assumption and not a fact because Sadie does not really know what does go on in her mother's life. She does not know because she does not care to know – at least not about what goes on in Lily's life now, in the present. She does not know how Lily fills her day or who her friends are or what she eats for dinner at night with Sadie's father. These are not the things that interest her about her mother. What does interest her are the things her mother would not want her to know.

So Sadie never does ask Lily how she fills her day or what she eats for dinner. But now, at this moment, she is making Sadie ask, 'Oh, what? What's the matter?'

Lily pauses before speaking. Sadie can tell how much she is enjoying this moment, when she has her full attention, because she so rarely has something to say her daughter wants to hear. And, as she sits at her desk in her new office, Sadie pictures her mother for a moment. She sees Lily's once-dark hair hennaed and gleaming in the light of the elaborately wallpapered hallway of a low-ceilinged bungalow which is full-to-bursting with decorations and ornaments. They are all compensations for childhood deprivation and things that Sadie loathes for Sadie is the child of a minimalist age. She thinks this as she pictures her mother standing by the fake wrought-iron telephone table in the bright gold hallway, holding the phone in the silence of an empty house full of objects.

'I didn't want to leave a message with the secretary – I wanted to tell you myself.'

'Uh-uh, tell me what?' Sadie's interest is fading – Lily is never quick. She is impatient again and wishes her mother would hurry up.

'Well, how do I put it? It's Amy.'

And Sadie is almost pleasantly surprised. 'Amy? Really? Aunt Amy? What about her?' She hears Lily catching her breath.

'Well, we had a call about an hour ago from her husband – from Pete. She's had an accident – a very bad one. Someone ran into her car. They don't know if she'll make it.'

There is a pause and Sadie waits, says nothing.

Her mother takes a deep breath and continues in a rush, 'Your father and I are flying out to Toronto. We're off to the airport in an hour or two – it's been a nightmare getting flights . . .'

Sadie does not know what has surprised her more. Her mother voicing those words 'flying out to Toronto', words she has never used before, or her own behaviour – keeping quiet while Lily is saying this and not taunting her mother the way she has always done for not demanding that she tell her about her family when it has always been clear Lily does not want to. What began for Sadie as a small child's curiosity about grandparents and aunts and uncles and cousins became a teenager's cruelty when she wanted to bait the woman who insisted and demanded and disapproved of anything she did.

Now it is no longer cruelty that makes her ask but a professional interest that she hasn't yet divulged to Lily. Even when her mother still manages to annoy her with her misconceptions of the world, Sadie does not ask about her family just to upset her, as she once did. Sadie asks her because she wants to know, needs to know, because she decided, as soon as she came here to this ancient university town, what her new research project would be. Sadie has decided she will use the story of her mother's family and, more precisely, the story of her mother's mother. Sadie wants to write about her, theorise about her, raise this woman, who is never, ever discussed for a reason she has never managed to discover, to a position of importance. She wants to write about the personal but Lily will not let her. And it comes to Sadie, as she holds the cream-coloured office phone with someone else's personal numbers still pasted to the handle, that she wants this trip, this excursion to meet her mother's family, for herself. She needs to go too, she needs to be by the bedside of an aunt she has no memory of meeting, she wants to see family she has never seen because she wants to write about them. So finally she says, 'You're really going out there?'

Lily clicks her tongue. 'Well, I haven't got much choice – she could die.'

And so she does it. Sadie takes a breath and asks the question, 'D'you think . . . d'you think . . . *Rubina* . . . could be there?' And now she has mentioned the unmentionable, on this dark and dreary morning of unwelcome interruptions, she has spoken her grandmother's name and she hears Lily's disapproval and shame speed to her through the telephone line.

'How many times? Can't you leave it alone, even at a time like this?'

Sadie is sorry and resentful all at once. She is a teenager again. 'Mum, it's not like that . . .'

But Lily will not let her speak. Her voice sharpens even more. 'For heaven's sake, Sadie, how often do we have to go through this? I can't believe that's all you can say . . .'

'I'm sorry – I just . . .'

'Can't you have a bit of consideration, just for once?'

'I was only asking – I need to know . . .' Sadie interrupts her but the line is dead. Lily has slammed down the phone. Sadie pictures her jamming it down on to its box. She is the bad daughter. She has upset her mother and she can only sigh, here, miles away in her office, and replace her own cream-coloured phone. She sighs because she knows what will happen later. It has happened so many times before, whenever she has mentioned her grandmother's name. Sadie will wait, she will feel guilty, she will call Lily back, she will apologise and her mother will accept her apology and then the two of them will pretend that the offence was never given, that the unmentionable was never mentioned. And they will go on as before, not asking each other questions until something like this accident happens or until Sadie is impatient or angry and then she will ask again – just like now, she will ask and the game will begin all over again.

And how absurd it feels to her now, alone in her office in her first professional post, that her own mother should upset her as much as the Obsolete Professor of the day before. And how much more absurd it will feel to be chasing Lily later to apologise, chasing her still for information that she will never give her daughter, when the reason that Sadie left home in the first place – she will never admit it to herself but it is there, the reason that she came here to this tiny ancient university, whose little town reminds her of a day trip many years ago – was to get away from her mother.

Tuesday, February 21st

It's very late. Almost midnight. John's asleep. I can't sleep. Not when I'm travelling. Never could sleep on planes. I don't know where to begin. How do I start? Can't put anything in order. The flight's delayed. Two hours at one end, waiting. Now we've been circling for ages like this. Who knows when we'll land? They never tell you anything. And the hotel's overpriced. Well, that's what happens when you try the first one. It'll be too grand. They must get commission. But we're in a hurry. And we couldn't stay at yours. Even though Pete wanted it.

Oh, I don't know what comes first any more – what to say first. Well, you come first, Amy, of course you do but I have to give it some order. Say it to you the way I'd explain it to someone. Yes, I can do that. Not the way I'd explain it to John. He'd jump in and tell me what bits he knew. I'd just get confused. So. I'll explain it to someone else – to myself first and to you, Amy.

Today. What was today? Today was getting on this plane. No, before that. Finding out you were in a coma. No, let me leave that for now. I'll deal with that in the daytime. When I see you. I can't think about that now. Wait till I see you.

So where do I start? How do I sort it? I need to say it all. Every detail. Everything. That'll help me sort it. I need to sort it. You're in a coma, Amy. I need to sort it. You might . . . die. No, stop that. So how do I start? I'll start when I saw you last. That's right – 1973. The last time I saw you, Amy, and . . . everyone. I'll only understand it if I start then. Not with today. So I'll start with the holiday. And that day – the day of the picnic. There, I've started already. I need to do this. Remember? The day of the picnic – twenty-one years and eight months ago? The exact date. Is this ridiculous of me? Do I need to go back? Yes, yes, I do. I need to go back twenty-one years and eight months exactly. So . . . start. Think back. Start at the beginning. Yes. When we arrived. It wasn't like today of course – not cold. Well, it wasn't cold for a start. And we weren't in a rush. Nothing like today. So start back then.

We'd been in Toronto, oh, six, seven days already? Yes, it was seven days. Me, John, Sadie and Campbell – the Scottish ones with the pale skin and the funny voices. Yes, I want everything. Say it all to myself. And to you, Amy. Think back. Remember. How strange our voices sounded. Even to ourselves. Pretty much from the off. Not just our voices though. That moment we got off the plane. The minute we stepped out into the heat. But no, it wasn't the heat. Not really. It was the smell. That was it. That's what I remember. The smell of newness. Everything was new. Fresh, clean, newness. Everything was gleaming. And the sun that white-hot way. A smell Glasgow's never had. Because nothing's ever felt new there. Oh, I could smell . . . what? Well, brand-new rubber tyres for a start. I could smell them burning on the tarmac. And lots of new hand luggage. That smell of scorching plastic in the heat. And all the freshly painted airport corridors. The silver steel doors. Everything brand new. Nothing with dust or dirt on it. Nothing old. Nothing smelling of years and years of the same.

It won't be like that now when we land. It'll be dark. And cold. Well, it's winter. And we've had our holidays, me and John. More now that Sadie and Campbell are grown up. I'm more used to it. That newness. It's wherever we go. We don't go to old places, dirty places. Just new clean ones. But that's what it was like then. How new it was. And your house too, Amy. That house, the same new feel. I remember. Couldn't take my eyes off that enormous cream fridge in the kitchen. And your basement! The whole size of the house – huge and all painted white. Apart from that horrible orange circled wallpaper you had on the wall. But it was the fashion. And those brown sort of oriental rugs on the floor. The Mexican-looking ornaments. It was a young house, Amy. Young people lived there. That's what it said. Not like me and John in our first flat – that always felt like an old people's place. I painted all the walls white, just like your place, Amy, but it always looked old-fashioned. You could put as many Mexican ornaments in it as you liked and it wouldn't be anything other than . . . oh, a damp tenement flat. In rainy old Glasgow.

Remember. Think back. In your garden, Amy. That red and silver bicycle you and Pete bought the twins. Oh, they loved that bicycle! Sadie used to ride round and round on it too. She and Campbell used to fight over it every morning. Over who got first go on it. But all those things you had . . . When had we last bought anything new then? Even for the kids. John's asleep. This isn't his worry. But I remember. The only new furniture we had for years was what? That teak bedroom set and a sideboard that we got when we got married. And the old house we bought. Big enough for Sadie and Campbell to have their own rooms, right enough, but nothing new in them – second-hand beds and reclaimed dressing tables. To afford the house, we cut back on everything else.

Staying at yours wasn't ideal, was it, Amy? I should have known that. Couldn't stop comparing everything you had with what we had back home. I knew I'd feel bad about it. It didn't help either. Not with you making it clear having us to stay wasn't good. Oh, Amy, you've always been difficult. Terrible of me to say that right now but it's true – you are. You've always been highly strung. I tiptoed around you all the time. Watching what to say. You lose your temper so easily. That's why you always smoked so much. Always a cigarette in your mouth – even when you were pregnant with the twins. One lit up in one room and then one in another and one in another. So that you always had one. No matter what room you were in. Oh, Amy.

I should have been a bit better prepared – that's all I'm saying. Big cream fridges aren't really a luxury. So I shouldn't have been jealous of what you had – not when Pete had just lost his job. It wasn't the best timing in the world, I know. Wasn't exactly what you had in mind when you asked us to stay. 'Come over, Lily. Bring John and the kids – it's been so long. Stay here.' Me and John in that guest bedroom on the first floor. Wee ones in Becka's room. You and Pete in your room. Ricky and Becka doubling up in Ricky's. And they were . . . well, more about them later. No, not the best time. Not with Pete out of work. I was used to making do but you weren't.

I tried to remind you how little we had. Remember? When we lived in Glasgow. But you couldn't. You wouldn't remember any of it. I wanted to be sympathetic. You were used to a lot better. Why should you remember what it was like not to have anything? But you'd been in such a bad mood. From the moment we arrived. Even at the airport. You were more cross about the flight being late than anything else. I did my best. You know I did. I kept us out your way. I've always been like that. Always tried my best. You know that. Because I was the oldest. Always the responsible one. Always the dependable one. At least, I used to be – once.

Made sure we were hardly ever inside. Any of us. The weather helped. And Sadie and Campbell were on their best behaviour. Bless them. They were so good. I was proud of them. John kept saying that. Kept saying my worrying about Pete's job was pointless. We wouldn't be there to see how it all turned out. Which was true. We wouldn't be. Even though I don't think I believed what I was saying.

That morning. Start from the beginning. Don't leave anything out. You leave something out and that'll be the very thing that explains it all, won't it? The one thing you need to piece it all together.

It was about nine – so hot already. The wee ones had to sit on the grass because the paving stones were burning. I gave them their breakfast – fresh orange juice and honey cereal with milk. Sadie asked for the butterscotch ice cream we'd had the night before. I said it was in the garbage can. She was going to get it out just the same. She meant it too. I was awful worried about that. Awful worried she'd be difficult when we got home if she got too used to all those things. I was short with her. I remember. It wasn't her fault. She went in the huff straightaway. Oh, Sadie and her wee huffs.

But they all got their breakfast that morning – in a bit of a bad mood and a bit of a hurry, true. But it was so they'd be done before you came in, Amy, and told them to get out of the kitchen and out of your way. There was too much to do. The picnic was a last-minute decision. When I think back now. If only the car hadn't overheated the day before on the way to Niagara. If only we'd gone there as we'd planned. If only, if only. Maybe things would have been different. I don't know. We didn't want to see the wee ones disappointed. That's understandable, isn't it?

I remember standing in the kitchen. Bending over the plates on the kitchen table. Looking at my hands. I was buttering bread for sandwiches but watching my hands. Such a deep brown they were. Never been that brown before – or since. So much sunshine. So strong. I wanted to show you my hands, Amy. You'd got too used to the sun now to notice how much it shone or how hot it was. I just wanted to remind you. That's all. How lucky you were to have it all summer long. Not just for an odd day here and there so you can never plan anything.

I was looking up from my hands when you came in. You went right to the back door. Kept your back to me so I didn't get the chance. That cigarette between your fingers. You wouldn't want reminding how lucky you were. Not at that moment. Not after that big row you'd had with Pete about him losing his job.

'This'll take Pete's mind off things, at least for a day, anyway.' I shouldn't have said that.

You coughed. I remember. Because of the cigarette or because of what I'd said? Well, I couldn't tell. Then you turned round and looked at me. The wee ones were behind you on the grass. Sadie was playing with Becka's hair. Campbell, with his freckled wee Scottish face and Ricky with his tanned wee Canadian one. So cute, they were. Both of them. Laughing away and floating bits of grass in their milk. They thought it was hilarious. I didn't want to look at your face, Amy. I knew what I'd see there.

'I'm damned if I'm going to have that kind of conversation

first thing in the morning before I've even finished my first cigarette.' That's what you said. Stubbed your cigarette out on the sink. You were never good in the mornings. Not as a wee girl and not as a teenager either. You got worse as you got older. All that smoking didn't help. Kept you slim but you were always skinny. I think it made your face look pinched – that hollow-cheeked look every time you breathed in. It was even on your face when you weren't smoking.

And you turned back to the kids and really let them have it. 'Campbell, Ricky, stop that! Sadie, leave Becka's hair, for crying out loud! I only just brushed it – I don't want to have to do it again!'

I couldn't get used to your accent at first. Mine's gone, pretty much. I still say some things. Sadie and Campbell tease me about it – garbage can and toMAYtoes – but you'd never really know I'd ever lived here. But you, Amy, not a trace – nothing Scottish left in you at all. And I hear that voice, shouting at my kids when they were only playing – not doing any harm. They weren't even making a noise. There was no need for it. I should have known there was more to it but I just put it down to the row with Pete. And your funny ways. I knew you weren't going to talk about it anyway. I remember looking past to Sadie. Sadie, sitting on the grass in that flowery wee cotton nightdress she had. Already hiking up to her knees. She'd grown so quickly in the last six months. And I tensed up when you shouted at her. Someone else telling off my own daughter? I hate that. I've always hated it. I'll tell them when they've done something wrong. Oh and Sadie. She just looked at you, Amy, with this big frown on her face. As if she hadn't really worked out yet who was the real boss when she was in your house, Amy – her mum or her aunt Amy. Standing up, her hands on her hips as if she was about to say something cheeky – which I'm sure she was. Then sitting back down. Sticking her hands under her bottom. Something so cute about it. Made me want to laugh.

Something serious and grown-up about it too. Sadie – she's always taken things too seriously. Even at six. She's got none of Campbell's sense of carelessness – that's the problem. Such a serious wee girl and she's serious now too. Too serious. I don't know what to say to her half the time. She would never put grass in her milk when she was three – not even as a joke. And she didn't like being told what to do. She didn't like being reminded she was just a wee thing. Which was exactly what you liked doing, Amy. Reminding her about it. And as much as possible.

Then Becka standing up to braid Sadie's hair. And me, waiting for you to blow up. 'Look at the influence your kids are having on mine.' You clicking your tongue like you did all the time. My best option was to keep the peace. I looked away. Went back to the sandwiches. I knew what that click meant. 'Where have all these kids come from? Why is my house full of folk?'

'Don't any of you know how to eat your food?' That was you, on the paving stones. Scooping Becka up from the grass. 'I'm getting her ready. I'll be back in a minute.'

What could I do? I waited till you'd gone back inside. Then I just sighed. Shook my head at Sadie. Sadie and her soft baby hair, falling out of those big, pink plastic rollers. I'd roll her hair in them before she went to bed at night. So she'd have curls the next day.

'You'll get us thrown out if you're not careful. Keep an eye on Campbell, will you, Sadie? There's a good girl or we'll never get this picnic ready.'

Best thing to do – just to get on with lunch. So I mashed up hard-boiled eggs in a bowl with a bit of margarine. The kids all loved that. The boys chasing each other about on the grass. Sadie pulling the rest of the rollers out of her hair. The kitchen hotter and hotter. No air conditioning then. Moving things out of the way of the sun before they melted. Pete and John were away somewhere. I didn't catch where when John got up. He mumbled something about it. Mary and Mike would be here soon with Baby Sandy. We'd need the food ready by then.

You came back in at last with another cigarette. Pulling Becka behind you. I didn't say anything. I wanted to know if you knew where Pete and John had gone. Didn't want to risk a worse bad mood. though. Not if you didn't have the answer.

'That's another thing we don't have yet,' was what I said instead.

'Hmmm.' You could be so aggravating sometimes, Amy.

'We might try and get a new fridge when we get back home – one that has a bigger icebox – but I can't see us affording a freezer as well just now. Not with them being so expensive. I don't know anyone at home who's got one.'

Was that bad of me? Talking about the prices of these things? With Pete being out of work? Maybe I'd lost any sense of what was the right thing to talk about and what was the wrong thing.

'I can't get over how much bigger everything is over here.' I just couldn't stop myself. I can be like that, sometimes. Especially when I'm nervous.

'And we'll have to renew the telly when we get back – I don't think the kids will stand black and white now they've seen colour.'

As if I'd said nothing at all. 'Becka, stay off the grass! And Ricky!'

Don't know why I kept going. 'D'you know, it would probably be cheaper for us to buy one here and take it back with us on the plane, than it would be getting one back home.'

Still nothing.

'Ricky, bring that in to me now! The bowl *and* the spoon!'

Damned if you're going to ignore me any more – that's what I thought. 'Can you imagine getting on the plane with a colour TV? I know – I'll leave one of the kids behind and take that in their place, what d'you think?'

Well, I got a reaction, didn't I? 'What? Sorry. Look, Ricky, just come in – Mummy needs to wash you. Come on, inside now! And don't get that dress dirty, Becka. Watch her, will you? I'll be back in a minute.'

Too much frank talking last night and now no talking at all. I waited till you'd left the kitchen. Finished the last few sandwiches. Yes, that's what I did. Sorted them into a nice tidy pile. Then went out to join the kids. Sadie was trying to make daisy chains. That way that . . . that way that we used to do when we were wee. Slitting the tops of the stalks. Threading the next one through. Campbell running round and round the grass on his little legs. Still quite new to walking but not scared. Banging into everything. His wee legs had a life of their own – couldn't stop them in time.

'Now, if we came back here to live, d'you think we'd have all this too?' It wasn't right of me to say that. So I said it quietly. Sadie concentrating on her daisies. Campbell couldn't hear me. So it was all right. My dreams, my plans. 'A big freezer and a proper garden? And a big house?'

'Would we have butterscotch ice cream?' Sadie looking like she wasn't paying attention when she was.

'Yes, sweetheart, we'd have butterscotch ice cream.'

And day trips in a car. Picnics with the whole family. You didn't put me off, Amy. Even with your moods. How could you? Sunny days, one right after another. All those new things. A new life. John had warned me. This was just a holiday – not a recce visit. We wouldn't be emigrating. He didn't want to live in Toronto. I didn't want to live there either, I told him. Just a holiday – I'd thought that all that day when I was packing in Glasgow. And all the way to the airport. And all the way over on the plane. Just a holiday. We wouldn't be coming over here to stay. Funny how, when you say words over and over again, they become meaningless. Meaningless, you know, without any meaning. What I didn't mean because it wasn't true any more. Only that day changed it, didn't it?

Sadie is waiting for something. She is waiting for her body to perform. Sometimes, in the past, she has forgotten she even has a body until someone or something reminds her that she does because she thinks, most of the time, that she only exists through words. Words, not bodies.

But Sadie has been more conscious of her body ever since she began seeing Richard, just a few weeks ago. It was at a postgraduate party that she made herself attend in a sudden, conscious effort to be different from how she had been since she arrived at the start of the academic year – to meet people and to make friends. She saw him watching her from the other end of the room as she chatted to a group of chemistry students and then he came over to her and offered her a share of his joint. He was not a postgraduate but a post-doctoral researcher. And new to this town, just like her. And now they have slept together half a dozen times since that first meeting and Sadie has been remembering her body ever since, remembering those parts of herself she forgets all about until they are in pain or don't work properly. And this remembering of her body means, just occasionally, a forgetting of words. Words still interest her – of course they do. It is just that it is hard sometimes to remember what they are for when she is in bed with Richard, when he touches her. The body chases words away and she doesn't try and stop it.

But now, in the middle of this windy, wintry day that the rattling windows of her office are only just keeping at bay, Sadie is thinking of her body without any of her recent pleasure. It is not working properly and suddenly an image comes into her head. It is an image that she has had before and she likes to chase it, just as she likes to chase her mother's story, because she thinks it should tell her more than it does and, every time she pictures it, she tries to see more clearly – she looks at the shading, sees the faces in the background, tries not to let anything slip by her. But, because it is not just an image, because it is also a memory, she knows that it is real because she knows that she was there, even though it is a memory she has added to every time she recalls it so she no longer knows how much is real and how much is imagined.

So Sadie cannot be sure that it really was a hot sunny day and that there were three youngish men there or that they all wore long shorts or that two of them had beards. Three youngish men of different heights and colouring, throwing a large, bright ball back and forth over the grass for four little children, two girls and two boys. She cannot be sure that there were four little children, any more than she can be sure that there were three young women there too or if they were sitting around a huge picnic hamper, talking in the sunshine or if one of them wore a huge hat to keep off the sun. And she cannot be sure at all of the older couple with them, sitting under the trees in the sunshine not far away, watching the children play. She stares and stares at the image in her head and sometimes the old couple get up and walk away. Sometimes the picnic hamper changes into a carrycot. And sometimes one of the young women has a baby in her arms. Because Sadie cannot be sure of what she pictures in her head, she cannot be sure of what is real. But she knows that the image is a family image.

Sadie knows all about theories of the family. She has read her Freudian and post-Freudian analyses of the family romance, full of push and pull, repulsion and attraction, rejection and embrace. Yet she has never quite understood the appeal of it for her – this particular family romance, this prelapsarian scene that has taken up a place at the back of her mind. She does not know why she likes it so much, why she toys with it, changes it now and then. Because she knows that she does change it, she knows that she enjoys doing that even if it hides any truth further away from her every time she changes something. Perhaps it is simply academic – its appeal for her. She wants to subject it to her theories – that is what it is. She wants to take her theoretical brush and wipe stroke after stroke over this picture, spoiling its innocence with knowledge. But Sadie does not believe that knowledge spoils things. She does not just believe that a little knowledge is a dangerous thing. She believes that a little knowledge is not nearly enough. Yes, that is what she believes – a little knowledge is not nearly enough.

And, now, she is waiting to know something else – a mystery about herself. It is late morning, just over twenty-four hours since her mother's phone call. Lily and John will have arrived in Toronto by now. It is another dark cloudy day and Sadie has to switch on one of the cheap lamps in the room. Along with the mugs, she purchased two lamps especially for her office from the same supermarket and she stares into space and thinks about the mixture of anxiety and excitement that lie at the pit of her stomach. Anxiety – over what her body has failed to do today, its appointed monthly day – and excitement – because she is a miserable being who is excited by news of a possible death in the family.

But it means something else, something more than a death 'in the family'. It is words – the last three words are what cause her excitement. And so, when Sadie sips her first cup of tea of the day and burns her tongue, just as she does every morning and every afternoon, because every morning and every afternoon she forgets – how is it that she can never remember? – that powdered milk doesn't cool anything down, the pain for once does not make her cross.

Family romance, dysfunctional family, family set-up, extended family, Oedipus complex, Monique Wittig, the maternal, Julia Kristeva, the abject mother's milk, the skin on the surface of milk, repulsion-attraction, mother-daughter conflict, passive-aggressive mothers, Mother Superior, what else, who hates their mother, films, books . . . Words not bodies. Sadie jots words down on the spiral notebook in front of her. Words that make her think she could turn a family mystery into research. Alice Walker's *In Search of our Mother's Gardens*. Nancy Miller's *Getting Personal: Feminist Occasions and other Autobiographical Acts*. Rita Felski's theory of the 'feminist confession'. Writers and theorists about the family who have elevated the personal and the confessional to positions of importance within academic studies – that is what Sadie wants to do. And she teases herself with the prospect like the wicked daughter she is. What a strike back at Lily it would be for not telling her enough! But she cannot do it without her. She knows she needs Lily's help – that her words are useless without her mother's co-operation. Only Lily can tell her about the personal history of her family. And so Sadie scores through her words, heavy lines in pen, criss-crossing back and forth. She knows there is a tiny hard centre inside her when she thinks of Lily and her grandmother,

Rubina, and about what must have happened one summer's day years ago. She will find a way – yes, she knows she will. 'The current proliferation in literary studies of autobiographical or personal criticism,' Nancy Miller writes. 'This outbreak of self-writing.' How wonderful it would be to discover and write about her own personal history – well, Lily's and Rubina's – and then critique that very history! And now Sadie is thinking how she will read, analyse, present on this topic – whether it will be a psychoanalytic or deconstructive or new-historicist approach . . .

Has anyone ever heard of any of these women?

The voice of another Obsolete Professor hits her as she runs through her list and the tip of her tongue stings still from the hot tea so that her head is full of clashing thoughts – why her mother never speaks about her family and how the rest of the department manages without fresh milk. Lily left them years ago – she left them behind in Toronto and came back to Scotland where she married Sadie's father, John. Sadie thinks this as she realises most of the department have their tea made for them by the secretaries in the office. Lily has never said why she left them although Sadie knows it had something to do with her grandmother, Rubina – a grandmother she only met once on holiday when she was too little to remember properly and, no, she could never ask the secretaries to make tea for her. Sadie hates the thought of the secretaries whispering behind her back.

'Do you know what that Dr Mathieson asked me to do? Can you believe the cheek of it? She can't be more than twenty-five and she's only just arrived.'

But she will have to face them to get her mail and, as Sadie's stomach flutters at the thought of braving their preserve for mail that belongs to her, the mystery of her mother's life and the little prelapsarian scene that always appears in her mind when she contemplates that mystery recede a little. She wonders how she would view the world if there was always someone to make tea for her. What assumptions she would make about what she could do and what she could say and how she could behave instead of having to think, 'What will I do about tea in my office?' and 'Where will I keep fresh milk if I don't have a fridge?"

When Sadie returned to the office yesterday at lunchtime, a bag of shopping from the supermarket in each hand, how odd it was because she'd never seen anyone in the department come back to their offices with a shopping bag in each hand – except for the secretaries. Her colleagues never have shopping bags because they never go to supermarkets – not at lunchtime, not during the working week. They have wives to shop for them and how Sadie must confuse them – a woman who is neither a wife nor a secretary even though the supermarket bags suggest she must be one or the other.

She has no supermarket bags with her this morning. She will wait until early evening and she is on her way home to go shopping. She will only carry her briefcase with her to work – nothing else, not even a small bag for a hairbrush or make-up. Everything she needs will be carried in the briefcase.

Sadie looks down at the briefcase on the heavy, scarred old desk, takes out her new black hairbrush and black plastic tube of lipstick and black plastic powder compact and puts them in the drawer. Then she takes out the essays that she marked so late at night and hasn't had a chance to look at again.

'More on the uses of poetic language . . .'
'A clear understanding of the poem . . .'
'What you might find helpful . . .'
'Well structured, concise . . .'

And she orders them into a shallow pile beside her computer. What should become her office is bare still. Along with the lamps and mugs, Sadie has bought a small, plain pale rug to brighten the ash-grey acrylic flooring. The bookcase is slowly filling up with newly acquired contemporary novels and books on theory that she is adding to the ones she already has. She is keeping a lookout too for any bright-looking posters advertising conferences – posters that she will save for a corner of the room. All of it is to help her make a claim here on this room that wasn't hers before. The room belonged to someone else who isn't here any more – only her colleagues don't like to talk about what happened to the promising young scholar who left one bright afternoon just like any other afternoon but didn't come back. She is Dr Sadie Mathieson. This is her office. She will not walk out on a summer afternoon and leave it behind for someone else to remove her posters and pack up her books and make way for himself. She is a serious academic and she wants to be taken seriously, even if she does have to shop in supermarkets at lunchtime and hasn't thought of the English-Channel-as-it-features-in-the-poetry-of-the-nineteenth-century for her post-doctoral research project.

Sadie drinks her tea faster and now she can no longer put off collecting her mail. She heads up the stairs from the basement to the ground floor and opens the door at the top of the stairs that leads to the main office. Inside are Mrs Finlay, a middle-aged, pencil-thin, militaristically tidy woman and her two younger, part-time assistants, both of them mothers with babies. They are all very polite to her. Sadie has insisted that they call her by her first name and not Dr Mathieson, the way they did on her first day which had just made her feel ridiculous. So they do but Sadie knows they will probably never joke about with her the way they do with the old professors who like to flirt with them and act the part of being hopeless, while they like to pretend that the entire department would fall apart without their typing skills to keep it all going.

You're such a superior cow, Sadie.

'Afternoon, Sadie – there's some mail for you!' It's Pamela, the youngest of the secretaries who sits nearest the door. She has a friendly smile and flat hair and she dresses sensibly from Marks and Spencer's. She is the same age as Sadie but she is a mother and the responsibility of it has made her look older than she is. Sadie is aware of this as she stands before her in her black pinafore dress that stops a good six inches above her knee and her thick black tights and black platform heels. The uniform of the perennial student, only now Sadie is a student who has gone over to the other side and she shouldn't still be dressing like this. She's already removed the nose stud she's had for two years and that is as much of a concession as she is prepared to make towards responsibility.

Pamela smiles at her and, because she wants to answer friendliness with friendliness, Sadie smiles back. 'Hi, Pamela, hope there's not something too exciting in the mail – don't think I could take too much excitement on a February afternoon.' Sadie wants to follow this up with something else light and funny because she doesn't know her colleagues yet at all and she misses ordinary, everyday conversation and the secretaries are the only women her own age so she must have some things in common with them. But, no, she can't think of anything to say at all. She just picks up her mail from the pigeonhole that has her name on it, written in black on paper Sellotaped to the little wooden ledge – so unlike the others, the permanent members of staff, who have their names engraved on the wood in gold – and turns and leaves with a forced, too-cheery 'Bye!' when suddenly, 'Sadie! Settling in all right?'

As she steps out into the hallway, the head of the department, the man who gave Sadie her first academic job, emerges from his office and catches her before she can run away. He is an abrupt man – not unkind but a little bit threatening in a bulky, excessive kind of way. She has hardly seen him since her interview

> 'And what do you think you have to offer that we should give you this job?'
>
> 'I'm a young woman and this profession needs young women.'
>
> Laughter. Not unkind.

but this is the second time in two days. The first was after the Obsolete Professor had insulted her and the Head had heard about it and had come to her office to apologise. It embarrassed her even though she hadn't been in the wrong and now, meeting him again so soon and remembering the easy, jovial way he had handled an apology to a lower member of staff, she's embarrassed once more because she doesn't feel it was his place to apologise. It wasn't his fault.

'Yes, fine, thanks – everything's great.'

'Good. Remember, if you need anything, just let me know. And I'll see you at the departmental meeting, tomorrow, two o'clock.'

'Oh, yes – I hadn't forgotten.'

Shit! What did I say that for?

And Sadie wonders at her lack of sophistication as the Head smiles and walks past her to the secretaries' office and she hears him make a joke and they all laugh. She made it sound as though she might have forgotten or that she'd only just remembered – that forgetting was even a possibility! It wasn't professional and now she just wants to hurry back to her office before she meets anyone else and she betrays herself again.

But, as she approaches the stairs to the basement, two more men appear – the youngest professor in the department, who is barely forty, and another colleague, who is less flamboyantly successful but still making steady progress, emerge from another room. The first is David Jamieson, a tall, thin man with bright red, schoolboy hair parted neatly to the side, and the second is James Brooks, shorter, stouter, younger, his thin black hair receding so rapidly that a little less seems to be sitting on his head each day, like a nest that has been abandoned and is gradually falling away.

Sadie likes them both. They have been courteous and encouraging to her on the two occasions when they have met her over the last few weeks. They both want to see her make a success of the post – she knows they do. She trusts their courtesy and their encouragement. She believes in those things.

'Ah, SAdie! I was JUST THINking . . .' begins Professor

Jamieson, who has told her to call him David but she still feels funny about that.

She smiles brightly and then less brightly, in case brightness is too superficial and not scholarly enough. 'Yes?'

'My SEcond year COURse – SHAKEspeare . . .'

Sadie nods.

'I was JUST THINKing you COULD LECture on *The TAming of the SHREW*. It's NOT until the END of term – PLENty of time to GET some PREparAtion in – and I THOUGHT it would be YOUR sort of THING.'

Ah, yes. It's 'her sort of thing' because it is a play with a vocal woman in it. A shouty woman. A shrew. And Sadie has studied vocal women, shouty women, shrews. She has a PhD on shrews – on Angela Carter, Joyce Carol Oates, Toni Morrison, shrews all three. She is an expert on these twentieth-century shrews – women who have spoken when they were not supposed to. So why shouldn't she give a lecture on the original shrew? Perhaps she is even thought of as a shrew herself although Sadie can't really believe that's possible. She has trouble speaking. She does not shout. She is not vocal.

The Taming of the Fucking Shrew.

'I'd love to. That would be smashing.'

Christ, I didn't . . . I didn't say 'smashing'?

And the thirty-something professor looks at her but not in an odd way so maybe he hasn't really heard her say 'smashing', which must be the least academic word she could have chosen. Maybe she didn't really say it – it's not a word she ever uses. Why would she say it?

'It's just . . . I mean . . . I think that would fit with some stuff I'm working on just now so, yes, that would be fine.'

He smiles and promises to give her a few more details in the next day or so.

Sadie can't think of anything else to say but, fortunately, James Brooks, who is married with a newborn son and has taken on a fatherly sheen, leans towards her in a conspiratorial way and says, 'Hope you're feeling a bit better after yesterday. Don't worry about John Middleton. He's always saying something inappropriate – it's just the way he is.'

James Brooks is smiling so Sadie wants to smile too but she can't because she still worries she has said the wrong thing and now the Obsolete Professor's remarks from before are pinching at her head, making her think that maybe he was right – maybe she is only good for teaching and for filling in at short notice and she won't be here for long because the kind of person who says 'smashing' in an academic context can't be the real thing. All Sadie can do is try to be mature about it, try to behave the way they would behave, say what they would say.

'Yes, I know. It's all said and done now, it doesn't matter. Really. I've come across it before – that way, that sort of . . .'

But she knows neither he nor David Jamieson really want to talk about it – they just want to make their own disapproval clear. Because, at that moment, she sees a flash of something in James Brooks' eyes – almost like surprise, surprise that she should be drawing this out. So she stops abruptly, smiles again.

'We mustn't keep you – we'll leave you to your mail.'

James Brooks raises his hands in a defensive gesture. David Jamieson has already moved on to greet the arrival of a student at the front door. The moment is past and it would be wrong to try to prolong it and anyway Sadie doesn't want to – it has taken quite enough to get through this small amount of conversation.

She is released and she hurries down the stairs to the basement and the safety of her office. And everything is just as she left it and she is faintly surprised by this. She almost expects her room to reflect her state of mind and to change when she changes but, of course, it does not. And so, when Sadie sits down shakily at her desk and notices that her heart is beating too fast and she puts cold hands up to feel the hotness of her cheeks, she heaves a sigh of relief that nothing has changed, that the room is calmer than she is. She puts the mail on the desk, breathes slowly. Yes, she is calm now, she can do this, she will take her time and weigh up the merits of speaking in public about a sixteenth-century harridan. And suddenly she remembers her mother's phone call all those hours ago and, for the thousandth time, yes, for the thousandth time in her life, she wonders what it must mean for a woman never to speak about who she is or where she is from.

Wednesday, February 22nd

Bad things shouldn't happen when the sun shines. It's freezing outside. I'd forgotten how cold the winters are here. All the snow. How do they manage? The hotel is warm. Overpriced, though, as I said. Very grand lobby but very basic rooms. At least they're clean. I'm so tired. I just wanted to come here straightaway. Here, to the hospital. As soon as we touched down in the early hours. But John insisted – 'You'll be no use to anyone without some sleep.' So we went to the hotel first. But I couldn't sleep. Not a minute. Seemed like ages before it got to one o'clock and I could get up. Come here. Come and see you. My wee sister.

It's too warm in here as well. Makes the cold outside all the colder. And the sun is shining through all the hospital windows. Making everything so bright. Shining. Shining on this clean, new, spotless hospital. On my chair – which is state-of-the-art, too. Nothing like at home. Nothing state-of-the-art in hospitals at home. Nothing new. Not that all this newness is helping you much, Amy.

There's been no change. You still won't wake up. Your face is so thin. I can hardly say it but I don't think . . . you're going to make it. My poor wee sister. So pale, so thin. Oh, to see you like this. You don't look strong enough for it. Poor Pete. The state he was in when we got here. He's not coping. Looks just the same though. But, you . . . you look so different. Your hair's all grey. I pictured you dark still. Like me. Keeping the dark in your hair. But you haven't. And your features. So pinched, small, fine. Tiny mouth, that long, thin nose. Not like me. But we still look alike, I think, after all those years. It's our eyes. We've got the same eyes so we've always looked like sisters. Maybe more than when I last saw you, even. Oh, Amy, I wish you would wake up – wake up and talk to me. Be cross with me. Complain about the food and the nurses. Shout at me for staying away so long. For being too scared. For not keeping in touch. For not forcing you to talk about it. Anything. John's away with Pete. He wants us to stay with him. But the kids'll be here soon. Ricky and Becka. Your kids, Amy. He'll need the room for them. And the house, your house. I don't think so. Don't think I can stay there. But they'll be back soon. Pete and John. I hate talking to you, to your face like this when you can't reply.

They say I should be telling you all my news. What I've been doing in Scotland. Since we last saw each other. That maybe you can hear me. That maybe it'll help.

How do I sum it up? When you're lying there in front of me? Can't hear you breathing. The machine does it for you. All the tubes. And the noises. I can't help thinking it's not really you. It's some sort of horrible joke. You'll come in and say hello. And I'll wonder why I'm sitting here, talking to a stranger. A stranger. It's been almost twenty-two years. Is that what we are then, too? Strangers. I suppose so. What do we know of each other now, Amy? I saw that one home of yours. The one you still live in. But you've never seen any of the homes I've lived in. Not one. The tenements. A four-in-a-block, once. Then a terraced house. And the bungalow John and I share now. Big wide rooms that are hard to fill up. What would you think of them? I wonder. We can afford things now. We can change the suite every five years. Get a brand-new one. Even if we don't need it. Just for the change. The one we have now is gold-and-red. I like warm colours. Always did, didn't I, though? Like my ornaments to match too. Candelabra in gold. Rugs in red. Paintings that I've chosen for their colours. Sadie complains. Too many things crammed into one space, she says. Books. Plants, real and dried ones. Holiday mementoes. Photographs of the children. Photographs of family pets. We had two cats – Pinky and Perky. They're dead now. Scented candles. Mirrors. Some antique pieces. Newspaper racks. Ashtrays. John still smokes – he won't give up. Bet you haven't either, Amy. Videos. Boxes for storage. CD racks. Oh, Sadie can't bear it. Clutter. She says that's all it is. But they're all my things. I won't throw any of it out. Bungalows are good for that. We have a huge attic where I can keep things. There's boxes of stuff up there. The house of our old age, is this bungalow. Everything in it from our lives together. And no stairs. So when we're too old and can't go up the stairs. Or too incontinent to be far from the bathroom. And won't have to go into a home. What a reason for buying a house! But we have to think of ourselves. Can't rely on family being there. Not when you're older. Who knows where Sadie will be by then? Or Campbell. Well, Campbell has big plans for after he graduates as an accountant but I don't think his plans include us. What are the twins like with you, Amy? I wonder what people think when they see Sadie. Or Campbell. John wasn't so ambitious. But he has two kids who make up for that. I worry about them. Because they don't tell me anything. Are Becka and Ricky like that, Amy? Silent with you too? Do you know them at all? You probably don't. But maybe

I'm wrong. Maybe when you wake up I'll see how like you they are.

So what I have done? In almost twenty-two years. Apart from raise two children, that is. Well, we were lucky. John's businesses survived. It was one recession then another but not for us. I never had to work more than part-time. Pin money. That's all it was. I was a receptionist. At a golf club. But it was too quiet. I like being around people. Did I always like people, Amy? Yes, I think I did. Don't think that would surprise you. It was too quiet, that place, though. So then after that, some volunteer work – I did that for twelve years. At a retirement home. People hate retirement homes. But, you know, Amy, I liked it. Never want to live in one myself, of course – who does? But older people, I liked them. Always made time for them. Always talked to them. About their lives. What they did. So many of them without families. Without sons or daughters. No one to talk to or ask them about who they were – who they used to be. I'd ask them, oh, for all their stories. And some of the things they told me. What lives they had. All ignored, all forgotten. No one to listen to them. Soon John'll retire. Then I suppose we'll do what retired people do when they don't have to worry about money. See the bridge club more often. Take a cruise. Spend winters in Spain. Make occasional visits to our kids. Who knows maybe even grandkids. When they can bear us.

Is your life as empty as mine is, Amy? Now. The way it is now. I wonder. I wonder if you feel the future doesn't have very much in it. Maybe that's also why I'm here. Talking to you. I'm using your accident as an excuse. That's what Sadie would say. If she knew what I was thinking. And you, too, Amy. That's just what you'd say. I wish you would wake up and say it. 'Don't use my accident as an excuse!' But the past is getting more interesting. Too interesting. Dangerous. Now that the future isn't. There's more of it, you see. Even if it is scary. Or maybe I'm here because I'm bored. I care about you, Amy. I wish you would wake up. But maybe part of me is . . . Yes, you're right. I'm – what? Enjoying this chance to come here? Enjoying it! Never mind what I say to Sadie about it. All she wants to know I don't want her to know. But I can say it for myself – remember it for myself. Maybe, if I remember it, I'll have an answer. To why it happened. And why I am the way I am. Restless. Bored. Lifeless.

Lifeless. I'm looking at you, Amy, and that's just how you seem to me. So I'll remember instead. Bring you back to life with a bit of reminiscence. So . . . I haven't seen you since that holiday – hardly at all after that day. If I keep going with this, I know what I'll have to mention sooner or later. *Who* I'll have to mention – *who* is the point of it all. But let's keep away from that for a while, Amy. Away. Away from us. So, the last time we saw each other. That holiday. That day. A sunny day, just like this. Except not like this. Hot, hot. A perfect sunny day. Perfect for a picnic. You don't expect bad things when the sun shines. Rows, maybe. Breaking something. Forgetting keys. That's what you expect at the most. Silly things. Not bad things.

Remember. Remember where I was. Getting Sadie and Campbell ready in your room. The yellow patterned bedspread. Pale curtains. No photographs on the little dresser. No decoration. No pictures on the walls. No little ornaments. Only the Mexican ones in the basement. All a bit stark for me. Made me long to hang up the ribbons I used for Sadie's hair. Anything. I would buy you something before we left, that's what I thought. Just a little something for the house. Make it more homey. Warmer. An ornament or a picture. Some little detail. Break up the plainness of everything. Bits and pieces you can get from markets. I can spend all day wandering around those markets. Something here, something there. All those little things you want around you to make it a home. And you had none of that, Amy. I wanted to give you some of that.

Anyway. Got changed myself. I remember. That brand-new yellow tunic top I really wanted to wear. Silly details. But I have to have everything. So here it is. And it's nice. To remember something like that in the middle of everything. So, it had flowers across it. The top. Remember. Little orange flowers with blue petals sewn in and tiny bits of fruit in red and white. And my big wide straw hat. With the orange and brown ribbon tied round it. Tied under the chin, just loosely. Like a big Mexican sombrero. And my flared jeans. Proper flares. Not like the ones they have now. Original flares. Terrible. Had hardly any shape at all. Didn't flatter me one bit. Not with *my* hips and thighs. Made me look enormous. But, when it's the fashion, you can't see past that sometimes. Oh and platform sandals too, of course. The last time I wore that outfit. You wouldn't know that, Amy. I never put that top on again. Almost as though I didn't want to. Not after what happened. Did you do that too? I wonder. Pack away anything that reminded you. I think you would have. Done more than that, even. I think you would have made a bonfire. Another one. Burnt everything. Of yours, this time. I bet that's what you did.

Anyway, so. Sadie and Campbell are all ready upstairs. Then Mary and Mike arriving. I could hear them in the kitchen. Mike such a loud man. Nice, very friendly. Couldn't do enough for people. But really loud. Born and brought up in Toronto. His family had been here for a couple of generations,

I remember. One of the few like that. Mary hadn't met him before I left. She'd have been . . . what? fifteen or so. And we didn't have the money to come over for the wedding. At least that was my excuse at the time. It wasn't Mary that was the problem. You know that. So this . . . It was the first time we'd had a chance to meet him. Maybe it was because he was so loud. That was why Mary seemed so much quieter. Always was the quiet one, wasn't she? Not the usual thing. Usually the youngest is the real mischief-maker. The one who gets away with more. But not Mary. You were our mischief-maker, Amy. When we were little. Mary just got upset if she thought she was going to get into trouble. She didn't like it. Always so trusting. But you and me, Amy, we never had to be warned about eating berries. Or going off with strangers. I was too sensible. You were too contrary. But Mary. We just feared for Mary all the time. She'd have gone off with Jack the Ripper if he'd smiled nicely enough at her.

Not that I'm saying Mike was Jack the Ripper – of course not. Just that Mary had a trusting nature. And maybe she wasn't the best judge of character. Mike was just so loud. Big hands. Big feet. So clumsy. He was always knocking things over. But not in a funny way. Not clumsy in a 'gentle giant' kind of way. More like he enjoyed slapping things about. Making a noise. Slapping his hand down on the table. Scared me out of my wits. I hated it. But Mary just seemed used to it. She never jumped or looked anxious. She never looked anything at all. Always in a bit of a haze. Like she wasn't there. I wonder what she's like now? And if Mike's any different. They're coming tomorrow, Amy. They live in Ottawa now. I don't even know if you know that. I don't know when you saw them last.

Anyway. Back to it. I heard Pete. And John. And the wee

ones running through the hall screaming away. I liked the noise, though. And the mess they made. It was homey to me, too. Your place was just that bit too pristine for me, Amy. A bit too clean and perfect. Made me cringe just the same, though, the noise. How you'd handle it. Well, you didn't really. You just smoked yourself silly. And we kept out of your way. Once we were at the picnic, though, you were a lot better. Why was that? Was it because of . . . Oh, I shouldn't do that. Shouldn't keep jumping ahead.

Well, now, Sadie wanted her new doll with her. I hadn't the heart to say no. Wish I had, though. Then maybe she'd still have had it when we got back. It was a Daisy doll, brand new. We bought it a couple of days before. Remember? Just after we arrived. Me and you, downtown, shopping. I couldn't resist it. Sadie loved her dolls. But she only had a few from that friend of John's mum in Glasgow. She had a granddaughter too. Sadie got some of her cast-offs. You have no idea what it was like for us then. You really don't. We didn't have a penny. Borrowed the money to get to Toronto and took ages to pay it back. No cheap flights then. Freddie Laker. That was all. We flew with him. He should have been bailed out. They shouldn't have let him go under. A lot of people could fly only because of him. Anyway, the doll. Sadie only had these old ones. The old hard plastic kind with legs that didn't bend. Daisy's legs were rubber so you could bend them. Make her walk properly. And the clothes for her as well. The little red platform shoes and denim dungarees. Sadie loved it all. She wouldn't let it out of her sight.

Stop.

All right. Better now. It's the doll. The doll upsets me. What I link it with. The last day. The last day I saw a doll! How silly is that, that that's what upsets me? But, when I think it's the last day . . . And, if I think about myself, that today could be the last day I see my family . . . or they see me. Do I look as old as . . . I don't know. It's hard to remember. I can't think back to when we were wee. When we were back in Glasgow.

I've lost the thread again. Oh, yes – Sadie and Campbell ready. Got changed myself. John arriving in the middle of it. He'd taken Pete out for breakfast. Talked after the row the night before. But he'd had no chance to tell me much because you knocked on the door. Right at that moment. It's why I hate staying in other people's houses. It's always like that. No privacy. It's ungrateful to ask for any when you're staying there for free. Although it never really is for free. You pay for meals and drinks and wee presents. Just to say thanks. It's all a bit . . . no, I don't like it. Never have.

Anyway, you knocked on the door. To say everyone was ready. We were packing up the cars. We were going to picnic on the other side of Lake Ontario. So it would be another bit of a drive. About two and a half hours if the traffic was good – three and half if it wasn't. Pete and you squeezing the four of us into the replacement car that the insurance company supplied because of your one overheating. Mary and Mike talking – everyone else must have been. The thought of being stuck in the back seat with you sulking and smoking all the way. And two bored kids going crazy in the heat. Not exactly the thing to make me rush downstairs.

But John talked me round. He always can. So we went downstairs. And it was mayhem in the kitchen. Pete was throwing the wee ones up in the air one after the other. As if he had all the time in the world. You were getting so angry with him. Mike was talking over the top all of this to Dad. Dad with the usual expression on his face. That's who Mary gets it from. That same dazed look – 'Whatever.' 'It doesn't matter.' 'That's fine.' – although, with him, it usually meant he was thinking about what he'd have for lunch – or maybe when he could have a beer – or watch some sports on TV. The business was over for him. He'd made enough money. Didn't need to work any more. Couldn't imagine Dad like that until I saw him that holiday, Amy. So overweight. Panting whenever he walked more than half a yard. But happy. He seemed happy. With the wee things. Some TV, some beer, some good food. And having us all around. He liked that. Loved having the children around him too. Happy families. Playing happy families for the first time in his life.

For the first time. The first time I'd seen us all like that, anyway. Even with all your moans and groans, Amy. And the row with Pete. And the crossness. We were a family. We were a proper family. The first time I'd thought that about us. How funny – that it should have been the day. The day I'd be glad about my family. That day I'd see what family was.

Funny. And all of us there messing about. Not doing things. Funny. The only person who was . . . who was actually doing anything. Not me. Not just then. Not when I'd just finished the sandwiches. I was giving John a kiss in the hall, I remember. We were kissing like a couple of teenagers. No, the only one who was actually doing anything was . . . Funny. I never noticed it before.

From the mercury-backed glass
Mother, grandmother, great-grandmother
Reach hag hands to haul me in

Sadie quotes this to herself as she stands in front of the mirror in the bathroom in the basement, just two doors along from her office. It is the end of the week but it has been another busy day, like the past few days, with yet another request from another member of staff to lecture on literary women.

> Word must have gotten round.
>
> *The Mill on the Floss*? I'd love to.
>
> Miss Havisham? Yes, she is fascinating, isn't she?
>
> What about twentieth-century women poets? You know, Sylvia Plath, Anne Sexton, Elizabeth Bishop?

It is slowly becoming clearer to her that it is just a matter of placing herself correctly – like crazy paving. She thought all she had to do was avoid stepping on the lines but it has been trickier than that. There are lines she can cross and lines she cannot – *must* not. Sadie is slowly learning who draws the lines and it is not her.

The mirror has lines – four lines that frame her face as she combs her soft, dark-blonde hair and applies her cherry-red lipstick. Four lines, even and straight, that suggest where its frame once was. Sadie thinks it might have been the type that once sat on a dressing table and could be angled up and down. The glass that the lines frame is so old and pockmarked it is difficult for her to see what she is doing. The mirror is precariously balanced behind the taps of a sink and is so low that Sadie has to crouch down to use it. It has been a hasty addition to the bathroom, which was designed, of course, at a time when no women were around to use it and require mirrors. So naturally there are no special machines decorated in pink flowers and dispensing little packages in bright colours either and there is no soap, no simple orange Pears bar which is what anyone might have expected, at the very least. There is only a toilet, a sink and a cream metal box that contains rough blue paper for wiping your hands. The toilet paper is of the slippery, shiny kind so Sadie has brought a supply of her own in to use, quilted, scented.

The mirror's lines do not move. It is not a feminine-looking glass, full of curves. It won't reflect Sadie back at herself with disturbing touches, hints that undermine and suggestions of other women. Sadie crouches down in front of the glass again and thinks of the poem but it does not have that depth for her. She is not three women – she is the only one to be seen. She does not see Lily when she looks in the mirror and she does not see her father either but, according to the poem, there is no room there for men. It is their mothers women are supposed to turn into, not their fathers. Sadie is supposed to turn into Lily. Lily is supposed to turn into Rubina. But Sadie doesn't know what Rubina looks like. Lily is dark, was dark, has hennaed hair; Sadie is dirty blonde, brown with streaks of lightness. Lily has a round face, like Sadie's father, she has even features like him too, and defining brows; Sadie's features are fine, her face is long. She cannot tell from looking at Lily what she will look like when she is old. There are no hag hands waiting to haul her into the mirror because there are no hags. Rubina does not exist – not for Sadie or for her mother.

Sadie wonders if she looks like Rubina.

> In me she has drowned a young girl, and in me an
> old woman
> Rises toward her day after day, like a terrible fish.

There is something waiting beneath the surface for her too – there is a terrible fish waiting to devour her, only Sadie will never see it, never know it, even when she is old herself, she will never know, she can choose to see only what she sees now, if she wants to. Sadie can choose never to grow old. Isn't that what everyone wants? Never to grow old?

She will ask Richard when she sees him – Richard who works on genetics. This is why she is crouched here, in front of the mirror. She is getting ready to see Richard again and she does not have time to go all the way back up the hill to the house to get changed as her teaching finishes so late on Fridays. So Sadie must stay in her work clothes but they are black, like her going-out clothes, so that does not matter. It is their seventh date now. He is a little older than her and he has an accent that comes from growing up in a faraway place where the sun shines all the time but it is not a good place to be and so he is here. After the first night she stayed over at his flat, he gave her his home number and his work number and his e-mail address so that Sadie would know she would be seeing him again, so that she could not mistake it, and she liked his enthusiasm, she was flattered by his need to make that clear to her. And as she crouches in front of the mirror, putting the last touches to her hair and face, she knows she was destined to meet him. Even though Sadie despises anything as fanciful as destiny and fate, 'soulmates' and 'better halves' – rejects it all as weak-minded and irrational – she still cannot help wondering if she was meant to meet this man who understands her fascination with a grandmother she doesn't remember. Who understands because ignorance of genetic history is dangerous – we must know more, not less. And she will ask him to explain again because she finds it hard to understand. She will not be distracted by the sharp dark lines of hair that run along his cheekbones or by the black eyebrow that rises when he looks at her as though she is a question he cannot answer – this time she will listen properly and she will concentrate.

Sadie smiles to herself as she straightens up and smoothes down her black wool dress. She will forget about hags and terrible fish and ponds like mirrors and about the long thin cardboard box with its potential blue lines that she forced herself to buy today and that is now lying in the drawer of her desk and that she has not had the courage to use yet. Yes, she will forget about that.

She opens the bathroom door to the silence of the basement corridor. It is six o'clock and everyone else in the building, except for the Head who always works late, has left for home. She picks up her coat off the bathroom floor because there is no coat hook for her to hang her coat on and switches off the light. She buttons up her coat, lifts her briefcase and hurries along the corridor to the white wooden latched door and lifts the latch and heads out into the bitter cold of an early

February evening. She is on time. It would not matter if she is a little late but she does not like to play games with people.

The Masthead is quiet when Sadie gets there. She glances at her reflection in the glass door in the hope that her face is not too red and her hair is still as it was when she looked in the bathroom mirror. And then suddenly she sees Richard, sitting in the half gloom at a far table near the back, reading a book by the light of the candle on the dark wooden table. Sadie pauses for a moment, imagines that he is not there to meet her, that she has not met him until this moment and she enjoys gazing at him until he looks up just as she approaches. He smiles a broad smile, showing even white teeth, puts his book down and gets up to kiss her. His lips touch hers softly and the touch startles her as though it hasn't happened to her before and, for a moment, she is too surprised to know what to do but then he moves behind her, takes hold of her coat and helps her shrug it off her shoulders.

'You smell nice,' he says, taking a sniff at her hair and Sadie smiles at him, not knowing what to say.

> You smell nice too? You're not supposed to notice how men smell.

'What would you like?'

'Dry white wine, thanks.'

They are playing world music in the bar, something Spanish, but Sadie forgets it as soon as he returns with her drink, sits himself down and takes up her hand. He has the most perfectly symmetrical face she has ever seen. His long, straight nose bisects his face exactly, there are no odd quirks, no bumps or lines or smudges, one eyelid is not slightly heavier than the other, one eyebrow is not finer or thicker than its opposite. He is a mirror reflection captured within his own features. If a line could be drawn down the middle of his face, the two sides would reflect each other and Sadie is fascinated by this. Her own face is so far from symmetrical – she has one eyebrow like a half-moon shape and one that is almost straight, her nose slightly veers to the left at the tip and her lips are full but not even. Richard has heavy features, not fine ones like hers, but his are a scientific success.

> What are the chances, what are the chances?

'So – good day?'

'Oh, well, just the usual, really.' Sadie shrugs. She does not want him to know yet how it unnerves her, her day. How its small terrors are to be found in the things someone other than Sadie Mathieson would find unremarkable, like the bathrooms that smell of old men, or the corridors that are frigid and cold or the suicide stillness of her office. So instead she says, 'My mum called again.'

'About your aunt? How is she?'

And Sadie is so pleased he has remembered. 'Yes. Oh, not good – she's still in a coma.' But that sounds cold and careless especially when she says it with the smile on her face that is always there when she is in his company so she adds, 'My mum's still not saying anything really. It's so annoying.'

He reaches across the table, strokes her hand lightly, looks into her eyes.

> I know what you want and it isn't to listen about
> my mum.

'Yeah, I had that too,' he says, 'for years.'

Now Sadie is intrigued. She leans back in her seat, raises her eyebrows. She is flirting with him now because he has said nothing about his family before even though she has asked but he has not told her and she knew he was being deliberately mysterious, that this was part of the game the two of them played – even though she does not like games. Sadie knows that this revelation is part of that game and she cannot decide whether to carry on playing and ignore his remark or to give in, admit her curiosity and let him think he is winning. Which would be a victory of a kind, she decides suddenly, so she does it, she gives in and asks, 'What d'you mean that you had it too?'

And it works, she is rewarded as he strokes his sleek sliver of a sideburn and says, 'It's hard to talk about.'

> Tell me tell me – I want you to tell me.

'Maybe it would help.'

He wants Sadie to press him, to beg him to tell her. She will have to decide how far she is prepared to go.

'You think?'

> I know you want to tell me – I know you do – just a little bit more.

'Sure, yes, of course,' is what she says but it's the last time she will press him. She will not beg him. And so she pulls back with, 'Unless it's too personal – I wouldn't want you to . . .'

And it works. Push and push and push, then pull back. He leans towards her, as if she is pulling him across the table by an invisible thread.

'No, no. I want to tell you.'

Tell me tell me – you won't regret it. How nice I'm going to be to you . . .

'Well, it's . . . I had a brother . . . years ago . . . he died.'

Sadie has framed her mouth to say what she must say – 'Oh, I'm *so* sorry.' – but he glances at her and his look stops her from interrupting him.

'He killed himself. It was when we were teenagers. He was in lots of debt – he owed thousands and he couldn't pay it off. I found him. I had to tell . . . my parents. My mother hasn't mentioned him since.'

And Sadie is appalled. This is not a game – how ashamed of herself she is at this moment. She wants to embrace him, hold him, tell him she can take the pain away but she doesn't know how to start or what to say and the table is between them. He withdraws his hand and lifts his pint glass and keeps his eyes on her. He is unemotional – there are no tears in his eyes. His voice did not shake when he told her about his brother – he did not betray a thing – and now Sadie doesn't know how to respond at all. She is flailing about, looking for the right things to say and do when he says, 'It's OK but it's hard sometimes.'

And she knows that he has said all he needs to say, that tonight she will go home with him again and she will hold him all night if he wants her to.

'So . . . back to you – your mum?'

His switch is too sudden. Sadie wants to talk about this, about his dead brother – about how he got over it, if he is over it, about how he is feeling. But she has to say something and all she says, all she can say is, 'Oh, well . . . I . . .'

He puts his hand on hers again and pats it, like a child's.

'I've thrown you a bit. Sorry. Don't worry about it. Everyone reacts like that. No one knows what to say.'

'No, no, you haven't. I mean it's fine . . . I just . . . my stuff's so trivial compared to . . .'

'No, it's not – tell me. Come on, let's go back to mine. Tell me on the way.'

They finish their drinks. It is still early and Sadie would prefer to stay in the pub but she doesn't object. How can she object to anything he wants now? How can she when he has won this game? She fastens up her coat, picks up her briefcase and together they head for the door. It is busier inside the Masthead now and the salsa music is louder, students have congregated over at the bar and near the door, where a pebble fire is shooting blue flames high up the flue. A part of Sadie still doesn't want to leave but she cannot resist him, his story and the sympathy he has awakened in her, and she forgives him his manipulation and follows him through the door.

'So, come on,' he says, putting his arm round her shoulders as they head over the cobbles towards the ancient brick archway that bisects the road. Sadie would prefer not to talk about this while they are walking but she knows that, once they are at his flat, there will not be much opportunity to talk seriously so she begins, talking quickly, not wanting to take up too much time as the walk will be a short one and she wants to finish before they arrive at his flat. 'It's something about my gran – my mum's mum. I've never met her. Well, I did – years ago, when we went over on holiday but I was only about six. They lived in Toronto, they emigrated there, my gran and grandpa, a few years after the war, with, you know, my mum, obviously, and her two sisters – Amy, the one who's ill, and Mary. I don't remember them either.'

Sadie looks up at him to see if he is listening and he smiles at her, pulls her closer. He is doing all the right things, things that men usually get wrong, she thinks. He is quiet, he is not interrupting her, he does not look impatient. Yes, he is doing all the right things.

'Well, at least, not very well. Mum doesn't talk about them. I know she didn't like it there, that's why she came back when she was old enough – about twenty. Then she met my dad over here, got married and everything. So that holiday we went on, it was the first time she'd been back there, when we went over. But something happened while we were over there, I know that. And whenever my brother or I asked about them all – you know, about our cousins and why didn't we ever see them, that kind of thing – she just said, "You don't need to know." So that made it all worse, of course – you want to know straightaway but she would never say. We got Christmas cards sometimes but never anything from my gran and then, one day, my dad told me that she'd done this awful thing, my gran. I'm not sure what exactly but that's why Mum wouldn't talk about it.'

Suddenly Sadie stops. The road is quiet and dark – there are hardly any cars and no one is about. The ground is wet in front of her and it makes her want to go back inside – be inside alone, at home. She is not sure she wants to confide any more in Richard for some reason and, as if he senses her resistance, his voice changes, it is less confident, he patronises her gently as if he is not quite sure of her,

'And d'you know why she did this "awful thing"?'

Sadie doesn't want to talk about it any more. He is not taking her seriously – he sounds amused. She really does want to be alone. He doesn't understand after all. She was wrong about him. He knows about genetics, about what is inherited and what is not. He knows how to get rid of what is inherited if it is bad – but that is all. If Sadie was bad, he would know how to get rid of her – if she was a disease, a chromosome too much, a brother in debt, bad genes. But that is the wrong thing to think and so she forces herself to reply, 'Not really. I've wondered – well . . . maybe I've got a theory or two.' She pauses for a moment, sighs. 'I think it's worth looking at . . . well, I mean, it's more than that. I want to write about it – it's research and it's personal too, so I suppose I want to know where I'm from as well. And . . . what she was like, my gran. You know, what she did, who she was. What did she do? Was it really like it sounds? You don't just do something "bad", whatever it is – not when you're a grandmother. There has to be a reason for it.'

They are almost at his flat. Sadie still doesn't want to go in. She is wondering how to tell him she has changed her mind – that she will go home by herself. 'So, you see, it's work but it's personal too.'

And I have to go home now.

When suddenly he turns to face her, puts a hand under her chin and kisses her.

I have to go home.

'I think you're amazing,' he whispers. 'I can't believe I've met someone like you in a stupid little town like this.'

I have to go home.

'No,' she says back, as he pulls her to him. 'Yes. Yes.'

Saturday, February 25th

Had to leave Mike and Mary at the hospital. I just couldn't look at Mary any more. All that crying. She won't stop. I can't cope with it. John's out getting dinner. I don't want to eat out. Or sit in the hotel restaurant. Just want to wash that hospital smell off me. Just want to be quiet. Here. Alone. Till John gets back. Couldn't sleep last night either. I'm exhausted. Too exhausted now though. Too exhausted to sleep.

Still no change in you, Amy. Three whole days and nothing. I don't think you can hear us. I don't believe what the doctors and nurses say. You can't hear me. The twins were here this morning. Babies they were, the last time I saw them. But they're good kids. Not kids any more though. But you know what I mean. And so like Pete! There's not a trace of you to be seen. They're broad. Blonde. Sporty. I can't see what connection they have to you at all. But they're good. And you're good, Amy. You're a good person, in spite of all your moods. You always were good. Really. Putting us up when we came over. Even when it wasn't convenient. I'm not sure I'd have managed that.

It's been a shock for Mary. Too much for her. Mary. Oh, Mary hardly looks a day older. Softer, slacker. A little bit wider at the hips. But still sweet-tempered, still quiet. Still trying not to cause a fuss. Still the same. Why didn't we keep in touch more? All of us. We tried. A wee bit. Well . . . she tried. She always phoned me at Christmas. Better than a card. But I never called her. Never called back. I let her call me. That was enough. Kept my family as far from me as I could. And now, seeing her – how little she's changed. I could picture her, that day – so easily. Made me want to cry. But she was crying so much, I couldn't cry too. Oh, Amy, why don't you wake up? Are you doing this deliberately? Are you really fine? Do you pull out all those wires and get up out of bed the minute my back's turned? It's just what you would do. But I'd forgive you if it meant you'd wake up.

Mary. And Mike. Mike isn't how I remember him – not at all. He's still big but a big, shuffling quiet man – not the heavy-handed man I remember, not the loud man. Which worries me, Amy, when I think about that day. Am I remembering it right? That's why you have to wake up. Mary can't help. I know she can't. She's too gentle to remember bad things. And we always shielded things from her – even when she was an adult, even that day. We kept her out of it. Would have driven me mad, that – two older sisters keeping me out of everything. We used to send her out the room. Remember? When we came over and had TV for the first time, anything we thought was too 'racy', we'd send her out of the room. Racy! To think what passed for racy with two teenage girls in the fifties! Not like today, obviously – they know everything today. No one gets sent out of the room now. I think they should – some things you just shouldn't see.

And some things you should. Maybe Mary should have been allowed to see more. Know more. It's why she won't remember. You'd remember it properly. I can ask John about details – physical ones, like how hot it was, how busy the park was. He'd help with that but not with personalities – not with the way people were. He'd never notice those things. You'd remember, though, and you'd know if I got it wrong too. We could argue about who was right and who was wrong because remembering by myself isn't right – I could get it wrong. I think I see it so clearly – I've been over it so many times – but is every time the same? Maybe, every time I remember it, I change something, remember something differently, just a tiny bit. But then another tiny bit and another and soon the whole picture's different. I could trick myself. The way you do with déjà vu – feels like you've seen it before but you haven't. A horrible day lasts forever but a wonderful day – you can hardly remember it because it passed so quickly.

When I think back, it goes slowly but, even then, not slowly enough – not when I remember it like this. Have to slow it down even more. Can't rush. If I rush it, what will I miss? If only you'd wake up, Amy!

Leaving – I was thinking about leaving and how you do it. How many times I've wondered . . . What goes through your head when you decide? If you decide? How long you keep it to yourself for? How you plan it? When? How? If you plan it or if it's spur-of-the-moment? If it sneaks up on you – a surprise? Surprise yourself – 'Oh, that's what I wanted all along.' – or if you've always known what you wanted? And just didn't let on – not for years. And what you give away or don't give away. If you seem different or if you just get on with everything as usual. Keep quiet. Don't complain. Don't say much at all. Don't say anything to anyone. Except maybe when you're angry and you can't help yourself – when it just comes bursting out of you? 'You'll be sorry when I'm not around. How'd you cope without me? Never cope without me – you're nothing without me.' And who's left behind? What're you left with? Especially if you have no idea, had no idea – not once, not in all the years, no idea that they're going to leave. Oh, not to know something that big about someone. Not to know what's to come. It's awful.

And then, when I think about the only one who was actually doing anything . . . Yes, that's where I was, wasn't I? Before. Funny, that. The only one who was doing anything.

What *she* was doing.

She was carrying out the bags of sandwiches.

There. I've said it. She – who this is all about. There she was, that morning, the she we all knew, the she who was our mother, carrying out bags of sandwiches. Such an ordinary thing to be doing, we hardly noticed. And going so slowly down the steps because she was wearing her high heels. She liked to look glamorous – when she was older, that is. But they weren't good for her at that age. Well, maybe she wasn't so old. Fifty? Fifty-three, I think. She liked looking smart, didn't she? She didn't always wear make-up, not when we were younger. Remember? Watching her putting on her lipstick at the mirror when she and Dad were going out? But she wore it all the time then – I noticed that. She had this beautiful gold powder case and a little gold-and-black make-up bag. And high-heeled shoes in that weather! And a summer dress – pale yellow with purple and pink flowers on it, a belt round the waist, buttons down the front, a pale collar – every detail of that dress, like it was the only thing I can remember her wearing. But it made no sense – none of it. I suppose, if there was anything . . . Yes, I would say she looked tired. And I was annoyed with you, Amy, and with Mary for letting her do all the fetching and carrying – and with Dad too. Although there wasn't much point starting on at him – he wouldn't bother. She could have been on fire in front of him and he wouldn't have noticed.

I shouldn't have said that. It's not fair. Not true, either. It wasn't that he took no notice. Not really. He just didn't want to see. That's it. He didn't want to see. Not when we were younger and not later, either. Didn't want to know if there was a problem. I didn't ever go to him. Did you, Amy? If you had a problem? My problem was her, of course. When I was younger. Couldn't tell him that. He didn't want to know.

And there he was, just as always, not noticing, not seeing. I couldn't stand it. Everybody busy with their own nonsense and nobody doing a thing.

'Come on, let's all load up the cars.' I remember saying that. Everyone listened to me, too. Which was something, considering how many of us were there. You ignored me, Amy, but I expected that.

You blew up all the same, though. You made an even bigger fuss than me. 'Pete, for God's sake, get the kids out of here! Put Becka down. You'll just make her sick. And where's Ricky? Ricky, get out from under there and don't pick up things you find on the floor. Pete! For God's sake, it's like I'm talking to myself. Are you listening to me?'

Nothing ever ruffled Pete. What a good-natured man. Even losing his job hadn't ruffled him. It wasn't his fault – it was just redundancy. The firm had gone out of business. It had been happening quite a bit over here then. Had been happening in Scotland for ages. But he worked with microchips. It was new – a new industry with lots of jobs. At least, that's all I could ever understand about it. But new businesses were sprouting up all over the place. It wouldn't be two minutes before he got another job. That's what *she* said the night before – just before the row. And I agreed with her, didn't I? Remember, Amy? 'He'll be fine – he'll get something else before you know it.' That's what she said.

And Pete, always so cheerful, 'Sure I will.'

She could say that. Once Dad got his own electrician's business up and running, she'd no worries. Neither had we. But I was in my teens by then. It was too late for me – all the shiny new appliances, the clothes, the brand-new cars, too late for me. Not enough to make up for everything she put me through. Not enough to make me stay.

So she thought it would be the same for Pete. Plenty of jobs, no money worries, a nice big house and that was it. Or was it? She didn't want to talk about anything bad, I remember that. Like she'd made up her mind. We were all settled – all her daughters. And that was that – her job done. She didn't want . . . what? To be bothered with our problems? But you're a mother. Your family's problems are always yours too.

Anyway. You just went for Pete, didn't you? Not her. You went for him. Why you did that I'll never understand. It wasn't his fault. And the awful things you said to him – right in front of us, too. 'I don't think I love you any more – I don't think I ever loved you. How could you let me down like this? Don't you ever get it right? What the hell's wrong with you?'

I could have died. How could you, Amy? But you weren't yourself, were you? I know something . . . about you . . . about that little family trait you've got . . . from her. I know. I was counting. Four, maybe five whiskies and you ate like a bird. John was upstairs. He didn't hear all that you said. *She* didn't say anything more – just poured herself another whisky. Yes, another whisky – I was keeping count of hers too. And you screaming at Pete, 'Why did I marry you? What was I thinking? You've never made me happy – not once!'

Oh, if John had ever said that to me, that would have

been it – over, no more. I'd have left and taken the kids. But Pete just took it all. You ended up crashing out of the room. Banging all the doors. Stamping upstairs. Throwing things. We could hear you down below – smashing the few objects you had in your room. Nothing we could do. I remembered your tantrums – it was just the same, just the same as when you were little. So I waited. Went up later to see if you were all right. But you wouldn't let me in. Had a feeling Pete slept on the sofa that night.

What am I saying? It wasn't serious. I knew that and so did Pete. You two were great together – are great together. And it wasn't as bad as it sounded that night. All couples row, especially in the early days – always about money too. All families have arguments. None of it means anything. It doesn't mean we're unhappy. It doesn't mean what you said – 'I don't love you – I don't think I've ever loved you.' You didn't mean you didn't love Pete. Of course you loved him. You wouldn't mean it – not with the kids and everything. Why can't people see? It's just letting off steam – nothing more than that. It isn't. You're with a person. Of course I didn't mean it when I said I would have left John if he'd ever said he didn't love me. Of course I wouldn't have. We'd have talked it out. That's what you do when you've made a vow to someone. You get on with it – even when it's bad. I would never have left him. Don't think that. I know you have to be able to tell the difference between what's real and what isn't. What's realistic – what you can expect. That's all that matters – that you expect the same. You understand that, Amy, that you expect the same. But then, what happens when you don't?

Except, of course, in a way she did. That's all I can see. Yes. Well, look at me . . . all these years later and I'm still angry. There's no resolution to it – no 'closure'. One of those American words they use for things now. Sadie can tease me about 'garbage can' but there are daft words like 'closure' – all the rage. There's been no 'closure' to it. That's why I'm still angry. When I think of her that day, helping out, carrying all those things out to the car, doing all that . . . 'Anything else to go in? Do we need anything else?' As though she cared – about us, about what we needed. And, all the time, it was all for something else. I should have seen . . . Oh, not just how tired she was but how *apart* from us she was. I wish I'd paid more attention. Never liked to look too closely at her, though. Her changes in mood upset me. I liked to pretend they weren't happening. I was a bit like Dad too, I suppose, in that way. If I looked too closely, I saw a side to her I didn't trust – like seeing another person, not the real person, not her. She was somebody else. Alcohol does that to you. If you drink enough of it, I mean, over long periods of time. I didn't know about the secret drinking – that it still went on. I did before – when I was younger, when I was living with you all, Amy. And you knew too, I think. But I'd forgotten. Didn't know how much worse it was after . . . after I left. There was no reason for it. Dad's work had taken off. They had fewer rows. No, no reason for it.

Would I have done something about the drinking if I'd known how bad it was? Maybe. Did I know? After I left? No. I couldn't have done anything anyway. I was too far away. And there was always a barrier between us. I was the good girl, the oldest daughter, the good daughter. I was the one who cared about her carrying bags out to the car on a hot sunny morning. But I didn't look any further than that. Maybe I was scared – too scared to look. Maybe there were just too many other things going on. Maybe I thought, if I just helped with things, that would do. Maybe I'm just making excuses, Amy. Who knows? It's impossible to say now.

So, anyway, what next? Yes, I got you and Mary to pick up the last bottles of juice to go into the iceboxes and carry them out to the cars. You were grumbling away, 'I can't keep my eye on everybody all of the time . . .'

I knew that you felt guilty because, when you went back to the kitchen, you were nicer to Pete. And you helped her down the steps. You've always looked so alike, Amy. Glad you can't hear me say that. You'd hate it. But you were – you and her. Both fine-featured. Slim. Her hair was dyed. But once it was exactly the same colour as yours. You've always had the same mannerisms too, the same way of holding yourselves – a bit off, a bit apart. She'd put her hand up as if she was warding you off her. And you do exactly the same thing. Or at least you used to. You know you did. Especially if you were telling some story about someone you didn't like. You and her – maybe the closest in our family, the most naturally alike. Could never say that to your face. I know you don't have any pictures of her any more. Before we left, you got rid of them all that day. I've still got some – keep them in a box. No pictures of the family on display – not our parents or you or Mary. Just the kids and us – me and John. We never mentioned her again. We kept in touch, at first, didn't we, Amy? Cards at Christmas – have I said that already? – until you discovered typewritten newsletters. Lots of information – like the family was a company. You were updating company events – so cold, remote. But we never spoke about anything in our cards, our letters – not about anything that mattered, just about who'd done this and who'd done that. We've never said a word about her. If we had done, I'd like to have known about things you'd noticed that I didn't. By the time

I *could* talk about it, it was too late – Dad was gone. I don't know because you never said but still . . . I know it killed him – that day. I know that day finished him. We should have talked. Maybe we would have – if I'd gone to his funeral, if I'd been there. But it was too easy not to go – to make money the excuse. John was expanding the business then. We were starting to do well but we needed every penny. So that's what I did. I didn't go. Five years after it happened. Five years. It took him five years to die.

I'm being melodramatic. It wasn't a melodramatic day. It was so mundane – family squabbles – the wee ones overexcited – wondering what we'd forgotten to pack – all of that. We got in the cars. We were to follow Mike and Mary so they headed off first. The traffic was OK, I think. Didn't really notice – had my hands full keeping the kids distracted in the back seat. You joined in a wee bit too. Pete and John were talking about where would be best to park. The heat . . . even with the air-conditioning on. I've gone through that whole day in my head – hundreds of times. If she'd been in the car with me . . . if we'd had a bit of time to talk on our own. I still want to know now, all these years later, and now I never will. How long she'd planned it all . . . why she picked that day . . . what was going through her head . . . how she thought we'd all feel . . . I don't think she thought about us at all. I think she was selfish. I think Dad was right. She just thought about herself and she didn't care about any of us. What a thing to do – to your own family. I'll never understand it. How she could have done it. Not even if I had her right here right now and she told me. And now, after all this time? Am I supposed to know? Am I supposed to know why it happened? Well, I know how – just not why. I don't suppose I'll ever know why.

Except of course, there was something. No, there was nothing. It was nothing. Stupid. What was I saying? Yes, leave. That's it. Leaving. How you can do it . . . how you can do it . . . Well, I suppose I know how you can do it, don't I, Amy? After all, I did it too. Did you ever forgive me for leaving? I wonder. Didn't think it mattered to you at the time but now? Maybe you did. Maybe you hated me for leaving. At least you knew – where I was going, when I was going. At least I told everyone. At least I said.

'Here, take one of these before you go up, will you, Sadie?' Pamela calls to her from the office as Sadie comes flying in through the department's front door, short of breath because she forgot about today's special departmental meeting because she did not see how it could be so different from the other monthly departmental meetings she has to attend and, even though she has run all the way from the library back to the department, she is almost late.

'What is it? Oh, sure.' Sadie grabs at the paper Pamela is holding out to her, her scarf gets in the way and she misses the catch. It flutters gently to the floor and, as they both bend down to pick it up, Pamela says, 'Actually, Sadie, you're the last one to go up. You wouldn't mind taking these up for me, would you? Just the minutes from the last meeting. Save me a trip, I've got tons to do.'

''Course – I'll just hand them round?' Sadie doesn't mean it to sound like a question, as though she wouldn't know what to do, but she just wants to make sure.

'Yes, thanks, Sadie!' Pamela hands the bundle of white paper to her and calls, 'Good luck!' over her shoulder as she heads back to her desk and Sadie pauses for a moment, looks up at the staircase ahead of her on the right and wonders why she might need good luck to attend a departmental meeting. But, today, the thought does not worry her – she has other things to worry her besides the meeting. There is the long, thin cardboard box still lying inside her desk drawer with its plastic-wrapped tube and possible blue lines that, every day her body does not perform, she comes closer to using. There is the aunt Sadie only vaguely remembers meeting years ago who is now lying so ill in a hospital thousands of miles away and who is not proving to be the catalyst for her mother – and so for her research – that she hoped she would be. Lily is no more forthcoming than she ever was and Sadie is beginning to despair of her research plans if her mother will not talk to her. The best she can do, she has decided, is to investigate a little herself. She will visit the place where her grandmother once lived. She will find out if anybody remembers her – if there is anybody who can tell her anything. It is exactly a week to the day since Lily first called her about Amy. But Sadie is anxious to get started. All the days she has spent here so far have been long ones – days that take their time to use up the light, days that contain so much that is new to her.

For instance, she has only been up to the top of this very staircase once – on the day that she came here for her interview. Sadie still does not know what the rest of this building is like – what the offices on the other floors are like or even whose offices they are. Monthly department meetings are held in a small room next to the head's office and she has noticed not everyone attends. Today she is sure they will all be there.

The library along the road is more familiar to her than her place of work but, for all that, she has discovered just today, as she was running along the grey street beside the sea, that a part of her is enjoying this newness, this strangeness. She is beginning to enjoy finding new things, remembering new places and people and names and faces. And, because she is beginning to enjoy this newness, she does not want to be worried by the cardboard package in her desk drawer which will soon prove to be an unnecessary purchase – she knows that it will – and she does not want to dwell on her mother's obstinacy and she does not want to be intimidated by the need for 'good luck'.

And so Sadie does not take offence at Pamela's request to hand round minutes, even though it ensures that, as the only woman at the meeting, she will be doing the job the secretary was supposed to do. All of it is fine.

> You can do this.

And so, as she makes for the stairs across the red-carpeted floor, she feels a surge of confidence. Sadie does not know where it has come from except that, last night, she was reminded of something. She was thinking of Lily and Rubina and mothers and daughters and it made her wonder about stories about mothers and daughters and the refrain would not go away.

> Does anyone know who any of these women actually are?

And now, today, at the foot of the stairs, remembering that again makes Sadie realise it is likely she will be the only person in the room above who knows what she knows. And that it is unlikely she knows nothing of what someone else knows – it is unlikely she will know nothing of Jonson or Wordsworth or Marvell. She will know something of Jonson or Wordsworth or Marvell. She will know enough. And, because she knows enough, she will be able to ask questions of other people about the knowledge they have and of which she shares just a little, she knows enough to ask informed questions, not to show herself up, not to expose a lack of learning.

But she will be the only person in the room who knows about her PhD shrews, about winged women and girl gangs and *Jazz* – who knows about 'feminist confessions' and self-writing and her grandmother. Except that Sadie does not know about her grandmother – not yet. 'The spectacle of a significant number of critics getting personal in their writing,' says Nancy Miller. If only Lily would talk to her about Rubina, then Sadie could be one of that significant number too. But how? How will she do it? How will she get her mother to talk to her? she wonders as she approaches the top of the stairs. And, yes, she can see right into the conference room ahead of her – such an inappropriately modern name for a room with old oak panels and old oak bookcases and white busts of men she's never heard of. And it should make her feel better – all this knowledge that she has already and is going to have, knowledge that no one else in that room will be able share with her. And it does make her feel better. It does not make her feel lonely and worried that her knowledge isn't the right kind of knowledge.

That is only a brief thought. It occurs to Sadie for no longer than a second – that thought, like the thought that her knowledge might be knowledge that isn't considered worth having. Only for a second. So, when she took the red-carpeted stairs slowly just there and heard the voices in the room at the top get louder and louder, until she could make out what the men there were saying through the open door, her face may have been red with all the knowledge she has that isn't wanted but it did not bother her. It did not bother her until . . . until . . . yes, until she walked through the door and realised that the only place left for her to sit was in between the head and

> Oh God, there must be somewhere else for me to sit.
> Will it look really bad if I pull another chair over?
> Shit, it will! I'm just going to have to . . .

'Excuse me, Professor Middleton . . .'

The well-fed, suntanned, wrinkled face, with strong blue eyes behind small-rimmed glasses, turns to her and looks at the empty chair she has indicated beside him. 'Do sit down! Do sit down! Everybody together!' He gestures with his hands in a way that is meant to be friendly and then he turns away. He is as embarrassed as Sadie is that she must sit next to someone who insulted her so recently and who was reprimanded for it.

'Erm . . . I have these – the minutes from the last meeting, Pamela asked me to pass them round,' she says to the head who is sitting on her right.

'Splendid, Sadie, thank you!'

But he does not take them from her or tell her what to do so she supposes that she must simply pass them round and she realises that to get his attention she will have to place a hand lightly on Professor Middleton's tweed arm and, when she does so, he turns to her in mild surprise and she smiles brightly and says, 'If you wouldn't mind, could you take one and pass them round?'

It is done. Sadie sits down now, opens her briefcase up beside her, takes out a notepad and a pen, tries to look like she knows what to expect from this particular departmental meeting. The conference room is full today – fifteen men and one woman are gathered. And Sadie, the one woman, is not here to serve tea and biscuits but to speak about students and essays and departmental aims and objectives and mission statements

> Mission statements? What the hell are mission statements? When did this place turn into fucking ICI?

along with everyone else, only she doesn't know what everyone else knows about essays and departmental aims and objectives and certainly not about mission statements.

> To boldly go where no man has gone before – world's most famous split infinitive – a mission statement if ever there was one. Something inherently male about mission statements. Then to boldly go where no woman has gone before – boldly, baldly, badly go.

And Sadie wants to giggle which wouldn't be right in this room where she is the only woman to think about mission statements and so she thinks about her shrews for some female company but 'Does anyone know who any of these women actually are?' won't leave her head. That refrain sings around her head today just as it did last night and yesterday afternoon and it won't leave. That is the problem with refrains – they depend upon not leaving, they rely on an inability to forget, that mental action that cannot be forced. Sadie hears it over and over again, this nasty little refrain that did not come from the Obsolete Professor sitting beside her. He didn't say it. He isn't the only Obsolete Professor in the world – Sadie has met plenty like him before. It came from someone else, another Obsolete Professor in a previous department in a previous university who was working on a book on Oakeshott – 'Now does anyone know who this man actually is?' He did say it and was quite proud to say it and he thought it was funny, too.

> Regular testing to keep academics up to date – that's what's needed, not bloody mission statements. Although not knowing about Oakeshott should definitely be one of the requirements for the job.

And this room is busy with the thoughts of men who won't know Sadie's shrews and won't help her at this precise moment when she feels that some mistake has been made after all, that the head is about look at her and wonder who she is and why she is here and she will have to explain to him that she had an interview, that she was offered the post, she is supposed to be here, she has a right to be here, it is right that she is here and he won't believe her.

'I think it's time we started, David,' the head nods to David Jamieson and tips his sheaf of papers up on to their side so that he can make an authoritative noise as he jostles them on the desk. Everyone looks at him and then at David Jamieson although Sadie sneaks a look at other faces around the table. It's the first time she has seen everyone in the department at the same time since her interview and she wonders how many of them she will recognise, how many of them she will remember from that day, so that, if any of them do speak to her, she can remind herself that they were there, they saw her.

And what Sadie sees is every colour in the rainbow on show around the table. Like multicoloured plumage, ties of varying shades of red, blue and green are displayed, along with jackets in an assortment of browns.

Who the hell knew there were so many shades of brown?

And there are some dark blues and even the odd bowtie and matching handkerchief in the top pocket. James Brooks bucks the trend with the absence of a tie, wearing only a plain pale blue shirt.

Ah-ha, new baby in the house – no time for crucial style decisions, then.

David Jamieson, smart and businesslike in a navy pin-stripe suit, appears harassed. He is in charge of this year's Research Assessment Exercise and he wants to improve the department's rating from a horribly average three last time round, four years ago, to a much more respectable four or even a five. Five is the highest rating – there really is no hope of achieving that but, with a little bit of bullying, he might make it to four. Sadie can tell he is determined to achieve it. But he is getting little help from the older members of staff who don't care about RAE ratings, which they view as a Thatcherite lesson in market forces and something that is beneath them.

'The REPutation of the dePARTment RESTS on our RAE RAting, and will diRECTly affect our FUNding,' Jamieson explains for the third time, a little less patiently with each effort and with his own peculiar stress pattern growing more pronounced. Professor Tom Dickson, the oldest and longest-serving member of staff, snores gently, his cleanly shaven chin resting on a dark woollen bow tie. Beside him, James Brooks is serious and supportive. Two more enthusiastic and ambitious lecturers, Alan Young and Benjamin Alexander, who Sadie's not yet spoken to, voice their support too but they, along with the head, are the only ones to get to grips with this new approach to funding. The rest of them – and, apart from the Obsolete Professor, Sadie barely knows the others by sight, never mind by name – employ schoolboy tactics to show how little they care. They whisper to each other, rustle their papers, gaze out of the window. The Obsolete Professor next to Sadie is talking to another member of staff quite loudly, even as James Brooks is adding his comments to David Jamieson's.

'There is the quite SERious matter of publication,' Jamieson begins again. 'Alan YOUNG and I will be GAthering DATA on PRESent and FORTHcoming publicATIONS. It is enCUMbent upon EVery member of staff that he subMIT a full LIST of all publicATIONS with full DEtails of works PUBlished since the last RAE.'

Sadie will ignore his use of the exclusive 'he' – after all, she thinks, as a temporary member of staff with her name Sellotaped on to her pigeonhole, this doesn't apply to her.

But suddenly David Jamieson directs himself to her, 'YOU aren't included, Sadie, but do let me KNOW all the same about ANY publicATIONS that you might have forthCOMing, in REFereed journals ONly, of COURSE.'

Sadie nods, embarrassed as the room focuses its attention on her, and she tries to say something but John Middleton has turned back to his neighbour and noise has begun again so she decides to say nothing but then one of the older staff members, whose name she doesn't yet know, interrupts loudly with, 'Quiet everyone! Quiet! Sadie has something to say!'

No, she doesn't. She is not sure of her voice. She doesn't have anything to say. It was a small point and it doesn't matter. It doesn't need to be announced and they're all waiting, looking at her, so she has to say what she was going to say after all and they will all hear her say, 'Yes, there is one due out in a refereed journal, in about two months' time. It's just a short article – I can tell you about it another time . . .'

And they stare – not in an unfriendly way, as though she had no right to speak, but with curiosity that she should be voicing the words she just has, as though she is an animal who has suddenly just started speaking and in the English language too.

'WONderful. WONderful. That's Excellent, Sadie, that is EXcellent.' And David Jamieson looks around the room at his colleagues as if to say, 'If she can do it, why can't you?'

And Sadie feels the hotness in her face

It's like being the school swot – this is ridiculous.

before the room returns to a normal temperature and they all look away from her once again. The irritation in the air is palpable – the head is throwing disapproving looks at John Middleton and his partner in crime, who are merrily discussing the merits of Islay whisky, and David Jamieson is hitting his hand hard down on thc old oak table as he speaks. Then he stops for a moment, looks down at his papers and begins to read from the first page. 'CondITIOns of the ReSEARCH AssESSment EXercise,' he reads out loud, with an insistence bordering on cheek, as though he is speaking to an unruly group of five-year-olds and Sadie feels it, she feels that, yes, he is being insolent to them all, no matter how long they have been here and how old they are. But finally he has their attention and the men next to her stop talking about whisky. Others stop looking out of the window and even Professor Dickson opposite her manages to wake up at this new and unpleasantly combative tone of voice in the room.

He gazes at Sadie in a puzzled fashion, as though he cannot quite remember who she is, and she smiles but he does not smile back. He is trying to figure it out – this conundrum in the middle of the conference meeting that is Sadie. And she stops smiling but he is still looking at her, his heavy grey eyebrows knotted together in frustration, and she looks away for a moment and then back again and he is still staring at her, still trying to puzzle out who or what she is. And she is cut up in front of him – she is a face, a body, hands, legs, feet that he cannot understand. He cannot understand what this *body* is doing here and suddenly, suddenly, Sadie sees a face, heavy eyebrows in a woman's face, not knotted in confusion but pointing upward in the centre, giving the woman a cautious, inquisitive look – how a woman looks when she does not know what to expect, how she might look when she is a body that isn't supposed to be there. An image from one of Sadie's favourite films. She sees the unplucked eyebrows of a repressed spinster daughter – 'the daughter of my old age' – as she slowly descends the stairs to be assessed by a famous psychiatrist. She sees a beautiful young girl's treacherous pout in close-up as she tells her mother how much she hates her for her lowly cleaning job. Bits of women's bodies up close – lips and eyebrows pursed or raised, all in fear or expectation of the worst or because they are bodies that don't belong. Angry, repressed daughters with their pouts and their fearful looks.

And this makes Sadie pick up her pen. She thinks of mothers and daughters, she thinks of Nanda Grey in *Frost in May*. She thinks of Virginia Woolf in *A Room of One's Own* when she said . . . what? What was it about 'no wealth to leave us'? A generation of women . . . bits of bodies – faces and lips and eyebrows . . . daughters between the wars.

Daughters who hated their mothers. May Sinclair wrote about it too. And Molly Keane. Daughters who hated their mothers. Daughters and mothers like Sadie and Lily and Rubina. Lily and the mother she never speaks of. Women and the mothers they *do* speak of. How they speak of them . . . Women with troublesome voices . . . Daughters with troublesome voices, troubling their mothers – 'Tell me about Rubina.' Troublesome daughters . . . Canada and Rubina and mothers and daughters . . . Sadie is not sure why they pull her to them – places and people she does not remember – but they *do* pull her. And she pictures her mother and it is not a memory this time – this time it is only some sort of imagining of her mother's hennaed head, perhaps bent down in sorrow at the bedside of a sister she has not seen for over twenty years, and Sadie wonders what she could be saying to her at this moment – what her mother could be saying to a sister who may not even hear a word she says . . . if she can even speak to her . . . if she can even say the words at all.

Rubina's era when she was growing up. 'Rubina's era' – Sadie scrawls the words on her notepad surreptitiously, under the desk, while David Jamieson carries on talking about research standards and she knows that something has come to her, in this room full of busts of old men. 'Rubina's era' – the twenties and thirties. Olive Higgins Prouty. Edith Wharton. Not winged women and girl gangs and jazz. Mothers and daughters and conflict. Not now. Not in the present day. Not her and Lily – 'Rubina's era'.

'I think that covers everything?' the head is speaking loudly over the scraping of chairs and coughing that has broken out and Sadie is woken out of her daydream by David Jamieson who makes his way past the chairs to her as she is picking up her briefcase. 'SAdie, I've LEFT the DEtails of the LECture I'd

LIKE you to give DOWNstairs and I was WONdering if you would be WILling to give a PAper at the END of next WEEK for the POSTgraduate SEMinar? THURSday EVening, seven o'clock. NOTHing too POLished – we're VEry informal. Just a little RUN-down of the REsearch you're WORking on just NOW?'

The coincidence startles Sadie into submission and she agrees before she has time to think of an excuse, 'Yes, yes, of course – I'd love to. That's very kind of you! Thank you.'

But, as she walks down the stairs beside David Jamieson, her head is full of mothers and daughters and an era she knows little about except for a few women writers. And Sadie is well aware that it is a little displaced interest. These mothers and daughters are what she will research because she cannot get at the real mothers and daughters she wants to write about but that is good. It is good to have a back-up plan – that is what this will be. She will not give up on finding Rubina – she will find her, she will locate her, she will go to the street where she knows her grandmother once lived – and, in the meantime, while she is chasing Rubina, she will write about mothers and daughters in fiction, from Rubina's era. It will bring Sadie closer to her. 'Self-writing,' Nancy Miller said. 'A proliferation in literary studies of autobiographical or personal criticism.' Sadie could even bring them both together – if she can find out about Rubina in time.

Yes, perhaps she can bring them both together and, with that thought in her head, Sadie lets herself in to her office but she will only be there for a moment because she wants to pick up her briefcase, button up her coat, turn off the light, lock the door behind her and head out along the cobbled, windy street that takes her to the library. It is already dark and the street is busy with students out from the last classes of the day and they jostle her accidentally as she makes her way along the narrow pavement, trying not to slip over on to the road, which is busy now with cars taking people home, but Sadie does not mind. She doesn't mind anything now because she is eager – eager to get to the library and look up a dozen women writers and plan, plan how she can impress.

Tuesday, February 28th

Still no change. It's been a whole week. Spent the weekend with Pete at your house – in spite of not wanting to. It was so difficult, Amy, going back there without you. It's all changed of course – the basement papered and painted differently. That's where we stayed, me and John. Pete insisted. We're not to go back to the hotel. I can't refuse him. So there we are, Amy, in the basement – the basement where Mum and Dad were staying that day because their place was being redecorated. Something like that. Not that it's anything like it was then. All carpeted now, soft lilac, with dried flowers in clear vases, violet duvet covers, violet cushions. Even the en-suite is different – just white now. It was yellow then. Your 'guest' room. No photographs anywhere but lots of your paintings – watercolours. I'd forgotten how good you were at those. Lovely to have them on the walls – like having you all around the room.

And the house, too. Your paintings all over it, Amy. And, now we're older, you know what? Our tastes are not so different. You like gold and red too. Your front room looks like mine. Not as much stuff – 'clutter', as Sadie would say. But we like the same things, the same colours. All still pristine, of course, but there's colour now – there wasn't much before – and it's warm. You have a warm house, Amy. You sorted it, didn't you? Your problems with Pete. You must have. It's a happy house. It feels happy – not the house of a family in trouble. You must have sorted it all.

And the kids – Becka and Ricky – you have such nice kids. So well-mannered. Easygoing. Thoughtful. Nothing too much trouble. Just like Pete. Nothing ruffles them. I looked for you in them. More of you. I wanted to see things – certain things – but I couldn't see. There's none of your . . . what? None of your nervous energy, none of your inventiveness – your unpredictability. But they love you. And you've been happy with them. You can see it. In your home. You need to get better for them, Amy. Don't leave them. Don't leave. They need you. I need you. Yes, I need you too. Don't leave me. I cut myself free. I know I did. Of all of you. But all it's meant is that I'm adrift. I don't know where I'm going. Or what to do. Don't want to know where Mum is now. Not after all this time. Or what she's doing. Or even if she's still alive. But I want to know you again, Amy. I want the chance to fix that, at least. I want us to sit in your front room. One evening, glasses of wine in our hands, talking about everything – like sisters are meant to. Which we never did. We never got the chance to know each other grown up. That was my fault, I know. Well, partly my fault. Not all of it, though, because there was something you never knew – something I never told you about. That day – the day of the picnic – after we left . . . 'After we left' – how easy it is to say. To do even. Just leave. It's what people do every day. Leave to go to work. Leave to go to the shops. Leave to go on holiday. Leave to have an affair. Leave to find yourself. People do it all the time. Leave for one reason or another. And, I suppose, that day . . . She chose that day to leave. It was just so easy, I suppose. Everything about it was easy. We packed up the cars. Headed off. Nice and smooth. No hold-ups in the traffic. No wrong turnings. No arguments about the best way to get there. We followed Mike and Mary. Got there easily by lunchtime although it *was* getting busy by then. You could see that half the families in Toronto had all had the same idea. What a wonderful park it is! A place that got that much sunshine shouldn't be so green but it was. How green I remember it! All that thick green grass, the huge oak trees and all the evergreens, hedges and bushes and flowers . . . It could have been Scotland, it was so green. Except for the weather, of course. Didn't make me feel homesick, though – just the opposite. Here was home – if I wanted to remember it that way. That's what it said to me. Oh, I hadn't said anything to John about staying although I planned to that day – as soon as we had a moment to ourselves. I was keeping an eye on things. Watching to see how it all went, in case there was a moment we could slip away – be by ourselves and not be noticed.

That's what you never knew – that I'd persuade John to emigrate, move back to Toronto. I'd thought about it all on the drive there – all the arguments I'd use to win him over. The weather's better. The standard of living. More jobs. Better jobs. Better chances for the kids. Family all around us. We'd be leaving friends but we could make new ones. What was the argument for staying in Glasgow? That it was where we were from. That it was what was familiar. But that was all. I tried to think up better reasons than that – to anticipate what he'd say – but I couldn't. Couldn't come up with a decent reason why we should stay. Why we shouldn't move away. His family. That would be it. That would the crunch. He was always close to his parents, John. And they were getting older. He had one sister but they weren't close and she was in Australia. So he'd be the only one to look after them in their old age. And, sorry, but I wasn't going to let them spoil it. Not going to let two old folk hold me back. They'd had their life. That's what I was thinking. They'd had their life. It was time for me now. Time for me to live mine. Here, in Toronto.

You'd be surprised, Amy, wouldn't you? To hear what I'd planned. And that I kept it a secret. That you never knew. Because I was the big talker in the family. Always babbling. Couldn't keep a thing to myself. The number of times you'd tell me off. 'I told you not to tell anybody!' I was rubbish at keeping secrets. Who your first boyfriend was – remember? I wasn't being mean. His name just slipped out – Dougie – one dinner time at the table. I really didn't do it deliberately. You almost killed me. Wouldn't speak to me for a whole month – remember? Why could I never keep a secret? You asked me that all the time. I don't know. I've never worked it out. Kept quiet about this one, though. Maybe that's what it is. Keep so quiet about one thing there's no will left for anything else. Everything else has to come out. There's always one big secret taking up so much space. So much effort to keep it that you can't keep anything else in.

Anyway, that's what I'd planned. And when we got there – the park – I had that planned too. We didn't walk too far from where we'd parked the cars mainly because we had too much to carry. And because *she* couldn't walk too far – especially not in those heels. Way too dressed up for a picnic. Dressed up. Dressed up. Of *course* she was dressed up. I know she liked to look smart but it was ridiculous. For a picnic. Her heels stuck in the grass. She slowed us all down. She must have known. She must have known she was dressing all wrong for a picnic. But dressing right for something . . . something else.

Maybe it was for us. The last time we'd see her and she

wanted to look nice for us. To remember her that way – smart and proper. Respectable. But I don't think so. Don't think it was for us at all. What she was going to do. That's what it was all for. She had to look proper for that. That was the reason for the heels and the lipstick. All of it so inappropriate – so *wrong*. How it glares out now. And none of us mentioned it. Nobody said, 'Isn't that a bit much for a picnic?'

I used to notice everything, Amy. Had a real knack for it when I was a girl. Do you remember? How much I liked watching things . . . people? I liked watching people and what they did. I could have watched people all day long. When we moved to the house on Victoria Avenue, my bedroom looked out on to the main road. I loved that – could watch the cars going by all day. Neighbours coming and going. I could see what Mrs Robertson was wearing when she went to the mall. Could see Mr Cohen driving past with his deliveries. Remember them. I liked noticing as much as I could. You keep as quiet and still as possible and no one knows you're there. Then you see everything. That's what I learned. It sounds sneaky, I know, but it wasn't – not really. I was just good at noticing things. *Was* good at noticing things. Used to be good at it. See that. Not now. It's all changed now. What changed it? When did I stop seeing everything?

Motherhood, I think. That's what changed it. Started only to see Sadie and Campbell. Didn't see anyone else. What my eyes were for. What every mother's eyes are for. Watching to make sure they didn't wander off. Campbell was always doing that. Watching to make sure they didn't get their clothes dirty. Or eat all the sweet things before dinner. Or get too much of the sun. Or get too over-excited. Can't watch a mother when you're a mother yourself. Grown-ups can watch themselves. Can't be watching them all of the time. Because, the minute you take your eyes off them – the wee ones, I mean – that's when they fall down or push someone or eat wild berries or talk to strangers or . . . You think they're the ones you have to watch because they're the ones who are in danger but not always – sometimes it's the adults we should be watching.

Anyway, that day – eight adults to four kids and a baby so taking my eyes off Sadie and Campbell for a minute or two . . . well, that would be all right. I knew it would be all right for me and John to slip away. I say that but I don't believe it – not really. After all I've said about watching them all the time. Just before we left for Toronto that summer, we took Sadie and Campbell to another park – one in Glasgow, near where we lived, at the top of a hill. Sadie wanted to run down to the bottom. John thought we could go down the path at the side instead of over the grass and we'd meet her at the bottom – only we didn't. When we got there, there was no sign of her. We were shouting and shouting but there was no reply – nothing. Didn't know what had happened or where she'd got to. Remember grabbing Campbell, trying not to cry. John ran back up the hill but she wasn't anywhere. Then – when he got to the top – he saw her, over in the distance. Talking to this young couple. Turned out she'd changed her mind halfway down the hill. Looked round to see if we were following. Panicked when she saw we weren't there. Run back up to the top. The young couple were so nice. But, when I think of it . . . if it hadn't been them . . . if it had been someone else she'd run into . . . someone not so nice . . . someone bad – it would only have taken a couple of minutes . . . just a couple of minutes . . . out of sight . . . for a couple of minutes. That was all. Out of my sight. I wasn't looking. Wasn't watching.

We're told now all we ever do is watch things. We're

all couch potatoes. Peeping toms. Curiosity killed the cat. We're nosy neighbours. Neighbourhood watch. We're all spectators now – 'voyeurs'. Yes, that's the word Sadie would use – voyeurs. Getting pleasure out of watching. Watching what doesn't concern us. But, you know, Amy, I don't think we watch enough. Like that day I took my eye off Sadie. Or we watch the wrong things. We look at the details. Think we'll learn all about a person from the perfume they wear or the shoes they have on. You see it in that new magazine – the one with celebrities and their houses. They had it in the retirement home. Very glossy. I never buy it. I read it sometimes, though. Don't know how people can buy it all the time. It's full of rubbish. That Meryl Streep wasn't wearing any make-up. That Dustin Hoffman had a ring on his third finger. As though that tells you anything. One wee thing like that. What detective stories play on too. It's what I'm doing now. As though this is a detective story too. Hoping that, if I go over every single little detail I can remember from that day, I'll find the reason hidden there – somewhere. I'll be able to solve the crime. Thinking that something she said or wore or did . . . something will give me the clue I need to what really happened. But details don't add up to that much. I've been over that day in my head so many times. Details don't tell me anything. So she was dressed up. So what? Details distract us or lead us down the wrong path. Details are bad for us – like anything, if we have too much of it. Makes us sick.

But I've started. And I want to do this properly. For you, Amy. And for me – for all of us, maybe. So, I'll look at the details then. I'll look at it all. The wooden picnic tables. The raffia hampers with the sandwiches and chips. Chips? Crisps, I mean! If Sadie could hear me . . . What else? Bottles of Coke in the iceboxes. Pete and John playing football with the kids with a big orange ball with black squares on it. Soft rubber, the size of my head. Does *that* detail help me? Is the clue to what she did there in a black and orange football? No.

But not all details are the same. Some are more important than others. It's working out which ones matter and which ones don't. How ruthless that is. Details that count and details that don't. What if *I'm* a detail that doesn't count? What if I'm not part of someone's big picture? That is a legacy of what she did. Leaving me with that feeling I've never been rid of. Do you have it too, Amy? How often I've wanted to ask you if you feel like an unnecessary detail – a bit of description in a story, an unnecessary paragraph . . . Or one tree too many in a landscape painting. What works of art we are! How little it takes to make us wrong . . . or too much . . . or not fit right. One wee detail and the masterpiece is ruined. But I don't know yet which details matter and which ones don't. So I'm keeping them all in. All the details I can think of – the right ones and the wrong ones.

But maybe . . . Now I come to think of it, it was something she said – a wee thing, a bit of detail in the conversation. You were talking about going back to work, now that the twins were a bit older. Pete didn't want you to. That's what was at the back of your argument the night before, wasn't it? I knew it was something else. 'He's got no idea,' you said. Pete and John were too far away to hear and anyway the kids were squealing so they couldn't hear us. Don't think you cared whether Pete heard you or not, though. Can see you exactly, Amy – every detail. You holding your cigarette that way – high up. Your head over to one side, looking up at the sky. How often she sat like that too. And her lighting up as well. Blowing the smoke away from Mary and the baby. That at least. Not as bad as you about the smoking. 'He's got no idea. I'm stuck at home all day – I need to get back to work or I'll die of boredom *and* we need the money even more now.'

John wouldn't have minded me working. But I wanted to stay at home – until Campbell was at school. Before I went to the golf club. And the retirement home. It turned out I didn't have to work. But I've told you that, Amy, haven't I. You should tell me – tell me when I've told you something you've heard before. Don't let me repeat it. Wake up and tell me.

'He gets out to his work – he sees his co-workers. I'm stuck inside with two kids all day and then he comes in and wants me to amuse him as soon as gets in the door.'

Mary laughed – high-pitched, light. 'I don't think Mike cares one way or the other,' she said.

You looked at her, Amy – such contempt. 'But you'll do exactly what he says, I'll bet, when the time comes,' you said.

I knew you thought the same about Mike as I did – that he might be a bit of a bully. But, Amy, there are ways of saying things – not like that, not straight out at the person. You'll just have them defending them and what's the point of that?

'Dad never minded you working, did he?'

You expected *her* to back you up, didn't you, Amy? Because it was obvious I wasn't going to. She didn't say anything, though, did she? She just sat there, blowing out cigarette smoke, fixing her sunglasses, smoothing out her dress, watching Sadie and Becka playing tig around the bushes. Not a maternal woman – not motherly. Not at all. Not ever.

'Mind you, he probably wouldn't have noticed if you'd been at home all day or if you'd been walking the streets, would he?' You weren't going to let it drop. Having a go at everyone that day – Sadie, me, Pete, Mary and now *her*. But she still didn't say anything.

Then she smiled at you, like you'd just given her the biggest compliment, and said, 'People notice more than they think.' That was all.

And you said, 'But you do think I should go back to work, don't you? It's not the nineteenth century, for Christ's sake. The twins can go to day care – they'll be fine there. Better that than hanging round me all day in a foul mood.'

Nothing worse for two wee ones than to be around you when you're like that, Amy, when you're in one of your moods. But it wouldn't help – not if I said so. So all I said was, 'I remember Mum working – remember? The butcher's? The chicken feet?'

She smiled. You laughed. So did I. Even though it wasn't that funny. A family joke – that butcher's. The customer who wanted a chicken with the toenails trimmed to use the feet for stock. We were poor but never that bad.

'I didn't mean she *never* worked – of course I remember that. I mean did Dad mind or not? Did he have a say in whether you did? Would he have noticed one way or the other?'

'That's a bit daft!' I couldn't help it – you were really annoying me and it was so hot. 'What d'you mean "did he notice"? How could he not have noticed? And it wasn't a question of minding – it was a question of having to work because there wasn't enough money. You don't get to "mind" when you're poor.'

You were mad at that, weren't you? So angry. So much for me, the good big sister . . . Me and my big mouth . . . And, as always, Mary tried to ease things over. Got more Coke out the icebox. Opened up some sandwiches. Gave you a beer. Yes, that helped. Didn't it, Amy? Beers for you. That would help you. Called the kids over. But *she* never said another thing. Never got involved in our quarrel. Just sat so distant – so removed from it all. Maybe she was glad to be getting away – away from all the noise and the arguing. *And* the family. Maybe she'd had enough.

Part of me . . . yes, a part of me can sympathise. *Really*! Times I could have seen John and Sadie and Campbell far enough. Could have put my coat on and walked out that door and never come back. I did leave – once or twice. In the early days. Oh, nothing serious. I'd never have left them all. Good girls don't. They don't abandon their men and their kids. I was always a good girl. No. Just a couple of times. After John and I'd had a row – about money or something . . . Just put my coat on and went for a walk – round the block, up to the park. But never to stay away – never that. Don't know how . . . how to do that . . . how to leave . . .

What am I saying? I hear you, Amy. Amy, wake up. I hear you. Yes, I left. Of course I know how to leave. That's what I did – I left. I suppose I've always left. Like mother, like daughter. I'm just as bad. I never thought about it like that before. Never thought that I did just the same thing as she did. But that's just what I did do – I left. I left you all.

On this damp, chilly Friday afternoon Sadie is walking slowly and carefully, as if she is in a dream. She has just woken up. It has been a long journey and now she is glad to be out in the open air just like this – even if it is raining. She is putting one foot in front of the other as though she knows exactly where she is going. Which she does know – of course she knows where she is going. Sadie is going to visit Lawrie Street, where her grandmother used to live.

It is not part of the paper she is due to give and Richard has already criticised her for taking valuable time off. She cannot just disappear off on day trips on a whim, he has told her, with some annoyance which she cannot understand.

> Why the hell do you care? It's not *your* research – it's not *your* paper.

But she does have a plan – Sadie has tried to tell him this. He tells her that it is not good to be divided between two different projects – that she must stick to one or the other. But she has told him she believes they overlap – that they are about the same thing. In her defence, she has cited Nancy Miller who says:

> Why personal criticism now? Is it another form of 'Anti-Theory'? Is it a new stage of theory? Is it gendered? Only for women and gay men? Is it bourgeois? Postmodern? A product of Late Capitalism? Reaganomics? Post-feminism? It might be possible, and the reflexes of my structuralist training make me contemplate the project, to construct a typology, a poetics of 'egodocuments' that constitute personal criticism: confessional, locational, academic, political, narrative, anecdotal, biographematic, etc. but is it really a good idea?

But Richard does not agree. He does not see that Sadie's mother-daughter authors were writing about themselves, were 'confessing' in their fiction. He does not see the connection with Rubina. He does not see the link.

Sadie had left his flat early this morning without having any breakfast because she knew he was still annoyed with her. So now, before she goes any further, she would like something to eat and she is putting one foot in front of the other not in the hope that her steps will take her somewhere to eat but in the expectation of it. Because she is here in the heart of the city she grew up in and she should expect it of the city – she should expect to find somewhere to eat on every corner, down every street. So she slowly passes by the posters decorating the construction site of the new concert hall and the *Big Issue* sellers who stand shivering in the cold by its wooden walls and the queues full of grumpy children and their parents at the bank's auto-teller beside it.

God, nothing can brighten up this place in the rain.

No, not the people, not the posters, not the new buildings full of glass meant to catch the light. And she knows, from her experience of growing up here, that it is better not to fight it.

Just go with it. Where's my umbrella?

Because Sadie knows that, whenever she dreams of this city when she is far away, she always dreams of it in the rain.

She walks away from the bus station then turns left and, as she turns, she passes first a large wine bar on the corner that is new. She hasn't seen it before – it is all wrought iron and wood inside. Then an old-fashioned pub, the kind with worn velvet seats and plastic flooring. Then she passes another wine bar before she turns to the right and heads past the cinema she used to go to as a child, an old coffee house and another new bar she hasn't seen before and then she reaches the next corner and there is a department store, an all-you-can-eat-for-a-fiver canteen, the door to a small Chinese restaurant upstairs and a McDonald's. Sadie walks slowly. She is taking her time. She just wants a sandwich or some soup. She wants to eat somewhere that is casual but comfortable but every place she passes seems too hard, too fast, too plastic, too busy, too noisy and she realises, as she walks along taking her time, how easy it is to forget what it is like to be in a city after only a few months away. She can feel she is already developing a small-town mentality and now she is back in the city just in time – before she had forgotten completely, before she had changed for good and couldn't change back again, before three cobbled streets felt like the whole world.

Sadie will not let the noise or the busyness of everyone around her put her off, even though she can feel it – the urge to run back to the bus station and wait for the next bus to take her back to her small town. She has a purpose here – she is here in the city to investigate. She will visit Lawrie Street and she will place adverts in local shop windows. She has already prepared the white oblong cards she has with her in her large black bag:

> Did you know a Rubina McAllister of Lawrie Street, 1940–1951? Part of family research project. If you have any information, please contact Sadie Mathieson at . . .

And she has worried about that address, worried that a university address would scare people away, but she didn't want to put her home address on a card so it will have to do.

If Lily was at home, Sadie would visit her. Or, if she had warned some old friends she was coming, she could have met up with them. But she never got around to it – she was too distracted. Yes, that's it, really. She doesn't want to admit to herself that she was afraid to contact any old friends – that, when she left, she didn't plan to come back and there is too much in the meeting of old friends, too much reminiscing, too much proving that she made the right decision, to want to see them. The city has gone on growing without her and her friends will have, too. They didn't need her to stay to carry on living and neither did the city – she can see how many people it has to take her place! And a small boy jostles her as she stands at the traffic lights. The green man has appeared but she is the only one not moving and this will not do. This *will* not do – she will have to wake up.

Sadie steps off the kerb and heads along the main

pedestrianised street, leaving behind her the squat, square buildings on the shopping concourse that startled her because, apart from a short visit to Glasgow to stay with her parents at Christmas, it has been months since she has seen a building that dates from after the nineteenth century. And Sadie thinks, as she steps off the kerb and heads further along the street, that this is a city Rubina has never seen. She thinks this as she progresses along the street and tilts her head back to look up at buildings she cannot remember ever having looked at before. Rubina left in the 1950s – Rubina wouldn't have seen the modern shopping concourse, Rubina would never have known about the new buildings or all of these shops and restaurants and bars and people surging along. And Sadie wonders, as she feels how strange it is to return, after only a few months, to the place she grew up in, what it would be like to return to a place you have not seen for almost fifty years, what would surprise you and what would not. But Sadie cannot really imagine it. She cannot know, even though she tries, because the things she would notice are not the things she would expect Rubina to notice. Rubina would not be surprised by modern buildings or shops or people – she would be used to them all from Canada. Rubina would be surprised by something else – something that her granddaughter cannot know because it would come from inside her, from her own memory, and Sadie has no access to that. And perhaps that is really what Sadie wants, why she is pursuing her grandmother after all this time, because she wants to know what she thought, she wants access to what was inside Rubina, to what she knew and thought and felt and saw, as though knowing and thinking and feeling and seeing all of that will somehow answer questions Sadie hasn't even begun to ask yet.

She really does not want to walk any further in this drizzle, though, her shoes are getting wet and so are her trouser hems and her umbrella keeps clashing with people squeezing past her. She must stop somewhere, anywhere – the first place she sees – and, on her left, she sees a large bar that also serves food. It is the kind of bar that serves food all day long and the music hits her as soon as she opens the door. It is only just past noon, early yet for lunch, so Sadie crosses an empty floor to a choice of tables, sits down at the one nearest the window so she will have something to look at while she eats alone and lifts the menu. They have soup – that will do. She might have a gin and tonic as well. Why not? Sadie changes her mind about the gin and tonic about five times. And she can't decide whether to stick to soup or have a burger or chicken fajitas and maybe some chips either. She changes her mind about the food five times too before she catches the attention of a waitress, a very young girl with dyed blonde hair piled up who is lounging by the bar, chewing gum.

This sort of thing is good for her, Sadie decides as she looks out of the window. It is good to be out, eating by herself, in a busy city, and not sneaking a roll on the way back to her office. Yes, this is much better for her. How unusual it is to be out and about, out in the open. She had not realised before how much she has been skulking about at work – yes, that is what she does and she will stop it. She will eat out sometimes when she gets back. She will be visible – she won't skulk behind university walls and in basement offices any more.

After she has eaten and after she manages to get the waitress to bring her the bill,

> This is taking longer than it did to eat the whole damn meal.

Sadie is outside once again and it has stopped raining. She is more awake now. The food has made her feel better – ready to tackle her visit, the short journey she will take to Lawrie Street. She has not been able to make up her mind whether to hail a taxi or try to find a bus to take her there. A taxi seems like cheating somehow. This is a quest, a mission, and it should be hard and fraught with danger, full of obstacles to be overcome and foes to be fought. No one on a mission simply takes a taxi and arrives at their destination without a problem. Sadie wants this to be more of a struggle than it is – she wants it to be worthwhile. But she has no idea which bus to get to take her there or where she would take the bus from. She has a city street map with her, though, and the sun is coming out. She can walk – it will not be too far. Yes, she decides she will walk, she will walk through the city.

Sadie consults her map. She will walk back along the pedestrianised main street, then across to the motorway underpass, which is only a few minutes away, and then up past an estate. She knows the one – she has seen it from the motorway many times and it is not a appealing prospect but she will stick to the main road that will take her all the way. And, from there, Lawrie Street is only a few streets further on. The motorway would not have been there when Rubina left for Toronto and nor would the estate so Sadie will not see what Rubina would have seen but she can try. So she crosses the street and begins to climb the steep hill. She decides she will try to see only those things old enough to have been here when Rubina was here. She will take a 1940s' tour of her city and block out anything else.

But that is harder than she realises. There is so much that is in her way. And Sadie is not sure how old some things are. Was the theatre she is about to pass here then? Rubina would never have gone to the theatre – she wouldn't have been able to afford it. And the old church at the end of the road that is now a council building would probably still have been a church fifty years ago but Sadie can't be sure. She is afraid she might go too far back and knock down buildings that might have been here after all – erase sights that Rubina would have seen.

The streets are less busy now as she approaches the motorway underpass. There are hardly any shops here and she is nervous of the underpass even in daylight but it is over quickly. She hurries past the colour paintings on the walls, garish and bright and affected by damp. There are dark streaks running up through the crude drawings and there is moss growing along the bottom. When Sadie comes back out into the light again, an overweight middle-aged woman approaches her and says, 'If it'll just hold off a bit more till the washing's dry . . .' as though she knows Sadie and it is part of a conversation the two of them have been conducting between them for a while.

Well, that's great for you, isn't it?

And Sadie smiles and nods at the woman who continues, 'You might know it – the minute it's on the line . . .', as she passes by. And Sadie cannot help it, she pictures her washing on the line, blowing in the chill breeze – large white underwear, a husband's huge shirts, because this woman's husband will surely be as enormous as she is, striped bed sheets and pillowcases all along one line and then the red T-shirt that belongs to the son who will still live at home because she is the kind of wife and mother who does everything for the men in her life, who washes and cooks and cleans for them so her son will not want to leave for a woman who does not do all those things for him, and the lacy teen underwear that belongs to the daughter who might be younger but who has just started her first job and dating her first proper grown-up boyfriend who picks her up at their tiny house in his flash new car. But Sadie knows that she has this failing, that she wants to believe that washing can say so much about a person because she believes in signs, that signs can tell her things and that what they tell her isn't always the truth. And, even though Sadie knows that they don't always tell the truth, she still believes in them anyway and that is Sadie's failing, that is her failing, and she knows that she is going to Lawrie Street looking for signs and, if she finds any, they will probably lie to her too.

But all the same, she smiles, she cannot help finding the overweight middle-aged woman and her confidences funny – it makes her smile that there are people in the world so willing to talk to anyone. And she pictures Lily's annoyance at it – her impatience with the imposition a stranger might make on her – and Sadie wonders if Rubina would find it an imposition or if Rubina would have been just such a middle-aged woman herself, if she would have been a middle-aged woman who spoke about her washing to strangers she passed on the street.

Sadie has reached the long main road now, the long road that will take her to Lawrie Street, and she is beginning to wish that she had taken a taxi. Her feet are sore and she doesn't like this road – it is huge and lorries and cars and buses thunder past her. The people she passes do not look at her in a friendly way – there are no more middle-aged overweight women willing to tell her about their lives. She passes improbably thin men with gaunt faces, who all seem to be wearing white tracksuits, and young girls with gold necklaces that dangle down over tracksuit tops and no one is dressed all in black the way Sadie is – no one looks anything like her. And she walks on, past the cemetery and towards the railway line, and there are shops here too – shops selling bits of things, not whole things but parts of other things that might have been broken or lost or stolen or never there in the first place. And she looks to the left suddenly and sees the place where the locomotive works used to be when Rubina was here. They are closed and empty now but they are the first sign she has of what her grandmother must have seen when she lived here and Sadie forgets the shops and the thin-faced men and she hurries along faster. She wants to get to Lawrie Street which must be close now. She would like to make sure but then she would have to take her street map out of her bag and the last thing she wants is to do that.

> I'd look like a tourist in my own flaming city.

But Sadie knows that Rubina lived near the locomotive works and the railyard – Lily mentioned it once, just once. She'd seen a newly built train and said what a sight it was so Sadie knows she must be close. And she wishes she had asked Richard to come with her to see this after all but she doesn't want to have to imagine his refusal.

> I'm too busy – I've got research to do. It's a waste of time.

And there, it's too late – she has imagined it, played it out in her mind and she is annoyed at him for refusing in her imagination a request she never made of him in real life. But this is not her imagination now. The side streets appear on the left and, no, they are not the tenement buildings that her grandmother lived in – they are small, grey houses that look as if they would fold up and collapse in a gale. But as Sadie makes her way over the main road, where the traffic never stops, halting three times as she crosses, she sees the street name on the front of the first house and, yes, there it is – it says, 'Lawrie Street'.

Sadie's grandmother never saw these houses but she would have walked along this same street on a day just like this – cloudy and breezy and promising more rain. And she starts to walk past the houses, looking for a shop – somewhere she can leave her cards – and there is one. There is a small newsagent's, with thick wire mesh on the front, set in between an off-sales and a bookie's, both of which have reinforced glass at the front.

Sadie stops for a moment.

> Can I just go in and ask them to put up my cards? Isn't that a bit mad? What if this is just a really stupid idea? Who says it's the kind of place where people answer questions about folk from fifty years ago?

In her sheltered little university town, Sadie has forgotten about the kind of places where people respond with wire mesh and reinforced glass. She has forgotten about places like this and, for a moment, she thinks that Richard was right after all and that she will have to turn round and go back the way she came with her bag still carrying the cards she made out so carefully.

But she can't bear the thought of that so she will go in. And Sadie pushes the newsagent's heavy door and smiles at the man behind the till who does not smile back at her.

'I wonder if you can help me?' she begins, as she approaches him.

The shop is dark inside. There are only two strips of lighting on the ceiling although the large freezer in the middle of the shop gives a bit more light. The man is bearded, foreign. He looks at her with suspicion and Sadie wonders how best to get him to agree to do what she wants him to. She bends down, opens her bag and takes out her cards.

'My grandmother used to live in this street, about fifty years ago. I'm trying to trace people who might have known her back then. I wondered if you'd be willing to put up some of these cards in the window or here at the till?'

Sadie speaks carefully but the man's face does not alter very much and she wonders if he has understood her. Then he looks at her cards, picks one up and smiles briefly. 'Yes,' he says, nodding, 'I can do that. Your family?'

'Thank you!' she says. 'Yes, I'm trying to trace my family – they lived here but they emigrated a while back.' Then suddenly she is shy of telling this man any more, even though he is friendly and smiling, so she says her goodbyes and is about to turn round and leave when she thinks that it might be better if she bought something so she stops and reaches for some chocolate on the counter in front of her and hands it over and he picks up the cards she has given him, places them on the till while he rings up her chocolate. Then points at the window. 'I will put them up today – in the window.'

Sadie thanks him again.

It is the same at the off-licence and at the bookie's. It has all been much easier than she thought and suddenly it is over – there is no more she can do. It was a simple task after all and she is tired and she wants to go home – home that is the small university town and she wants to be there now. She walks back along Lawrie Street as it begins to get dark. And Sadie will go to the train station across the road, she will take the train back into town and she will get on the bus and she will go home. She has done what she can. If there is anybody still left on this empty, grey little street from fifty years ago, then they will see her cards and, with luck, they might even get in touch with her and tell her something about Rubina.

Friday, March 3rd

I'm sorry, Amy – sorry I didn't come yesterday. They've told us, you see, no point in being here every minute. I know why, too – it's because they don't think you'll wake up. That's why they say it – I know. But there's always someone here with you. Don't worry, Amy – you're never alone. And now that Mike and Mary are here and Becka and Ricky – all your family – all here . . . John and I decided – well, John thought it would be a good idea – for us to have a break from sitting watching you so we had a day out. I'm sorry. I had to just get out, walk about. Freezing though it is, I don't care. We needed it – both of us. You'd understand, wouldn't you, Amy? Couldn't bear another minute of that hospital smell. Just to get out, away. It was only a day. And I wanted to see how different the city is now. We went downtown. Downtown. Twenty-two years. It's still . . . what I liked then, only better now – more glamorous. All the shops – much better ones now. Couldn't afford any of them, though – all those designer names. We walked all along Bloor Street. Bloor Street . . . What a treat to come downtown! Remember, Amy? All the shops and the museums. Had lunch just at the corner of Yonge Street. Some bits still a bit scruffy. A bit – bohemian. Not for us – me and John. But it was a good walk, even with the snow. Down past Victoria

University and back up University Avenue with all the students.

I've never walked so much. But I wanted to see it all – remember. Everything so clean. I expected changes – of course I did – from when we were last here. The airport is huge – not the little stopover that I remember from before. And we haven't seen much so far. Forgive us, Amy. We've just been going from your place to the hospital. We drive in a hired car the same journey every day. We hadn't seen anything downtown at all so we took the train yesterday – a double-decker train – all the way in to Union Station. So clean. And there we were right in the middle of it, like a couple of tourists. John insisted on the CN Tower. It didn't feel right to be sightseeing – not when you're like this – but John insisted. So forgive me, Amy, but I just needed to forget, just get away – even for a few hours. I needed it.

And now I keep thinking Sadie would love it here – all the bookshops, all the buzz. She could go to Victoria – like a piece of history in the middle of all this newness. Beautiful old buildings. All the green. Yes, I suppose it's still like that for me – new. What I want to see. Newness. I've no desire to go and visit our old homes. The old street we used to live on. Victoria Avenue. Up in Riverdale. Our old school. No, don't want to see any of that. I like looking at the things I haven't seen before. Seeing what is different. Yes, Sadie would like it here. Maybe she would be teaching at Victoria now. If . . . if I'd come back. If that day I'd . . . you know – been able to carry on with what I'd planned.

Dad used to say there were too many women in our family. When we were little. It was just a joke – he meant it as a joke but I wonder if that's what he really thought sometimes. Especially after what happened. After there was . . . what? One less woman in our family? Ironic. Did he, Amy, did he say it? Not as a joke any more. Did he say it bitterly, like a criticism? Or like it was our fault? Mine and yours, Amy? Mary's too? Maybe he started to think, after she left, if only we'd been boys . . . All boys – like the Robertsons. Remember them, Amy? My friend – Charlie Robertson? Well, now, I wonder where you are now, Charlie. What you're doing? If you got married? Had kids? I hope so. Hope you did.

Maybe, if we'd been boys, Mum'd still be here. If we'd only been boys, we'd still be a family. Maybe that's what Dad thought afterwards. But I've always thought it's the women who keep a family together. The women who do all the phoning and the writing – the keeping in touch. It's why our family fell apart. Because we couldn't. The women – we couldn't keep in touch. It was up to us but we couldn't do it. Women arrange everything – the family get-togethers, Christmas, birthdays. Men never do. They don't bother. So, if I didn't bother and you didn't, Amy, and Mary tried but not enough . . . Not then – so that was that.

It's the women who fall out too, you see. It's women who have the rows. Cause problems and upsets. If you and I had been boys, Amy, we'd probably have gotten along much better. But we let our family down. Yes, we did. That's what we did. But, still, it's the women who understand what family means – I think so. I might have turned my back on everyone. I did, yes, that's what I did to you but not to my own family – not the one I made myself. That's the family I make all the effort for. Even though I hardly know them – not any more. My own son and daughter . . . I'm the one who calls, who writes, who arranges everything. Who drags them back home for

Easter and Christmas and birthdays, no matter what they're doing or where they are.

It's why this generation – well, Sadie's generation – why they've got the problems they have. Why I never know what to say to her any more – my own daughter. She never visits us except when she needs something – or wants to torment me. Asking about *her* – about Rubina. She doesn't bother with Campbell at all. Doesn't care. I don't know why. But she doesn't value family, not properly. She wants to know something about her family but she doesn't want to know *us*. Our mother – Rubina – she's just . . . What? Some little mystery to my daughter. And yet she's the only link – she's all we have between us, the only thing I know that draws her to me. If I wanted to . . . You know, I've thought this so many times. If I wanted to, I could do it – could dangle Rubina in front of Sadie like a big juicy carrot. No more need for the stick. You see? No more nagging. No more emotional blackmail – 'Your dad's not been well. Couldn't you come and visit?' But to use our mother . . . It would be just as bad.

No, I couldn't do it. Sadie – she doesn't care about her family at all. Doesn't value us – like most young women her age. They're all after what they can get – career, money, nice things, travel – and they're so demanding about men. If he doesn't have a good car and a good job and if he isn't the most handsome man alive, who's famous . . . then they're just not interested. There's going to be a lot of very lonely women in a few years. Not like us, Amy. We didn't ask for the impossible, did we? Sadie will be unhappy and that makes me sad. I wish I could tell her – wish I could warn her. She expects too much. She should be looking for someone nice, getting a home started, having kids of her own. A good career is all very well but it's not going to look after you in your old age, is it?

What am I saying, Amy? That Sadie values family less than my own mother did? No, I don't think that's true. Sadie wouldn't – she wouldn't be like that. Not if she had her own wee ones. She wouldn't abandon them. Not even once they were grown-up. Abandon them. What a word! That's stayed with me – never left me. Maybe I was born with it. A sense of abandonment. Born to people who abandon and were abandoned. We were a family of people who left, after all. Left Scotland for Canada – emigrated. Part of a great bunch of exiles. What is it they call it now? 'The Scottish Diaspora' – a very grand name for a not very grand flitting, if you ask me. That's what we did – we flitted. We might not have sneaked out in the middle of the night with bills owing but we left. Abandoned everyone else for the sake of a better way of life for ourselves – even though it was the right thing to do. You don't stay on a ship you think is sinking. You get off it. You save yourselves. What Mum and Dad did – saved us. Made sure we had chances – opportunities that they never had. What leaving is all about – creating more opportunities for yourself, giving yourself a chance. Maybe that's what Mum thought she was doing that day. Getting away from us. Abandoning us. Saving herself. Giving herself a chance she'd never had.

I've still no sympathy for what she did, though. I wonder if it made her happy – eventually. If she made peace – with herself and her decision. If it worked out for her. If she missed us. If she ever regretted it. Not seeing her own grandchildren grow up. Not knowing them. And you, now, Amy. If she's still alive. If she knows her second daughter can't wake up. If that'll make her step out of the shadows and appear. If she's still alive. I hope she's dead. No, I don't – that's wrong. It's what I thought though in the days just after . . . I was angry then.

Or maybe she was so sick of us all. Maybe she never looked back. Just skipped off and lived the high life. No responsibilities. No worries. She'd reached that point when a family becomes too much – when it suffocates who you are. We all do, we all reach that point – sometimes. But still . . . To do it, to actually do it – the way she did, that day . . .

Where was I? That day . . . Oh, yes. You were going on about going back to work and all that. Then what? Nothing much. Quiet. We sat around. Ate our sandwiches. Drank our Cokes. Remember? Laughs. We were laughing – rows forgotten. I'm sure I'm not wrong. I'm sure I've got that right – a family having fun. That's what we were. That day . . . Then there was John taking lots of pictures as usual – of the kids playing, of Pete and Mike fooling around with them. But that's when we got our chance – me and John – after he'd taken his pictures. I told him I wanted a word – just a quiet one. He looked surprised but he knew I wasn't angry. Just a bit of a chat, away from everyone – that's all I wanted. And he said, 'Fine.' So we got up after a bit. Nobody noticed. You didn't, Amy. Don't think Mum did either. Maybe she did – maybe that's when she took her chance. Maybe, if I'd stayed – if I hadn't gone off with John, if I'd stayed and we'd talked – she wouldn't have done it, couldn't have done it. But then, as John says, I couldn't be there all the time, could I? That's what he says now – when I get like this. But it doesn't help because I could have – I could have been there all the time. And then I might have stopped it. If *only* I had been there all the time . . .

I bet you think that too, Amy. Bet you think, 'If only

. . .' too. If only you had watched more – watched her. But everyone was fooling around, acting up, playing. Well, except Mum and Dad. But they were watching the wee ones. Dad was egging them all on. It's such a happy memory. I make it sound so bad, don't I, Amy? What with your tantrums . . . But it wasn't like that. It *was* happy. A happy time . . . So much better at the time. And then it all got spoilt by what happened next. If I think that it was so bad, all of it, then I won't understand myself. Or why I wanted to come back. Because I *did* want to – I really did.

I keep saying you never knew that, Amy, but it's true. You never knew how much I wanted to come back. That I had planned it all. And how far I'd got, too. Me and John walking up that little path, up to the botanic gardens. So hot, we didn't walk far. Started it, oh, just in my usual way. You know, asked him how much he was enjoying the holiday. 'Isn't it nice being around everyone?' 'Aren't Sadie and Campbell enjoying themselves?' All those sorts of things – lots of questions I knew he'd have to say yes to. I'd worked them out in advance, how I was going to put it to him. I'd just say it, straight out. 'What d'you think about living here?' 'What d'you think? D'you think there are good opportunities here? For the kids, I mean. What about you?' Not very subtle – no – but that wouldn't matter.

Remember? Yes, I remember exactly. Walking hand in hand along the little path – like when we first went out together back in Glasgow. What a beautiful day! It seemed like all the families in Toronto were there too. Have I said that before, Amy? Kids everywhere. Remember? And these big mixed groups that I loved – still do. Cousins and aunts and uncles all together. That's what I've missed – everyone spending time together. Yes, there are quarrels – and arguments and huffs and tantrums – but there are games and food and sharing and having fun and feeling like you're part of something, something bigger than yourself but the same as yourself too. A big group of friends together isn't the same – not the same as a big family get-together with people who have the same eyes as you or the same mannerisms or who laugh at the same things. I love it that Sadie has Mary's eyes and that Campbell and Ricky have the same laugh. I love that Dad's love of cars has passed on to Campbell. I even love that I see traits of Mum in you, Amy. Even now – even after all that's happened. After what she did.

It's what I said to John – all of that. Poor soul! What chance did he have? How do you fight that? He suggested I might not like it – the reality of being so near my family, on a permanent basis. But it wasn't just that. It was the standard of living. He could see that. He could see how much better things were here. Oh, he had a few objections. About education, 'A Scottish education's admired around the world, Lily.' And about values, 'Don't you think it's all a bit materialistic here?'

Willy Loman and Biff. Sadie isn't the only one who knows about books. I've read Arthur Miller. We did it once. The play, *Death of a Salesman* – amateur dramatics. I only joined them for one season, our local group – too many arguments, too much backbiting. I didn't have a big part but it was fun being part of something. And I kept seeing it in that play – Willy Loman and his values. Keeping up with the Joneses. Biggest adverts must mean better products. He got it all wrong, Willy Loman – what he wanted for his kids, for his family. John worried about that. He wasn't sure, not about those aspects of it all. But I reassured him – I did – that I knew we could resist anything we didn't approve of out here because there was plenty we didn't approve of back home. And, you know, Amy, it's the way of the world. Things – having things. I like having things. I don't value them over people but I do like having things. So, yes, I know about values – I know what's important. I don't get it wrong or out of proportion. I'm not Willy Loman. That's not me. And I convinced him, John. He agreed to give a move some thought. He actually said, 'You're right, you know, Lily – it might be the best thing to do after all.' And that's when I knew that that was it. I knew that we'd be moving. All those years after I'd left, there I was planning to come back.

You'd have been so surprised, Amy, to have known that's what was in my head that day – especially after the way I'd left in the first place. How much of that do you remember? We were what? Just squabbling teenagers then. Didn't tell you my reasons. And that summer, when I'd come back after thirteen years away – back with my family and my kids – you didn't ask me. I suppose you just thought, 'Oh, that's what Lily wanted to do.' Never heard you say you missed me after I left. You didn't write much. Mary did – a lot. And Mum did too – all the time. Funny that – when she was the main reason I left. Because I wasn't happy – not when I was young. You knew that, Amy. I didn't know what I wanted to do – no big career plans, stopped going out with that boy I'd been seeing . . . Can't even remember his name now. Isn't that strange? Something beginning with an S . . . Simon? Stephen? Stuart? Maybe something Scottish like that. Scott? Oh! Can't remember. Maybe I'd been hoping he'd propose. Take me away from it all – even though I didn't love him. But it became clear he wasn't going to or at least not soon enough for me. So that was that. The start of the sixties. No 'free love' or 'flower power' for us, eh, Amy? We just missed out – born just too late for all that. And I was a good girl. And, maybe because I'd been the oldest when we left Scotland, I could still remember it – only in a foggy sort of way. Romantic, a *Brigadoon* vision.

I was running away but it didn't seem like that – not at the time. I wasn't getting on with her – Mum – not at all. And, in those days, well, unmarried women didn't live on their own. There were no close school friends I could move in with. Most of them lived at home until they got married. That's what happened back then. Remember, Amy? Sadie hardly believes it. She doesn't believe it. She does all that feminist stuff but she doesn't know. It's all theories to her. She doesn't know what it was like. But that's how it was. Even in Toronto – especially in Toronto. Immigrant families – you worked hard to do well. Showed how well you could do. Showed how much the country needed you. So no one would ever say, 'We don't need you here. Go back to where you came from. We don't want you.'

But I thought, if I went back to Scotland by myself, then I'd have no choice – I'd have to live on my own. Mum tried family. Tried to get me to stay with some distant relations I'd never met but I wouldn't. And it just began to seem more and more exciting to me – moving away, going back. The only jobs were nursing or secretarial so I opted for nursing. It all made sense. I'd enrol at nursing college, get a qualification, have a career.

The more I thought about it, the more I liked it. And Mum liked it too, the minute I suggested it. Dad didn't want me to go but Mum couldn't wait. It's true – she was happy I was going. Not just because we didn't get on. That wasn't all. I made her uncomfortable. She made me nervy. She used say, 'Curiosity killed the cat!' all the time when I was wee. Accuse me all the time – 'Sticking your nose in where it's not wanted.' Maybe we were just at that age. I was almost twenty. She was in her early forties. Not a good age – not for mothers and daughters. Sadie and I at that age . . . hardly a civil word between us. What about you and Becka, Amy? I wish I'd kept in touch. We could have exchanged experiences. Helped each other, our daughters.

But I left. That day I sailed. All of you on the pier. Waving to you from the *Queen Mary*. Had a bit of a cry when I saw you all like that. Mum hugging Mary because she was crying. That girl – *such* a crybaby. Wee Mary. And Dad – the sad look on his face, pressing money into my hand before I walked up the gangway. And you, Amy – your angry, thin, handsome little face so like Mum's. Like to think you missed me a bit but I bet you didn't. You'll have had fun – after I left. And I wasn't sad long. I was too excited. Going back to Scotland . . . a career . . . a nurse . . . living on my own . . . What I was going to do with my life . . . Places I'd see . . . People I'd meet . . . Things I'd do . . .

But none of that happened. I'd only been at nursing college six months when I decided it wasn't for me and I chucked it in. When I think of the jobs I did after that . . . So awful and so badly paid. Sometimes I wonder how I survived but then I met John. John! How sophisticated he seemed to me! A businessman already – well, he ran his own finance company and he had big plans to expand it. We hadn't been going out that long when I got pregnant with Sadie. I should have gone on the pill but that was all new then and so John and I got married. We would have anyway – even if I hadn't been pregnant, I mean. We loved each other. But still . . . Perhaps we wouldn't have got married so soon. Who knows?

I didn't miss much about Canada, not at first. I noticed how grimy things were back in 'the old country', yes. And how rare new cars were. How few people had TV – still the radio. I missed the weather. Blistering-hot summers and freezing-cold winters – I loved the extremes. Couldn't get used to all the rain – not to begin with. But I was happy. It had been the right decision to leave – to leave you all. I didn't regret it. Not until that summer I came back. And the picnic. I'd left my family behind – abandoned them to be by myself, to do what I wanted to do. So what's the difference then? Between me and Mum? I know, Amy. You'd be the first to point it out to me. I know. But it's *not* the same – not the same at all. I didn't just disappear. And there I was, thirteen years later, longing – yes, longing – to come back. I'd had enough of Scotland. Done *Brigadoon*. Wanted back. Back to what felt like home. Toronto. My family. My mother. Who I'd been getting on with so much better since I'd been away. And even now, on this holiday, things were fine. She was a different woman from the one I left behind thirteen years ago – more sophisticated, more closed-off. And less quick to anger, more tolerant – like she had accepted things. And so it just made what she did seem all the more awful, I think. So much more *shocking*. It came right when nobody expected it.

That was us that day – strolling along that path, me and John. Felt like we hadn't a care in the world. Everything was sorted. Everything was OK. How I wish that walk had lasted forever. Wish I could just take that walk and make it my life. A single moment of complete happiness. The calm before the storm. A moment of ignorance. Before you know the truth. 'What the eye doesn't see, the heart doesn't grieve over.' But sometimes you have no choice. Your eyes are forced open – then you have to see. Someone up there must have been laughing at me – known what I was about to see. Was forced to see. Looking down at me. Pointing a finger. Laughing. 'You think it's all worked out, don't you, Lily? How could you be so stupid?' How *could* I have been so stupid, Amy? We were all so stupid – all of us.

'Sadie, is that you?'

> Shit! I thought I'd have the place to myself – I'm not up for conversation.

Jackie, one of the girls Sadie shares her house with, hears her key in the lock. The weekend has been quiet after her trip to Lawrie Street. She didn't really expect to hear anything so quickly but she is still disappointed that she hasn't – even though it is only Tuesday. And she is beginning to think that Richard was right – that she was wasting her time when she has her paper to think about. It is two weeks since Lily left for Toronto and two days since her last conversation with her mother. Tonight, Sadie is tired. Tonight, she knows that she can't put it off any longer, what it is she has to do. And she has to do it before she can see Richard again.

'Yes, it's me,' Sadie calls back. 'Be with you in a minute.'

There are three of them in the house. Jackie and Maria are graduate students, both in science. Maria is older – from Spain where she has left behind her family and her fiancé to come and study in this tiny frozen little place by the sea. Jackie is younger – she is a local girl who is too old to live with her parents any more but has not found the confidence to leave the town she has outgrown. So Maria is biding her time until she goes home; Jackie is biding her time until she can leave it. The tension between them sometimes flares up in petty rows about toilet rolls and cleaning duties but, generally, they are good friends and the house has a harmonious atmosphere.

Jackie is coming out of the kitchen just as Sadie steps into the tiny, lilac-wallpapered hall and, before she can escape upstairs to her bedroom, Jackie has demanded that Sadie listen to her suggestion and, because it is a convivial one and she means well, Sadie is not rude to her – she does not insist on her time alone even though it is a Tuesday night and she is tired and she has 'things to do'. She smiles and takes off her coat and follows Jackie into the living room.

The house they rent together is a modern one on a new estate, just on the edge of the town, so all the rooms are small and the ceilings are low. The wallpaper is pastel coloured with the same lilac shade throughout the house and a floral border running across all the walls. The artificial carpet has shiny tight curls in violet, its colour the colour of a flower and thereby serving only to emphasise its distance from anything natural. The furniture is cheap and plastic – the beige chairs in the long, narrow kitchen – or cheap and velour – the blue-and-lilac three-piece suite in the main room, which also has a television set and a coffee table. It is an utterly cheerless house without any pretence to character or quirkiness – in fact, quirkiness has been excised so thoroughly from the house's straight lines and mean proportions that Sadie has trouble recalling how the house actually looks every time she leaves it and, every night when she returns to it, she experiences the same tiny shock of recognising something she daily finds impossible to recall.

'Well, we're all going to the Masthead later and you really have to come,' Jackie continues as Sadie sits down on the sofa and begins to pull off her black leather boots. 'There's a big crowd of us girls from the lab going – you have to come along too.'

Jackie's dyed blonde hair hangs limply on either side of sharp cheekbones and her buck teeth protrude slightly as she forces Sadie to agree to something that is the last thing she wants. She only wants some time alone so that she can do what she has to do and then she will have a large glass of wine. She does not want to be with a big crowd in a noisy pub. It is the last place she wants to be.

'Maybe,' Sadie surrenders and then she stands up in her stockinged feet and heads for the living-room door. 'I've got a really horrible headache – it's been a busy day. And I might be seeing Richard – I'm not sure.'

'All the more reason to come out with us,' Jackie shouts over her shoulder as she returns to the kitchen. Sadie hears a plastic carton being stabbed at with a fork and the microwave door ping open – Jackie's dinner. Sadie hasn't thought about dinner. She doesn't think there is any food in the kitchen for her. She will have to order in or go and get some. But the thought of feeding her body right now, when it is doing what it is doing, does not appeal to her.

She heads upstairs and opens the door of her room. Sadie has the smallest bedroom in the house – and it is also the cheapest one. There is just enough room for a short single bed, complete with pale pink duvet patterned with an impressionist darker pink, and a single chest of drawers. It is a child's room that is empty of childish things. The owner of this house had a child and Sadie thinks that this pink room must have been the girl child's room. She has found that she has to hang any clothes that she cannot fold up on the hook at the back of the door. And she has to pile sweaters that she cannot fit into the chest of drawers on top because there is no wardrobe – children don't need wardrobes. Sadie has no pictures or ornaments of any kind in her room – nothing to change the bleak pinkness of this girl child's room – and, anyway, Sadie doesn't like excess. So, for all its drab air and its childishness, the room suits her in a way. It is clean, it is tidy and it isn't threatening in any way. It lets her come and go as she pleases without demanding very much of her – just a little tidiness, that is all. It does not lure her in with a warm glow and a soft carpet, silently chiding her every time she leaves because she has somewhere better to go. It is a room without those kinds of feelings – because it is a girl child's room.

But, tonight, Sadie wishes that it wasn't because that is the last thing she wants. She doesn't want to be in this relic of a child's room. She has grown-up things to do. And now it is time. So she sits on the edge of the narrow bed in the gloom of a single tiny lamp, lifts up her briefcase and takes out the long cardboard box that she has been transferring from briefcase to desk drawer and back again for so many days. She cannot postpone this moment any longer – she knows that. So she opens the box at one end and takes out first the long plastic package and then the printed leaflet. 'Pregnancy Test. Accurate. Simple. Fast. Please read this leaflet carefully before beginning your test.'

'Sadie, come and see this – it's hilarious!' Jackie calls to her from the sitting room downstairs where the TV is playing loudly.

'Just a minute!' Sadie calls back but she hears the front door open downstairs and Maria coming in. A diversion for Jackie – Sadie will no longer be the focus of her attention. But it is better to be sure so she gets up from the bed and opens the door.

'I'm just going to have a quick bath!' Sadie calls out as she slips across the hall with her package and a towel and closes the bathroom door behind her. She pauses for a moment in the bright, white bathroom with its net curtains and flowery towels and matching bathmat. But the objections she is waiting for do not come and so she sits down on the lid of the white plastic toilet seat and looks again at the instructions on the leaflet. 'With the tip pointing downwards, hold the absorbent sampler in your urine stream for 5 seconds only. It is important not to exceed 5 seconds.'

The possible result is temporarily forgotten as Sadie struggles to understand how she should time five seconds exactly. Will it matter if it's six seconds? What if she only makes it for three or what if she misjudges and makes it six or seven? How can she tell precisely without a watch with a second hand, which she does not have? This detail makes her want to forget it all – it makes her want to push the plastic tube with its two clear windows back inside its packaging. Forget all about it, have a bath, go to the Masthead, meet Richard. The test is impossible – it is asking her to meet conditions that are impossible.

'This pregnancy test is a simple and easy to use home pregnancy test that will give you a clear, accurate result in only 1 minute. You can use the test at any time of the day from the day that your period is due. When you are ready to begin testing, remove the test stick from the foil wrapper and take off the cap.' How positive the words are! It is asking for impossible conditions but in such positive language that it almost sways her, it almost makes Sadie think that it is on her side. 'Simple', 'easy', 'clear', 'accurate', 'only'. 'When you are ready to begin testing . . .' As though it is an experiment – some scientific thing that has nothing to do with her, nothing to do with her life, so why should she bother with it? It is almost urging her to throw it away, it is almost telling her that this is unnecessary – look, it says, how impossible this is! I am asking for five seconds precisely. How can you do that, Sadie? I am 'simple' and 'easy' and 'clear' and 'accurate'. How can you need to do anything? Throw me away, forget about me, get on with your life, Sadie. You have far more important things to think about than me.

'Remove the sampler from the urine stream and keep the test pointing downwards for a few seconds. Replace the cap if you wish.' But, no, she shouldn't listen to it. Sadie knows she has to do this. She has been prevaricating for too long. It is only a test and she is good at tests – she has always been good at tests. She hasn't failed a single test in her life and she is not going to fail this one.

'A blue line should appear in the oval window. This indicates that the test is complete and has worked correctly. If there is a blue cross in the square window, you are pregnant. If there is a blue line in the square window, you are not pregnant. Discard the test after 10 minutes.' Lines and crosses. Oval windows. Square windows. Arched windows. What's through the window today? *Play School*. The oval window. The round window. Sadie always liked the round window best when she watched *Play School*, when she was little, so it does not surprise her that it is the square window which will give her the answer. The square window was always the mean window – she never liked the square window.

Sadie sighs suddenly – it escapes from her as she lifts the lid and sits back down on the white plastic toilet seat. She can have only five seconds, no more. She will try but she doesn't think she can manage. She should have had a drink of water first but it clearly says, 'Excessive fluid intake immediately before testing may dilute the pregnancy hormone.' So she will not have any water and then suddenly, after a moment or two, she is all right and she has to pull the plastic stick away quickly as she fears that more than five seconds have passed and then the test will not work. Sadie wonders how long she will have to wait but she wonders only for a brief moment as the window reveals itself faster than she expected it to. A dark grey curtain is pulled past across the dusty little square window first and there it is – before it even has a chance to show a line in the oval window to let her know that the test has worked, there it is.

> Shit, shit, shit, shit, shit, shit.

A blue cross in the square window.

The test has worked.

It tells Sadie that she is pregnant.

'This test has been shown to be more than 99% accurate in clinical trials which makes it as accurate as a doctor's test.' Sadie stares at the square window. The leaflet warns her that, in some squares, the cross can be faint but her cross is very clear. There is no doubt about it. She thinks that maybe she has it the wrong way round and she reads the instructions again, just in case the cross in the square window means that she is not pregnant. She cannot believe that all those positive words, all the 'clear' and 'accurate' and 'simple' and 'easy' and 'only' words, can have meant this.

She turns the leaflet over, looking for more words – judgemental words, condemning words.

> Where are the sentences that read, 'You stupid fucking idiot – you're pregnant. What the hell's Richard going to say? You've only known him for a few weeks.'?

A laugh escapes from her as she thinks this. Where are those words, 'stupid' and 'careless' and 'mistake' and 'no'? Sadie can't see them. But the leaflet doesn't have to say them – the blue cross says enough.

> Right. OK, then. Well, that's shit – it's shit! Stop. Don't cry. Don't panic. Breathe. Take a deep breath . . . and again . . . and another one . . . just like that, in and out, in and out . . .

Sadie gets up from the toilet seat and goes over to the bath. When she reaches out to turn on the taps she is surprised to find that her hands are shaking. The hot water shoots out straightaway, scalding her fingers and she snatches them back, collapses on the white flowery bathmat beside the bath. She sits on the mat, rests her head against the side of the bath and watches the steam gather on the white floral tiles.

> It doesn't matter – forget about it. Another test. It doesn't matter. Doctor . . . blood test . . . It doesn't matter. Tell Richard – no, don't tell Richard. It doesn't matter.

She unbuttons her black shirt and unzips her black trousers and leaves them in a pile beside the bath – socks, bra, pants, all just in a heap. The bath water is too hot but she doesn't feel it as she steps into the bath and lies down and lets the heat turn her pale body pink. Sadie is not someone who has ever spent much time thinking about her body. She cares about her appearance, yes – she has cared about that for a long time now – but, as she looks down at the pinking skin of her legs and arms, the tips of her breasts just above the water, the pink of her stomach, her thighs, her hands, she realises that she has never really thought about her body. Not really thought about it. Words, not bodies, are what have always interested Sadie.

She has never thought about what her body was for, what it might do for her one day. She has accepted it as long as it worked, as long as it did what she told it to do. She never thought much about its cells, its tissue, its muscles, its nerves. If someone asked her to point out where her ovaries were on a drawing of the female body, she'd have a hard time getting it right. The reproductive aspects of her body, what makes her body female, Sadie has never given more than a moment's thought to until now, when they have let her down. Hormones. Ovaries. Womb. Fallopian tubes. Uterus. Fertility. Pregnant. Words, not bodies.

And, as she lies there, in the hot unscented water that will slowly cool, it comes to her that she only needs to know the words. She does not need to know the body after all. The body is a tool. The body is a device. The body is a prison, a trap, a confining, defining space. The body is something to view or not to view. It is something to use or not to use. It is something to know or not to know. She has a choice. Lying there pinking in the hot water, she either needs or does not need knowledge of this body. If a part of the body has let a person down, then the best thing a person can do is to ignore the body. The best thing a person can do is not to give the body the attention it is obviously craving. A person must not let the body divert him or her from words, from research, from important projects. The body can set a trap for an unwise person and it is only unwise people who fall into such traps. A person should, therefore, not fret about the future. A person should not fret about blue squares and what they mean. A person should not fret about any of these things because the body does not matter. A person should say nothing to anyone at all because there is nothing for anyone to know. The reproductive function of the body does not matter. It is not the kind of future a person wants. A person does not want a future controlled by the body, by mere biology. And so a person should ignore the body. That will be best. A person does not want a future of bodies. A person wants a future of words. Words, not bodies.

Jackie bangs on the bathroom door. 'Hurry up! I need to get ready too. We're off in half an hour – you'd better be coming!'

Sadie splashes the water as she starts to sit up. 'I'll only be a minute. Wait for me – I think I'll come after all. I won't be long.'

'What about the lovely Richard?' Jackie teases her, calling from her room.

'Oh, I'll leave him till tomorrow.'

'Girls' night, then?' Jackie calls through the door again.

Sadie gets out of the bath, starts to towel herself dry. She picks up her clothes, the leaflet and the plastic tube, wraps the damp towel around her body and opens the bathroom door to find Jackie standing there. Sadie smiles at her. 'Girls' night,' she says.

'Great. Maria, get a move on!'

Jackie closes the bathroom door and Sadie heads back to her room to get dressed. She throws the plastic tube and the leaflet into the little wicker waste paper bin beside her bed. She will go out tonight to the Masthead. It will be a girls' night.

PART TWO

1950–1953

Lily knows what it means to see red and she doesn't like it very much. Mammy says it when Granny comes. 'That woman – she makes me see red, so she does.' Mammy gets angry when she sees red. When Granny says something like 'This isn't the tea I'm used to!' or complains about what Lily is doing or what she's wearing, Mammy doesn't smile the way she does when other visitors come. That's because Granny makes her see red and seeing red is a bad thing.

Lily wonders about this because she can see red now too. She is peeking through a torn hole in the curtain and she can see red. It's a faded red but it's still red and Lily wants to giggle because she knows it's not what Mammy means when Mammy says she can see red and she thinks that's funny. But Mammy doesn't think it's funny when she sees red so Lily tries to frown the way that Mammy does when she sees red. She presses her lips together and scowls at the brown curtain hanging in front of her face. But then the red that she can see moves a bit and so she stops frowning and leans in closer to the hole. The red she can see is a real red – not like Mammy's red – and Lily knows that isn't real in the same way. This red is a real red wool dress, with bends and twists in it every time it moves.

Lily's not supposed to be here. Mammy would see red if she knew she was here. Lily wants to giggle again now because it sounds silly, seeing red the way she can when it's not what Mammy means. Lily doesn't really know why one red is more real than the other – she just knows that it is. The red dress she can see, through the hole in the curtain, is real and the red that Mammy sees when Granny comes isn't. Then she wonders if maybe Mammy gets so angry that her eyes go red inside and that's what she means so it is a real red then and Lily closes her eyes tightly and rubs them with her fingers so she can see it too. But all she can see is darkness and some funny shapes and it starts to hurt so she stops.

Lily knows she can't make any sounds at all because, if she does, she'll get caught and she's not supposed to be here. This is Mammy and Pappy's bed she's sitting on and she and Amy and Mary all know that no one's allowed in the recess but Mammy and Pappy. Mammy's left things at the end of the bed that Lily knows she's not supposed to see but they're out on the line all the time or up on the pulley so she can't see why it matters if she sees them or not. There's a pair of brown stockings with a bit of darning at the toe and a big white stiff thing with hard bends in it that she knows is called a girdle. Lily likes the word girdle. It makes her think of cakes and running fast – milk that curdles and carts that hurtle – and now she's forgotten that she's not supposed to be here, on the bed in the recess behind the curtain, because she wants more words that rhyme with girdle, only she has been through the alphabet twice in her head now and she can't think of any more.

Amy and Mary are outside – that's where Lily should be too. Pappy told them to go out and play because he had things to do but she sneaked off when Amy and Mary ran out the front door and down the stairs. Pappy wouldn't be about. She knew that because, when he had 'things to do', they were never things that he had to do in the house. They were always things he had to do somewhere else and they sometimes made Mammy see red as well. Mammy wasn't back from the shops yet so she knew the recess would be quiet and she could sit on Mammy and Pappy's bed and look at the picture.

Lily likes looking at the picture that sits there on the shelf above the wooden headboard. She turns her head away from the hole in the curtain to look at it again. Mammy and Pappy were sent it last year when Auntie Jean moved to Canada. It's a black and white picture of a house standing on its own – a big square one with two windows either side of a big front door, just like the ones she draws at school. There's nothing beside the house except for lots of dirt on the ground and a fence at the back and, in the far-right hand corner, she can just see the edge of another house, running white down one side. Auntie Jean and Uncle Bill are standing at the front door of the house. Auntie Jean is Mammy's sister but she doesn't look like her – Auntie Jean has yellow hair and Mammy's is dark. Auntie Jean's hair is flying away from her in the wind. She is wearing a pair of trousers – something that Lily has never seen Mammy wearing – and she is smiling. Uncle Bill has his arm round her shoulder and he is smiling too. Lily thinks they must be smiling because they live in a house that doesn't have any neighbours – and because they have no closes and no creepy dunnies. That's what Mammy said. She said they just had lots of space of their own and that Auntie Jean's two, Alice and Iris, each had their own rooms. Lily and Amy and Mary would have a room of their own and have a bed each too, instead of having to share one big bed between them, Mammy said. That's what they'd have if they went where Auntie Jean is. 'Jean's always been the smart one.' And Pappy smiles when Mammy says that but he doesn't say anything. If Mammy thinks that Canada is such a grand place, then it must be and so Lily thinks Canada is be a grand place too.

Her leg is getting a bit sore now and Lily wants to move it but it's bent up under her other leg and the big bed will squeak if she moves and then they'll know she's here. She squints at the curtain again and wishes that Mammy washed it more often because it smells so much. She can smell dinner from last night and porridge from this morning – all mince and oats. It's a smell she doesn't like – it stops her feeling hungry even when she hasn't had anything to eat for ages. She sticks out her tongue to touch the curtain just for a minute, to see if it tastes as bad as it smells. Mammy cut a piece out of it for Mary when she was a baby for her to suck on and Mary carried it about with her all the time and would never let Mammy wash it. It smelt horrible too and just thinking of it now makes Lily whip her tongue back in again. The curtain tastes sharp and salty – even worse than old mince and oats.

The red wool dress moves again and Lily stops thinking of words that rhyme and curtains that smell. She closes one eye and opens the other wider to peer through the hole in the curtain a bit more. She knows who is wearing the red dress. It is Mrs MacIver who lives across the close. Mrs MacIver is standing in front of the fireplace in her red dress. Lily can just see her top half and Mrs MacIver's dark hair. It is curled at the sides and pinned back and it looks greasy which is not like Mrs MacIver, who always looks so smart when she comes over to visit. Mrs MacIver isn't wearing lipstick like she usually does and her face is red too, almost as red as her dress. Lily thinks that must be because she is standing in front of the fireplace and she is too warm. It is springtime and the days are bright but it can be cold – sometimes as cold as winter – and so Mammy still makes sure there is a fire even if, like today, it is almost dying out. The fireplace is where Lily and Amy were last night, when Mammy was rubbing their knees with a cloth because they were dirty. The fire was jumping and cracking – that's another red she could see so it must have been angry too. 'That's the Germans,' Mammy always says when the fire makes that noise and Lily and Amy giggle even if they're a bit scared of the fire and the Germans who would get them in their beds at night – well, that's what Mammy has told them.

Lily has a dim memory of ages ago when some boys from another street made a big dummy out of old clothing and stuffed it and hung it from a lamp post with a big noose around its neck. Mammy had told Lily that it was Hitler and the boys were celebrating because the war was over. But even though the war was over ages ago, Lily still wonders if the Germans can get her when the fire is angry and cracking.

The fire is almost out now and Mrs MacIver is standing in front of the fireplace and Lily knows Mrs MacIver almost as well as she knows Mammy because Mrs MacIver comes in every day. Mrs MacIver gives Lily sweets all the time now. She couldn't give her any before, she says, because of the war. That was to do with the Germans too. Because of them, they didn't have any sweets. Sometimes Mrs MacIver gives sweets to Amy or Mary if Lily's not there but Mammy says that's not the real reason Mrs MacIver gives them sweets. Mrs MacIver gives them sweets, Mammy says, because she doesn't have any wee girls of her own. Lily likes Mrs MacIver for having no wee girls of her own to give sweets to. It's why she always smiles at Mrs MacIver and pretends to herself sometimes that she is Mrs MacIver's wee girl instead. But she doesn't do that very much in case Mammy can tell and she gets angry. Maybe that's why Mrs MacIver comes in every day – because Lily's really her wee girl and Mrs MacIver wants to see her.

But Mrs MacIver's already been here today, just for a bit this morning, talking to Mammy before she went for the messages. So Lily doesn't see why Mrs MacIver's come in again. And on a Saturday – because Mr MacIver is at home on a Saturday. Lily doesn't like Mr MacIver and, when she thinks of him, she gets the same feeling she gets when she has to do something she doesn't like, like run through the dunny by herself. Lily wonders if Mrs MacIver likes him. He is very big and fat and his red face is always wet and he calls Mrs MacIver 'woman' in a way that sounds as if he is seeing red, just like Mammy does when she's talking about Granny so it's not just because of Mrs MacIver's dress. Pappy never calls Mammy 'woman' except when he's laughing and so is Mammy and everyone knows he's joking. But Mr MacIver is never laughing when he says it so Lily can only think he doesn't mean it as a joke and she doesn't think that's very nice for Mrs MacIver. She wouldn't like to be married to Mr MacIver and she doesn't understand why Mrs MacIver is married to him. Maybe her Mammy told her she had to and Lily wonders what she would do if Mammy told her to marry a man like Mr MacIver. Lily decides she would run away. If Mammy told her to marry a Mr MacIver, she would pack up some of her clothes and her dolls and some sweets and she would run away.

Maybe Mr MacIver isn't home today or maybe Mrs MacIver has sneaked out and he hasn't noticed and that's why Mrs MacIver is here. She must have sneaked out because Lily can hear Mrs MacIver sniffing now, just the way that Mary does when Amy's hidden the little doll that Mammy made for her out of old material of Pappy's. Mary isn't really crying, though, and Amy knows that but all the same, when Mary starts, Amy always has to go and get it from under the bed or from inside Pappy's shoe or wherever it is she's hidden it. That's just how Mrs MacIver is sniffing but Mrs MacIver hasn't lost her doll because she doesn't have any wee girls and only wee girls have dolls. Mrs MacIver is speaking very quietly now as if someone might hear her through the kitchen and even through the close into her own house. Where there isn't anybody to hear what Mrs MacIver's saying but maybe Mrs MacIver wants to whisper anyway, just in case.

Maybe Mrs MacIver wants to go to Canada like Auntie Jean and she can't because she's not smart enough and that's why she's crying just now in the kitchen. Lily can hear Mrs MacIver sniffing 'not right' and 'why' and 'would' and she can see her hands reaching across her chest, over the gold buttons that run down the front of the red dress that isn't as red as it used to be. It looks like a red that wouldn't be so bad if that was the red that Mammy saw when Granny came because it's so faded. A faded red might be a red that made Mammy smile even, instead of making her angry. Lily blinks and rubs her eyes. She can't hear any more what Mrs MacIver is saying but she knows it must be bad. She wishes she could get up and leave but there's no way out of the recess without being seen and then she would be in more trouble.

But then, suddenly, Lily notices there isn't any crying any more. There isn't even any sniffing. There's a softer sound, a gentle clicking noise. She recognises it. When Mammy puts them all to bed at night, her and Amy and Mary, that's the noise she makes when she kisses them all goodnight. Lily squints through the hole in the curtain again to see who is kissing Mrs MacIver and for some reason she thinks she knows what she will see even before she sees it. Someone is kissing Mrs MacIver and Mrs MacIver is kissing them back, gently at first then harder. Someone is stroking Mrs MacIver's hair, then pulling on it and Mrs MacIver reaches up to touch an arm, an arm in dark blue wool, a dark blue wool cardigan that Lily saw Mammy putting on this morning.

Canada is a place across the ocean. Canada is a place across the ocean with Red Indians. Canada is a place across the ocean with Red Indians who kill bears and men with their bows and arrows. Canada is a place across the ocean where Mammy wants to go even if it does have Red Indians – although Mammy has told Lily that that isn't true. It was Davey across the road who told Lily about the Red Indians – Davey with the callipers. He showed her the Red Indians in his comic so it must be true. Canada is a place across the ocean with Red Indians who have dark, angry faces and wear bright feathers in their hair. That's just nonsense Mammy said when Lily asked her about the Red Indians and Pappy laughed. 'I'm no' living in a wigwam – not on your life!' he said. Canada is a place across the ocean that Auntie Jean went to. Canada is a place across the ocean that Auntie Jean went to because it has lots of 'opportunities'. That's what Mammy said before Lily was sent out with Amy and Mary because Mammy and Pappy wanted to talk and they would just be in the way.

Lily thinks about 'opportunities' when they go down the stairs together. Mary and Amy push each other to see who's going first through the dunny. Lily thinks about 'opportunities' because it's another one of those words that she has to ask about. There are so many words she has to ask about. There are words she hears at home, there are words she hears at school. There are even words that she hears on a Sunday when she goes to the Band of Hope at the church and they show slides of angels and sing hymns and talk about 'testaments'. Lily doesn't know what 'testaments' are. She doesn't know if Jerusalem is a place across the ocean, just like Canada, and if she would have to sail to get there. She would like to ask about 'opportunities' and 'testaments' and the ocean but her Sunday School teacher, Mrs Morrison, doesn't like her to ask questions. She gave Lily into trouble for asking questions one day. 'Wee girls aren't supposed to ask so many questions,' Mrs Morrison said. One time, when Lily did ask a question, Mrs Morrison said she was cheeky and pulled at her hand and smacked it with a ruler. It wasn't very sore but it made Lily want to cry anyway because she'd done something bad. Mammy's always telling her she's not a bad girl – she's a good girl – so she couldn't see why Mrs Morrison would say she was. She doesn't know who's right – Mammy or Mrs Morrison – but she thinks it must be Mammy because Pappy says that Mammies are always right – except today or when Mammy mentions Canada. That's when Pappy says over and over again, 'You know I'm right, you know I'm right.'

Pappy wants to move to a new house but it's not in Canada across the ocean. The house that Pappy wants them to move to is in the country. This house in the country that isn't in Canada has two bedrooms and a living room. Lily doesn't know what a living room is so she asks and Mammy says it's where you sit with your visitors. Lily thinks that must mean it's for Mrs MacIver, then, when she visits, or for Granny, when she visits. Lily doesn't want to move to the new house where Mrs MacIver and Granny will visit and have a room to themselves. If they go to Canada, they won't have any visitors because they will be too far away for Mrs

MacIver and Granny to visit. Pappy doesn't see why they have to go to Canada when they can move to this new house but Mammy still wants to go. She says she wants to do what Auntie Jean did and go to Canada because Canada is a place with 'opportunities'.

They are out of the dark dunny and across the backcourt which is bright with sunshine. The buildings are black beside them and they throw shadows on to the stones. Lily looks down at the ground and tries to step on the shadow bits. It's the Easter holidays. They have all afternoon. Pappy has given her some money and Lily tells Amy and Mary they will go along to Mario's for ice cream first, then to Paddy Ower's park. Mary starts to jump up and down and shout about ice cream. Lily wonders if they have ice cream in Canada. She knows that it is cold in Canada sometimes because Auntie Jean has written and told Mammy about all the snow they get every year. So, if it is cold there, they must have ice cream. This makes Lily want to go to Canada even more.

'Ice cream, ice cream!' shouts Mary.

Lily takes her hand because they are out on the street now and she has to watch her on the street. Mammy says, 'Mary's only wee.' Lily is a good girl. She is a good big sister and good big sisters hold their wee sisters' hands – even if their hands are sticky and dirty. Lily, the good big sister, leads Mary and Amy along to the right and past five other closes to the end of Lawrie Street. The end of the street is a cul-de-sac. Lily and Amy and Mary know all their neighbours on their own side of the street but they don't know the ones across from them on the other side – except for Davey, the boy with callipers. Lily knows what callipers are because Mammy told her she was lucky not to have to wear callipers and that she must always be nice to Davey because of his callipers. When she and Amy went to his birthday party last year, Lily asked Davey about his callipers. Lily asked if they were heavy and that was why he walked so badly. But Davey said no, they helped him to walk. Lily didn't believe him. Lily didn't believe the callipers helped him and she was going to tell him to take his callipers off.

But then his pappy came in with a special camera. He closed the curtains even though it was daytime and made the room dark. Lily and Amy were excited. It was like being at the Kinema on Saturday mornings. Davey's pappy showed black-and-white Mickey Mouse films that flickered on the wall. Amy loved it and pestered Pappy for weeks afterwards for a special camera that showed Mickey Mouse films but Pappy just laughed as usual. 'I'm no' made o' money.' Lily thinks now in the street that, if they went to Canada, then maybe Amy could get a special camera. Maybe that's what Mammy means when she talks about 'opportunities'. Amy would have a special camera that showed Mickey Mouse films and Lily would like a brand-new doll's house – if that's what 'opportunities' mean. She asked for one last Christmas but Santa brought her a little set of saucepans and a bright red iron instead. She liked the saucepans and iron but they weren't what she asked for.

Lily and Amy and Mary climb up the steps at the end of the street and the steps take them up on to another street. It rained last night but the sun is so warm that the ground is almost dry. Bits of moss grow on the walls of the tenements and along the ground, where dandelions flower. Someone has drawn a line of chalk along the wall, just about Lily's shoulder and she wonders if this was to see how tall someone is, just the way Pappy marks how tall she is or Amy or Mary, with chalk on the wall where their heads stop. But it is hard to wonder for very long because the street is so noisy, with people tooting and shouting and tram bells ringing. This is the busiest street Lily knows. There are always cars and trams and buses on this street. It is the only street that leads to the park, which is on the right, and to the school and the church and the big railyard on the left so they have to go this way but Mammy always tells them they have to be careful.

Only Lily and Amy go to the school. Mary is too little for school. 'I want her to start school in Canada,' Lily heard Mammy say to Pappy, just before they went out. She has to hold on to Mary's hand tight now that they're up on the busy road because Mary's only wee. Because she's only wee, she might get knocked down by a tram if Lily lets go of her. Mary's hand is sticky because she never washes her hands even though Lily does, all the time. Lily likes washing her hands because Granny gave her special soap at Christmas. Amy is asking for a comic instead of ice cream but Lily's in charge of the money and she tells her they'll only get what she says they can get.

Lily doesn't tell Amy or Mary about being in the recess the day before. She is a good girl and she doesn't tell. Good girls don't tell. So she doesn't tell Amy or Mary that she saw Mrs MacIver. Mary is too wee to tell, anyway. Lily doesn't tell Amy that she might not take any more sweets from Mrs MacIver the next time she comes. She doesn't tell Amy that she doesn't think she can be Mrs MacIver's wee girl after all. She doesn't tell Amy that she thinks Mrs MacIver must just say that. She doesn't tell Amy that she waited in the recess until there was no one there to see her and catch her or that she ran along through the lobby and locked herself in the toilet. She doesn't tell Amy that she pretended she'd been there all along or that she took one of Amy's dolls with her.

Amy wouldn't like that. She doesn't tell her that she sat and played on the cold floor of the toilet until Pappy knocked on the door and asked who was in there and if whoever it was was planning to stay in there all day. She doesn't tell Amy that, when she came out, that's where he thought she'd been all the time and so she didn't say anything about what she saw or about Mrs MacIver because she's a good girl and good girls don't tell. Then Mammy made them all jam sandwiches and scrubbed their knees by the fire in the kitchen as usual and they all listened to the radio. But Mammy didn't laugh at any of the jokes and she was cross with Pappy for laughing at them. So Lily didn't like to laugh at them either even though Amy and Mary did. When Lily and Amy and Mary were in bed later, Lily could hear Mammy and Pappy in the kitchen – 'I don't want to stay here', over and over again. And the sound of crying which she knew must be Mammy because pappies don't cry – not even when Pappy hurt his leg, when he got knocked down by a tram on his way home from work and he couldn't walk for weeks. Lily has never seen Pappy cry – not even when his own pappy died and that just left Granny.

But that was last night and today Mammy isn't crying. Today Mammy is very serious and, when she said Lily must take Amy and Mary out, Pappy looked up to heaven, which isn't a nice thing to do. Lily isn't sure why looking up to heaven isn't a nice thing to do but Pappy told her once that, when people look up to heaven and they're angry, it's not nice. So Pappy is angry and not being nice. But he still gave them some money and now they're sitting on a wall outside Mario's ice-cream shop in the sunshine, smelling the coffee smell that comes from his shop and eating big creamy ice creams. There has even been enough money left over to buy

Amy a comic from Mr Terence's newspaper shop next door and they read it – except Mary just pretends to read because she can't read yet because she's too wee. It's a scary comic. Amy likes scary comics best – ones with lots of zombies and ghosts. Amy likes the pictures mainly and doesn't read the words so Lily reads the words out loud and won't let Amy turn the pages until she's finished. Lily is good at reading. Amy isn't good at it at all and Mary can't do it yet – she's too wee. Being good at reading makes Lily feel grown up. She is like Mammy because Mammy is good at reading. But then Lily is suddenly not sure if she is like Mammy at all and, when Amy asks her if there will be comics in Canada, Lily says she isn't sure. So she tells Amy she should take some with her when they go, just in case.

Lily has black-brown hair and Amy has brown hair and Mary has black-brown hair too. Lily and Amy look more like sisters, though, than Lily and Mary or Amy and Mary. Everybody who knows them tells them that – even Mario in the ice-cream shop and Mr Terence in the newsagent's. Lily has red shoes on and Amy has red shoes on and Mary has red shoes as well and they are all wearing thick cardigans. Lily's was knitted for her by Mammy, Amy wears one that Lily used to have and Mary wears one that Amy used to have.

Then Lily looks up and sees Wilma McLaughlin coming towards them. Wilma has fair hair. She is wearing new shoes and she is wearing a dress but no cardigan. Her fair hair is curled like a grown-up's, like Mammy's, and isn't in ribbons like Lily's or Amy's or Mary's. That is because Wilma is much older than Lily and it's also why her shoes are new. She is not their sister and Lily is glad Wilma is not their sister. Lily watches Wilma coming towards them and remembers the last time she saw Wilma. Lily was outside in the backcourt just a few days ago. She had gone out to play with her dolls just before teatime even though it was getting dark and suddenly she saw Wilma outside, against the back wall, with Jimmy Leitch. Jimmy was pressed up against Wilma who didn't have new shoes on then and she was making a funny noise and Jimmy was moving up and down against her, groaning. Then old Mrs McKenna above opened up her window and threw water over them. 'Worse than animals ye are! Here – that'll sort ye!' Wilma didn't see Lily then. Lily ran away with her dolls so Wilma doesn't know that Lily saw. But Lily hasn't spoken to her since she saw and she thinks – like she does about Mrs MacIver – that, if she went to Canada, she wouldn't have to see Wilma again either.

'Can Ah hae some?' Wilma asks when she comes right up to them and points at their ice creams. Wilma is always asking for things even though she is older and has new shoes.

Lily and Amy and Mary each shake their heads. Mary shakes hers too much and her bit of ribbon comes out of one of her bunches and Lily jumps down from the wall and bends down to pick it up. Mary is never tidy – not like Lily and Amy – and that worries Lily because they are sisters and she wants them to be the same and not like Wilma. Wilma sits down where Lily was sitting and Lily scowls at her.

'Ah've goat an apple – Ah'll swap it fur yur ice cream,' Wilma says.

Lily shakes her head at the tiny, hard green pip in Wilma's hand. She knows it's from the apple tree behind the old bunkers where some of the boys from school play at being soldiers. Mammy has told them they can't eat those apples. Those apples are only for cooking. Amy says no to Wilma as well but Mary thinks about it. She likes apples – even hard, bitter little ones. Sometimes Lily and Amy give her the stumps of their apples to suck on when they're finished – that is how much Mary likes apples.

'Aw right.'

So Mary hands over her ice cream and Wilma hands over her apple. It's even got some brown bits on it but Mary won't care about those. Lily would care about them. Lily hates the brown bits. She bites them out with her teeth then spits them out on the ground if she finds any – but only when Mammy and Pappy aren't there to see her. She doesn't know why Mary likes them so much.

'We're gaun' away,' says Amy.

'Fur yur hoalidays?'

'No, furever.'

'Whaur to?

'Maybe the country, maybe Cannayda.'

'Whaur's Cannayda?'

'Over the sea.'

'Can Ah come wi' ye?'

'Ah'll have to ask but Ah don't think so. Ah think it's jist us.'

Wilma sits down on the wall beside Mary but Lily doesn't want Wilma to join them – not after what she saw Wilma and Jimmy doing in the backcourt. Lily puts her arm around Mary and tries to pull her away without Wilma noticing but Wilma does notice.

'Whi's up wi' ye?'

'Nuthin'. We've got tae go.'

'Whaur ye gaun'?'

'Paddy Ower's,' says Mary before Lily can think of something that Wilma wouldn't like so that she won't follow them. Lily doesn't want people to see her with Wilma. Lily knows Wilma is a bad girl. If people saw her with Wilma, they might think Lily is a bad girl too and maybe that Amy and Mary are bad as well. If people saw her with Wilma, they might think that Lily does what Wilma does. Even though it was only Lily and Mrs McKenna who saw her. And even though she doesn't think Mrs McKenna knew it was Wilma she was throwing water on. Mrs McKenna can't see that well. Mrs McKenna lives too high up to see. She was too high up to see who she was throwing water on.

But Wilma won't be put off. She trundles along behind Lily and Amy and Mary, once they've jumped off the wall. Wilma licks at Mary's ice cream as they go. Lily turns round but she doesn't like the way Wilma eats the ice cream. Wilma flicks at it with her tongue and giggles and squeals. Lily is annoyed at Wilma now and she frowns in the hot sun. Now she has to look away from Wilma. Lily knows she isn't being nice but it's hard not to show what she thinks of Wilma. Lily knows everybody knows what she thinks because her face turns red and then they can see what she thinks. So, if Lily thinks, 'Go away, Wilma – I don't like you', then Wilma will see it and know. So she turns her face, which is hot and red, away so that Wilma can't see what she thinks.

They leave the coffee-smelling ice-cream shop behind and go past the cobbler's shop where Mr Siskesky works. They must always be nice to Mr Siskesky because Mammy says that 'his people have suffered'. They walk past the newspaper shop too. The newspaper shop is where they buy bullseyes and dolly mixtures and mint sherbet and black-and-white striped balls and penny sherbet dabs and cinnamon sticks and liquorice root that turns their teeth yellow. Lily wonders if they will be able to buy these sweets in Canada across the ocean.

They carry on down the street and finish their ice creams. Lily is hot now – she wants to unbutton her cardigan but she doesn't. Instead, she watches Mary kick at the dust on the pavement and she tells her not to scuff her shoes. Wilma points at her new shoes that don't have dust on them. Lily doesn't like Wilma's new shoes either although Mary does. They are almost at Paddy Ower's park and Lily hopes that Wilma will change her mind about coming with them.

'You'll mess up your new shoes in the park,' Lily says.

'Nah, Ah willnae.'

'You will. It's mucky in the park.'

'No, it's no'.'

'Aye, it is. It's real mucky.'

'No, it's no. An' ma shoes'll be fine.'

Lily is about to say that Wilma will get into trouble from her Mammy if she gets her shoes dirty but she doesn't get the chance to because right then, when she is about to say it, Mary pulls at her hand and Amy says, 'Oooooooh.'

There is a big crowd of people cheering at the end of the street, just in front of the park, across from the railyard. Mary jumps up and down and Amy asks Lily what it's all about but Lily doesn't know. Wilma doesn't know either even though she is older. Lily wants to know why all these people are there but she has to be careful of Mary – she's only wee. She thinks maybe they should turn back. But Amy runs ahead and now Lily is running with Mary to catch her up, shouting out, 'Amy, Amy!' and Wilma is behind them.

The crowd bars the entrance to Paddy Ower's and it's moving towards Lily and Amy and Mary. As they get closer, all the people in the crowd are shouting and cheering. They are cheering at something that Lily is too small to see. She and Mary run faster along the street to where the crowd begins and they catch up with Amy at the edge of the crowd but Lily is still too small to see. She isn't scared any more. She wants to see what is happening. A big, red-faced woman with a bright headscarf turns to the man beside her and nudges him out of the way. 'Let the wee lassies through!'

There are more cheers and a huge grinding noise, louder than Lily has ever heard before. It sounds like a monster is caught. A monster is caught and wants to be set free. Lily knows all about monsters – she has read about them. But monsters aren't real – that's what Mammy told her when she was wee, when she couldn't get to sleep in case the monster got her. There can't be any monsters out here in street or people wouldn't be cheering.

And then the crowd laughs. Lily pushes through with Amy and Mary, past pockets and jackets and legs and big heavy boots that some men wear even in summer. And, when she comes to a gap in the jackets and legs and boots, she sees it. She sees the monster, she sees a great, enormous metal monster and the wagon pulling it is groaning with the weight of it.

'What is it, Lily? What is it?' Mary wants to know.

And Lily knows what it is. 'It's a train, Mary – it's a new train!'

It shines bright and green in the sunshine on top of the special wagon and the crowd roars again as it slowly rolls past on its way to the docks to be shipped across the sea.

'It's a new train and it's going to Canada, Mary!'

Lily wants to cheer with the men and women standing beside her and Mary jumps up and down as much as she can in the tiny space there is for her.

'It's going where we're going! That's where we're going!'

And Lily can see the giant locomotive being lowered down

on tracks in a new land across the ocean – a land of white houses and grass and opportunities across the ocean – just before it sets off on its way, far away. And she knows that, when she goes home, Mammy will have won and, just like the big train, they will be standing at the docks soon enough. They will be standing at the docks and they will be ready to leave forever.

There are so many words she hears in this new country – 'wait up' and 'darn' and 'gees' and 'cripes' and 'oh brother' and 'holy smoke'. She hears Edgar saying them all the time even though Mammy has told him to mind his language – 'No' in front of the girls, now.' But Lily likes hearing Edgar talk. She likes hearing how different his voice is, how smooth and gentle it is, even when he is cursing. And she knows that some of the new words she has heard are curses and she shouldn't know them but she still likes the sound of them and, at night in bed, she whispers to herself over and over again 'darn' and 'gees' and 'holy smoke'.

They are all living at the top of a big house in their new country. It is a great big house that is much bigger than their home in Lawrie Street but it is not just for them. They live at the top of it and they have to climb lots of stairs every day, much more than they used to. Because it is a bigger house, Mammy and Pappy now have a room of their own and don't have to sleep in a recess in the kitchen but Lily and Amy and Mary still have to share one big bed in a room together. The bed they share is bigger, though, and so is the room. They still have to eat and play in the kitchen because there isn't another room for them – there isn't a living room here for visitors. That's because of Edgar. When Edgar is asleep, he is in his own room in the attic, which Lily heard Mammy say should have been for the girls. But Edgar is their lodger, Pappy explained. Edgar wasn't living in the attic when they first came, two weeks ago. He didn't sleep in the attic – he slept in the room that is now Lily and Amy and Mary's room. Edgar was here when they arrived. Pappy was supposed to have found a house for them by the time they got here. That was why he came out to Canada before Mammy and Lily and Amy and Mary did. That was why he left them last year and Mammy slept in the recess all by herself. But, when they all got off the boat and when they saw Pappy on the docks, when they saw Pappy waving at them in a bright, patterned shirt they hadn't seen before, with a wide-brimmed hat on his head that they hadn't seen before either and he was smoking a big cigar and when he said he would take them to their new home and when he took them to their new home and they met Edgar, then Mammy stopped holding Pappy's hand and told him, 'It won't do, it won't do.' So they don't have their own new white house yet like Auntie Jean's but Pappy has promised Mammy that they will have one soon.

Lily lies on her and Mary's and Amy's bed in the dark, pushing Amy every so often. Mary wriggles in her sleep and it annoys Lily so she pushes her away too. It is very hot. The whole house is very hot and it is worse because they are near the top and heat rises to the top. Edgar explained this to her. Even the hottest day in Lawrie Street that she can ever remember was not as hot as this. Lily thinks about how much hotter it is in this new country and she thinks about how much brighter it is too – how much greener the grass is, how much bluer the sky, how much browner the ground. She thinks about how much bigger the trains are here – big and silver – and about how many cars there are – shiny and bright with curves and bends and in all sorts of colours.

She thinks too about the miles and miles of forests she saw when they sailed up the huge river when they came here – the huge river Mammy told Lily and Amy was called the St Lawrence. Mammy had to say it about three times because Amy kept forgetting its name because she was too excited to listen to Mammy. And Lily had stood on the deck of the boat and looked out for Red Indians in the forests. She looked for them all the way up to the docks and all the way on the big silver train from Quebec City to their new home in Toronto. All the way on the train, she watched for Red Indians. She wanted to ask Pappy about them – if he'd seen any – but he was asleep on the seat with Mammy beside him, their heads drooping against each other, holding hands. Pappy had taken off his hat and Lily could see a big streak of grey in his dark hair that she hadn't seen before.

But she never saw any Red Indians then and she hasn't seen any in their new home of Toronto either. Davey with the callipers would be sad to know there aren't any Red Indians in Canada after all. Davey had wanted to give Lily his silver pistol in case she should have to shoot any Red Indians. But, even though Lily had told him she wasn't scared of Red Indians and had given him his pistol back, she was scared of them when she stood on the deck of the boat and looked out for them. That's when Lily imagined the wild whoops and yells of the Red Indians on their horses and the bright feathers in the hair and the bloody scalpings they would all get if she, Lily with the silver pistol, didn't shoot at them first. And she had wished then that she had taken Davey's pistol after all.

But there weren't any Red Indians. In fact, there weren't many people about at all when they stopped at the docks or when they got on the train. Pappy said it was too early in the morning and people would be at work and that they would see plenty of people in the next few days but Lily has only been to the shops round the corner from their new home with Mammy and Amy and Mary since they came and she still hasn't seen lots of people.

Their house is like all the other houses. Lily saw that all the houses had things like big letter 'H's on their roofs and, when she asked Pappy what they were, Pappy said the big letter 'H's meant televisions. 'Every house has got one – even ours,' Pappy said and Lily and Amy and Mary had run up the flights of stairs, with Pappy shouting directions all the way, right to the top of the house to see if it was true – to see if the big letter 'H' on top of their house meant they had a television. And, when they got to the top of all the flights of stairs, sitting there, in the kitchen right where the radio used to be in their old home in Lawrie Street, was a television of their very own.

But Lily hasn't watched the television very much, even though she would like to watch it every day. Lily has been too busy helping Mammy wash everything they have brought with them and she and Mammy have been washing everything in their rooms as well. 'Has anything in this place ever seen a cloth? How could you men stand to live in this pig-sty?' Mammy said about twenty times. Lily is busy because she is a good girl and she is a big girl now too. She is not wee like Mary and she is bigger than Amy.

Amy and Mary were sick at first because they couldn't stop feeling they were rolling, even though they weren't on the boat any longer. Lily felt sick at first too but she didn't want to say so. Lily liked being on the ship and, even though she wanted to see their new house, she was sad to have to leave it. Lily liked the proper sit-up dinners they had every night at a big round table, with lots of round tables beside them where other mammies sat with their children and some tables had pappies too. She liked having to be smart and clean and wear her Sunday-best clothes just to have her dinner. And she liked working from the outside in with the knives and forks beside her plate – she had never had two knives and two forks before to eat her dinner with. And she liked the big icebergs she and Amy saw one day when they were walking on the deck and the way that the sun shone on them – it made her blink it was so bright.

But she didn't like it when a sailor, with marks on his skin and a red moustache, told her that the big icebergs could sink a whole ship – even one like this, even the SS *Atlantic*. 'Did no one ever tell you about the *Titanic*?' he asked. To Lily, the icebergs didn't look big enough for that and she didn't believe him and told him so but the sailor said that, underneath the water, the icebergs were even bigger – that the biggest, most dangerous part of them was hidden away. Lily didn't like the way the sailor had winked at her when he told her this and said, 'Wee lassies want to watch that.' The sailor didn't wink in the way that Pappy winked at her when he said something to annoy Mammy or to make her laugh. The sailor's wink was a funny sort of wink and Lily didn't like it. She didn't like it when he pinched her cheek either and bent down close to her and said very quietly, 'You're a bonny wee lassie – I bet you're a good girl.' Lily wished then as well that she had taken Davey's pistol after all. Then she could have shot at the sailor if he'd winked at her again. Even though she is a good girl and good girls don't shoot at people with pistols.

But she didn't have to shoot at him because, every time she saw him, she could hide. That was the best thing about the ship, she and Amy decided. There were loads of places to hide. When Lily and Amy played hide-and-seek – without Mary because she's too wee – they took ages. They hid inside the kitchens or under tables in the dining rooms or anywhere on deck, underneath tarpaulins and in between double steel doors and behind funnels. At first, it could take all day for them to find each other but, by the end, they knew each other's favourite hiding places too well for it to last all day.

Lily lies in bed where it's too hot and she wonders what Davey with the callipers is doing right now and she wonders about Wilma McLaughlin and Mrs MacIver and Granny, too. Wilma didn't ask to come with them after all but Lily heard Mrs MacIver talking to Mammy and Pappy one day. 'It's a great chance – I wish I was going too.' And she was glad that Mrs MacIver wasn't coming with them. Granny was too old to come with them, Mammy said. Lily doesn't really miss Wilma or Mrs MacIver or Granny, she thinks, as she pushes Mary away again and throws the sheet off her – it's too hot even for a sheet – but she does miss Davey, just a little bit. If she thinks about never seeing Davey again or never eating ice creams at Mario's or never saying hello to Mr Terence, then she thinks she might cry, just a little bit.

So because she doesn't want to cry – 'Good girls aren't crybabies,' Mammy told her when they got on board the big boat on the day they left – she thinks about tomorrow instead and about her new job. Edgar has got Lily a job in his friend's grocer's shop. She will start tomorrow morning. She will measure out things for customers. She will measure out flour and sugar and beans and all sorts of things for Edgar's friend's customers. Lily is very proud that she will have a job. She will only have a job on Saturdays and sometimes after school. But she thinks that it will not be long before it is the holidays and it will not be long before she can leave school forever and she can work in Edgar's friend's shop all the time. Then she will be like Mammy. She will be like Mammy because Mammy has a job now too. Two days a week, Mammy works all day in a butcher's shop round the corner from their house.

Last night she came in all red and laughing. Her eyes were all bright and her brown hair was shining. It was only her second day at the butcher's shop but she was laughing. Pappy had been at home with Lily and Amy and Mary because he wasn't well enough for work that day and they had made cakes in the garden out of dirt and leaves and flowers and grass.

Mammy came in just in time for dinner, bright and shining. 'You'll never believe this!' she said.

Pappy loved her being all bright and shining and he kissed her. Edgar was in the kitchen and he laughed too when Mammy told them about the customer who asked her for a whole chicken and for the nails to be trimmed off the chicken's feet. 'What does anybody want to trim a chicken's toenails for?'

Mammy laughed and Pappy laughed and Edgar laughed and Lily laughed too – although she didn't really know why.

Then the butcher told Mammy that the customer wanted to use the feet for stock and that's why she wanted the nails trimmed.

'That's no stock I'll be havin',' Pappy said and Edgar said something about 'immigrants and their ways not meaning you folks'.

Lily wanted to ask about immigrants and their ways but she was too busy imagining a big pot of soup bubbling on the stove with chicken feet sticking out of the top.

There is so much here that is new to Lily. As well as the

chicken feet and Edgar's cursing and the talk of immigrants that she doesn't understand, there was a hurricane. It happened on the second day after they arrived. Lily was coming back from the shops with Mammy and Amy and Mary and a lady with bright red hair came rushing out from the house two doors along from them, right out on to the street, yelling, 'You gotta all get inside! You gotta all get inside!' She shouted this at Mammy but Mammy couldn't understand what all the fuss was about and she didn't believe the red-haired woman when she said that a hurricane was on the way.

'It's no' even windy,' Mammy said, pulling Lily and Amy and Mary around her and looking funny at the red-haired woman. Lily knew Mammy didn't believe her but the red-haired woman kept on at them, even trying to push them along the road.

'I saw you yesterday. You've just arrived. You're from Scotland?'

Lily liked the way the red-haired woman spoke – she sounded just like Edgar. Lily was tempted to say 'cripes' or 'gees' but she knew Mammy would be angry if she used Edgar's bad words.

'There's a hurricane on the way – you gotta get inside!' The red-haired woman was flapping at them, pushing Mammy's back along the road to their house with the big oak tree in the garden – that's how Lily remembered which was their house in the first days, the big oak tree in the garden. Then, just as Mammy was about to say something to the woman, a great big raindrop appeared from nowhere and suddenly there were lots of raindrops, huge and warm – warm rain, raining down on them, soaking them all, and they ran shrieking into the house.

Lily was so excited. She watched out of the window up

high and shouted, 'Mammy! Mammy!' when she saw the next-door neighbours' rabbit hutch just lift up and disappear with the wind. 'It's just like in the *Wizard of Oz*!' Lily shouted to Mammy but then she wished she hadn't said that because Mary heard her and started to cry. Mary thought that the Wicked Witch of the West was coming to get them on her broomstick and that their house would spin up and round and round. Amy told her she would be all right, their house was much bigger and, anyway, Mary didn't have any ruby slippers. But Mary wouldn't stop crying. Mammy was all white-faced and worried every time the walls shook with the wind and she gave Lily and Amy and Mary some milk and the biscuits that Edgar calls cookies that she had just bought at the shops. But Lily wasn't scared of the Wicked Witch of the West and she wasn't scared of the hurricane. She got a chair and stood on it so she could see it all and that's when she saw their neighbours' rabbit hutch disappear altogether. Their neighbours weren't at home. Lily said to Mammy that maybe they should have taken the rabbit hutch in with them but Mammy said they weren't to know.

Mary was still crying even after the wind had stopped yelling at them all and stopped trying to make the house fly up into the sky. So Lily and Amy shared Mary's milk and cookies between them and Mammy made some more tea. Mammy made the tea and then Mammy got up on the chair Lily had used and reached up to the top of the big kitchen dresser and took down a clear bottle with dark liquid inside. Mammy unscrewed the clear bottle and poured some of the dark liquid into her cup of tea. Lily knew that was what Mammy sometimes liked to put in her tea but only mammies could have it – that's what Mammy had said when Lily had asked for some too once. Only mammies could have it – not even pappies – and she wasn't to tell Pappy. Lily was a good girl and good girls don't tell pappies what mammies have sometimes.

One day, back in Lawrie Street, when Mammy was next door at Mrs MacIver's, Lily had made Amy help her drag the stepladders out of the cupboard in the lobby. She stood on them to get the bottle from the top of the even bigger dresser they used to have there. Lily was scared of getting into trouble but she wanted to know what was in the bottle. She poured some of it into a cup and tasted it but it tasted horrible. Lily thought maybe it was better in tea, the way Mammy had it, but she couldn't lift the kettle off the stove. So then she tried mixing it with some milk. But, when she mixed it with milk, it was even worse. Lily decided it must be special medicine that Mammy took and that it was just for mammies after all and that she and Amy would have some when they were mammies too.

When Amy had a taste, she said, 'It tastes as bad as medicine but Mammy takes it every day – even when she's well.' So Lily and Amy couldn't decide what kind of medicine it might be.

They only just got the bottle back on the dresser and the ladders back in the lobby cupboard in time before Mammy came back. Mammy knew Lily and Amy had been doing something bad. Mammy could tell by the guilty look on Lily and Amy's faces. But they didn't tell her what it was. That wasn't good. Lily was a bad girl. She doesn't want to be bad girl again.

Lily is still awake even this late and even though the house is silent and even though Mary has stopped wriggling. She is still too excited about her new job at Edgar's friend's shop tomorrow. She will have 'soda pop', Edgar says, if she is a good girl and works hard. Lily knows she will be a good girl so she knows she will get to have some 'soda pop'. Mammy says she mustn't spend all her money on it, though. Mammy says she must save up what Edgar's friend pays her and then she can buy the new doll's house she wants. But Lily isn't sure she wants a new doll's house any more. Lily is thinking about saving for something else. Lily thinks she would like to save for a bicycle. She would like to save for a bright, shiny new bicycle all of her own that she can ride along their street and then along the new street when Pappy finds them their white house just like Auntie Jean's. She will buy the shiniest newest bicycle to ride past their white house just like Auntie Jean's and everyone in the street will say, 'Look, that's Lily. Isn't she lucky? Lily is so lucky to have such a bright, shiny new bicycle.' And she will be lucky – Lily will be the lucky one just like Pappy always says she is. And she will have lots of friends and she will come top in all her classes at school and she will have 'opportunities'. Because, now that she is here, now that she is living in this new country where they say 'darn' and 'gees' and 'cripes', she has learned what 'opportunities' are.

She asked Pappy about it when they arrived – on their first nigh when they had gone to bed after their dinner, which was food Lily hadn't seen before. They'd had cold pink meats and brown bread with seeds and nuts and juice that was fizzier and pinker than the juice they had at home – the 'soda pop' that Edgar said she can buy with her money from the grocer's. When Pappy came in to kiss them all goodnight, it was very late and they were all in bed and Amy and Mary were both fast asleep but Lily was still awake and she reached up and patted the grey streak in Pappy's hair and he smiled and told her how much he had missed his girls and that they were the most important things in the world to him and that he would never leave them behind again – not for anything.

And Lily asked if he wouldn't even have to leave them for the opportunities. And Pappy had had tears in his eyes and Lily thought that pappies couldn't cry and Pappy said, yes, he had to leave so they could have opportunities – so that his girls could have a good chance in life and not be like him or Mammy. And, when Lily asked if that's what opportunities meant and Pappy said, yes, it meant that they would all have nice homes when they grew up. And Lily asked if that meant even Mary – even though she's only wee – and did it mean they would all marry nice men – not like Mr MacIver. No, not like Mr MacIver, Pappy said. They'd never want for anything and that's what they'd do when they were all mammies too with wee girls of their own. And, as Pappy smoothed her hair back, Lily closed her eyes and tried to picture herself as old as Mammy with a house like Auntie Jean's and lots of wee girls beside her that looked just like Mary. And then she heard him sniffing and sniffing again and he whispered, 'Lily is the lucky one – Lily is my best girl,' so that Lily knew, before she fell fast asleep, that she was still a good girl. 'I missed you too, Pappy.'

Lily steps on 'June bugs' on her way to Mr Cohen the grocer's shop and the 'June bugs' crunch and crackle then splatter like broken eggs on the ground and that makes her squirm. She steps on 'June bugs' after she watches the iceman deliver the big block of ice that he hacks off with his ice pick for their icebox. Dripping water all the way, he carries the block of ice from his ice truck up the stairs and through to the kitchen but there is no other way to get it there. The iceman is an 'immigrant' but, although Lily knows what an 'immigrant' is now – an 'immigrant' is someone who leaves the country where they were born to live in another country, Pappy says, just like Mammy and Pappy and Lily and Amy and Mary – she knows that the iceman isn't a 'DP' and neither is she and nor is Amy or Mary or Mammy or Pappy. And she knows she wouldn't like to be a 'DP', which is what she sometimes hears children shouting, because 'DP' means 'Displaced Person', Pappy says, and that isn't the same as an 'immigrant' because a 'Displaced Person' has to leave the country they were born in and an 'immigrant' doesn't have to leave but wants to leave. And somehow having to leave is worse but Lily isn't sure why.

Sometimes children in the street shout 'DP' at the women who come into Mr Cohen the grocer's shop. Lily nearly always sees the same women every day and, when she was first there, they asked Mr Cohen who Lily was in a language Lily didn't understand and which Mr Cohen told her later was called Hebrew. And the women bought 'cantaloupe' and 'melon' and 'gefilte fish' and 'matzo balls' and 'holishkes' which were all things Lily hadn't heard of before either but now she has worked in Mr Cohen's shop three times and she knows what everything is, which makes her feel very good. And some of the women who come into Mr Cohen's shop have numbers on their arms but she has been too shy to ask them why. So she has waited to ask Mammy and Mammy says bad people did it to them. Lily wishes she'd asked Pappy instead but Pappy is out working and Mammy will have to do even if she is tired after being at the butcher's shop. Lily doesn't know what is bad about having a number on your arm and why bad people would be bad to do that and so she asks Mammy if she should ask Mr Cohen for a number too but Mammy smacks her hand when she says that. 'You're a bad girl to say that! Don't you ever say anything like that in Mr Cohen's shop.' So Lily is a bad girl even though she knows what everything in Mr Cohen's shop is. She wishes she'd waited till Pappy came home.

Lily is not in Mr Cohen's shop today but there are still 'June bugs' on the ground. Lily doesn't step on any on her way out of the house with Amy and Mary and Edgar. It is Sunday and the sun is hot and shining and Edgar is taking Lily and Amy and Mary out in his 'automobile' for 'milkshakes'.

Mammy and Pappy have had a big row. Mammy was shouting, 'Why did I ever marry you?' and crying at the same time. And Pappy was shouting back, 'Well, too late – you're stuck wi' me now!' Then Mammy picked up a jug from the dresser and threw it on the kitchen floor where it smashed and Pappy said, 'You're no' the only one who can break things!' and he picked up a teacup and threw it on the floor too and, although it was smaller, it made more noise because Pappy threw it so hard. Lily and Amy and Mary were all in the kitchen. They couldn't get out because Mammy and Pappy were in front of the door and Mary was crying.

'Look, you're upsetting the wee one,' Mammy said but Pappy picked up another cup and smashed that as well.

Then Edgar came to the door and said very quietly, 'Come on, girls. I'll take them out for a while.'

Lily and Amy and Mary and even Mammy have hardly seen Pappy all week. Edgar says it is because Pappy has two jobs. 'I'm working all the hours God sends. Isn't that enough?' he says. And Mammy is working too. 'Nothing's changed,' Mammy says back. 'It's still the same – what's it all been for?'

And, when they get into his blue 'automobile', Edgar tells Mary, who is scared and crying, that 'sometimes your maw and paw need to be by themselves.' Edgar says he is getting under Mammy's feet too but he says it with a big smile and doesn't look bothered about being under Mammy's feet so Lily is not scared and crying like Mary. And she is not scared and crying because she has never been inside an 'automobile' before and she lands on the slippery seat with a bump and laughs. But still she doesn't like it when Mammy and Pappy are shouting at each other and breaking things. Mammy and Pappy used to shout at each other when they lived in Lawrie Street and Lily thinks that maybe it is because they are moving again.

Lily and Amy and Mary sit on the back seat of Edgar's blue 'automobile', which doesn't have air conditioning, he says, because it is an old wreck but they wind the windows down and let their hair blow as Edgar drives them 'downtown' for 'milkshakes'. They haven't been 'downtown' yet and Lily can't imagine what that means. But soon they leave behind scraps of land and brown stony streets to travel along by the lake instead – the placid blue lake where Lily can see boats with sails – and then clean, grey pavements appear that Edgar calls 'sidewalks' and Lily peers out to look up at the tall glass buildings called 'skyscrapers'. They are in the heart of the city, Edgar tells them, and Lily is excited because they haven't been into town before. In her excitement at all the people she sees, hurrying along the streets even though it is a Sunday, Lily forgets about Mammy and Pappy having a row.

When, at last, they get to a bright pink shop Edgar calls a 'store', Edgar stops the car at the 'sidewalk' and lets them out of the back seat. Mary has stopped crying – she is excited too. They scamper into the pink store that has lots of tables and benches and a big silver counter. They sit down straightaway at one of the tables. Then a lady in a pink uniform comes over and Edgar orders a 'Canada Dry' for himself and strawberry milkshakes for Lily and Amy and Mary. While they wait for their pinky milkshakes to arrive, Edgar gives Mary some 'cents' to play music on the big colourful jukebox in the corner of the shop and Amy goes with her.

It is a special occasion because tomorrow Edgar is leaving the house and, the day after that, Lily and Amy and Mary and Mammy and Pappy are moving to their new home, which is only a block away, and, the week after that, it is Lily's birthday. Lily will be ten. And, even though the new house will not be a white house like Auntie Jean's, it will be their own house. There will be no stairs and Lily will have a room all of her own because Mammy said ten-year-old girls had to have their own rooms and Amy who is nine and Mary who is six will share one. And they will have a bathroom, with a proper bath so they don't have to wash in a basin in the sink any more.

Lily tells Edgar this while Amy and Mary choose some music but soon they are back, pushing each other and squirming on the bench beside Lily. But Lily doesn't pay any attention to them. Instead, she is watching Edgar now.

Edgar isn't telling Amy and Mary to stop squirming because he is too busy talking to a lady who has just come in to the store.

'Eddie, honey!'

To Lily, the lady looks like a lady from a film. She is a lady from a film who calls Edgar 'Eddie', which Lily hasn't heard before. Neither Mammy nor Pappy calls Edgar 'Eddie'. Lily decides it must be because the lady is a special lady from a film. She has very red lips and a pink short-sleeved top on and a big white skirt and white high-heeled shoes. She is carrying a pale pink bag and, when Edgar offers her a cigarette, she sits down beside him on the bench opposite Lily.

She gives Lily a wink and says, 'Hey, cutie!'

Mammy sometimes wears lipstick too. Lily used to watch her get dressed sometimes when she and Pappy went out to the Kinema or the Princes', back in Lawrie Street, but Mammy never wore lipstick as red as this and never during the day. The lady has her hair curled like Mammy's but it is shinier and tidier than Mammy's is. It doesn't look quite real to Lily.

Lily doesn't think she should be watching Edgar and the lady but she is too interested. All of a sudden, Edgar doesn't seem quite real either. He smiles very widely, showing all his teeth, and he keeps smoothing his hand over his brown slick-backed hair and touching his moustache which looks tidier today than it usually does. Edgar is looking the tidiest Lily has ever seen him. He has a brown short-sleeved shirt on that she has never seen and he wears brown-and-cream checked trousers called 'pants'. Lily and Amy and Mary didn't believe Edgar when he first told them trousers were called 'pants' and, even now, they still giggle at the thought of grown men walking about in their underwear. But Edgar thinks he is in a film too, Lily decides, and that is why he is behaving in this way that isn't quite real. He is playing the hero – he is like Errol Flynn in *Robin Hood*. He smiles the way that Errol Flynn smiles at Maid Marian and he will rescue the lady if something bad happens to her.

But it doesn't look as if anything bad will happen to her. The lady is too happy. She is laughing at everything Edgar says, 'Eddie, honey, you just kill me!'

Lily watches the lady hit Edgar playfully on the arm, which Edgar seems to like because he blushes slightly when she does this. Lily tries to smile a big smile the way that the lady is doing and she tries to imagine saying to Edgar when they get back home, 'Eddie, honey . . .' But she can't imagine saying that to Edgar. She would only say that to Edgar if she wanted to marry him and she likes Edgar very much but she doesn't want to marry him.

But perhaps the lady wants to marry Edgar. Perhaps that is why she says, 'Eddie, honey . . .'

Edgar is offering to take the lady to see a film called *Rancho Notorious* on Monday night and Lily is surprised when the lady says, 'Why, Eddie, I believe that night I'm setting my hair.'

Lily knows what setting hair means because Mammy does it sometimes but she doesn't think Mammy would ever tell Pappy she couldn't go to the Kinema because of it. Lily is surprised because she thought the lady liked Edgar and she doesn't understand why she would rather set her hair than go to the pictures with him. But then the worry is over when the lady says, 'I'm free on Tuesday.' and Edgar says he would like to take her to the film then.

When the lady finally gets up and leaves, after giving Edgar a big red kiss on his cheek, which he has to wipe away, Lily asks Edgar if he is going to marry the lady. Edgar bursts out laughing. 'Hold on there, princess!' Edgar tells Lily that the lady's name is Cora and she is very nice but he 'ain't planning to marry anyone just yet'.

Lily asks if Cora is a film star like Judy Garland and Edgar bursts out laughing again. 'She wishes she was a film star!' he says.

Lily tells Edgar that her favourite film star is Judy Garland and Edgar says he likes her too. But Amy, who has stopped pushing Mary, hears this and she spoils it for Lily by saying, 'You said you liked Elizabeth Taylor best.'

Lily blushes but Edgar says, 'I wouldn't say no to Elizabeth Taylor myself!' And so Lily isn't worried that he will think she is silly.

Edgar doesn't want to talk about the lady any more because now he asks Lily how school was this week and even though Lily would like to know why Edgar isn't planning to marry anyone, not even the lady, she tells him about school. Lily and Amy have both been to the same school, even though there isn't long until the holidays begin. Lily wasn't scared, she tells Edgar, even though she was the only Scottish girl in her class. At lunchtime, the other children made her say the word 'girl' again and again until it didn't mean anything and they all tried to roll their Rs the way that she did. Lily is pleased that they couldn't do it as well as she did. Some of the other children can't speak to her at all and she can't speak to them because they don't speak the same language. The school is a much bigger one than the school they went to near Lawrie Street and Lily says she has never seen so many different-looking people before.

Edgar tells her some of the girls and boys in her class will be Chinese and some of them will be Japanese and some of them will be from Poland and some of them will be from Norway and some of them will be from Germany.

Lily tells him that her teacher is a very tall woman called Miss Draper and she is English. But Miss Draper told the class when Lily arrived that 'everybody is Canadian now'. Lily tells him that Miss Draper said they must all be 'good Canadians'. Lily wants to be a good Canadian and that is why, every night, she writes down, in a little notepad that Edgar has given her, the words she hears him using. Except for the cursing bad ones because Mammy would be angry if she wrote those down. And she writes down all the other new words she hears too. She writes everything down so that she can speak like a Canadian and be a good Canadian girl. Then she makes Amy and Mary say the words she has written down so that they can be good Canadian girls too.

Edgar says that is right – they will be good Canadians. And then he tells them to get ready because they have to go home. He finishes his Canada Dry and takes some money out of his pocket for the waitress and they all leave the store and get back into the automobile. As they sit in the back seat with the windows down, Lily shouts to Edgar she will be a film star one day just like his friend, Cora, and Edgar says, 'I don't doubt it for a minute, sweetheart.'

Lily knows that films aren't real but she wishes that they were. She wishes she lived in a film and that, right now, she was on her way back to the land of Oz or the jungle in the

Jungle Book or, best of all, to Sherwood Forest where Errol Flynn can rescue her from the Sheriff of Nottingham and she can wear a long dress with a veil just like Maid Marian. But she isn't going there now because that isn't real although she still thinks it must be real somewhere. Somewhere in the world, Errol Flynn is fighting the Sheriff's men and, if she knew where that was, then maybe she could live there. And sometimes that would be nicer than where she is living just now – not because she doesn't like living in Toronto and she wants to have her own room, very much, as Mammy has promised, but because she is on her way back to a house she won't be living in for very much longer where Mammy and Pappy have rows and where they break things and Lily hoped that wouldn't happen in Toronto the way it did in Lawrie Street.

Edgar drives back to the house a different way – not along the shore but through lots of little streets. He says he wants to show them more of Toronto and they drive past streets with magic lanterns hanging from the wires between the buildings, and funny-coloured houses in pink and blue and yellow and more schools and churches and shops. It takes them longer to get home and, by the time that they do, both Amy and Mary are asleep on the seat. Lily has to wake them up as they stop at the garden with the tree outside. But Mary won't wake up so Edgar has to lift her out and carry her, through the garden and in the front door and up all the flights of stairs. Lily and Amy look at each other as they climb the stairs but it is all very quiet and when they finally get in their own door they hear only quiet voices inside. Lily is holding Amy's hand and she gives it a little squeeze and smiles an it's-all-right smile at her. She is the good big sister and she will not tell and she will look after them all.

She will not tell but she will keep looking. When Pappy opens the door to let them in, Lily looks first at the kitchen floor for the broken things but they are not there any more.

'Did you have a nice time, girls?' Mammy asks. She is smiling although her eyes are red and she takes Mary from Edgar. She sits with her asleep in her lap and says, 'My poor wee sleepy baby.'

Edgar says they were good as gold and Amy starts to tell her about pinky milkshakes.

Pappy says, 'And how's my Lily?'

And Lily just smiles. She wants to tell him about Cora, the film star who Edgar will marry – she really does. That is much more interesting than milkshakes but she is a good girl and good girls don't tell so she says nothing. And then she asks if Pappy will take them to see *Rancho Notorious* too.

And Edgar bursts out laughing. 'That's my hot date gone!'

Mammy says she'd like to see it because she likes Marlene Dietrich but Pappy says, 'No, that's too old for wee girls.' But then he says he will take them to see *Singin' in the Rain* instead.

He asks if Lily has finished packing for their big move and, when she says no, he tells her to hurry up because they are having a special tea for Edgar before he leaves and there won't be much time for packing tomorrow, after she comes home from school.

Lily is a good girl. She takes Amy into their room and Amy immediately lies down on the bed and falls asleep. But Lily doesn't start to pack anything away. Instead, she takes her notebook and pen out from under her pillow then goes and sits down by the door and listens to the adults talking in the kitchen. She wants to hear more words that Edgar might use that Mammy wouldn't like. She writes down 'downtown' and 'milkshakes' and 'hot date'. One day she will put the words together and write a story about a girl called Lily who sailed across the ocean to live in another country with Errol Flynn in Sherwood Forest. It won't be real – it will only be a story and she knows that stories, like films, aren't real. But, somewhere in the things that she knows, there is a blurring so that handsome princes who wake sleeping princesses with a single kiss are not real but men with bows and arrows who fight in Sherwood Forest just might be. Some stories are more real than others and, if she was to write about a girl called Lily who sailed across the ocean to live in another country with Errol Flynn in Sherwood Forest, part of that would be real because it was true – she *is* Lily and she *did* sail across the ocean to another country. She just doesn't know about how real Errol Flynn is because she hasn't met him or been to Sherwood Forest. But she has seen him. She has seen him on the screen at the Kinema. She has seen him in a film.

So she understands that what she sees is sometimes real and is sometimes not so real. There are no smashed plates on the kitchen floor but she knows that Mammy and Pappy smashed them because she was there and she saw them. She could write a story about a girl called Lily who crossed an ocean to another country because she saw . . . because she saw something . . . because she saw something that might have been real . . . only the next day, when she looked for a sign of it, there was no sign anywhere. Just like the smashed cups, it had been swept up, out of sight, and now she still wonders about what she saw once and if she ever really saw it at all.

Lily stops at the candy store and buys a Tootsie Roll and some Lifesavers with the quarter Pappy has given her. Charlie is with her and he buys a Shopsy's hot dog. It is Saturday and it is very cold. There is snow on the ground. It has been snowing since long before Christmas. Lily has never seen so much snow before. Lily wears her new red earmuffs that Pappy gave her three days ago for Christmas to keep her ears warm and a red scarf round her neck – a new red scarf that Mammy knitted specially for her – along with red woollen mittens that Mammy made too. Amy wanted a red scarf and red mittens as soon as she saw Lily's but Pappy said that Lily was his Little Red Riding Hood and only she could have a red scarf and red earmuffs and red mittens – especially now that she is such a big girl, now that she is ten and soon, when she is thirteen, she will go up to the big school, the Collegiate, which is where the big girls go and where Lily wants to go most of all. Lily opens up her Tootsie Roll and bites into it, crunching the middle bit and letting the sweet chocolate sauce ooze inside her mouth.

Charlie doesn't wear earmuffs – he has a hat. He wears a blue woollen one, which he pulls down over his red curls, and he has a blue scarf to match. They are Christmas presents from his Mammy and Pappy only Charlie doesn't call them that. He calls them 'Mummy and Daddy' and, when she talks to Charlie, Lily has been trying to remember and call Mammy and Pappy 'Mummy and Daddy' too. Charlie has very thick boots that Lily doesn't have. She just has shoes and she wishes she had boots too because already her toes are cold from the snow on the streets and they have only been outside for a little while so far.

Lily and Charlie are on their way to the ice rink in Cedarvale Park, which is four whole blocks away. Lily has never been so far away without Mammy or Pappy and she has never been ice-skating before but Charlie is with her and he will show her what to do because Charlie has been ice-skating lots of times before.

Charlie is Lily's new friend and he lives on Victoria Avenue too. He leaves his house on Victoria Avenue very early in the morning every day to deliver the *Toronto Telegram* all over Riverdale and, once he is finished, he meets Lily in front of her house on Victoria Avenue and, every morning, they walk to school together. They are in the same class at school although Charlie is near the top and Lily has to work hard to catch up with him. Lily likes school and so does Charlie and Charlie wears a tartan scarf every day to show everybody that he is Scottish. Charlie likes being Scottish and says he will go back to Scotland when he is older. Lily isn't sure if she wants to go back – she has only just got here – but she thinks, if Charlie goes back one day, then she might go back with him.

Today, Charlie has a whole dollar with him, from all his newspaper rounds, but he tells Lily he will not spend it all as he is saving to buy his first car – a 'hot rod' – for when he is sixteen. He just brought the dollar with him today to show Lily what a whole dollar looked like because she had told him she had never seen one before. Mr Cohen has said he will let her take money from his customers when she is older and then she will see lots of dollars – lots of 'bucks', as Charlie calls them.

Charlie waves the dollar in front of Lily as he boasts about the 'hot rod' he will buy one day and she tries to snatch it from him but he is too quick for her. And he runs down the road, too fast for Lily, who is laughing too much to run. Mammy and Pappy have met Mr and Mrs Robertson who are Charlie's parents and they have said it is all right for her to be friends with him. That's what Mammy said before she went away. Mammy said Lily could be friends with Charlie. Then Mammy went away and Lily thought it was because she was friends with Charlie but, when she asked Pappy, he said it wasn't because of Charlie – it was that Mammy just needed a rest and she would be back soon, she would be back in time for Christmas. But she still isn't back, not ever for Christmas, so Lily has had dinner at Charlie's three times a week because school has finished for the holidays and Mammy is still away having a rest.

Charlie has two younger brothers – just like Lily has two younger sisters. They are called Jimmy and Stewey, which is short for Stuart, and they have paper rounds too – even Stewey, even though he is only wee – and they give some of the money they make from their paper rounds to Mrs Robertson for their keep, which Lily doesn't have to do. Lily keeps the money she makes from Mr Cohen's shop for herself and she is glad about that – she is glad she can keep all her money to herself even if she does not earn as much as Charlie and is not saving for a 'hot rod'. Charlie has a Scottish voice like Lily but Jimmy and Stewey sound Canadian. Lily wonders if Amy and Mary will soon sound Canadian too.

Jimmy and Stewey are very funny – they make Lily laugh at dinner time when they steal potatoes off each other's plates when one of them isn't looking. Mrs Robertson always sees them but she never shouts at them the way Mammy would if Lily or Amy or Mary took potatoes off each other's plates. Mrs Robertson just smiles and shakes her head. Then she gets up from the big table in the kitchen where they are all eating and she takes more potatoes from the pot on the stove and gives them to whoever has had their potatoes stolen. When Lily goes to Charlie's they always eat at the big table, which Lily never does at home because Pappy sometimes doesn't come home till very late because of his new job – sometimes not until after Lily has gone to bed. At Charlie's house, once they have had dinner at the big table, they all go through to the living room and sit round the TV and watch the *$64000 Question* quiz show together because Mr Robertson likes to watch it all the time and, before it comes on, they laugh at Percy Saltzman telling the weather with his bit of chalk that he throws up in the air at the end of every weather report. 'Some day you're going to drop that, Percy!' Mr Robertson says every time and, every time, Lily and the Robertsons laugh when he says it.

Lily likes being at Charlie's with Mr and Mrs Robertson and Charlie and his younger brothers. Mr Robertson is at home more often than Pappy is. Sometimes he is at home for whole days at a time but Mrs Robertson doesn't seem to mind as sometimes she is out because she is working too. Mrs Robertson cleans rich people's houses and, when she comes home, she tells them all about the fancy things she has seen – like the big white piano in one man's house and the four-poster bed with gold drapes in another. Mr and Mrs Robertson are always happy and sometimes they kiss each other in front of Lily and Charlie and Jimmy and Stewey, which Charlie and Jimmy and Stewey hate. Lily likes being at Charlie's even though his house is much the same as

Lily's. His house has three bedrooms, one for him, one for Mr and Mrs Robertson and one for Jimmy and Stewey – just like Lily's. It has a garden too with grass and flowers in the summer, which Charlie looks after because he likes gardening so much. Lily's garden is just a patch of brown earth as her house is so new no grass has had time to grow. She would like to learn how to plant things and Charlie has said he will show her. Because Charlie's family have lived in their house for longer than Lily's family have. The Robertsons' house has lots of things in it although most of their things are old – like the chairs in the living room that have bits of wire poking through the armrests – and some of them are broken – like the grandfather clock in the hall that doesn't tell the time – and some of them are messy – like the big baskets of washing that are always sitting in the kitchen and spilling out over the floor. But Lily likes everything even if it is all messy and broken. It is never like that at home because Mammy said she wanted everything new in their new home and now, if something gets broken, Mammy throws it away.

Lily wonders if that is why her home seems empty and Charlie's is always full. There are always people at Charlie's house. He has cousins and aunts and uncles who came over to Canada from Scotland too and, when they come to Charlie's house, they play music and his uncle Robert plays a guitar and his uncle David plays a fiddle and they all sing songs. Mrs Robertson likes to have her family round her as much as possible, she says, which Lily thinks is funny because Mammy is always saying the reason she left Scotland was to get away from her family, except Auntie Jean. Lily thinks that, if Mammy's family was like Charlie's family, then she would like to have them in their house all the time too because Auntie Jean doesn't play music and Lily wonders if maybe some day she will ask Mammy if Charlie's uncle David and his uncle Robert can come and play music in their house although she cannot quite picture that in her head.

Sometimes Mrs Robertson asks Lily how Mammy is and Lily always says very politely, 'She's very well, thank you.' – even if Mammy is not well. Lily doesn't like lying to Mrs Robertson who is very friendly and who cuddles her sometimes when she and Charlie come in through the kitchen door and she has been baking cakes and she lets them lick the bowl with mixture left in it. And she says to Lily, 'I always wanted a wee girl!' and Jimmy and Stewey say, 'Eeeuugghh – girls!' at the same time and Mrs Robertson laughs at them and tries to cuddle them too but they won't let her. Lily likes being cuddled by Mrs Robertson. She has a smiley face and red curly hair, just like Charlie's and Stewey's, and she wears glasses that are rose-tipped at the ends which turn up like little wings. Even though Lily doesn't like lying to Mrs Robertson, sometimes she does tell her things that aren't true which makes her feel bad but it is only so Mrs Robertson will say, 'My wee lamb!' and give her a cuddle so Lily thinks it can't be so bad to say things that aren't true sometimes and that she isn't a bad girl to do that.

Charlie says all girls are stupid but he doesn't think Lily is stupid like all girls and that's why he can be friends with her. Charlie says that Lily is smart. Lily can climb trees and chop firewood and sing along to Fats Domino. Lily is a good girl.

So, today, Lily and Charlie are going ice-skating and, afterwards, Lily will have her dinner at Charlie's house because Mammy is still away having a rest and Pappy said Lily could stay at Charlie's for dinner and then Mr Robertson and Charlie could walk her home as they always do. Pappy is at home with Amy and Mary who are too wee to go ice-skating. Lily had asked Pappy if he could take them ice-skating but he wasn't very well when she asked because it made him angry. 'Are you kids never happy? Always wantin' this an' wantin' that! Is nothin' ever good enough for you?' But Pappy only gets angry with Mammy, not with them, so he can't be very well at all and maybe he needs a rest too. Maybe Pappy will go away for a rest while Mammy is away and then it will just be Lily and Amy and Mary . . . And this makes Lily feel happy because she thinks, if Pappy and Mammy both went away for a rest, then they could all stay with Mrs Robertson who would then have three wee girls.

Lily knows it is not nice to think it but she likes it when Mammy goes away. She likes it when Mammy is having another rest. Pappy is always sad when Mammy goes away but only at first and then he is happy too and they do things they could not do if Mammy was there – they make French toast with maple syrup for tea and forget to wash the dishes and Pappy makes them all hot chocolate with milk just before she and Amy and Mary go to bed, which they are not allowed to do if Mammy is there because Mammy says it gives them nightmares if they eat just before they go to sleep. But Lily never has nightmares when she goes to sleep after eating French toast and maple syrup and drinking hot chocolate so she thinks maybe Mammy just doesn't like the mess they make with all the pans and dishes and bowls.

Pappy has said that Mammy will be back soon from the place where she is having a rest. The last time Mammy went away, she was away for a whole week and Pappy had to do everything. Auntie Jean has come to the house a couple of times to help Pappy because he is so tired but Lily knows that Pappy doesn't know where Mammy is having a rest because one night, after she and Amy and Mary had gone to bed, Lily got up again and sat on the stairs very quietly and watched through the open door of the living room and she could see Pappy leaning forward in his chair with his head in his hands and he said to Auntie Jean, 'I don't know where she is, Jean – I don't know where my own bloody wife is!' And Lily thought that Pappy was bad because he had told Lily and Amy and Mary that he knew where Mammy was having a rest and that wasn't true and he didn't say it to get a cuddle like Lily does with Mrs Robertson because Auntie Jean wasn't giving Pappy a cuddle. Auntie Jean was walking up and down in front of Pappy. 'Rubina's always been that flighty. I thought being here would have calmed her down a bit.' And Lily didn't know what flighty meant but she knew it wasn't good because Auntie Jean was angry. Lily wanted to ask Mrs Robertson the next day what flighty meant but she didn't. Lily was afraid of what Mrs Robertson might say it meant.

It must mean that Mammy doesn't like their new house and Lily thinks that's maybe because she doesn't have her own room all to herself, like Lily has. Mammy has promised Lily she will have lots of lovely new things for her own room. Sometimes Mammy cries when she comes into Lily's room late at night and promises her lots of new things and Lily smells Mammy's special medicine and she knows that that is what makes Mammy cry. Or it must mean that Mammy doesn't like the new car which is an Austin and which Pappy says is almost the best and which Lily and Amy and Mary all help him to wash every Sunday morning. Or it must mean that Mammy doesn't like Pappy's new job even though Pappy wears a suit and a tie every day which he never wore before and Lily thinks he looks like men on TV and his hair is slicked back too and it is grey now all over, not just one bit streaked in the middle.

'Does your Pap . . . Daddy wear a suit every day?' Lily asks Charlie now that she has caught up with him. She is panting hard. Charlie is a little bit taller than she is and he likes to walk on the outside of the sidewalk so he takes bigger strides.

'Hmm. No,' says Charlie. Then he adds, 'Well, sometimes.'

'Will you wear a suit when you leave school?' Lily scuffs at the lumpy brown ice on the sidewalk. There is more snow to come but not today, according to Percy Saltzman. Today is just very cold but there will be no more snow.

'Sure will,' Charlie says, trying to sound Canadian in his Scottish voice and smiling at the future when he can wear a suit.

'I'd like to wear one,' says Lily although she says this partly to make Charlie laugh, which he does.

'Ha-ha! Don't be silly – girls can't wear suits! You'll have to wear a dress,' he says, bending down to pick up some slush with his bare hands.

Lily knows what he is going to do with the slush so she pushes him as he bends down and shouts, 'Can't catch me, can't catch me!' all the way down the street until Charlie does catch her.

But he isn't mean – he doesn't wipe the slush all over her face as Lily saw some boys do to girls at school yesterday – he just throws it a bit lamely and it lands on her red earmuffs.

They are almost at the park. Lily can see lots of tiny coloured lights in the distance over the whiteness of the snow and she hears the noise of people, like a great buzzing, which must mean that a lot of people are skating there. She and Charlie are excited now. They run into the park, over the snow which powders about them and it slips inside Lily's shoes as she runs but she doesn't mind because she wants to see the people skating and she wants to be skating too and then she sees it – the big white circle that girls and boys are skating on, the bobbled hats and scarves and short skirts and woolly sweaters and shrieks and tumbles and trips and swoosh and slice and how elegant it looks. And Lily stumbles as she follows behind Charlie all the way to the edge of the ice rink and there she is – right up close to it all – and she stares, entranced by the skaters who fly by her, red and blue and green all blurring together.

'Come on, we can get skates over here,' Charlie says as he pulls at her arm and they hurry over to a queue of people waiting to hire skates. When it is their turn, Charlie hands over their money and then he shows Lily how to lace up the dark leather skates properly and he laughs at her when she tries to stand up in them and immediately falls over.

'Look – do it this way,' he says and he shows her how to bend her legs properly and soon she is walking and only wobbling a little bit on her way over to the edge of the ice rink. There is such a lot of noise that Lily and Charlie have to shout to each other to be heard and Lily can hear other people shouting and some are squealing as they fall over and some are calling to their friends, 'Hey, look at me!' as they fly past and some are very serious and going very fast with their arms behind their backs and some are laughing as they look like they are trying to swim, their arms and legs out at all angles. And Lily hopes that she will look like the serious ones when she starts to skate but it is not easy – the blades are too narrow. How can she move on them? They slide away from her as soon as she puts her foot down. And Charlie is away – he is away on the ice, skating away. And Lily lands on her bottom as her feet slip from under her and she thinks she might cry but then Charlie appears again and she can't cry in front of him. And he laughs and pulls her up. 'Look, watch me – do what I do!' And Lily can't get it – she tries but she can't get it. She moves her foot and she stubs her skate on the ice or it slips out from her heel and she keeps trying but she can't get it and then suddenly her boot glides over the icy bumps instead of stumbling against them, suddenly her other foot follows and glides too and she is off. She moves one foot then the other and she is skating. She is not skating very far and soon she stumbles again but she skated – she *really* skated. And she scrambles up to start again – to glide again – even if it's only for a few steps. But this time it's even better and she skates – she skates like Charlie who is whooping beside her. 'Now you've got it! Now you've got it!' And she is skating and she can look up for the first time since she stepped on to the ice and she can see the people flying past her but she is one of them – she is skating too.

It is getting dark but the coloured lights round the rink only grow brighter and the big arc lights are shining down now so that Lily can see everyone's frozen breath, hazy under the light, and even the stalls selling burgers and hot dogs and hot coffee and hot chocolate are lit up too. Lily's legs are aching and her ankles have never felt so heavy but she cannot stop. She wants to keep going, to skate faster and faster, and Charlie tells her to be patient – she is trying to do too much too soon – but Lily is having fun, she is laughing and skating and the lights are sparkling all around her and she looks and she sees . . .

And what does Lily see?

Who does Lily see?

Lily sees Mammy.

Mammy.

Mammy's here!

Mammy is here which means she can't be having a rest any more. Lily can see her on the ice, staggering a little bit. It *is* Mammy – Lily recognises her blue coat with the fur around the top and her dark hair, in a bun at the back of her head. And Mammy is laughing as another lady holds her up and they both slip and slide at the edge of the ice rink. And Lily is about to shout and she starts to skate over to Mammy but then suddenly two tall men with flying scarves and woollen pullovers stop just by Mammy and the lady and one of them bends down to Mammy and offers her his hand and she puts out her hand to him and he steadies her as she laughs still and blushes.

Lily stops and holds on to the side of the ice rink and she stops and she stares at her mother who is being helped off the ice now by the tall man with black hair and the other lady friend follows them with the other man. Lily doesn't recognise any of them so she doesn't think they are family. Something tells her they are not family. And suddenly Lily is very confused because Pappy is at home by himself and he is worried about Mammy and Mammy isn't having a rest – she is out skating. And Lily thinks Pappy wouldn't know Mammy was out skating like this or he would be here skating too.

'Hey! Wotcha doin'?' Charlie stops by Lily with a big skoosh, raising ice as he skids on his skates.

'Nothing,' says Lily. 'I'm cold. I'm going home.'

'But we've still got time left before the hour's up.' Charlie isn't happy – he's looking at his watch. 'We've still got ten minutes.'

Lily shakes her head. Her mouth is set and she is starting to skate away from him.

Charlie skates after her. 'What's up, Lily? You feelin' all right?'

But still Lily doesn't say anything and she stumbles all the way back to the edge where she can get off the ice and take off her skating boots and hand them back in for her own shoes.

'You had enough?' Charlie looks worried then he grins and says, 'Girls. Might have known!'

But Lily won't laugh and she won't be teased. The man takes her skating boots and gives her her shoes and she puts them on. They are cold and damp but she doesn't care.

'I just want to go home,' she says as she ties the laces on her shoes. 'My pa . . . my daddy'll be waiting for me.'

'But I thought you were having your dinner at ours,' says Charlie.

And Lily shakes her head again. 'No. I can't. I have to get home.'

Charlie looks cross now. 'Mum'll wonder what's wrong,' he says. 'She'll think I've upset you.'

But nothing he says can sway Lily and she gets up and starts to walk over to the park entrance. She will go home by herself if she has to – she knows the way home – even though Pappy would be very angry if he thought Charlie had left her to walk four whole blocks by herself. But she doesn't have to walk by herself – Charlie is walking beside her and he tries to cheer her up by falling in the snow a couple of times and making slushy snowballs and throwing them at parked cars. But she doesn't laugh at any of it and, by the time she is back on Victoria Avenue, Charlie is cross with her again and he says goodbye.

And, when Pappy opens the door, Lily runs into the house and he calls after her, 'How was the ice-skatin', pet?'

And, because Lily is a good girl and good girls don't tell, Lily shouts back, 'Oh, fine!' as she runs into her room and shuts the door behind her.

Lily has been a bad girl. She has been telling stories. She has been saying things that aren't true. She has been telling stories to all sorts of people. She has told Mrs Robertson that Mammy slipped on the ice and broke her leg. She has told Miss Draper at school that Pappy has left and gone back to Scotland. She has told Mr Cohen that Mary is ill in bed at home and might never get better. And she has told Charlie that she is getting a dog, that they are moving to California where Zorro lives and that Pappy has won a prize on the *$64000 Question* quiz show.

None of it is true and now Lily has been found out. Mammy has found out about Lily telling stories and now Mammy is very angry and she is not speaking to her. But Lily doesn't care. She is alone in her bedroom where Mammy has told her she must stay until she learns not to tell lies and she can hear Mary laughing at *Howdy Doody* on the new TV in the living room where Amy has gone with all her new dolls.

Mrs Robertson came round to the house yesterday with a big pot of soup because Lily had told her that Mammy broke her leg and Mr Cohen asked Mammy how Mary was when she came to take her home from the shop.

Lily has been a bad girl but Lily has been a foolish girl too because she should have been more careful about what she said and who she said it to. Lily has been a bad girl but she is not sorry. Lily sits on the edge of her bed with the pink coloured blankets and she opens up her lined notebook. Lily thinks of other stories she can tell. Lily doesn't want to stop telling stories – no matter what Mammy says or how long Mammy says she has to stay in her room.

It is almost spring. The snow melted last week after lasting for months and months and other people's gardens are beginning to show little green shoots of flowers – other people's gardens but not hers, not yet. Pappy said they could plant some bulbs this week and they might flower in the summer. So now, when Lily looks out of her bedroom window just beside her bed, the ground is brown just as it was before the snow fell. She stares at the brown ground and the longer she stares at it the more convinced she is that she can see flowers there – yellow daffodils and purple pansies, pink roses and bluebells. Then she remembers Pappy told her they were too late for daffodils and bluebells this year so she ignores the blue and the yellow in her mind's eye and concentrates instead on the purple and the pink. She pictures a swing too, sitting on the luscious green grass they will soon have, and a red bicycle, just like the one Charlie has, just beside it. The sun is shining on the brown earth and that will make it green – Pappy said flowers and plants need the sun to make them grow. Lily leans on the window ledge, her chin in her palms, and pictures cycling round her garden in the summer on her red bicycle while Pappy and Amy and Mary watch her and clap and cheer.

Mammy isn't in this picture. Lily is enjoying making up stories that don't have Mammy in them. Yesterday she wrote in her lined notebook about three sisters who run away and are caught by Red Indians. The day before she wrote about a girl and her pappy who lived together in a big house full of dogs and cats and rabbits – just like the one the hurricane took away. And, the day before that, she imagined what she and Charlie would do if they found themselves in the middle of the desert and had to survive on rats and mice for food.

Lily doesn't write any stories about mammies, except the one about the ice rink. That was her last story with a mammy in it. The mammy in the story about the ice rink was bad. She had run away without telling anyone where she was going and, while everybody worried about where she was, she went to the ice rink with her friends. Then, when she was in the middle of skating across the ice, a great big crack appeared and she disappeared under the water and was never seen again. And then the ice froze quickly so that nobody knew what happened to the mammy who ran away – only Lily knew. Only Lily knew that the mammy in the story about the ice rink was trapped under the ice forever.

Lily doesn't care about the other stories she has been telling. They are stupid stories – stupid stories about broken legs and sick sisters – and Lily was surprised by how easily she was believed. Each time someone said, 'Oh, my dear, that's terrible!', she thought she must think of something else to tell. And she would think of something else to tell and then she would tell it and it was as easy as telling Mary what to do. Charlie didn't mind about the stories she told him – he thought they were fun. Mrs Robertson had looked very surprised when she came over with the soup and Mammy answered the door. But she didn't shout at Lily – she just smiled at Mammy and said, 'I must have got it wrong.'

Lily wishes Mrs Robertson was her mammy. She wouldn't have her own room or new pink blankets on her bed if she lived at the Robertsons' but she thinks she will ask Mrs Robertson the next time she sees her if she can stay all the time, not just for dinner. And she imagines getting up every morning in the Robertsons' house, just before Mr Robertson goes to work building houses and Mrs Robertson goes to work cleaning rich people's houses, and making breakfast for Charlie and Jimmy and Stewey before they all go to school.

But then she stops imagining anything because she hears a noise coming from the kitchen downstairs. It sounds as if something big has fallen over and then she hears shouting and Mary is crying. She wonders if she should get up and look but then she hears the back door shut and when she looks out of the bedroom window she sees Amy and Mary are in the back garden. Amy has picked up a spade and is trying to get Mary to do the same but Mary is sniffing and wiping her face with her fists.

Lily waits for a moment. Then she hears them. The footsteps on the stairs – stumbling footsteps, knocks and bumps and curses whispered. She wonders if the steps will go past her bedroom but then they stop just at the door outside and Lily sits still on her bed and stares at the closed door.

Then suddenly the bedroom door opens. The bedroom door opens and it is Mammy. Mammy is standing in the doorway. She has a funny look on her face. Lily knows the look on her face – it is the one Mammy has when she has too much of her medicine – and Lily looks back at Mammy, whose hair is tied in a bun at the back of her head but it is unravelling. There are thick strands of Mammy's dark brown hair lying on her shoulders and Lily looks at the hair on Mammy's shoulders, at the hair lying on her green sweater, as Mammy steps into Lily's room and slams the door behind her.

'And what d'you think that's . . . What've you've got there, eh? What's that, eh? Young . . . lady?'

Lily looks first at Mammy and then at her lined notebook.

'Nothing.'

She tries to shut the lined notebook but Mammy is too quick for her. 'Oh, no – oh, no you don't, you little besom. Give that to me.'

'It's nothing.'

'I don't care what it is – give it to me! Right now! I mean it – I won't tell you again!'

But Lily shakes her head and holds her lined notebook to her chest and then suddenly Mammy crosses over to the bed in a flash and shoots out her hand and makes a grab for it and tries to pull it away from Lily and the steel rings that keep the pages together hurt Lily's fingers as she clings on to the lined notebook.

'You evil wee girl, give me that now! Is this where you write it all down, then? So it is. This is there where you plan out all your little lies. You're a wicked, wicked girl!'

Mammy shouts this at her and Lily is trembling and she wants to cry but, even though her throat is sore and she feels the tears at the back of her eyes, she still holds on to her notebook and Mammy starts to shout again and to slap at her hands. She tries to prise Lily's fingers apart and hits them, over and over again.

Lily is crying now, 'That's sore, that's sore, Mammy!'

And then Mammy stops and she stares at Lily and her eyes are glazed as she looks at Lily. And then she raises her right hand all the way up and brings it down, giving Lily the hardest slap across her cheek that she has ever had in her life. The slap knocks her right on to her back and she's sprawling across the bed. And the notebook finally slips out of her fingers as her hand automatically goes up to her cheek and Mammy grabs the notebook, opens the pages and starts to read.

The only sound is Lily sniffing as she lies on the bed, waiting for Mammy to stop reading, but Mammy doesn't stop – she turns one page then another and another. And finally she looks at Lily and Lily thinks that her mammy hates her.

'What the hell is this?' Mammy hisses at her, moving over to Lily on the bed. Lily pulls back, up against the wall, but Mammy still moves forward, pushing the notebook right up at Lily's face. 'What is this about the ice rink? What did you see? WHAT DID YOU SEE?' Mammy starts to scream at Lily again and then she pulls at the pages of the notebook, rips them out and starts to tear them up into little pieces and, as she throws the pieces of paper at Lily on the bed she shouts, 'You wee bitch! You wee bitch! You tell anybody about this and I'll kill you! So help me, I'll kill you, you evil wee girl! I wish I'd never had you! I should've given you away when you were born – I wish I'd never had any of you. You're the worst girl in the world! D'you hear that? D'you hear me? You're the worst girl in the world and I hate you, I hate you, I . . .'

Then Mammy stops screaming and bursts into tears and falls down on to the floor. And Mammy is lying on the floor. She is crying and hitting the side of the bed and saying, 'Oh, Lily . . . oh, Lily . . . Mammy's sorry, Mammy's so sorry . . .'

And Lily doesn't move – she's crouched on the bed, up against the wall, keeping as still as she can. And she hears Mammy crying and Mammy coughing and it goes on for ages, the crying and the coughing, and Lily still doesn't move and then finally Mammy is sitting up and Lily sees the big black smudges under Mammy's eyes. And her hair is loose now – it is all over her shoulders and in her eyes and in her mouth. 'Oh, Lily,' Mammy says and she wipes under her eyes with her fingers and tries to push her hair back from her face and still Lily sits, still she doesn't move a muscle. 'You don't understand, you don't understand . . . I'm so sorry!'

And Mammy is up on the bed too now and she lunges at Lily who shrinks down but Mammy is not hitting her – Mammy has her arms round Lily and she is hugging her tightly and crying and saying, 'My wee girl, my wee girl . . . forgive me – I didn't mean it . . .'

And Lily is crying again too and she says, 'It's all right, Mammy, it's all right – I never saw anything. I won't do it any more – I won't tell stories any more. I'm sorry, Mammy, I'm sorry!'

And she's pressing against Mammy's shoulder and Mammy is crying and shaking and she hugs Lily more tightly. 'My wee baby, my good wee baby . . .' and they sit on Lily's bed like that for ages and ages and ages and they don't say any more.

When Lily wakes up and opens her eyes, it is dark in her room and Mammy has gone but Mammy has put a big blanket round her on the bed and she is warm and cosy under the blanket. Lily rubs her eyes and decides she should sit up. The little pieces of paper that Mammy threw at her before are not there on the bed any more – they have all gone from the bed and the floor – and her lined notebook is gone too. Lily touches her cheek, which is tender and sore, and then she pushes the blanket away and gets up from the bed and goes over to the bedroom door. When she opens the door, she hears the quiet murmur of the television in the living room and she quietly pads down the stairs and stands outside the living-room door. She cannot decide if she should go in or not but finally she pushes the door open a little bit. Mammy is sitting in the new white chair by the fire watching the television. Her hair is tidy now and she gives Lily a big smile when she sees her.

'Hello there. Shh! Amy and Mary are in bed. Come on in. Are you hungry? D'you want me to get you something to eat?'

Mammy gets up from the chair and comes over to Lily, who is not sure at first what to do when Mammy approaches her, and she shivers slightly but then Mammy's arms are round her and she hears Mammy whispering to her, 'I'm sorry about before, Lily. Let's not tell Pappy when he comes in. My best wee girl.'

Lily says, 'All right, Mammy.' And Mammy gives her an extra hug. Lily is so happy that she is Mammy's best wee girl again.

Mammy pulls away and smiles at her. 'Things,' she says to Lily as she kneels in front of her and looks at her straight in the eyes, 'are going to change, Lily. We're all going to be very happy from now on. Me and Pappy and you and Amy and Mary. We're all going to be very happy. Mammy won't be going away ever again.'

And Lily smiles at Mammy because everything is going to be happy and they will be just like the Robertsons after all and she won't tell any more stories and Mammy won't get angry ever again and Mammy won't go away.

Mammy gets up, smiles at Lily and says, 'So what d'you want to eat? What's your favourite? Piece and jam and a glass of milk?' And Lily nods and Mammy pulls her gently over to her chair by the fire and sits Lily in it and says, 'Then just you wait there, sweetheart, and I'll go and get it for you.'

And later, when everybody is in bed fast asleep, Lily creeps downstairs and goes into the kitchen by herself for another glass of milk. She very quietly pulls a chair from the table over to one of the kitchen cabinets and stands on the chair and opens the cabinet. She moves aside the bags of sugar and tea and feels behind them but it is gone. Mammy's special medicine isn't there. Lily gets down from the chair then very quietly carries it back to the table.

PART THREE

1995

Don't forget to look up, look up, look up.

And because Sadie cannot forget, because she does not need that voice to remind her, she does indeed raise her eyes from the sheaf of papers on the desk in front of her and looks at her audience.

Sadie has not been in this room before so she could not have known from her position on the raised dais how the light would blind her and it throws her, this dazzling light – it makes her return to her papers, leaf through them as though she is checking they are all there when she knows, of course, that they are even though she cannot see what she is doing because of the light still stained on her retina. So she keeps flicking, waiting for the focus to return, while the room buzzes.

Writers like Vera Brittain in *Testament of Youth* . . .

. . . expected to return to their parents' homes . . .

. . . harm done by their mothers . . .

. . . 'a host of human vampires' . . .

Odd phrases catch her eye as her vision becomes normal once again and she says them silently to herself, wincing at the thought of speaking them out loud.

> . . . malevolent mother figures in *The Old Maid* and *Now, Voyager*. Both stories were made into films starring Bette Davis as . . .

But it is too late to correct them now,

> . . . popularity of women like May Sinclair . . .

now that she is here.

> . . . the theme appears again and again throughout . . .

And this time, when Sadie looks up, she avoids the overhead light and faces, instead, the mixed group before her. She is surprised to recognise one or two of them: a young girl from her first-year group, noticeable for her very curly red hair and pale face, pale eyelashes, a face beautiful four hundred years ago when it was perfect for soft oil portraits but too delicate for photography or TV or film; the postgraduate student she keeps seeing in the main office for some reason or another; a young man with long black curly hair that is thinning already and which he constantly flicks back over his shoulders. His full lips pout as he does so, as he strokes his chest, adorned and, yes, 'adorned' is the only word that will do for this piece of purple velvet material slashed at the neck and sleeves, with the hand-made slogan 'Desiring Machine' on the front. He whispers to the thin blonde boy beside him, whose blue-and-white striped top hangs loosely across his shoulders – with no fat to catch hold of and cling to, it billows gently every time the door opens and causes a draught and Sadie cannot help thinking that it must be a very light top and that he must be very cold even though the room itself is too warm and she has had to remove her black cardigan.

> . . . First World War gave a generation of young women the opportunity to leave home and set up on their own – share a flat with friends or colleagues.

Sadie says this quietly to herself as she watches the Obsolete Professor coming through the door. She is surprised to see him here and he nods at her as he approaches David Jamieson, who is so tall, even when he is sitting down, that he has to bow his head to hear what others are saying to him. James Brooks is sitting beside him and he smiles encouragingly.

> The majority of the writers I am researching during this period are middle-class women writing for a middle-class audience . . .

As Sadie runs it through in her mind, she sees that next to him is Benjamin Alexander. She still has not spoken to him. All she knows is how highly regarded he is, as a former British Academy scholar and Oxford graduate, and that he industriously publishes at least three articles in refereed journals every year and one book every other year. He does not smile at her even when he catches her eye so Sadie looks back down at her papers.

> In England, May Sinclair's *Mary Olivier*, Radclyffe Hall's *The Unlit Lamp* and Antonia White's *Frost in May* all show the effect of a malevolent maternal influence on young women . . .

And then she looks away again for a friendlier face this time. But she does not recognise the rest of the slowly assembling audience at all and, as she has never attended even a postgraduate seminar here before, Sadie has no idea of the standard expected of her.

It is cold outside. The blindless windows behind her audience are black holes crossed with white, like ghostly crucifixes, and she fixes on them – on the condensation that is gathering already as the room fills – and she realises there is no fresh air coming in and, for a moment, she thinks she might be sick.

> 'What had our mothers been doing then that they had no wealth to leave us? Powdering their noses? Looking in at shop windows? Flaunting in the sun at Monte Carlo?'

But, no, the nausea passes. She blinks and David Jamieson smiles at her and nods.

The first few moments before speaking are always the longest.

> This is just another lecture,

Sadie knows that it will be over sooner than she thinks. And she will begin in a moment and, as soon as she does, she will forget how tired she is right now. She will forget that she has been researching and writing constantly for five days and that it is still not ready – her paper – but it will do as a work in progress.

She will forget that her work has been the perfect excuse not to spend time with her flatmates when they have tried to take her to the Masthead with them. She will forget that it has been the perfect excuse not to speak to her mother when she calls from Toronto and leaves messages telling her not to worry but there has been no change and Amy still hasn't woken up – the perfect excuse not to tell her mother where she has been or to ask her about Rubina which she knows she must do and which will only increase her anger.

Sadie will forget too that her work has been the perfect excuse not to see Richard who is approving of her sudden industriousness because he wants a girlfriend whose scholarship he can take seriously – status is important to him. But he is anxious, all the same. Sadie can tell he is anxious that it will be too long before the two of them sleep together again and she is not sure when she will be able to do that because work has been the perfect excuse not to think about sleeping with him at all – not to think about what her body is doing to her.

Yes, it has been the perfect excuse to forget all of that and she will forget still more as soon as she begins and the only things inside her head will be the words of her paper and the subject matter of writers who were famous decades ago and so she must begin and so . . .

> There are two consistent motherly 'types' that emerge from the novels of this period . . .

There is silence as the whispering stops and Sadie is

unsure whether to stand or remain sitting but she does not move. She smiles at the faces in front of her and clears her throat and begins, with only a trace of hoarseness in her voice as she announces her title, '"Mother–Daughter Conflict in Novels by Women Between the Wars".'

There is another silence and Sadie realises that is because she has stopped speaking. She must open her mouth and begin all over again. She must say something else. Yet it has taken all this effort just to say the title out loud and suddenly she notices how wet her hands are. Damp patches have appeared at the edges of the paper she is holding in front of her but she will keep them still, she will not tremble, she will not let them see her tremble.

> Shit, shit! Should have remembered slides or something – photographs, film stills, visual aids, visual fucking aids.

'I don't have any visual aids although I will be referring to some film work,' Sadie begins again. Her voice is dry and she gives a cough. 'I haven't quite decided on my approach yet. I'm looking at a number of different writers of different capabilities and influences – Olive Higgins Prouty, for example, was influenced by Freudian analysis and Radclyffe Hall by the "inversion" theories of the contemporaneous eugenicists – so it may be that one approach won't suit them all. Ultimately, it's the theme of mother–daughter conflict and the time period that links them – although diversity is part of the appeal of the project.'

Sadie forces herself to look at her audience now and smile but nobody smiles back. So at least they are taking her seriously and so must she and so she must begin for a third time – all these beginnings . . . She must take another breath and say, 'It was during the First World War that young unmarried women were able to live alone while employed – maybe as nurses or in munitions factories – without society's disapproval.'

> Rules about public speaking. Keep your head up. Don't speak too quickly. Take pauses between points. Visual aids. No, remember? Don't have any visual aids. Damn it, damn it! Should have got something – photographs, anything. Shit graphs, figures, statistics . . . how many went back home?

And so she will make the point before anyone else does. 'Part of my research will be to investigate the social conditions many women were writing about in their fiction – how many women lost their jobs, how many women returned to the parental home and so on – immediately after the First World War ended in 1919 and until the beginning of the Second World War in 1939. For many middle-class women, the twenties and thirties were two decades of domestic imprisonment and their jailors were their mothers.'

> Slow down, slow down. Look up – don't forget to keep eye contact, don't lose them. It's too dry. Should have started with a joke, something funny or dramatic – an anecdote, a death, anything.

And Sadie's hands are shaking and her foot is tapping while she sits and she feels the sweat run down her spine which makes her worry that, when she stands up and turns round, there will be a dark line running down the back of her black shirt. And, almost as soon as she has begun, she is in the middle of her paper and now her worry is that she has mentioned too much too soon and she will not have enough left to fill the required thirty minutes. Because now she has already mentioned Edith Wharton and Virginia Woolf and the debt mothers owe their daughters and she has discussed repressed spinsters in *Now Voyager* and *Mary Olivier* and she has praised Molly Keane and Elizabeth Bowen for depicting mothers who trap their daughters inside 'the Big House' and she has pointed to the work of Willa Muir, Catherine Carswell, E. M. Delafield, Lettice Cooper, Mary Lavin. And she has read aloud an extract from a letter, sent to *The Times* in 1914 – a forewarning of what was to come.

'"They drain the life blood of those who are their nearest and should be their dearest . . . the widowed mother with a daughter of any age from twenty to fifty . . . she must come when she is called, go where she is sent, walk or drive cheek by jowl with the vampire who saps her vitality, write her letters, pay calls, 'do' the flowers, exercise the dog, order the dinner, pay the wages, engage and dismiss her servants, count the linen, keep the books and, to speak generally, run the house for the vampire's convenience from the vampire's point of view . . . The vampire has them by the throat and, slowly but surely, squeezes the life out of them and drains them of youth and joy and hope . . ."'

And now Sadie cannot help but focus on Professor Middleton, whose eyelids are drooping and whose chin is failing to resist gravity's pull towards his chest, as she says as brightly as she can, 'To sum up, the main type of motherly control is represented by the "passive-aggressive" kind of mother. The secondary type is more directly aggressive in her approach. In Antonia White's 1933 novel *Frost in May*, for instance, it is the figurative mother, the Mother Superior, who crushes the spirit of her pupil, Nanda Gray, with physical and verbal abuse.'

Sadie pauses.

> Ask for questions. Slow it down – see if they're listening to you. You old sod, go and fucking sleep somewhere else!

'Any questions at this point?'

> Please ask a question, please ask a question – anything, I don't care.

'Desiring Machine' has his hand up and Sadie nods gratefully in his direction. 'Yes?'

He shakes his curls and flicks them back over his shoulder. Then he looks around him as he says, 'Aren't you just conforming to a stereotype about the pathology of women and mothers in particular? I don't see what's new about this.'

Before Sadie has time to take back her silent thanks of gratitude in the wake of his question, there is an outbreak of whispering and some giggling. Feet are shuffling on the floor, papers are being rustled and members of the audience are turning towards each other.

> You're losing them! Get them back – get their attention back to you.

So she coughs loudly but it is no use – no one hears her. 'Desiring Machine' is saying something else that she does not catch and it causes laughter from his companion beside him which infuriates Sadie but there is nothing she can do.

And then, all of a sudden, Professor Middleton heaves a great sigh, turns towards the student and says loudly and pointedly, 'Perhaps, laddie, you might get your hair cut if you're planning to attend university seminars?'

And there it is, just what she needed – complete silence. Although perhaps not quite like this – shocked and confused and outraged and stifling laughter.

> Jesus Christ, save me from pompous old bastards and student show-offs! This is too fucking much.

And so, now, this is the moment to act, to get the moment back, to capture their attention and, before anyone else can reply, Sadie says quickly, 'Sure, of course we've been demonising mothers ever since Eve ate the apple. But I'm not just reinforcing a good mother/bad mother dichotomy. There are complex versions of the two categories I've described. I'm not saying this is a rescue project. I don't believe those mothers were misrepresented. But there were serious reasons why these women wanted to keep their daughters at home. We shouldn't underestimate the power of the maternal bond and how difficult it was for these daughters to break that bond.' Sadie is out of breath. Suddenly she is aware again of how hot the room has become but she has done enough – the room is quiet again and the audience has turned to her. She is not just the speaker – she is in charge. This is *her* seminar and she will not have it hijacked by Obsolete Professors and know-it-all students.

And now Benjamin Alexander is leaning forward in a

tweed jacket that is too old-fashioned a fabric for a man in his early thirties. He is stroking his light-brown beard with one hand and repositioning his glasses with the other. It is an action that obscures his face and should make Sadie suspicious but she is welcoming his contribution even before she has heard what he has to say.

> God, please just let me go now – 'were now to die, were now to be most happy' or something like that. *Othello.*

'Do I dare,' Benjamin Alexander begins, in a long, slow drawl with perfect enunciation, 'do I dare suggest . . .' He coughs suddenly. 'Eheurgh, a link with the Gothic? Do I dare suggest the Gothic's attempts, eheurgh, to figure in painting and poetry and prose, eheurgh . . .'

> Oh, Jesus, get on with it! Give him a fucking Strepsil.

'the troubled seck-su-ality of young women, eheurgh . . .'

> Ah, that's your thing, is it? Sex? Female sexuality – of course.

'their fears and neuroses that, of course, today is understood in the kind of psychological terms, eheurgh, that the Gothics simply did not have – naturally enough . . .'

> Of course – he's a Romantic. Might have known. This is his area. Right, OK, I see where he's going with this. Hurry up, for God's sake, before we all die.

'What I mean to say is, eheurgh – what I would like to point to is the daughters' resistance to their mothers, which is a resistance, of course, to the fully grown female body, eheurgh. We see that the focus in Gothic painting, of course, is on breasts, pubis, luxuriant hair . . .'

> What the hell does nineteenth-century painting have
> to do with twentieth-century novels?

Benjamin Alexander pauses for a moment to lick his lips and clear his throat once again. He looks up at the ceiling, strokes his sparse beard and then continues, 'All are signifiers of sexuality, eheurgh. Which are all indicators, of course, of the shadow of death that lingers over puberty.'

> You wank over paintings of virgins in white with
> goblins sitting on their chests – I bet that's just what
> you do. And all in the name of academic pursuit.

As he drags out this last sentence, his voice increases in volume, as though he has captured the essence of Sadie's paper, and he sits back in his chair and resumes a stroking of his beard.

But she must pretend that she does understand. She must nod and smile anyway. She must not say out loud what it is she is thinking. How glorious it would be if she could tell Benjamin Alexander what she really thinks not just of his comments but of him. But Sadie does what she should and instead says, 'Yes, you could argue that resistance to adulthood is there, of course, in these young women's animosity towards their mothers. But it doesn't account for their longing to be free of their mothers, to stand on their own two feet, to be out in the world. Not to be trapped at home means to be grown up – no longer a child.'

Benjamin Alexander is disappointed by Sadie's answer. It is not titillating enough. She has poured cold water over the fire he has tried to fan into being. Her paper lacks sex, sensuousness. There are no bodies – only words. Sadie can read this failure on her part on his face. And he raises his eyebrows dramatically and turns to James Brooks as if he is about to say something disparaging.

But the pale young woman with the red curls intervenes instead and says, loudly and nervously, 'You said you didn't see what was new about this?' She is ignoring Benjamin Alexander's contribution entirely, which makes Sadie want to cheer, and instead she is addressing herself to 'Desiring Machine'. Ever since Professor Middleton's remarks, he has been flicking his hair with greater intensity and is now pouting his full lips at her – lips Sadie suspects may bear the faintest trace of pink lipstick. 'I haven't come across anything on these women before. Why shouldn't we be looking at them?'

'I didn't say we *shouldn't* be reading them,' Desiring Machine replies, in a bored voice. 'I said we've seen the maternal used to demonise women before. It's not the writers that's the problem here – it's the approach.'

> Fuck, here we go again! Be nice – don't be patronising.

But, before Sadie has a chance to reply, the girl with the red hair speaks. 'Why *can't* you apply the same methodology to a group of writers you've never come across or who've never been grouped together like this before either?' she asks angrily.

'I'm not saying you can't . . .'

And, this time, Sadie interrupts Desiring Machine herself before he can say any more. 'Your criticism – that this isn't a new approach – tends to be one that crops up again and again when people are looking at women writers,' she says. It is a cheap shot and Sadie knows it but she doesn't care. She has had enough of this. 'Nobody complains when a "new" study of fathers and sons, say, in Joyce or Lawrence or Proust comes out. Yet it's the same methodology that's used over and over again. Or haven't you noticed that?'

> Nope, failed. Wasn't nice, was patronising. Now they'll hate me.

But Sadie is wrong. She is surprised when two young women, from the back of the room, applaud her remarks and she blushes at the noise and the thought of support when she is not used to it and she does not know how to respond. Then Desiring Machine shrugs and holds up his hands as if to say, 'What you gonna do?' But suddenly she does not need to respond as David Jamieson is asking about mixing high literature with popular work – something, he has to admit, he has felt increasingly compelled to investigate himself. James Brooks wants to know more about the use of stream of consciousness in these writers he has never heard of and even the blonde boy with the sailor top betrays his companion by voicing his excitement about studying the films of Bette Davis.

'I'd like to thank Sadie for a most interesting talk,' David Jamieson finally says as he stands up and claps, which sets off a small round of applause that can only make her smile with relief. And suddenly four or five students are up on the dais talking to her – they are demanding to know what she thinks of this and that and whom – and, as she tries to answer them, they insist that they must all leave together because it is almost nine o'clock and they want to take her to the Masthead and buy her a drink. And Sadie is saying yes, she will join them, and she picks up her papers and puts on her coat because she has forgotten that she cannot drink and that smoky atmospheres are not good for women in her condition because she has forgotten what her condition is – even though she has spent five days researching and another hour this evening discussing her new project.

Her new project – which is all about mothers.

Wednesday, March 8th

I imagine if I'd stayed. I do it a lot – probably too much. I wonder what would have happened if we'd come back and lived here, if that day had turned out differently. What would I be doing now? Maybe nothing different. Maybe we'd be friends, Amy. Maybe you wouldn't have been driving that day and then you wouldn't be lying here. Maybe we'd be out together, right now, shopping, having lunch, doing things that sisters do. Maybe our kids would have been friends. Picture it, a different life – friends, sisters, mothers.

It's a stupid thing to think now – you can't turn the clock back, can't change what's happened. And I am stupid to think it – stupid. But, sometimes, I just wonder . . . I can't help it. I play with the thought of it. Growing up here, our kids – Sadie and Campbell. They'd have family. John's sister Ann never had any kids and she moved to Australia with her husband years ago. Have I said that before? Not that we saw them much even when they were here. We don't have any family. Not any more. That's what it feels like. Maybe if we did, Sadie would . . . No – it's stupid. What family? I'm just imagining things. We did it that day too – imagined all sorts of things. And got it all wrong, of course. We were stupid, weren't we, Amy? That day. And I'm stupid now – thinking that, if I go over all this, somehow you'll know and it'll make you wake up. I know it won't but I can't help it. How sad it is for you, for me, for all of us. How sad it was then too. I keep thinking about myself on that day – me and my pathetic little dreams. I really thought it would all work out, you see. I thought that *John* was the problem. He was the big obstacle I had to overcome. If only I'd known – John was the easy bit. He was what I'd prepared for but it's always what you don't expect, isn't it? What you can't prepare for, what you can't see coming. Fate. God.

I don't believe in God – not any more. I did then, years ago. I went to church when I went back to Scotland – went every Sunday. And, after I got married, I still went – even though John didn't – right up until that holiday. I believed, you see, in the right things – that, if you worked hard and behaved properly, you'd avoid bad things. I've always thought that bad things wouldn't happen to me if I was good. But I wasn't always good. I was pregnant when I got married. So that was bad. I was always worried that that was why Sadie and I don't get on. I did a bad thing. Good girls don't get pregnant first – not before they get married. Oh, now they do of course but not then. Good girls didn't do that then. And I was a good girl. Maybe Sadie is a punishment. Maybe that day was one too. What Mum did to us was a punishment – for behaving badly, for being too curious, for not waiting.

No, I'm being self-centred, Amy. It's not all about me, is it? And I don't believe in those sorts of things. Fate and God and everything – that there's something out there. Not any more. And, no, I don't believe that you're punished – not for anything. Bad people get away with things all the time. She did. She got away with it. She was allowed to disappear. What was her punishment? Never to see us again? I don't think it could have hurt her as much as it hurt us. I don't think so. Maybe having to go back, back to Scotland after all – maybe *that* was my punishment.

I just had no idea what was coming, you see, Amy. I was so happy, walking back that day through the park – back to you all. Humming a little tune, me and John hand in hand. And then we came to the end of the path, out into the green. I didn't know what I was looking at – not at first. We'd left you all . . . oh, sitting or playing or just enjoying the sunshine. It was a happy scene. Happy. All around us, everything happy. And then we came back. I couldn't believe it. It was just mayhem, utter mayhem. Everything was all over the place – the rugs, the food, the hampers. Garbage everywhere. Remember, Amy? You couldn't forget it. The wee ones all crying. Becka and Ricky, their wee faces all red and wet. Sadie, with her arms around Campbell, rushing up to us as soon as she saw us. What a fright they gave me. They didn't know what was wrong. They just knew something was. I thought at first someone had died. That's how bad it was. That's what I really thought. It was Mum or Dad – heart attack. Or the baby – but then I heard him crying. And Mary – do you remember? How frantic she was? Panicky. Everybody was shouting. You, Pete, Mike, Dad – all of you shouting and running about all over the place. And none of you would tell us what was wrong – not for ages, it seemed. I kept shouting at you all, 'What the hell's going on?' Nobody listened to me. I thought you'd all gone mad. Then finally you told me, Amy, what I hadn't noticed.

Mum was missing. Nobody had realised. Me and John, well . . . we could only have been away . . . oh, two hours at the most. That was all. It's not so long. Look what you can do in two hours these days. Fly to another country. Leave the city and be out in the countryside. Getting away from it all. Getting away. Disappearing forever. That's all the time it takes. I'd told Mary where John and I were going so she wouldn't worry – not about us. But Mum hadn't said anything – not a thing to anyone. Mary was the first one to notice she wasn't there. She said it was just after John and I had gone. Dad was playing with Ricky. Campbell and Pete were kicking a ball around. You were braiding Sadie and Becka's hair. Remember? Mike sitting down by Mary, whacked out with all the running around. I can see it – just as if I was there, as if I was there at the very moment you all discovered she was missing. I can see it. I can see Mary turning her head round, her hair, long and straight – reddish brown down her back. And her thin pale blue shirt. She was still breastfeeding. That shirt was all wrong. That's what I kept thinking. Isn't that stupid? How that shirt showed leaks. It was too thin. What a thing to remember! But it's what I remember the most – Mary and that pale blue shirt. I wanted to cover her up – get a cardigan, anything. Those big dark patches spreading. And right then, too. Right at that moment. And then, when she'd turned to speak to Mum and she just wasn't there, I can see it.

Mary was in such a state but I calmed her down – calmed you all down, didn't I? I said we'd got it wrong – she wasn't missing, she wasn't lying dead somewhere. She'll just have gone to the toilets, I said, just along the trail, and then probably decided to go off for a wee walk herself. That's what I said. None of you believed me. I didn't believe me. I had a feeling. Me and John away off like that, planning out our future – that we'd come back and live with you all again – coming back along that path so happy, so happy. I should have known it would never happen. But I wasn't going to let go of it that easily – wasn't going to give up my wee dream just like that. So I kept saying it: 'She's just wandered off somewhere. We're getting in a state about nothing.'

But then, when Mum didn't come back after twenty minutes and thirty minutes and forty . . . Mary left the baby with Mike. She was the first to go and look again but Mum definitely wasn't there. She hadn't gone to the toilets or, if she had, well . . . she wasn't there any more.

That's when we all started to get really worried. Mike raced back to the parking lot to see if she'd . . . oh, gone back to the cars for some reason. Maybe she'd be there waiting for us. No good reason why she should be but you don't know, do you? When something like that happens, you don't know what to think. Dad was convinced she'd had an accident or been mugged or attacked and left for dead – awful things. All the worst things go through your head. He'd wanted to call the police – right there and then. So, by the time John and I got back . . . well, it was different. We all had to split up to look. Dad went with Mike. I was with you. Pete was with John. John and I didn't know the park. Mary stayed with the wee ones, trying to calm them, feeding the baby.

We must have looked . . . oh, for at least two hours, was it, Amy? Did it feel longer than that? Can't remember. You were so angry with her for going off by herself. I kept saying to you that maybe that's not how it is – maybe she'd taken a funny turn. You'd said she'd had these odd moments recently – odd turns when she didn't seem to be there. It had happened a few times before we came over. You'd be talking to her, you told me, and then she'd ask you what you'd been saying – as though she hadn't heard any of it. And forgetting things – she'd forget everything. Not just the odd thing like where she'd left her book or her glasses but serious things – like leaving the rings on the cooker on or not locking the front door when she went out. She left it wide open the day before we arrived, you said. Anything could have happened. Becka or Ricky could have just wandered out on to the road. They could have gone off with strangers, anything. And drinking – she was drinking again. I knew it. I'd noticed it. I told you that. You said it'd been going on for ages – the whole time she and Dad were staying with you and before that too. You said that sometimes you were frightened to leave Ricky and Becka with her. She was too distracted – like she wasn't there.

So we thought she'd just gotten lost – had an attack of amnesia. Or maybe, at the worst, it was the onset of some kind of dementia – that's what we thought, wasn't it? Even though I didn't want to think it. She wasn't that old – not old enough for that. But it can happen younger. Or maybe it was something else but just as bad – cancer, a brain tumour . . . Really, that's what we were thinking – all those awful things. That's what we thought, didn't we, Amy? Illness. She was ill. And nobody had noticed. She was ill – maybe dying – and we hadn't even noticed. How we blamed ourselves. How terrible we felt. Such bad daughters. Not caring, not looking when our mother was so ill all that time. Remember? Searching through the undergrowth – ridiculous – even though the bushes couldn't have hidden a cat, never mind a grown woman. Stupid searches. Thinking that she might be hiding somewhere even, in a distracted state – not knowing what she was doing.

It was awful. Ages before we got back to Mary and the wee ones. We were back first. Then Pete and John came. And then Dad was back too, insisting – he was shouting – we had to go to the police. Right now. We couldn't wait any longer. He wouldn't wait. None of us could understand it. What could have happened? She'd just vanished into thin air. *The Lady Vanishes.* We asked everyone we could if they'd seen her. 'She's about fifty, slim, good-looking with dark hair, in high heels and a floral dress.' But nobody saw her. How could nobody have noticed her? Not even one single person? Everyone was just too busy. Yes. People with their own families. You only see your own, don't you? But we hadn't even done that. We hadn't even kept our eyes on our own family. Nobody, not one of us, had noticed a thing.

I'll never forget the guilt. And the fear. The worry. And getting worse all the time. As bad as if it had been Sadie or Campbell. No, that's not true. Mum was a grown woman. It's not the same with your kids. I'd have had worse thoughts if it had been one of them. I'd have been hysterical. Not guilty or worried. I'd have been out of my mind. So what does that say about me then, Amy? Or are all mothers the same, do you think? Children are the most important things in their lives. Nothing else but our kids – you live for nothing else but them.

And how could I ever forget that drive back from the park? Not for as long as I live – I'll never forget it. It's a recurring dream I get whenever I'm anxious or worried about anything. I'm in a car. It's hot. The windows are down. I don't know where I'm going. I'm not driving but I don't know who is. And we keep getting lost. We can't find the right road. We go down street after street. Then suddenly it's dark. Lights are on but it's so dark everywhere. And then we start to run out of petrol. I always wake up just when the car stops. I'm somewhere I don't recognise and I'm alone. I'm alone in the car in the dark and I don't know how to get home.

I wonder how often you've had nightmares, Amy – about

it all. Maybe you never have. Maybe you put it all away so deep down it never comes out – not even when you're sleeping. I thought I'd done that too but I know I've just been fooling myself. You can't stop your dreams, can you?

We went straight from the park to the police station to report Mum missing. Even now, saying those words, it makes no sense – no sense at all. Remember? It took so long. All the details they wanted – it just took forever. That police station – so clean, like everything here, modern, clean, air-conditioned. But we couldn't all stay. Someone had to take the wee ones home. It was getting late. They were exhausted – poor wee things. So Dad waited with John and Mike and Pete. And you drove me and Mary and the kids back to your house. Remember Mary not crying? The panic was over. The crybaby of the family too shocked and scared to cry. That upset me too. Sadie and Campbell were awful – tired and crotchety. 'When's Daddy coming?' 'Why isn't Daddy coming home too?' 'He'll be back later, pet. Don't worry.' Sadie just wouldn't stop with all her questions. And Ricky and Becka weren't much better – complaining all the way home, fighting with each other about who got to sit next to the window, wanting some juice then not wanting it. It was all I could do not to lose my temper. I was so angry and scared too – like Mary. But I was never like Mary. You'd never think we were from the same family, would you? Maybe *you* would, Amy. I always looked after her, didn't I? I was always the good girl – the good big sister. I was, wasn't I? But we're not alike – not at all.

Only, halfway back on the journey home, Sadie realised she'd left her Daisy doll behind. But we couldn't go back. It was too late. I promised I'd get her another one. And I did – when we flew back to Scotland. But I always wish we'd gone back for it – I just do. Somehow, I still think, if we'd gone back for the doll . . . we'd have found Mum too. It was like she was just lost or just something we'd forgotten, left behind at a picnic . . .

You drove as fast as you could even though it made me nervous. You're a terrible driver, Amy – always were. You don't take care. And look what's happened now to you. Ironic, isn't it? Horrible and ironic. But that drive back, it seemed like ages. Every traffic light was red – of course it was – every lane we were in was the slowest, every Sunday driver was out on the road that day. Crawling along, miles of traffic for hours – it was awful. I thought we'd never get there. The sun was setting but it was still boiling hot. Misty, smoky, orange air – like the end of the world, the end of it all. A beautiful sunset to end the perfect day is what there should have been. But we did get home – eventually. It was almost dark by the time we got back. We were exhausted. We put the wee ones to bed straightaway. They were all asleep in the car by the end. We carried them out, one by one, put them all in your and Pete's room – all four of them – on that great big double bed you had, all of them together. Like four little sleeping babies, little cherubs – not a care in the world between them. All safe and sound, home with us. Not lost, not abandoned, not left behind and all alone. 'Down a lane a lonely figure sadly wept upon a stone, little fieldy mouse was lonely left behind and all alone.' Sadie used to recite that when she was little – only about two years old at the time. And the whole book – she knew it by heart. 'Left behind and all alone.' Baby Sandy was down too – asleep in the cot. Then we sat in the front room. Couldn't eat a thing. We started on the booze instead. Even Mary had a drink – even though she was breastfeeding. I hate whisky but I drank more of it that night than I ever have in my whole life. I haven't touched it since.

It was you, Amy, who went into the basement. One minute we were all together in the front room – not talking, just sipping our whiskies – and then you were gone. Downstairs. I still don't know why you did that. You never explained. Never told me why. Never spoke about it after that night. So all I can do is guess. You were looking for something, maybe. Or you wanted to be among Mum's things – sentiment, perhaps. Or hope . . . I don't know what made you do it. Sitting, waiting for the men to come back, like we were three war widows – maybe that was it. Maybe it was just too much for you – too depressing, too little action. You needed to do something. You just wanted out of the room, didn't you? Away from me and Mary – I know, I know. Or maybe you just wanted to tell yourself that Mum was safe. That she'd be all right.

And that's when you found out. I heard you scream. That horrible noise you made – like a wounded animal. And then me, running out of the front room, along the hallway, down into the basement. Mary followed behind me. We were bumping into things – drunk by then, clumsy. I almost fell down the stairs. Remember? The light was on. It was all whiteness and so bright. And there you were, standing at the wardrobe, with the wardrobe door wide open. You were shaking, red-faced, crying with anger. I'd never seen you like that.

You could hardly get the words out. 'Her clothes . . . Mum . . . some of her clothes are missing . . . and the small suitcase.'

I didn't get it at first. I thought you were trying to tell me something crazy. That someone had kidnapped our mother –

thoughtfully packing a few items of clothing, first, of course, before taking her away. Or that she'd been abducted by aliens – aliens who'd need her clothes as well. Or that she'd gone on holiday and somehow forgotten to tell us.

Then I saw the dressing table. Mum's favourite perfume – that was gone too. You started yanking open all the drawers. Almost all her underwear was gone as well. And the little ceramic box where she kept her jewellery. She'd had it for years. It was a present. Remember? From us – from me and you and Mary. We'd saved up for it. We were only young – our pocket money. It was a Mother's Day present. And a couple of pairs of shoes were missing too.

'Isn't there a note? Some kind of a message?' I remember saying that and you shaking your head. You were throwing things out of drawers now. Flinging them across the room – over the bed and all over the floor. I had to stop you – actually had to hold you back. Mary was crying now – the crybaby of the family. At last she could cry.

'Stop it!' I was shouting at you. You were shouting back at me. I had to do something to make you stop. You were too strong for me. I couldn't hold you.

I tried to reason with you. 'We'll never find out what else she's taken with her if you do this!'

But you didn't care. 'What the hell does it matter what she's taken? She's gone – don't you get it? Our fucking mother has gone without telling anybody why or where she's going. That fucking bitch has gone!'

Then you collapsed on the bed. Oh, I never heard crying like it. And me trying to comfort you when I was crying so much myself. And Mary was just sitting on the stairs sobbing her heart out.

'She can't have.' That's what I said – wouldn't believe

it. 'There's bound to be some explanation. It must be something else. What about those odd turns you said she'd been having? You said she was behaving oddly. Couldn't that be it?'

But, you know, Amy, I didn't believe it myself – not even when I was saying it. I knew as soon as I saw the jewellery box was missing. Funny, isn't it? I saw what wasn't there. Yes, that's right – what wasn't there, not what was. Funny to see an absence – not a presence. You shouldn't be able to 'see' it at all – not once something's gone. But then how else do you notice it's gone? To miss something, it has to have been there in the first place – like the photographs. There had been two of them – by Mum's side of the bed – one of Campbell and Sadie that we'd sent over last Christmas and one of Ricky and Becka, an old one, when they were just newborn. I remember the photos from the few times I'd been in that room before she went. My eyes were just drawn to pictures of kids I suppose. You're like that when you have wee ones of your own. But there were no other pictures. No photographs of her own kids – none of me or you or Mary, none, even, of her and Dad. That's strange, isn't it? When I think about it now. At the time it just seemed . . . I don't know. I didn't think it meant anything – not at the time. You don't think photographs by someone's bedside are that important. Don't wonder why some are on display and others aren't. Or why some are taken when someone leaves forever.

Hurry, hurry! I must hurry or I'll be late!

But something is holding her back. Something is pulling at her. She is not strong enough to fight it and it is slowing her down. It is dark on the street. She is facing downhill on the way into the town and she should be running here where the road dips down but she can't run. Then suddenly she wakes up. Richard is lying beside her, snoring softly. Sadie is gasping for breath as though she has been battling some unseen monster in the dark. She wants the light on so she reaches round to the lamp on her side of the bed. She sits up in the dim light of Richard's tidy bedroom, blinks at the sleeping computer in the corner and the orderly boxes of books and papers that surround it. The books that Richard likes are on display on the top of his bookshelves, the others he leaves in the boxes beside the computer. Sadie stares up at the books and, for once, does not notice the titles but something else instead. They are all in alphabetical order. She squints at them and her eyes move down the shelves to the LPs at the bottom. They are in alphabetical order too.

Somewhere at the back of Sadie's mind she knows she has registered this before. That is why she hasn't told him yet. He may have sexy sideburns and a beaten-up leather jacket but he lines up his books and his LPs in alphabetical order. His room is spotless even though this is an old house and everything in it is borrowed or bought second-hand. He likes Arnold Schwarzenegger films but disapproves of Sadie watching soaps because they are an insult to her intelligence and she should know better. He cut up slices of avocado and drizzled Italian dressing over them once, a dish he was appalled to learn she hadn't tried before and so, even though she loathes avocado, she swallowed it down because Richard doesn't like to see food go to waste.

Richard does not like waste or mess or complications – of any kind. Sadie is only now learning just how much he likes order. The order of genetics – simple lines leading somewhere. He is not a man – and she is surprising herself when she realises this – she wants to be tied to for ever.

Sadie takes a deep breath and sips some water from the glass beside the lamp. She can't push it out of her mind even though she told herself that she would – even though she said she wouldn't think about it and she would ignore what her body is doing. But how can she? How can she when, only yesterday, after a leisurely weekend and an easy beginning to the week, David Jamieson stopped her in the corridor to invite her to dinner with a visiting academic.

'I was ONce a STUdent of MADeleine Bower,' he had explained, just as something made her stomach turn over – something that made her think she might faint there, right in front of David Jamieson. But it didn't happen. No, it didn't happen. Her body didn't let her down – not yet. And so she had to work hard to listen to him as he said, 'I THInk it would BE to your adVANtage to MEET her after she's spoken here toMORrow. WOULD you like to COME to DINner afterwards?'

But she was fine after all. She did not betray anything. Her body did not betray her.

'Thanks, yes, I would,' she said, without gushing. She sounded like a real academic – yes, a real academic, not the fake one that she has been all this time, the fake one who would have gushed foolishly at the thought of dining with the Madeleine Bower. And, even better, she was able to add, 'I've read *Siren Sounds* so I'll look forward to asking her about it.' Measured, measured, Sadie is always measured now. There is no more gushiness, there are no more foolish remarks. She is learning – she is learning how to act.

And David Jamieson had nodded approvingly and said, 'SPLENdid,'

And Sadie could not keep the smile from her face all day because not only had she given a well-received paper just a few days ago but she had also been invited to dinner with one of the country's most famous female academics, the author of *Siren Sounds: Women's Voices in the Work of Jane Austen, Fanny Burney and Maria Edgeworth* (Claridge Press, 1978), a landmark study about the difficulty of speaking. It was a reward for her good work. David Jamieson was rewarding her by inviting her to meet Madeleine Bower, the same Madeleine Bower who wrote about women's voices when a woman's voice in literary criticism was an accident, nothing intentional at all. She'd been writing about women's voices in academia when women's voices in academia were usually only heard offering to make tea or type papers. Madeleine Bower was one of those troublesome women who headed out and wanted other women to follow her. And Sadie cannot wait to meet her. When she does, it will endorse the success of her paper, it will grant her that sense that, at last, her academic life is a success too, that she is right to be here, that she belongs here.

Yes, that is right, Sadie tells herself as she puts the glass back down on the table quietly so as not to disturb Richard and slips back under the covers. Richard has not woken up at all. He is still snoring gently and, as she looks at him just before she switches off the lamp, she reminds herself that it is voices that matter – words not bodies.

Sadie is late – she must hurry. Her hair is still damp as she tries to rush across the cobbles to the restaurant where David Jamieson is waiting with Madeleine Bower. But rushing across cobbles is impossible and she catches her heel just as she reaches the edge of the pavement. Her mind is on the conversation she had with Lily, just moments before she left the house.

> 'I've been trying to get you all day. Didn't the secretaries tell you I rang?'
> 'Sorry, Mum, it's been non-stop teaching all day.' A lie.
> 'Well, things are still the same here. We thought – last night – that she was improving. Her eyelids fluttered. We thought she was coming out of it.'
> 'I'm sorry, Mum, really.' But Sadie has to go – Madeleine Bower is waiting.
> 'You sound out of breath. Have I caught you at a bad time?'
> 'No, it's just . . . I've got a meeting on – couple of academics.'
> 'At this time?'
> 'It's dinner.' With Madeleine Bower. But Lily would not know who that is.
> 'Well, I won't keep you.' Sharp tone that Sadie hates.

It's not her fault. She has a life. Madeleine Bower is waiting. 'There's nothing else?' She doesn't mean it to come out like that but it does.
'What else should there be? Isn't Amy being in a coma enough?'
'Sorry.' How many times has Sadie apologised now? Get going – she has to get going. She has to leave.

And she reaches out her hand as she feels herself pitching forward but, no, she is steady after all and doesn't fall. Madeleine Bower is waiting close by and family, the only family Sadie is interested in, is what her mother refuses to discuss with her so Sadie must stop thinking about it all. She must concentrate on the here and now, on her meeting, on dinner, on first impressions, on making a good impression.

Without another stumble, she reaches the door of the restaurant, a stocky, two-storey building well suited to North Sea breezes with its thick walls and reinforced windows. It's a new restaurant, bringing fusion food

to a town that still thinks prawn cocktail is exotic, ha!

And she sees them already sitting at a table inside. David Jamieson is talking to Madeleine Bower who is at his elbow. He is talking with great seriousness and, opposite him, Sadie can see one of his graduate students, Archie Something – she doesn't know his last name – nodding constantly as he speaks.

Right then, here goes.

Sadie steps inside and immediately a female student from

one of her tutorial groups, Anouska, she can't remember her last name either, with her Scandinavian blonde hair tied back in a ponytail, appears and smiles at her. 'Hi, Dr Mathieson!' she says and she takes Sadie's coat and leads her to the table.

'SAdie!' David Jamieson stands up inelegantly and hurries round to the opposite side of the table to pull out a chair for her.

Sadie will not be seated beside Madeleine Bower or even directly opposite. This disappoints her immediately but it will be all right. It will be all right because here she is – here she is in the presence of this important woman whose hand she is now shaking. And Sadie looks down into a face she recognises because, although Madeleine Bower is taller than Sadie, she is seated and Sadie is standing. And then Madeleine Bower smiles at her. She shows even teeth in a broad, full-lipped smile and her large hooded eyes are half-closed as her faces creases and Sadie is honoured – yes, honoured – to meet her. But, of course, Sadie does not say that. She does not say how honoured she is to meet this large woman in her late fifties with expensively hennaed hair who is wearing a beautifully cut jacket that moves without seeming to crease. Madeleine Bower shakes Sadie's hand and, at that moment, she is exactly as Sadie expected – she is all dynamism and style and purpose. And, for a split second, Sadie falters. She is too intimidated – she does not believe she is good enough to be here – but she smiles nevertheless because she is hoping that, when she smiles at Madeleine Bower, it will be enough.

'I'm sorry I'm a wee bit late.' Sadie has begun with an apology that reminds her of her conversation with her mother and it isn't how she wanted to begin at all and she feels suddenly self-conscious about her accent – she sounds like someone she doesn't want to be, someone she isn't.

'It's FINE. We haven't ORdered yet. SAdie, this is PROfessor MAdeleine BOWer. PROfessor, this is Dr SAdie Mathieson, one of our NEWest apPOINtees.'

Madeleine Bower blinks her heavy-lidded eyes slowly and Sadie pulls her hand back too quickly and it accidentally jostles the professor's glass of water. It ebbs from one side to the other and, for a moment, looks as if it will tip over completely but, no, Sadie is lucky and it doesn't topple – nothing is spilt and Madeleine Bower behaves as if she hasn't noticed it so perhaps everything is all right, perhaps everything is perfectly fine.

Anouska, the blonde student, comes back to take everybody's order. The room is dim, lit only by soft orange lights and candles on the table. Wine is brought over and Sadie takes a large sip – it will relax her. And she asks them all in the accent which is now disturbing her – she doesn't know where it has come from and it makes her voice sound so strange – to go back to the conversation they were having before she interrupted them with her arrival.

'PROfessor BOWer was just EXplaining about her REcent stay at PRINCEton,' David Jamieson tells her.

Sadie smiles even though she hasn't been invited to call the professor by her first name and that is a barrier, straightaway. So she asks to hear more from 'Professor' Bower

I rrreelly I woood rreelly like t' heeer mower.

And Sadie really doesn't understand what is wrong with her voice. The graduate student beside her, Archie, is very quiet. She has seen him once or twice in the department. He is sickly looking and pale but he is intelligent and Sadie is glad she is not the only younger person at the table.

'Yes,' Professor Bower begins once again and the table is silent.

Sadie wonders if the reason her voice sounds strange to her is because it is not anything like the professor's voice which is deep and full and round-vowelled. Sadie takes another sip of wine and wishes she had been to the States too so she had something to contribute.

> Berkeley, Ithaca where else do they publish? MIT? There must be another one. What are all the Ivy League ones? Yale, Princeton, Cornell, Harvard . . . What's the other one? Damn it! Can't even remember that.

'We were in Washington for just over a year. My husband was on sabbatical there, of course.' Madeleine Bower nods to David Jamieson, who nods back.

Sadie wonders who her husband is and if she should know who he is. Yes, she should probably know who he is but perhaps it won't matter because soon she will be discussing her work – she will be discussing pioneering work that upsets stale old departments and then it will not matter that she does not know who Madeleine Bower's husband is or what he does.

'It was extremely refreshing. Quite a change from Oxford – a much greater mix of people. It can be quite tiresome only being surrounded by academics.' The professor pauses and everybody laughs – including Sadie although she doesn't know why. It has taken almost five minutes for Madeleine Bower's to enunciate her last sentence in her round-vowelled voice and any possible joke has been anticipated well in advance but still they all laugh. And it seems to Sadie that she is laughing too loudly – she can hear her voice over everybody else's – and she feels suddenly vulgar, suddenly wrong for this setting and this conversation.

'Yes, very pleasant. A much greater mix of . . . middle-class people.'

And now Sadie wonders, because she does not know if it is her imagination or if it has really happened, whether Madeleine Bower really looked directly at her when she said 'middle-class people'.

But it cannot be her imagination because the professor follows it with a hurried, 'Of course, I do realise that is still very narrow.' And, when she says that, she looks Sadie square in the eye so Sadie cannot mistake it. She has heard Sadie's voice, she has made her judgement, she knows where Sadie belongs, she knows why Sadie Mathieson, of all people, might find 'middle class' too narrow.

But Sadie still cannot quite believe that it matters because it is the quality of her education that counts, surely? Sadie believes it is the work she is doing that counts because it is the work that Madeleine Bower does that counts for her. And she believes that, because the professor is a woman in a male-dominated profession, she will want to help her.

'SAdie gave a WONderful PAper here just a FEW nights aGO,' David Jamieson announces suddenly and Madeleine Bower turns benevolently in Sadie's direction.

'Really? And is it going to be published?'

'Yes, well, it's early days but I think there might be one who's quite keen,' Sadie ventures even though she only received this tentative assurance recently and over the phone so she cannot be completely sure.

'Who?'

'Oh,' Sadie smiles and gives the name of the small academic publishing house she contacted the other day and then Madeleine Bower does a strange thing. She bursts out laughing.

'With them?'

Sadie doesn't know what she means. She is confused – she doesn't know what to say.

'My dear, that's practically vanity publishing! Can't you get somebody better?'

And Sadie looks at David Jamieson who has the decency to be embarrassed for her and she still doesn't know what to say but Madeleine Bower is looking at her, waiting for an answer.

'Someone else must be interested, dear, surely. What did you say you were working on?'

Sadie mumbles a few words about mothers and daughters and Madeleine Bower laughs again.

'Ah, well, there it is. Rather narrow, I think. You might want to reconsider. Something less . . . questionable, academically speaking?'

'Well,' Sadie begins again. She still wants Madeleine Bower's approval, even after this, so she adds hurriedly, 'I'm really interested in personal writing – you know, theorising autobiographies, diaries, that kind of thing. I know it's very big in the States right now . . .'

Madeleine Bower's features do not move. '*Was*, I think,' she says gently.

And now, as she picks up her glass of wine, Sadie knows that, because Madeleine Bower has moved on now – she is attending to Archie – in that moment, she knows that, of course, this woman will not help her. Of course the professor is not that woman, so much higher up the career ladder, who will look at Sadie and think, 'I must help her – I must help this young woman who is on her own here because, once upon a time, I, too, was on my own.' Of course she is not that woman Sadie believed her to be – of course not. She is the woman who has looked at Sadie in the black trousers and black shirt that she bought from a high street chain store and she is the woman who will not want Sadie on her side. She will not want Sadie on her side because Sadie's voice gave her away the minute she spoke, because Sadie's clothes gave her away the moment she appeared, because Sadie's research gave her away the moment she discovered it. And Sadie understands, in that moment, that Madeleine Bower is not a woman who will help other younger women in the same profession because Madeleine Bower is a woman who is frightened and resentful of other younger women in the same profession.

And then it happens.

Sadie reaches for another sip of wine but her glass is already empty and they have only brought the bread rolls so far. But then Anouska, the blonde student, appears with the starters and Sadie orders another glass of wine as the dishes are placed on the table and everybody exclaims over how nice they look.

And Sadie reaches for the glass jug of water in the middle of the table to keep her going until the wine arrives.

But the glass jug is heavier than she thought it would be.

She cannot hold it properly. The glass handle is slipping from her grasp. The jug is falling. She cannot stop it. She doesn't have the strength to hold it.

Then, suddenly, Sadie brings her other hand up to steady the jug. But, no, she has saved the moment – nothing spills and she heaves a sigh of relief, smiles and pulls her hand back and then . . .

Smash!

She knocks over David Jamieson's almost full glass of wine. It tips sideways as it heads to the floor.

Sadie watches it fall, fall so slowly that, if she could move just a little bit, she would surely have had time to catch it. But, no, it crashes as it hits the parquet and red wine spills purple on the floor.

Everything happens at once. David Jamieson is standing almost immediately. 'NO, no, it's FINE – it MISSed me completely!'

Anouska, the blonde student, rushes over. 'I'll clear it away – please don't worry!'

And Sadie gasps, horrified. 'I'm so sorry! That was *so* clumsy of me!'

And Archie mops up a few drops that landed on the table before the glass smashed.

Madeleine Bower says nothing but smiles at the scene in a distracted kind of way.

> You bitch! You *absolute* bitch!

Sadie catches her eye and she knows she cannot make a joke of it all. If she was with friends, this would be funny. But Sadie is not with friends.

David Jamieson sits down, half-smiling at her, and Anouska, the blonde student, reappears with another glass of wine for him and another one for Sadie, which is somehow even worse. She must seem drunk enough already and yet here is more.

'COULD have been WORse,' David Jamieson says,

cheerfully. 'ANYway, MADeleine, you were SAYing About WASHington . . .'

It was a minor thing – to break a glass. Madeleine Bower begins to speak again and Sadie tells herself it was nothing, it was nothing, but, even so, it wouldn't matter anyway. And it does seem that it is soon forgotten.

The main course arrives, Sadie's head is fuzzy now with past anxiety and more wine that she shouldn't have drunk of course but, all the same, she starts, incredibly, to feel better. The food is passable, comments are made on changing fashions in restaurants and Archie has exchanged a few words with Madeleine Bower by now and so Sadie must move beyond apologies. She must show that her voice and her clumsiness are not what define her and that her research is not what the professor insists it is. This is her chance and so, by the time dessert arrives and she is on her fourth glass of wine, Sadie at last feels confident enough to ask Madeleine Bower about her research and in a more combative manner. Let Madeleine Bower defend her work. Even though, of course, she no longer has to, Sadie is determined she will make her defend it. The professor is a specialist on Jane Austen. Sadie knows a lot about Jane Austen – she is very fond of Jane Austen – so this is safe territory. But, when Sadie asks her question, she cannot think of narrative or mise en scène, she cannot think of anything except to ask what the professor thinks of the recent film of *Sense and Sensibility*.

It is, Madeleine Bower makes clear, 'designed wholly for the American market'. Her eyelids are almost completely shut and her lips are wide with what almost looks like a white line around them which has the effect of spreading them out more. Sadie's lips are full but uneven, of course. She decides she doesn't want to say anything more with her funny voice and her uneven mouth. She certainly doesn't want to ask whether being designed for an American market is good or bad – she suspects that it is bad – but then . . .

What the hell – it's all shot to pieces anyway.

And Sadie decides to tell the professor a story.

'It's really quite funny,' she begins and, even through the reassuring haze of wine, she knows that it won't work but she can't stop – she can't stop a verbal crash that's going to be even worse than knocking over a glass of wine. 'It was just when I was working in this bar last year, the manager called his girlfriend at home when we'd all finished to say when he'd be back late – we were having a lock-in and it was about one in the morning. But she wasn't mad at him for being so late because it turned out it was her day off. When he came off the phone, he asked us to guess why she was so happy. A bottle of wine and six hours of Mr Darcy!'

Madeleine Bower looks at her.

'She'd been watching a video of *Pride and Prejudice,*' Sadie explains.

There is no response.

David Jamieson decides that he should offer up a smile and Sadie tries to turn what she has said into something academic. 'Isn't it interesting how Jane Austen has been completely repackaged for a modern audience?'

But it doesn't work. Madeleine Bower sees through her now – she sees right through Dr Sadie Mathieson and her story – and she is appalled to think that she might be expected to know anything about bars and girls who watch videos on their days off. Madeleine Bower knows as much about bars and girls who watch videos on their days off as Sadie does about the middle-class mix of Washington. Madeleine Bower doesn't need to know – she doesn't need to know anything about Sadie or her world, about what she thinks or what she does. Sadie is all wrong and Archie, the graduate student, is far more impressive than she is. David Jamieson gave her a chance but she couldn't take it – she couldn't take it and use it properly.

Eventually, after a little more conversation which has returned to the subject of the American university system, the bill is brought and Sadie is surprised when she looks at her watch to see that it is not nearly as late as she thought.

Madeleine Bower announces she is tired and will be going to her hotel and everybody says goodnight and Sadie retrieves her coat and steps out into the night with David Jamieson and Archie, who say their goodbyes and, because they live in the same street, they leave to get a taxi together. So Sadie is left alone with her disappointment and disillusion.

She hears noises coming from down the street. It is a group of students heading for the Masthead – two girls and three boys. They're laughing as they push each other a little and one of the girls is picked up by two of the boys and carried along in an arm basket.

The street is quiet once they are gone. It is dark and cold and the old-style streetlamps reflect on the cobbles, shining and slippery. Sadie doesn't want to go home but she has nowhere else to go. Richard is working late in the lab and Jackie and her friends are at a party. So she will go home. She will go back up the road to the cheap house she shares, where she will sit down, pour herself another glass of wine even though that is the last thing she should allow herself to have and she will think about what she is going to do.

Sunday, March 19th

It's been three days since . . . There was nothing more they could do. You'd never wake up. That's what they kept saying. Over and over, as if we didn't understand what they meant, as if it was confusing – not simple. They made Pete decide. He had to do something. He kept thinking – machines. They'll be needed. By the next person who comes in after a car crash.

Three days – since they switched off the machine. After Pete said yes. And you left me, Amy. You stayed asleep and you left me.

You've left all of us. How could you leave us? How could you? I can't believe I'm saying this. I can't believe you won't ever speak to me again. I won't ever see you. Never. Why couldn't you have woken up? I want to blame you so much! For so many things, Amy. Oh, for not waking up – that's just the start. I want to shout at you. Scream at you. Hit you even. My bad little sister – always so bad. Amy. Wish you were here so I could scream and yell at you. For leaving me – just like she did. For leaving without saying goodbye. Why couldn't you say goodbye? Would that have been so difficult? Say goodbye! Let someone know why you're leaving! Don't be so damn selfish! Think of others for a change. That's what I want to shout at you. Think of others for a change.

And now you've left before I've finished. You're leaving

me to finish this on my own and I'm never going to forgive you for that. No, I don't mean that – you know I don't. I forgive you, I forgive you. I have to finish. Have to finish this. On my own – John has left me on my own. He understands – always understands – always knows. And your kids, Amy, Becka and Ricky, and Pete – the poor souls. If you could have seen them . . . The state of them . . . How could you leave them on their own? All alone – without you. How could you? How could she? How could she have done it? Left us on our own – without her. You're just as bad as she was, Amy. I mean it. Yes. You are. No, I'm sorry. Of course I am. You're not like her. Oh, but you've left us, Amy. You've left us all. And now I'll have to finish it – without you.

So I'll finish it. Properly. What I remember. That night. What I remember of you. Your fury. Out of control. Smashing things. Tearing clothes. I was afraid, Amy. Afraid of you. I couldn't control you. I wished Pete was there. And John and Dad. Too many women. I wished they'd hurry home so I wouldn't be left to deal with you on my own. And deal with her on my own too. You weren't helping. How you managed not to wake the wee ones . . . You didn't want to wake them – I remember that too. In the middle of all the smashing and the tearing, you didn't want them to know. I didn't want them to know. Didn't want them upset. They'd seen enough at the park. It's not good for wee ones to see adults so out of control. If they see it too often, they think it's all right. But how they never heard you . . . The noise you made! Too shattered by it all, I suppose. They slept through the whole thing.

Because you and me, Amy, we knew. We knew that she'd gone for good. And that she'd gone because she wanted to go. Nobody had kidnapped her. No aliens had abducted her.

She wasn't away for a little trip. That's what Dad wanted to believe at first. When he got back from the police station, he looked about eighty. Terrified. Frail. Old. He wouldn't see it. 'She's been very tired lately – that's all. She's decided to have a wee break. You know, like she used to do.'

Yes. I remember those 'wee breaks'. She'd go off – sometimes for days – when we were little. Only I knew about them. I saw them. Saw her. Dad never knew where she'd gone but I did. Just like this time. And this time I knew as well. It was for good, this time. I don't know why – I just knew. Maybe it was from the things that were missing – they were things you'd take if you weren't coming back.

That was an awful night. Trying to calm you down, Amy. I only managed it with more of the whisky we'd brought over. Finished the whole bottle. Poor Pete didn't have a clue what to do. Mary was just confused once she'd calmed down – like Dad. Kept saying it must be a holiday. 'She wasn't thinking. Mum's been a little off lately. Maybe it's the change. That might be what it is.' Didn't she say something about it? Night sweats or something? That might be it. And Dad would nod, and Mary would nod back. We sat that night in your front room, Amy. Thinking of the friends we could call. The neighbours. Any other relatives.

'Was there a favourite place Mum liked to go? Someone she'd go to when she was upset?' I remember asking that – wanting to join in the pretence. That it was all just temporary. Dad kept saying she would write or phone. He wouldn't leave your front room. Not even to sleep. You had to make up a bed for him on the sofa – in case she phoned and he missed it. The basement didn't have a phone connection.

Then, when he saw the mess you'd made of their room, of

her things . . . 'She might have left a note! You stupid, stupid woman, Amy! How'll I find it now?'

Dad hardly ever shouted at us – not even when we were little. And there he was, yelling at you, Amy. And you just turned round, walked back up the stairs. Said nothing for the rest of the night – or the next day. How we got through those next few days I'll never know. Like living a nightmare. Dad wouldn't eat a thing. You smoking so much – one cigarette right after the other. Even worse than usual – before one had finished you'd started another. There were too many of us in the house – Mary and Mike stayed on too, waiting for a call or a letter. And us all getting on each other's nerves. The wee ones didn't have a clue what was wrong. How could they? No one explained anything to them. They knew something was up, though. Only Sadie asked. She was the oldest. She knew her grandmother wasn't there. 'Where's Gran? When's she coming back? Did we leave her at the picnic? Has she got my Daisy doll with her?'

I can hear her wee voice now – as if it was yesterday. But what could I say? I didn't have anything to say. None of us did. You were impossible, Amy. Just impossible. Fighting with Dad over her clothes. You binned them all. Put them in a steel container. Set fire to them. Remember that evening? Three days after she'd gone. You'd been drinking too. I'd been out with John and the kids all day. We needed to get away from the house. Get Sadie and Campbell away too. Your wee ones as well as ours. I don't think there was a single moment – not a single moment in the whole day – when I didn't think about her, about what she'd done. We went to the animal park. Let the children feed the deer. The baby goats. Greedy little goats. Made us all laugh. Laughing – after what had happened? It seemed incredible. But you know what wee ones are like.

Becka running away when one of the baby goats started nibbling her hair. So cute, so funny. She wouldn't go near them after that, though – not even the smallest ones. She'd learned her lesson.

And then, when we came back, all that black smoke pouring out of the back garden . . . We could see it halfway down the street. And you on the ground, crying. Dad trying to throw water on the clothes. Pathetically running back and forth to the kitchen for water. Pete just standing there. He'd no idea what to do. All Mum's clothes ruined. Dad was crying too. I couldn't bear it.

John insisted, eventually, that we go back to Scotland as we'd planned – even if Mum still wasn't back. The police couldn't do much, they said. They'd look but we got the feeling they wouldn't look too hard. They thought the same as me and you, Amy, that she'd left. 'Done a bunk.' Only, why now? Why now when Dad was retired from the business? When everything was easy? When there were no more worries?

I didn't want to stay in Scotland – I still wanted to come back. But I wouldn't let it happen, couldn't – not now. She'd left us. Well, then, to hell with her and her new country. I didn't need her. And I didn't need it. I wouldn't even let John mention it again. Nothing more was said – no more about emigrating. We'd stay put. I wasn't going to give her the satisfaction of coming back and waiting, just waiting, every day, for a knock on the door. Or a phone call. Or a letter. And that's what I'd have done if I'd come back to Toronto – I'd have sat and waited. She'd have ruined my life. But she ruined it anyway because now I had to stay where I didn't want to stay. And I couldn't go where I wanted to go.

It's terrible thing to hate your own mother. Did you, Amy? I'll never know now if you hated her too. Not for what or who she is. I never hated her for that. I didn't always get on with her, maybe, but I didn't hate her – not until that day, the day of the picnic. From then on, I hated her. I think you might have too. If you didn't, you would have called more often. I'd have called you. We'd have been like sisters are meant to be. But we were too busy hating her.

Our last day there . . . Remember? Mary and Mike were leaving the same day.

'What will you do about Dad?' Mary asked, standing in the doorway, holding baby Sandy. Worried sick. 'He can't go back to that big apartment all on his own.'

He wasn't Mary's problem or mine – or yours, for that matter. But you were a good girl, Amy. You were a good girl. You let him stay – as long as he wanted to. And he stayed until the day he died . . . five years later. Five years in the basement with her things. He wouldn't go back to their apartment even though it was all finished – all redecorated. But he wouldn't go back without her. And he wouldn't let you touch her things again. I knew that – Mary told me. You didn't make him go back but you never told me why not, Amy. Afraid we'd all see how soft you were? And we'd take advantage? You did the right thing – the good thing – but it didn't bring us together as a family the way tragedies are supposed to. The way a death is supposed to. And that's what it was like – a death. We never saw her again – our mother.

Your funeral has been arranged. Cremation, of course. You were always practical, unsentimental. John and I will leave the day after. Becka and Ricky are both going to say something, bless them. They are good kids. Not kids, grown-ups now of course. Must remember – stop calling them that. And Pete is holding up, Amy. They'll be all right. They will manage without you. They'll manage.

Oh, what am I saying? As if they can, as if they can just go on when a mother dies, when a wife dies – when she's just not there any more. Dad was never the same. I knew it even from far away. I'd call him sometimes – at odd times when I felt sentimental and not angry. It was never at the right times, though – never on Mother's Day or on her birthday – always an odd day, a day that meant nothing. Dad would phone me, though. Every year, in June – on that day. Just to let me know she was still missing, still disappeared. As though it was a surprise. As though he thought one year it would be different. As though one year he'd have something different to tell me. And then, of course, the year I didn't hear. You always said it killed him – her going. Well, it was a slow killing, then. Five years – five years and three months after she left, he left too.

Oh, no. No more of that. No more 'leaving'. I'm sick of talking about leaving as though they might come back. They died. Mum and Dad. He died. She died. That's what I tell myself. I never saw him after the picnic either. I spoke to him. I wrote to him. But I never set eyes on him again.

I told myself stories, though. Bet you did too, Amy. What were yours? I'd love to have known. Mine stayed the same. They never changed. I had four. Four stories – two bad, two good and all ludicrous. She'd been having an affair all this time with someone else and now they were free – that was on a bad day. Or she'd discovered she had a terminal disease and didn't want us to see her suffer – that was on a good day, a day I was feeling especially generous. She hated us all along and couldn't stand to see any more of us – bad day. She was being threatened by someone and didn't want them to hurt us – good day. Ludicrous – all of it. But, see, Amy, see how it switches. From hurt to protection. She wanted to hurt us, she wanted to protect us. Just one or the other. All black and white – I can't see any grey. Can't see what could have been grey, what could have blurred the lines – made a different story.

Because I didn't *want* to see – I didn't want a different story. Bad or good – that's it. What I really think, though, what I really think deep down, is that she always wanted to leave – always. She never planned to stay with us so long, never expected to stay so long. Then one day she woke up and just thought suddenly, 'What am I doing here?' *Sleeping Beauty. Snow White and the Seven Dwarfs.* It's what happens when the princess wakes up. Sleeping changes things. That's what I think it was like. She'd been sleeping and she woke up and just thought to herself, 'I'm not supposed to be here. This isn't my life. My life was supposed to be something else – something else entirely. I was never meant to be married. I was never meant to have three girls. I was never meant to live this life.' And that story is my romantic story – when I'm feeling that I want the truth, when I want to know what's real. I still read romances – isn't that funny, Amy? Remember how we used to read them when we were girls? Over and over again, our favourite ones. Yours was the painter story – the painter looking for the perfect subject to paint. That was an unusual one. Mine wasn't so unusual. The handsome prince, a handsome prince masquerading as a poor woodsman – I loved that sort of thing. Still do. People pretending to be something else. Not to lie or cheat or hurt anyone – just because their own selves were too much for them. They need something else – something simpler. *The Prisoner of Zenda.* Fake princes. *The Prince and the Pauper.* I never had the nerve to pretend to be something or someone I wasn't – if nerve is what it takes – but I like the idea of it.

I never really knew what to say to Sadie, though. She actually thinks – no, thought – that she'd be here, Rubina. That her grandmother would just pop up from nowhere – that she'd appear by your bedside, Amy. Well. It's too late for that – too late for Mum to show now. It's been too late for a long time. Maybe she's dead now too. She'd be in her seventies so she could still be alive. I wonder what she'd look like if she *is* still alive somewhere. No. Stop that! Sadie always has to get it going, always has to start. I don't know where it comes from. Why she wants to know. And to think . . . Mum would be here . . . It's my own fault – I should have talked to her about what happened. Then she wouldn't be so curious. Like giving wee ones a taste of wine when they're wee and don't like it – then they won't be mystified by it later on, will they? You stop them having a treat now and then but it's no good. McDonald's, sweeties – they'll just be desperate for them when they're older if you do that. Think that they're a big mystery. Not smoking, though. Can't give a wee thing a cigarette – not even to put them off. But that's different – that's peer pressure, being 'cool'. What was being 'cool' for us, Amy? Simple things – music, hairdos, that special underskirt I got when I was sixteen, the one that made your skirts stick out, just like in the films. What did they call them then? Can't remember.

Amy. I can't remember – and I can't ask you to remember it for me.

No news is good news, no news is good news, no news is good news . . .

And that is all Sadie can think – a little cliché repeating itself inside her head, as she sifts through her Monday mail with extra care.

It is late, Sadie has been in the library all day because term has almost ended for the Easter break and she has been able to spend the last few days reading more women writers from the twenties and thirties – even though she has been worried about her research ever since Madeleine Bower dismissed it. She is sure she will find more comfort in the personal, whatever the professor said about it, which is why, today, Sadie is looking so frantically through her mail. There must be something – someone *must* know something. But, once again, she is disappointed. No one has replied to her adverts, no one can tell her about Rubina.

And Aunt Amy is dead – her aunt Amy who she barely remembers. Lily was very quiet on the phone last night, until Sadie told her why she wanted to ask her about Rubina. It was for research, she told her mother. The personal, self-writing, it's all huge, she said. She could write about Rubina's life. Academics are going crazy for this sort of thing, she said. Feminism has made the inner life of a woman

– any woman, not just literary women – suddenly worth talking about.

Well done, Sadie! Nice timing.

She has been telling herself that all day – ever since Lily slammed the phone down on her yet again. So now she has one research project that has been dismissed as frivolous by a senior academic she respected and another research project that cannot begin until her mother speaks to her or someone from Lawrie Street contacts her. She doesn't need written proof, she doesn't need diaries or letters or journals – not that Rubina would have been sophisticated enough to keep a 'journal' – she only needs words, spoken words, someone to talk to her about her grandmother. Oral history is part of the personal. She can work with stories and hearsay, gossip and rumour – all of it will work. The personal doesn't need the written to authenticate it.

But, without even the spoken, Sadie knows she is caught between two dead ends and now she does not know what to do. Richard does not understand her distress. He still phones her every night when they do not see each other but she knows how disappointed he will be, one day soon, when he realises his mistake. Sadie has not disappointed him yet but she knows that, when she does, it will not be because she is a fraud. She has not misled him. She has never let him think she is someone she is not – even if she feels that somehow she has – but, when he finds out his mistake, he will be angry with her and will want to blame her for misleading him. When Sadie tells him how her body has let her down – let them both down . . . But she is not a fraud.

When are you going to tell him? When are you going to tell him?

Sadie must shut out that voice, must not think about her body just now. Words not bodies – that is what she must remember. She knows there is not really enough between her and Richard for things to go much further. They have come to the end of the road.

What's wrong with me? Can I only think in clichés all of a sudden?

But he is so determined they are right for each other that she is ignoring what he will do when she tells him. And, yes, all right, she *will* have to tell him.

When are you going to tell him? When are you going to tell him?

No, she can't tell him. When everything else seems to be going so wrong, she must have some success in her life. Sadie just cannot admit another mistake to herself. Not that Richard is a mistake . . . She cannot admit that her relationship with him has been a mistake – just like this post, just like her research, just like her relationship with her mother.

Sadie rests her elbows on the desk and sinks her head on to the palms of her hands. It has begun to snow outside and it is pitch dark but the lamp beside the computer on her desk gives the room a warm glow and she thinks about the next day when she will go on a short teacher-training programme, organised by one of her colleagues, which is to be held at a five-star hotel in the country. Yes, colleagues – that word slips easily by now. Surely that is a mark of success? She is attending a programme organised by a colleague. It is only two days long but she is eager to go – she wants the break away from this small town.

She glances at the mail on her desk again then looks up to watch the snowflakes flutter past the window. She should be heading up the road.

There is a knock at the door.

Sadie looks at her watch, she is surprised that it is already almost seven and she realises how hungry she is. She considers ignoring the knock. Her door fits tight with the hard carpet so it lets no light slip out to betray she is there but then, for some reason – for some reason she will not be able to fathom later on, when she will blame herself and wonder,

> Why did I do that?

for some inexplicable reason, Sadie clears her throat and says loudly, 'Come in!'

It is Maurice. He is a final-year student from her contemporary fiction class. He is very tall and broad with dark curly hair and he is wearing green combat trousers, Doc Marten boots and a camouflage jacket. His face is greasy, pasty. He doesn't look right and Sadie frowns as he enters clumsily. His frame is too big and heavy for her office. He's barely through the door and already he fills the space and suddenly her desk seems to be squashing her.

'What can I do for you, Maurice?' she says in a voice that is more cheery than she feels.

And he doesn't reply. He paces up and down, his heavy boots beating against the carpet, and she experiences a sense of unease that she cannot quite place. Why does he not answer her? She closes her book and is starting to pick up a few papers from her desk when he stops pacing and turns round to face her.

'It's about the essay – I need some more time. Some stuff's been happening.'

'All right . . .' Sadie is puzzled but she is also tired and hungry and she resents his intrusion at this hour. She was thinking of her research and how things have been going and she doesn't want to know what the 'stuff' may be. She doesn't want to know because then it will hold her up and she should be home and packing for tomorrow. 'How long d'you think you'll need?'

Maurice says nothing. He just looks at her and then begins to pace again.

It occurs to Sadie later that she didn't ask him to sit down but she doubts he would have done that anyway

Why didn't I tell him to stop pacing about?

Maurice's face is wide at the temples, his eyebrows are dark and thick and he has a strong jaw – he has the kind of indestructible face she has seen a lot of since she arrived here – but his lips are dry and cracked. And he is sweating – Sadie can smell him from behind her desk. The smell of him is filling the room and it is not a human smell. It is an animal smell – it is a strange sort of animal smell and she realises how little it belongs here in her office. She wants to tell him to get out. Suddenly, she has an irrational desire to tell him to get out

Why didn't I just tell him to leave?

and she has to choke it down as he swings back over to her desk.

Now he is looking down on her and he says, 'I've got it with me – what I've done so far. It's on a disk.'

Sadie raises an eyebrow at him. She does not like having to look up at him.

Why didn't I stand up? Why didn't I stand up?

And she does not understand him – not yet. 'Well, I'd rather not have an unfinished essay,' is what she finally says and, when Sadie thinks back over it later, she wonders if she was too sharp, too angry, too authoritative – or not authoritative enough – or if she was too strong – or not strong enough – or if she was wrong, how she was wrong, just wrong. 'I'd rather you took the time to finish it – it'll be better for your end-of-year marks too.'

Maurice stares at Sadie as she says this. He is frowning hard and then suddenly he raises his fist and slams it down on the old wooden desk. It happens so quickly and the noise of it is so loud that Sadie starts in her seat and blinks quickly at him. He is staring at her as though he is drunk, as though he cannot quite see her, but she doesn't smell any alcohol on his breath and that makes it worse.

'Bit of a problem about that. Yep. Bit . . . of . . . a . . . fucking . . . problem.' As he says this, he leans over the desk towards Sadie, right over towards her face. His face is so close to hers that she can see the pale freckles on his skin – his pale skin stretched over his short nose – and she can see redness on the rims of his eyes. And then, suddenly, he breaks away and begins to pace back and forth once again, over the thin carpet, from the sink to the door and back again. He has a heavy tread – he is well built and his heavy boots make his tread even heavier.

The office feels too hot. Sadie wishes she could open the door for some air but the possibility of opening the door is not one she has – she knows she will not be allowed to open the door. She says nothing. She waits.

Just be calm, Sadie, just be calm.

'And that fucking problem is . . . a fucking bitch who calls herself my girlfriend.' Maurice is from Morningside in Edinburgh and there is something wrong with a young middle-class man from Morningside using the kind of language he is using. It is incongruous – it doesn't fit – but he doesn't stop. 'She's been fucking someone else and guess who that is? One of my fucking friends. Yep. One of my fucking mates.'

Sadie isn't here. She isn't here because this isn't real. She is not trapped in her office by an angry middle-class student who is using words like 'fucking' and 'mates' and 'bitch' and who seems to be directing it all at her.

Maurice slams his fist into his hand and then he comes over to her desk again, leans towards her and glares. Then he pulls away, rubs his fist against his cheek. He looks at Sadie side-on, slyly. 'She told me about it at the weekend. Just sidled up to me, you know? The way a fucking cat does – rubs itself up against your leg. Know what I mean? Just like that – like a fucking cat. Rubbing herself up against me. As easy as that. As easy as spreading her fucking legs. Fucking bitch.' He says these last words quietly and deliberately and looks directly at Sadie while he is saying them.

And something switches inside her brain, a mechanism clicks in her head, and, in that moment, she knows what she needs to do and she will remember this moment later and for a long time and she will recall how thankful she will be for that little click, that little warning she gave herself, when she thinks back later and torments herself with thoughts of what might have happened without that little click going off inside her head to tell her what to do. Because, in that instant, Sadie knows she will not react. She will not show anything. She will not show anger or embarrassment or awkwardness. And, most of all, she will not show that he has made her afraid of him – even though she is afraid of him. She knows that is why he is speaking to her like this. It is because he *can* speak to her like this. It is because he knows she cannot stop him. It is because he knows she is here alone and that is why he has come to her office so late. And she will not show panic. She will not show how afraid she is that he hates her so much. No, he doesn't even know her. He has barely even spoken to her before but he hates her because of what another girl has done and Sadie will have to keep calm and not be afraid and she will have to think about what she is going to do.

'Have you spoken to anyone about it?' Sadie keeps her voice light and it works.

For a moment, he is caught off guard. He looks surprised – it wasn't the response he was expecting. 'What? No. No.'

> Don't look away. Keep looking at him, keep looking at him, keep looking at him.

The room is too small and he is blocking the door. There is silence outside – everyone has gone home. The snow is falling and it is dark outside and everyone has gone home. Sadie doesn't want to look at his face any more – the wide temples and the set-apart blue eyes that are staring at hers right now and are making her feel sick – but she keeps control, she keeps her voice light and she forces herself to hold his gaze. 'I didn't have exactly the same experience but . . .' is what she says slowly. This is what she must say.

> Identify with him – you are like him. You are not like his girlfriend – you are just like him. You are a person – not male or female. You are just a person.

'my boyfriend cheated on me when I was in my final year. Not with a close friend but with . . . someone I knew. I don't know everything you're going through but . . . it did help me to speak to someone. I went to the SRC – they gave me the name of someone . . . Well, it helped me, anyway.' Sadie offers this information casually and she shrugs as she finishes. None of what she has just said is true but Maurice cannot know that and, for the first time since he walked in to her office, he seems to see her, he is interested and the angry look on his face has eased – just a bit, just a very tiny bit.

And he says, 'That happened to you, then?'

Sadie nods and prepares to stand up. She can't stay sitting down any longer. She can't sit there feeling threatened in her own office. She has to get up.

> Stand up, stand up.

And she takes her eyes from his face at last and looks down at the desk and picks up the book that she had in her hand when he walked in and, yes, she must, she has to take this step, she has to step out from behind the desk because the desk will not protect her. 'It doesn't take forever to get over it,' Sadie says, still light, still casual, 'it just feels like it. It's all

I can tell you. It helped me to get some counselling. But you might be different. Might be worth a try anyway.'

Maurice looks confused suddenly and he runs a hand through his dark, greasy hair. 'Do you think so?' His threatening manner is gone.

'Tell you what – give me the disk with what you've done so far. I'll mark it if you can't finish the essay in time.'

He looks down at his trousers and then he takes the disk out of his pocket. 'Can you print it up now? I'd rather keep the disk if that's OK.'

She doesn't want him there a minute longer. She hoped he would hand over the disk and go but she has to agree and so she takes the disk from him. She goes back to her desk, puts the disk in her computer, clicks open the file and presses print. Then she gets up and says, 'I'll just be a minute.' She doesn't have her own printer. All the computers in the basement offices are connected to one central printer in the room next to hers so Sadie must walk along the dim corridor and switch on the light in the printer room and listen as the paper winds through. Then she must walk back along the corridor and back into her office. She would give anything to be able to head for the door and leave – get out into the snow and run away from him before he changes back, before he forgets who she is and what she has told him – but that is impossible.

Everything's fine. Everything's fine.

She can go back, it is quite safe.

So Sadie goes back and opens the office door. He is there, standing facing the door, and she hands him back the disk.

'Thanks,' he says but, for a moment, for a single moment,

there is that look in his face again – that pasty, odd, nasty, sly look – and she needs to deflect it, she needs to do something about it quickly because he is about to say something else.

'Well, think about the counselling. Don't worry about deadlines – they're the least of things right now. OK?' And Sadie turns her back on him and picks up her briefcase. It takes everything to turn her back on him and she waits for something to happen – she waits for it but, no, the moment is gone. He just wants to get away and then he is out of the door and she hears him trample down the passageway, his heavy boots kicking against the old white wooden door as he leaves the building.

She puts on her coat, packs up her books and papers in her briefcase, takes out her umbrella and wraps her scarf around her neck. Then she checks everything in her office is all right – as though things might have leapt out of their places in the time that Maurice was here which already feels like hours. She switches off the light and locks the door. She walks down the dim corridor to the door at the end, lifts the latch and steps out into the darkness and the snow. She can't believe he is not there waiting to jump at her, that someone is not there to strike her or pull her down, but there is no one in the darkness and the quiet – just Sadie. And she puts up her umbrella with hands that are shaking and steps out into the street.

The house is empty when she gets back – Jackie and Maria are still at the lab. They have left a note to say they will be late and have apologised in advance in case they wake her up when they get back. Sadie has to get up early for the teacher-training programme tomorrow. The coach leaves at 8.30 from the university so she should get an early night but, before she has even taken off her coat, she has already opened a bottle of wine, which she should not drink, and she knows she will finish it, even though she shouldn't, before she can think of going to bed.

'For the last role-playing session, I want you all to stay in your groups of six. I want you to imagine that three of you are established members of staff and that three of you are brand new. What advice would you give? What do you think you should be told? Put your preferences in colour-coded bullet points – red for most important, green for second most important and so on – and we'll compare results when you're finished.'

The woman running the teacher-training session has almost exhausted herself with her enthusiasm for role-playing, colour charts and bullet points – an enthusiasm that has been met so far by lethargy, cynicism and embarrassment by most of the room. But, for Sadie, this is the kind of mundanity she needs. She welcomes the banal, the trivial, the petty, the glorious uselessness and ordinariness of it all after the strangeness of the evening before – a strangeness that even an entire bottle of wine, consumed in just under an hour, couldn't dissipate. None of the day's sessions have covered what she should do in the event of a threatening student who makes obscene remarks in her office. There have been plenty of 'workshops' dealing with racial difference, the need for visual aids when giving a lecture and how to deal with lazy or work-shy students who won't hand in their work on time but nothing, not a word, on what a young woman on her own in her office should do when a student twice the size of her threatens her.

As she joins the others at the plastic table in the low-ceilinged room that the hotel reserves especially for conferences and sessions just like this, Sadie is reminded of that play, the one that has been causing so much fuss in the press – the play that has audiences cheering and booing and that has provoked so many arguments. *Oleanna*. She hasn't seen it herself – she has only read reviews and articles about how it has struck a blow for 'put-upon men', how it has 'set relations between men and women, students and teachers, back years', how it is 'cutting edge', how it is 'reactionary bullshit'. A young female student falsely accuses her male professor of rape and, as a result of her accusation, he loses both his job and his wife. When the student finally harasses him one time too many, the professor turns on her and punches her in the face. Sadie has read that some people in the audience cheer when he does this.

Sadie thought this teacher-training day might help. She hoped it would give her an answer to the question – the question of how to behave when a student is threatening – but it has offered her nothing and she wonders about people cheering at a woman being punched, at a portrayal of male insecurity, when she has just experienced the very opposite. And she is waiting, in fact, she is expecting, surely, she is going to see, she is going to hear, right now, in this room full of academics – men and women, laughing and joking and wanting their five-star meal with wine – she is going to hear someone tell her how it is done and why it is done and what she can do about it.

'Sadie! Glad you could make it,' calls Peter Martinson, the organiser of the session from her department. The session has drawn to an end and nothing, of course, nothing has helped her and she, along with the rest of the group, is released to freshen up before dinner. And, as Peter Martinson calls to her, he's smiling. He rushes over to her, his large frame warning others to step out of the way. His large hand is pulling a young woman by his side. Sadie hasn't spoken to him much before but he is a friendly man and she knows he got married late in life to a local woman who owns a bookshop in the town.

His voice booms at her, 'I wonder if I can introduce you to Elizabeth? She's had a queer sort of experience with one of your students recently – Maurice Something. What's his last name, Elizabeth? Anyway, I thought you might be able to help her, Sadie – she's in a bit of a to-do about it, aren't you, Elizabeth?'

The woman standing in front of Sadie has prematurely greying hair, even though she can only be a few years older than she is.

'I don't believe this,' Sadie says excitedly to Peter Martinson, as she shakes the woman's hand. 'I just had a really bad time with him last night. He was in my office – he was in quite a state . . .'

But Peter Martinson simply beams at her, slaps Elizabeth on the back and quickly turns away. 'Don't you two girls get gabbing and miss dinner, now!'

Sadie blinks at his retreating back and looks at Elizabeth. She does not know what to say so she smiles and raises her eyebrows.

'Shall we go to the bar?' Elizabeth suggests, politely. She is wearing small, round-rimmed glasses and has the beaky kind of look caused by a hooked nose and too much reading but it's the sort of look that is associated with bookish people so, at first, Sadie thinks she might be timid but her voice is strong and she is direct. She guides Sadie along the pink-carpeted floor to the tiny bar in the corner, outside the main dining room.

'I just can't believe it,' Sadie says again, shaking her head, once they are both seated at the bar. The corridor is quiet and the barman has poured their drinks before retiring to a storeroom to finish a cup of coffee. 'He really was in my office last night and he threatened me.'

Elizabeth nods, takes a sip of her gin and tonic. 'He came into my office three days ago. I teach modern history.'

Elizabeth is dressed all in grey. She is wearing a grey woollen suit so she is not like Sadie. She is not still wearing some kind of student dress – all black – and she is not too young or too flimsy to be here. She has an English accent – she has probably been to Oxford. She is exactly the kind of woman that Sadie is sure her department would like – even the Obsolete Professor – and yet, with all of that, with all of that to help her, she has the same problem. She is nothing like Sadie – she probably would not even like Sadie if they were in the same department or if they had met under other circumstances but, right now, they have something in common, something that is crucial.

'He looked very strange. I didn't know what the matter was with him but I could tell something was up straightaway. He started by arguing with me about the essay questions I'd set – said they were too obtuse and he couldn't understand them. And then he started going on about my accent.'

'Your accent?

'Yes, he started saying all these strange things about how "posh" I was and that I had a problem with class – that I was just a snob who didn't have a clue. I was furious. I just argued back. I told him my father's family were all from Durham and they were all involved in mining – said that I'm not some middle-class princess. But he wasn't having any of it. He started shouting at me – actually shouting. It was terrifying. I thought he was going to hit me.' Elizabeth stops and takes another gulp.

'I just shouted back and told him I'd report him to the head of department and I did that yesterday. I'm not teaching him again – I want him out of my class. I'm not having that from a student – not from anybody. Did he do that to you too?'

Sadie shrugs a little bit. 'No, he wasn't shouting so much – he was weird though. I thought maybe he was on something when he came in – he had this weird look about him. Anyway, he told me he couldn't finish his essay on time because of personal stuff, which turned out to be that his girlfriend had two-timed him with his friend. But he was pacing up and down my room, really angry and he made a couple of remarks – sexual remarks, you know. Obscene.'

But already it doesn't seem so bad, already Maurice is smaller than he was, already he is shrinking as Sadie thinks of him in her office, because she can share him now and she will speak to her head of department too. She will have him removed from her class. She will support this woman's experience with her own and together they will make sure that he never treats anyone like that again. It is because they are both young, because they are both women, Elizabeth says, and, although Sadie knew that already, she doesn't say so because this is the first time she has felt support in a place and in a job that have both been lacking support for months and only now does she realise how much she has missed it.

And, when Sadie goes back to the department two days later, she makes an appointment with her head of department and, when she sees him and tells him what happened that night in her office and what happened to Elizabeth too, her head of department laughs and suggests Sadie take up self-defence classes and that some of the female students in his class would put the fear of God into him. And, when she persists, he says finally that she doesn't have to teach Maurice again if she doesn't want to but he makes it very clear he thinks she is making a very big fuss over something very, very small.

Tuesday, March 21st

Can't sleep. I keep having bad dreams. I just want to get away – before the funeral happens. I don't think I can handle it. But John thinks I should stay. I can't decide. Don't know what to do. What should I do, Amy? Help me decide what to do for the best. It wasn't like this with Dad. There was no choice to be made then. We couldn't afford to come over for his funeral. Couldn't leave Sadie and Campbell. But, no, that's not it. No, to be honest, I didn't want to come over. Didn't want to see everyone. Not even you, Amy. Not then. But this is different. It's different with you. I should stay. I know that. Pete would be upset. He wouldn't understand. He would think I hated you – my own sister. I don't want him thinking that.

And John . . . He doesn't understand why I need to leave now or why I haven't phoned Sadie – not since the other night when she told me what she wants to do, why she keeps on asking about Mum. I know why she did it when she was younger. I know she did it to annoy me. I know that. We were so different. She was always in her own wee world. If I'm honest, it was Campbell who got all my attention. He wasn't well when he was a baby. I didn't get to hold him for long when he was first born. He was a bit premature and he had jaundice. He was in an incubator for days and so I couldn't cuddle him – it stays with you. So, when they were growing up, well . . . I left Sadie to herself, didn't I? So it's all my fault. All my fault. I'd always wanted a boy. No more girls – too many girls. Yes, it's true. I was disappointed to see Sadie when she was born. She wasn't what I wanted. Maybe she sensed it. Of course she did. How couldn't she? Bad mother. I'm a bad mother. And as she grew up . . . Oh, I couldn't see anything in her. Features, I mean – in her features. Where was Rubina's smile? Her eyes? Her face? There was nothing of her in my own daughter. And it was funny – I resented her for that. Suppose it's because I like it – seeing family resemblances. But you'd think I wouldn't want to see her, wouldn't you? Not in my own child. But suddenly I did. I'd look at her and think. Where's my mother gone? Campbell was easy – so much easier in comparison. He's the spit of John. There's nothing of her in him. But I wasn't looking for it. Nothing of the McAllisters at all. He was safe. Like John. Safe for me. The boy I'd always wanted. I give in to him all the time. Now, I know I do. I know that's bad. Bad mother. I'm a bad mother. Breaks my heart that he comes to see us so little. Dundee – it's not so far away. He could see us more often. See his mother more often. After all I've done. After all I've cared. Loved.

I complain to John about him all the time. 'You'd think he could give his own mother a ring now and then.' I know he has a girlfriend. Patricia – I think that's her name. Not that he ever mentions her. Well, hardly ever. And we haven't even met her. Not yet. Don't know if we ever will.

What about Sadie? She never talks to me about her boyfriends. I know she has them but she never tells me about them. Never did. Never confided in me about anything. Maybe I was glad about that. Once upon a time. Not sure I wanted to know. Didn't want to get involved. I'd like it now, though

– if she came to me with something. Is it too late? I'd ask her but she can be so prickly. If she thinks you're nosying about in her affairs. I think sometimes she took that job just to get away from me. I do. Oh, can I really be surprised? I haven't made any effort with her – not really. And now I'm being punished for it. There she is. Wanting to get her nose in *my* affairs. Wanting to know all the grubby details just so she can publish them in some book. How dare she! She doesn't care – not about me or about Amy. She just cares about herself. That's all she cares about. Turning my mother into research. Who does she think she is? How dare she. Can't get through to John how angry I am. 'It's all in the past now. Where's the harm?' John thinks it's all right. Doesn't see what's wrong with it. Well, he would if he had my memories.

Anyway, who wants to know about a sad old woman? And that's all she was – just a sad lonely old woman who abandoned her family one day at a picnic. Who cares what happened to her? I don't. I don't care where she is or what she's doing. Sadie doesn't care either. I know that. She just wants to use her for her precious career. And she wants *me* to help her do it. How could she? How could she even think about it? Washing your dirty linen in public – that's what they used to call it. Theorise about it, she said. That's what she wants to do. Write up Rubina's story and theorise about it. What kind of theories would she come up with? That's what I'd like to know. I can just imagine. Something disgusting. It's all so trendy nowadays. Deviancy we used to call it. Deviancy. It was better then when you didn't know what people got up to. How dare she. She'd want to drag all that out into the open. She'd love to find out her grandmother wasn't just Mrs Ordinary after all.

No, I won't think about it. Never think about it. Never

remember. Makes my stomach turn to think of it. I won't have people feel sorry for me – look down on me. What would the neighbours say? What would they think at the bridge club? 'Oh you never go and you can't stand them anyway,' that's John – I can hear him now. But that's just what Sadie doesn't think about. She doesn't think how it would make me feel if it all came out about my mother. What I don't think – won't think. How I would feel in front of the world. Everyone knowing. Where's your mother gone, they'd ask. That's what people would ask. And more than that – once they knew. That's why she left you all.

Yes, I know. I know why she did it. I know why she left. Oh, Amy, Amy. I hope you never knew. I hope it was just me – just me who saw, just me who knew. I'll never tell. Never tell anyone. Not John. Not Sadie – especially not Sadie.

She doesn't know what it would be like. I've never given her any reason to be ashamed of me – she has no idea how that feels – but sometimes she behaves as if she is. Just the same – as if I was just the same. She'd soon know all about it if I was. But then she'd probably like that. She could go on one of those TV programmes. Confess it all. Why she's so messed up now. It's all because of her mother. Yes, it's all my fault. Honestly. What did I ever do to her? Why can't she see the damage it'll do? To all of us. The damage it did do.

When we came back to Scotland, I wouldn't let the kids out of my sight. I don't know why – just had this fear that they'd be taken off me as well. There was that song, too. The one with the line 'Where's your mama gone?' I've been hearing that song in my head ever since Sadie's call. It was playing when we got back to Scotland. It was on the radio for months – that whole summer. Middle of the Road, the group were called. 'Far, far away' – oh, the irony of it! You couldn't have planned for it. 'Last night I heard my mama singing a song . . .' and that silly chorus – 'Chirpy-chirpy, cheep-cheep'. It keeps going round my head. 'Woke up this morning and my mama was gone . . .' It was like they knew – like somehow some silly pop group on the hit parade knew what had happened to my mother and they were singing about it. Such a cheerful, silly little song. What a strange thing to set to music – just wasn't right. But it was played everywhere. Stewpot Stewart Something his name was. The DJ. Sadie and Campbell loved his show. He played all the kiddies' favourites. 'Nelly the Elephant packed her trunk and said goodbye to the circus, off she went with a trumpety-trump . . .' 'The Runaway Train' – 'The Runaway Train came down the track and she blew . . .' What was it about that time? Everything seems to be about leaving – everything's about running away.

I remember Sadie saying once – about the only time she ever mentioned a boyfriend to me. She had been seeing some boy from her lecture class when she was a student. George McKenzie was his name. And, suddenly, there was this band had a big hit – Goodbye Mr Mackenzie they were called. I always remember that name. It was just when she and George split up. Can't remember the song but I remember the name of the band. Remember her laughing about it. But I didn't laugh. You couldn't have planned it. And she said she came across that book for the first time – *After Leaving Mr Mackenzie* by Jean Rhys. Like there's someone up there watching you – having a little bit of a laugh at your expense. I loved *Wide Sargasso Sea.* Not a patch on *Jane Eyre* of course. I was disappointed at first when I realised it wasn't what I was expecting. Then I read it – loved it. Sadie's not the only one. I read good things too sometimes – not just silly magazines. She doesn't need to turn her nose up at me – at my friends, at the bridge club. Social climber she called me once – just because I like to have the right friends. It's important to me. She doesn't know what it's like when you're not considered important.

No, she isn't worried about me or about what people will think or about what happened to Rubina. And as for Campbell . . . Well, he won't bother. You know. I haven't phoned him at all. Not since we've been here. John wants to call him. But I don't. Won't let him do it either. I'll wait till we get back – if I can be bothered. Might not – might not phone him ever again. Or Sadie. What would she care? She doesn't care. Might be dead myself for all she cares. She hardly showed any interest in you at all. When you're the one who's lying . . . you were the one . . . Oh, Amy. All she wants is to know about Rubina – that's all she's interested in. So I won't call her. She can just wait.

And John doesn't understand me. Because, of course, I don't tell him, do I? Don't talk to him about it. Don't talk to him. Don't talk to Sadie. I'm talking to you, Amy, but it's too late. We had the chance. If you'd only come round . . . then we might have . . . Who do I talk to now, Amy? Who wants to hear my story – your story? What she did. Why she did it. What happened. Well, apart from Sadie, that is. Sadie wants to know. Can't tell her. Won't tell her. I'm going to have to face the fact that I don't trust my own daughter. How angry I am with her. But, beneath that, I don't trust her with it. It's why I haven't told her. Why I haven't told anyone – not even you, Amy – about things that happened, things that I saw. Just me. Only me. *I* saw them. Don't think I can talk about any of that – not even after all this time. Don't trust anyone with it.

It's not a good thing, not to trust. I've never even told John. It didn't matter. Childish things. Things that happen when you're a child. You just put them away. Wrap them up. Hide them under the bed. No one needs to know. If things have changed – if it's not the same – then why bring it all out into the open? Maybe families *should* have secrets. Why should it all be out in the open? It's the way things have to be these days. All those talk shows, chat shows. What are their names? *Oprah. Rikki Lake.* Reveal. Confess. Expose. Private things dragged out into the public. Who cares? Who wants to know? All that fighting. Telling everything. Affairs. Lovers. Why would you want everyone to see that? To know how unhappy you are? We all want people to know now if we're not happy. We're not asking them to do anything about it. We just want people to know. Sharing, they call it. But they're sharing things other people don't want. At least I don't want it. I don't want other people's misery. Let them keep it to themselves. I'm with the Queen. That was her era. You kept your lips sealed, your mouth shut. 'Careless talk costs lives' – that's what the posters said. Don't blab.

Although I do – I am a blabber. I've said that before, haven't I? It's true. Haven't blabbed about this though. Because I pretended it didn't happen. Pretended none of it happened. Mum was different then – when we were wee. It was easy to forget after I left. Couldn't do that while I was still here. I tried but I couldn't do it. It was only after I left, after I went back to Scotland . . . Then I could forget it. Could write to her. As though she was a different person. Not my mum from years ago – a new mum. Could make her into the mum I wanted to – from a distance. Then coming back here – after all that time. Things so different. Well, we were both grown-ups then. I was a mother too. Had my own kids, my own husband, my own house. Things were different. She was different. And so was I. I think . . . I thought . . . that maybe we understood each other then. So the holiday . . . well . . . That was why I thought I could come back. Live here with my family. The one I'd made and the one I'd left behind. Bringing them both together. Because we understood each other. But I was wrong. That's what that day, the day of the picnic, showed me – that I never understood her. Not when I was wee and not when I was married, grown-up, with wee ones of my own.

I did something yesterday, Amy. I went back to our old house after all. I said I didn't want to. I was lying. I did want to. Wanted to see it. But it's not there. The street is the same. Has a different name now but it's still a suburban street. The houses are different though – all one-storey, wooden, painted pale, with those huge cars in the front. What do they call them? Like big Range Rovers. Can't be warm in winter, wooden houses. When we stayed here, they were all brick houses – end of the last century. Must have been one of the oldest parts of the city.

Of course, I say 'our old house' – I mean the first one. Not the one on Victoria Avenue, not that one – the shiny new one. No, I always mean the first one – the one where the lodger was. Edgar. That's the one that sticks in my mind for some reason. Why would that be? It's not as if we stayed there the longest. And it's not where things changed for me – got better. But it's the one that we came to first and it's the one I'll always remember best because of that – the tree in the front garden, all the stairs up to the top, too hot in the summer . . . Who knows what it would have been like in winter if we'd stayed there. But, for some reason, I like it. I wish it *was* still there. I wish I could have seen it one last time. Wish I could do a lot of things – change a lot of things.

And it does not matter, *it does not matter*, it must not matter. Nobody thinks it matters – not Jackie or Maria with their lab friends and joint projects, not Sadie's head of department with his colleagues and students who respect his authority, not Richard with his confidence in himself and the world around him which is only waiting for him to explain it all. Not Richard who says to her, 'He didn't actually do anything, did he, Sadie?' when she gets back from the teacher-training programme and tells him what happened in her office the night before she left. And Sadie tries to tell herself every morning, as she repeats her routine on her way into the department as if nothing has changed, that it does not matter. It does not matter that her office does not feel safe. It does not matter that she still has to teach Maurice for a few more weeks until the end of term because she'd be making too much of a fuss otherwise when really it does not matter, it does not matter . . .

But, *if* it does not matter, then why does every day that Sadie spends in her office now feel so wrong? If it does not matter, why will she be reading in the library today instead of in her office? If it does not matter, why does it feel like an affront to behave as if nothing has changed?

'He didn't actually do anything, did he, Sadie?'

If it does not matter, why does she find it harder every morning to walk over the cobbles on the main street to her place of work, a place that has been invaded and made strange for her by someone who has never even been punished for what he did.

> 'He didn't actually do anything, did he, Sadie?'

If it does not matter why does she want to leave? Because Sadie *does* want to leave. She wants to pack up her books into cardboard boxes, collect her papers and roll up her posters, put away her kettle and her mugs, go back to the house she shares and pack up her clothes, put everything in boxes and then leave them all, leave her books and papers and clothes behind for others to send after her, and go back to where she came from because she was never meant to be here in the first place.

It has taken Sadie such a long time to feel that she should be here. Oh, not here – in this particular university, in this particular office – but here in an academic world where the paintings of former chancellors and principals down through the centuries adorn the walls.

> 'Yes, it really has been that long.'

Here, where select college clubs offer up red leather-backed chairs in palely lit, wood-varnished rooms.

> 'Is that the only white wine you have?'

Here, where older men in tweed jackets suspiciously eye any younger men who wear their hair too long or too short unless they are younger men they have personally spotted for their potential and encouraged.

'And what about the young women?'

But Sadie never did work out how to find a place here. Her alma mater didn't want her – it spat her out as soon as it could because she wasn't the right kind of person, she wasn't doing the right kind of research, she didn't know how to find a place. Her alma mater was another university with the paintings and wood-varnished rooms and men in tweed but it rejected her while this one wanted – well, they seemed to at first. Her alma mater only liked younger women of a certain class who wrote about Wordsworth climbing up Cheddar Gorge; it liked younger women of a certain class who wrote about feminism while wearing short skirts and brushing imaginary dust off the arm of a tweed jacket held out for support.

Everyone has a history and this one is Sadie's but it is not the history she planned for herself because she was a good girl, once upon a time. She did her degree, got a good enough class to study at postgraduate level. She stayed at the same university because it was home to her and she was used to it and she wasn't sure where else to go. And she started her research, quickly gave one paper, then another and another. She studied abroad for a time, on a special grant, and she came back with her findings but then there came the day when she was to present what she knew in front of the department.

It was a bright day, in early June, and it was still bright at six in the evening. The new postgraduate common room was full of light and Sadie sat at the large desk, in front of the audience. And she gave a thirty-minute reading of her work. But an elderly, overweight professor, too used to spotting the talent and resenting his position being usurped by newer colleagues, challenged her on a point of interpretation.

'Show me where it says that! Go on, show me where it says that in the text!' he'd shouted at her, as he waved a copy of one of the novels she was critiquing above his head.

Sadie did not have a copy of the novel with her. She did not think she would need it. She did not expect to be accused of misquoting, of misinterpreting. Interpreting differently – yes – but interpreting wrongly, reading wrongly – no. She did not expect a professor to shout at her in full view of an audience. But he did. And she was rescued by a younger professor who did have a copy of the novel with him. He was able to do her job, to read out the offending passage – which is what she should have done. But it made little difference to the older professor anyway – even when her interpretation proved to be the correct one after all.

Sadie wasn't a good girl any more. She was a bad girl – not a dangerous bad girl or a subversive bad girl, just a stupid bad girl. There are the right kinds of good girl and the right kinds of bad girl. And she has researched . . . It is only now dawning on her – it is only now coming to her as she sits here in the warm, yellow glow of the library where she has taken to working more and more because her basement office doesn't feel safe any more – it is only now that she realises that she may have researched the right kinds of bad girl but, in doing so, she became the wrong sort of bad girl herself because she didn't read properly after all. The old, overweight professor was right. She didn't read the real histories of those trail-blazing women and see them properly. She didn't see why winged women and girl gangs and *Jazz* should make the grade and why she should not. She was the wrong sort of bad girl – the sort of bad girl who wants to do something different but who wants to be accepted too, the sort of bad girl who says no but who still wants to be loved anyway. And only now is Sadie realising what those histories were telling her. All this time, she has been trying to fit in. All this time, she has been trying to correct a mistake – the mistake of her alma mater. She thought this new post, this first position in this small university town, would correct the mistake she made when she ignored the lesson of what happened to women who tried to do something different. But it hasn't worked because Sadie can't change who she is. She can't become the right sort of bad girl and she left behind being a good girl far too long ago to return to it.

It is still very cold outside. She sees through the window that the frost hasn't melted and it is getting foggier. The library is busy today and it is distracting but she had no teaching this afternoon and she is counting down the minutes until she can leave and go back to the house, missing out her office altogether. But Sadie is refusing to let herself run away just because she wants to. So she will stay here for only a few minutes more and then she will leave, and she will go back to the department, collect her things from the office, check her mail.

Still, she is thinking about leaving – properly leaving – and how and when she can do it. Her contract has three months to run, as does the lease on her room. She will not see Richard again if she leaves now and goes back to the city – 'Long-distance relationships never work.' She may not get another job if she leaves before this one is finished. She will not get a good reference.

And then Sadie knows, of course she does, that she will

not leave. Not yet. She is not the right sort of bad girl – like Rubina, she thinks suddenly. And, just as suddenly, she is not alone. Rubina was the wrong sort of bad girl too. She knows it – all of a sudden, she can tell.

What worth does the personal have? Sadie can hear her voice – Rubina's voice, as she imagines it to be. And Rubina is asking her who will be interested in her story if Sadie packs up her belongings and leaves this small university town without saying goodbye? She will not even be the first to do it – the man who had her office before left one day and did not come back, she remembers that. He left, he was done, it was over for him and, if Sadie leaves now, she will only be the second person to leave her office and not come back so she must see it out. She is afraid but she must see it out and maybe, if she keeps going, she can find out what or who it was made her grandmother leave one sunny day too and never come back.

So Sadie gets up from her warm booth in the library and makes a familiar trip down the yellow-carpeted stairs, passing students in the hallway whose boisterousness alarms her as they jostle each other with their bags. And she checks out her book at the desk and collects her coat and opens the library doors on to the main street for the fifteen-minute walk along the cobbled street to her office. The day is dull with fog. The east-coast temperatures are sharper than she is used to but at least it is drier. She does not miss the rain but she will never get used to the sharpness of this wind and she wraps her arms around herself as she passes the tiny baker's shop, the supermarket, the bookshop, the post office, the chip shop, the shop selling antiques – the shops she passes every day on her way to work but that look different to her now.

She already knows she will not run away but she will

not stay here either. She will stay for long enough and then she will go. When she gets what she needs, then she will leave.

There is a letter waiting for her when she gets back to the department. It arrived in the second post but she was in the library when it was delivered and Sadie wonders if Pamela or any of the other secretaries have noticed that she is never there for the second post now, that she does not spend so much time in her office any more. But they do not give anything away, not a thing, as Pamela says brightly, 'Some post for you, Sadie! And your mother called and asked if you could phone her back.'

Sadie thanks her, takes the unusual-looking letter – unusual because it is handwritten, not typed, so it must be personal, not official – and goes down the dark stairs to the basement where the narrow corridor is silent and poorly lit. And she does not think of anything as she walks along to her office, she does not think of anything as she takes out her key and opens her door and switches on the main light – she prefers too much light in her office now, no more desk lamps – and she closes the door behind her. It cannot be locked from the inside and, as she has so often done lately, she pictures fastening a chair under the handle but that is melodramatic so she doesn't ever do it.

'He didn't actually do anything, did he, Sadie?'

The envelope is pale yellow and smells of old-fashioned flowers like roses – the kind of flowers that nobody plants any more because it's too much like hard work and they take a long time to get established. Sadie opens it carefully and pulls out the sheaves of folded handwritten paper that are also pale yellow and smelling of roses. The writing is carefully looped and cursive, without punctuation.

62 Lawrie Street

Dear Dr Mathieson

My name is Moira Barr and my aunt Euphemia MacIver was a neighbour of your grandmother Rubina McAllister they used to live across the close from each other my aunt used to talk about her all the time she was always glad to get a letter from her from Canada they were great friends I still live on Lawrie Street in one of the new houses they built in place of the tenements my aunt never took to them as much shes been dead for two years but I have kept a lot of her things even her letters from your gran Im sure will still be there Im sorry if its all in a bit of a mess we never got round to sorting it all out but youre welcome to come and look whenever you like I don't work any more so Im at home most of the time if you want to phone me first my number is 0141 888 9119

Yours

Moira Barr

Thursday, March 23rd

Can't stop crying. I'm worse than Mary. One minute, I'm angry, furious – with you, with John, with Sadie, with her. I switch from one person to another all the time. Over and over again. The same stuff in my head. All the same thoughts. Angry thoughts. Like you were all just put on this earth to make me miserable. That's what I honestly think sometimes. That you died just to spite me, Amy. How ridiculous I am! A ridiculous old woman – that's what I'm turning into. Turning into her. Our mother. Now *that*'s a frightening thought. See what you've escaped, Amy, by dying? But then maybe you left just like her. Maybe you crashed into that van deliberately. Maybe you knew he'd had too much to drink – that driver. Maybe he was swerving on the road. Maybe you just thought, 'Now, now's the time. He'll do. He's a worse driver than me. He'll hit me. He'll do some damage.'

Stop.

There. Better now. I won't know what was in your head any more than I'll ever know what was in hers. But I don't think you would have chosen to leave your kids behind – and Pete. No. You wouldn't. You're not like her – not enough. But your funeral? Do I have to go? I'm running away again. Amn't I, Amy? I'm running away. From the things I should do. Your funeral tomorrow. Of course I'll wait. Of course I'll go to your funeral tomorrow. Never thought I'd be saying that. Thinking that. Doing that. But I will do it. All this anger – it's not good for me, not good for anyone. So tomorrow I'll be there. With Pete and Becka and Ricky and Mary and Mike – we'll all be there. For you. To say a last goodbye. Because that's what you do – you say a last goodbye and then you can grieve properly. Put it all behind you, get on with your life. That's what they say on all those programmes. Move on.

And then what do I move on to, Amy? Now that it's all over and you've left. Well, I suppose I'll leave too – leave here, this country, and go back home. Where I belong. That's what I'll do. And I'll carry on doing the same things. I'll maybe meet the bridge club more often. Maybe I'll have friends over more often. Maybe I'll find other things to do with my day apart from keeping the house clean. That's what I do, Amy – I clean the house. Every day, every room. I clean things that aren't dirty. Clean things that couldn't be any cleaner. You could eat your dinner off the floors – off anything. John says that all the time. Tries to stop me. He thinks it's unhealthy to be cleaning so much. What a man! Most husbands would be glad of a wife who kept everything so spick and span. Does he have to find fault with everything I do? No, that's not fair. Of course he doesn't. He's only trying to help. I shouldn't get angry with him – shouldn't get angry at all. But it's just that . . . It's all I have to do with myself all day. It never changes. And it doesn't matter. Who cares how clean it all is?

Stop.

Not again. Just can't stop the tears. Self-pity – that's all it is, just self-pity. Because there's no answer, is there? I don't have an answer to what I should do with myself – now that my family are grown and away and don't need me. But I need to do *some*thing. I don't think I can go back. Don't think I can even get on the plane. Back to that street. That house. All the same things. When something so big has happened. When you've left us, Amy. I'll be rattling around by myself all day while John keeps himself busy at work. I can't do it – can't get through it. Not unless I've got something else. Something else to *do*. Sadie is always telling me to do something – something that matters to *me*. But what? What does the world need me for? Need us for? Did you ever wonder about that, Amy? Or were your days too full to wonder about it. With things you had to do. So you never had to wonder what women our age are for. What can we do? If we don't have grandchildren to look after? Or a career to keep going? I should have had a career. Maybe Sadie's right doing what she's doing after all. But, still . . . I still want to be useful and not just sit back and do nothing. I want to be useful. Yes, that's what it is. I want to do something useful.

And so.

I should do it.

I should tell Sadie.

Tell her what I remember.

What I knew.

What I saw. What I think I saw.

What harm can it do now? Not to you, Amy. No more harm to you. And I don't think your kids are bothered. They are too much part of this world, here – too new, too shiny. They won't be affected by it. But Sadie will. Sadie wants to know and it will affect her. Make her think about what she has learned. So I should tell her.

I will tell Sadie.

And she can use it.

There – *that*'s my use, my purpose. What I will tell her. About what I saw . . . when I was wee . . . back home. About

Mum and . . . our neighbour . . . Yes, about that woman and . . . about the other 'friends' she had – the ones over here. The days she disappeared off, leaving us by ourselves – me and you and Mary and Dad. About where she really was . . . About what she was really doing and who she was really doing it with. I'll tell it all. *There*. Serve you right, you old bitch! Leaving us. Serve you right.

Stop.

No, I can't. Even saying it . . . It's not right. I don't want to. Don't want Sadie knowing all this. I don't want anyone knowing this. There's no point. Just because I'm angry . . . Don't want to go over it all. Raking over the rubbish, washing dirty linen in public – all of that. I don't want to do it. Don't want to use my mother's grubby little secrets just to give me something to do, give me a connection with my daughter. It's not loyalty – no. Not to her. I'm not protecting her memory – nothing like that. I just don't want . . . What do I want? What is it I want to do? What is useful?

I'll find her.

That's what I want to do.

After all this time, all these years.

We never did it. I'll do it.

I'm sorry, Amy.

It's what I have to do.

That's why I'm still here. Why I'm over here. Why you had your accident. Why you're dead. Oh, that's nonsense. John would never let me think that. Rubbish, he would say. But maybe it isn't. Maybe I'm here for a reason. None of us tried. We never looked. Not beyond telling the police that day. None of us went looking for her. Not even Dad. He just sat and waited. Waited for her to come back like all those other times. He didn't know what else to do. And I was too busy. I had my own family to look after. I couldn't have chased after her then. None of us knew what to do. So we just did what we'd always done – all the times she'd left before. We just waited for her to come back. She knew that's what we'd do – that we wouldn't come after her. Learned behaviour – that's what it was. Wasn't natural, not doing anything. We should have . . . would have if we'd been brought up differently. Placed ads in papers. Contacted authorities in other cities. Hospitals. Private detectives. Anything. That's what we should have done and we didn't do it.

So that's what I'll do now. I'll tell John. He has to postpone the flight.

Maybe she can't be found. Maybe she's dead. It'll be easier if she is – to find her, I mean. How I can say that? And so calmly. 'If my own mother's dead'. But it *will* be easier. Can check records here. There must be records if she's dead – somewhere. She might have left, though. Emigrated. Gone back to Scotland. Or somewhere else. Anything of course. Why would she have stayed here? So she might even be alive. I have to find out. Have to start the search for her. Just to find out what happened. Where she went that day.

And I'll tell Sadie that I'm looking for her, for my mother.

We can do it together if that's what she wants for her research.

And for me. And for you, Amy.

I'll start here. I'll tell Sadie I'm going to start here. See what I can find out. Then, when we go home, I'll carry on. There's that thing on the computer – the internet, I think it is. Sadie uses it all the time. She says it tells you everything – everything you want to know. It's all there. Well, that's what we'll do when I get back. If I don't find anything here, we can look when we get back. And there'll be more time. We can take our time. It's all a rush here. We've only a few weeks or so at the most but maybe we could stay a bit longer. Where do I start? Local offices. That's where I should start. There must be a coroner's office. And hospital records. I'll ask Pete. Pete'll know about how things are done here. Now.

'Last night I heard my mama singing a song . . .' Then I can get started. 'Woke up this morning and my mama was gone . . .' I'm going to find her. Whatever happened to her, I'll find out. Find her. I'll tell Sadie. We can do it together. We can find her together.

And what a relief it has been for Sadie to have this excuse, this reason for leaving the small university town and getting back to the city once again. The bus is almost there. This time, she will take a taxi to Lawrie Street. She is in a hurry – she wants to know what Moira Barr has to tell her.

It was a huge surprise – Moira Barr's letter. Sadie could not have hoped for written evidence. Oral history was the most she could have expected. But now, this – a written record when she needs words. Words, not bodies.

And, when she realised this, she had a second surprise – a second surprise because she suddenly found herself caring about her grandmother, wanting to protect her from too much observation. Now that she is so close at hand, Sadie wants to protect her from the outside world. She still wants her to be the subject of her research but suddenly she cares about who she was and what she thought and how she lived her life and how she felt and what she knew. Sadie cares about the *person* – not just the subject. Words, not bodies. What she has always believed. But her grandmother was a living, breathing body. Sadie does not want words to betray her.

And so she is making this journey excitedly, tentatively, worried about what she might find, worried that she finds too much, that she finds too little, that what she finds is wrong, that what she finds may be the key to unlocking it all.

It is Tuesday. Sadie hasn't heard from Lily since she told her she wanted to use Rubina's life story for research. Self-writing. Words and bodies. Coming together – that is what it is about. The word *and* the body. Rubina's own words will let Sadie see what she looked like. And she couldn't understand why Lily was so angry – not now, not when Sadie can explain it all properly to her. She really thought that all she had to do was just explain it properly to her mother. But she couldn't phone her back and tell her about Moira Barr's letter – not after all the things Lily said to her. Sadie didn't even want to phone and ask about Aunt Amy's funeral – whether she should send something, a card, a wreath, and where to send it to – so she hasn't done anything. She has convinced herself that this is a better tribute to her aunt – this visit, this discovery she is about to make.

The Easter break has begun so Sadie has all the time in the world. Depending on what she finds at Moira Barr's house and how long she has to stay there, if she misses the bus back, she has decided she will let herself in to her mother's house. She still has the key and she can sleep the night there. She will not phone Richard to tell him she will be staying in the city. He does not call her every night now, the way he did at the beginning. There are more things about her that he does not like. He has begun to tell her this with regularity.

She doesn't know the difference between nitrogen and nitrate. 'God, who does?' She sometimes wear the wrong clothes. 'Don't like yours all the time either.' She doesn't read the right books, watch the right films . . . She is not the quirky arty girl in black he thought she was when he first met her. She is a girl who has the wrong taste in things, the wrong knowledge about the world. Wrong for him, anyway. Sadie can tell he is beginning to feel disappointed in her and she is not as dismayed by this as she should be because she knew, right from the start, that he would be one day – she expected this disappointment to come in him. And not from anything that has changed between them, apart from the occasional complaints about her clothes or her books or her choice of films. He is just as interested in her body as he was – they still have sex as often as they did at the start, once at night and once in the morning. But every night and every morning, Sadie is shocked to find herself getting bored with the routine of it. From a passionate beginning to a routine action – isn't that how all love affairs begin and end? She wonders this as the end of the motorway approaches and the bus makes a turn into the city centre. Now Sadie can predict exactly where Richard will touch her first and where he will touch her second and where he will touch her third and fourth and last. She can tell how much pressure he will use and when. Like an exercise workout, there are steps to be followed and he follows the same steps every night and every morning.

The evening before, he was on the phone for a very long time. Sadie rang three times from her office and, each time, it was engaged and, when she finally reached him, he said, 'We don't have to speak to each other every night, do we?' which amazed her as he was the one who insisted on calling every night. When Sadie told him she was coming here today, he was cross. His favourite film is on TV at night. '*Withnail and I* – it's my favourite film and you have to see it with me. If you're going to understand me, you have to watch that film with me.' But she will not be watching it with him because she will be here. And Sadie knows, somewhere at the back of her mind, that this will be seen as an irrevocable step. So perhaps she will have to decide soon whether she is willing to give up on Richard altogether – perhaps before he gives up on her.

And yet, in spite of how different they are from each other, he has given her a sense of continuity in a new place, he is there every day, their sex life is routine but she needs some routine, and perhaps she needs the promise of a future of routine too. 'Let's rent a flat together next term' was what he said to her the night before last and that was a commitment in spite of it all, in spite of how different they are from each other. And Sadie agreed. She was happy to agree – happy to commit to a man who gave her routine, even as she knew she disappointed him.

And perhaps too, at the back of her mind, was that thought she doesn't allow herself to think. It was there when he said it. She could not help but think it. 'Does that mean he'll be there if I tell him? Will he still be there if I tell him?'

And now, as the bus comes to a halt inside the grimy, badly-lit bus station that even on a sunny day cannot greet its visitors with a welcome smile, Sadie wonders if she is happy with the only answer she can be sure of because all the answers are the same. 'No, he'd leave.' But they are not well suited. 'Yes, he'd stay.' But they are not well suited.

The time is approaching when she will have to decide what to do. But it will not be today – she will not decide today while she is engaged on another subject altogether. She has to give each subject its own time and attention. The time for one is approaching but the time for the other is here so that is what she must attend to – the one that is here, here and now.

And so, when Sadie steps down from the bus and looks over to the taxi rank, she is pleased to see there are no queues. And she takes the first black cab straightaway. She bumps down on the flat back seat and the black cab shoogles its way over the bridge and on to the main road leading to Lawrie Street where she walked not so long ago. A lot has happened to her since she was last here and thinking that selfish thought catches her. It's not that a lot has happened to *her* at all – a lot has happened to someone else. Her aunt Amy has died – death is a lot to have happened to a person, not what Sadie has been through. And soon she is there – she is here outside Moira Barr's grey little house on Lawrie Street. And she pays the driver and gets out of the cab.

'But, afore I get tae aw that, we'll hae a cup o' tea.' Moira Barr has a gravelly voice, a smoker's voice that sounds like a man's.

Sadie says thanks and Moira gets up from her easy chair. Her once-dark curly hair has grey streaks running through it. Sadie can't help noticing this because of her own mother's attitude to her hair. But Moira Barr must be a good few years younger than Lily. She must only be in her late forties but she looks like a woman twenty years older and, as the woman shuffles stiffly out of the front room, Sadie puts that down to hard living, as well as a poor diet and, of course, the constant smoking. Moira had greeted her with a cigarette in her hand when she opened the door. Sadie has been trying hard not to cough in the smoky little room. She does not mean to be so judgemental but there is something at stake here and it is making her feel ungenerous.

As soon as she entered that tiny front room, Sadie felt herself slipping into Rubina's world and all she would like is for Moira Barr to tell her what she wants to know and to leave her alone with it and not to interrupt her. It was not hard for Sadie to slip back in time. It would not be hard for anyone to do this in a room full of mementoes from another era. And so, when Moira Barr left her tiny front room and went into the kitchenette, Sadie got up from the settee and took a closer look at the old-fashioned glass cabinet that stands in the corner and noticed inside it a wedding gift from 1937. She could see, printed on the large art-deco style bread plate, in orange and black lettering, the words 'To celebrate the wedding of Euphemia Watson and Alexander MacIver, June 12th 1937'.

She is still staring at it now, as she hears the kettle's strange hum in the kitchen – strange because she never thought there were still kettles in the world that hummed when the water boiled. The cabinet, made of beautifully carved wood, is glass-fronted with a full set of china inside it. Moira Barr has inherited this from her aunt, Sadie must suppose. It is not the kind of thing you could buy new now and its outdatedness gives her a sudden warm feeling that her own grandmother must be close by. In between the plates and cups, Sadie sees little silver shoes and silver spoons – more mementoes of a happy day so long ago – along with a smaller, more flowery dining set, this time with the words 'Moira MacIver and David Barr, 1st July 1968'. And on top of the cabinet are faded black-and-white photographs of what may be Moira Barr's parents. At least Sadie hopes they are Moira's and not her husband's and she hopes that one of the women she sees in the photograph is Euphemia MacIver, her grandmother's friend. And she peers at the unsmiling faces, trying to find a clue that isn't there.

And then Sadie's gaze passes round the rest of the little room to more antique photographs on the mantelpiece above the gas fire, the little ornaments of dogs, the furry black woollen dog pulled over a bottle so that it is sitting up, begging for a treat. In the corner behind the easy chair, there is even an old-style radio, from the fifties, standing on its own legs, with a sliding door and huge knobs underneath faded red lines.

'Can I give you a hand?' Sadie calls loudly, remembering her manners.

But Moira Barr is not as frail as she looks. She hears her perfectly and replies, 'Nae need!' as she enters the room with a tray carrying two china cups and saucers, a china teapot, a china milk jug and china sugar bowl and Sadie thinks how strange the taste in fashion is. She doesn't know anyone who uses china any more and she wouldn't think of buying it for her own house if she had one. She shakes her head as Moira MacIver offers her sugar and sits back down in her easy chair, a cup of strong, milky tea in her hand. Sadie is sitting uncomfortably on the edge of the poorly sprung velour settee that has decorated white lace things on the back of it and she is trying to remember the word for these things – not doilies but they look like them.

Moira Barr takes a sip of her tea, swallows and holds her head up. 'Aye, so, then. Euphemia MacIver wis ma auntie, ma faither's sister-in-law – well, it wis Effie she was known as. I telt you she died two years ago. The back room there's fu' o' her things. You can hae a wee look in a minute. There's a whole bunch o' letters fae yer gran, Rubina. They were awfae great pals. Some of thae letters go right back tae the fifties – when Rubina'd jist left for Canada. And they go right on up, over twenty years, so they do. Aye, but, they were awfae great pals. Mind you, I dinnae ken hauf o' whit they gae on aboot. Me 'n' Davie, we had a look through them but we couldnae mak heid nor tel ae half ae it. So you're mair than welcome to them. They're no' in any order, mind. I nivir goat around tae sortin' it aw oot.'

'No, of course,' Sadie says and, for something else to add because it seems rude just to come here and read this stranger's aunt's private mail without giving something back herself, she asks, 'What was she like, your aunt? What did she tell you about Rubina?'

'Oh, jist aboot the rer times they had!' Moira Barr shakes her head and purses her mouth.

Sadie knows for certain that she has had a hard life. She has nothing very much to smile about and is honest enough not to pretend.

'Gaun' up the dancin', that kind ae' thing. That's whit she used to tell me aboot when Ah wis wee. Mainly during the war, when the men were awa'. Ma uncle Alec wis in Africa somewhere fur maest ae' it. Effie moved to Lawrie Street jist afore the war an' yer grannie moved there just efter she did. They never had any weans ae' thir ain, ye see, Effie and Alec. Ah wis always ma auntie's favourite.'

Sadie nods eagerly, wanting to hear more.

'Aye, well, Ah wis sayin' . . . ma auntie. It wis surprisin' she had such a great pal. She wisnae the friendliest sort. She nivir hud many friends – jist yer grannie. Ma uncle – he wis a kinda difficult man. Liked a drink, ye ken?'

No, Sadie doesn't but she nods as if she does.

'She wis a'ways a quiet woman, didnae go out much – well, my uncle didnae like her to. He liked her whaur he could see her – ken whit I mean? Dunno whaur he thought she'd be gaun but that's the way he wis. Ma auntie wis a gentle soul. She worked hard but she wis a'ways a gentle soul.'

'What else did she tell you about Rubina?' Sadie

doesn't want to be rude but she is not so interested in Effie MacIver's marriage – not if it does not shed any light on her grandmother's life.

'Well,' Moira Barr says, after a pause and the lighting of another cigarette, 'Ah a'ways remember her sayin' aboot Rubina comin' fae a wee village, oot by Stirling, an' her nae knowin' much about the city afore she goat married. Effie wis different – she'd grown up here so it wisnae new tae her, aw the trams and the picture hooses and the dancing an' that. So they'd go out, every Wednesday, ma auntie said, tae see a film – she loved her films, ma auntie did. Greta Garbo wis her favourite but ye'll see that soon enough.'

Sadie wants to stop her at this point and ask what she means, but Moira Barr is on a roll and doesn't want to stop.

'Anyway, auld Mrs Coates frae doonstairs, Ah remember her too – she would babysit Rubina's weans and on Saturdays sometimes an' aw so they could go the dancing up the High Street. Even though the blackout wis oan. Ma auntie always said she had the best time of her life when they waur neighbours – her and Rubina.'

'And this was mostly when my grandfather was away? What happened when he came back?' Sadie asks.

'Ah dinnae ken aboot that bit. Effie nivir said much aboot him or efter the war – she just talked aboot when the men were awa'. I think it wis ma auntie's only chance tae huv a bit ae' fun.'

Sadie is getting impatient. She wants to see her grandmother's letters for herself now and Moira Barr isn't telling her enough. She is a red herring. She can't paint her grandmother for her – she doesn't know enough. But Sadie is not sure how to interrupt her now. The older woman is enjoying having her attention and she doesn't want to lose her guest to the papers in a back room but Sadie has to be firm and so she takes a breath and in the middle of Moira Barr's next sentence about her uncle Alec having a firm hand and she says, 'Would it be OK . . . I mean would you mind . . . if I had a look at the letters now? I'd love to see them – especially after what you've told me.'

Moira Barr frowns and then gets up from her chair with pain. 'Aye, well, it's jist through here,' she says.

And Sadie follows her through the glass door behind her chair and into a tiny dark room that has only a small narrow window at the far end. An old dining table and chairs sit in the middle of the room and that is all – apart from the boxes and boxes that are everywhere.

As Moira Barr switches on the brash overhead light, Sadie gasps at the sight of them all. There must be about twenty cardboard boxes piled on top of each other. Coats and dresses are strewn across the tabletop and there are several pairs of worn, dark pairs of ladies' shoes on the floor.

'We nivir use this room,' Moira Barr says, 'so we've jist kinda left it aw. We'll be gein' it tae a charity shop or somethin' soon so it's jist lucky you goat us in time.'

Sadie smiles at her even though her heart sinks at the number of boxes in the room and she hopes that she will not have to go through them all. 'Are the letters in any one place?' she asks, almost expecting the worst.

But Moira Barr does not disappoint her and says cheerily enough, 'Oh, aye, they're aw in that box ower there. An' a couple o' photies too – o' Effie and yer grannie.'

'Photographs? Of my grandmother?'

> Jesus fucking Christ! Why the *hell* didn't you show me them first?

But Sadie can't believe it. For all her sudden fury at this woman who is standing at the door like some sort of ancient mythical crone of a gatekeeper between her and the treasure she is seeking, she can't believe she is finally going to see what Rubina looks like and she can barely stand still, can barely hold herself from tearing the boxes open as Moira Barr shuffles slowly over to a large box in the corner and opens it.

'Aye, it's this one right enough,' she says, pulling something out. She stands up. 'Here,' she says and she hands Sadie a small framed black-and-white photograph.

A young woman, who looks nothing like Sadie at all, smiles back at her, a cloche hat hiding her dark curls, as she stands with her gloved hands crossed over in front of her, in her long, fur-trimmed coat, with trams just discernible in the background. It is Rubina. It is Rubina! She looks nothing like her granddaughter or her daughter Lily but Sadie can see a resemblance to her aunt Amy – or, rather, what she remembers of Amy. Rubina is tall and slim, with high cheekbones. She has a nervous face. An artist's face, Sadie thinks as she looks at it – not the kind of face to be hidden out of the way in a tenement in an old city. Rubina's smile is nervous too although that may be because she was not used to having her photograph taken and Sadie wishes she could ask her, ask her why she was nervous and why she was smiling.

'Aye, well, I'll leave ye tae it,' Moira Barr says, as Sadie sinks down on her knees to rifle through the rest of the box. 'Yu're welcome tae huv whitivir ye want. We'd only be giein' it awa' or throwin' it oot.'

Sadie barely hears her as Moira Barr lights up another cigarette and carries on talking for a while – until she realises she will get nothing more from her guest and leaves the room quietly. Sadie's hands are shaking and she doesn't want to lay the framed photograph down but she has to if she wants to see everything else and so she does and she lifts back the flap of the cardboard box, takes out more photographs and pulls at the first handful of papers on the top.

It is over. Sadie has spent three and half hours in this ugly little room reading almost every word of every letter her grandmother wrote to her neighbour Effie MacIver, starting in 1951 and ending in 1973. And, now that it is over, she wants to cry because she cannot believe what is in front of her. She has been through everything, she has read it all and she cannot believe it. When Moira Barr told her that she and her husband had read some of the letters but that they couldn't understand a word of them Sadie had assumed that it was because they weren't as educated as she is, that they didn't know what to look for or they couldn't decipher the handwriting. She told herself all sorts of patronising things when Moira Barr first made her remark but now, three and a half hours later, Sadie can see what she means – because she can barely understand a word of them herself.

Her grandmother wrote to Effie MacIver in code.

Her letters were not completely in code – many of the sentences run on or are unfinished or skip from one unrelated topic to another which would be hard enough for anyone to follow but not impossible. No, it is the code that defeats Sadie. And it is not a silly childish code that substituted letters for numbers or made words up – not that sort of thing at all. In the early days, there are plenty of mundane, bland statements about the weather, the cost of things like renting apartments or school clothes and then the description of a new car as the years go on and money improves. But they are the kinds of statements anybody might make – they are not peculiar to her grandmother and they tell her little about her life to distinguish it from a million other lives. No, it is the phrases – the odd little phrases, the *same* odd little phrases – that keep cropping up over and over again and that make no sense at all that force Sadie to realise Rubina is writing to her friend in code. In a private code, an intimate one, one that tells outsiders nothing because that is what codes are for.

Sadie can't understand any of it and she wants to cry because here she is, her grandmother, in this ugly little room, and this is all she has of her and it might as well be nothing because she is not talking to her granddaughter. How foolish she was to think she could be talking to her. She is talking a private language to the only other person in the world who could understand her and that person is not Sadie. It is not her.

Saturday, March 25th

It's been bothering me all day – since the funeral yesterday. Oh, Amy, you'd have been so proud if you could have seen them – Becka and Ricky. They did so well, so well. They loved you so much. And all the folk there! Faces I haven't seen in years. They hadn't seen you in years either. Just heard about you. Saw the notice in the paper and wanted to come. Neighbours way back when we were in Victoria Avenue. I hardly recognised the half of them. And one of your college teachers was there. I can't remember her name but she must've been about eighty. Said you were her best student. Always so original – marked for greatness, she said.

That didn't happen, did it? It doesn't – not when the wee ones come along. Always wondered where you got that from, Amy – your artistic talent. I was proud of you too yesterday. Seeing all those people. Don't think half that many would turn up for me. Or will when it's my turn. Maybe they would. I don't know. Doubt it. I'm not good. Not the way you were. You were better than me, Amy. You and Mary – both of you. I was the bad one. I wasn't the good girl you thought. The good girl I thought.

Stop.

I can't go on like this. Couldn't. Last night, you see, I told John about my plans. Just those at first – my plans to look for her. It's been you, Amy, you've done this – see what you've done! But I don't mean it. It got it all started, though. The minute I told him, it all started. Couldn't stop it. So much of it. Just came flooding out. So I told him what I never told you – or anyone. I told him what nobody knows. I'm a blabbermouth, yes, but not when it's doing me harm – oh, no. Then I can be *very* careful. I'm a bitter horrible old woman and that's why. But John, my John, I thought he'd hate me. I hate me. Or I did – not now. He wasn't shocked. Not about the first part, anyway – the part about Mum. Well, who's shocked nowadays? But he said he always thought it might be something like that – not that exactly that but something that couldn't be mentioned. Not then.

You see that's what I think, Amy. That's why she left us. We were grown up. We were married. We had our own families. Mary'd just had Sandy. We were all safe. She'd done her job. It was her time now. And she knew we wouldn't understand. Couldn't. If she'd tried to tell us, tried to explain. Remember all those letters, Amy? The letters from Glasgow? From our old neighbour, Mrs MacIver? She wrote to Mum all the time.

But that's not it – not what I had to tell John. It wasn't her. Mum didn't leave us for her. I know that. Effie MacIver never left Scotland. I know – I checked . . . oh, a few years ago. She was an old lady, still living in Lawrie Street. But she wrote to Mum every week – every week those same envelopes, that same writing. I don't think Dad bothered. I don't think he noticed. He was too busy working – too busy worrying about the businesses. Maybe he was off having his own fun. Who knows now? But I noticed them. I noticed them all. I told you I was good at that – remember? I noticed everything.

And then there were the other ones. Don't think you ever saw them. When she got a letter every day for over a fortnight? It was the time I was ill. I'd started that silly office job. I was just eighteen. Remember? I'd been begging to leave school and I'd seen the ad downtown. Downtown! Me, working downtown! I was so excited. I bought a pencil skirt. Remember it? No more girls' clothes for me. I was a grown-up at last. I couldn't wait.

Well, I came down with the flu. Remember? After only two weeks. Couldn't believe it. Proper flu – not a bad cold. They always talk about flu nowadays but that's not what they mean. Couldn't get my head off the pillow for a whole week. Mum dragging me into the bathroom, making me take cold showers to keep my temperature down. I just slept all the time. Never been so ill. But then it lifted. Remember? The first time I could eat something. Wanting that whole plate of roast potatoes and chicken Mum made? And you all standing round my bed, watching me eat my first meal for days and cheering when I had my first mouthful. But I couldn't eat it or hardly any of it – my stomach had shrunk so much.

Anyway, I was at home for another week – in bed the whole time. But I was getting bored – I'd read all my books. Oh, Amy, what did I do? John just patted me on the back when I told him. Poured me a glass of wine and said it wasn't my fault. I was a teenager. That's what teenagers do – they do stupid, selfish things. But it's not what they do. I bet Sadie would never have done anything like this.

It was me, you see. When I was at home, I saw them in her hand – those letters. Every morning, I saw her picking them up – the same envelopes every day, with the same writing. Not from Glasgow – not Effie MacIver. Someone else. But it was just the same. Happening all over again. Mum would get a letter every morning and off she would go. I'd be home all day by myself. I minded that – Mum going out every day when I was still ill. She never told me where she was going. I was bored. That's my excuse. This is my confession, Amy. What I did. Because it was wrong. I just wanted to know, that's all – where she was going, who was writing to her every day.

So, one morning, after she'd gone, I got out of bed and went through to her and Dad's room. I didn't think there'd be anything there. She surely wouldn't keep anything there – not where Dad might've found it – but I rummaged about anyway. Nothing – couldn't find a thing.

Then, when she came back that evening, that's when I did it. She was always back in time. She'd have bought me something. Some treat to cheer me up, she'd say – something nice to eat or a lipstick. She'd be all chatty and happy. She'd come up to my room, sit on the end of the bed and take off her little pillbox hat. Remember? The red one? She was so smart those days – well turned-out. And so happy! I loved her spending time with me. We'd just chat. She'd give me my present – whatever she'd bought – and I'd always love it. She had taste. And she would always fuss – make sure I was comfortable. It was the closest we ever were – when I was ill, when she was looking after me. Just me and her. No one else. I had all her attention. Just for once.

And I suppose. I didn't want anyone else taking it, taking my mum away from me. I resented it – those days she'd spend away from me. I'm confessing, Amy, so I'll tell the truth. It wasn't boredom – that's not why I did it.

So she'd come back – always an hour or so before Dad and you and Mary – come up and speak to me and then get started on dinner. But, this time, before she went down to the kitchen, I said I'd run out of . . . you know . . . sanitary napkins. I knew she didn't have any. I'd already been through her stuff. I knew there was nothing there. And I couldn't go to get any – I wasn't well enough to go outside yet. So she said she'd send Amy or Mary out when they got back. I said I couldn't wait for that – I needed something right there and then.

She trusted me, Amy. She was happy. She was in love, I think. Yes, I think she *was* in love with someone. She was glowing that way – you know? And she believed me. She said she'd get the potatoes on and, if I'd go downstairs and watch them, she'd go. And then she left – with just her purse. She didn't take her handbag. Why should she? It was only the end of the street she was going to. I knew she wouldn't take it with her.

And the minute she was gone. I grabbed her bag. And there they were – all these letters that she'd been getting – tucked away in the pocket of her handbag. I shouldn't have done it – it wasn't right. But I wanted to stop it – she was *ours*. She said she wouldn't leave. Even if sometimes it had been better when she was away – those times when we were wee. But she'd promised me she'd never do that again and she didn't. She was always there – she kept her promise. And she seemed happy with us. Dad was happy. We all thought everything was all right, didn't we?

I knew I didn't have very long till she came back. But I only needed an address and there it was – right at the top of each letter. Funny that – being so formal in a love letter. Writing your address at the top – just habit, I suppose. I still do it. Address on top right-hand corner, 'Yours faithfully' at the bottom – even though Sadie says it's 'Yours sincerely' nowadays. But the address was there on every one. Showed she was respectable – this woman who was writing to my mum, just another respectable wife and mother. She mentioned a daughter in one letter. So there must have been a husband. I didn't read the letters that closely. I started one or two. But I couldn't go on. It was shocking. Because it was a woman writing these things? Would I have been more shocked if it had been a man? I don't know. Maybe. All I knew was that her name was Gracie. I didn't know her last name. She signed herself 'Your darling Gracie'.

It was the same things mostly. They were short letters – demanding, tender, frank. But there was a build-up in them – I could see that. She was building up to something. She wanted to take Mum away from us. You could see it. She was pushing for it. Any minute now, that's what she'd be writing next. Maybe that's what they talked about. When they saw each other every day. I don't know. I was only eighteen. Everything's black and white when you're eighteen. This was wrong. That was what I thought. I didn't link it with Mum, exactly – not my mother. But I knew. I saw it when I was wee – I saw her with Mrs MacIver. I always knew but I wanted it stopped.

Oh, what did I do, Amy? If I hadn't, what would have happened? What did it matter? I would be leaving myself, anyway, soon enough, wouldn't I? I wasn't going to be staying even if I hadn't worked all that out then. So why did I do it? I just wanted it to stop. I didn't care. I just wanted it stopped.

So I did it. I copied down her address from the letter. I didn't know her surname but I didn't need it. The address was enough. Without a surname, maybe he would get it – the husband. Maybe he'd read it first. Then I put the letters back just before Mum got home – all dazed and happy still. Giving me a hug in the kitchen for watching the potatoes. Helping me back upstairs till dinner time. Then, later, kissing me goodnight. Telling me how proud she was of me for getting that job. Saying how well I was going to do.

I don't know if she ever knew that I wrote my note. I did it in big capitals – not like my writing. 'I KNOW WHAT YOU'RE DOING, GRACIE. LEAVE RUBINA MCALLISTER ALONE. IF YOU DON'T STOP IT, I'LL TELL EVERYONE.' Can you believe it? The melodrama. The spite. What a wicked, wicked thing to do. But I was scared, Amy. It frightened me – all of it. I put the note in an envelope. Next day, when Mum was out as usual, I nipped out and posted it and then waited to see what would happen.

Nothing happened – not at first. Couldn't watch for the mail every day – not once I was better and had gone back to work. But, one afternoon, I came back home when I wasn't supposed to – a late lunch break – and Mum was there. She wasn't out – not the way she'd been before. She was at home. I tried coming back unexpectedly a couple of times and she was always there. I got hold of her handbag a couple of times too. The letters were all gone. The Glasgow ones kept coming but I never saw any of the other ones again. Her glow had gone too. It was over. She was quiet – not miserable but the light had gone out of her.

And I couldn't stand it so I left, went back to Scotland. Free of it all – of her, of what she did, who she was . . . I was *so* ashamed – of her, not of myself. I still thought I'd done the right thing, you see, Amy. Do you see? Do you understand? I thought I was right – for a long time I thought I was.

Then, the day of the picnic . . . When I'd forgotten all about it, when all I thought about was my own happiness – what I wanted – that's when she left. And it was my fault. If I hadn't done what I did all those years before, maybe . . . Well, maybe she would have left back then and it would have been bad – yes, it would have been bad – but maybe she wouldn't have sneaked off. Maybe she'd just have told Dad she was leaving but she wanted to stay in touch or something like that – I don't know. But that day, Amy, that day, she left the way she did because she didn't want anyone to know. Because she knew what would happen if someone knew – someone would tell. Isn't that what my note threatened to do? I don't think she ever knew who sent it. Maybe she thought they might still be around, might still be keeping an eye on her and the company she was keeping. Ready to spoil it all for her. Yes, I bet that's what she thought – some stranger, some nosy neighbour, someone who knew all about her, someone she didn't know. When, all the time, it was me – only I wasn't there to keep an eye on her. I'd left so she could have gone any time and I wouldn't have known. She could have had as many letters as she liked but she wouldn't have dared – not any more. She didn't know who it was watching her so, one day, she left too. And, if I get the chance – if I find her – maybe I can say sorry. It's too late to say sorry to you, Amy, too late for you but maybe, if I find her . . . Maybe it won't be too late to say sorry to her . . . for what I did.

Greta's hat was crooked . . .
Marlene sings off-key . . .
Greta never laughs . . .
Marlene pencils in her brows . . .

It is two days since Sadie's visit to Moira Barr and these phrases have not left her mind. All the way back on the too-warm bus to the little university town, they ran through her head and it continued as she walked up the hill to her shared house. Maria had taken the opportunity of the Easter break to return to Spain and see her fiancé and Jackie was away for a few days with two other girls from the lab so Sadie had the house to herself and, for half a moment, as she let herself into the dark, cold hallway, she had thought of calling Richard. He is an expert on DNA, on breaking genetic codes. He would know how to break this code. But she resisted that thought, she didn't want to call him for anything, especially not this and later, as she sat in the front room on the cheap velour sofa with the letters she didn't understand sitting on her lap, Sadie realised that his expertise was not the kind of expertise she needed. She needed her own not his. She realised that she was, in fact, far better equipped than he was to interpret her grandmother's words. Because interpretation, not decoding, is what is needed and she has been interpreting words all her adult life.

And so now, in her office, on this bright, sunny Thursday morning, two days after she sat in Moira Barr's gloomy little back room, she has spread her grandmother's letters all about the floor. There is hardly a spot on the carpet that is not covered by Rubina's delicate, spidery hand and run-on sentences, hardly a letter page that has not been abused by Sadie's highlighter pen.

She has photocopied everything which was something that divided her opinion. It was a professional action – treating her grandmother's words as just another text – but it was an impersonal one too and she knows already how personal this is becoming for her. And so, reluctantly, Sadie had lifted her yellow highlighter pen and scored through the first mention of the first odd phrase that took place right in the middle of a sentence about plants:

We went out to look at a new site where they are building new houses. They are being bought up very quickly by all us new arrivals Greta's hat was crooked there are no flowers anywhere, just lots of brown earth.

Sadie sits back on her haunches, trying not to squash the pages at her feet, and she is captivated by the luminous yellow lines she has drawn on sheet after sheet – lines that appear without warning and without any regularity of any kind over years and years of correspondence. Her grandmother is not a highly descriptive writer. She does not take much time to describe her new world or her family or her home, except to note everyday and general details. There is nothing to indicate when a peculiar phrase will appear but Sadie is beginning to understand a little more. She is beginning to interpret the details about her grandmother's life that she has omitted to mention. She is beginning to understand about 'self-writing', about the dual nature of a woman's life. Yes, she is beginning to understand all about that . . .

> Haven't you told him yet?

all about the public and the private –

> Haven't you told him yet? When are you going to tell him?

the things you can say and the things you can't.

And the things that Rubina could say were the ordinary things, the details of a life lived by a wife and mother from the 1950s to the 1970s, in another country from the one she was born in. That is what Rubina is telling Sadie in her letters – that is what she is permitting her granddaughter and anyone else who might be listening to hear. *Things are cheaper here so we have been able to buy most things for the girls brand new* Rubina reveals in one, at the end of 1955. Then, a year later, *We have found another new house not so small as the last one and a bigger garden* and then *I made my own curtains there is a very nice shade of mauve that I managed to pick up from the general store near to our home* and so it goes on and, if it wasn't for *Greta never laughs* coming straight after that mention of mauve curtains, Sadie would have consigned her grandmother and her life and her letters to the dustbin.

But she is learning. This is her public life – in case anyone else but Effie MacIver should one day read these letters, in case her friend's drunken husband back in Scotland should one day come across them, Sadie supposes. As she picks up one page and then another, she wonders idly

What if they'd been e-mails?

and she tells herself that she has been very lucky that these letters have been saved and that she only has to interpret them correctly to find out what happened to her grandmother because she is certain that what happened to her is linked to the kind of person she was and that these letters can still reveal that.

And so Sadie will go through them all, line by line, for as long as it takes her. She will pore over every word. She is already relishing this chase after Rubina because she believes and it is a romantic notion, she knows, but she believes that Rubina wants her to know and to find her. This is what Sadie is here for – the granddaughter who interprets words for a living.

She realises quickly, of course, that Greta and Marlene mean Greta Garbo and Marlene Dietrich. She remembered Moira Barr telling her that Greta Garbo was her aunt Effie's favourite film actress but Sadie cannot see any more to it than that. Rubina does not call herself Greta or Effie Marlene or vice versa. They are not pseudonyms for each other, however much the poignancy of two young women from the same tenement in Scotland giving themselves the alter egos of two of the most glamorous film stars the world has ever seen appeals to Sadie. No, when Rubina writes *Greta's hat was crooked,* she suspects that the phrase hints at something taking place in Rubina's life that she is not happy about. The letters that contain this phrase tend to be more downbeat with the domestic details sounding like complaints – *There is a great wind here through the summer and nothing is ever clean for long. It gets so dusty* – and they are more distracted too – *What was I saying? Oh, yes, well, we have been very busy with the new car* – and most of her sentences are unfinished before she begins another topic, as though something distressing has happened. And only Effie will know what that distressing thing is – only Effie will understand the ringing of the bell, the red flash of light, the warning that comes with *Greta's hat was crooked.*

Sadie's grandmother liked her word games then, she thinks as she gazes at her words on the floor. She does not know what all that word play means but she is beginning to know some things, gradually. Like a palimpsest, her grandmother's life is leaving its traces, barely detectable under the cover she has arranged for herself, but it is present and detectable all the same. And, when she writes *Marlene pencils in her brows,* the letters with this phrase often come after a long gap because Rubina did not write at regular intervals. Sometimes almost a whole year passes and Sadie wonders, as she puts the pages into chronological order on the floor of her office, if Rubina had written something or done something to her friend that Effie took offence at because these letters with *Marlene pencils in her brows* are slightly recalcitrant in tone. They are almost appeasing – as though Rubina is apologising for the long gap in time since she last wrote without actually saying so.

Yes, Sadie knows some things and she is getting closer to knowing more although the most important question the letters pose – why write in code at all? – is only partly answered by the reasoning that it is just people with something to hide who try to disguise their meaning. By now, Sadie has read and reread the very last letter a hundred times. Short in comparison to the others, it is the most peculiar of them all and it is dated May 1973, just a few weeks before Lily and John with Sadie and Campbell arrived in Toronto on holiday.

Effie,
How is your hair? You must tell me because I am thinking of a different shade or maybe a different colour altogether not because I want to have a change Greta never laughs although sometimes I think that would be good. But what do you think? I should do it is not my suggestion you know how these things are someone sees you with an outfit you haven't worn for a while and they say Greta never laughs you should change it but I have thought about it and I don't want to but maybe you think it would be better for me to take another's Greta never laughs or I will be sorry if I don't you see how it is because it isn't just me and maybe it's too late. What should I do? I should leave it just as it is and see what happens when they all see the grey there but will it make me look will they all the grey can I bear it all the grey Greta never laughs you know about the grey and I have always coloured it ever since and thought I always would and up until now that has been fine and no worries at all but now I have to change it I'm told. So what do you think I should do?

Your friend
Rubina

All Rubina is concerned about in this letter is her hair, which Sadie cannot understand. She doesn't understand why it matters so much or why her grandmother should sound so confused, so torn between colouring her hair or leaving it as it is

Christ, it's only about a hairdo!

even though Sadie has a thing about her hair and so does Lily and so, presumably, did Rubina. That is where Sadie gets it from – her concern about her hair. So perhaps, Sadie tries to reason with herself, it is not surprising her grandmother should make such a fuss about something so trivial when much more important things were taking place, like the impending visit from a daughter and her family – a son-in-law and grandchildren she had never seen. Perhaps that is just the way she was. But that is too literal for Sadie. She knows, deep down, that this letter is not about hair.

No, it is not about hair.

Haven't you told him yet?

The telephone is ringing. It is late now and Sadie is surprised to hear it but, when she scrambles over her grandmother's letters on the floor and picks up the receiver, it is Pamela's voice she hears. 'Sadie, do you have a moment?'

What the bloody hell is it now?

'What? Oh, yes, sure,' she says. The department is like a seaside town during winter – shut up and empty of people. She didn't expect to be disturbed at all; she doesn't want to be.

'The head wants to know if he can come down and have a word?'

Sadie gazes at the floor covered in letters.

Shit, shit, shit!

'I can come up and see him if he likes.'

A pause, a hand placed over the receiver, words spoken in the background. 'No, that's OK, Sadie, he says he just wants to pop down and see you for a minute or two.'

Fuck, fuck, fuck!

'OK, that's fine.'

'Bye.'

'Bye.'

She has about thirty seconds to clear the floor before he appears. It's not long enough to pick up all the pages in chronological order so all the time she has spent today sorting them out will be wasted. She will have to pick everything up just anyhow. She will have to hurry and she can hear the door at the end of the basement corridor squeal open and the head's heavy tread as he makes his way along the corridor. And Sadie is crushing the pages as she snatches them up from the floor, while trying to figure out why the head should want to see her, of all people – she who has only a few months of her contract left to run. But she has no time to think about this as she hears him stop outside her office just as she picks up the last letter.

Shit, the mugs and those books and . . . oh, fucking hell!

There is a knock at the door and Sadie shouts, 'Come in!' as she runs to her desk and crams the letters into the desk drawer.

The head opens the door. Sadie hasn't seen him since she complained about Maurice. She is not afraid of him – she is just startled to see him. She is always startled to see him – he has that sort of effect on her.

He is smiling at her. 'Sadie!' the head booms at her from the doorway. 'Just a quick question.'

Sadie is halfway out of her seat already but he motions her to sit back down as he cups his hands behind his back and takes a few purposeful steps over the thin grey carpet to her bookshelf.

'Yes, yes,' he says, as he bends down, squinting at a few titles, before standing up straight and looking up towards the high windows. 'Yes, Sadie, I'd say you've settled in very well here, don't you think?' Now he turns to look at her, his pale blue eyes fix her as he smiles again.

'Well . . . I . . . well . . . thank you,' she says, stammering slightly but not from her previous beginner's sense of inadequacy. Sadie is not a beginner any more. She has nothing to prove.

'Yes, yes – we all think so,' the head rushes on, turning away from her again to gaze round the room once more. He stops at the sink, with its dirty mugs and moves on quickly, back to the bookshelf. 'And it looks as though I'll have enough money to continue the post – extend it for twelve months. I take it that's something you'd be interested in?'

He is looking straight at her once again and this time Sadie blushes. She feels the redness flush across her face as she struggles for the right words which do not come.

'No need, Sadie, no need! I can see that would be fine,'

he nods as she opens her mouth to speak. 'We can discuss the details later. I don't think there should be any need for paperwork – it's just a continuation of your existing contract – but I'll check with Personnel.'

He is already at the door. 'Won't keep you any longer. Good to see someone's in their office. Some of our colleagues seem to think everything stops for Easter! See you later.' And he is gone.

It is too strange for Sadie to take in. For a moment, she is held by the image of herself here, in this office that is now undeniably hers, for a full year more, completing more research, writing more papers, creating more opportunities to get her name into refereed journals.

> 'I'd say you've settled in here very well.'

Forget that student. Forget the lack of companionship. Forget everything that has happened over the last couple of months. Forget it all because they want her to continue here.

> 'You've settled in very well.'

And then suddenly she thinks of Richard – of seeing him possibly for another year. She can fix whatever is wrong between them. She is not a phoney. She is not going to let him down. She is not a mistake he has made. And that is when Sadie looks down at her stomach, at the back wool pinafore dress that grips her tightly in the waist and which she imagines is straining at the seams even though that can't be possible, even though it has only been weeks rather than months. And she has done nothing about it – she must do something about it, she must tell Richard, she must go to the doctor, she must sort it out, she must fix it, she must make it possible that she can carry on, she must sort it out, she must, she must. And she is out of her chair, standing up. She is not sure what to do. Go to the practice on the main road? Or should she call Richard and ask him to meet her first? But she will go, she will go now. Yes, that is what she will do.

That is what she will do.

But the telephone is ringing again. Sadie has her coat on and it makes her jump but she hesitates. She does not leave after all. No, she picks up the phone instead. Something inside her is expecting to hear the head's voice telling her that it was all a mistake – of course he hasn't offered her a job for another year – but it isn't the head she hears. No, the voice she is hearing now is her mother's voice. It is Lily.

'Sadie? Is that you?'

'Mum? God, yes.'

Shit! I don't believe this.

Lily's timing has never been good and Sadie marvels at her ability to call at just the wrong moment.

'Are you all right? You sound all out of breath.'

'No, yes, I'm fine. How are you?' She doesn't want to discuss anything with her mother – not about the job offer, not about Rubina, not about Richard, not about . . .

'Fine, fine!'

Lily's voice is unusually cheerful and Sadie stops what she is doing. She cannot leave just yet. She has to sit back down instead. She starts to unbutton her coat.

'The funeral was . . .'

And Sadie is reminded immediately that she hasn't asked about it. She has barely thought about it but she cannot tell her mother why that is.

Lily continues, 'Well, what can you expect from these things? It was horrible but it was all very well handled. I think that's the best thing you can say.'

She stops and Sadie rushes in with, 'You sound OK, though? You don't sound *too* upset.' Immediately Sadie wishes she could take back what she has just said. It sounds callous and now Lily will be difficult. She will criticise her daughter's reaction or accuse her of being tactless which Sadie is – Lily is right to say that she is.

But Lily does not say those things. Instead, she says, 'No, well, I think that's because . . . well . . . I've come to a decision and I think it's helping me through things. I've discussed it with your father and he agrees with me so we're going to be staying on a bit longer here – another couple of weeks. And that's partly why I'm phoning you.'

Sadie is not sure that this day could become more confusing or surprising and she is not really following what her mother is saying so she replies, almost absent-mindedly, by saying, 'Oh? Why's that?'

'Well . . .' Lily takes a big deep breath. Sadie hears it from the other end of the phone and she imagines her mother gathering her strength. She doesn't like the sound of this all of a sudden and she is preparing to hear something she doesn't want to hear, when her mother suddenly says, 'Can you come over? I know it's your Easter break, isn't it? So it should be possible for you to get over here for a week or two, shouldn't it? Don't worry about money if that's a problem. Your dad and I can book you a flight from here or we can get some money to you – whatever you need . . .'

'What d'you want me over there for? The funeral's over. Why, what are you asking me . . .' There is a pause as Sadie stops.

Lily says nothing.

Sadie has offended her. She has asked for her only daughter's support and she has been thoughtless and insensitive. Why can she never say the right thing to her mother?

Then suddenly comes, 'I'm looking for Rubina and I wondered if you'd like to come over and help me?' Lily says this quite calmly – as though it is the most natural request in the world. She waits for a second, pauses for Sadie's reaction. Then, when she hears nothing, she asks urgently, 'Sadie? Are you there? Did you hear me?'

> I'm looking for Rubina. I'm looking for Rubina.
>
> Haven't you told him yet?
>
> 'You've settled in very well.'
>
> 'Greta never laughs'

Sadie fights to clear her head of the voices. She is frightened that she is about to blurt one of them out. She has to think . . . think . . . what she should say . . .

'When did you decide this? What's happened?' is all she can manage. It is breathless and she doesn't sound like herself.

There is another pause and she can hear another voice in the background, saying something she can't make out, and Lily hurries on, 'I'll call you later and explain properly. But I've decided to go and look for her. I never told you . . . what happened on holiday. I know you know she disappeared . . .'

'Well, I've gathered that much,' Sadie says. She does

not mean to sound rude but her head is still clearing of all those phrases, all loose and unconnected words, and she is impatient to hear what else her mother has to say – yes, for the first time, she is impatient to hear what her mother has to say.

'Yes, it was at a picnic, in Ontario Park.'

The picnic. 'Yes,' Sadie says and now her head is clear at last, now she is excited, and she says, 'I remember it. We were all there, weren't we?'

'Yes, we were,' Lily says. 'Look, I'll speak to you about this a bit more tonight but one minute she was there, the next she was gone. We did go to the police but they never traced her. It wasn't kidnapping or anything dramatic like that. She just went of her own accord. We knew that. But we never really tried to find her. No, we never really did . . .' Her mother's voice trails off or perhaps it is the connection that suddenly sounds much fainter and Sadie needs to be there, she needs to go.

'Mum? Mum? You still there?'

There is a small sound and then, 'I'm going to have to nip out for a while but I'll call you later tonight at home, will I? There's . . . something else – other things I should tell you. Think about it anyway. All right, Sadie?'

She needs to go – it is time for her to go. 'Yes,' she says. 'Yes, yes, OK, I'll speak to you tonight, Mum. I'll come over . . .'

> 'Greta told him . . .'
> 'Haven't you settled in?'
> I'm looking for Richard.

The voices garble and jumble together as the connection is

cut off and Lily does not hear Sadie's last words. And, as she puts the phone down in the silence of her office, her head is spinning because of all the things she hasn't said, all the things she hasn't told her mother, about Rubina's letters and the job offer and Richard and about being pregnant.

Words, not bodies.
Words and bodies.

She needs to go.

It is gloomy in her office all of a sudden and she realises how late it must be but her heart is doubling its beats. It is painful and she needs to sit down. She will have a cup of tea since she doesn't have anything stronger to hand and she goes over to the sink and fills up the kettle. She will drink some tea and she will be calm again. Her mother wants her to go to Toronto . . . to help her look for Rubina . . . when Sadie has Rubina here, in her desk – a Rubina she cannot understand.

Words and bodies.

She pours some hot water into a mug and drops a teabag into it. She thinks, yes, it is time. She needs to go. It is time for her to go.

And so it is late and Sadie is about to pack a large suitcase that she purchased only a few hours ago. Jackie, who has just returned from the city with her friends, is concerned that she is packing everything she has here. 'Does this mean you're not coming back?' And Sadie has had to reassure her that yes, she will be back but not for about three weeks and, after that . . . well, she is not sure, she cannot say. But Jackie should not worry about the rent, she tells her as she heaves her suitcase on to the bed and begins to lift up clothes that are strewn on the floor, because she will pay her share until the end of the lease whatever she decides to do and she will do her best to give her enough notice so that she and Maria can find a new flatmate. Jackie is not happy about this, Sadie can see but, short of signing it in blood, there is nothing else she can do to reassure her so this will have to do.

And so it is late but it is not late in Canada – she still has time to phone her mother. Lily will be waiting for her at the airport when she lands, some twelve hours from now. Sadie has time to phone her and tell her what she has still not told her about Moira Barr and Effie MacIver and Rubina's letters and the job offer and Richard and the pregnancy. The pregnancy. Words and bodies. But she is not sure. Families shouldn't have secrets – that's what she believed. She knows she should tell her mother about the meeting with Moira Barr at her house in Lawrie Street. And she knows that she should tell Lily what Moira Barr said and that she should tell her about the letters . . .

And so it is late and all the things Sadie knows she should do are making her yawn as much as the late hour and she sleepily folds another sweater and places it on the pile inside her suitcase. Families shouldn't have secrets. She has been angry with Lily all these years because she kept things from her and now Sadie is keeping things from Lily. There is a scene in her head – a picnic with mothers and fathers, girls and boys, a grandmother and a grandfather, all together on a hot summer's day. And, after all Sadie has read of Rubina's letters, that scene has not changed. It is still a picture of innocence before the fall. Rubina did not hate her family. She did not run away. She loved them. Sadie is sure of that. She is sure that that is what they will find, Sadie and Lily, when they read her letters properly together.

And so it is late and Sadie knows she will only have a few hours to make up her mind about it all. She leaves the rest of her packing for the moment and tiptoes downstairs, in her stockinged feet, so as not to wake up Jackie and Maria who have already gone to bed. She goes into the kitchen, snaps on the light and pours a glass of red wine from the bottle on the counter. No, she thinks, she will not be coming back. She will pay the rest of the lease that she owes but she won't be coming back – not to live here. She will come through from the city for the last few teaching sessions she still has in the third term and for any departmental meetings and invigilating of exams but she will not be accepting the offer of the job. Sadie will not be coming back.

And so it is late and that is what she has decided even though, when she met with Richard earlier this evening, she was cowardly with him and she let him believe that she would be back.

> 'It's only a few weeks. I'll send you a postcard!'
> 'Well, that's very big of you, Sadie. Thanks very much. Don't miss me too much, will you?'
> 'Oh, don't be like that. It's not really that long.'
> 'Maybe not to you but I'm not sure I'll be able to . . . well, all I'm saying is . . .'

But he didn't say it. He didn't say what she knew he was thinking – that he wouldn't be waiting for her. Sadie knows that he is tired of her and that, before she returns for the third term, he will have met someone else – if he hasn't done so already. And she feels a little sad about that, as she stands under the strip light in the kitchen in the silence, sipping her red wine, even though it has helped make up her mind about yet another question. No, of course she will not be telling him. She will not be telling him anything. What is it all for, she wonders. Coming to this strange little university town. Pursuing knowledge. She will have no friends, no colleagues, no job, no flat, no boyfriend if she leaves now and doesn't come back. All of them will be gone if she doesn't come back.

And so it is late and Sadie switches off the kitchen light and takes the half-empty glass back upstairs with her. Suddenly she thinks that she will investigate the academic situation in Toronto when she is over there. That is something she can do. She will see what the universities over there are like. She will see what kind of research they are carrying out. She will see if there is a way for her to fit in, if she can find a way to be who she wants to be, in a city with all her relatives. With her family. Perhaps she could work on a general sort of project – the lives of Scots who emigrated after the war. Perhaps she will be able to tell her grandmother's story and, if not that one, then she may find others she can tell. Perhaps there will be lots of personal stories that she can put together – a collage of experience that will rescue her faith in the personal. Yes, Sadie smiles to herself as she switches on the bathroom light and runs water gently from the tap in the sink. That will rescue her project. She should have known there would be a way – a way that might even rescue her.

And so it is late when she finishes her packing.

She will not phone her mother after all. She will wait until she arrives there, in Toronto, before she decides what to tell and what not to tell.

She will wait until she sees Lily and then Sadie will know what it is she really wants to do.

NURSING RESEARCH METHODOLOGY

Issues and Implementation

Edited by
Peggy L. Chinn, RN, PhD, FAAN
State University of New York at Buffalo

AN ASPEN PUBLICATION®
Aspen Publishers, Inc.
1986
Rockville, Maryland
Royal Tunbridge Wells

Library of Congress Cataloging in Publication Data

Nursing research methodology

"An Aspen publication."
Includes bibliographies and index.
1. Nursing—Research—Methodology. I. Chinn, Peggy L. [DNLM: 1. Nursing.
2. Research—methods. WY 20.5 N9746]
RT81.5.N8745 1986 610.73'072 86-10857
ISBN: 0-87189-373-8

Editorial Services: Ruth Bloom

Library of Congress Catalog Card Number: 86-10857
ISBN: 0-87189-373-8

Printed in the United States of America

1 2 3 4 5

Table of Contents

Editorial Review Board

GRAYCE M. SILLS, RN, PhD, FAAN
Ohio State University

MARY CIPRIANO SILVA, RN, PhD, FAAN
George Mason University

A. MARILYN SIME, RN, PhD
University of Minnesota

JUDITH A. SMITH, RN, PhD
University of Pennsylvania

JEAN L. STAIR, RN, EdD
Visiting Nurse Association of Metropolitan Detroit

MARJORIE STANTON, RN, EdD
D'Youville College

ORA L. STRICKLAND, RN, PhD, FAAN
University of Maryland

ARDIS R. SWANSON, RN, PhD
New York University

CHRISTINE TANNER, RN, PhD
University of Oregon

GERTRUDE TORRES, RN, EdD
D'Youville College

INEZ TUCK, PhD
University of North Carolina at Chapel Hill

ROBERT W. TUCKER, PhD
Arizona State University

ANN M. VODA, RN, PhD
University of Utah

LORRAINE O. WALKER, RN, EdD
University of Texas at Austin

JEAN WATSON, RN, PhD
University of Colorado Health Sciences Center

RETHA V. WELLONS, RN, PhD,
University of California, San Francisco

CAROLYN ANTONIDES WILLIAMS, RN, PhD, FAAN
University of Kentucky

JANET A. WILLIAMSON, RN, PhD
The Pennsylvania State University

PATRICIA WINSTEAD-FRY, RN, PhD
New York University

D. JEAN WOOD, RN, PhD
University of South Carolina

MARY M. ZIEMER, DNSc
Villanova University

Contributors

IVO L. ABRAHAM, RN, PhD
Assistant Professor
Nursing, Psychiatric-Mental Health
Frances Payne Bolton School of Nursing
Case Western Reserve University
Cleveland, Ohio

DAVID G. ALLEN, RN, PhD
Assistant Professor
School of Nursing
University of Wisconsin-Madison
Madison, Wisconsin

JOAN M. ANDERSON, RN, PhD
Associate Professor
School of Nursing
University of British Columbia
Vancouver, British Columbia

PATRICIA BENNER, RN, PhD
Associate Professor
School of Nursing
University of California-San Francisco
San Francisco, California

KAREN WALTON BUDD, RN, PhD
Assistant Professor and Clinical Nurse Specialist
Frances Payne Bolton School of Nursing
Case Western Reserve University and University Hospitals of Cleveland
Cleveland, Ohio

NORMA P. CHICK, PhD
Senior Lecturer
Department of Nursing Studies
Masey University
Palmerston North, New Zealand

JACQUELINE F. CLINTON, RN, PhD, FAAN
Director
Center for Nursing Research and Evaluation
University of Wisconsin-Madison
Madison, Wisconsin

W. RICHARD COWLING, III, BSN, MS, PhD
Doctoral Program Coordinator and Assistant Professor
Frances Payne Bolton School of Nursing
Case Western Reserve University
Cleveland, Ohio

NANCY L. DIEKELMANN, RN, PhD
Associate Professor
School of Nursing
University of Wisconsin-Madison
Madison, Wisconsin

LAURA COX DZUREC, RN, MS, PhD Candidate
Case Western Reserve University
Cleveland, Ohio
and
Assistant Professor
Nursing of Children
Kent State University
Kent, Ohio

BONNIE J. GARVIN, RN, PhD
Associate Professor
The Ohio State University College of Nursing
Columbus, Ohio

BARBARA A. HEDIN, RN, PhD
Assistant Professor
Department of Nursing
Virginia State University
Richmond, Virginia

MAEONA K. JACOBS
Associate Professor
College of Nursing
University of Utah
Salt Lake City, Utah

CAROL W. KENNEDY, RN, PhD
Acting Chairperson
Department of Life Span Process
The Ohio State University College of Nursing
Columbus, Ohio

BARBARA J. KERR, RN, MSN
Assistant Vice President, Medical/Surgical Nursing
Patient Care Services
Southwest Washington Hospitals
Vancouver, Washington

HESOOK SUZIE KIM, RN, PhD
Professor and Dean
College of Nursing
University of Rhode Island
Kingston, Rhode Island

HARRIETT J. LIONBERGER, RN, DNSc
Consultant-Integrative Nursing and Instructor for Consortium of the California State University, Region 12
Napa, California

MARIE L. LOBO, RN, PhD
Associate Professor and Director/Chairperson
Nursing Care of Children
Frances Payne Bolton School of Nursing
Case Western Reserve University
Cleveland, Ohio

M. JUDITH LYNAM, BScN, MSN
Assistant Professor
School of Nursing
University of British Columbia
Vancouver, British Columbia

KATHLEEN M. MCKEEHAN, RN, PhD
Postdoctoral Research Fellow
The Ohio State University College of Nursing
Columbus, Ohio

AFAF I. MELEIS, PhD
Professor
Mental Health and Community Nursing
University of California-San Francisco
San Francisco, California

PATRICIA MOCCIA, RN, PhD
Associate Professor and Chairperson
Department of Nursing Education
Teachers College
Columbia University
New York, New York

JANICE M. MORSE, RN, PhD(Nurs), PhD(Anthro)
Professor of Nursing
University of Alberta
Edmonton, Alberta, Canada

PATRICIA L. MUNHALL
Associate Professor
Graduate Program
Hunter College-Bellevue School of Nursing
New York, New York

PHYLLIS R. SCHULTZ, RN, MN, MA, PhD
Assistant Professor of Nursing Administration and Community Health
University of Colorado Health Sciences Center
Denver, Colorado

DONNA SCHWARTZ-BARCOTT, RN, PhD
Associate Professor of Nursing
College of Nursing
University of Rhode Island
Kingston, Rhode Island

MARILYN L. STEMBER, RN, PhD
Associate Professor for Research and Evaluation
School of Nursing
University of Colorado Health Sciences Center
Denver, Colorado

ORA L. STRICKLAND, RN, PhD, FAAN
Associate Professor and Doctoral Program Evaluator
School of Nursing
University of Maryland-Baltimore
Baltimore, Maryland

CAROLYN F. WALTZ, RN, PhD, FAAN
Professor and Coordinator for Evaluation
School of Nursing
University of Maryland-Baltimore
Baltimore, Maryland

DELOIS PITTMAN WEEKES, RN, MS
Doctoral Student
Family Health Care Nursing
University of California-San Francisco
San Francisco, California

MAY L. WYKLE, RN, PhD
Associate Professor and Chairperson/Director
Psychiatric Mental Health Nursing
Frances Payne Bolton School of Nursing
Case Western Reserve University
Cleveland, Ohio

Preface

Nursing literature has recently reflected a growing skepticism about the methods and ways of science. When the notion of nursing science first began to appear in journals and textbooks, the primary issue of concern was whether or not scientific development was a worthwhile goal for a practice discipline. There were few published expressions questioning the worth of science itself; the concern was whether science development in nursing was necessary, or would serve to improve practice. As graduate programs in nursing proliferated, and nurses began to acquire doctoral-level research training, it became increasingly clear that research in nursing was here to stay, and that the methods of science would at least help nursing acquire some standing in the academic community.

Today the practice value of nursing research is widely recognized, and the development of theory is advancing to the point of influencing the conduct of nursing in a growing number of practice settings. However, it also has become increasingly clear that a longstanding suspicion among nurses may have validity—that science itself may not be as sufficient as its proponents have claimed. Nurse scientists, nurse philosophers, and philosophers of science began to publish insights about the fundamental assumptions of science and have questioned the value of the methods of science as suitable for nursing's problems.[1]

This book emerged in the context of the debate. The chapters that are included resulted from the submissions for the April 1986 issue of *Advances in Nursing Science* (*ANS*), which focused on methodological issues. The topic was first publicized on the "Information for Authors" page in October 1984. As the deadline for article submission neared, it was clear that not only was there significant interest among nurse scholars on this topic, but also that the quality of work being done was excellent. The 90 or so articles that were

submitted addressed fundamental philosophical issues, broad issues concerning theory development, general issues of research methodology for both quantitative and qualitative approaches, and specific reports of research completed that used a selected methodological approach to solve a nagging problem. Each article was reviewed by three members of the *ANS* editorial review board. Those that met the criteria for publication in *ANS*, as judged by at least two of the three reviewers, have been published in *ANS* 8:4 and in this book.

The articles chosen for publication do not resolve the fundamental debate over the worth of scientific methods; nor do they offer easy formulas for solving related problems. They are, however, examples of the scholarly work being done by nurses and reveal how various nurses are addressing issues that they encounter in their particular research and theory development. Some of the writings offer alternatives to the traditional scientific paradigm and include suggestions for the scholar who is interested in pursuing a different approach to knowledge development. Others propose ways of solving the dilemmas and limitations of the scientific traditions while remaining within those traditions.

The contributions are thought-provoking, instructive, and inspiring. While I was collecting the material for this book and the journal issue, it struck me that nurse scholars have clearly moved beyond the stage of "oughts" and "shoulds" in methodological writing. A substantial level of actual work is now being done to develop approaches and methods that are consistent with what we think we should be doing—what we *are* doing. More than anything else, the writings reflect the results of that work and point toward a wide diversity of directions for future development.

Peggy L. Chinn
August 1986

NOTES

1. A number of articles and books published in the early 1980s focus on this issue. Two articles published in *Advances in Nursing Science* are Silva MC, Rothbart D: An analysis of changing trends in philosophies of science on nursing theory development and testing (1984;6[2]:1-13), and, Tinkle MB, Beaton JL: Toward a new view of science: Implications for nursing research (1983;5[2]:27-36).

Chapter 1

Methodological Issues in Nursing Research: Beyond a Wax Apple*

Patricia L. Munhall

Bronowski[1] tells us that science is the search to discover unity in the variety of nature and the variety of our experiences. Poetry, painting, and the arts are the same search. This author attempts through the language of poetry to search for the sense experiences of living through contemporary methodological issue questions in nursing. The intent is to move beyond the issue of issues and to discover some sense of unity. The question is raised implicitly why our wonderful scholarship has evolved into a search for structural truth rather than dynamic meaning.

When Prufrock sang his love song
"politic, cautious and meticulous:
full of high sentence, but a bit obtuse"[2(p241)]
he asked us
have we become etherized
are we measuring our lives in coffee spoons?
Making issues out of methodological's yields
obfuscation
Struggle to the surface from didacticism
to the freedom
of possibilities
of uncategorizing
the colors of time, space, & being (even in the
fourth dimension)

---

*Reprinted from *Advances in Nursing Science* (1986;8:1-5), Copyright 1986, Aspen Publishers, Inc.

> "Everything is alive: what we call dead is an abstraction."[3(p174)]

Wax apples
analogue models, systems, stages, symmetry
tasteless, dry, but perfect in stability
and lifelessness
definitions, like wax apples
limit possibilities

> "There are more things in heaven and earth than are dreamt of in our hypothesis, and our observations should be open to them."[4(p127)]

Anxiety tolls us miserably
Ultimately says Tillich[5] *from fear of death*
So we grope with what
stubbornly remains a mystery
Let's make the unknown, known
Let's create five stages to do it in.[6]

Go now (as in the bible) to the podium
and search ye for the truth
Take the knotted, anomalous, confounded
world
and make it orderly & sometimes predictable
but report occasionally on an N. of I.

We come and go
Are we pre-paradigm or metaparadigm?[7]
or no paradigm and a
research tradition[8]
Are we qualitative or quantitative
Are we empiricists, historicists or past it
all?[9]

> "Dichotomy is the usual pathway to vulgarization. We take a complex web of arguments and divide it into two polarized positions—them against us. We then portray them as a foolish caricature of extremes in order to put us in a better light."[10(p7)]

And thus we create ideologies,
"isms" and schisms
I like to do this sometimes,
sometimes though it goes too far
to a diversionary extreme
while people (holistic beings) suffer.

> "We re-search and re-search to the point that we know less and less about more and more, failing to recognize the relevance or irrelevance of what we are studying."[11(p47)]

99% of bicycle owners also have telephones
is this lawfulness, determinism or causality?
If this is causality,
is it causalism, acausalism or semicausal-ism?[12]
Or is it happenstance
More important perhaps, is it important?
I'm not value free
and while so, I can still be a scientist
Laudan[13] *says so*
I believe he has read feminist literature
so I think it's OK to have an "ism"
so long as I don't equate it to "truth"

> ". . . since we have come to the understanding that science is not a description of "reality" but a metaphorical ordering of experiences, the new science does not impugn the old. It is not a question of which view is "true" in some ultimate sense. Rather it is a matter of which picture is more useful in guiding human affairs."—Willis Harman[14]

Worldviews abound, concepts defined
Human being—a biopsychosocial being[15]
Nursing Client—biopsychosocial adaptive system[16]
Human being—an irreducible, negentropic energyfield[17]
Nursing Client—unique, total, open system[18]
Human being—a self care agent[19]

What is proposed has naught to do
with truth
It has to do with perception,
interpretation,
unconscious wishes
and stipulation.

Somehow we know this esthetically
we see beauty in different things
but where it comes to science
is it anxiety, the fear the apple
will not live forever
that prods us to seek the definition

Scheffler[20] *stipulating about definitions*
says
there are three kinds
the stipulative
the descriptive
the programmatic

Interpretation yields the stipulative
"this is how I see it"
Wishes yield the programmatic
"this is the way I think it should be"
and the descriptive
is what is in your dictionary

Go again to the podium
and emerge in contradictions,
hold in your head
two opposing ideas, or maybe three, four
ideas like real apples
vary, unlike supposed "facts"

> "Sit down before fact like a little child, and be prepared to give up every preconceived notion, following humbly wherever and to whatever abyss Nature leads or you shall learn nothing."—T.H. Huxley[21]

Polemics, to what end
New ideas need not immediately
polarize
Though an oppressed group might
tea party together, horizontally violent.[22]

> "But there are times when two or more research traditions, far from mutually undermining one another, can be amalgamated, producing a synthesis which is progressive with respect to both the former research traditions."[13(p103)]

Is there one best way
Is there one best outcome
When we focus our lens
on the literature of "issues"
concerning methods, a way of doing something
Wax apples are juggled about.

> "The perfect method, by definition, leads us on a path of examining small segments and parts of reality apart from the whole and is based on the assumption that a segmented analysis of the parts will yield knowledge of the whole."[11(p27)]

However wax apples are not real
and cannot, like imperfect ideas
be expanded to assist
people (unified wholes) with their suffering
or pursuit of happiness.
Surrounded by them, one could die.
Trouble started in Eden over a real apple
some might say, but
interpretation of that infamous event
has yielded that it was a gift
from on high, called
self determination
We seem though (understandably considering the anxiety)
to want rules and corresponding rules
We seem to search for truth
Impregnable citadels
Where the hopes, fears & loves
of human beings (self care agents) are distracting

Should nurses study nurses
Should nurses be a concept
within a metaparadigm (or whatever)
Should research be basic and applied
or only applied, or just basic
or in neon lights proclaiming
"CLINICAL."

These are some observations
These are some feeling states
What is written thus far is
stipulative
What is now offered is
programmatic

Rather than focus on definition and choices
let us inquire into their construction
their simultaneity
their complementarity
their interdependency
their conjunction

Even as I think a contradiction
emerges
mocking
my attempt to make sense out of
a very dangerous
world, but this always happens

Comparing and contrasting
the either/or nature of choices
is I think pedantically useful
especially when a student
says
"why can't it be both ways?"

Is this programmatic thought
conciliatory
Sterile reductionistic philosophies
would say so,
I, in fact, admire their quest for clarity
if it stops before impoverishment.

> "One important sign of intellectual maturity
> is self consciousness."[9(p59)]

Or in our rising consciousness
we can do as Kierkegaard,
"to create difficulties everywhere"[23(p194)]
This is the beginning of wisdom
to acknowledge the spell
of historical contradictions.

Yes this is conciliation
an ethic of ambiguity
an attempt to build some bridges
to present dichotomies
not to choose between
but to angle in for varying images

> "Insight announces itself in mental images. Newton's conception of gravity and Einstein's notion of the constant speed of light came to them as perceptions, as images, not a hypothesis or conclusions drawn from logical deduction. Formal logic is secondary to insight via images, and is never the source of new knowledge."[24(p144)]

Let us not make methodological issues
another issue for
the
submissive aggressive syndrome[22]
the
differences should lead to discourse

We do not have to do anything
according to a male prototype
including an offense and a defense
Nor do we have to be linebackers
at conferences, lining up to question and
tackling the jugular

Let us spend some time
epistemizing
but remembering again Prufrock
"In the room the women come & go
Talking of Michelangelo"[2(p239)]
Could that be us?

We're in this together
to assist individuals (open systems)
with problems of disease (alteration in
wellness) of
development (evolution), loneliness, anxiety
hunger
We need not create these problems among
ourselves

Our different angles
enlarge our promise
are to be summative
not negating
but engaging us in
our community of endeavors

I found a wooden apple yesterday
The cost was $4.99
More than the real fruit
this saddened me
though it is no longer fashionable
to be a hippie

Don't we have a karma?

REFERENCES

1. Bronowski J: *Science and Human Values.* New York, Harper & Row, 1965.

2. Eliot TS: The love song of J. Alfred Prufrock, in Perrine L: *Sound and Sense,* ed 2. New York, Harcourt, Brace & World, 1963.

3. Bohm D, cited by Smith H: Beyond the modern Western mind set. *Teachers College Record* 1981;82(3).

4. Chronbach L, cited by Reichardt C, Cook T (eds): *Qualitative and Quantitative Methods in Evaluation Research.* Beverly Hills, Calif, Sage, 1979.

5. Tillich P: *The Courage to Be.* New Haven, Conn, Yale Univ Press, 1952.

6. Kubler-Ross E: *On Death and Dying.* New York, Macmillan, 1970.

7. Conway ME: Toward greater specificity in defining nursing's metaparadigm. *Adv Nurs Sci* 1985;7(4):73-82.

8. Silva MC, Rothbart D: An analysis of changing trends in philosophies of science on nursing theory development and testing. *Adv Nurs Sci* 1984;6(2):1-13.

9. Thompson JL: Practical discourse in nursing: Going beyond empiricism and historicism. *Adv Nurs Sci* 1985;7(4):59-72.

10. Gould SJ: Science and Gender. *The New York Times Book Review* 1984;2:45-49.

11. Chinn P: Debunking myths in nursing theory and research. *Image* 1985;17(2):45-49.

12. Wilson LM, Fitzpatrick JJ: Dialectical thinking as a means of understanding systems-in-development: Relevance to Roger's principles. *Adv Nurs Sci* 1984;6(2):24-41.

13. Laudan L: *Progress and Its Problems: Towards a Theory of Scientific Growth.* Berkeley, University of California Press, 1977.

14. Harman W: *Symposium on Consciousness.* New York, Penguin, 1977.

15. Johnson DE: The behavioral system model for nursing, in Riehl JP, Roy C (eds): *Conceptual Models for Nursing Practice,* ed 2. New York, Appleton-Century-Crofts, 1980.

16. Roy C, Roberts SL: *Theory Construction in Nursing: An Adaptation Model.* Englewood Cliffs, NJ, Prentice-Hall, 1981.

17. Rogers M: Nursing: A science of unitary man, in Riehl JP, Roy C (eds): *Conceptual Models for Nursing Practice,* ed 2. New York, Appleton-Century-Crofts, 1980, pp 329-337.

18. King IM: *A Theory for Nursing: Systems, Concepts, Progress.* New York, John Wiley, 1981.

19. Orem DE: *Nursing: Concepts of Practice,* ed 2. New York, McGraw-Hill, 1980.

20. Scheffler I: *The Language of Education.* Springfield, Ill, Charles C Thomas, 1960.

21. Huxley TH, cited by Dossey L: *Space, Time, and Medicine.* Boulder, Colo, Shambhala, 1982.

22. Roberts SJ: Oppressed group behavior: Implications for nursing. *Adv Nurs Sci* 1983;5(4):21-30.

23. Bretall R (ed): *A Kierkegaard Anthology.* New York, Modern Library, 1936.

24. Bohm D: *Wholeness and the Implicate Order.* London, Routledge & Kegan Paul, 1980.

Chapter 2

Theory-Free Observation: Fact or Fantasy?

DeLois Pittman Weekes

Theory and observation are essential to the development of nursing science. Although this fact is generally accepted by nurse scientists, these tools tend to be viewed as absolutes belonging to different, distinct categories, as dichotomous opposites. The tendency to discriminate, divide, and dichotomize entities is an illusion that originates in a measuring and categorizing mentality. This type of mentality creates intellectual distinctions and opposites that can exist only in relation to one another.

One important sign of intellectual growth is the recognition that all things and events perceived by the senses are interrelated, connected and are but different aspects or manifestations of the same ultimate reality. When this type of intellectual awareness occurs, theory and observation cease to be viewed as dichotomous opposites and are seen as interconnected, interrelated, and interdependent complementarities.

This chapter demonstrates the importance of theory-free observation to nursing science, explores salient arguments from the philosophy of science, shows how scientific philosophies have influenced the current view of theory and observation in nursing science, and proposes a dialectic unity-of-opposites view of theory and observation.

SIGNIFICANCE TO NURSING

Because a great deal of nursing theory has been rationally, rather than empirically, derived, the relationship between theory and observation is important to nursing science. Questions regarding the existence and meaning of theories and constructs are being raised by many in nursing (e.g., Conway,

---

Note: The author would like to thank Susan Gortner, RN, PhD, FAAN, Associate Dean, Research and Professor, University of California-San Francisco, for her comments on earlier drafts of this manuscript.

Gortner, Silva and Rothbart).[1-3] These questions include: What relation does theory have to the empirical world (observation)? Are the constructs and concepts of theories illusion or reality? These questions are reflected in Newman's[4] comparison of Schlacter and Roger's explication of the construct of "personal space." This construct cannot be observed directly and does not exist apart from a subjectivistic, as well as relativistic, frame of reference. That is, the description of personal space depends on observation and theory. In fact, as concepts become more abstract, their reality basis becomes less empirical and less capable of being directly measured. Thus observation depends increasingly on indirect means and theoretical definitions.[5]

PHILOSOPHY OF SCIENCE VIEW OF THEORY AND OBSERVATION

Philosophers Who View Observation as Theory-free

The question of the relationship between observation and theory is embedded in the philosophical orientation of empiricism. The proponents of empiricism give the key role of inquiry to observation rather than to reason.[6] For example, in the 17th century, Roger Bacon argued for knowledge gained by "direct inspection"—unbiased observation. He further asserted that through unbiased observations, regularities among phenomena could be discerned. John Locke contributed the tracing of ideas to experience and the identification of "being" with the "perceived" to empiricism. According to traditional empiricists, the ultimate source of all knowledge is observation, and observations have meaning in and of themselves—apart from any theory. Furthermore, theory is said to have meaning only to the extent that it can be translated and connected with observation language.

Reese[6] traced the progress of the empiricists into the 20th century, where some became known as logical positivists. The core group responsible for developing the tenets of logical positivism were those philosophers who gathered in Vienna in the 1930s. The view espoused by the Vienna circle group has been labeled the "Received View (RV)."

The positivist RV philosophers attempted to purify philosophy of science of all nonempirical elements. They developed a language of science that relied heavily on formal logic. Hence the name "logical positivists." The key arguments of the RV positivists, according to Gortner,[7] were that (1) observables or sense objects are the source of all knowledge, (2) the real statements of truth are contained in the observables, and (3) nonobservables are only testable vis-à-vis the observables and the formal rules of logic. There was a general denial by the RV positivists (scientists and mathematicians) that theories could be explanatory. They felt that there were no such things as a priori theories or laws, and thus no external truths.

The RV positivists argued for theory-free observation based on the belief that the senses do not err. They suggest that errors occur only when the information gained through the senses is interpreted from the framework of some specified theory and meaning attached to the observations.

Philosophers Who View Observation as Theory-laden

The positivist RV dominated philosophy of science from the 1930s to the 1950s, but in the early 1960s, a wave of criticism began. In attempting to increase logical rigor, the logical positivist RV had become more detached from the reality that scientists sought to know. Thus there began a movement to bring philosophy of science back into line with the actual practices of scientists.[3] The changes initiated as a result of this movement are reflected in an altered view of observation and theory; that is, rather than being viewed as theory-free, observation began to be viewed as theory-laden.

The notion of theory-laden observation was popularized in recent philosophy of science literature by Hanson.[8] According to Hanson, observation is largely influenced by theory, which acts as a lens, affecting what is observed. He posited two theses regarding the theory-ladenness of observation. The soft thesis stated that theory is inherent in observation statement; that is, in order to make an observation statement, one must use general terms (place the statement in a general category). In so doing, one is using theory. Consequently, the observation statement is theory-laden. The strong thesis stated that theory is built into the individual's perceptual mechanism as background knowledge, and this background knowledge acts as a lens or filter, influencing what is observed. Thus observation is unavoidably theory-laden.

To further establish the theory-ladenness of observation, Hanson advanced the following argument regarding what it means to "see:" two persons viewing the same phenomenon "see" the same thing in one sense (neutral sense of "see"), but in another sense they do not. Hanson[8] and Kuhn[9] indicate that it is from the latter sense of "see" that scientific data is obtained; that is, two persons viewing the same phenomenon do not begin their observations from the same point. Each person enters the observation arena with different experiential, educational, theoretical, and philosophical agendas. Thus they cannot make the same observations because they do not "see" the same thing.

Hanson's notions regarding what it means to "see" have been rather soundly criticized by Kordig.[10] The criticism stems from Hanson's equating the terms "sees that" and "knows that." Hanson's discussion revolves around two persons observing the sun. Although both see the same object (sun), one sees it from a geocentric theoretical perspective and one from a heliocentric perspective. Thus Kordig argues that if "sees that" equals "knows that," one

would be led to conclude that the observer who sees the sun as mobile (geocentric) is correct. In order to accept this notion, the widely accepted heliocentric view would need to be abandoned.

Because it is unlikely, according to Kordig, that Hanson really does subscribe to a geocentric view of the world, he would say that seeing the sun as mobile is wrong. Therefore, "sees that" cannot be equal to "knows that." Thus Kordig's conclusion that Hanson's argument relative to "sees that" and "knows that" is fallacious.

Although Kordig does criticize Hanson's conclusions regarding seeing and knowing, he does not indicate any disagreement with Hanson's basic premise, which is that observations are theory-laden and that particular theories determine what is seen.

A similar point is made in atomic physics, in that the properties of an object cannot be discussed in isolation, since they have meaning only in the context of the object's interactions with the observer. In support of this notion, Heisenberg[11] states that "what we observe is not reality itself, but reality exposed to our method of questioning." The observer decides how he or she is going to set up the measurement of particular phenomena, and the type of measurement determines, to some extent, the properties of the observed phenomena. Each observer installs his or her chosen measuring equipment, and as a result, although looking from the same point in the same direction, two scientists will "see" different things. Thus each person observes through his or her own set of spectacles, that is, experience, education, theory, and philosophy.

In discussing the theory-ladenness of observation, Maxwell[12] uses the analogy of looking through a vacuum composed of a window pane, glasses, binoculars, and a microscope. Based on this analogy, it is suggested that the degree of theory-ladenness of observations is related to the level of the vacuum at which the observer is functioning. For example, the first level is that of the window pane, which is viewed as the level at which observations are influenced and guided only by the observer's unique experiential and educational frame of reference. That is, the observer's experience and education provide the perspective from which observations are made. Glasses constitute the second level, which is seen as the level at which observations are directed by guiding concepts. That is, specific concepts are selected to guide observations of particular phenomena. The third level is that of binoculars. Binoculars are viewed as the conceptual model level. At this level, observations are guided by a set of loosely organized ideas and concepts. The microscope constitutes the final level. It is viewed as the theory level, or the level at which observations are made within the framework of tightly organized concepts, propositions, and hypotheses.

The substantive theories and concepts of science are both the cause and the result of empirical observations. Even the collection of data (empirical

observations) cannot proceed without some implicit or explicit set of categories to drive it.[13] Thus observation does not and cannot exist in isolation. The needs of observation are met by theory. It is theory that provides observation with a point of view, an object, a task, etc. Consequently, theory performs dual functions; it provides a statement about reality and a perspective from which to interpret reality.

INFLUENCES OF PHILOSOPHIES OF SCIENCE ON NURSING SCIENCE'S VIEW OF THEORY AND OBSERVATION

The influence of the logical positivist RV on nursing science has abated. However, according to Suppe and Jacox,[14] the vestiges of that influence as it relates to theoretical-observational distinctions can still be seen in recent nursing literature (e.g., Bohny,[15] Hardy [16,17]). For example, current theoretical discourse in nursing includes a preoccupation with making observations that are more contextual and less biased by theory. This preoccupation is most evident in the writings of the qualitative nurse researchers—the phenomenologists, the new paradigm advocates, and the grounded theorists (Oiler,[18] Omery,[19] Benner,[20] Tinkle and Beaton,[21] Benoliel[22]).

A number of these qualitative nurse researchers assert that the overlay of theory onto observations will result in distortion or misapprehension of the real world that nurses seek to know. Thus there is the quest to liberate observations from the biases of theory (make them theory-free) in order to obtain a clearer picture of reality. Such liberation from bias would enable the nurse to make observations in the client/patient care area without any preconceived notions regarding what would be found.

The push for this approach to observation arises out of a felt need to let the empirical world dictate what emerges, rather than superimpose a priori expectations on it from a theoretical frame of reference. There is the belief that when observations are made vis-à-vis theory, the door is opened to interpretation (to relativism). This relativism stems from the variations among theories and the possibility that no theory provides an accurate reflection of reality.

Other nurse investigators suggest that it is impossible to separate theoretical and observational terms (e.g., Gortner,[2,7,23] Jacox[24]). They assert that there is no such entity as theory-free observation; that is, all observation is theory-laden. Thus any attempt to separate the two constitutes a false dichotomy.

In addition, Jacox[24] states that a researcher always works back and forth between theory and observation. Sometimes the work is more of one and less of the other, but the researcher always travels between the two camps. It is time to move beyond this "emperor's clothes syndrome" in claiming that

observations are theory-free and acknowledge that they they are theory-laden. Gortner's[2] suggestion that nursing science goes full circle from a problem situation to observation to inference and "conjecture" and back again to observation further supports Jacox's claims.

In practice sciences, knowledge is sought toward some purpose. In nursing, according to Kim,[25] that purpose is the promotion of individual health. This purpose cannot be fully achieved without generating knowledge at the descriptive, explanatory, and predictive levels. Observation made apart from theory is mainly directed toward descriptive knowledge. Theory serves as the intellectual tool that adds meaning to phenomena of interest to nursing science and facilitates generation of explanatory and predictive knowledge.

In the effort to generate descriptive, explanatory, and predictive knowledge, nurse scientists have attempted to clarify the relationship between theory and observation. For example, Chinn and Jacobs[5] developed an empirical observation continuum. On this continuum, the more concrete concepts are thought to be empirically referenced, and thus relatively independent of theory. On the other hand, the more abstract concepts are said to rely on indirect measures, and thus to be more dependent on theoretical referents. Independence is an example of an abstract concept. One cannot directly, or even indirectly, see independence. Instead, traits and behaviors are observed within a given context, and the inference is made that independence exists. The traits and behaviors used to measure or observe independence are theoretically alleged to be associated with the concept, and each behavior is designated as an empirical indicator for it.

The effort to label and name things, events, ideas, and other empirical realities is also seen as an attempt to clarify the relationship between observation and theory. This approach is illustrated by Kim,[25] when she suggests that real world phenomena need to be symbolically described by concepts. The concepts may refer to abstract or concrete phenomena. Thus empirical observations are converted to theoretically derived symbolic statements having varying degrees of theory-ladenness, depending on their level of abstractness. That is, as concepts become more abstract, they become increasingly dependent on theory for observation or measurement.

The philosophy of science RV has had a significant influence on nursing science's view of theory and observation. For example, both of the approaches discussed would have appeal primarily for theorists and researchers who adhere to the empiricist tradition, since they attempt to designate levels or degrees of association between theory and observation and do not consider the dynamic interrelatedness of the two.

DIALECTIC UNITY-OF-OPPOSITES VIEW OF THEORY AND OBSERVATION

The division of the world into separate objects and events is not a fundamental feature of reality, but an abstraction devised by the human species' discriminating and categorizing intellect.[26] The belief that things can be separated into distinct opposites that can exist only in relation to one another as dichotomous opposites is, as indicated, an illusion.

Rather than erect a theory-observation dichotomy, it would be far more productive to view theory and observation from a dialectical perspective. Tolman[26] points out that the word dialectic has been used historically to mean different things. For example, the ancient dialectic, as used by the Greek philosopher Zeno of Elea, meant the act of debate or conversation. Hall[27] defined it as a method of seeking, and sometimes arriving at, the truth by reasoning. The modern dialectic is defined in the Hegelian sense as a unitary or integrated developmental process having the characteristics of (a) qualitative transformation, which includes both quantitative and qualitative changes, and (b) opposition, opposites forming a unity yet each remaining clearly distinguishable from the other. The latter definition forms the basis for dialectic as it is used in this analysis.

The Hegelian dialectic allows for the integration of theory and observation into a unitary whole (although perhaps not in equal proportions). The result, of course, is qualitatively different from the two basic components. However, the integration more closely approximates the actual relationship between theory and observation.

Using Wald's[28] view of dialectic, theory and observation could be conceptualized as interdependent complementarities, independent and yet inseparable. Hence, when interacting, they interpenetrate each other so that each modifies and is modified by the other. Such a conceptualization might help to uncover theory-observation complementarities heretofore unnoticed, and thus maximize their usefulness in knowledge generation.

The external world does not exist as an independent, separate entity into which the individual inserts herself or himself. Rather, the external and the internal world are merely two sides of the same fabric, into which threads of all forces, events, forms of consciousness, and their objects are woven into an inseparable net of endless, interconnected, interdependent, dynamic relations.[29]

A Unity of Opposites

The conceptualization of theory and observation as a dialectic also encompasses the notion of the unity of opposites. This notion comes out of the Eastern world view that suggests that opposites are actually different

aspects of the same phenomenon.[29] The essence of this view is the awareness of the unity and interrelation of all things and events. All phenomena are experienced as manifestations of a basic oneness. Therefore, all things are seen as interdependent and inseparable parts of the whole, as different manifestations of the same ultimate reality. Because all opposites are viewed as interdependent, conflict between them can never result in the total victory of either, but will simply reflect the interplay between the two. A "good" researcher does not undertake the impossible task of striving for theory-free observation, but seeks to maintain a dynamic balance between the two. There is also a continual awareness that all phenomena are interconnected, interrelated, and interdependent, and as such cannot be observed as isolated entities, but only as integrated parts of the whole. A dialectic unity-of-opposites view of theory and observation such as the one proposed negates the need to erect observational-theoretical dichotomies. It enables nurses to cycle back and forth between the two in the process of examining conjectures and exploring the unknown.

Strategies That Support the Dialectic Unity-of-Opposites View

No solution can be effective without adequate support. The two strategies discussed here are conceptualized as forming an intellectual support system for the proposed dialectic unity-of-opposites solution. No single strategy is more crucial than any other. Thus the order of presentation does not imply priority or degree of importance.

The initial strategy to be considered is the maieutic art of Socrates. This strategy guides the investigator to ask questions designed to destroy traditional or fashionable prejudices and false beliefs.[10] Consequently, it facilitates the search for truth by helping to debunk and criticize cherished beliefs.

The potential prejudices of theory can further be ameliorated by the strategy of constantly searching for counterinstances or negative cases. In so doing, the true essence of the empirical world is more likely to be observed. This strategy is referred to by Descartes as systematic doubt—a method of destroying false prejudices of the mind in order to arrive at a closer approximation of the truth. Such doubt is a useful means of dealing with the inevitable biases associated with observing through the spectacles of theory.

SUMMARY AND CONCLUSIONS

This chapter has dealt with the relationship between theory and observation and the degree to which observation is, or should be, theory-free. The analysis demonstrates that observations cannot be made separate and apart from theory.

The view of nurse scientists relative to theory and observation has been significantly influenced by philosophy of science, particularly the positivist RV. In response to this influence, some nurse researchers have either (a) established observational-theoretical dichotomies a la the RV, (b) established observational-theoretical distinctions with the aim of making observations more contextual and less biased by theory, or (c) avoided establishing observational-theoretical distinctions, choosing rather to view observation as inevitably theory-laden.

Based on the analysis presented in this chapter, it is suggested that nursing science approach observation and theory as a dialectic unity of opposites involving (1) clinical observations evaluated in light of available theory, (2) present knowledge (theory) evaluated from the perspective of clinical observations, and (3) completed studies evaluated in light of both. This approach allows, as well as corrects, for the fact that observation is theory-laden. In addition, it clearly explicates the relationship between theory and observation; that is, theory drives observation, and observational findings shape the development of theory, and the two form the core of an observational practice discipline.

Several implications for nursing are inherent in acknowledging that observations are theory-laden:

- Gortner[7] points out that nursing science is and may continue to be primarily an observational science and a practice discipline to which both observation and theory are essential tools. Therefore, nursing must evolve concepts derived vis-à-vis both theory and observation, as only concepts derived in this manner are appropriate to a practice discipline. In addition, unless nursing's concepts can be empirically referenced in practice, theories built on them cannot be applied in the practice arena.
- Because nursing is primarily a practice discipline, it seeks to know individuals in all their uniqueness and particularity. Nurses cannot accomplish this task by approaching scientific investigation as detached, naive examiners of observables; rather, they must approach it as informed scientists aided by theory. One also needs to remember that there are few, if any, absolute truths. In fact, truth may be somewhat like an onion, with many layers that need to be revealed. The only way to reveal succeeding layers is through the conjoint use of theory and observation.
- Whether one views science as systematic conjecture,[30] as puzzle solving,[9] or from the definitional perspective of other philosophers of science, theory and observation are tools used by science to generate knowledge regarding phenomena of interest. Neither is individually capable of adequately meeting the needs of nursing science. Thus it is necessary that

they be used as dynamic interdependent parts of a single whole that is capable of revealing succeeding layers of truth.

REFERENCES

1. Conway ME: Toward greater specificity in defining nursing's metaparadigm. *Adv Nurs Sci* 1985;7(4):73-81.

2. Gortner S: Knowledge for a practice discipline: Philosophy and pragmatics. Keynote address for the Annual Meeting of the American Academy of Nursing, Minneapolis, Sept 26, 1983b.

3. Silva MC, Rothbart D: An analysis of changing trends in philosophies of science on nursing theory development and testing. *Adv Nurs Sci* 1984;6(2):1-13.

4. Newman M: *Theory Development in Nursing.* Philadelphia, FA Davis, 1979.

5. Chinn PL, Jacobs MK: *Theory and Nursing: A Systematic Approach.* St Louis, CV Mosby, 1983.

6. Reese WL: *Dictionary of Philosophy and Religion Eastern and Western Thought.* Atlantic Highlands, NJ, Humanities Press, 1980.

7. Gortner S: Logical positivism and its legacy. Paper presented at the University of California School of Nursing, San Francisco, October 1983c.

8. Hanson NR: *Patterns of Discovery.* Cambridge, Cambridge University Press, 1958.

9. Kuhn TS: *The Structure of Scientific Revolutions,* ed 11, 2(2). Chicago, University of Chicago Press, 1970.

10. Kordig CR: The theory-ladenness of observation, in Klemke, et al (eds): *Introductory Readings in the Philosophy of Science.* Iowa, Prometheus Books, 1980, pp 164-168.

11. Heisenberg W: *Physics and Philosophy.* New York, Harper & Row, Harper Torchbooks,1958.

12. Maxwell G: The ontological status of theoretical entities, in Klemke, et al (eds): *Introductory Readings in the Philosophy of Science,* Iowa, Prometheus Books, 1980, pp 175-187.

13. Roberts M: On the nature and condition of social science in Daedalus. *J Am Acad Arts Sci* 1974;103(3):47-64.

14. Suppe F, Jacox AK: Philosophy of science and the development of nursing theory, in Werley HH, Fitzpatrick JJ (eds): *Annual Review of Nursing Research.* New York, Springer Publishing Co., 1985;3:241-267.

15. Bohny B: Theory development for a nursing science. *Nurs Forum* 1980;19:50-67.

16. Hardy M: Theories: Components, developments, evaluation. *Nurs Res* 1974;23:100-107.

17. Hardy ME: Perspectives on nursing theory. *Adv Nurs Sci* 1978;1(1):37-48.

18. Oiler C: The phenomenological approach in nursing research. *Nurs Res* 1982;31(3):178-181.

19. Omery A: Phenomenology: A method for nursing research. *Adv Nurs Sci* 1983;5(2):49-64.

20. Benner P: Uncovering the knowledge embedded in clinical practice. *Image* 1983;142:36-41.

21. Tinkle M, Beaton J: Toward a new view of science: Implications for nursing research. *Adv Nurs Sci* 1983;5(2):27-36.

22. Benoliel JQ: The interaction between theory and research. *Nurs Outlook* 1977;25(2):109-112.

23. Gortner S: The history and philosophy of nursing science and research. *Adv Nurs Sci* 1983a;5(2):1-8.

24. Jacox A: Competing theories of science. Paper presented at the Forum on Doctoral Education in Nursing, Seattle, June 25, 1981.

25. Kim HS: *The Nature of Theoretical Thinking in Nursing.* Norwalk, Conn, Appleton-Century-Crofts, 1983.

26. Tolman C: Further comments on the meaning of dialectic. *Hum Dev* 1983;26:320-324.

27. Hall T: Dialectic, in Edwards: *The Encyclopedia of Philosophy*. New York, Macmillan, 1967.

28. Wald H: *Introduction to Dialectical Logic*. Amsterdam, Editura Academei, 1975.

29. Govinda LA: *Foundations of Tibetan Mysticism*. New York, Samuel Weiser, 1974.

30. Popper K: On the sources of knowledge and of ignorance. *Conjectures and Refutations: The Growth of Scientific Knowledge*. New York, Harper & Row, 1963, pp 3-30.

Chapter 3

Three Paradigms for Nursing Research: Methodological Implications

David Allen, Patricia Benner, and Nancy L. Diekelmann

INTRODUCTION

Methodological disputes in nursing research are often framed in practical or technical terms. For example, the discussions around quantitative versus qualitative research are often presented as a choice of which data-gathering techniques one should use for a particular study. In many of these accounts, a hierarchy is stated or assumed: quantitative data is preferable, but qualitative research may be a helpful, preliminary step to developing quantitative information. This chapter reexamines these distinctions by placing them in the context of the philosophies of science from which they arose. By discussing three central positions in the philosophy of science—analytical empiricism, Heideggerian phenomenology, and critical social theory—in terms of the research they produce, one can make intelligent, informed, and flexible methodological decisions. Further, the hope is that this discussion will make clearer that all *three* positions generate fruitful nursing research and that it is not a matter of one or two being superseded by another. All three, for example, are explanatory and not "merely" descriptive, and all three can incorporate qualitative and quantitative data gathering and analysis, albeit to different ends. Thus a pluralistic vision of research methodology can do much more to enlighten us about the universe of nursing than any single model.

To facilitate the understanding of similarities and differences, the three philosophical schools are discussed separately but using a common outline. Each section concludes by taking a particular research question—the role of experience in nursing education—and explicates that question from the point

of view of the philosophical school being discussed. It is hoped that this common ground will help to clarify the theory and method distinctions among the three paradigms.

EMPIRICAL-ANALYTIC PARADIGM

The empirical-analytic paradigm dominates the broader scientific community (especially in the United States) as well as nursing research. Indeed, its tenets are often assumed to be those of "science" itself. Many central features of this position are familiar to most researchers: the emphasis on theory, the centrality of observation and measurement, the ideal of experimental designs. Some of these will be reviewed briefly in the discussion of "Underlying Assumptions," "Definition of Knowledge," "Purpose and Value of Theory," "Organization, Categorization, and Definition of Objects," and, finally, a discussion of researching "The Role of Experience in Nursing Education" (a similar outline is used in discussing Heideggerian Phenomenology and Critical Social Theory).

Underlying Assumptions

An important assumption of this paradigm is that the world is structured by lawlike regularities that can be identified and manipulated. This assumption about the world pertains to research in the physical as well as the biological and human sciences. There is no difference in theory and explanation between the study of humans and that of objects

It is assumed that human behavior—that is, the social affairs of people—is structured by lawlike regularities that can be identified and manipulated, as can objects in the physical world. In nursing education research, for example, the use of this paradigm assumes that the teaching and learning of nursing operate on the basis of lawlike regularities that can be manipulated to achieve more effective or efficient teaching and learning. Although we and our colleagues in education have not yet been able to identify these laws, this can be attributed to the youth of research in education, indeed research in the social sciences. The assumption, however, is that given the time and resources, one day how students learn nursing will be understood through the development of theory, that is, identification of the lawlike regularities that can be manipulated to improve nursing education.

In this paradigm, theory is considered to be universal and not bound to the specific context in which it is formulated. The universal statements of scientific theories are usually termed laws. Statements that express laws must have the syntactical form of universal conditionals—"If X, then Y."[1] In empirical-analytical science, objects and events are analyzed as dependent

and independent variables. Empirical-analytic science investigates the regularities among them.

A simple law would be "if X occurs, then Y will be the effect." In highly developed theory, there are principles or rules of inference that can be deductively arranged to describe the interaction of the parts. By studying the effects of several preoperative nursing interventions on the patient's postoperative course, the ideal would be to find a single intervention that in all instances reduced the rate or severity of postoperative complications.

The theory of universality is linked to a theory of observation. According to this paradigm, the truth or falsity of statements about observations does not depend on the truth or falsity of theories, and theoretical disputes can be resolved by reference to agreed-on observation statements. A statement can only be properly regarded as scientific if its truth or falsity can be ascertained by means of theory-neutral observations.

Finally, this paradigm assumes a world that is ordered—one that can be broken down into a system of independent variables. These variables exist as distinct and analytically separable parts that interact as a system to produce human behavior yet can be studied independently of one another.

As a consequence of these assumptions, research is expected to meet strict standards in defining distinct variables in terms of simple observations. Thus anxiety is defined as a score on a particular scale or as a certain level of circulating catecholamines. Measurability is stressed in part as a function of the need for reproducible, theory-neutral observations.

Definition of Knowledge

The empirical-analytic paradigm stressed the importance of formalizing knowledge. Knowledge is generated when measurable hypotheses can be tested and reproducible findings used to make improvements in theory. Variables of theory must be operationalized into precise and distinct definitions.

In this paradigm, the knower can be completely differentiated from the known. The comparison and manipulation of variables is to confirm or falsify hypotheses as they relate to the development of theory. Preciseness of variables and reliability of measure assume importance in defining and limiting the scope of empirical-analytic theory. Quantification of variables exposes ambiguities and contradictions. This preciseness and the necessity to quantify variables with a commitment to observations as objective necessitate the assumption of both ontological and epistemological privilege.

Under the assumption of ontological privilege, objects that can be observed have more valid claim to existence. Thus terms belonging to observation language, and only such terms, can be regarded as making genuine reference to items in the physical world. Only such items can properly be said to exist.

These observational statements can be verified or falsified without reference to the truth or falsity of theoretical statements.

Of primary importance is the epistemological claim that those objects that can be observed can be known with more certainty that those that cannot. Thus the truth or falsity of statements containing only observational terms can be known with total certainty, or at least with far greater certainty than those containing nonobservational terms. In addition, there is in this paradigm a commitment to observations as objective that encourages a requirement of mathematics in theory construction.

Purpose and Value of Theory

The goal of this paradigm is quantitative theory whose ultimate purpose is to provide control through explanation and prediction. Scientific explanation is a form of deductive argument. It provides the basis for explaining or predicting the phenomenon described in the conclusion. Empirical-analytic theory enables one to predict an event that has not occurred and to explain that even after its occurrence.

There is a distinction, however, between theory and practice. People create, discover, or invent theories about behavior.[2] These systems are assumed to be separate from practice. In this paradigm, it is not assumed that nurses will consciously use this knowledge to guide the practice of nursing. Thus there exists an important distinction between theory and practice.

Empirical-analytic theory is descriptive of what exists. It espouses neutrality regarding human interests. That is, how people use the theory to guide practice is a question not of science, but of ethics and politics. In this paradigm, the value in theory is in its universality; because of this universality, it is the closest approximation of truth and is distinguishable from nonuniversal, politically and historically contingent human interests.

In summary, the fundamental purpose of empirical-analytic science is control. Through confirming and falsifying of hypotheses in which objects and events are dependent and independent variables, the regularities among them are identified that allow one to control the practice of nursing through the ability to explain and predict. Although this paradigm has as its central interest control through explanation and prediction, it does not follow that nurse researchers personally value the ability to control.

Organization, Categorization, and Definition of Objects

In empirical-analytic science, sophisticated concepts and techniques that can be formally expressed are central. Briefly, objects in this paradigm are distinguishable from any individual's perception of them. Thus research using

terms like nonverbal emotional expressiveness and affective sensitivity assumes that these terms are no more dependent on an individual's perception of what it is or should be than arterial oxygen pressure levels are. These characteristics must be precisely defined with both reliability and validity of measurement.

Similarly, when studying the best way to teach a complex set of behaviors, like how to administer parenteral medications, the assumption is made that studying small parts of the process will ultimately result in understanding the reality of the entire event. The organization and categorization in this paradigm are assumed to be additive; each study contributes another part and, when viewed in totality, constitutes the reality of the object or event.

The Role of Experience

The study of experience, in this paradigm, is usually treated as if experience were a trait, a possession of the person based on the past. Although there are a number of competing theories to account for how the person learns from experience (e.g., cognitivism, behaviorism), the rational-empirical paradigm contributes the view of the person as a subject who represents external objects. This Cartesian tradition is a particular epistemological view of a world made up of minds and matter. Minds more or less approximate reality through mental representations, and intelligibility is won through rationality. Because this paradigm treats experience as a trait, most research analyzes the "present state" best and has more difficulty depicting historical influences or the impact of future goals on present activity. Experience is thus reduced to distinct observables, such as age or degree preparation, or the number of times a particular activity was performed. Relationships between these variables, such as degree preparation and the achievement scores on state board exams, can then be expressed to establish causation. The goal, in this instance, is to predict the outcome on board scores based on degree preparation. Research in this area holds true for all times and places, that is, any state board exam and any baccalaureate grade. One goal, then, of research on experience in nursing education is to identify the lawlike regularities that exist that can be manipulated to, in this case, help students to pass boards.

Theoretical terms in this paradigm must be expressed as observable events. Therefore, role strain or anxiety can be reduced to a series of observations that are neutral, that is, interpretation-free. And they can be used in all instances to describe the event.

HEIDEGGERIAN PHENOMENOLOGY

Underlying Assumptions

The underlying assumption of this paradigm is that the study of pragmatic activity, that is, everyday understanding and practices, and the study of relational issues are distinctly different from the study of objects, as in the natural sciences, or even biophysiological events on the tissue and cellular level.[3]

The view of the person in this paradigm breaks with the Cartesian subject/object, mind-body distinctions. In the Heideggerian view, to be human is to be-in-the-world, to participate in cultural, social, and historical contexts. This is a relational view of the person, and "human nature" is not considered fixed. The person is self-interpreting through and through, and these self-interpretations are not individually generated, but are handed down in the language and cultural practices. Social practices and perceptions are already laden with interpretations. For example, Caudill and Weinstein[4] found that Japanese and American babies were distinctly Japanese and American by the age of four months. It seems that all the child-rearing practices of the Japanese embody meanings and interpretations of the sort: the infant is an independent creature that must be civilized and made dependent. By contrast, the child-rearing practices of American mothers embody the understanding that the infant is a dependent creature that must be made independent. Underlying all interpretation-laden practices and self-understanding handed down through language and culture is the notion of "The Background."[5] This full-blown notion of the background preunderstanding is one of the major distinctions between Heideggerian phenomenology and critical theory, which is discussed in the next section. This background cannot be made fully explicit; nor can we get completely clear about it or clear of it. Consequently, purely neutral, noninterpreted observation is impossible.[6] The background gives us the conditions for our actions. This background makes human beings different from computers, which always must build up the story element by element, whereas human beings come with a story—and a history.

Definition of Knowledge

In this paradigm, meaning resides neither solely within the individual nor solely within the situation. Meaning is a transaction between the two so that the individual both constitutes and is constituted by the situation. This position expects commonalities and recurring similarities and dissimilarities, but unlike analytical empiricism, it does not look for these recurring similarities and differences in laws, mechanisms, structures, and processes that are unrelated to meaning. No higher court than meaning, or deeper

explanation than meaning, exists in this paradigm. Explanation is making meaning as apparent as possible, not simply juxtaposing two sequential events ("If X, then Y"). However, meaning is not based on private meanings given by individual subjects or on consensus of private meanings (intersubjectivity). Meaning is shared and handed down culturally through language, skills, and practices and is directly perceived by the individual. Experience is always already interpreted—it is never perceived as sense data to be interpreted by a subject.[6]

Explanatory knowledge is not expected, ultimately, to lie in mechanisms, laws, structures that are ahistorical and free of value and interpretation. All of knowledge is not necessarily explicit. Human beings have embodied ways of knowing that show up in skills, perceptions, and sensory knowledge and in ways of organizing the perceptual field. These bodily perceptual skills, instead of being primitive and lower on the hierarchy, are essential to expert human problem solving, which relies on recognition of the whole. These perceptual skills are missing with purely structural, conceptual, and mechanistic aspects of knowledge capable of being simulated by a computer. This paradigm is concerned with the ontological basis for knowledge, that is, the conditions for the possibility of any way of knowing.[7]

Purpose and Value of Theory

Theory is viewed as a skeletal, deprived view of reality that is drawn from everyday practical activity and knowledge. Theory is always context-specific, not universal. Thus some knowledge may be generated by developing a theory from practice and then extended and refined by testing that theory in practice, but there was knowledge *in* the practice before the theory was derived. For the beginner, typically, formal theory is used to direct the learner to the accurate region of the problem, to direct the cue sensitivity and approach to the problem. As expertise is gained, the theory is refined and taken over by practical knowledge so that the theory is elaborated, changed, or discarded. Highest levels of skilled performance are achieved when the performer uses past concrete experiences as a perceptual lens. The actual comparison of similar and dissimilar situations is far more complex than any explicit formal model because it has nonspecified globally recognized aspects. It follows, then, that the range and complexity of the theory useful to novices and experts will be different.

Organization, Categorization, and Definition of Objects

Theory, in this model, does not ascribe to criteria developed by Socrates and elaborated by 17th-century scientists, such as explicitness, abstractedness, discreteness, systematicity, prediction, and completeness. Theory takes

on a new prospect, since the aim is to describe family resemblances, prototypes, exemplars, or paradigm cases that convey contextual, relational, and transactional explanations and interpretations.[8]

Critique of Other Paradigms—Similarities and Differences

From the perspective of this paradigm, the goal in the human sciences, particularly in studying health and illness, is to get beyond the purely intentionalistic descriptions, as in cognitivism, and the purely stimulus-response descriptions of behaviorism. Of interest in studying human behavior is the role of cultural practices, skills, and meanings, the role of the situation, and the role of the body in addition to beliefs, values, and intentions.

Everyday understanding, meanings, practices, relational concerns, and skilled activities are the focus of study in this paradigm. The actual practices of clinicians take on new significance,[9] as does the practical knowledge gained by patients living with an illness. Patients who learn how to manage chronic symptoms or accomplish remarkable recoveries may possess practical knowledge not yet captured by a purely theoretical account of the disease. There are patterns or regularities (knowledge) in the practices of clinicians and the struggles of people with chronic illness. These regularities can be expressed numerically as frequencies or analyzed as covariance. The crucial differences for hermeneutics lie at the kind and level of description and explanation. What is important about the patterns is the meanings or interpretation they reflect, and the explanation of those patterns lies in the meanings that shape them. Teleological explanations are used to account for human agency and historicity. Thus in studying social activity, both description and explanation are grounded or constituted by meaning, but that does not make their study inimical to quantitative techniques. Rather, what is claimed for quantitative techniques and their derivative role in explanation varies from the analytic-empiricist's account.

The Role of Experience in Clinical Knowledge Acquisition

Experience has a dialogical character in the hermeneutical phenomenological paradigm. Experience, as understood by Heidegger and Gadamer,[10] is not longevity or mere passage of time, but the turning around, or refining, of preconceptions. This position holds that one never approaches a situation without a preunderstanding. This preunderstanding has different levels of specificity, which Heidegger outlined as the forestructure of knowledge. Experience is one step away from fluid, nonproblematic skilled performance because there is a discrepancy or a disruption that causes one to reflect on the activity and to come to terms with why expectations are not met by the performance or the situation. Heidegger departs from the tradition that

detached, objective knowledge is preferable to knowledge acquired through involved practical activity. In fact, he posits that involved skilled activity precedes theory.

To examine the nature of a hammer, to use Heidegger's example, in terms of its objective properties, such as heaviness, density, smoothness of the metal, is not to understand hammering. Furthermore, these properties can only make sense in relation to the task of hammering itself. We encounter the world through involved activity. With breakdown or incongruency we notice or have an experience that causes us to reflect on the breakdown or unmet expectations. Distortion is created when we mistake the description apparent in breakdown for normal functioning. In nursing education, experience is often distorted through the misguided belief that telling is teaching, or that the procedural steps given to the beginner adequately describe the flexible performance of the expert. It is a misguided notion to think that it is possible to confer everything the student must know in principles, theories, and directions, or, in a less extreme form, that you can tell students *all* the cues that they should notice. Although all this instruction is helpful, it is not the same as noticing cues in their relative importance to a particular patient's history and illness trajectory and the particular patient care context. Passing a nasogastric tube on a mannequin in a skills lab is not the same as inserting a nasogastric tube on a thin anxious patient, or on an obtunded obese one, or as deciding when the patient might be better off without the tube.

The paradigm of knowledge that values reflective, detached, objectified knowledge and distrusts involved practical activity ignores the knowledge that resides in the working out of knowledge in skilled performance. Knowledge that is highly context-dependent and relational is overlooked or oversimplified. This does a great disservice to the complexity of actual nursing practice, when the nurse must frequently weigh the important against the important.[9,11]

Given this view of experience, the study of clinical practice must be done in realistic practice settings, and time must be given to examine what the situation challenges, teaches, refines, alters. Practice becomes a place to interact with and refine theory, not a place where one naively gives theory priority and expects to apply or match it with practical situations. Theory provides the foreknowledge that raises questions and points to relevant behaviors, signs, and symptoms. But knowledge and ways of knowing are not exhausted by theoretical understanding; therefore, practice itself is seen as a repository of knowledge and takes on a new importance. Clinical practice is no longer a mere shadow of reality that may or may not match up to the idea posed by theoretical understanding. Instead, expert practice is an important original source of knowledge. Expertise in this model is a hybrid of theoretical knowledge (knowing that) and practical knowledge (knowing how to).

As expertise develops, the nature of theory that will actually provide a heuristic, or an understanding, also changes. The theory useful to the beginner cannot rely on holisitc understanding, a sense of salience, or graded qualitative distinctions (connoisseurship) because these can only be acquired through experience.[9] With expertise, the most relevant theories can have relational and context-dependent formulations. They can be more interpretive. Necessarily the rules generated in a theory for experts about pragmatic activity and relational issues will be conditional rules that will hold only as long as all other things remain equal or when there is consensus between the practitioner and the patient about what the goals of health care should be. The rules could never be context-independent, as is the ideal for rational/empirical theories.

The model of the person differs from the cartesianism of the empirical paradigm. The individual is not capable of being a passive receiver of noninterpreted stimuli; or to put it another way, brute, or "raw," data is not a possibility. Anything that is perceived is already meaningful owing to the active nature of perception. Unlike that of the cognitivists, this position does not hold to a mental representation theory of the mind. That is, the mind is not full of programs, rules, symbols, or templates that are then matched to reality.

The person can have direct access to situations because of concrete memories and perception of similarities with dissimilarities from past events. This view of knowledge dictates that clinical learners be systematic record keepers of what they learn from experience. When a clinical situation teaches the clinician something new about helping, or about signs and symptoms, this should be preserved. The good clinician does this informally, but this model predicts that systematic record keeping of clinical knowledge in the form of paradigm cases and other forms of practical knowledge will enhance the systematic growth of clinical knowledge.[9] For example, over time, clinicians would have clusters of paradigm cases around issues, such as recognizing early signs of septic shock, or around maintaining a healing relationship with patients who are depressed or discouraged. Such systematic record keeping could begin in the undergraduate years and continue. A notebook of paradigm cases would provide the clinician advancing to research with a wealth of significant clinical questions and issues for research. Research can only be enriched by such a seedbed of recognizable clinical knowledge.

This view of experience has implications for clinical evaluation. In the quest for objective evaluation, educators have increasingly moved to written works as a means of evaluating clinical practice. Part of the reason for moving to written care plans or written case studies for clinical evaluation is based on the need for "objective" evidence that will bear scrutiny during a grievance procedure. Descriptive anecdotes of actual clinical practice are considered too subjective, especially in a litigation-conscious environment.

Consequently, we have ceased to evaluate clinical practice and are currently evaluating the ability to document it. The ability to document our practice is a necessary skill, but it is not the same as actual skilled performance. A return to direct observation, clinical diaries, narrative descriptive accounts of actual practice, and teacher-taperecorded or -written descriptions of actual practice are essential tools for the evaluation of actual clinical performance.

CRITICAL SOCIAL THEORY

Underlying Assumptions

Critical social theory is part of the tradition of scientific theory that includes Thomas Kuhn, Karl Popper, Ludwig Wittgenstein, and Hans-Georg Gadamer.[12,13] This tradition stands in sharp contrast to the foundationist assumption of analytic empiricism that there is a "foundation" of pure fact, i.e., theory-free observation, that can always be appealed to for questions of truth. Instead, critical theory and hermeneutics maintain that standards of truth or evidence are always social. In other words, the criteria that scientists (or anyone) use to separate knowledge from fiction or mere belief are always based on social conventions, on a negotiated agreement, not on some transcendental appeal to "facts" against which one can supposedly measure the validity of an assertion. These conventions or agreements change historically (forming what some call "paradigms").

If standards of truth for a given community of scientists are based on their consenting to a negotiated agreement about what they will accept as evidence or knowledge, it is obviously of the utmost importance that their agreement be as rational, as uncoerced as possible. Rationality in turn entails two central values: autonomy *and* responsibility. One must be autonomous in the (ideal) sense of free of any conscious or unconscious constraints because the whole community must base its decisions on the best possible argument. If I am afraid to say what I believe because of an unconscious fear of authority or a conscious fear of retribution, then the interests of truth and rationality are not served. But I am also *responsible* for creating social conditions in which others can speak their minds as freely as I can. If I personally intimidate or socially threaten, then again the community (and therefore I) will suffer from not having heard all possible positions before deciding on the best one.[14]

Critical theory labels its interest in creating conditions of autonomy and responsibility an "emancipatory" interest.[12] That is, its central interest as a theory is in emancipating speakers from conscious or unconscious constraints in the hopes of making community life more rational.

Another central assumption of critical theory—and here it is in agreement with the hermeneutic perspective—is that social life is structured by meaning, by rules, conventions, or habits adhered to by individuals as social beings. To

understand the patterns or regularities that structure human activity is to comprehend the meaning or conventions underlying that activity. Critical social theory differs from hermeneutics by its interest in the relationship between the meanings—including embodied activity—and social structure or power. Meanings are negotiated, but the negotiation is often one-sided. Social meanings, for example, the meanings in the discourse of sexuality or gender, are closely tied to social domination.[15] There is, then, according to critical social theory and hermeneutics, a radical difference between explaining physical events and explaining human activity.

Definition of Knowledge

Knowledge is warranted belief. That is, knowledge is separated from personal opinion by the "warrants" or evidence that can be used to support that belief. These warrants, as the previous section suggested, are historical conventions negotiated by a community. Knowledge is not discovered, it is created. Knowledge of social activity is cognizance of the meaning that social actors use to structure their world. It is always contextual, not universal, because how one acts depends on how one interprets the context in which one is acting. Interpretation is grounded in the last instance on language. Language is socially and historically variable, so knowledge cannot be universal. There is no ahistorical foundation for knowledge. Although the empiricist claims that the contents of observation constitute such a foundation, no observation can possibly support ascribing such status to observations. The privileging of observation by the empiricist is itself a *theoretical* position that cannot be supported by appeal to observation. All knowledge is theoretical in the sense that it is grounded in interpretation. Many critical theorists would agree with the Heideggerian position that theory is derivative from, but at the same moment corrective of, implicit understandings.

Purpose and Value of Theory

Critical theory argues that one cannot separate theory and value, as the empiricist claims.[16] Every theory is penetrated by value interests. The empirical-analytic theories are structured by an interest in *control*, just as critical theory is structured by an interest in emancipation. Because theory—as a systematized understanding of social activity—is the basis of understanding, including understanding the contents of observation, there is a close linkage between theory and knowledge. Theory makes knowledge—as warranted belief—possible. The value of theory lies in making shared meanings as explicit as possible and in suggesting ways in which they limit autonomy and responsibility. Nurses, for example, organize much of their occupational identity and many educational practices around various mean-

ings of "professionalism." Yet these meanings can constrain as well as facilitate nursing's movement toward autonomy and responsibility.[17]

Organization, Categorization, and Definition of Objects

Objects are defined and organized through language. Language is the means by which we "carve up" the universe by identifying which features we will attend to, which will be relegated to "background" or context. Cultures vary in their definition and organization of objects. In this sense, order is social, created by meaning, which is in turn made possible through language. One aspect of this process to which critical social theory attends is the way meaning is created and sustained. Certain institutions—in our society, education and media—are central to the production of meaning. These institutions are controlled (not in an uncontested way, however) by certain interest groups, who can produce a vision of reality favorable to the perpetuation of their interests. In other words, the social production of meaning is not equally distributed among social classes, genders, or races. This in turn blocks the possibility of "rational"—autonomous and responsible—social discourse. Advertising media, for example, communicate restrictive definitions of men and women. To the extent that a woman internalizes these definitions into her own concept of what it is to be a feminine, her social reality can be restricted and controlled.[18,19] A central political struggle concerns control over these meaning-generating institutions, which is why research grounded in critical theory is so central to research in nursing education. Nursing education is a primary shaper and conveyor of the meaning of nursing and, consequently, of how nursing participates in other social meanings, such as "The Family."[20]

The Role of Experience in Nursing Education

When reflecting on the role of experience in nursing education, critical investigations attend as much to *how* meaning or knowledge is created and passed on as to *what* specific knowledge is transmitted. For example, when current "knowledge," such as Maslow's model, is passed to students as empirical fact, and when students are rewarded or punished on the degree to which they treat that knowledge as truth, problems are generated on at least two levels. First, the analytic-empirical paradigm encourages viewing information as fact, as neutral information torn from its theoretical and historical context. The social meanings or experiences that *generate* the patterns theorized by Maslow are seldom discussed. The patterns—even assuming they are accurately described—are presented as self-contained. Second, this decontextualization of knowledge encourages a pedagogical model in which acquisition of meaning and experience is treated as a passive process.

Students are reinforced for taking a passive stance toward authority, and they are blinded to the process of negotiation that underlies the emergence of that knowledge as well as to the controversies surrounding it.[21] Similarly, when attitudes and behaviors are sanctioned as "inappropriate" or "unprofessional" with no analysis of how or why those standards have become dominant, students are unprepared to recognize the extent to which clinical experience, what is to be defined as legitimate nursing, is controlled by others, such as administrators and doctors.[17]

If a hypothetical researcher grounded in the empirical-analytic paradigm then researched the outcomes of this educational experience, the conclusion might be an assertion of covariance: when students are exposed to Maslow or professionalism under certain conditions, they score well on an exam or are able correctly to identify professional and unprofessional activity. The patterns exist because of shared meanings, but the sharing is possible because of preexistent interpretations (such as the American ideal of the autonomous individual or the capitalist vision of unalienated labor in a situation where an individual worker controls the means of production). Without this context, the empiricists' covariance would disappear. Further, even if the hermeneutic scientist made those meanings as explicit as possible (including their historical roots and historical alternatives), and it turned out that all the students shared an understanding of "free market individualism," one would need an analysis of the consequences of sharing that interpretation. Such an understanding would include an analysis of its impact on nursing as a gender-segregated occupation and would be essential to developing an agenda for change. The choice of methodological technique, then, depends on what *kind* of description/explanation is being sought. There is no "ultimate" description or explanation apart from purposes or intents.

But the experience—the meaning—of nursing is intimately tied to the social processes that legitimate nonnursing meanings as well. Our social definitions as men and women, our social placement in class hierarchies, and our existence in a sexually stratified workplace all influence how we experience nursing and how we encourage others to experience it.[22]

What is essential about experience in nursing education is that students learn to analyze the sources of their own interpretations, to question and resist the predefined meanings we educators encourage them to adopt, and to develop the tools to negotiate a world of nursing in which the twin goals of autonomy and responsibility are achievable. From the point of view of research in nursing education, critical theory reframes the dilemma concerning the value-laden nature of education. Interpretation and values are inseparable, including the interpretation of what it means to be scientific as well as what it means to be a nurse.

CONCLUSION

The preceding discussion, it is hoped, helped to clarify why methodological decisions need to be made in the context of the philosophic position from which the research emerges. Statistical data, for example, can be used in all three paradigms. In the analytic-empirical paradigm, such quantitative techniques can serve both descriptive and explanatory purposes. Their central function in hermeneutic and critical research is descriptive. On the other hand, the hermeneutic and critical positions would argue that empirical-analytic research should be restricted to quantitative techniques only when meaning is not a factor in the emergence of patterns—cellular level oxygenation studies, for example. Any research on human activity must, they would suggest, take meaning into account, if only as a premise (as in much statistical social science). Hermeneutic and critical social research differ in matters of emphasis and explanation. Hermeneutics—for example, Benner's clinical research[9] or recent studies of nursing textbooks[23]—attends to explicating implicit meanings. Critical theory focuses on the relationships between those meanings and the social ideal of autonomy and responsibility. The *techniques* they use—statistical analysis, diaries, textual analysis—vary with the social domain being interrogated. Certainly a fully dimensional field of nursing research needs to take all three philosophical paradigms into consideration in debating methodological choices.

REFERENCES

1. Keat R, Urry J: *Social Theory as Science.* London, Routledge & Kegan Paul, 1975.

2. Popkewitz TS: *Paradigm and Ideology in Educational Research.* New York, Falmer Press, 1984.

3. Benner P: *Stress and Satisfaction on the Job: Work Meanings and Coping of Mid-Career Men.* New York; Scientific Press, 1984.

4. Caudill W, Weinstein H: Maternal care and infant behavior in Japan and America. *Psychiatry* 1969;32:12-43.

5. Dreyfus H: *Heidegger, a Commentary on Being and Time.* Cambridge, Mass, MIT Press (in press).

6. Taylor C: Interpretation and the sciences of man, *Rev Metaphys* 1971;25(1):3-34, 45-51.

7. Guignon CB: *Heidegger and the Problem of Knowledge.* Indianapolis, Hackett Publishing Co, 1983.

8. Dreyfus H: Why current studies of human capacities can never be scientific. Berkeley Cognitive Science Report No. 11. Berkeley, Institute of Human Learning, University of California, January 1984.

9. Benner P: *From Novice to Expert: Excellence and Power in Clinical Nursing Practice.* Menlo Park, Calif, Addison-Wesley, 1984.

10. Gadamer G: *Truth and Method.* London, Sheed & Ward, 1970.

11. Dreyfus H, Dreyfus S, Athanasiou T: *Mind Over Machines.* New York: Macmillan Free Press (in press).

12. Allen D: Nursing research and social control: Alternative models of science that emphasize understanding and emancipation. *Image* 1985;17:2, 58-64.

13. Bernstein R: *The Restructuring of Social and Political Theory*. Philadelphia, University of Pennsylvania Press, 1978.

14. Habermas J: *Legitimation Crisis,* McCarthy T (trans). Boston, Beacon Press, 1975.

15. Coward R: *Patriarchal Precedents.* London, RKP, 1983.

16. Habermas J: *Theory and Practice,* Viertel J (trans). Boston, Beacon Press, 1973.

17. Allen D: Professionalism, occupational segregation by gender and the control of nursing practice. *Women and Politics* 6:4 (in press).

18. MacKinnon C: Feminism, Marxism, method and the state: An agenda for theory. *Signs* 1982;7(3):515-543.

19. Allen D, Wolfgram B: Nursing, therapy and social control: Feminist-science and systems-based family therapy. Paper presented at Meeting of Midwest Nursing Research Society, Minneapolis, April 1984, *Women's Health Care International* (in press).

20. Allen D: Nursing and oppression: A feminist analysis of representations of "The Family" in nursing textbooks. Paper presented at Meeting of Society for Research in Nursing Education, San Francisco, January 1984, *Feminist Teacher* 2(2) (in press).

21. Culley M, Portugesje C (eds): *Gendered Subjects: The Dynamics of Feminist Teaching.* Boston, RKP, 1985.

22. Allen D, Whatley M: Nursing and men's health: Some critical considerations. *Nurs Clin North Am* 1986:21(1).

23. Diekelmann N (ed): *Issues in Nursing Education—Critical Perspectives* (in press).

Chapter 4

Can Nursing Theory Be Tested?

Maeona K. Jacobs

INTRODUCTION

The theoretical literature in nursing is replete with directives to guide its theory-testing endeavors.[1(p27),2(p83),3,4] Yet, in a recent issue of *Advances in Nursing Science*, editor Chinn questions and challenges our ability to deliver on the rhetoric. Chinn notes that despite a call by writers and reviewers for an issue entitled "Testing of Nursing Theory," with advance information encouraging a wide variety of "testing" approaches, articles were not forthcoming.[5] Although there are notable examples of theory-testing research in the nursing literature,[6–8] this editorial indicates that we remain focused on analysis and critique. Thus the fundamental question "Can we test nursing theory?" needs to be raised. Moreover, we need to consider what the "test" of our theories should be.

To begin considering the possibilities, let me suggest that the answer to this question is not yes *or* no, but yes *and* no, *perhaps*. The intent of this statement is not to interject humor, but to call attention to the kinds of analyses required to even broach the question. Simply, if by nursing theory and by testing theory we mean a certain sort of thing, the answer may be yes: we can test nursing theory. If, on the other hand, we take alternate meanings for nursing theory and its test, we may have to answer no: nursing theory cannot be tested. Our analysis of the question must illuminate how embracing a given method of theory-testing affects theory development, and the converse, how specific approaches to theory construction determine testing possibilities. Regardless, however, of how we view nursing theory and testing processes, and therefore, how we attempt to answer the question "Can nursing theory be tested?" there are problems and issues related to testing theory that need to be raised. This chapter considers problems and issues inherent in using a hypotheticodeductive model for testing nursing theory, primarily those

related to *establishing meaning for concepts*. It also argues that *problem development* and *concept analyses* are central to deductively developing theory that can be tested and that is useful for solving nursing problems. Before considering an answer to the question "Can nursing theory be tested?" some clarification of what is meant by nursing theory is important.

THE NATURE OF THEORY

Fundamentally, theory is an abstraction of reality that serves some purpose.[9] To make a common analogy, theory "maps" reality. A difficulty with this metaphor is that for some, it conveys a singular approach to the development and use of theory—an approach that claims theory seeks to provide explanatory knowledge. Maps, however, serve multiple purposes and so does theory. Maps not only describe a territory, but also provide a means for making decisions and comparing the utility of various decisions in relation to some goal. Theoretical maps are conceptual; that is, they use symbols, usually words, that have some shared meaning within a domain. Theoretical knowledge is also mediated; that is, it "goes between" sensory experience and our organized understanding of it. The symbols constituting theory are interrelated to "mirror" the shared generalities of empirical reality. Empirical phenomena are taken to mean sensory-dependent events, that is, reality phenomena that are known by some reference to sense experience.[10(p72)] The notion that phenomena are empirical does not equate with objectively observable and measurable data. Empirically experienced phenomena may also be normative. That is, we can directly experience, or know empirically, highly normative phenomena, such as independence, and in this sense, independence is said to contain both empirical and normative elements. In sum, empirically based phenomena, symbolically represented and systematized into a certain form, constitute theory. The organized abstraction of empirical reality called theory may represent an actual or presumed state of affairs: what *is*, or a more normative state of affairs, what *ought*. Reality experiences also may take forms that defy theoretical organization.

The various forms that theory can take and its multiple purposes are reflected in its definitions. An analysis of these forms and purposes for theory as derived from definitions has been set forth by Chinn and Jacobs[9] and Meleis.[11(pp25–29)] For our purposes, the general definition of theory as an organized abstraction of reality will suffice. That is, although various conceptualizations of theory and arguments about their adequacy do exist, an analysis of those arguments is not central to raising the issues about testing considered here.

THE NATURE OF NURSING THEORY

If theory is a systematic, purpose-oriented abstraction representing reality, nursing theory is theory that can be justifiably related to some nursing purpose. This notion is circular and ambiguous, yet appropriate. It is intentionally ambiguous because what comprises the nursing domain is unclear. It is appropriate because it acknowledges existing unclarity and requires that theory have some identifiable purpose. Identifying purpose for theory in turn will ultimately serve to help clarify the domain of nursing. Thus if it can be argued that a theory serves a reasonable and accepted purpose for nursing practice, broadly defined, it is taken to be nursing theory. This definition of nursing theory is meant to exclude nursing metatheory, that is, theory devoid of nursing content, such as theory about the nature of nursing theory. The considerations raised in this chapter do not require fine discrimination between theory as nursing or nonnursing, or conceptual frameworks as theory or only theorylike. Thus nursing theory would include such diverse formulations as Roy's Adaptation Model,[12] Rogers's Conceptual System,[2] King's Theory for Nursing,[13] Selye's Stress Theory,[14] Becker et al.'s Health Belief Model,[15] Rotter's Locus of Control Theory,[16] and Rawls's Egalitarian Theory of Justice.[17]

TRADITIONAL THEORY-TESTING APPROACHES

Because traditional approaches to testing theory still permeate the nursing literature, they do merit consideration. If we have not been overly successful in evaluating our theories, an examination of why there is a disjunction between what we advocate and what we do is in order. Traditional approaches to theory testing are taken to mean those associated with the well-known hypotheticodeductive model. This model requires that concepts embodied in deductively developed theory be represented in reality and assessed, certainly by observation and preferably by measurement. Once reality referents are "measured," a judgment about the extent to which "reality" linkages correspond with theoretical linkages can be rendered, usually using statistical models. For this testing approach, not every theoretical linkage need be tested to "accept" a theory, but the extent to which an empirical reality is explained is central in designating a theory "tested." Within this model, then, the primary goal of developing and testing theory is explanation, that is, elucidating why and how reality connects and functions. Explanation is of value because it leads to prediction, with the ultimate vision of controlling or producing outcomes. Whether or not the theory is useful in any way is of secondary concern.

Within the hypotheticodeductive model, research and theory are closely linked, at least in principle, and theory is postulated to grow by accretion

through hypothesis testing. The ghostly vestiges of the hypotheticodeductive approach to generating knowledge, which has its roots in the logical positivist tradition, remain in nursing.[18] Although we may acknowledge in nursing literature that empirical testing of theories can and does include assessing subjective data, the attempt is often to translate subjective data into numbers for statistical manipulation, rather than to report it "as is" for the knowledge that it represents. We need to ask if qualitative research methods are generally denigrated, with preference given to experimental designs with their inferential statistical models.

The hypotheticodeductive model has been useful for developing theory of a form that "mirrors" an existing image of reality and is not useful for testing theory that attempts to set forth what ought to be, as in normative ethical theory. This does not mean that we are unable to deductively test theory that sets forth norms. We *can* assess the extent to which theory that makes obvious normative claims *does* represent reality. This is not to assert that we can use empirical data to justify norms, a longstanding issue in metaethical theory.[19,20] In sum, what has been characterized as a traditional testing approach, that associated with the hypotheticodeductive model, will be useful to examine how well an actual empirical reality is described, explained, or predicted and to what extent a supposed empirical reality actually does exist. Simply, within this model, tests of nursing theory can answer if the theory's claims, whether normative or factual, correspond with an empirical reality.

Nursing is bound to have a great deal of difficulty with this approach to testing theory. A central reason why difficulties arise when the hypothetico-deductive approach is attempted relates to problems of defining reality referents for concepts. This is especially problematic given the broad nature of nursing concepts and the longstanding commitments to holism that these concepts represent. If we hold this view of theory testing, we should not be surprised if our testing literature is sparse. The disjunction between what we value in nursing, holism, and what research within a traditional model requires needs to be resolved.

DIFFICULTIES ASSOCIATED WITH TRADITIONAL THEORY-TESTING APPROACHES

As noted earlier, traditional approaches to theory testing require isolating a theory statement, referencing the concepts, and statistically validating whether reality, thus referenced, "matches" the theory. This in turn requires designating a meaning for the concept. There are many possible choices.

Within the hypotheticodeductive model, the assumption is that concepts contained in theory can be defined in a universal way. The guiding formal logic for exact definitions required that they fit models of necessary and sufficient conditions for the existence of the phenomena. Settling on *a*

definition ensured, in principle, that the theory would be stable, narrow in scope, and testable and would predict with a high degree of probability. Defining terms synthetically with definitions containing simple terms fitting models of necessary and sufficient conditions was not successful. If it could be accomplished at all, the definitions were analytic, that is, tautologies that were essentially useless for generating knowledge of empirical reality.

Even the most empirical of terms appearing as concepts within theory will not lend themselves to *a* definition, that is, one that can endure across contexts and through time, for the minute a definition is attached to a term, counterexamples can be offered. For this reason, empirical concepts, even the most highly empirical, are said to be normative to a degree. Highly empirical concepts, that is, those close to an observed empirical reality, simply do not lend themselves to objective universal definition. Whether the definition is or is not "right," which is a normative judgment, is argued on the basis of the theoretical context in which the concept is located.[21(p58)]

Given the problems of defining any concept, the breadth of concepts embodied in what are often identified as nursing theories poses special difficulties. Problems arise because these broad concepts are highly abstract and normative. For example, *adaptation* is often cited as a central nursing concept and can be used to illustrate the difficulties encountered in testing theory if direct referencing of theoretical relationships embodying the concept is required. Adaptation, although used for illustration, is not an endorsement of its value or disvalue for nursing; it is merely an example. Roy characterizes an adaptive response, which is taken to mean a positive adaptation, as a response that maintains integrity. Roy further characterizes integrity as survival, growth, reproduction, and self-mastery.[1(p43)] An adaptive response, for Roy, constitutes the goal for the client, and the nurse is to promote it. It seems plausible to suggest a theoretical premise for testing that embodies this concept. For example, action X promotes an adaptive response. If, in traditional fashion, this statement is to be tested, integrity must be assessed, since this is what adaptation theoretically implies. But what is integrity? Even defined in relation to self-mastery, survival, growth, and reproduction, its nature is not objectively self-evident. Thus what we define as integrity in order to test the theoretical statement may differ from what we would want to define as integrity when the theory is applied. When testing theory embodying such normative concepts, we could conclude that nursing action X in situation A *does* promote integrity, as a Type I adaptive response. But when we encounter situation Y, we may desire a Type II adaptive response as integrity, and our test of the theory does not guide us in this second situation. A failure to fully comprehend the normative element in determining conceptual meaning for both high empirical and very abstract concepts might lead to the conclusion that tested theory will endure if the matter of designating a universal meaning can be accomplished.

It is difficult to disagree with the premise that meaning for concepts is not self-evident, and therefore must be assigned by a normative judgment. But although meanings are arguable, and legitimately so, is it not possible to agree on a reasonable meaning and then use that meaning to test relationships within theory? This, it seems, is an appropriate approach, especially if conceptual meaning is established in relation to a well-developed nursing problem and concepts defined are highly empirical. However, it must be recognized that we have a tradition in nursing of concern for the whole person, and the highly normative, abstract concepts in our theories capture and reflect this. We resist attempts to designate reality referents for concepts because they narrow our focus, and we search for holistic measures of nursing phenomena. Given these values and proclivities, designating meaning for concepts will be rendered difficult.

Some have advocated that we test theories within conceptual frameworks, thereby openly acknowledging the difficulty of referencing concepts and determining the linkages contained in our broad frameworks.[22(p26),23(p20)] Although this approach may make designating conceptual meaning somewhat easier, since concepts *within* theories are probably narrower in scope than those contained in the parent conceptual framework, designating meaning will still be problematic. It will be problematic regardless of whether we claim to test theories some would call conceptual frameworks, test theories within conceptual frameworks, or test narrow theories apart from any overriding conceptual guide. In sum, the hypotheticodeductive approach to generating theory will not lead to stable, easily testable construction. If the meaning of concepts is not self-evident, but designated arbitrarily (not to imply unthinkingly) in relation to some context, one cannot make any claims that the theory will not be discarded as other conceptual meanings are necessitated by changes in the problem.

Difficulties related to defining concepts need to be raised because much of our rhetoric about testing theory, replicating research, and explaining and predicting reality *does* imply a need to have universally acceptable conceptual meanings, that is, specifying *a* meaning. It implies that definitions *can* occur independent of nursing problems or other relevant contexts. Although we may have reasonable success in designating definitions for some concepts within the nursing domain, that process will always be problematic in deductively testing nursing theory.

The multiple other issues linked with use of the hypotheticodeductive model are not developed here. Problems related to fundamental philosophical assumptions about empirical reality related to the approach have been well developed in the literature.[24,25] Also, it needs to be acknowledged that deductively testing theory goes beyond processes of designating meaning for concepts. This operation, however, which *is* requisite for testing theory, is centrally problematic in that difficulties here will reflect into other aspects of

theory testing, including measurement of referents and verification using statistical models.

TOWARD TESTABLE THEORY

Given the foregoing discussion of difficulties encountered when theory-testing methodologies require designating conceptual meaning in the face of broad nursing concepts, what are the alternatives? Should we abandon discourse about this approach to testing, attempt to develop more testable theories, or continue to attempt such tests in relation to our broadly formulated theories?

To abandon considered discussion of the hypotheticodeductive approach to testing theory in nursing, at least until we have carefully examined whether or not some utility can be extracted from it, does not seem wise. To the extent that some aspects of reality are understandable, at least partially, through sensory experience and those sensory experiences are organizable in relation to some nursing purpose, the approach has merit. To what purpose, then, should these abstractions about reality be organized?

Stating that theory, in this case deductively formulated theory, ought to be organized in relation to some nursing purpose is a powerful and controversial claim, but hardly a novel one. Although traditional scientific theory sought to explain reality and relied on underlying notions of causality that are seriously questioned, if not rejected, today, there is no reason to embrace the notion that events in empirically observed reality cannot be meaningfully related. We may be able deductively to develop and test theory that is useful for realizing significant nursing goals. Such theory may assist us directly, by providing the understanding necessary to bring about valued ends, or indirectly, by furnishing information about the empirical world. Laudan has suggested that theory be viewed as a problem-solving tool and that the "test" of theory relates to its adequacy in solving important empirical problems.[26] This reconceptualization of traditional scientific theory de-emphasizes the requirement that theory explain reality and relocates significance, as validity, in problem-solving utility. Because problems change, the adequacy of theories for solving them will also alter.

Theory as a problem-solving tool perhaps has its most well-known nursing proponents in the work of philosophers Dickoff and James, who define theory as a conceptual framework invented to some purpose.[27,28] Their purpose for theory was production of a normative end. Traditional scientific theory was an important ingredient for bringing about desired states of affairs but was not sufficient for practice utility. Dickoff and James's practice metatheory has its advocates but was never widely embraced. The controversy over Dickoff and James's metatheory continues, while utility, which they specifically address, is a criterion for theory evaluation cited by many nursing

metatheorists.[29–31] Utility is achieved when some significant nursing problem is addressed by theory. If a measure of utility is to accrue from our theories, we need specifically to attend to the purpose they address. Two theoretical processes in particular deserve attention: problem development and concept analysis. Choices made with regard to problem development and concept analysis will in turn determine whether our theories can be meaningfully tested, which is presumed important to increase utility for some sorts of theories.

CHOOSING A PROBLEM

Considerations related to problem development include not only the choice of problem, but also how the problem is analyzed, or framed. Problem choice should consider both the scope of the problem to be developed and the domain of nursing. Fortunately, there are guidelines within nursing that are helpful for choosing problems. For example, human responses to illness have been identified as an appropriate focus for nursing in the American Nurses' Association *Social Policy Statement*.[32] Donaldson and Crowley have suggested three themes for nursing enquiry that they derive from theoretical work in nursing. These themes include (1) principles governing life processes, well-being, and optimum human function; (2) behavior patterning in environmental interaction in critical life situations; and (3) processes for affecting positive health status changes.[33] Nursing theory has also been analyzed for areas of agreement with the suggestion that their shared focus is management of patient environment interaction.[34] These examples hardly exhaust the literature, for there is much general direction for making choices about the scope and domain of nursing problems.

There is no streamlined approach for designating meaningful problems within the framework of these general guides. The decision about problems that are worth our efforts ultimately will come from within ourselves, that is, our practice. Once we begin to generate, by theoretical work, a research tradition, that tradition may evolve guidelines for problem choices. For now, our individual and collective judgments about problem choices should reflect consensus about their importance. But what sorts of problems are important? The work of Johnson et al. related to decreasing pain experiences by informing patients about what to expect is cited as an example.[35,36] Many kinds of pain are clearly a response to treatment; pain management is a longstanding concern of nurses; and the problem applies to a variety of clients in multiple settings.

Another important consideration in choosing problems is whether the problem should exist within a practice arena. There is value in beginning with a problem for nurses where they practice. However, this value does not preclude theory development that evolves understanding, or generates

knowledge, about empirical reality. If one begins with a clinically grounded problem, basic knowledge about empirical reality can be generated in relation to that problem, not in isolation from it. Thus linking theory that provides basic understanding of reality to a problem increases its chances for utility.

PROBLEM DEVELOPMENT

Initial decisions that focus theoretical work on a specific problem portend the challenge of developing the problem in meaningful relationship to nursing. Initial decisions about "what problem" will alter and flex as development continues. Problem development helps to assure, according to Adams, that we do not "set in motion a set of solutions-causing problems requiring solutions, ad infinitum.[37(p7)] The necessity of clearly developing problems preparatory to initiating research is well accepted, yet problem development seldom receives consideration as a theoretical endeavor. In stating problems to guide theory development, approaches like that advanced by Diers, who suggests that problems be stated as discrepancies, are favored.[38] Discrepancy statements, according to Diers, assert that some phenomena exist that ought not exist. That is, the normative aim for nursing is explicitly acknowledged. Approaches to problem identification and statements that suggest that problems are difficulties, or irritations, imply a normative alternative but do not boldly state it. Stating the normative goal is not deemed important because, once acknowledged, we can, in principle, manipulate reality to produce it, although this is not such an ignoble aim. Manipulating reality, assuming we could, to produce a normative end is of concern when we fail to understand that, being normative, that end will be constituted differently for different persons and situations. Stating normative ends, defining them in a narrow singular fashion, and then developing theory useful to bring those ends into existence is not what is intended in goal identification. Rather, asserting an ought and examining it in the context of a problem will illuminate its normative nature and bring us up against the reality of our claims to "test" theories interrelating normative concepts. It will, in short, help us to understand what our theories can and cannot do!

Multiple schemes for the development of problems are developed in the literature.[39–41] Generally, they involve analyzing factors and phenomena affecting the problem and clarifying its domain and scope. Although attention should be given to the "universe" of elements affecting the problem, the theorist should attend to those phenomena and interrelationships within the problem that are modifiable by nurses. For example, in developing a problem around acute pain, the theorist might consider the effect aberrant anatomical structure has on its occurrence but would recognize a nurse's inability to surgically alter structure. The theorist might consider, in more detail, other means to alter pain experiences, such as imagery, which is within

the scope of nursing practice. In the final analysis, a well-developed problem can constitute deductively formulated nursing theory, for it structures and relates concepts and ascribes meaning to concepts by way of their contextual placement. Moreover, the goal of the theory is made explicit if a discrepancy statement of the form suggested by Diers is set forth. If the problem analysis proceeds around a difficulty or irritation, the goal may be implicit but is, nonetheless, identifiable.

If problem development, thoroughly and carefully done, constitutes theory, we again ask, "Can *this* theory, which, for want of a better characterization, is dubbed *problemtheory,* be deductively tested? Can it be more easily developed beyond its initial formulation, or more readily linked to other theory?" A thornier question is, "Can such theory be tested in relation to our broad conceptual frameworks, as suggested by some metatheorists?"[22,23]

TESTING PROBLEMTHEORY

If we take a liberal view, rigorously developed problemtheory may be considered "tested." If such theory is useful for solving problems and providing understanding, we may legitimately question the need to proceed further. Assuming, however, that some problemtheory will require testing for refinement and clarification, the familiar difficulties of designating conceptual meaning arise. Transforming a nursing problem into theory by developing it within a specific concept facilitates the designation of conceptual meaning. In problemtheory, concepts to be defined are already framed within a bounded context and that context suggests their meaning. A suggested meaning, although helpful, will not suffice, and the problem of designating meaning for deductively testing such theory remains. A central theoretical operation that helps to clarify our choices about testing problemtheory, as well as other forms of theory, is concept analysis.

CLARIFYING TESTING APPROACHES THROUGH CONCEPT ANALYSIS

Nursing has a metatheoretical literature related to Concept Analysis and its variants,[9,42,43] as well as some reported analyses of nursing concepts.[44–47] The appearance of this literature supports the premise that conceptual meaning is an invention, a deliberate choice from among alternatives. Concept analysis provides a framework for assigning appropriate meaning to concepts. In concept analysis, criteria are generated and used to determine the "existence" of the concept in the context in which concept is assumed to be "present." Concept analysis constitutes definition by criteria that are formulated by rigorous cognitive processes. Criteria may be quantitatively

measurable or assessable qualitatively. They may reflect self-reports of clients or be inferred by an observer. Some criteria for concepts may need to be evidenced for all instances of a concept, whereas others may be selectively present as the context alters.

Concept analysis allows for shifts in meaning across situations but also has potential to identify criteria generic to multiple settings. Concept analysis renders obvious the flaws of assessing concepts in a singular manner, for multiple criteria usually evolve when concepts are analyzed. Concept analysis illuminates the normative elements within concepts, for often the existence of a criterion can only be assessed by reports of feelings based in individual perceptions of what is good. Simply, concept analysis provides a basis for making reasoned choices about what to assess and how to assess it.

Testing criteria for concepts is facilitated when concepts are drawn from developed nursing problems. For example, if criteria for the concept of dependency were identified, a clinically based assessment of dependency, as identified by clinicians, could be attempted. Moreover, there is potential for criteria modification based on what is clinically observed. If criteria for concepts do not reflect what is evident in instances of dependency as clinically noted, theoretical utility is decreased.

CHOOSING A CONCEPT FOR ANALYSIS

Guidelines for making decisions about which concept to choose for initial analysis may be problematic, although as the problem develops, a single concept usually begins to emerge as centrally important. This concept is a suitable beginning point. The phenomenon of a singularly important concept emerging as analysis proceeds is similar to that described for grounded theory approaches, in which core concepts generate from empirical data.[48] When multiple concepts, usually not more than two or three, do seem equally significant, other considerations can guide the selection. These include previous development of the concept, its significance for solving additional nursing problems, potential for linking the concept to available nursing theory, possibilities for clinically testing the concept's criteria, and availability of resources to support further work.

Concept analysis can also provide information basic to decisions about testing theory within conceptual frameworks, or accomplishing other forms of theory-theory linkages. One variant of testing theory within conceptual frameworks involves invoking conceptual linkages within the parent framework to guide the selection of relevant theory for testing.[23] For example, Roy's conceptual framework links the concepts of focal stimuli and maladaptation.[12] This variant of testing theory within a conceptual framework would involve either locating or deducing theory containing concepts that represent Roy's construction of focal stimuli and maladaptation,

determining how those concepts are linked within the theory, and empirically assessing them to determine if the theory reflects the conceptual linkages within the parent framework.

The suggestion that our conceptual frameworks provide general guides for the selection and development of testable theory seems innocuous. If, however, our intent is to meaningfully interrelate theories under an overriding conceptual scheme by testing theory to determine if it represents the intent of the conceptual framework, a central task emerges. We need to justify the location of theoretical phenomena "under" or "within" the conceptual framework. This task is facilitated by concept analysis, for if meanings for concepts are not compatible, it is difficult to justify subconcepts as compatible with parent concepts. Clarification of meaning resulting from analysis is also basic to assuring that philosophical assumptions basic to the various theoretical perspectives are compatible.

Assume, returning to the issue of testing theory within conceptual frameworks, that four concepts are involved: two within the broad framework and two within the theory. We want to determine whether the meanings for concepts within the framework, and their vertical and horizontal linkages evaluated in relation to their meaning, justify locating some theory within the framework. It seems plausible to expect that, after analysis, shared criteria for concepts within both thc broad framework and the theory would emerge to justify the theory's location "under" and "within" the given framework. There are several difficulties with this approach to interrelating theories and conceptual frameworks, however. First, the domain and context for application of broad conceptual frameworks, and concepts located within it, are expansive. Thus it is difficult to identify aims that give form and direction to the analysis without significantly altering the framework. When concepts and aims are identified, they are broad in scopc, resulting in a convoluted and protracted analysis. Second, if criteria for concepts in our broad frameworks can be elicited, criteria for the concept embedded in the theory may be shared only partially, if at all. To say that criteria are shared implies that they assess a given aspect of reality in a compatible manner. If sharing occurs between criteria that are deemed essential for an instance of the concept, then the framework-to-theory linkage can be justified. Often, however, criteria for the concept to be located within a theory only partially reflect essential criteria for the concept contained in the framework, or the extent of sharing is unclear, and we have little justification for linking the theory to the framework. Finally, and perhaps most important, concepts in broad frameworks, if analyzed, are likely to generate highly normative criteria. Locating theory, especially highly empirical theory, under frameworks embodying highly normativc concepts requires that wc deal the epistemological question of how empirically testable and normative theory interrelate. The foregoing considerations are also significant when theories are deduced from conceptual

frameworks for testing. Unless conceptual meaning in the parent framework can be clarified, it will provide little guidance for deduction processes.

This interpretation of testing theories within conceptual frameworks, with its emphasis on concept analysis, would accrue positive benefits. First, the normative nature of broad concepts in our frameworks would be clarified, and their utility to guide practice reassessed. Clarification of meaning provided by analysis would subsequently increase the utility of frameworks for generating theory and guiding conceptualizations of nursing problems.

In sum, concept analysis is invaluable for elucidating the normative and empirical nature of our nursing concepts and guides meaningful comparisons for purposes of linking theories, testing them, and enhancing practice. Ellis has eloquently suggested that "when we understand the issues surrounding such terms as health, patient/client, and environment we can clarify their meaning and develop a system to transmit nursing knowledge."[49] Although understanding issues surrounding concepts certainly can clarify meaning, the process is circular. Concept analysis, or the process of clarifying meaning, will in turn illuminate the issues surrounding the testing of our theory.

CAN NURSING THEORY BE TESTED?

The question has brought us full circle, but the answer has not changed: *yes* and *no, perhaps.* To the extent that (a) our theories represent well-developed nursing problems, (b) the concepts contained within them are analyzed and clarified, and (c) those concepts are empirically accessible, we *can* test our theories. We can deductively test their reality basis and their utility to solve problems, the more traditional view of theory. They can also be assessed for problem-solving utility apart from any traditional test of their reality basis. That is, if a deductively developed untested theory works to solve problems, it can be considered "tested." Such reasoning requires that we carefully formulate the problem as theory and be able to recognize reality events as criteria for the concepts, whether more normative than empirical or more empirical than normative. We can, as Laudan notes, expect theories to be modified and discarded as history gives rise to new problems.[26]

The time for nursing to carefully evaluate its theoretical endeavors is now and will continue to be now. The suggestions in this chapter are offered to that end, for we must continually examine how well theory advances practice and abandon traditions that are not useful. Discarded traditions, however, merit reexamination within new historical contexts so their useful features may be reclaimed.

REFERENCES

1. Roy C, Roberts SL: *Theory Construction in Nursing.* Englewood Cliffs, NJ, Prentice-Hall, 1981.

2. Rogers ME: Theoretical Basis of Nursing. Philadelphia, FA Davis, 1970.

3. Batey ML: Conceptualizing the research process. *Nurs Res* 1971;20:496-508.

4. Dickoff J, James P: Researching research's role in theory development. *Nurs Res* 1968;17:204-206.

5. Chinn PL: From the editor. *Adv Nurs Sci* 1984;6:ix.

6. Gill BP, Atwood JR: Reciprocy and helicy used to relate mEGF and wound healing. *Nurs Res* 1981;30:68-72.

7. Floyd J: Research using Rogers' conceptual system: Development of a testable theorum. *Adv Nurs Sci* 1983;5:37-48.

8. Harper DC: Application of Orem's theoretical constructs to self-care medication behaviors in the elderly. *Adv Nurs Sci* 1984;6:29-46.

9. Chinn PL, Jacobs MK: *Theory and Nursing: A Systematic Approach.* St Louis, CV Mosby, 1983.

10. Beck LW, Holmes RL: *Philosophic Inquiry,* ed. 2. Englewood Cliffs, NJ, Prentice-Hall, 1968.

11. Meleis AL: *Theoretical Nursing.* Philadelphia, JB Lippincott, 1985.

12. Roy C: *Introduction to Nursing: An Adaptation Model.* Englewood Cliffs, NJ, Prentice-Hall, 1976.

13. King I: *A Theory for Nursing.* New York, John Wiley, 1981.

14. Selye H: *The Stress of Life.* New York, McGraw-Hill, 1956.

15. Becker MH, Drachman RH, Kirscht JP: A new approach to explaining sick role behavior in low income populations. *Am J Public Health* 1964;3:205–216.

16. Rotter JB: Generalized expectancies for internal vs. external control of reinforcement. *Psychol Monogr* 1966;80:609.

17. Rawls J: *A Theory of Justice.* Cambridge, Mass, Harvard University Press, 1971.

18. Webster G, Jacox A, Baldwin B: Nursing theory and the ghost of the received view, in Grace HK, McClosky JC (eds): *Current Issues in Nursing.* Boston, Blackwell Scientific Publications, 1981,pp 26–35.

19. Frankena WK: The naturalistic fallacy. *Mind* 1939;48:464–477.

20. Moore GE. *Principa Ethica.* Cambridge, Cambridge University Press, 1903.

21. Kaplan A: *The Conduct of Inquiry.* New York, Thomas Y. Crowell, 1964.

22. Fawcett J: *Analysis and Evaluation of Conceptual Models of Nursing.* Philadelphia, FA Davis, 1984.

23. Newman MA: *Theory Development in Nursing.* Philadelphia, FA Davis, 1979.

24. Silva MC, Rothbart D: An analysis of changing trends in philosophies of science on nursing theory development and testing. *Adv Nurs Sci* 1984;6:1–13.

25. Munhall PL: Nursing philosophy and nursing research: In opposition or apposition. *Nurs Res* 1982;31:175–77.

26. Laudan L. *Progress and Its Problems.* Berkeley, University of California Press, 1977.

27. Dickoff J, James P: Theory in a practice discipline: Part I. *Nurs Res* 1968;17:415–435.

28. Dickoff J, James P: A theory of theories: A position paper. *Nurs Res* 1968;17:197–203.

29. Stevens BJ: *Nursing Theory: Analysis, Evaluation and Application,* ed. 2. Boston, Little, Brown, 1984.

30. Ellis R: Characteristics of significant theories. *Nurs Res* 1968;17:217–22.

31. Thibodeau JL: *Nursing Models: Analysis and Evaluation.* Belmont, Calif, Wadsworth, 1983.

32. Nursing: A Social Policy Statement. Kansas City, MO, American Nurses' Association, 1980.

33. Donaldson SK, Crowley DE: The discipline of nursing. *Nurs Outlook* 1978;25:113–120.

34. Flaskerud JH, Halloran EJ: Areas of agreement in nursing theory development. *Adv Nurs Sci* 1980;3:1–7.

35. Johnson JE, Fuller SS, Endress MP, Rice VS: Altering patients' responses to surgery: An extension and replication. *Res Nurs Health* 1978;1:111–121.

36. Johnson JE, Kirchhoff KT, Endress MP: Altering children's distress behavior during orthopedic cast removal. *Nurs Res* 1975;24:404–410.

37. Adams JL: *Conceptual Blockbusting,* ed. 2. New York, WW Norton, 1979.

38. Diers D. *Research in Nursing Practice.* Philadelphia, JB Lippincott, 1979.

39. Ackerman WB, Lohnes PR: *Research Methods for Nurses.* New York, McGraw-Hill, 1981.

40. Wandelt MA: *Guide for the Beginning Researcher.* New York, Appleton-Century-Crofts, 1970.

41. Brink PJ, Wood MJ: *Basic Steps in Planning Nursing Research.* North Scituate, Mass, Duxbury Press, 1978.

42. Walker LO, Avant KC: *Strategies for Theory Construction in Nursing.* Norwalk, Conn, Appleton-Century-Crofts, 1983.

43. Norris CM: *Concept Clarification in Nursing.* Rockville, Md, Aspen Systems, 1983.

44. Forsythe GL: Analysis of the concept of empathy: Illustration of one approach. *Adv Nurs Sci* 1980;2:33–42.

45. Hall BA: Toward an understanding of stability in nursing phenomena. *Adv Nurs Sci* 1983;5:15–20.

46. Carlson CE, Blackwell B: *Behavioral Concepts and Nursing Intervention,* ed. 2. Philadelphia, JB Lippincott, 1978.

47. Crawford G: The concept of pattern in nursing: Conceptual development and measurement. *Adv Nurs Sci* 1982:5:1–6.

48. Stern PN: Grounded theory methodology. *Image* 1980;12:20–23.

49. Ellis R: Conceptual issues in nursing. *Nurs Outlook* 1982;30:406.

Chapter 5

Analogy between Phenomenology and Multivariate Statistical Analysis

Laura Cox Dzurec and Ivo L. Abraham

This chapter demonstrates the consistencies between a quantitative methodology—multivariate statistical analysis—and a qualitative methodology and philosophy of science—phenomenology. We argue that there is potential for integration of both quantitative and qualitative methodologies in a single study and that such integration can answer important nursing questions.

A shift in the emphasis of nursing thought and nursing research from a perspective that dichotomizes quantitative and qualitative research methods toward a perspective that encourages use of both strategies simultaneously is evident in the nursing literature.[1–3] As Goodwin and Goodwin state, the choice of research procedures, including design, sampling plan, instrumentation, data-collection methods, and data analysis techniques, should match the research question and be optimally efficient, powerful, valid, and reliable.[2(p378)]

As nurse researchers better define and understand the nature of science and of nursing, it becomes possible to better define and understand the nature of the research that will allow us to theorize about nursing. That research will necessarily address questions that are not amenable to either qualitative or quantitative methodology alone.

The dichotomy between qualitative and quantitative research methodologies has a historical component, as Silva[4] discusses. From the Age of Greece (500 B.C. to 300 B.C.) until the Industrial Revolution, all knowledge was designated as philosophy. With the Industrial Revolution, however, came a knowledge explosion that divorced science from philosophy. This division was based on seemingly incongruous modes of understanding reality. To the philosopher, understanding of reality continued to be the product of intuition, introspection, and reasoning. The scientist, with a new wealth of information,

on the other hand, based understanding of reality on cause and effect. Investigation in the realms of science and philosophy sought to answer dichotomous questions; hence research methodologies similarly diverged, a major difference represented by the absence of experiment in philosophic inquiry.[5] Scientific and philosophic inquiry became viewed as incompatible, proponents of scientific investigation, using quantitative methodology, claiming that philosophic endeavor is without rigor or measurable outcomes, and therefore of limited value; proponents of philosophic inquiry, using qualitative methodology, claiming that the scientist fails to take into account the totality of the reality to be described.

Within nursing research and theory development, there exists a characteristic aspect that perpetuates the qualitative-quantitative methodology dichotomy accompanying the split between science and philosophy. Review of the nursing research literature from 1950 to 1982[6] and of the nursing theory literature from 1964 to 1976[3] demonstrates that research and theory development within the discipline of nursing have a fairly consistent commitment to logical positivism, one philosophy of science. This philosophy of science is characterized by empirical, that is, five-sense perceptible, evidence. Although Goodwin and Goodwin[2] argue that research methodology is not necessarily linked with a particular paradigm (i.e., philosophy of science), one can state that, generally, nursing research questions addressed using qualitative methodology, those questions that consider meaning-in-context, are not amenable to the logical positivist philosophy of science. Within logical positivism, evidence is characterized as "observation statements derived from theoretical statements in a hypodeductive system of explanation."[7(p19)] The significance of this notion becomes apparent as one recognizes that review of nursing's paradigms conducted by Fawcett[8] revealed the integral nature of human and environment as a consistent theme across nursing paradigms. As Reeder discusses, evidence that is acceptable within logical positivism "does not reflect the integral nature of human and environmental fields."[7(p9)] Philosophies of science other than logical positivism—historicism and phenomenology, for instance—might be more appropriate for investigation of philosophical questions in nursing.

Silva and Rothbart[3(p9)] note that theory development from 1976 to the present is characterized by trends somewhat different from those typical of earlier theory development in nursing. Specifically, there exists a continued and relatively stable commitment to logical empiricism (positivism), although a beginning trend toward historicism is apparent; a revision of several conceptual frameworks for nursing and the introduction of some new frameworks; a questioning of the adequacy of strictly quantitative research methods to test nursing theory deductions.

In this chapter, we argue that the particulate perspective resulting from the artificial, and inappropriate, dichotomy between science and philosophy

arises from failure to acknowledge multiple potential philosophies of science underlying research. Science, viewed solely within the logical-positivist framework, fails to adequately address the full range of questions relevant in nursing research. Other authors[2,3,6,7,9] have suggested this notion as well. It is our contention that nurse researchers potentially can use both quantitative and qualitative methodologies within one study, as Goodwin and Goodwin[2] suggest, to answer relevant nursing questions. We argue, in addition, that optimal use of the full range of potential methodologies requires that nurse researchers recognize the philosophy of science to which they ascribe in their conduct of research. Thus we present here a demonstration of the consistency between phenomenology, a philosophy of science and qualitative research method, and multivariate analysis, a quantitative research method.

We begin with a description of phenomenology and then address the premises of selected multivariate analytic procedures. In the final part, we discuss consistent features of phenomenology and multivariate analysis.

PHENOMENOLOGY AS A PHILOSOPHY OF SCIENCE AND QUALITATIVE RESEARCH METHOD

Since most debates surrounding the quality of research methods address the assumptions and goals underlying the methods and the theory and perspectives of the methods,[10] we will discuss the nature of phenomenology as a philosophy of science and a qualitative research method. Clarification of the assumptions and goals, theory, and perspectives of phenomenology will clarify its nature and its utility for research in nursing.

The phenomenological movement was founded by Edmund Husserl (1859-1939). Although other philosophers added to and changed Husserl's original conceptions of phenomenology as presented in 1933,[11] Husserlian phenomenology, specifically, is addressed in this chapter.

As a philosophy of science that admits everyday experience as evidence, phenomenology focuses on investigation of consciousness of the world. According to Husserl, life and world are integral, and consciousness is always directed to the world. Therefore, "consciousness and world experienced first hand is not conceivable or imaginable apart from each other."[6(p110)] Whereas other philosophies of science—logical positivism, for example—limit acceptable evidence to five-sense perceptible data that are consistent with the three-dimensional (Newtonian) concepts of space, time, and causality, phenomenology admits evidence "comprising all items and objects as they present themselves in prescientific experience and as they present themselves prior to their scientific interpretation."[12(p17)] Objectivity, a condition of the object of study, not of the researcher's techniques, is founded in subjective experience.[13] "The world of possibility is broader than the possibility for the conditions of knowledge represented by the categories of Kant, and is infinite

but nonetheless effable (knowable). Accordingly, Husserlian phenomenologists consider all that is perceptible, conceivable and imaginable on equal terms."[6(p283)]

As a research method, phenomenology is no less rigorous than other research methodologies. The procedures used by the researcher, however, are different from those commonly used by researchers ascribing to logical positivism. The rationale for choice of research procedures is to allow the researcher to match them with the research question and provide optimally efficient, powerful, valid, and reliable information, as Goodwin and Goodwin[2] discuss.

The goal of the researcher using the phenomenological method is to uncover human understanding of reality as it is experienced in life.[14] Theoretical assumptions underlying this goal are that the human and the environment are integral and that access to knowledge about the integral human being is gained by rigorous investigation of consciousness of the world. Methodological assumptions underlying the goal are that one can holistically describe subjects' consciousness of the world through participant observation and qualitative description of findings,[15] and that spoken and written language provide an accurate description of lived experience.[16] Truth is viewed as a composite of individuals' perceived realities and is conceptualized as changing and context-dependent rather than as fixed and inviolate.

The researcher investigates subjects' consciousness of the world by bracketing (suspending what is known about an experience), intuiting (viewing the experience from an unrestricted perspective and becoming absorbed in it), analyzing (identifying recurring elements in the experience in retrospect), and describing (conveying what has been found).[15] As a participant observer, the research determines answers to questions about the research phenomenon by establishing rapport with subjects and interacting unobtrusively with them.[10] Questions planned initially in the study may change as the researcher finds that they do not address the reality described by subjects.

Data are analyzed in terms of recurrent themes and hypotheses. Through careful analysis of texts of researcher-subject interviews and interactions, narrative data are reduced to meaningful units of "revelatory phrases"[17] that appear to represent the subjects' major ideas. Specifics of the conduct of research, including the nature of the interaction between researcher and subjects, are included, again to present the integral nature of human and environment to the reader.

As a philosophy of science and a research methodology that assumes human-environmental integrality, phenomenology appropriately addresses questions about the integral human and environment. Such questions may not be amenable to five-sense restricted data such as that required by other philosophies of science.

MULTIVARIATE STATISTICAL ANALYSIS

Multivariate statistical analysis is chosen for presentation here because it offers researchers the most complete selection of quantitative empirical-inferential procedures and techniques for application in nursing research. It permits comprehensive comparisons of people and interventions on both simple and complex outcome criteria. It also permits sorting out of relationships among variables or among people, most often in a mode that is relatively easy to comprehend. Techniques reviewed include multivariate significance testing (T-squared, MANOVA [multivariate analysis of variance], profile analysis), principal components analysis/factor analysis, cluster analysis, discriminant function analysis, and canonical correlation analysis. The criterion for distinguishing between uni/bivariate and multivariate statistics used in this chapter is multiplicity of dependent variables. Hence multiple regression is not included (yet its applicability is similar to that of canonical correlation analysis).

Because we are interested in the simultaneous and comprehensive analysis of multiple dependent variables, a system for mathematical notation and manipulation of sets of dependent variables is required. Such a system is matrix algebra, the mathematical basis of multivariate analysis. In matrix algebra, sets of dependent variables are represented in aggregate units called vectors. A vector is the representation of two or more interrelated outcome variables and is used as the basic unit in subsequent computations. Matrix algebra, more generally, avoids fragmentation of interrelated issues into separate quasi-independent ones when, in fact, truthfulness would be served if studied under consideration of these relationships.

Multivariate significance testing comprises procedures for comparing two (Hotelling's T-squared) or more (MANOVA) groups of subjects on a set of interrelated variables. If these variables constitute a profile, the groups may be compared more informatively using profile analysis, a technique for investigating differences in dimensional profiles.

In certain instances, groups may not be known a priori, and inquiry may therefore be focused on identification of these groups. Accessing this information entails two processes. First, there is the search for subjects who are similar to one another with respect to several dependent variables, while different from others. Cluster analysis is a technique that, as the term implies, clusters subjects on the basis of similarities and dissimilarities. Second, we may want to describe specifically how these groups differ. This may be done using discriminant function analysis, a procedure for describing similarity and discriminating among dissimilar groups.

Factor analysis (and principal components analysis as a part of factor analysis) is concerned with the underlying structure among variables observed within a sample of subjects and often is used to determine

dimensions and subscales of instruments. Marascuilo and Levin cogently point out that factors should not be understood as "mathematical and statistical entities, but as real-world human characteristics, such as intelligence, fear, self-concept, locus of control, anxiety, androgyny, verbal ability, musical aptitude as well as many other.... variables that cannot be measured in the same, direct manner as physical characteristics.[18(p252)] The naming of factors is a crucial component of factor analysis because it permits the researcher to describe phenomena as they appear in their fullest breadth and depth.

The purpose of canonical correlation analysis is to describe all possible associations between two sets (or vectors/matrices) of variables. Intuitively, it is best understood as the multivariate extension of the product-moment correlation, which describes the associations between two single variables.[19] Canonical correlation analysis may therefore be understood as a technique to model the relationship between two aggregates of interdependent variables. Its major use is to examine how variables hold together as an entity. It has been used widely in research on holistic phenomena.[20]

THE ANALOGY

At first sight, the preceding sections on phenomenology and statistical analysis may appear quite disparate, particularly if one views qualitative and quantitative methods as dichotomous. This section argues that the traditional dichotomy has little to do with inquiry itself, for inquiry has its roots at a suboperational level, that is, at a level that hierarchically precedes that at which a particular approach is considered, espoused, and adopted. Indeed, inquiry is inquiry, regardless of methodology. We study phenomena because we are, so to speak, driven by a desire to know and a desire to apply knowledge to the enhancement of human beings, environment, health, and nursing.

Rather, the dichotomy has more to do with the tenacity of the separation between science and philosophy, a separation based on too narrow a definition of both terms. "Major 'habits of mind,' approaches to the world, ... are extensions of habits of thought that emerge and are developed in the practice of an occupation, profession, or craft"[21(p1)] The dichotomy between science and philosophy, and the resultant dichotomy between quantitative and qualitative research methods in nursing as in other disciplines, is a habit of mind that has developed from nurse (and other) researchers' commitment to logical positivism to the exclusion of other philosophies of science. The resulting particulate perspective fails to adequately address the full range of relevant nursing questions.

The philosophy and methodology of phenomenology demand that one describe phenomena as they are experienced in an effort to understand

"reality," itself a context-dependent composite of lived experience. Such an approach to description is generally considered subjective and less appropriate than more objective methods of data analysis within the framework of logical positivism. Within that framework, objective quantification enhances the value of a research study, and multivariate analysis is viewed, quite simply, as the most advanced quantitative method available to reduce the complexity of data. Yet, in considering the phenomenon of multivariate analysis, one can identify much subjectivity couched in terms of researcher responsibility for appropriate use of this particular methodology. For example, Marascuilo and Levin identified appropriate conditions for selection of multivariate techniques for data analysis. "In some situations, multivariate methods constitute the only rational approach to a research problem, (but) whether or not a potential multivariate problem is analyzed 'multivariately' is a function of the researcher's perceptions of the problem and corresponding desired substantive interpretations of the data."[18(p2)] In other words, for the researcher using multivariate analysis, as for the researcher using phenomenology, meaning is not inherent in data as they are analyzed, but is implied by the researcher's view of "reality" and the construction of reality to be conveyed in a given situation. Hence attribution of meaning to objective data collected using either multivariate analysis or phenomenology is a subjective task.

As previously discussed, multivariate analysis may be used to reduce data complexity, to discriminate between groups on the basis of multiple attributes, or to identify and describe relationships between groups of variables. The aims of phenomenology as a research method are similar, as comparison of the two approaches to data analysis demonstrates.

For example, cluster analysis, a technique for reducing data complexity, addresses the problem of devising a classification scheme that identifies groups of subjects or variables with similar characteristics. The technique involves naive description of variables or subjects and clusters of those, explanation of the cluster phenomenon, and matching of an appropriate data-collection methodology (for example, hierarchical, optimization, density or mode-seeking, or clumping techniques) with appropriate data. Choice of an appropriate clustering technique is based on the potential for generation of meaningful data. Data generated require substantial researcher interpretation to determine which subjects or variables cluster together.[22] The subjective nature of this objective technique for reducing data complexity is apparent. The researcher using "analyzing," the phenomenological operation discussed by Oiler,[15] might approach smaller data sets in a manner similar to multivariate cluster analysis, comparing and contrasting recurring elements to identify their relationships to one another. For multivariate analysis, as well as for phenomenology, degrees of both objectivity and subjectivity influence findings.

Factor analysis, a second multivariate technique used to reduce data complexity, identifies distinct bodies of information and can be used to establish conceptual meaningfulness of data. It differs from cluster analysis in that it yields dimensions on which each variable loads, rather than groupings of variables or subjects. The simplest possible structure of data, that is, the outcome of factor analysis, is, finally, determined by the researcher using subjective manipulation of data sets to establish conceptual meaningfulness. Factor analysis allows data to be conceptualized as human characteristics, as Marascuilo and Levin[18] discuss. The naming of factors is the responsibility of the researcher, allowing for description of characteristics as they appear to the researcher. This approach to description is consistent with the method of phenomenology. Factor analysis allows the researcher to approach a phenomenon with no preconceived expectations or categories and to use the method of phenomenology to make "things whose meanings seem clear, meaningless, and then, discover what they mean."[23(p189)] Factor analysis supports introspection by leaving in the hands of the researcher those decisions that are subjective: how to put the data together, how to enter it into the analytic process (that is, how to define the variables in the computer program), how to interpret the data once the computer has acted on the information communicated to it, and how to name the outcomes. It allows for simplistic description of phenomena as they are experienced through identification of recurrent themes and hypotheses. Identification of central characteristics is identified by Paterson and Zderad[24] as a technique useful in describing phenomena. The technique is used in multivariate analysis and phenomenology alike.

A third multivariate technique with aspects analogous to phenomenology is canonical correlation analysis, a major use of which is modeling. As in the cases of factor analysis and cluster analysis, there are determinations about canonical correlation that are left to the researcher, for example, determination of the significance of the correlations and interpretation of the meaning of each linear combination.[20] These researcher-defined outcomes, in combination with characteristics that render canonical correlation associative and not causal in nature, suggest that canonical correlation might be a useful tool in research that would bridge the chasm between quantitative and qualitative methodologies. As a technique that assists with description of relationships among sets of variables, canonical correlation analysis allows the researcher to classify variables in a manner similar to that used by the phenomenologist.

In short, the subjective descriptive techniques of phenomenology have objective components as the objective descriptive techniques of multivariate analysis have subjective components. The researcher, recognizing a philosophy of science that accommodates both quantitative and qualitative methodologies, can also recognize the complimentarity between the two methods. Rather than espousing one method as appropriate and, subsequently,

rejecting the other as inadequate, a researcher cognizant of the philosophy of science espoused can use both qualitative and quantitative methods simultaneously to validly address questions not appropriate to either methodology alone. Although not appropriate for all nursing inquiry, phenomenology used in conjunction with multivariate analysis does allow one to ask and to validly answer questions that address meaning in context for large sets of data or when multiple variables are involved.

To summarize the analogy between phenomenology and multivariate statistical analysis, we have developed a table that highlights similarities and congruencies of the two methods of data analysis. Table 5-1 lists aspects of both approaches to data analysis according to two categories, philosophy and methodology. To summarize, from the phenomenological perspective, the

Table 5–1 Analogy between Phenomenology and Multivariate Statistical Analysis

Phenomenology	Multivariate Analysis
Philosophic Analogies	
• Emphasis on intentionality, researcher connectedness with phenomenon	• Matrix algebra forms an interrelated, comprehensive data set as devised by the researcher
• Nonspatial, nontemporal, noncausal nature of phenomenon	• Potential for nonspatial, nontemporal, noncausal analysis of phenomenon
• Objectivity in the relationship between phenomenon of study and researcher	• Objectivity achieved through quantification tempered with researcher-determined meaningfulness
Methodologic Analogies	
• Explanation and understanding sought through reflection	• Explanation and understanding sought through quantification and meaningful structure
• Bracketing, intuiting, analyzing, describing used to extract information; meaning inherent in researcher's view of reality	• Elimination of error variance, factor analysis, cluster analysis, discriminant analysis, canonical correlation used to extract information; meaning inherent in researcher's view of reality
• Recurrent themes are identified	• Recurrent themes are identified

researcher views phenomena and is integral with them. Similar emphasis can be detected within the multivariate analytic perspective, where matrix algebra forms the basic mathematical strategy. Data constitute an interrelated, comprehensive set determined by the researcher. The data are integral with the researcher. Three major assumptions of the phenomenological method are that phenomena are noncausal, nonspatial, and nontemporal. Although most scientists think of multivariate quantitative methods as causal, spatial, and temporal, this is a matter of a priori-defined assumptions. In other words, multivariate statistics can describe phenomena posited to be causal or noncausal, spatial or nonspatial, and temporal or nontemporal, depending on the assumptions of the researcher. The phenomenological method, although often criticized for its presumed lack of objectivity, is highly concerned with the accuracy of conclusions drawn. In that capacity it parallels multivariate statistics, in which objectivity, tempered with researcher-determined meaningfulness, is of primary concern.

Analogies also can be drawn at the methodological level. Both scientific approaches are concerned with the pursuit of understanding and explanation. Using the phenomenological method, the researcher uses reflection. In multivariate analysis, reflection is also present, structured and governed by quantitative rules and researcher-imposed meaningfulness. The phenomenological technique of bracketing, an effort to suspend what is known about a phenomenon, finds its equivalent in the multivariate statistical effort to eliminate error variance and maximize the explanation of true variance. Further, the techniques of intuiting, analyzing, and describing have cognitive analogs in multivariate analysis, specifically in the techniques of factor analysis, cluster analysis, discriminant analysis, and canonical correlation. Both the researcher using phenomenology and the researcher using multivariate analysis seek to extract what is most informative about the phenomenon of study and about the subjects experiencing the phenomenon. A major methodological aspect of phenomenology is identification of recurrent themes and universals. Again, a similarity with multivariate analysis is apparent. Using multivariate hypothesis testing, the researcher attempts to identify the consistency with which certain phenomena, events, or themes occur and may occur in the future. Furthermore, aggregate entities of information, comparable to phenomenological themes, may be found in the techniques of factor analysis and cluster analysis.

SUMMARY

From this discussion, then, it is apparent that the traditional dichotomy between qualitative and quantitative research is more a matter of "the eye of the beholder" than of "the mind of the scientist." Indeed, what scientists do, regardless of the approach chosen, appears to be consistent and similar from

one to another. It is hypothesized that science is a basic human inclination and not a matter of adapting a particular "appropriate" strategy.

Omery[25] suggests that the researcher using phenomenology accept as valuable the accurate description of an experience that the data provide; accept all data as they appear and study the data in such a way that they are not influenced by the researcher; interpret a comprehensive meaning from the data; use no preconceived notions, expectations, or frameworks to guide the data collection and analysis; report data in natural language and collect data in a natural setting. These notions are not unlike the assumptions underlying multivariate analysis. Used appropriately, that is, with the researcher assuming responsibility for determining meaning from findings and judiciously applying the techniques in a statistically and substantively meaningful manner, multivariate analysis and phenomenology can address important questions about phenomena relevant to nursing that are not amenable to either technique independently.

REFERENCES

1. Reichardt CS, Cook TD: Beyond qualitative versus quantitative methods, in Cook TD, Reichardt CS (eds): *Qualitative and Quantitative Methods in Evaluation Research.* Beverly Hills, Calif, Sage, 1979, pp 7-32.

2. Goodwin LD, Goodwin WL: Qualitative vs. quantitative research or qualitative and quantitative research? *Nurs Res,* 1984;33:378-380.

3. Silva MC, Rothbart D: An analysis of changing trends in philosophies of science on nursing theory development and testing. *Adv Nurs Sci,* 1984;6(2):1-13.

4. Silva MC: Philosophy, science, theory: Interrelationships and implications for nursing research. *Image* 1977;9:59-63.

5. Smith JA: The idea of health: A philosophic inquiry. *Adv Nurs Sci,* 1981;3(3):43-50.

6. Reeder F: *Nursing Research, Holism, and Philosophies of Science: Points of Congruence Between E. Husserl and M.E. Rogers,* doctoral dissertation. New York University, 1984. University Microfilms No. 84-21, 466.

7. Reeder F: Philosophical issues in the Rogerian science of unitary human beings. *Adv Nurs Sci,* 1984;6(2):14-23.

8. Fawcett J: The metaparadigm of nursing: Present status and future refinements. *Image,* 1984;16:84-87.

9. Tinkle MB, Beaton JL: Toward a new view of science: Implications for nursing research. *Adv Nurs Sci,* 1983;5(2):27-36.

10. Bogdan R, Taylor SJ: *Introduction to qualitative research methods: A phenomenological approach to the social sciences.* New York, John Wiley, 1975.

11. Husserl E: Cartesian meditations, Cairns D. (trans). 1933. Reprint. The Hague, Nijhoff, 1960.

12. Gurwitsch A: *Phenomenology and the theory of science.* Evanston, Ill, Northwestern University Press, 1974.

13. Torbert WR: Initiating collaborative inquiry, in Morgan G. (ed): *Beyond Method.* Beverly Hills, Calif, Sage, 1983, pp 272-291.

14. Kohak E: Idea and experience: Edmund Husserl's project of phenomenology, in Ideas I. Chicago, University of Chicago Press, 1978.

15. Oiler C: The phenomenological approach in nursing research. *Nurs Res* 1982;31:178-181.

16. Kestenbaum V: The humanity of the ill. Knoxville, University of Tennessee Press, 1982.

17. Lanigan RL: Semiotic phenomenology of rhetoric: Eidetic practice in Henry Grattan's discourse on tolerance. Washington, DC: Center for Advanced Research in Phenomenology and University Press of America, 1984.

18. Marascuilo LA, Levin JR: *Multivariate Statistics in the Social Sciences: A Researcher's Guide.* Monterey, Calif, Brooks/Cole, 1983.

19. Achenbach TM: *Research in development psychology: Concepts, strategies, methods.* New York, Free Press, 1978.

20. Laessig RE, Duckett EJ: Canonical correlation analysis: Potential for environmental planning. *Am J Public Health* 1979;69:353-359.

21. Bensman J, Lilienfield R: *Craft and consciousness: Occupational technique and the development of world images.* New York, John Wiley, 1973.

22. Kruskal JB, Landwehr JM: Icicle plots: Better displays for hierarchical clustering. *Am Statistician* 1983;37:162-171.

23. Blumensteil A: A sociology of good times, in Psathas G. (ed): *Phenomenological Sociology: Issues and Applications,* New York, John Wiley, 1973.

24. Paterson J, Zderad L: *Humanistic Nursing.* New York, John Wiley, 1976.

25. Omery A: Phenomenology: A method for nursing research. *Adv Nurs Sci* 1983;5(2):49-63.

Chapter 6

Methods: A Reflective Model

W. Richard Cowling, III

INTRODUCTION

The recent emphasis on a fundamental critique of the predominant logical positivist stance and its accompanying empirical-analytic approaches, although justified, has spawned a great deal of uncertainty about methods appropriate for advancing nursing science. Critiques of traditional approaches to science applied to nursing research have led to the following conclusions:

1. Empirical-analytic modes of inquiry are inconsistent with the predominant philosophical tenets of nursing.[1,2]
2. More specifically, the prevailing methods used by researchers in nursing are context-stripping[3] and do not attend to the holistic nature of human beings.[4]
3. The empirical-analytic mode of inquiry contains problems and fallacies worth consideration that can be characterized as major myths that impede creative approaches to methodology.[5,6]
4. Multiple modes of inquiry are necessary for the advancement of nursing science.[7,8]
5. Nursing scientists adhere to models of science and perspectives that have important implications for the nature and limits of their research.[2,5,9]

Although the emphasis on these issues and concerns have heightened our awareness of the methodological fallacies of some traditional approaches to science, there has been a lack of emphasis on evaluation criteria for selecting research strategies that arise from various models of science.[5] Evaluation criteria are relevant to the acts of choice and decision making faced by the

researcher. In nursing research texts and courses, there is often a simplistic approach to selecting methods for research, with no attention to epistemological considerations. Often a linear perspective of scientific knowledge is suggested in which qualitative methods are advocated for areas in which little knowledge exists, and quantitative methods for more advanced fields of knowledge.[7,10] The standard criteria for selecting methods that still receive major attention are appropriateness to the research question, technical adequacy, and reliability and validity.[11]

The typical solution to evaluating research methods is to use a foundational solution. A foundational solution to the problem of evaluating research methods encompasses the notion that there is a universal, singular evaluative perspective from which claims of *different* research strategies can be assessed.[12] One example is the application of criteria for evaluating positivist research to all kinds of knowledge claims arising from various research strategies. "In other words, the kind of knowledge for which positivist researchers seek is seen as defining the nature of knowledge per se."[12(p392)] Another example would be the application of a set of criteria based on assumptions of a naturalistic or postpositivist paradigm[13] to all knowledge claims arising from various research strategies. A final example of a foundational solution is to advocate a synthesis of criteria based on assumptions of two scientific paradigms, such as positivism and postpositivism, and, again, apply them to all forms of knowledge claims from whatever research strategies.

The difficulty with the foundational solution to evaluating research strategies is that the criteria inevitably favor those research strategies that are consistent with the assumptions that generate such criteria.[12] "It is simply inadequate to attempt to justify a particular style of research in terms of assumptions that give rise to that style of research."[12(p15)] In other words, evaluation of the validity or contribution of different research strategies in terms of the ground assumptions of any one set, or a singular synthesized set, of those strategies is a self-justifying process.[12] The foundational solution hinders the development of research strategies aimed at producing different forms of knowledge and impedes the recognition and exploration of a full range of choices concerning methodology open to the researcher.[12]

The difficulty inherent in finding a foundational solution to evaluating research strategies is one of relativism. More explicit, because it is not possible to find an independent set of criteria to evaluate research strategies in an absolute sense, all evaluative efforts encounter a relativism. Relativism implies that one research strategy may be more effective for a specific purpose than for another.[12] Thus Morgan advocates an evaluative stance that reframes the traditional view of knowledge as foundational, which can be evaluated in an absolute way. The reframing involves dealing with relativism as an inevitable feature of the process through which knowledge is

generated.[12] In reframing our view of knowledge, evaluation of research strategies is not a quest for absolute judgment, but a concern with exploring and understanding the significance of research strategies.

The thrust of this chapter is to explicate the approach to analyzing and evaluating research strategies advocated by Morgan[12] that goes beyond a foundational solution. Such an approach has relevance for dealing with the current methodological diversity and uncertainty in nursing science today. Morgan's[12] approach is twofold, involving analysis of research strategies as modes of engagement and evaluation as a reflective explorational and conversational process.

RESEARCH STRATEGIES AS MODES OF ENGAGEMENT

The view of research strategies as modes of engagement encompasses the notion that method is part of a wider process that involves a perspective of the situation being studied. Methodology is selected or favored because of implicit or explicit assumptions about what we are trying to do in our research. Research as engagement stresses the importance of understanding the network of assumptions and practices that link the researcher to the phenomenon being investigated.[12]

The mode of engagement reflects a logic or strategy of research that is embodied in these assumptions and practices. Instead of focusing on the merits of different kinds of methodology, the researcher considers the significance and merits of different logics of research when analyzing research strategies. The choice is not one of method alone, but involves choice between modes of engagement entailing varying relationships between theory and method, concept and object, and researcher and researched.[12]

Morgan[12] argues that the logic of different research strategies can be decoded through systematic analysis of the modes of engagement. He has provided a framework for doing this for social science that has been modestly adapted for nursing science (Table 6–1).[12(p21)] The framework focuses attention on the way ontological and epistemological premises favor distinctive research practices. Components of the framework include the constitutive assumptions embodied in a basic paradigm, the epistemological stance expressed in the form of metaphors, and the favored methodology that functions as a puzzle-solving device for bridging the researcher's image of a phenomenon and the phenomenon itself.

Constitutive assumptions form a foundation of inquiry reflecting a view of the world embedded in an ontological perspective, inclining the researcher to see and interpret the world in a selective way, and providing rationale for chosen research strategies.[12] From these constitutive assumptions, a basic paradigm can be identified. Morgan[14] defines paradigm based on Kuhn's[15] use of the term specifically as "alternative realities." Paradigm is used in "its

Table 6–1 Analytic Framework for Research Strategy

Focus	*Framework for Analysis*
Constitutive Assumptions (paradigms)	Rationale for particular research strategy grounded in assumptions (explicit or implicit) concerning ontology and human nature that define researcher's world view. Provide foundations of research practice inclining researcher to see and interpret the world and nursing from a particular perspective. By identifying researcher's assumptions, we can identify the basic paradigm that serves as foundation of inquiry.
Epistemological Stance (metaphors)	Scientific knowledge shaped by the way researchers attempt to concretize ground assumptions that underwrite work. Images of a nursing phenomenon, usually expressed in terms of favored metaphors, provide means of structuring inquiry, guiding attention in distinctive ways. Image favors a particular epistemological stance (certain kinds of insight understanding and explanation more appropriate than others). Different ground assumptions expressed in images give rise to different grounds for knowledge about nursing.
Favored Methodology (puzzle solving)	The image of a phenomenon to be investigated provides the basis for detailed scientific research concerned to examine, and perhaps operationalize and measure, the extent to which detailed aspects of the image characterize the phenomenon. Image generates specific concepts and methods of study through which knowledge of the phenomenon can be obtained. Methodologies are the puzzle-solving devices that bridge the gap between the image of a phenomenon and the phenomenon itself. Methodologies link the researcher to the situation being studied in terms of rules, procedures, and general protocol that operationalize the network of assumptions embodied in the researcher's paradigm and favored epistemological stance.

The logic of a research strategy is embedded in links between all above factors.

Source: Adapted from *Beyond Method: Strategies for Social Research* (p 21) by G Morgan with permission of Sage Publications, Inc, © 1983.

meta-theoretical or philosophical sense to denote an implicit or explicit view of reality."[14(pp606–607)]

Included within paradigms are various schools of thought that are composed of theorists who subscribe to relatively coherent perspectives. Within schools of thought, there is acceptance and use of different kinds of metaphor that serve as a foundation of inquiry.[14] Research strategies are used to operationalize the detailed implications of the metaphor defining a

particular school of thought and are evidenced in many specific texts, models, and research tools.

In organizational theory, the predominant metaphors are machine and organism.[14] In physics, Jones[16] has identified space and time metaphors as significant to the field of inquiry. Health and development metaphors seem to predominate the discipline of nursing. Awareness of how specified puzzle-solving activities are linked to these metaphors congruent with a view of reality helps the theorist to appreciate his or her role in relation to the social construction of scientific knowledge.[14]

Research as modes of engagement places particular emphasis on metaphors as a tool for analysis. Morgan[12] argues for analysis of the logics of different research strategies as embedded in assumptions and epistemological stance and the linkage between them. The decoding of the logic proceeds from an identification of the favored metaphors.

Metaphors make the world concrete by symbolically giving it form, enabling the person to structure the world in meaningful ways.[17,18] This view assumes that humans attempt to objectify the world by subjective processes, rather than to receive, uninvolved, an objective world through external events. Words, names, concepts, ideas, facts, observations are not merely external "things." They reflect conceptions derived from a selective and meaningful form of noticing the world. "The scientist on this score, like others in everyday life, draws upon symbolic constructs to make concrete the relationships between subjective and objective worlds, which captures only a pale and abbreviated view of either."[14(p610)]

Metaphorical thinking is viewed as a basic way of symbolizing used to forge knowledge and experience. Metaphor produces its effect through a crossing of images, often transferring meaning from one situation to another. Metaphor embodies processes of comparison, substitution, and interaction between images, leading to new meaning.[19]

According to Morgan,[14] the scientist's world view is essentially metaphorical and expressed in language and concepts that serve as a filter and structure for perceptions about the subject of study. The world view of the scientist is also expressed in the metaphors that are implicitly or explicitly chosen to develop a framework for understanding phenomena of interest.

The metaphor generates an image of a phenomenon as well as an image for studying a subject.[12,14] The basis for detailed scientific research is in attempts to discover the extent to which features of the metaphor are found in the subject of inquiry. Methodologies are chosen to examine, and perhaps operationalize and measure, detailed implications of the metaphorical insight. Morgan[14] points out that any one metaphorical insight provides only a partial and one-sided view of the phenomenon to which it is applied. Thus perhaps any selected research approach may be limited as well in its ability to capture

the phenomenon. However, the possibility may exist for multiple metaphorical insights that complement the fuller study of a phenomenon.

A broadening of perspective and flexibility of approach to research is brought about by an appreciation of the metaphorical status of scientific theorizing. Greater attention is warranted toward the links between theory and method, and the range of methodological approaches for investigating different metaphorical standpoints.[20]

Example of Modes of Engagement Analysis, with Emphasis on Metaphorical Content

In Morgan's[12] book *Beyond Method: Strategies for Social Research,* 21 research strategies are analyzed in detail by proponents of these strategies using the modes of engagement framework. The example of quasi-experimentation presented by Cook[21] is offered here to demonstrate the modes of engagement framework because it is a common strategy used in nursing research. Particular emphasis is placed on metaphorical content to clarify the role of metaphors in the epistemological stance of this strategy.

In describing the ontology of quasi-experimentation, Cook[21] deals primarily with the assumptions related to causality and human cognition and motivation. Examination of the ontological statements concerning causality reveals a major constitutive assumption that the "real world of causal agency" is made up of large systems, with subsystems or parts, and that these systems are complexly interdependent. This ontology is evident in the use of such statements as "It seeks only to discover those parts of the real world in which causal relations exist and in which manipulating one thing predictably causes another to change,[21(p79)] and such phrases as "total set of contextual dependencies,"[21(p79)] "complexly interdependent systems,"[21(p79)] and "nature's dependable causal levers"[21(p80)] to describe nature and reality. In addition, the existence of phenomena termed "micromediating processes" is a central assumption of the nature of causal agency in the real world. This is the assumption that a process occurs between the time when a variable has varied and the time when more distal outcomes of interest have been observed.

Other key assumptions evident are (a) there is an internal and external world; (b) "the external world is probabilistically ordered in its essence";[(p80)] and (c) there is a real world of nature (which is the concern of quasi-experimentalists) and an artificial world of the laboratory (which is the concern of experimentalists).[21]

In terms of cognition and motivation, these constructs of social behavior are viewed as major in social sciences.[21] Cognition and motivation are manifested in the form of intentions, meanings, understandings, preferences, and desires. Cook[21] asserts, however, that what is unclear is how cognitions

and motives are "real" parts of the external world rather than invented construction.

The epistemology of quasi-experimentation encompasses three broad areas: (1) objectivity, (2) verification and falsification, and (3) being public and critical. The epistemological stance is difficult to summarize briefly, but the major tenets are presented. Objectivity represents "intersubjective verifiability across heterogeneous perspectives."[21(p82)] Theory neutral measurement is impossible because "observations are impregnated not with a single theory, but with multiple theories."[(p83)] Reliability (based on critically explicating and minimizing or equalizing biases) and multiple operationalism (incorporation into the test of a variable all alternative interpretations of a measure or set of measures) are central aspects of attaining objectivity.[21]

Specifically, the role of verification and falsification are used to *probe*, rather than to *prove*, causal relationships. Verification and falsification involve verifying that the data conform to a particular causal hypothesis and falsifying "all identified interpretations of the data pattern other than the one that is provisionally preferred."[21(p85)]

The importance of being public and critical rests on the epistemological idea of inevitable infallibility of knowledge of the external world."[21(p89)] Further, public exposure represents for Cook[21] a form of critical falsification because it can suggest limitations of the work not available from self-criticism alone.

In terms of favored methodology, three mechanisms are advocated to achieve the aims of research.[21] The first is an experimental design that will rule out threats to internal validity. The second method is measurement, often coupled with statistical analysis, to also rule out threats. And the final method is termed by Cook[21] "critical common sense," which is "one of the means whereby *possible* alternatives are assigned approximate *plausibility* value"[(p92)] in interpreting findings.

To summarize, quasi-experimentation, according to Cook,[21] is "probablist-realist in a fallibist model"[(p83)] and concerns itself with "knowledge about structural factors in society or persons that cannot be readily changed."[(p93)] Cook also describes it as "largely an OXO framework in search of valid causal inference."[(p93)] The logic of quasi-experimentation can best be ascertained by an examination of linkages between constitutive assumption (ontology), epistemological stance, and favored methodology. The assumption of causal connectedness between parts of a system is the major ontological theme. The epistemology of quasi-experimentation offers a foundation for applying methods. For example, because knowledge is gained through falsification, experimental designs can be implemented to falsify interpretations of data that are not causally connected. There is congruence between ontology, epistemology, and methodology.

The obvious metaphorical content in the quasi-experimentalist approach deals with the ontological nature of causality and the epistemology of objectivity and falsification and verification. Cook[21] refers to Cronbach's idea of "causal forces" existing in "systematic configurations" and McGuire's reference to a "pretzel-shaped reality." But even without these metaphorical references provided by others, the repeated references to causality as a "force" or a "lever" are obvious metaphorical referents in Cook's own writings about quasi-experimentation. Repeatedly, there is reference to quasi-experimentation as a "probe" of causality. Contextual dependencies and micromediating processes add to the image of the nature of reality described metaphorically. The mental image of the quasi-experimentation as a "probe" into vast complexity of reality conveys the notion that, at best, part of reality can be tapped but not all of it. Like a needle probing for samples of blood, quasi-experimentation taps a sample of reality. This also helps to explain why one quasi-experiment is insufficient in the total picture of verification and falsification.[21] Other metaphors that were recurrent in the epistemological stance[21] provide keys to how scientific inquiry should be structured to attain insight, understanding, and explanation. Some are phrases and some are single words. Examples are observations impregnated with theories; intersubjective reliability; triangulation, pattern; and threats. Although these can be viewed as mere phrases or words with specific definitions, the implication of assessing them as metaphors opens a wider window on the researcher's ontological perspective and can serve to clarify the intent of favored methodology.

REFLECTIVE EXPLORATION AND CONVERSATION

The modes of engagement model of research strategies provides a foundation for analysis of the methodologies that extends beyond method alone. It provides the substance for analysis through metaphorical language but does not include criteria for evaluation and selection of methods. A process of reflective exploration and conversation to accomplish evaluation requires, as stated earlier, a reframing of our view of knowledge. Morgan's[12] approach is particularly useful because it accommodates the diversity inherent in social science as well as nursing science.

The fundamental problem in establishing criteria for evaluating the significance of different approaches to research is recognized; "it is not possible to determine the validity or contribution of different research strategies in any absolute sense in terms of evaluative stances that draw on the same assumptions as do any of the research strategies examined."[12(p370)] Examples of attempts to evaluate research based on foundational criteria include (a) the positivist's claim that knowledge must be grounded in "empirical data" because the world is ultimately an objective reality, as well

as (b) the phenomenologist's claim that subjective reality is central because the locus of reality is in the knowing subject.[12] Given this major difficulty, and not desiring to adopt a foundational claim, the search for evaluative criteria rests on relativism. In a positive sense, evaluation should be aimed at the possibilities that relativism signifies.[12] As noted earlier, relativism applied to the research enterprise means that one research strategy may be more effective for a specific purpose than another and cannot be evaluated in an absolute, foundational way. Further, relativism brings with it the requirement of reflection as central to evaluating a research strategy, that is, reflecting on its nature, its possibilities, and its consequences. The process for accomplishing this reflection involves exploration and conversation by the researcher that lead to greater understanding.[12]

The terms reflective exploration and reflective conversation are metaphors for framing an approach to research inquiry that facilitate reflective understanding and action. The emphasis on critical reflection is aimed at helping researchers to orient action in a context of the relations in which such action is set, consequences of that action, and of alternative actions.[12] The shift is away from seeing the researcher as a technical functionary in pursuit of a prespecified form of knowledge toward seeing him or her as a reflecting actionary choosing appropriate paths of action, considering the nature and consequences of such actions in a much larger context.[12]

Morgan[12] implies that reflective exploration naturally leads to reflective conversation in multiple ways. First, the research process represents a form of social interaction with the phenomenon being studied that may involve new insights about appropriate research strategies. Second, different research strategies can be viewed as different "voices" about the nature and status of knowledge. Third, researchers can collectively engage in reflective conversation about the nature and claims with deliberate attempts to minimize commitment to a favored point of view. This is crucially needed in nursing today for the same reasons that Morgan[12] has advocated it for social science, "to explore diversity as fully and critically as possible without prejudging the issues involved."[(p375)]

Reflective exploration and conversation can take various turns, leading at different times to synthesis, compromise, consensus, transformation, polarization, or simply clarification and improved understanding of differences.[12] The emphasis must be on open exchange with regard to different points of view concerning research, with the goal of edifying dialogue. Conversation among participants should facilitate exploration rather than constrain it. This requires that participants take a somewhat detached stance in regard to their usual presuppositions, giving attention to "the nature and implications of what they and others do in their research and the consequences of the knowledge they generate."[12(p375)]

Conversation can begin anywhere and explore many themes according to the structure imposed by participants.[12] Morgan points out that the conversation will prove edifying as long as participants feel a sense of genuine involvement in the issues under exploration and use the conversation to reflect on the views they hold and to act on any significant conclusions that are generated.[12] The component areas of the modes of engagement analysis presented earlier can serve as the content for conversation. Of particular significance are the nature and consequences of the assumptions that frame different modes of inquiry.[12]

Reflection on one's favored research strategy in relation to other research strategies leads to greater clarity about the nature, strengths, and limitations of the favored strategy. A means of developing and refining research strategies becomes possible.[12] Such an approach encourages "an attitude and activity that is sensitive to the merits of diversity."[12(p381)]

Moving away from the assumption that research is aimed at generating a foundational knowledge obliges us to recognize that research is more than a technical process. It also suggests the inappropriateness of taking a stand for or against methodology without consideration of underlying constitutive assumptions and logic. It becomes possible to recognize many meaningful ways of evaluating claims and consequences of knowledge gained from research. Our view of knowledge may be broadened to include knowledge to explain empirical facts, to help us understand meanings, to allow us to act more appropriately, to empower in a liberating way, and to reveal links between everyday reality and the structural logic that produces and reproduces that reality.[12] Most important, it forces us to acknowledge the human consequences of research worth considering in selection of research strategies.

IMPLICATIONS FOR NURSING SCIENCE

The recent upheaval among nursing scientists about what should be accepted as valid methodological approaches to the study of phenomena of concern to nursing has spawned a great deal of scholarly dialogue but limited resolution to foundational criteria for selection of research strategies.[1–9] The preceding approach to the analysis and evaluation of research strategies was presented to offer a deliberative way of increasing dialogue among nursing scientists and is, of course, open to criticism. Allen[5] has noted the omission in the literature of any detailed discussion of criteria that might be used in adopting a view of science. Even more clearly, the entrenchment of researchers into camps and the absence of sharing perspectives on common phenomena of interest impede the advancement of nursing science.

A major implication of the approach to analysis and evaluation of research strategies in nursing is a detailed attention to the constitutive assumptions

that underwrite the logic of them. Inherent is an expanded awareness of the logic for research strategies rather than merely a more basic understanding of the techniques of doing or applying strategies. Learning about and choosing research strategies will become a different process with this shift in emphasis, requiring that we become more sophisticated in the analysis of ontological and epistemological perspectives.

Another important implication is the potential for moving beyond some of the more fundamental debates about theoretical structures in nursing and whether or not nursing has a paradigm. This can be accomplished by the attention to metaphor advocated by Morgan.[12,14] Metaphors may be a crucial link into the theoretical structures that are embodied in research and will enable us to critique more specifically the appropriateness of such structures for the purposes of nursing science. In addition, metaphors may provide a substantive foundation for analyzing the historical inclinations of nursing research. These processes can begin in nursing only when we first identify the metaphors that dominate our fields of inquiry. Revealing metaphors could occur through analysis of research in the field of nursing.

Although individual aspects of the modes of engagement model have significant implications, the model itself has far-reaching implications for nursing science. Using such a model enables us to attend to the research strategy through its constitutive assumptions and metaphors rather than having to begin with the application of external criteria. In other words, the model offers a framework for knowing the research strategy and its logic in detail before we apply evaluative criteria. It is hoped that such a process could be more broadly integrated into decision making concerning nursing research, both in education and in practice.

The call for reflective exploration and conversation about research that is inherent in Morgan's[12] approach shifts the emphasis for methodological considerations in nursing science to one of significance, based on consequences rather than on absolute judgment of merits. As Morgan[12] notes, this implies that responsibility for the conduct and consequences of research falls directly on the researcher. But reflective exploration and conversation can be an exemplar for doing and teaching research in nursing as a collective issue for consideration by nursing scholars. Whether or not an individual or a collective issue, the emphasis on the significance and consequences of our research strategies forces us to face equally such crucial questions as, "What will be considered significant scientific inquiry in nursing? How will we deal with the significance of knowledge, not only epistemologically, but also ideologically, politically, ethically, and morally?"

SUMMARY

If nursing scientists are to call for multiple modes of inquiry to accommodate the evolution of a scientific knowledge base for nursing, we need to attend to the analysis and evaluation of them is some systematic way. The approach offered by Morgan[12] provides a framework for analysis and evaluation that does not succumb to the temptation of an evaluative perspective based on foundational claims of knowledge. It also addresses what is so sorely needed in nursing science today—reflective conversation—not to create uniformity so much as to promote improved diversity.

REFERENCES

1. Munhall PL: Nursing philosophy and nursing research: In apposition or opposition? *Nurs Res* 1982;312(3):176-177, 181.

2. Tinkle MB, Beaton JL: Toward a new view of science: Implications for nursing research. *Adv Nurs Sci* 1983;5(2):27-36.

3. Newman MA: Editorial. *Adv Nurs Sci* 1983;5(2):x-xi.

4. Newman MA: *Theory Development in Nursing.* Philadelphia, FA Davis, 1979.

5. Allen DG: Nursing research and social control: Alternative models of science that emphasize understanding and emancipation. *Image* Spring 1985;17(2):58-64.

6. Chinn PL: Debunking myths in nursing theory and research. *Image* Spring 1985;17(2):45-49.

7. Fawcett J: Hallmarks of success in nursing research. *Adv Nurs Sci* 1984;7(1):1-11.

8. Silva MC, Rothbart D: An analysis of changing trends in philosophies of science on nursing theory development and testing. *Adv Nurs Sci* 1984;6(2):1-13.

9. Smith MC: Research methodology: Epistemological considerations. *Image* 1984;16(2):42-46.

10. Polit DF, Hungler BF: *Nursing Research: Principles and Methods,* ed 2. Philadelphia, JB Lippincott, 1983.

11. Kerlinger FN: *Foundations of Behavioral Research,* ed 2. New York, Holt, Rinehart, & Winston, 1973.

12. Morgan G: *Beyond Method: Strategies for Social Research.* Beverly Hills, Calif, Sage, 1983.

13. Lincoln YS, Guba ED: *Naturalistic Inquiry.* Beverly Hills, Calif, Sage, 1985.

14. Morgan G: Paradigms, metaphors and puzzle solving in organization theory. *Adm Sci Q* 1980;25:605-622.

15. Kuhn TS: *The Structure of Scientific Revolutions.* Chicago, University of Chicago Press, 1962.

16. Jones RS: *Physics as Metaphor.* New York, New American Library, 1982.

17. Cassirer E: *Language and Myth.* New York, Dover, 1946.

18. Cassirer E: *The Philosophy of Symbolic Forms.* New Haven, Conn, Yale University Press, vols 1-3, 1955.

19. Black M: *Models and Metaphors.* Ithaca, NY, Cornell University Press, 1962.

20. Morgan G, Smircich L: The case for qualitative research. *Acad Mgmt Rev* 1980;5:491-500.

21. Cook TD: Quasi-experimentation: Its ontology, epistemology, and methodology, in Morgan G (ed): *Beyond Method: Strategies for Social Research.* Beverly Hills, Sage, 1983, pp 74-94.

Chapter 7

Measurement of Research Variables in Nursing

Ora L. Strickland and Carolyn F. Waltz

The development and use of sound measurement tools and practices in nursing research studies are germane to the further development and advancement of nursing knowledge. Yet measurement has not been given the attention it warrants in nursing. How well and how effectively variables are measured within a study are directly related to its internal validity. If the approach to the measurement of a variable is not clearly developed, evolved systematically, and followed closely, then the variables will not be measured precisely. This results in larger amounts of error being introduced into the measurement process than when a more systematic approach is used.[1] The processes for measuring research variables specify the rules used to assign numbers to represent the amount or kind of specified attributes under study[2,3] and are a central requisite when assessing the validity of findings. Internal validity is indeed the basic minimum without which any research study is uninterpretable and the results made questionable.[4]

In an analysis of research journal articles published between January 1980 and September 1981 that focused on the investigation of clinical or educational outcomes of nursing practice, Waltz and Strickland[5] found the state of the art for measurement of nursing outcomes to be somewhat disappointing. They noted a number of violations in the use of sound measurement principles and practices, a heavy reliance on paper-and-pencil tests and self-report measures, and a general lack of clarity and specificity regarding measurement approaches used. This chapter builds on and updates the earlier work and presents some findings of an analysis of tools and devices used to measure nursing research variables in articles published during 1984 in three major nursing research journals. In doing so, it focuses on (a) the characteristics of tools or devices used for the measurement of nursing

---

Note: This information was presented at the International Council of Nurses 18th Quadrennial Congress, Tel Aviv, Israel, June 1985.

research variables and (b) the application of measurement principles and practices in nursing as reflected in the selected journal articles.

PROCEDURE

In order to assess instruments used for measuring nursing variables, 1984 research articles from three nursing research journals that were most cited by core nursing journals from 1981 to 1983[6] were selected for content analysis. It was the view of the authors that since articles published in these journals were cited most often and were subjected to peer review, their contents serve as a barometer of what nurses are doing in the area of measurement, as well as what is believed to be important for sharing through journal articles regarding the measurement properties of tools with other members of the profession. Those articles that provided original quantitative or qualitative research findings and that described research procedures and instrumentation within the text of the article were included. Research reviews and theoretical papers that were not presented as original research investigations were not included in the analysis. A total of 99 articles were reviewed, with 54 (54.5%) from *Nursing Research*, 16 (16.2%) from the *International Journal of Nursing Studies*, and 29 (29.3%) from *Research in Nursing and Health*. The articles represented a wide variety of research studies, which were categorized based on criteria adapted from Gortner, Bloch, and Phillips[7] and Bloch.[8] Table 7–1 presents the categorization of the articles according to the primary focus of each as well as the frequency of each category. The one article in the "other" category was on a health education program for firefighters. A total of 215 variables and 238 tools or measures were assessed.

The researchers developed a content analysis form designed to (a) specify characteristics of published nursing research studies that used measurement tools, (b) delineate the reported application of measurement principles and practices, (c) identify research variables studied, and (d) identify the characteristics and metric properties of measurement tools based on information provided by the articles reviewed. Items on the content analysis form and criteria for assessment of articles were generated based on content, principles, and practices propagated by measurement textbooks.[2,3,9–11] The content analysis form was submitted to two doctorally prepared content specialists who had preparation and experience in measurement and nursing research. A content validity index of 1.00 was obtained, which indicated perfect agreement by these experts that the items on the tool adequately sampled the specified domain. The interrater reliability of the tool was assessed by random selection of five articles for content analysis by two raters. An interrater reliability of 0.92 resulted, which was determined by the percentage of agreement between raters. The content analysis form generates descriptive

data. Therefore, findings are reported in terms of frequencies and percentages.

FINDINGS

Of the 215 variables measured in the 99 studies, 85.1% were measured with one tool; 9.3% were assessed by two tools. As can be seen in Table 7–2, up to six tools were used to measure a variable. Hence the majority of variables were measured by only one device. In those studies in which more than one tool was used to measure a particular variable, this most often was done to measure different dimensions of a global variable. For example, the variable health status might be operationalized to include psychological and physical dimensions, which would require the use of several tools for its assessment.

Each variable was assessed in regard to whether multiple indicators were used within a tool or measuring process. This is an important consideration because one-item measures or measurements based on a single observation do not usually sample a content domain adequately and are more amenable to measurement error. Hence the reliability and validity of the results could be drastically reduced. It was disappointing to note that 30.2% of the 215 variables were not measured using multiple indicators.

The conceptual framework of a measuring tool or device communicates the meaning and properties of the concept or variable that the tool measures. Researchers need to ensure that the conceptual basis, or the meaning of the

Table 7–1 Primary Focus of Articles

Category	*Frequency (%)*
Applied clinical or nursing practice	25 (25.3)
Fundamental	42 (42.4)
Nursing education	11 (11.1)
Nursing services delivery	8 (8.1)
Research on the profession of nursing	2 (2.0)
Development of research methods or tools	10 (10.1)
Other	1 (1.0)
Total	99 (100.0)

Table 7–2 Frequency of Tool Usage in Measurement of Variables

No. of Tools Used	*No. of Variables Measured (%)*
1	183 (85.1)
2	20 (9.3)
3	5 (2.3)
4	5 (2.3)
5	1 (0.5)
6	1 (0.5)
Total	215 (100.0)

concept measured by each tool they use in a study, is consistent with their intended meaning as well as with the overall theoretical framework for the study. For example, if attachment is conceptualized within a study as "feelings of an emotional tie or bond to another individual," then it is most appropriately assessed by obtaining information about one's reported feelings for another during measurement. If one were to limit its measurement to the observation of attachment behaviors, then the measurement of the concept would not be in concert with its conceptualization in the study. The analysis of the 238 tools assessed indicated that specific conceptual frameworks were identified for only 48 (20.2%) of the measures within the context of the 99 research articles. When the fit or congruence of the tool's conceptual framework or purpose was considered in relation to the conceptual framework of the study, 4.6% were clearly inconsistent. In 39.5% of the cases, it was not possible to determine the consistency between a tool's conceptual framework or purpose and the conceptual or theoretical basis of the study because of inadequate information. For 55.9% of the tools, consistency between the conceptual basis of the tools and that of the study was apparent.

The measurement framework of a tool guides not only its design, but also the interpretation and use of the scores generated by the tool. The norm-referenced approach is used when the interest is in assessing the performance or attributes of a subject relative to that of other subjects in some well-defined comparison group. On the other hand, criterion-referenced measures are used to determine a subject's status, usually with respect to some predetermined criterion or performance standard.[3] Based on the description of tools provided in the articles reviewed, the content analyzers were unable to determine the measurement framework of 57.6% of the tools; 22.3% were norm-referenced; 12.6% were

Table 7–3 Types of Measure

	Frequency of Use (%)
Achievement/Cognitive	12 (5.0)
Attitudinal/Perceptual	123 (51.7)
Behavioral/Performance	27 (11.3)
Physiological	47 (19.7)
Record review	23 (9.7)
Combination	4 (1.7)
Other	2 (0.9)
Total	238 (100.0)

criterion-referenced; 4.2% used a combination of the two frameworks; and for 3.4%, specification of the measurement framework was not applicable.

When the developer of the tool or device was considered, it was found that the majority of tools used in the studies were existing nonnursing tools, with 52.9% in this category. A total of 8.8% were existing nursing measures, and 37.0% were developed by the investigators for use in the study. Modifications that either combined or altered existing tools were reported for 1.3%. Most of the tools measured attitudinal or perceptual variables, with 51.7% in this category. Percentages for other categories are shown in Table 7–3.

The approaches used to obtain data for each tool were considered, and these are shown in Table 7–4. Because so many of the tools relied on self-

Table 7–4 Approaches Used To Obtain Data

	Frequency of Use (%)
Direct observation	33 (13.9)
Indirect observation	5 (2.1)
Self-report	135 (56.7)
Content analysis	26 (10.9)
Objective instrumentation	55 (23.1)

Note: Some tools used more than one approach. Indirect observation included the use of tape recordings and video cassettes. Objective instrumentation included the use of heart rate and blood pressure monitors and objective tests.

Table 7–5 Format of Tool or Device

	Frequency of Use (%)
Anecdotal record or critical incidents	1 (0.4)
Checklist	15 (6.3)
Chemical measure	1 (0.4)
Criterion-based categories	46 (19.3)
Essay	2 (0.8)
Interview—face to face	32 (13.4)
Interview—telephone	2 (0.8)
Microbiological measure	0 (0.0)
Multiple choice	11 (4.6)
Physical measure	48 (20.2)
Projective measure	0 (0.0)
Questionnaire	79 (33.2)
Q-sort	1 (0.4)
Rating scale	73 (30.7)
Review of documents	24 (10.1)
Semantic differential	3 (1.3)
Short answer	13 (5.5)
Survey	14 (5.9)
True/False	5 (2.1)
Vignettes	15 (6.3)

Note: Some tools used more than one type of format.

report for obtaining data, it is not surprising that the most frequently used format for tools was the questionnaire (33.2%), followed by rating scales (30.7%). Physical measures were characteristic of 20.2%. Low frequency of use was noted for other biological measures, such as chemical measures (0.4%) and microbiological measures (0%). Criterion-based categories were

used as a format for 19.3%, and review of existing documents were used by 10.1%. As can be seen in Table 7–5, a variety of other formats also were used.

Reliability and validity are essential characteristics of any measuring device or method and determine the degree of confidence that one can place in measurements. The metric properties of measures should be assessed each time they are used to determine whether they are functioning as intended. The types of reliability and validity data of tools reported in the selected research articles were noted, as well as the sources of these data. In this study, reliability and validity data were considered to be included when a notation about the type of procedure was reported along with the results or an index. Some authors only mentioned that other researchers had previously assessed the reliability and validity of tools without giving any further information. Such data was not considered reliability and validity evidence in this study.

The reliability of a measuring device refers to the consistency with which it assigns scores to the attribute of interest. Approaches to the estimation of reliability were designed to answer the question "What is the self-correlation of the measuring device or method?"[11(p373)] No reliability data were presented for 58.4% of the measures. The most frequent types of reliability assessed were test-retest (15.1%), internal consistency reliability (15.1%), and interrater reliability (13.9%). Table 7–6 presents a summary of the types and frequency of reliability data reported.

Few articles included reliability data for tools within the context of the current study. As indicated in Table 7–7, only 20.6% of the tools had data provided that reflected its reliability within the current study. Sixteen percent reported reliability data from previous studies, and only 1.7% supplied information regarding reliability from both the current study and previous studies.

Validity also is an important consideration when using a measuring device. It has to do with the question of whether the scores or results obtained actually measure what they are intended to measure. As noted in Table 7–8, the majority, or 58.0%, of tools did not have validity data reported. The type of validity most often reported was criterion-related validity, with this type of validity provided for 22.3% of the measures.

Table 7–9 presents the sources of validity data for the measures used. When validity data were provided, they were more often reported for the current study in the form of content validity. Only 2.1% of the tools had validity data provided for both the current study and previous studies.

In many instances, it was noted that reliability and validity information was not considered concurrently for a measure. Because reliability is a necessary but not sufficient condition for validity of a tool, this reflects some researchers' lack of sensitivity to this fundamental measurement principle. In a few instances, authors inappropriately labeled reliability and validity procedures and cited evidence for the reliability and validity of tools that was not appropriate.

Table 7–6 Reliability Data Provided

Type	*Frequency (%)*
None	139 (58.4)
Test-retest	36 (15.1)
Internal consistency	36 (15.1)
Parallel forms	2 (0.8)
Split half	8 (3.4)
Interrater	33 (13.9)
Intrarater	2 (0.8)
Instrument calibration	6 (2.5)
Item analysis	3 (1.3)
Other	2 (0.8)

Note: More than one type of reliability data was reported for some tools.

Table 7–7 Reliability Data Sources

	Frequency (%)
Current study	49 (20.6)
Previous studies	38 (16.0)
Both	8 (3.4)
Unable to determine	4 (1.7)
Reliability data not provided	139 (58.4)
Total	238 (100.1)

Note: The percentage total of 100.1 reflects rounding of percentages to the nearest 10th.

DISCUSSION

Given the data obtained from the nursing research articles reviewed, several implications are evident. First, nurses have not given adequate

Table 7–8 Validity Data Provided

Type	*Frequency (%)*
None	138 (58.0)
Face validity	13 (5.5)
Content validity	32 (13.4)
Construct validity	34 (14.3)
□ Contrasting groups	15 (6.3)
□ Hypothesis testing	5 (2.1)
□ Multitrait/multimethod	2 (0.8)
□ Factor analysis	12 (5.0)
Criterion-related validity	53 (22.3)
□ Concurrent	43 (18.1)
□ Predictive	10 (4.2)
Other	5 (2.1)

Note: More than one type of validity data were reported for some tools.

Table 7–9 Validity Data Sources

	Frequency (%)
Current study	51 (21.4)
Previous study	40 (16.8)
Both	5 (2.1)
Unable to determine	4 (1.7)
Not provided	138 (58.0)
Total	238 (100.0)

attention to the application of basic recommended measurement principles and practices in the journal publications of their research. When the results of this study are considered in relation to those present earlier by Waltz and Strickland,[5] no improvement in the application of measurement principles

and practices is evident. Almost one third of the researchers relied on one-item tools or single indicators to assess research variables. Because single indicators cannot be expected to adequately sample the conceptual domain of a concept, they allow for the introduction of more measurement error into scores. This has important implications for the advancement of nursing knowledge, since the validity of the study results are called into question.

Only about one fifth of the tools had specific conceptual frameworks identified, and a relatively large proportion did not have their purposes or conceptual frameworks described well enough within the context of the article for a fair assessment to be made regarding the compatibility of the tool with the study's conceptual framework. However, almost 5% of the tools clearly were not consistent with their study's conceptual framework and did not measure the concept in a manner consistent with that which was intended. This raises a question regarding the type of description that should be provided about the conceptual basis of a tool within the context of a published research journal article. Enough information should be given so that an opinion can be derived regarding the tool's usefulness for addressing the study's research questions or hypotheses. The fact that some tools were found to be incompatible with their study's conceptual framework highlights the need for an adequate description of a tool's purposes and conceptual basis within an article so that a fair assessment can be made by the reader regarding the appropriateness of the tool(s) used and whether an appropriate link between conceptualization and research methods exists.

Because the measurement framework of a tool indicates how its scores should be interpreted, it is important that the measurement framework of each tool be communicated. For more than half of the tools there was not enough information provided to determine whether they were norm-referenced or criterion-referenced. An awareness of the measurement framework of the tool often is needed to determine the appropriateness of statistical methods used for data analysis as well as for interpreting results. More clarity about the measurement framework of tools used within a study would enhance the reader's ability to make assessments about study results.

In most cases, reliability and validity data were not reported, either concurrently or within the context of the research presented. This indicates that nurse researchers are not adequately attuned to the need to rigorously assess measures used to operationalize variables. The citing of inappropriate evidence for reliability and validity indicates the need for nurses to increase their knowledge on the topic. Rigor in the assessment of metric properties of measuring tools and methods, and the selection and use of tools with evidence of good reliability and validity will allow for the placement of a higher level of confidence in the findings and interpretations drawn from nursing studies.

A second major implication of the findings is that efforts need to be made to generate and share more nursing measurement tools. A relatively small

percentage of existing nursing tools were used in the articles reviewed in comparison to tools developed specifically for the studies surveyed and existing nonnursing measures. This signifies a need not only for further development and use of existing nursing measures, but also for the continued development, modification, testing, and dissemination of new nursing measuring tools that address concepts from the nursing perspective. As noted by Waltz and Strickland:

> If nurses make a concerted effort to share resources by selecting, further modifying, and testing existing measures rather than constructing their own, and/or pooling resources to simultaneously develop and test a measure or set of measures in a variety of settings with varied and different populations, much progress can be made in this area.[5(p59)]

Another important point that the results of this study emphasize is that nurses continue to rely heavily on using only one tool or approach to measure a variable on attitudinal or perceptual measures and on self-report measures. Although attitudinal or perceptual measures are important in nursing, the relatively low incidence of use of other types of measures, such as behavioral or performance measures, record review, and physiological measures, results in a limitation in the scope of nursing research studies and findings and may reflect a narrow perspective about the type of measures that are useful for building nursing knowledge. It also is possible that the time and expense associated with developing and using other types of measures, eg, observational and physiological measures, are deterrents to their use. The frequent use of a single approach to measurement within the context of nursing studies reflects a reluctance by nurse researchers to actively integrate and apply nursing's broad scientific base within research studies. As suggested by Waltz and Strickland,[5] because nursing is a biopsychosocial science, nursing research problems need to be studied from this broad perspective through the simultaneous use of various types of measures that assess physiological, psychological, and social variables. Studies that focus only on one or two variables or use a single approach to the measurement of variables do not contribute as much to the extension of nursing knowledge as one with a more comprehensive thrust, since biological, psychological, and social variables seldom occur in isolation, are often related to one another, and change together.

The results of this study highlighted a number of gaps in the use and reporting of measurement practices and procedures. The extent to which the editorial policies of the journals included in the study affected the results is not fully known. A review of these journals' editorial and manuscript guidelines reflects an emphasis on sound research methodology that encour-

ages the reporting of measurement procedures and reliability and validity evidence. The same measurement issues and problems were reflected when comparisons were made between journals. Therefore, it is not likely that editorial policy had a significant affect on the results. Journal publishers can only print what is submitted to them and deemed appropriate by manuscript reviewers. Thus editorial review panels may need to place more emphasis on measurement issues when reviewing research manuscripts. More critical reviews of journal articles by readers and editorials such as those done by Ventura, Hinshaw, and Atwood[12] and by Knapp[13] could facilitate efforts in this area.

To summarize, nurse researchers, editorial review panels, and readers of research articles need to place more emphasis on measurement principles and practices. Tools designed to measure nursing variables need to be developed and then tested with various populations and in a number of studies. Because an understanding of sound measurement principles and practices is an essential component of a nurse's repertoire, more emphasis needs to be placed on measurement content during the nurse's education, particularly for nurse researchers.

REFERENCES

1. Strickland OL: *Measurement: An Essential Component for Evaluating Continuing Nursing Education*. Atlanta, Regional Action for Continuing Education in Nursing Project, Southern Regional Education Board, January 1983.

2. Nunnally JC: *Psychometric Theory,* ed 2. New York, McGraw-Hill, 1978.

3. Waltz CF, Strickland OL, Lenz, ER: *Measurement in Nursing Research*. Philadelphia, FA Davis, 1984.

4. Campbell DT, Stanley JC: *Experimental and Quasi-experimental Designs for Research*. Chicago, Rand McNally, 1963.

5. Waltz CF, Strickland OL: Measurement of nursing outcomes: State of the art as we enter the eighties, in Field WE (ed): *Measuring Outcomes of Nursing Practice, Education and Administration: Proceedings of the First Annual Southern Council of Collegiate Education for Nursing Research Conference*. Atlanta, Southern Regional Education Board, 1982, pp 47-62.

6. Garfield E: Citation patterns in nursing journals, and their most-cited articles. *Curr Contents* 1984; 27(43):3-12.

7. Gortner SR, Bloch D, Phillips TP: Contributions of nursing research to patient care. *J Nurs Admin* 1976;6(3):22-28.

8. Bloch D: Conceptualization of nursing research and nursing sciences, in McCloskey JC, Grace HK (eds): *Current Issues in Nursing*. Boston, Blackwell Scientific, 1981, pp 81-93.

9. Anastasi A: *Psychological Testing,* ed 4. New York, Macmillan, 1976.

10. Martuza V: *Applying Norm-referenced and Criterion-referenced Measurement in Education*. Boston, Allyn Bacon, 1977.

11. Guilford JP: *Psychometric Methods,* ed 2. New York, McGraw-Hill, 1954.

12. Ventura MR, Hinshaw AS, Atwood JR: Instrumentation: The next step. *Nurs Res* 1981;30(5):257.

13. Knapp TR: Validity, reliability and neither. *Nurs Res* 1985;34(3):189-192.

Chapter 8

A Hybrid Model for Concept Development

Donna Schwartz-Barcott and Hesook Suzie Kim

As early as 1973, Hardy[1] began highlighting the role of concepts as basic elements in theory development for nursing. In so doing, she drew on a longstanding tradition of theory development in the social sciences. For many years, social scientists[2–4] have been depicting concepts as the "building blocks" of theory and conceptual analysis as an essential step in theory development. Yet it is only recently that this step has gained major attention within the nursing literature.

In line with this intensified interest, a number of nursing scholars have proposed various approaches to analyzing concepts relevant to nursing. Most of these scholars have approached concept analysis as essentially either a theoretical or an empirical process. For example, approaches to concept analysis by Hardy,[5] Stevens,[6] Kim,[7] and Forsyth[8] are all basically theoretical. Varying sets of criteria are used to compare, contrast, and evaluate the usefulness of any one concept. The research literature and empirical referents at times are drawn on to augment the analysis. This approach has been used primarily for evaluating or refining existing concepts. In contrast, phenomenological,[9] grounded theory,[10] and ethnographic[11] field research approaches are basically empirical. Empirical observations are used as the principal source of data for identifying new concepts, as in the case of grounded theory, or in concept definition and refinement, as in the case of phenomenological and ethnographic approaches.

A hybrid model is proposed in this chapter. It interfaces theoretical analysis with empirical observation, combining the rigors of both approaches. The model involves steps used to identify, analyze, and refine concepts in the initial stage of theory development and is most applicable to applied sciences in general and to nursing specifically. Because the approach draws heavily on insights generated in clinical practice, it is especially useful in studying significant and central phenomena in nursing. Theoretical development based on this model at the initial stage thus can include concepts having both analytical and empirical foundations.

A HYBRID MODEL

Figure 8–1 is a diagram of the overall model and its major components. The model, which combines theoretical and empirical elements, is composed of three phases: a theoretical phase, a fieldwork phase, and an analytical phase. As the label denotes, the initial phase is largely theoretical, although it draws heavily on experiences from clinical practice. During this phase, Reynolds's[12] analytical approach to concept analysis is used to begin the literature search, the analysis, and the selection of a working definition. The second phase, which overlaps partly in time with the first phase, emphasizes the empirical component of the process. It uses field research methods to collect qualitative data for further analysis of the selected concept. Schatzman and Strauss's[13] guide to field research is used directly for the overall structuring and sequencing of steps in this phase. Reynolds's analytical approach helps to undergird the collection and analysis of data. Wilson's[14] analytical approach is brought forth as potentially useful in steps 3 and 4

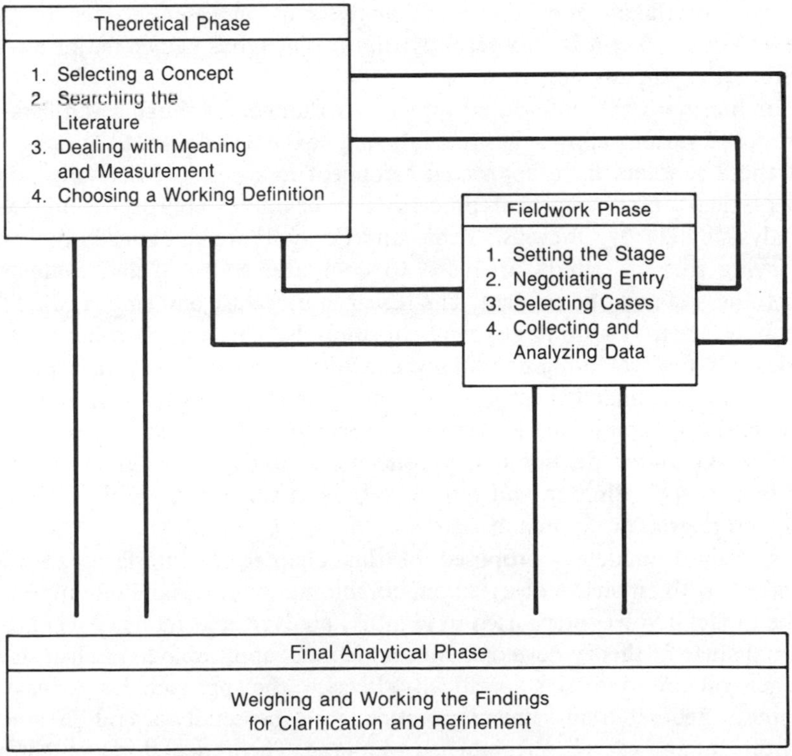

Figure 8–1. A Hybrid Model to Concept Development

(selecting cases, and collecting and analyzing data). Phase three includes the final step in interfacing the initial theoretical analysis with insights gained from the empirical observations. Here again, Reynolds's and Wilson's analytical approaches help in finalizing the analysis and suggesting possible alterations or refinements of the concept.

Theoretical Phase

The principal focus in the theoretical phase is on the development of a foundation for the later phases of refinement and analysis. This includes the selection of a concept, initiation of the literature review, a mapping out of essential elements of definition and measurement, and the delineation of a working definition.

Selecting a Concept

The selection of a concept for study has been approached by nursing scholars in various ways. Some, such as Hardy,[15] Panzarine,[16] and Brownell,[17] have drawn directly from existing concepts in other disciplines. Others, such as Norris[18] and Leininger,[11] have drawn on identified but underdeveloped concepts from the nursing literature. More recently, a few have begun to generate new concepts directly out of nursing practice or research. Whatever the approach taken, one needs to give some initial consideration to ways of enhancing the probability of selecting a concept relevant to nursing.

The use of an encounter drawn directly from clinical practice can be used to great advantage. It can help to guide later theoretical and empirical analyses and, most important, to assure a nursing perspective. Some of the best encounters are those that are unexpected and leave the nurse feeling frustrated, horrified, angry, embarrassed, or bewildered. For example, a graduate student who was visiting a elderly client in a nursing home for the first time had the following experience:

> The foyer of the new, modern nursing home was filled with residents. At first glance it seemed to be full of potential hostesses, appropriately attired and positioned to offer a warm welcome to incoming visitors. But, as she entered a step further, moved toward one or two, to nod or smile—expecting in part to be ushered in or at least directed to her client—she discovered distant looks, vacuous smiles and aimless muttering.

She was surprised to discover that the initial image of social activity and animation among the elderly in the foyer was only a mirage. What was particularly disconcerting and saddening was the lack of human interaction among a group of individuals who appeared to need such interaction.

By filling in details related to the setting, people involved, and words exchanged, one can use such an encounter to begin to ferret out a relevant concept(s). By placing emphasis on *describing* the encounter rather than on trying to *explain* it, one can help to avoid premature interpretation. For example, much of the value of the early observations of the elderly group of residents in the foyer of the nursing home would have been lost if one inserted the word "senile" before elderly. "Confusing mutterings" would be much more descriptive of the encounter than the single term confused. The single term tends to imply that these individuals were always confused or spent most of their time in a state of confusion—an interpretation that would have been erroneous given later observations.

Given a relatively full recording of the encounter, it can be reexamined for possible concepts to be used for labeling and further understanding the unexpected or problematic aspect of the encounter. The following questions can be used to focus one's attention on the existing pool of potentially relevant concepts from other disciplines and nursing, thus drawing on two of the approaches mentioned earlier for concept selection. What might be happening here? It there a single concept, such as withdrawal or noncompliance, that provides a relatively accurate label of the focus of concern? What kind of explanation might a physiologist or psychologist give? How might a sociologist or anthropologist explain this encounter? Last, but not least, how might other nurses explain the encounter? It is not necessary to strike on a single concept immediately. Initially, it is important that consideration be given to the wide range of possible scientific concepts or explanations that might help to illuminate this particular encounter. In the encounter with the elderly, one scholar may see indications of disorientation or withdrawal or some combination of these in the faces and actions of the elderly. Another might see evidence of senility, sensory deprivation, or disengagement. It is not unusual, at this point, to be confronted with a number, even an overabundance, of potential concepts for further examination. In the case just mentioned, five potentially relevant concepts were identified.

There are additional steps that one can take to focus on a single concept. First, one can begin to ferret out concepts that may be more useful as independent variables than as dependent variables. At this point, it is easy to confuse descriptive and explanatory uses of a concept. For example, in the case just mentioned, senility, sensory deprivation, and disengagement were being used primarily as concepts to explain the behavior observed among the elderly in the foyer. Second, one can arrange the remaining concepts by degree of plausibility. One may want to refer back to the initial encounter to review the details in light of the concepts now being considered.

In some cases, one still may not be able to draw on any one or two existing concepts directly. Instead, one may have a series of concepts, none of which seems to capture fully the image of reality that is of interest. In one situation,

for example, a nurse was feeling harassed by picayune, seemingly illogical and endless demands of a patient who had chronic obstructive lung disease. These demands often were accompanied by abusive language. The patient had a lengthy history of admissions related to his disease. He was well known to the staff. No amount of effort on the part of the nursing staff seemed to increase patient satisfaction or comfort. As one nurse described it:

> In cleaning up the bedside table—I moved the Kleenex box—he demanded it be replaced—he demanded it should be moved another quarter of an inch to the right. The bell would ring once or twice every fifteen minutes. The level of H_2O connected to the O_2 tank was down one-quarter inch, one inch above the level for refill. Mr. J. wanted the water refilled. The function and operation of the water apparatus were explained. Mr. J. nodded in seeming agreement. In five minutes the bell rang again. Mr. J. wanted the H_2O refilled.

It was not clear whether one was dealing with forgetfulness, autocratism, manipulative behavior, hostility, fear, neurosis, a sense of helplessness, or just open, interpersonal conflict between patient and nurse. All seemed to capture an important "reality" in this situation, but at the same time, none seemed to reflect its essence of fullness.

Given this kind of situation, it may be best to go ahead and create a new concept as a basis for tentative exploration in the field setting. Then, later, if one discovers an appropriate existing concept, one can simply discard the initial one. It is highly likely that the initial analysis and field data will be useful in examining and refining the existing concept.

Searching the Literature

A successful review of the literature requires a systematic approach. It is essential that one begin with a set of questions that will provide an initial direction for the search: What is the essential nature of a concept? How can its essence be defined clearly? How can it be fleshed out so as to enhance its measurability? As these questions suggest, the initial review of the literature needs to focus on central questions of definition and measurement. Later, after one is well into the fieldwork phase, the focus will shift to the subtle elements of definition and measurement.

Dealing with Meaning and Measurement

Once one has a few definitions in hand, one can begin looking for major points of contrast and similarity. With a concept such as creativity, one will be confronted with a variety of definitions. For some scholars, creativity is an

aspect of *cognitive* functioning, a way of thinking. For others, it is an intrapersonal and interpersonal *process.* May[19] speaks of it as an *encounter* between an "intensively conscious human being with his world." But for Rogers,[20(p5)] creativity is a "novel relational *product* growing out of the uniqueness of the individual on the one hand and the materials, events, people or circumstances of his life on the other." Creativity, as a concept, thus is considered as a *process* of interaction between a person and his or her environment, as a *product* of interaction, or as an interpersonal process. This kind of comparison gives one some idea of the amount of consensus among users of a particular concept and leads to what Reynolds[12(p15)] refers to as the degree of intersubjectivity of meaning.

Choosing a Definition

Once major points of agreement and disagreement have become apparent, one needs to select or generate a definition for a further detailed examination. Selecting one that seems congruent with one's initial thoughts will help to maintain a nursing perspective; however, a tentative posture with respect to a selected definition can provide open-mindedness in the refinement process.

Fieldwork Phase

The fieldwork phase is aimed at refining a concept that has been analyzed in the theoretical phase. Refinement at this phase involves an empirical validation of a concept through a method of qualitative research. As outlined in Figure 1, phase two begins with setting the stage and continues through the negotiation of entry, selection of cases, and collection and analysis of data. These steps certainly are not unique. They are the basic steps in any qualitative research that draws heavily on participant observation. Schatzman and Strauss provide an excellent overview of each of these steps in *Field Research: Strategies for a Natural Sociology.*[13] The proposed model has adopted these methods of field research for concept development in nursing. This phase involves a transformation of clinical practice into qualitative research.

Setting the Stage

The focus in this step is on the selection of a fieldwork site and identification of major questions to guide the fieldwork phase. The selection of a site is somewhat critical to assuring a nursing perspective. A listing of the potential range of patient populations or patient care situations in which one would expect the concept to be relevant will help to clarify core elements of the concept as well as its likely generalizability within nursing.

For example, in an initial literature review, withdrawal was repeatedly and explicitly linked with elderly people and those who were mentally ill. Earlier observations of elderly in nursing homes suggested that withdrawal might occur with considerable frequency in almost any long-term institutionalized patient population. In addition, withdrawal seemed to be more common than indicated in the research on the elderly and the mentally ill populations. At times, it seemed like an almost normal phase—one that most patients pass through in trying to cope with any illness. It appeared, then, that withdrawal may be present with some frequency in a variety of institutional settings, ranging from prisons, mental hospitals, and nursing homes to extended ambulatory care centers and hospices. It also may be experienced relatively frequently among the chronically ill and the elderly in noninstitutionalized settings.

Two essential criteria should guide the selection of a population and a setting: (1) the likelihood of frequent observations of the phenomenon under study and (2) the appropriateness of participant observation as a method of gathering empirical data.

One or two major questions can be used to link the concept with a specific patient population or a setting. For example, with regard to withdrawal, one might be interested in the presence of withdrawal among elderly individuals, especially with regard to whether or not there is a progressive nature to withdrawal. At the same time, it is apparent that one must deal with the ambiguities inherent in trying to identify any one patient as being "withdrawn." Questions guiding the fieldwork phase should address (a) the essential defining elements of a concept; (b) the differentiating elements, separating the central concept from similar concepts; (c) the measurement criteria that may be developed for the concept. The questions may be extended to search for explanatory ideas as the fieldwork progresses.

Negotiating Entry

It is easy to disregard the subtleties of gaining access and legitimation to the selected population or setting demands until it is too late. In *Field Research*, Schatzman and Strauss[13(pp18–33)] cover the intricacies and complexity of this type of negotiation in much detail—especially as it applies to formal and highly complex organizations such as the hospital.

Selecting Cases

Decisions regarding with whom to speak and how to focus one's observations in the field depend on (a) the unit of analysis under study and (b) the degree of clarity and intersubjectivity found in the initial review of literature. The unit of analysis depends on the concept. It most likely would be at the individual level for a study of withdrawal among the elderly or at

the dyad level for a study of the use of touch among couples attending Lamaze classes. Other concepts that may be studied at the dyad level include empathy, attraction, and anger. Empathy and anger are also illustrative of concepts that may be studied at multiple levels. A small group could be a unit of analysis, if one were focusing on empathetic interaction *among* group members. An entire *unit*, such as a floor in a nursing home, might be the unit of analysis, if one were looking for the presence of multiple patient roles and their patterns of interaction.

A complete sample is unnecessary with this model of concept analysis. Three to six individuals, three or four dyads, one or two groups, and one floor or ward may be appropriate. The selection of any one individual, couple, group, or floor will depend on the degree of definitional clarity gained in phase one. If the essential features of the concept are relatively clear, one or two indicators can serve as a basis for selection. If the essential features of the concept are not clear and no indicators are apparent, one may want to use Wilson's[14] typology for concept analysis as a basis for selection. This typology has been described by a number of nursing scholars. Briefly, the typology begins with the *model case*—one that absolutely reflects an instance of the concept. As Wilson notes, this is the instance in which we hear ourselves saying, "Well, if that isn't an example of so-and-so, then nothing is." Second is the *contrary* case. It represents a case that is absolutely not an instance of the concept: "Well, whatever so-and-so is, certainly it is not that." Third is the *borderline* case. It appears as the "odd" or "queer" case. It helps highlight elements that make for a "true" case. The typology ends with the *related* case. This one helps to clarify the central concept by identifying the criteria for a related concept.

Collecting and Analyzing the Data

As any qualitative research text will attest to, there are innumerable ways of collecting data. Some, however, such as questionnaires or highly structured interviews, are too closed-ended to allow for the probing and the dialogue that are needed in order to clarify the meaning and the nature of the concept. Other methods, like participant observation and unstructured interviews, may be more useful because they tend to facilitate multiple observations and in-depth probing and dialogue. Some combination of participant observation augmented with periodic in-depth interviews has been used successfully in our studies.

The notation system for recording proposed by Schatzman and Strauss,[13(pp94–108)] which includes Observational Notes (ON), Theoretical Notes (TN), and Methodological Notes (MN), guides the researcher into possible analytical distinctions at the point of recording. The observational notes "are statements bearing upon events experienced principally through watching and listening. They contain as little interpretation as possible, and

are as reliable as the observer can construct them." This is the who, what, when, where, and how of the phenomenon and identifies who said or did what under what circumstances. Quotation marks can be used to identify the exact words, phrases, or sentences that occurred in any one conversation. Otherwise, one can use the apostrophe for less accurate quoting or simply paraphrase as best as can be done. The theoretical notes are used to go beyond the "facts." One can consciously interpret, infer, hypothesize, or speculate about the possible meaning of the observations. One's instructions to oneself are included under methodological notes. This notation system encourages free-flowing and yet systematic recording and organizing of the data. It makes for easy retrieval of key observations and is conducive to continual analysis and reflection.

As is apparent from the notation system, data collection plunges one into the analysis phase. Collection and analysis of data go on concurrently with every other step under the rubric of the theoretical note. Nevertheless, about one half to three fourths of the way through the fieldwork phase, one needs to begin to pull out and organize the data that are most relevant to the concept. Wilson's[14] typology of cases can be helpful here. This can then serve as a basis for refocusing field observations and for more focused, in-depth probing as one moves through the latter half of this phase.

Final Analytical Phase

During the analytical phase, one steps back from the intensity and details of fieldwork and reexamines the findings in light of the initial focus of interest.

- How much is the concept applicable and important to nursing?
- Does the initial selection of the concept seem justified?
- To what extent does the review of literature, theoretical analysis, and empirical findings support the presence and frequency of this concept within the population selected for empirical study?

For example, a subsequent fieldwork with withdrawal tended to support the *presence* and *importance* of psychosocial *withdrawal* among residents in a nursing home setting. At the same time, the fieldwork suggested that, although the phenomenon existed frequently, withdrawal was not necessarily inherent in the adjustment process. In addition, the review of the literature and empirical findings altered an earlier perception of withdrawal as a predominantly negative process. It became apparent that withdrawal can be a positive factor by providing a "time-out" period for energy renewal and in maintaining one's self-dignity as well as gaining some control over the

immediate environment, even when that environment reflects the dictates of a total institution.

At other times, one may be less convinced of the relevance of a concept after fieldwork than one was before. Sometimes it is not so much that one's findings do not support the existence of a particular concept as it is that a new concept or reformulation of the initial idea emerges out of the empirical observations and analysis.

If the importance of the concept is supported, then the next step is to reconsider the findings in light of the concept's *definition* and *measurability.* One may want to begin by going back to the initial, tentative definitions, the listing of key elements in one's analysis of these definitions. How do the definitions compare and contrast with the empirical findings? It may be that one definition stands out as more useful than another. Yet, in still other situations, the empirical findings may lead to a new way of measuring a concept or to suggest refinements in existing measures. Sometimes empirical findings may simply raise the need for different indicators, given the lack of support for existing ones.

As the concept becomes clarified, refined, and redefined through the entire process, the final question involves linking the concept to a possible explanatory framework. A refined concept has to be put into a theoretical box as either an independent or a dependent variable for an explanation in the nursing perspective.

REFERENCES

1. Hardy ME: *Theoretical Foundations for Nursing.* New York, MSS Information Corp, 1973.

2. Hempel CG: *Fundamentals of Concept Formation in Empirical Science.* Chicago, University of Chicago Press, 1952.

3. Pelto PJ: *Anthropological Research: The Structure of Inquiry.* New York, Harper & Row, 1970.

4. Hage J: *Techniques and Problems of Theory Construction in Sociology.* New York, John Wiley, 1972.

5. Hardy ME: Theories: Components, development, evaluation. *Nurs Res* 1974;23(March-April):100-107.

6. Stevens B: *Nursing Theory: Analysis, Application and Evaluation,* ed 2. Boston, Little, Brown, 1984.

7. Kim HS: *The Nature of Theoretical Thinking in Nursing.* Norwalk, Conn, Appleton-Century-Crofts, 1983.

8. Forsyth GL: Analysis of the concept of empathy: Illustration of one approach. *Adv Nurs Sci* 1980;2(January):33-42.

9. Lynch-Sauer J: Using a phenomenological research method to study nursing phenomena, in Leininger MM (ed): *Qualitative Research Methods in Nursing.* Orlando, Fla, Grune & Stratton, 1985, pp 93-108.

10. Atwood JR: The phenomenon of selective neglect, in Bauwens E (ed): *The Anthropology of Health.* St Louis, CV Mosby, 1978, pp 192-200.

11. Leininger MM: Ethnography and ethnonursing: Models and modes of qualitative data analysis, in Leininger MM (ed): *Qualitative Research Methods in Nursing.* Orlando, Fla, Grune & Stratton, 1985, pp 33-71.

12. Reynolds PD: *A Primer in Theory Construction.* New York, Bobbs-Merrill, 1971.

13. Schatzman L, Strauss AL: *Field Research: Strategies for a Natural Science.* Englewood Cliffs, NJ, Prentice-Hall, 1973.

14. Wilson J: *Thinking with Concepts.* London, Cambridge University Press, 1969.

15. Hardy ME, Conway ME: *Role Theory: Perspectives for Health Professionals,* New York, Appleton-Century-Crofts, 1978.

16. Panzarine S: Coping: Conceptual and methodological issues. *Adv Nurs Sci* 1985;7(July):49-58.

17. Brownell MJ: The concept of crisis: Its utility for nursing. *Adv Nurs Sci* 1984;6(July):10-21.

18. Norris CM: *Concept Clarification in Nursing.* Rockville, Md, Aspen Systems, 1982.

19. May R: The nature of creativity, in Anderson HH (ed): *Interdisciplinary Symposia on Creativity.* New York, Harper & Row, 1972.

20. Rogers R: Toward a theory of creativity, in Anderson HH (ed): *Interdisciplinary Symposia on Creativity.* New York, Harper & Row, 1972.

Chapter 9

Model Building As a Strategy for Theory Development

Marilyn L. Stember

Model building is a logical theoretical and methodological process with the intent of clarifying and testing relationships and communicating them more effectively. In this activity, ideas are represented diagrammatically and mathematically, resulting in the development of structural models. Structural models are tested, using the results to refine the original model. In the model-building process, assumptions and conventions are used to build simple to complex models that are translated into simultaneous mathematical equations, evaluated empirically, and, subsequently, refined.

USE OF MODELS

Although many nursing scholars have acknowledged the role of models in theory development, research, and nursing science,[1–9] little attention has been given to the specific process of model building in nursing. Differences in usage of the term model may have contributed to the lack of attention to these strategies. In everyday language, models refer to precise replications of an object, such as a model car or a model airplane. On other occasions, the term is used to describe an ideal, such as a "model nurse" or a "model home." In the scientific community, similar diversity of definition exists. Sometimes models are used to label the most global or general theoretical specifications. At other times, models have precise requirements in terms of structure and form. As a result, the term is often loosely applied.

Models in both everyday and scientific usage provide a means of exhibiting, examining, observing, and teaching the structural relationships of many realities that cannot otherwise be observed. For example, a model of the human heart is helpful in demonstrating its structural entities (eg, chambers, valves, vessels) as they exist in approximate size and position. More elaborate models of the heart have circulating blood showing the process of blood flow

through that organ and adjacent structures. Even though the elements in such a heart model move, the forces that move the blood from chamber to chamber are contrived. Further, the parts of the heart model themselves do not replicate the organic substances from which they are made, nor do they possess the neurological fields that are actually present. Thus, although a cardiac model has great utilitarian value in studying the various movements and relationships of entities in the heart, it does not fully explain the components themselves, the reasons for the movements, nor does it demonstrate all functional relations thought to exist. A model does, however, provide an important means of communicating what a scientist has in mind when speaking of an entity or a structure or a process. A model represents some aspect of reality, concrete or abstract, in a structural, pictorial, diagrammatic, or mathematical form.[1] In models, attention is focused on the structure and functional relationships rather than on in-depth properties of the subject matter.

In nursing, various types of models have been developed. Sometimes nursing models order existing knowledge or concepts. At other times, relationships between known objects or events are conceptualized through models for the purpose of greater clarity and understanding. Most of the models in nursing are at the global or abstract theory level rather than at specific testable theory level. Many nurse scholars have argued for more explicit models to guide practice, education, and research.[10–14] A more precise methodology for building specific theoretical models is needed.

ASSUMPTIONS

Structural model building is based on a number of philosophical and mathematical assumptions. This type of theory construction and empirical analysis has also been called causal modeling,[15–17] path analysis,[18,19] simultaneous equation models,[20,21] or multivariate time-lag series, depending on the scholar or the discipline. The philosophical orientation is empirical, rational, and naturalistic.[22,23] This method is particularly well suited to addressing the classic definitions of theory[4,11,24–27] as it contributes to the scientific aim of obtaining coherent sets of verified relationships useful for description, explanation, and prediction.

The underlying statistical concepts and assumptions also need to be examined.[19–21,28–31] Because the method is based on the general linear model, ideas such as linearity, additivity, recursiveness, and uncorrelated error terms must be understood. Although computer programs are now more widely available to facilitate the mathematical solutions, the theorist-researcher must be clear about the assumptions required in this form of model building.

One term that needs clarification is the term causal. In this model-building strategy, causal is not meant as a cause and effect per se, but as a statement

encompassing probability of relationship, that is, the likelihood of a change in a second event given a change in an earlier event.[16] The probabilistic meaning and implications of structural models are best revealed through an understanding of the independence constraints. Independence is one of the fundamental notions of probability and statistics. The joint behavior of two or more random variables can be expressed in terms of independence. The question is, Are two parts of the model related or are they independent?

Because the purpose of a model is to describe and explain any association or departure from mutual independence exhibited by the variables, in its simplist terms, departure from mutual independence can be described by noting whether or not any association (eg, correlation or a qualitative analog) is present. For example, many models are expressed in terms of joint marginals or conditional independence. More sophisticated models seek to explain observed associations in terms of the overall sets of relationships between the variables. Some explanations involve what is termed a causal ordering and others do not. The causal models with such an ordering can be divided into those known as recursive causal models (those that specify that A comes before B, which comes before C) and the remainder, nonrecursive models (also called models with reciprocal causation, in which the ordering of A, B, and C are recognized as a cycle).

CONVENTIONS

Standard conventions facilitate a common referencing system. Variables are usually named from X_1 to X_n and are numbered in order as they occur or happen in time. This allows for simplicity in diagrams as well as ease in writing mathematical equations.

Relationships can be associational, directional, or causal. Associational relationships are indicated by a straight line connecting the variables, as in Figure 9–1. This indicates that the two variables are related but neither one directs or influences the other. A directional causal relationship, as shown in

Figure 9–1. Associational Relationship

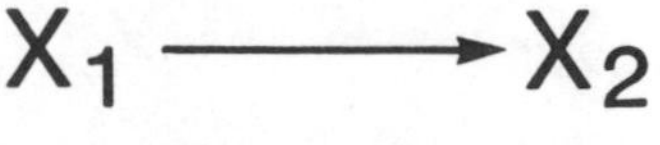

Figure 9–2. Directional Causal Relationship

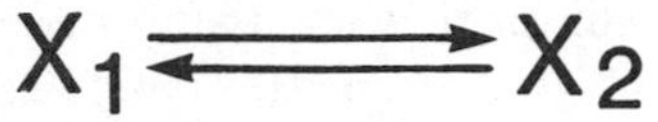

Figure 9–3. Reciprocal Causality

Figure 9–2, is noted by an unidirectional arrow going from the antecedent (causal) variable to the variable on which it is thought to exert influence. This means that a change in X_1 is likely to lead in a change in X_2. Reciprocal causality is indicated by two directional arrows (Figure 9–3). This states that a change in X_1 is likely to lead to a change in X_2 but that X_2 is likely in turn to lead to a change in X_1. Often these diagrams are useful in depicting regulating mechanisms where when one variable increases to produce an increase in the second variable, the increase in the second variable will lead to a decrease in the first variable.

The nature or kind of relationship is symbolically indicated by a + or a – along the arrow (Figure 9–4). This indicates whether variables are directly positively or negatively (inversely) related. If no direct relationship is hypothesized, the convention is that no lines are drawn connecting the variables.

The verbal statements describing the model directly correspond with the pictorial diagram of the model, and both are always equivalent to the mathematical statement. Diagrams have been used as visual aids to define and help interpret relationships in an independence model for the joint distribution of a set of multinomial or multivariate normal random variables.

MODEL FORMS: SIMPLE TO COMPLEX

Five major forms of models are associated with this approach to model building. The simplist form is a noncausal model. Figure 9–5 shows a four-variable noncausal model. This noncausal model requires that X_1, X_2, and X_4 be mutually and conditionally independent given X_3. Thus the pairs [1,2] [1,4] and [2,4] are only linked by way of X_3, and it can be said that X_1 and X_4 are independent given X_3. In this case of simple independence, the model could be statistically analyzed by what is often known as partial correlation models. If the conditional associations are zero or not statistically different

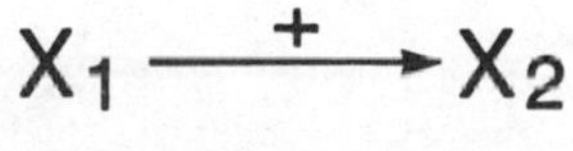

Figure 9–4. Symbol for Kind of Relationship

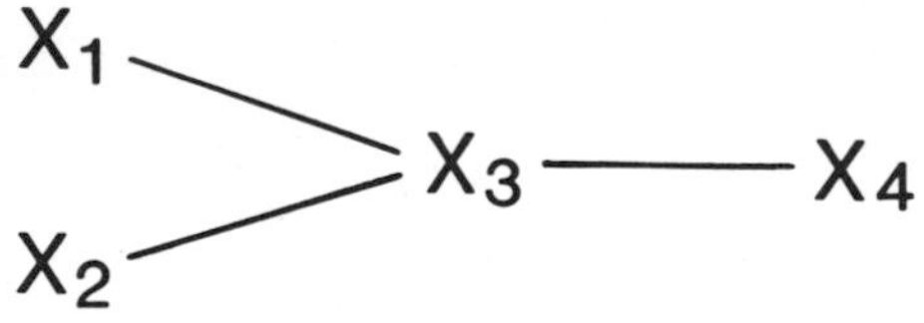

Figure 9–5. Noncausal Model

than zero, it is concluded that the independence constraints exist as specified. In structural modeling, the general analytic scheme is known as maximum-likelihood estimation. Given the assumptions of multinomial and multivariate normal distributions, maximum-likelihood estimates of each path coefficient are made for each possible relationship, and an overall likelihood ratio test statistic evaluating the model's goodness of fit can be used.

Figure 9–6 is a multiple causation model. It is a simple recursive independence model of four variables with the following a priori causal relations: X_1, X_2, and X_3 are possible causes of variable X_4. This can be recognized as a familiar multiple regression-type analytic problem that could be written as the equation:

$$X_4 = b_{41}X_1 + b_{42}X_2 + b_{43}X_2 + e_4$$

A third model pattern is multiple outcomes rather than multiple causation. It is diagrammed as shown in Figure 9–7. It can also be observed that for multivariate normal random variables satisfying this model form, the following equations can be written:

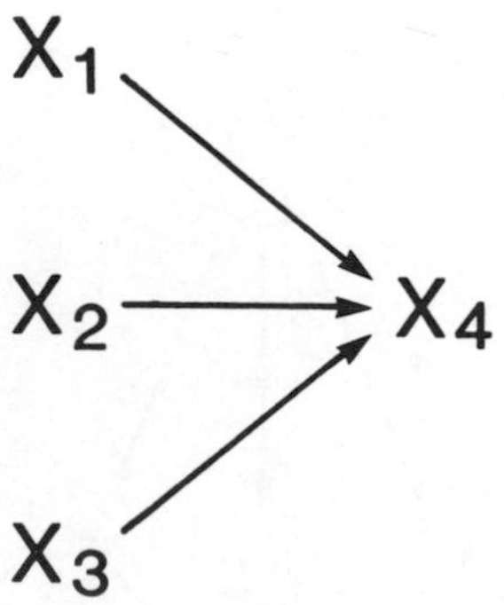

Figure 9–6. Multiple Causation Model

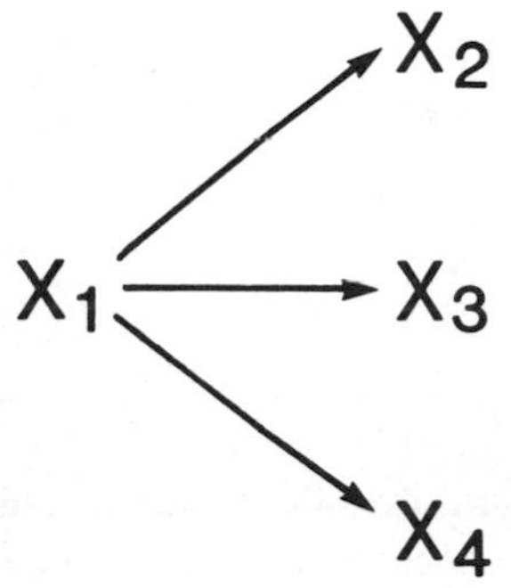

Figure 9–7. Multiple Outcome Model

$$X_1 = e_1$$

$$X_2 = b_{21}X_1 + e_2$$

$$X_3 = b_{31}X_1 + e_3$$

$$X_4 = b_{41}X_1 + e_4$$

Figure 9–8 is another model form in which the variable X_1 is unobserved. This model form is called a latent variable model or a multiple indicator model. Within the multinomial framework, this model is known as a latent-class model[32] with a single latent variable X_1 and manifest variables X_2, X_3, and X_4. Under multivariate normal assumptions, with the single factor X_1, this is also known as a multiple indicator or factor analysis model. A host of specialized techniques are devoted to solving the problems of estimation and testing. In structural modeling, special algorithms have been developed to

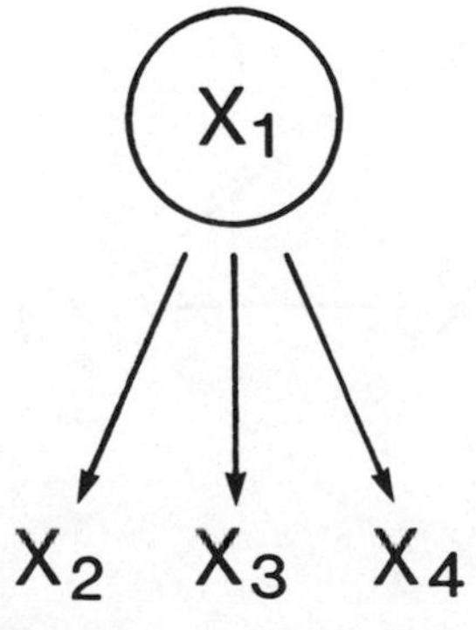

Figure 9–8. Latent Variable Model

estimate how well each of the observed variables measures the unobserved variable.

Another model form involves the notion of staged causation. Figure 9–9 shows a staged recursive model. This model form can be considered as a four-variable model with simultaneousness. X_1 and X_2 are exogenous variables; that is, they are determined by variables outside the model. X_3 and X_4 are endogenous variables; that is, they are determined by variables in the model. Changes in X_1 and X_2 will lead to a change in X_3, a change in X_3 will lead to a change in X_4, and a change in X_2 will lead to a change in X_4, independent of the influence of X_3. The following equations also represent this model and, when simultaneously solved, yield the unknown parameter estimates:

$$X_1 = e_1$$

$$X_2 = e_2$$

$$X_3 = b_{31}X_1 + b_{32}X_2 + e_3$$

$$X_4 = b_{41}X_2 + b_{42}X_2 + b_{43}X_3 + e_4$$

where it is expected that $b_{41}X_1$ will be zero.

The last representative model form is the staged nonrecursive model. Consider the same four-variable models, but add a reciprocal or feedback effect of X_4 on X_3. The diagram for this model is shown in Figure 9–10. Nonrecursive causal models with reciprocal causation and interdependent properties have been the subject of considerable discussion. Attention has focused on their meaning and interpretation, as well as on the complex methods required to fit them. The usual pattern is that many nonrecursive structural models can be reduced to block recursive form, treating variables that are reciprocally related or part of a causal cycle as a single block

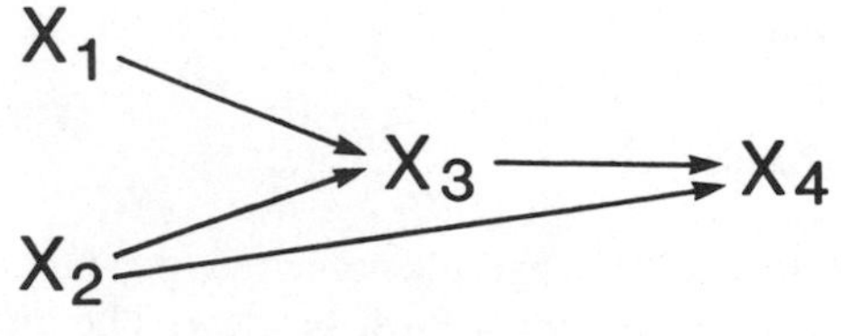

Figure 9–9. Staged Recursive Model

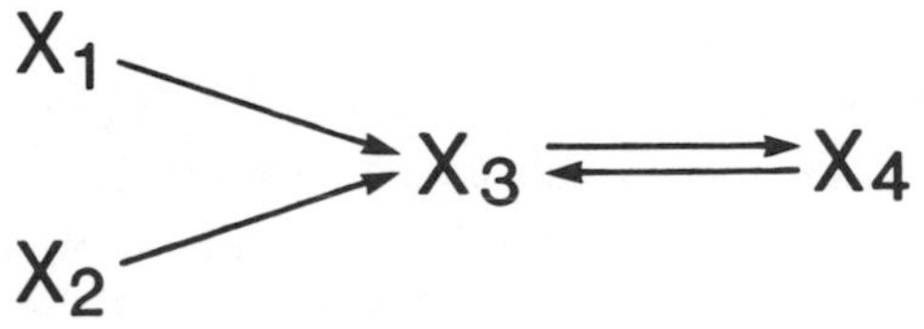

Figure 9–10. Staged Nonrecursive Model

variable. Then the relationships between elements of the blocks are described in terms of additional marginal independence constraints.

Models use or combine one or more of these five structural patterns. Thus models can include causal or noncausal relations and single or multiple antecedents or determinants. The possibility that each of a pair of variables may be a direct cause of each other is also permitted. Although the analysis of each model form may be understood by most researchers, when several patterns are present in the same model, the analysis is complex. Indeed, the model is always analyzed as a unit. The analysis becomes increasingly complex as the models contain more forms or types of relationships.

STEPS IN MODEL BUILDING

With some understanding of the underlying assumptions, conventions, and model forms, the theorist-researcher participates in a five-stage process of model building. The structural modeling approach requires the researcher to:

1. construct a clear, precise model.
2. translate model into simultaneous equations.
3. collect data.
4. evaluate empirically.
5. refine the model.

Specification of a Model

The first step is to decide what phenomenon the model is intended to represent. The purpose of the model must be clear. The model builder must be familiar with both the theoretical and the empirical work in the area, as well as having a clear understanding of the concepts within the model. It is likely that some concepts have been analyzed to a much greater extent than others. It is also likely that there has been more empirical testing of some

relationships in the model than of others; perhaps some have not been tested to date. Past research findings, conceptual frameworks, experience, logic, and creative energy go into the specification of the model.

Once the variables are chosen as a result of their relationship to the main phenomenon of interest, the order of their occurrence must be delineated, that is, which variables come first, second, third, and so on in the chain. It is helpful to think of the specification of variables in terms of time. In a recursive model, succeeding variables cannot influence preceding variables. Early-determined variables are listed in the first (t_1) period. An example of the placement of eight variables is presented in Figure 9–11. Preceding from left to right, it would be clear that variables or events in t_4, for example, occur after events in t_3.

The next stage in the specification of the model is to delineate relationships between variables in the model, considering whether a direct positive or direct negative relationship is expected or whether no relationship is hypothesized. The entire set of relationships must be considered. The form that models take varies, beginning with the case in which all variables are observed and no causal relationships are presupposed and moving toward the most general case involving both unobserved (latent) and observed variables and relationships that may be noncausal, unidirectional causal, or reciprocally causal. More than one model may be specified, allowing comparison with one another.[33]

Graphs are drawn to indicate the relationships between the variables implied by the model. The graphs play a role in visualing the effects, both direct and indirect. A sample hypothesized causal model is graphically presented as a diagram in Figure 9–12. Following the usual conventions, causal relations postulated among the eight variables in the system are

---

X_1			X_6
X_2	X_4	X_5	X_7
X_3			X_8
(t_1)	(t_2)	(t_3)	(t_4)

Figure 9–11. Temporal Ordering

represented by unidirectional arrows extending from each determined variable to each variable dependent on it. The sign along the arrow is the direction of the relationship. When no direct effect is postulated, no arrows are presented. The rationale for these relationships is based on existing theory, logical connections, and research findings. Because no feedback is specified, these variables, when connected, form a recursive system. Each of the possible relationships could be thought of as an individual hypothesis, and in this example, there are 22 hypotheses to be tested.

Translation into Simultaneous Equations

The model must be translated into a set of simultaneous mathematical equations. An equation can be specified for each variable in the preceding model:

$$X_1 = e_1$$

$$X_2 = e_2$$

$$X_3 = e_3$$

$$X_4 = b_{41}X_1 + b_{42}X_2 + b_{43}X_3 + e_4$$

$$X_5 = b_{51}X_1 + b_{52}X_2 + b_{53}X_3 + b_{54}X_4 + e_5$$

$$X_6 = b_{61}X_1 + b_{62}X_2 + b_{63}X_3 + b_{64}X_4 + b_{65}X_5 + e_6$$

$$X_7 = b_{71}X_1 + b_{72}X_2 + b_{73}X_3 + b_{74}X_4 + b_{75}X_5 + e_7$$

$$X_8 = b_{81}X_1 + b_{82}X_2 + b_{83}X_3 + b_{84}X_4 + b_{85}X_5 + e_8$$

Data Collection

The next stage is usually data collection. The model specifies the variables that require measurement. However, modeling can be done after a study has

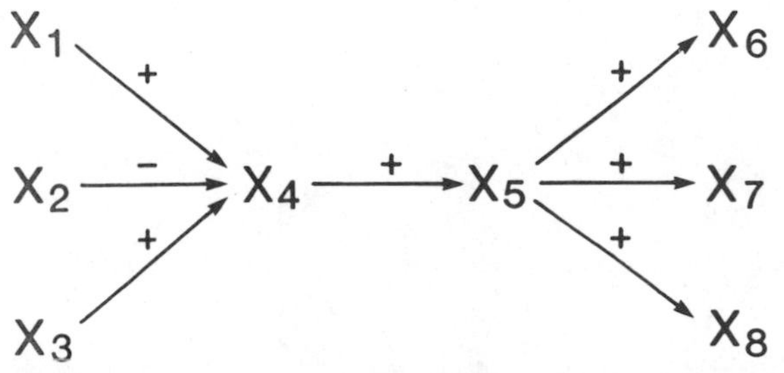

Figure 9–12. Hypothesized Structural Model

been completed (eg, using secondary sources of data). Sources of data for models can use multiple data-gathering strategies. Measurement issues are important, and every effort needs to be made to improve quality, reliability, validity, consistency, and completeness of the data. Multiple indicators can be built into the model and tested as part of the latent, unobserved variable schema.

Empirical Evaluation

The basic purpose of evaluating a model empirically is to determine the fit between the model and the data. The usual analysis for simple models is one of the least squares (OLS) or two-stage least squares (2SLS) procedures, none of which requires a multinomial distribution for the variables.[34] However, estimating the parameter by maximizing the likelihood (ML) is an efficient method under most of the assumptions. The evaluation of independence models for multinomial distribution uses several complex statistical theories. With the advent of efficient algorithms for calculating the maximum-likelihood estimates under log-linear models for multinomial probabilities, the task has become simpler. LISREL and RAM are two examples of these analytic computer programs.

While a maximum-likelihood procedure can be used to address the fit of a model and a set of data, it is becoming more popular to compare the fits of one model with at least one other competive or alternative model.[33] Under some circumstances, as in exploratory studies, the theorist-researcher is interested in making comparisons between successive numbers of a nested sequence of models. In this situation, it is advisable to keep track of the increment in the likelihood ratio (LR) statistics as well as the overall statistic.

In recent years, a number of authors have pointed to the need for further work on structural models for qualitative data.[29,35,36] Some traditional models for quantitative data (eg, those that can be solved with systems of equations or some linear regression analyses) have no immediate analogs when the data are qualitative. Some promising work also has been done for creating workable analogs for qualitative data. Even models with qualitative data, unobservable (latent) variables, lagged effects, two-way reciprocal relationships, and other complexities can now be fitted with available computer programs. Thus the theorist who is interested in model building of this kind can concentrate on the probabilistic meaning and scientific appropriateness of the model and its alternatives with greater confidence that the numerical problems can be efficiently solved.

Model Refinement

Only recently has attention been paid to the problem of deciding how a poorly fitting model should be changed to improve the fit between the model and empirical observations.[37] Flaming and Stember[38] identified five major strategies for improving the empirical fit of a model: (1) measurement, (2) nonlinear transformation, (3) removal of variables, (4) addition of variables, and (5) respecification. These strategies are reviewed and the outcomes of our model-building effort are reported to provide examples.

The model we refined is a model for understanding why certain segments of the population supported certain air quality control strategies. We developed and tested an initial structural equation model in 1977 using a sample of 400 residents. In 1980, a similar study was funded by the Environmental Protection Agency.[39] In the interim between the two studies, we refined the model. In order to test the refined model in the second study, a sample of 600 residents was selected from the six-county target population. Using a random dialing method, households were identified and respondents were chosen and interviewed by telephone following a predetermined protocol. Measurement of variables in the model was accomplished by modifying the instrument used in the 1977 study.

Measurement

The first potential for increasing the explanatory power of a model is improving measurement. Measurement errors have been demonstrated to have an effect on the ability of the model to explain variance. Cochran[40] discussed the effects of such errors on the squared multiple correlation coefficient, R^2. When errors are independent and a multivariate normal model is assumed, the effect is that R^2 is reduced to the region of $R^2 g_y g_w$, where g_y is the coefficient of reliability of Y and g_w is the weighted mean of the coefficient of reliability of the Xs.

How valid and reliable were the measures in the 1977 study, and how could they be improved? One strategy for eliciting data to estimate measurement properties is to construct multiple indicators. Allen's[41] canonical factor regression method for constructing composites was used in our studies. It requires canonical factoring to determine the weights and provides formulas for estimating the psychometric properties.

From the measurement information in the 1977 survey, decisions were made about construction of items for the 1981 survey. If the composite was satisfactory in 1977, the same questions were used. If the composite was good and involved many items, one or two of the worst items were deleted for efficiency. Finally, when the psychometric properties were unacceptable in 1977, new measures were developed. To compare measurement error from 1977 to 1981, tables of factor loadings, commonality estimates, factor score

coefficients, and reliability and validity coefficients were examined, showing an overall improvement in measurement.

Nonlinear Transformation

A second strategy of model refinement is nonlinear transformations. Path analysis of structural equation models is based on the general linear model. Thus if relationships are actually curvilinear, but represented as linear, the actual association may not be recognized and the R^2 is likely to be attenuated.[31,42] Nonlinear relationships can be handled in the model through mathematical transformations and representations. Power polynomials are one method of fitting nonlinear relationships. Cohen and Cohen[42] argue that usually the first two or three powers (X^2 or X^3) to be added to the equation will suffice.

In our data, scatterplots were examined to identify the shape of relationships. By examining the residuals, some possible relationships were tentatively located that could be better represented by the addition of a quadratic function. We tested this by adding the function and examining the incremental change in R^2. For example, representing age in both linear and quadratic terms increased the percentage of variance explained (R^2) in income from 5.6% to 19.8%. This statistically significant increase of 14.2% demonstrates the improvement in specifying the shape of the association.

Removal of Variables

A third potential for refinement is trimming variables from the model, thus making it more parsimonious.[43] By examining the coefficients in a path diagram, it is possible to identify variables that have no causal linkages. However, seldom will the path coefficients be precisely equal to zero. Sampling fluctuations and minor violations in various assumptions (ie, perfectly reliable measurements) usually preclude this. The problem is deciding when a path coefficient is negligible and can be treated as zero. Heise[18] suggested that absolute values be used for deciding what is sufficiently "small" rather than statistical significance. If not, when samples are small, large coefficients could be treated as negligible. Alternatively, if samples are large (as they should be for these analyses), a coefficient could be statistically significant, even though it is in fact small in absolute value.

A simplified path diagram with the findings from the initial model (1977 data) was drawn. One variable clearly was unconnected; it was not explained by the other variables in the model and did not contribute to explaining the central variable of interest. This variable was removed from the model for efficiency and parsimony.

Addition of Variables

Another strategy for model refinement is to ask, Should any variables not yet included in the model be considered for possible inclusion? Duncan[21] suggested that the basic difficulty with a model may reside, not in its mathematical form, but in the variables that enter into it. Weaker aspects of our model were examined and other relevant variables were identified. For example, adding the variable "Knowledge About Air Pollution" increased the amount of explained variance in "Belief Air Pollution Is Health Hazard" by the increment of 8.2%

Respecifying the Model

Finally, respecification can be considered.[44] However, it should be done with caution. The importance of a priori theory in model specification is paramount. In the initial model, we took a social psychological approach that suggested that demographic and socioeconomic characteristics determine values that people hold, and values are important contributors to beliefs. Beliefs in turn are likely to predict behavior. The reality, however, is perhaps more complex. The sequence may not necessarily occur in the hypothesized progression; feedback loops may exist. Where temporal ordering was difficult to justify, variables were blocked and respecified in the same temporal space.

DISCUSSION

Model building has been described as a theoretical and methodological activity in which a structural model is developed and tested to clarify relationships and communicate them more effectively. The use of structural models facilitates the identification and organization of knowledge in a selected domain. The model simplifies and, by so doing, assists in ordering important variables and specifying their structural relationship to one another. Although fullness of substance may not be achieved, the economically articulated organization of elements can make contributions.

This process encompasses both theoretical development and the empirical analytic methodology. It also has the advantage of clearly showing the theorist-researcher how to move precisely between the theoretical model and the empirical world. As a process, the structural model-building strategy is retroductive, having inductive and deductive elements. It requires that theory building and research do not occur in isolation, responding to the demand for research-theory-practice linkages. Model building, then, is an important theory-building strategy in nursing.

Although model building is not advocated as *the* strategy of choice for theory building in nursing, it is suggested as one important strategy. Many nurse scientists have suggested that at this critical point in our development,

it is too early to select one strategy for theory building.[4,13,22] Silva and Rothbart[45] suggest that research traditions should not be seen as competitive, trying to mutually undermine one another, but as collaborating toward the goal of solving scientific problems.

If we examine the current development of nursing science, we can observe theory building and research studies from one tradition or another, and we also see many studies that combine qualitative and quantitative methods. Yet in many publications, the battle between the two dominant approaches continues without full appreciation of the contributions of each and without recognition of the potential of a convergent exploration in nursing science. Chinn and Jacobs[4] caution that nothing is more detrimental to the development of science than individual scientists claiming that their own particular approach is the only one or the right one. I concur with Gortner[22] that the profession would be unwise to reject scientific techniques because of fear of dehumanization or concerns about the validity of analytic approaches. Different strategies will yield varying products, each contributing to the development of nursing theory. Multiple strategies for theory building and multiple modes of disciplined inquiry are needed if nursing is to be a scientific, humanistic profession.

REFERENCES

1. Bush HA: Models for nursing. *Adv Nurs Sci* 1978; 1(November):13-21.

2. Carper BA: Fundamental patterns of knowing in nursing. *Adv Nurs Sci* 1978; 1(October):13-23.

3. Chance KS: Nursing models: A requisite for professional accountability. *Adv Nurs Sci* 1982; 4(January):57-65.

4. Chinn PL, Jacobs MK: A model for theory development in nursing. *Adv Nurs Sci* 1978; 1(October):1-11.

5. Hardy LK: Nursing models and research—a restricting view? *J Adv Nurs* 1982; 7(September):447-451.

6. Hardy ME: Perspectives on nursing theory. *Adv Nurs Sci* 1978;1(October):37-48.

7. Jacobs MK, Huether SE: Nursing science: The theory-practice linkage. *Adv Nurs Sci* 1978; 1(October):63-73.

8. Kim HS: *The Nature of Theoretical Thinking in Nursing.* Norwalk, Conn, Appleton-Century-Crofts, 1983.

9. Walker LO, Avant KC: *Strategies for Theory Construction in Nursing.* Norwalk, Conn, Appleton-Century-Crofts, 1983.

10. Bilitski JS: Nursing science and the laws of health: The test of substance as a step in the process of theory development. *Adv Nurs Sci* 1981;4(October):15-29.

11. Bohny BJ: Theory development for a nursing science. *Nurs Forum* 1980;19:50-67.

12. Craig SL: Theory development and its relevance for nursing. *J Adv Nurs* 1980;5(July-August):349-355.

13. Fawcett J: The relationship between theory and research: A double helix. *Adv Nurs Sci* 1978; 1(October):49-61.

14. Johnson M: Some aspects of the relation between theory and research in nursing. *J Adv Nurs* 1983;8(January):21-28.

15. Blalock HM: *Causal Inferences in Non-experimental Research.* Chapel Hill, University of North Carolina Press, 1961.

16. Blalock HM: *Causal Models in the Social Sciences.* Chicago, Aldine-Atherton, 1971.

17. Costner HL: Utilizing causal models to discover flaws in experiments. *Sociometry* 1971;34:398-410.

18. Heise DR: Problems in path analysis and causal inference, in Borgatta EF (ed): *Sociological Methodology 1969.* San Francisco, Jossey-Bass, 1971.

19. Land K: Principles of path analysis, in Borgatta EF (ed): *Sociological Methodology 1969.* San Francisco, Jossey-Bass, 1971.

20. Goldberg AR, Duncan OD (eds): *Structural Equation Models in the Social Sciences.* New York, Seminar Press, 1973.

21. Duncan OD: *Introduction of Structural Equation Models.* New York, Academic Press, 1975.

22. Gortner SR: The history and philosophy of nursing science and research. *Adv Nurs Sci* 1983; 5(January):1-8.

23. Suppe F: *The Structure of Scientific Theories.* Urbana, University of Illinois Press, 1977.

24. Burr WR: *Theory Construction and the Sociology of the Family.* New York, John Wiley, 1973.

25. Dubin R: *Theory Building.* New York, The Free Press, 1969.

26. Reynolds PD: *A Primer in Theory Construction.* Indianapolis, Bobbs-Merrill, 1971.

27. Stinchcome AL: *Constructing Social Theories.* New York, Harcourt, Brace & World, 1968.

28. Bielby WT, Kluegel JR: Statistical interference and statistical power in applications of the general linear model, in Heise DR (ed): *Sociological Methodology 1977.* San Francisco, Jossey-Bass, 1977.

29. Fienberg SE: A note on fitting and interpreting parameters in models for categorical data, in Schuessler KF (ed): *Sociological Methodology 1979.* San Francisco, Jossey-Bass, 1978.

30. Heise DR: *Causal Analysis.* New York, John Wiley, 1975.

31. Stolzenberg RM: The measurement and decomposition of causal effects in nonlinear and nonadditive model, in Schuessler KF (ed): *Sociological Methodology 1980.* San Francisco, Jossey-Bass, 1980.

32. Hauser RM, Golderberg AS: The treatment of unobserved variables in path analysis, in Costner HL (ed): *Sociological Methodology 1971.* San Francisco, Jossey-Bass, 1971.

33. Specht DA, Warren RD: Comparing causal models, in Heise DR (ed): *Sociological Methodology 1976.* San Francisco, Jossey-Bass, 1975.

34. Fox J: Simultaneous equation models and two-stage least squares, in Schuessler KF (ed): *Sociological Methodology 1979.* San Francisco, Jossey-Bass, 1978.

35. Manski CF: Structural models for discrete data: The analysis of discrete choice, in Leinhardt S (ed): *Sociological Methodology 1981.* San Francisco, Jossey-Bass, 1971.

36. Hildebrand DK, Laing JD, Rosenthal H: A prediction-logic approach to causal models of qualitative variates, in Heise DR (ed): *Sociological Methodology 1976.* San Francisco, Jossey-Bass, 1978.

37. Muircheartaigh CA, Payne C: *Model Fitting: The Analysis of Survey Data,* vol 2. New York, John Wiley, 1977.

38. Stember ML, Flaming KH: Causal modeling for predicting perception of air pollution as a health hazard. *Proceedings of Envirometric 81.* Washington, DC, Government Printing Office, 1981.

39. Flaming KH, Stember ML: *Public Opinions About Improving Air Quality: The Technical Report.* Denver, Applied Sociological Research Team, 1982.

40. Cochran WG: Some effects of errors of measurement on multiple correlation. *J Am Stat Assoc* 1970;65:22-34.

41. Allen MP: Construction of composite measures by the canonical-factor-regression method, in Costner HL (ed): *Sociological Methodology 1973-1974.* San Francisco, Jossey-Bass, 1977.

42. Cohen J, Cohen P: *Applied Multiple Regression/Correlation Analysis for the Behavioral Sciences.* Hillsdale, NJ, Lawrence Erlbaum, 1975.

43. Neter J, Wasserman W: *Applied Linear Statistical Models.* Homewood, Ill, Richard D. Irwin. 1974.

44. Saris WE, de Pijper WM, Zegwaart P: Detection of specification errors in linear structural equation models, in Schuessler KF (ed): *Sociological Methodology 1979.* San Francisco, Jossey-Bass, 1978.

45. Silva MC, Rothbart D: Philosophies of science on nursing theory development and testing. *Adv Nurs Sci* 1984; 6(January):1-13.

Chapter 10

Causal Modeling: A Heuristic and Analytic Path to Nursing Knowledge

Karen Walton Budd and Kathleen M. McKeehan

Causal modeling is a useful heuristic and analytic tool for nurse scientists as they set about the task of discovering and explaining relationships among nursing phenomena. The development of nursing knowledge consists of two reciprocal stages: a theory-building stage and a theory-testing stage. Causal modeling as an heuristic device fits within the theory-building stage, and as an analytic device, it fits within the theory-testing stage. The theory-building stage involves the processes by which the phenomena of the discipline are identified. Concepts are clarified and defined, and relationships between and among the concepts are postulated. Causal modeling is particularly useful in this stage as an heuristic device for intuiting such relationships.

The theory-testing stage is where measurement procedures are worked out and links are established from the theoretical speculation of the first stage to physical measurement operations.[1] In this second stage, causal modeling as an analytic tool is useful for testing the hypothesized relationships. Cumulative nursing knowledge is built when attention is paid to the reciprocal nature of both stages.

An assumption being made by the authors is that nursing research, for the purpose of building nursing knowledge, is based on carefully explicated theoretical frameworks and statements. These propositional statements may be developed as a result of placing a nursing perspective on the phenomena encountered by nurses in their practice; or they may be based on existing theory and frameworks and emerge as a result of restating the postulations of the theory in a nursing context. The usefulness of causal modeling for both

---

Note: The authors gratefully, acknowledge Marthe Cook, PhD, for her creative approaches in teaching causal modeling.

approaches to nursing knowledge development is discussed in this chapter, which is divided into two sections corresponding to the theory-building and theory-testing stages. Examples of both a newly developed theoretical framework in nursing and an existing theoretical framework from another discipline placed within a nursing perspective are used to demonstrate causal modeling.

THE HEURISTIC PATH OF CAUSAL MODELING

As an heuristic device, causal modeling is a way of thinking that manifests itself in an arrow diagram. According to Hardy,[2] nurse researchers need to examine the syntax of theoretical notions guiding their research by using a diagram to depict linkages between variables. Hardy proposes that this visual diagram provides a means of evaluating internal consistency and logical adequacy of the framework guiding the research. Hardy's diagraming may be referred to as causal modeling.

Causal Relationships

Whether or not it is made explicit, no observation is made without guidance by theoretical notions. At the very least, observations are categorized by their relative importance to the observer, since it would be impossible to observe everything at the same time. At the most, categories or concepts are related to one another in an attempt to bring order and understanding to our observations. Understanding develops as one attempts to relate concepts, then attempts to find a temporal sequence in the relationship, and, finally, attempts to identify other concepts that may be important to the relationship.

Philosophers have been struggling for centuries for a consensus on the meaning of causation. Positivists stress three criteria for inferring cause: (1) covariation between presumed cause and effect, (2) temporal precedence of the cause, and (3) the need to rule out alternative interpretations for a possible cause and effect connection.[3] Covariation, time order, and nonspuriousness have become the key words to the causal mode of thinking.[4]

The first two criteria of causation, covariation and time order, are seldom difficult to establish. It is the third, nonspuriousness, that has distinguished experimental from nonexperimental research and has led to the superiority of the experimental method in determining the causation of one variable by another. The random assignment of manipulated and controlled conditions enables the researcher to determine explanations of causation and to be reasonably certain about the criteria that characterize causation. The problem faced in a practice discipline such as nursing is that the setting for experimental research is frequently artificial and often does not have external

validity. In addition, social behavior in general does not have an easily isolated single cause,[4] but instead has a "web of causation."[5] Causal modeling provides a solution to this problem. Rather than controlling confounding variables by the randomization process, such variables are identified on theoretical grounds and formally placed in a model in a causal ordering pattern.

The Causal Modeling Process

As nurse scientists work toward understanding the nursing situation, it is useful to follow three initial steps: (1) identify the phenomena, (2) define and label the phenomena, and (3) conduct an in-depth review of the literature concerning the phenomena. Either an existing theoretical framework is found that explains concepts related to the phenomena or a new framework is constructed. In either case, a careful reading of the literature usually produces a "systematic listing of all important concepts or variables and theoretical propositions linking these variables."[6(p29)]

At this point, it is often possible to construct a causal model that depicts the major variables and their postulated linkages. Causal modeling as a heuristic tool becomes important at this step because "thinking causally about a problem and constructing an arrow diagram that reflects causal processes may often facilitate a clearer statement of hypotheses and the generation of additional insights into the topic at hand."[7(p8)]

The three criteria for a causal relationship can be visually depicted in a causal model. Covariation is displayed by linking concepts with arrows, and the type of relationship hypothesized is indicated by positive or negative signs. Time order is shown by displaying antecedents to the left of the concepts that they are thought to precede. The issue of nonspuriousness is addressed by depicting direct and indirect causal relationships as well as spurious noncausal relationships. At this first stage, it cannot be determined which of the linkages is stronger with regard to effects. The results of path analysis in the next stage will indicate relative strength of the relationships.

Two Examples of Causal Modeling in the Heuristic Stage

The following examples illustrate causal modeling derived from a newly developed framework and causal modeling using a nursing perspective applied to an existing theory developed in another discipline.

Newly Developed Framework

Budd[8] set out to explain the attainment of psychosocial health during high-risk pregnancy from a holistic health perspective. The extant nursing literature of the high-risk maternity experience depicted the tension inherent

in the experience as additive to the tension of the psychosocial developmental stage of pregnancy, preventing the attainment of psychosocial health. Viewing high-risk pregnancy from a holistic health perspective led to the postulation that tension of both the high-risk experience and the developmental stage of pregnancy is integrated with previous experience, motivations, and goals. Psychosocial health then, would be achievable regardless of the pregnancy risk designation.

A review of the literature organized by the two holistic categories of (a) transaction with the environment and (b) integration of environmental experience with self-knowledge led to the postulations and theorems found in Table 10–1. Arriving at the final set of propositional statements involved a cyclical inductive-deductive process with critical review of the literature and clinical experience. Blalock[6] was used as a guide for the format of the propositional statements; the theorems became the hypotheses of the theoretical framework to be tested. A causal model was developed that depicted the major variables: self-coherence, perinatal risk designation, coping, mood, and psychosocial health during pregnancy, and their relationships proposed by the theoretical framework. The model is found in Figure 10–1.

Table 10–1. Assumptions, Axioms, and Theorems of the Budd Theoretical Framework

A. Assumptions

1. Pregnancy is a psychosocial, developmental stage.
2. Psychosocial health during pregnancy is achieved by accomplishing psychosocial developmental tasks.
3. Achieving psychosocial developmental tasks involves transaction with the environment and integration of that transaction with previous experience, motivations, and goals.

B. Axioms involving transaction with the environment

1. Transaction with the environment will produce cognitive structures or schemata.
2. Transaction with the environment involving appraisal of stressors will produce arousal of the autonomic nervous system, tension, and negative affect.
3. Arousal of the autonomic nervous system, tension, and negative affect produces affective-oriented and problem-oriented coping behavior.
4. Because it does not change the environment or the stressor, affective-oriented coping perpetuates arousal.

Table 10–1. Continued

5. Because it involves changing the environment, problem-oriented coping leads to accomplishment of psychosocial developmental tasks.
6. Designation of perinatal risk indicates the presence of factors that are appraised as stressors.

C. Theorems involving transaction with the environment

1. Perinatal risk designation will be related positively to affective-oriented coping.
2. Perinatal risk designation will be related positively to problem-oriented coping.
3. Problem-oriented coping will be related positively to psychosocial health.
4. Affective-oriented coping will be related positively to negative mood.

D. Axioms involving integration

1. Stimuli are appraised by the self-schemata system according to correspondence with its structure.
2. Arousal is produced by appraising stimuli as challenging, harmful, or threatening to the goals and motivation of the self-structure.
3. Knowing the goals and motivations of the self-structure allows one to interpret the meaning of a stimulus in terms of its correspondence with the self-structure. (Such interpretation is labeled self-coherence.)
4. Knowing the goals and motivations of the self-structure allows one either not to interpret a stimulus as a stressor or to identify a means to cope with the stressor.

E. Theorems involving integration of transaction with the environment

1. Self-coherence will be related inversely to perinatal risk designation.
2. Self-coherence will be related positively to problem-oriented coping.
3. Self-coherence will be related negatively to affective-oriented coping.
4. Self-coherence will be related positively to psychosocial health during pregnancy.
5. Self-coherence will be related inversely to negative mood.

Existing Framework

McKeehan[9] was interested in the decision-making capabilities of clients as they planned for continuing care posthospitalization. Results of a review of the literature revealed a theoretical framework by Janis and Mann[10] that contained variables that intuitively fit her target population. The Janis and

Mann model focused primarily on the variables of risk, hope, and time and their impact on vigilant information processing. Vigilant information processing was considered by them as the essence of decision making. According to Janis and Mann, the variable of freedom of choice indirectly affected vigilant information processing by directly affecting the variables of risk, hope, and time. Additional findings by Abramson, Seligman, and Teasdale[11] indicated that a lack of freedom of choice directly affected vigilant information processing by producing a feeling of helplessness in individuals. McKeehan designed a model based primarily on the theoretical notions of Janis and Mann but also incorporated research by Abramson et al. on human helplessness. Figure 10–2 illustrates her model and Table 10–2 lists the nine hypotheses represented by the paths in her model.

Once these causal models were developed, the next step was collecting empirical evidence to test the hypotheses that were derived from the theoretical frameworks. The analytic part of causal modeling is that testing process.

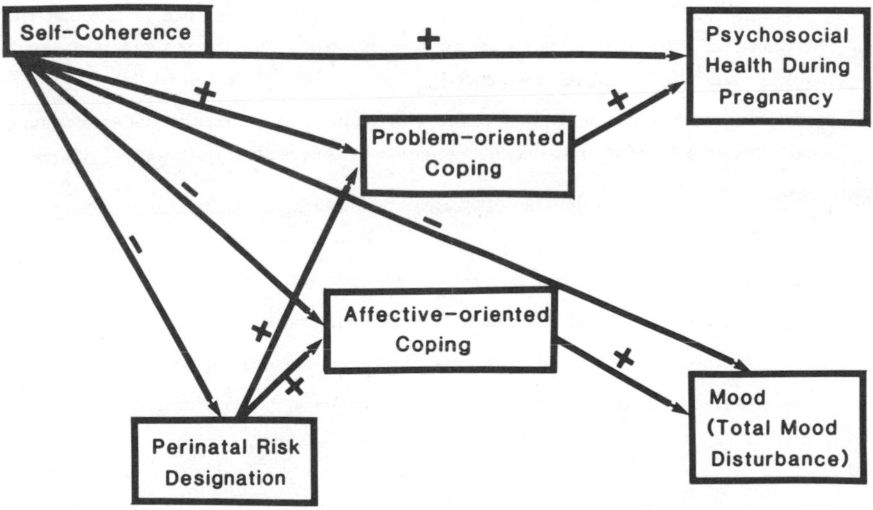

Figure 10–1. Psychosocial Reproductive Health

Source: Reprinted from *Perinatal Risk Designation, Self-Coherence, Coping and Mood: Relationships to Psychosocial Health during Pregnancy*, unpublished doctoral dissertation by K Budd, Case Western Reserve University, 1985.

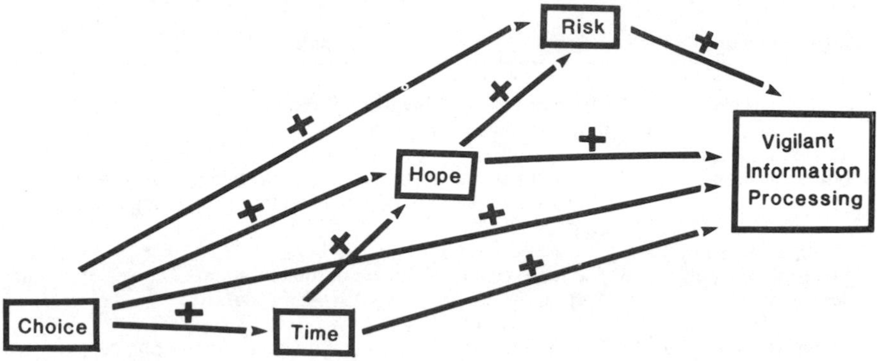

Figure 10–2. Decision Making by Clients

Source: Reprinted from *Decision Making by Clients Planning for Continuing Health Care*, unpublished doctoral dissertation by K McKeehan, Case Western Reserve University, 1985.

THE ANALYTIC PATH OF CAUSAL MODELING

According to Pedhazur,[12] the scientist's task of explaining phenomena is actually one of explaining the variation of phenomena in terms of observed or induced changes in supposed sources or the variation. Statistical analysis of data that measures the magnitude of the relationships between variables in causal modeling is called path analysis. Path analysis was developed by Wright[13] "as a method for studying the direct and indirect effects of variables hypothesized as causes of variables treated as effects."[12(p578)] It is becoming a dominant technique in social research[4] because of the ability it affords the investigator to disentangle relationships and test theoretical expectations about relationships.[14]

Path analysis is a method for specifically analyzing the extent to which the nonspuriousness criterion of causation has been met by the causal model. A correlation matrix will help the nurse scientist to determine the first criterion of causation: whether a relationship exists between variables. The second criterion, time ordering, has been addressed in the causal model by the placement of the variables and is determined on theoretical grounds. The third criterion, nonspuriousness, or ruling out other causes, is addressed in causal modeling by decomposing the correlations between variables. Path analysis leads to a determination of whether an independent variable's effect on a dependent variable is direct, indirect, spurious, or a combination of these.

Table 10–2. Hypotheses of the McKeehan Model

Variable Linkage	*Hypothesis*
Choice to Risk	1. The more clients are aware of their freedom of choice, the more they are aware of the seriousness of alternatives.
Choice to Hope	2. The more clients are aware of their freedom of choice, the more they are aware of the hopefulness that a satisfactory alternative exists.
Choice to Vigilant Information	3. The more clients are aware of their freedom of choice, the better their ability to process information vigilantly.
Choice to Time	4. The more clients are aware of their freedom of choice, the more they are aware of the adequacy of time to search and deliberate.
Hope to Risk	5. The more clients are hopeful that a satisfactory alternative exists, the more they are aware of the seriousness of the risks of alternatives.
Time to Hope	6. The more clients are aware of adequate time to search and deliberate, the more hopeful they are that a satisfactory alternative exists.
Risk to Vigilant Information Processing	7. The more clients are aware of the seriousness of risk alternatives, the better their ability to process information vigilantly.
Hope to Vigilant Information Processing	8. The more clients are hopeful that a satisfactory alternative exists, the better their ability to process information vigilantly.
Time to Vigilant Information Processing	9. The more clients are aware of adequate time to search and deliberate, the better their ability to process information vigilantly.

Estimates of the magnitude of the linkages between variables, the path coefficients, are obtained by regressing each dependent variable on variables to its left. The resulting betas are the path coefficients. For example, to obtain the estimates for the linkages of the Budd model (Figure 10–3), X^2 was regressed on X^1 in the first regression run. In the second run, X^3 was regressed on both X^1 and X^2, and so forth, until five regression runs had resulted in estimates for all hypothesized linkages.

By tracing paths in the diagram using a set of tracing rules,[4,7,12] it is possible to decompose the zero-order correlation between two variables. Or, in other words, it is possible to determine how much of the variation in the dependent variable is caused directly and indirectly by the independent variable, and how much is due to the spurious noncausal effect of a third variable. The decomposition of correlations among variables depicted in the

X_1 = Self-coherence

X_2 = Perinatal Risk Designation

X_3 = Problem-oriented Coping

X_4 = Affective-oriented Coping

X_5 = Psychosocial Reproductive Health (Total)

X_8 = Mood

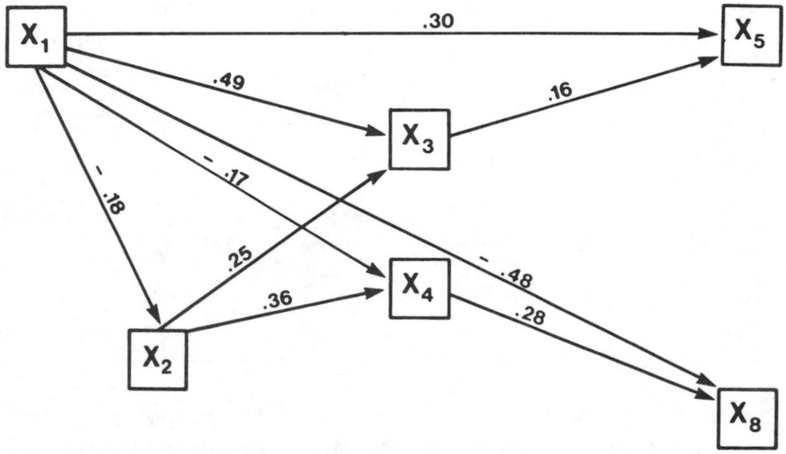

Figure 10–3. Path Analysis of Psychosocial Reproductive Health

Source: Reprinted from *Perinatal Risk Designation, Self-Coherence, Coping and Mood: Relationships to Psychosocial Health during Pregnancy*, unpublished doctoral dissertation by K Budd, Case Western Reserve University, 1985.

Budd model are found in Table 10–3. The path coefficients on the McKeehan model were obtained using the same approach.

Testing the Validity of the Model

Four approaches to testing the validity of a causal model are presented. Each approach has a specific use, and in many instances, it is wise to apply all four approaches to a model. One approach is to assess the model's ability to reproduce the zero-order correlation matrix by using the path coefficients. "If

Table 10–3. Decomposition of Bivariate Covariation for the Budd Model

Bivariate Relationship	*r*	*Direct Effect*	*Indirect Effect*	*Spurious Effect*	*Total Effect*
X_1X_2	−.18	−.18	None	None	−.18
X_1X_3	.45	.49	−.04	None	.45
X_1X_4	−.23	−.17	−.06	None	−.23
X_1X_5	.37	.30	.07	None	.37
X_1X_8	−.54	−.48	−.06	None	−.54
X_2X_3	.16	.25	None	−.09	.16
X_2X_4	.39	.36	None	.03	.39
X_2X_5	−.05	None	.04	−.07	−.03
X_2X_8	.29	None	.10	.10	.20
X_3X_5	.30	.16	None	.14	.30
X_3X_8	−.18	None	None	−.16	−.16
X_4X_5	−.12	None	None	−.03	−.03
X_4X_8	.39	.28	None	.11	.39

the model was specified correctly, then (except for measurement error and sampling error when relevant) the empirical correlation between any two variables should be numerically equal to the sum of the simple and compound paths linking the two variables."[7(p36)] The Total Effect column of Table 10–3 contains the correlations reproduced by the Budd model.

Two problems exist with this approach to testing validity. First, although slight inconsistencies in the correlation coefficients are to be expected, there are no criteria for judging slight from large inconsistencies. Second, it is impossible to use this approach to test the validity of a model if no paths are missing because regression with all possible variables entered will always reproduce the zero-order correlation matrix among those variables.

The second approach to validity testing, referred to as theory-trimming, is particularly useful when all possible variables have been entered in the regression run. With this approach, the path coefficients are tested for significance using a *t* or *F* ratio. Any path or beta coefficient smaller than a specified level of significance is "trimmed," or deleted, from the model. All paths of the Budd model were significant at the .05 level, so none were trimmed. Two paths in the McKeehan model were not significant and were deleted. Figure 10–4 depicts the McKeehan trimmed model.

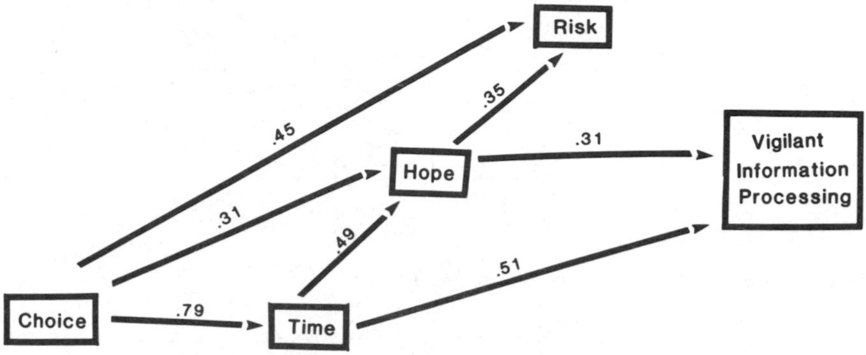

Figure 10–4. Trimmed Model of Decision Making by Clients

Source: Reprinted from *Decision Making by Clients Planning for Continuing Health Care,* unpublished doctoral dissertation by K McKeehan, Case Western Reserve University, 1985.

The third approach for testing the validity of a causal model involves testing the significance of paths that either were never included in the model or were trimmed from the model. Omitting a path between two variables implies that the magnitude of the path coefficient is zero.[7] Therefore, the test is to determine whether the beta is zero when all possible variables are entered in the particular regression run. The dotted line paths of the models in Figures 10–5 were nonsignificant, indicating that the models were correctly specified.

Finally, Pedhazur[12] suggests a X^2 goodness of fit test for models with deleted paths that uses properties of the zero-order and reproduced correlation matrices or the expected and observed correlations. This is the fourth approach for testing the validity of a model. The null hypothesis for the X^2 is: the reproduced correlation matrix of the trimmed model is the same as the zero-order correlation matrix. Failure to reject the null hypothesis indicates that the correlation matrix reproduced by the model closely approximates the original correlation matrix. The X^2 for both models of Figures 10–3 and 10–4 were nonsignificant, indicating that they were correctly specified.

In summary, causal modeling is a useful heuristic and analytic tool for generating knowledge in the discipline of nursing. The causal mode of thinking stimulates the search for causal relationships among the network of nursing phenomena and the development of theoretical frameworks. Path

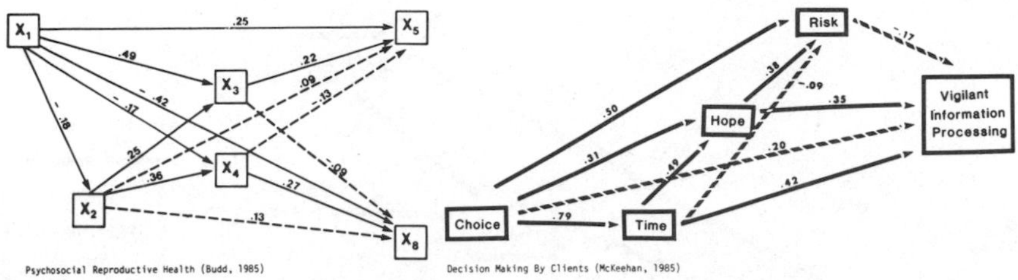

Figure 10–5. Validity Testing of Causal Models

Source: Reprinted from *Perinatal Risk Designation, Self-Coherence, Coping and Mood: Relationships to Psychosocial Health during Pregnancy* by K Budd and *Decision Making by Clients Planning for Continuing Health Care* by K McKeehan, unpublished doctoral dissertations, Case Western Reserve University, 1985.

analysis of data collected to measure the phenomena assists the nurse scientist to determine whether the causal model correctly reflects reality.

REFERENCES

1. Blalock HE: *Conceptualization and Measurement in the Social Sciences.* Beverly Hills, Calif., Sage, 1982.

2. Hardy ME: Perspectives on nursing theory. *Adv Nurs Sci* 1978;1(1):37–48.

3. Cook TD, Campbell DT: *Quasi-experimentation: Design and Analysis Issues for Field Settings.* Chicago, Rand McNally, 1979.

4. Bohrnstedt GW, Knoke D: *Statistics for Social Data Analysis.* Itasca Il, FE Peacock, 1982.

5. Friedman GD: *Primer of Epidemiology,* ed 2. New York, McGraw-Hill, 1980.

6. Blalock HE: *Theory Construction; From Verbal to Mathematical Formulations.* Englewood Cliffs, NJ, Prentice-Hall, 1969.

7. Asher HB: *Causal Modeling,* ed 2. Beverly Hills, Calif., Sage, 1983.

8. Budd K: *Perinatal Risk Designation, Self-Coherence, Coping and Mood: Relationships to Psychosocial Health during Pregnancy,* doctoral dissertation. Case Western Reserve University, Cleveland, 1985.

9. McKeehan K: *Decision Making by Clients Planning for Continuing Health Care,* doctoral dissertation. Case Western Reserve University, Cleveland, 1985.

10. Janis TL, Mann L: *Decision Making: A Psychological Analysis of Conflict, Choice, and Commitment.* New York, Free Press, 1977.

11. Abramson LY, Seligman ME, Teasdale JD: Learned helplessness in humans: Critique and reformulations. *J Abnorm Psychol,* 1978;87(1):49-74.

12. Pedhazur EJ: *Multiple Regression in Behavioral Research,* ed 2. New York, Holt, Rinehart & Winston, 1982.

13. Wright S: The method of path coefficients. *Ann Math Stat,* 1934;5:161-215.

14. Polit D, Hungler B: *Nursing Research; Principles and Methods,* ed 2. Philadelphia, JB Lippincott, 1983.

Chapter 11

Nursing, Education, and Emancipation: Applying the Critical Theoretical Approach to Nursing Research

Barbara A. Hedin

> The profession of medicine has a vested interest in that which has potential to affect its profits. Medical wives and nurses have this potential—their "cooperation" can improve business and increase profits, but their opposition may diminish and threaten the enterprise. The medical profession's habit of protecting what it has by paternalistically limiting full development of nursing potential in the health care field is a direct result of physicians' fear of losing control of their business.[1(p27)]

> Inherent value, humanness, is reserved for certain classes, races, for the male sex; their power-over others is thus legitimized . . . . The pain of all of us who are seen as the other . . . the rainbow of different races, religions, and ethnic heritages; all women . . . is not just the pain of direct discrimination, it is the pain of being negated again and again. It is the pain of knowing that our concerns will not be addressed unless we bring them up ourselves, and that even then they will be seen as peripheral, not central, to culture, to art, to policy.[2(p6)]

These statements are representative of some of the many constraints on individual and group potential that are being experienced today. These constraints are increasingly being put into words, and as this is done, their nature and origin become clearer. But the problem then becomes one of how

people can transcend them. Naming them is only the first step, albeit an important one. In the fields of nursing, nursing education, and health care, numerous problems and constraints are being named. They are economic, political, and social in nature.

For individuals to live together in society means that there will be restrictions on individual and group freedoms in order that group goals—that is, the common good—may be pursued. Hence there always have been, and always will be, constraints. However, as society changes, these constraints, of necessity, also change. One set of relations will be replaced by another. Just as the relationship between a parent and a young child changes to that of a parent-adolescent relationship over time, so too must the structures and relations of society be constantly reexamined as progress within society occurs. So long as the old relations remain in effect after a change has been effected, they act as constraints on individual and group potential.

There is, however, resistance to such change. That ways are outmoded is difficult to recognize because they are seen to be "the way things are," as "natural." Alternatives are therefore difficult to visualize. In addition to this, the traditional structures are often supported by those in power who do not want them to be seen through. Through critical thought and action, however, changes can be achieved.

Nursing has begun to recognize this, and increased discussion in the nursing literature reflects the need for new, broader perspectives that would reveal different understandings of reality and ways of dealing with it. This includes the realization that culture, health, and science itself are all socially constructed and not given, objective phenomena. Among approaches being used to uncover this are (a) the phenomenological approach, an explication of the lived world as it is experienced[3]; (b) the critical theoretical approach, which aims to analyze the cultural context, identify those constraints, organizations, and structures that are outmoded, and replace them with those that are more freeing[4]; and (c) the feminist approach, the elucidation of the systematic discrimination against women and the movement to transform the structures that perpetuate this, as discussed and used by a growing number of nurse researchers.[5–7]

This chapter provides an example of how the second of these methods, the critical theoretical approach, which Jurgen Habermas has brought into the mainstream of social philosophy, was used to analyze a current issue in West German nursing education. It is based on the belief that nursing research is directed toward increasing emancipation of individuals by the removal of unnecessary and unjust constraints. Such research is needed at different levels both in the development of therapeutic procedures and at the broader level of analysis of social, political, and economic issues. It is hoped that a concrete example of this method will provide an understanding of its relevance to nursing.

DESCRIPTION OF THE STUDY

The research focus of the study was the social, economic, and political factors that affect the nursing education system in the Federal Republic of Germany (FRG) and how those factors perceived as constraining could be transcended.[8] An incident in West German nursing history was sought that would shed light on the broader research question. After a review of the German nursing literature and discussions with German nurses, the short history of an experimental program at the Free University of Berlin, "*Modellversuch*: The Development and Testing of a Three-Year Course of Study for Instructors in the Health Professions," was selected.

This program was funded by both the state and the national government from October 1976 through June 1982 for the purpose of preparing instructors in nursing at the university level. This was the first nursing program to occur at a German university for which a bona fide university degree was awarded on completion. Its staff made efforts to establish it as a permanent course of study at the Free University on completion of its funding as an experimental model. The efforts failed and the program came to an end in June 1982, despite a waiting list of more than 100 candidates. The various factors effecting the failure were analyzed within a critical theoretical framework. Only those details of the research study that are relevant to the discussion of the method and methodology are discussed.

The study of constraints on nursing in the FRG, also a Western, industrialized, capitalist nation, reveals parallels to nursing in the United States and, through another cultural perspective, provides insight into similar problems in both cultures. Crosscultural study, however, is not a necessary condition for, or even characteristic of, the use of the critical theoretical approach.

THEORETICAL BACKGROUND

Overview of the Critical Theoretical Approach

Critical social theory as presented by the theorists of the Frankfurt School offers a critique of human activities from the standpoint of their constraining or enabling effects on individuals' efforts to create "the good life," that is, a life free from domination. Critical social theory is a "reflective critique of socially unnecessary constraints of human freedom"[9(p15)] that exposes the mystifications of conventional society that dominate human potentialities. Critical theory stands in opposition to traditional theory. Traditional theory accepts the organization of a social system as given. On the other hand, critical theory is an immanent critique of the social system, and it brings contradictions to the level of consciousness for consideration and transforma-

tion that otherwise remain opaque and seem natural. As such, it draws from reconstructed Marxism and concerns itself with a critique of positivism. It provides an alternate understanding of theory that includes attention to historicity and the explication of relationships among interests, knowledge, and action.

Origins of Critical Social Theory

While the critical theorists diverge from Karl Marx's position in *A Contribution to the Critique of Political Economy*, his book nevertheless serves as a paradigm for a critical theory of society and offers important insights into human reproduction, society, and human relations.[10] Marx gives a historical materialistic interpretation of reality, that is, one that views society as being historically determined. Humans are seen as historical beings who act in a concrete, historical context and who are agents of their history as well as products of it. This results in a dialectical two-sidedness of socialized organisms that sets them above nature. They are able to transform their past into conscious action toward the future, whereas other animals live only in the here and now. It is not the consciousness of humans that determines their existence, but social existence that determines their consciousness. However, this consciousness is then capable of transforming the real world by practical intervention. Fundamentally, then, historical materialism is an analysis that realizes the critique of society.

Another concept central to Marx's works is that of human alienation. The relationship between the material basis of life—work—and individuals' conceptions of themselves as social beings is distorted, producing a reification of social relations, that is, a reduction of human relations to objects. Alienation occurs on several levels: alienation from the product, alienation from work, alienation from other people, and alienation from self. In alienation there is an objectification and externalization of the individuality that makes people conscious of themselves as human beings. The social structure of capitalist society forces people to work in such a way that their human qualities are suppressed and they cannot relate effectively to one another. To Marx, this was an objective reality whether or not the workers themselves were aware of it. As a result of this, social interactions are systematically reproduced. Individuals cannot fully realize the potential of particular roles (eg, what it means to be a mother, father, wife, friend), and these roles are fulfilled automatically with no spontaneity, reflection, or authentic individuality. The problem for Marx was how to turn people, reduced to empty individuality through the alienation processes mentioned earlier, away from purely private interests and preoccupations, to be united with the community.

The aim of Marxism is the production of a qualitatively new social structure, based on the freedom of all, rather than the dominance of a few, in which all individuals could fulfill their individual needs and achieve social well-being. "Fragmentary, imperfect, disfigured man is incapable of transforming himself into a total man; he can only do so through society as it develops."[11(p23)] People cannot hope to develop into free individuals in a repressive society, in an environment in which they are socially, politically, or economically oppressed. Hence the importance of a framework with which to analyze and criticize the existing social structure, so that it might be transformed into one allowing more freedom, and the importance of dealing with the question of how to unify those with such an interest.

Critique

Although the meaning and use of the word critique have varied substantially over the years, the critical theorists use it to mean "a reflection on a system of constraints which are humanly produced: distorting pressures to which individuals, or a group of individuals, or the human race as a whole, succumb in their process of self-formation."[12(p18)] This view emanates from Hegel's concept of reflection leading to a liberation from coercive illusions.

Traditional Theory *v* Critical Theory

A fundamental, organizing principle of the critical theorists has been their opposition to the use of positivism in the realm of social theory. They maintain that the separation of the subject from the object of knowledge is illusory and that use of positivism in the social sciences subverts scientific truth.

An examination of several of the suppositions of traditional theory as compared with critical theory might elucidate this further. Traditional theory serves to maintain existing social relations; it is embedded in the work organization and division of labor by which the given social system maintains itself. It uses an atemporal, discursive logic and tends to be atomistic, ahistorical, and reductionistic. Critical theory is an immanent critique of capitalist social systems, and it aims to transform the present reality rather than maintain it. It sees the individual as creator of historical reality. It postulates what is and what could be. It seeks not to prescribe goals by existing life forms, but to allow humans, with all their possibilities, to work these out for themselves.

Individuals functioning within the traditional theory paradigm assume that humans passively perceive facts that are preformed and natural, rather than, as critical theorists propose, that humans produce their own historical way of life in its totality. Natural scientists, for example, do not see that facts are

socially constituted through the historical character of the perceived object and through the historical character of the perceiving organ. However, as maintained by critical theorists, there is an active subject involved; facts are not ultimate, but conditional.

The critical theorists are intent on maintaining the connection between action and theory. They realize that the creation of a purely intellectual world constituted by facts contributes to the continued control by existing societal arrangements by presupposing and accepting them as initial conditions. Rather, the focus of research must be a critique of domination, a recognition of those existing structures that exploit, alienate, and repress people. Theory emerges from, yet transcends, human relations and allows for a reconstitution of reality in a more emancipated way.

Historicity

A further important element of the critical approach is historicity, the conceptualization of the role of history in the life of the individual and society. Empirical scientists' practice of taking a "slice of reality" and studying it in the here and now with the assumption that this reveals the full meaning of a particular phenomenon has been found to be inadequate for study in the social sciences. Gadamer states that the *Geisteswissenschaften* (the cultural, or human, sciences) can be liberated from their obsessive identification with the procedures typified by the natural sciences only if the historic character of their object is acknowledged as a positive moment in their understanding rather than as an impediment to understanding.[13] The concept of hermeneutic situation is needed for this type of understanding; that is, that individuals must be conscious of their own prejudices so that the text can assert its own truth against them.

Historicity is also the perspective that enables individuals to view themselves as historical beings, as people who are a link between the past and the future and who see themselves as playing a vital role in shaping events to come.

Interests Guiding the Discovery of Knowledge

Jurgen Habermas, in his presentation of critical social theory, states that there are different interests guiding the discovery and development of knowledge. Knowledge pursued in a *technical interest* is for prediction and control; knowledge pursued in a *practical interest* is for the development of self and mutual understanding; and knowledge pursued in an *emancipatory interest* is for liberation from outmoded relationships and structures.[14] All three types of knowledge are necessary for the development of a society in

which individuals are enabled to function as whole persons; no one type of knowledge is superior to the others.

Operating Within the Critical Stand

To operate within the framework of critical theory, therefore, is to hold the belief that the phenomena of life cannot be fully comprehended unless they are related to the historical and contextual whole, that is, to the social structure conceived of as a global entity.

Critique reconstitutes the existing social order so that the possibilities that are present in it can be visualized. The intent is to promote conscious emancipatory activity. Such a comprehensive critique is called for, since the existence of an autonomous individual is essentially interdependent with the existence of an emancipated society.

The value of the dialectical method in such a schema is readily evident because of its reliance on holism and its refusal to accept the structure of existing reality as given. The dialectical method emphasizes the understanding of change and transformation through the identification of contradictions in existing situations. To engage in dialectical thinking is to recognize that there is an interdependence, an interpenetration, a unity of opposites. Applying this to the research cycle means that one looks for the contradictions in a situation as a guide to what is going on and what is likely to happen.[15] It acknowledges that movement and change occur through contradiction; life centers around a theme and then around a countertheme that is excluded but implied. To move requires a radical restructuring toward a new synthesis. Nothing is resolved; rather, it is a movement between opposites.

Also of use in such a method is an understanding of hermeneutics, the theory of the interpretation of meaning. It acknowledges that human expressions contain a meaningful component that has to be recognized by subjects and transposed into their own system of values and meanings. Although the natural sciences are concerned with explanation and consider a theory of explanation necessary and sufficient for a theory of knowledge, hermeneuticists contend that something more is needed in a method to account for the intentionality and purposiveness of humans than mere explanation or description offers. Herein lies the basis for the emphasis of hermeneutics on meaning and understanding.

THE CRITICAL THEORETICAL APPROACH

Although there is no specific method of critical theory, David Held outlines several general steps for proceeding with a critical theoretical

approach. These are offered here as a starting point for discussion of the approach used in this study. In critical theory, Held suggests the following:

> begin with an object the nature and meaning of which is in question;
>
> employ "dialogue," as in traditional hermeneutics, as an essential means of gaining data and exploring possible interpretations;
>
> move beyond traditional interpretative techniques, because subjects' accounts of their behaviour include meanings which remain opaque due to distortion and repression;
>
> explain the opaqueness through explanation involving causal connections. Such explanations can only be constructed with reference to a general theory (itself) formulated within terms provided by a metatheory—systematic reflections on the nature of the object domain under review, for instance, identity formation and ideology;
>
> test the general theory by reconstruction of individual cases (life histories in psychoanalysis, specific societies for critical theory) and examine whether or not it has the capacity to reveal and dissolve distortions of communication.[16(p324)]

To list and discuss these steps separately implies that they are carried out in a linear sequence. There is much overlap and interaction, however, between the various phases of the process, and the sequence should be understood only as a general direction. That is, the first step does need to be accomplished before the last, but what occurs in between is open, fluid, and interactive.

Begin with an Object . . .

As in any study, the object of the study must be clearly delineated and described, taking into consideration its nature and meaning. One may compare this phase of the critical theoretical approach with the identification of the problem in traditional research, that is, the formulation and delineation of the problem inclusive of the literature review. In this particular study, the object was the explication of the West German nursing education system and its connectedness to its context. The nature and meaning of nursing; nursing education; the social, economic, and political factors affecting these; and the

social, economic, and political context of West Germany were important to this explication.

Employ "Dialogue" . . . and Move Beyond Traditional Interpretative Techniques . . .

It is difficult, particularly in these phases, to separate the steps from one another. Dialogue is used in both collecting and interpreting the data, and there is a constant movement back and forth between collection and interpretation of data.

Dialogue, as used here, is the hermeneutical conversation between the interpreter and the text, involving equality and active reciprocity. The interpreter dialogues with the data while collecting, analyzing, and interpreting it. New meanings emerge, and phrases that have always been ignored suddenly come alive and demand explanation. The same data that yielded the interpretations now seem to question their very validity.[8]

The researcher spent 18 months over a three-year time span (June 1982 through September 1984) in the FRG collecting data for the study. On her arrival in June 1982, she had some knowledge of the German language and culture from an earlier three-year residence there. The first several months in Germany were spent in intensive language study and in study of German history and culture. This was obtained through readings in German history, especially documentaries on Germany since World War II, as well as through readings dealing with the social, economic, and political status of the country in the 1970s and 1980s, the time period preceding and including the existence of the experimental program. Immersion in the culture and study at a German university were also part of the researcher's familiarization process, that is, one of participant observation. German newspapers, television, and varied cultural experiences were part of this as well, all engaged in for the purpose of achieving an understanding of the total context and a historical overview of the setting of the study.

Because of the lack of information on the West German nursing system in English, this type of data could be obtained only firsthand in the Federal Republic. The first contacts for interviews were made with the German Nurses' Association and a convenience sample of nursing schools. Names of individuals in the major nursing organizations, such as the German Union of Nurses' Associations, the Diakonie, and the trade union, were obtained in order to achieve a triangulation of perspectives on the situation of West German nursing. The interviews dealt with the structure of nursing and the nursing education system, the status and role of nursing within the health care system in West Germany, the strengths and weaknesses of the existing education system, and trends and issues in West German nursing. The researcher was a member of the German Nurses' Association throughout her

stay in Germany and attended several continuing education offerings for nurses as a means to gain insight into concerns and issues in West German nursing and to meet and talk with nurses informally.

Formal interviews were semistructured and lasted for an average of one and a half to two hours. Questions in the first several interviews were necessarily broad and open-ended, for example, "Would you describe the structure of the West German nursing education system?" "Where do the funds for the programs come from?" and "What are the entrance requirements?" As the interviews proceeded, the questions became more specific and focused on the education for instructors of nursing, details of the German nursing law, the content of the basic and postbasic nursing education, and other related areas.

Data regarding the specific research question dealing with the noncontinuation of the experimental program were obtained chiefly from seven individuals involved in the planning, development, and leadership of the program, two individuals in the government administration, and the written reports from the program. Before the first interview dealing with this subject, the Final Report of the experimental program and several articles pertaining to the program were read. Questions at the first several interviews were wide-ranging, dealing with the conceptualization of the program, its various phases, and the strengths and weaknesses of it. Semistructured interviews were conducted, with the questions often emerging within the interview itself. The first individual interviewed was a research assistant in the program, and this person was asked for names of other individuals with whom to speak. This process was repeated in each of the interviews. The researcher read all reports of the program, and content from these served as the basis for further questions. Once again, individuals whose perspective would differ regarding the circumstances surrounding the noncontinuation were sought to obtain a broad understanding of the situation and the factors affecting it.

The attempt was made to develop questions, and an interview process, that were dialectical. This meant asking questions about what actually occurred as well as the possibilities of what could have been. As the data were reviewed after each interview, additional questions were formulated to explore new areas and to seek validation of interpretations that were being made.

The interviews were taped and the content transcribed. After each interview, the researcher listened to the tape and made notes on the content and circumstances surrounding the interview. A content analysis of the data from each interview and from the written sources was done and categories formulated for the data. The interviews and written sources were reviewed several times and analyzed for additional categories and meanings. They were reflected on as a whole, complete unit. A "dialogue with the data" was engaged on. The researcher immersed herself in the data and "walked around inside of it" seeking the meanings and interpretation. New interpretations

were held up and allowed to be questioned by the data: "Does it fit?" "Does it make sense?" The interpretation was then revised based on these new insights. It is particularly in these last actions that one enters into a movement beyond traditional interpretative techniques, with the search for contradictions and an analysis and reflection on these as a key to future directions.

In this study, the data from three time periods were analyzed to understand what factors in the social context affected the noncontinuation of the experimental program. That is, data dealing with the conceptualization of the program, the implementation of the program, and the time during which efforts were made to have the program established as a permanent course of study at the Free University of Berlin were collected, analyzed, and interpreted. Contradictions and opposing forces within and among these phases were sought and analyzed.

Perhaps a few more words about "the search for contradictions" might be enlightening. It is important to incorporate this perspective of the research approach into the data-collecting phase as well. That is, one can uncover contradictions in any data set, but it is helpful to formulate the questions and tools of the study so that this search is purposeful. There are two main areas that it is helpful to hold in one's consciousness when doing this. These are the search for opposites and the identification of the actual *v* the possible. Perhaps looking for opposites is the clearest and most easily understandable of the two. The search for positives *v* negatives, enabling *v* constraining factors, conservative *v* liberal forces: these fall into the first category. When seeking the actual *v* the possible, a general format for asking questions is to ask, "Why?" eg, "Why is this chair sitting here?" and to ask a question addressing another possibility, eg, "Why is it *not* sitting over there?" Examples of questions used in this study are (a) "Why did the experimental program occur at the FUB? Why did it not occur at another university, such as Hamburg or Heidelberg?" (b) "Why did the experimental program come into being at this particular time? Why did it not occur ten years earlier?" (c) "Why does nursing remain a mission of the hospital in West Germany? Why does it not occur as a mission of the university?" Both questions in each grouping supply slightly different views of the same issue and help one to break away from seeing only that which is, to visualize what might also be or have been.

Explain the Opaqueness . . .

At this point in the research process, a theory that refers to the domain under review, that has itself been developed through systematic reflections on the nature of the object, is used to explain the opaqueness of the situation

under study. In this instance, Paulo Freire's theory of cultural action was used.[17,18]

An analysis of the situation concerning the noncontinuation of the experimental program demonstrated the constraint that society had on the development of nursing and nursing education in the FRG. It depicted the influential role that those outside the nursing profession had on nursing for their own ends. This situation revealed that decisions were based not on the good of the professional group involved or their development and contribution to society, but on other technical motives. It was an act of prescription of the behavior of one group by another, an act of exploitation of a group. The situation was named as one of oppression.[8] Freire's theory of cultural action was used to make sense of the situation studied in the research. The theory and its various descriptive tenets were laid over the data and its interpretation in order to illuminate what occurred and to determine the direction for what needs to be done to transcend existing constraints on nursing education in the FRG.

Freire's work consists of four major elements. The first is a description of oppressed group behavior and its dialectical opposite, the behavior of the oppressors. The second component is his conceptualization of the education process either as a tool of conformity to present social structures or as an instrument of liberation to supersede these. The third component, evolving from the former, is a dialogical method of inquiry that is used to learn about the group to be educated to work with them rather than to manipulate them. The last element of his work is a discussion of theories of cultural action, which he distinguishes as being either antidialogical and resulting in cultural invasion or dialogical and leading to cultural synthesis. In this particular study, a nursing education that is "freeing" was outlined as the basis to overcoming the consciousness that is prescribed for nurses—and women in general—by others, in order that they may develop a critical consciousness that allows them to perceive themselves not merely as objects in the world, but as subjects who can intervene and shape reality.

Test the General Theory . . .

This study incorporated only the first four steps as described by Held and listed at the beginning of this section and not the final one, "Test the general theory by reconstruction of individual cases (. . . specific societies for critical theory) and examine whether or not it has the capacity to reveal and dissolve distortions of communication."[16] This final step has implications for future research in this area. I visualize this being done through the selection and analysis of several incidents in West German nursing history to see if the theory is generally applicable and offers direction for the transcendence of constraints.

CONCLUDING REMARKS

The steps of the critical theoretical approach have been described and examples given of how they were implemented in the execution of a research study seeking to uncover and transcend the constraints on West German nursing education. It was said earlier that there is no one specific methodology to be used. In this research study, an ethnographic approach was used—the effort to understand the culture, a situation, from the perspective of the participants—using semistructured interviews, participant observation, and review of written sources to collect data. Content analysis, categorization of data, reflection of the data, as well as a hermeneutic-dialectical analysis with an emphasis on uncovering contradictions were used in the interpretation of the data.

To limit the approach to only these methodologies—or others that one might specify—would be an error. It is not the mechanistic application of any particular methodology that can lead to emancipatory insight, but the use of methodology in a manner consistent with the philosophical beliefs of the approach that is most important. That is, the analysis of issues with emphasis on context and historicity for the purpose of leading to increasing emancipation of individuals and groups is of essence. In this case, the research process itself is praxis—critical reflection on the ends and means of activity for the purpose of transformation. It is a means of consciousness raising, in which theory and action become one, through its problem-posing nature.

REFERENCES

1. Lovell MC: Silent but perfect "partners": Medicine's use and abuse of women. *Adv Nurs Sci* 1981;3(2):25-40.

2. Starhawk: *Dreaming the Dark.* Boston, Beacon Press, 1982.

3. Omery A: Phenomenology: A method for nursing research. *Adv Nurs Sci* 1983;5(2):49-63.

4. Allen DG: Nursing research and social control: Alternative models of science that emphasize understanding and emancipation. *Image* 1985;17(2):58-64.

5. Chinn PL, Wheeler CE: Feminism and nursing. *Nurs Outlook* 1985;33(2):74-77.

6. McGrory A: Women and mental illness: A sexist trap? *JPN Ment Health Ser* 1980;18(ptl):13-19.

7. MacPerson KI: Osteoporosis and menopause: A feminist analysis of the social constraints of a syndrome. *Adv Nurs Sci* 1985;7(4):11-22.

8. Hedin BA: *Nursing Education, Constraints, and Critical Consciousness: The Birth and Death of a* Modellversuch *in West Germany*; dissertation. University of Utah, Provo, 1985.

9. Shroyer T: *The Critique of Domination.* Boston, Beacon Press, 1973.

10. Marx K: *A Contribution to the Critique of Political Economy.* New York, International Publishers, 1970.

11. Fisher E: *Marx in his Own Words.* New York, Penguin Books, 1970.

12. Connerton P (ed): *Critical Sociology.* New York, Penguin Books, 1976.

13. Gadamer HG: The historicity of understanding, in Connerton P (ed): *Critical Sociology.* New York, Penguin Books, 1976.

14. Habermas J: *Knowledge and Human Interests.* Boston, Beacon Press, 1971.

15. Rowan J, Reason P: On making sense, in Reason P, Rowan J (eds): *Human Inquiry: A Sourcebook of New Paradigm Research.* Chichester, England, John Wiley, 1981.

16. Held D: *Introduction to Critical Theory.* Berkeley, University of California Press, 1980.

17. Freire P: *Education for Critical Consciousness.* New York, Continuum, 1970.

18. Freire P: *Pedagogy of the Oppressed.* New York, Continuum, 1970.

Chapter 12

The Dialectic As Method

Patricia Moccia

Nursing's quest for the perfect method is being abandoned as researchers recognize that there are a variety of ways to investigate questions, and that the nature of the question is a significant factor in choosing from among the alternatives. The monopoly once enjoyed by quantitative methods has recently been shaken as an increasing number of researchers have turned to qualitative ways thought to be more appropriate and adequate for their concerns than the reductionist approach has shown itself to be.[1(pl–27),2] Nurse historians, phenomenologists, and feminists, among others, have contributed to nursing's knowledge base through studies that have sought to describe, understand, and explain human phenomena rather than to control, predict, or manipulate them. Most recently, there has been a call in the literature for further expanding nursing's repertoire with the addition of critical theory, which has been described at some length,[3] and the dialectic, which, until now, has had only limited discussion.[4–6]

Arguments for the dialectic include (a) its potential as a more productive and accurate method of inquiry than those less focused on the dynamic, relational, and contingent character of human processes; and (b) its potential contribution to the understanding of Rogers's conceptual system and other holistic models and to the resolution of the quantitative *v* qualitative debate.[4(p25),5(p33),6(p72)] Additional arguments have been made for more detailed study of a dialectic that is specifically developed within a Hegelian-Marxist framework as it shares a similar unitary world view with nursing, provides for a desired internal coherence between such a perspective and a method of inquiry, and includes assumptions of the dynamic nature of existence that parallel nursing's.[5(p36),6(p73)] Because of nursing's search for additional methods, the interest in the dialectic in general, and a Hegelian-Marxist interpretation in particular, the following will identify and discuss the basic assumptions and laws of such a dialectic, illustrate its approach to inquiry by comparing and contrasting dialectical and nondialectical ways to study the same problem, further assess the dialectic's relevance to theory

development in nursing, and identify questions that emerge from the discussion.

ASSUMPTIONS OF THE DIALECTIC

Despite the logical arguments for investigating a Hegelian or Marxist dialectic, such an approach might still seem far removed from nursing's usual modes without further explanation. Hegel's identification as a philosopher seems less problematic in this respect than that of Marx, who is generally associated with political science, economics, and historical materialism (accurately) or with the domestic and international policies of such countries as the Soviet Union and the People's Republic of China (less accurately). Neither of these popular perceptions or misperceptions are obviously relevant to nursing's concerns but for three factors. One, by its own admission, nursing is concerned with people as biopsychosocial beings, the nature of their environment, and the relationships between the two. Therefore, knowledge about the relationships between people and their social, political, and economic systems, which are inarguably constituent elements of the environment, is as potentially helpful to nurses as the study of the relationships between people's health and their biology or psychology. Two, the assumptions of a Hegelian-Marxist philosophy further extend dialectics' relevance to nursing. Both Hegel and Marx grounded their dialectic in a philosophy that emphasizes the interdependent relationship shared by the totality's parts no matter how widely disparate they might seem.[7,8] Although the disciplines of nursing and political science might *appear* to have little, if anything, to do with each other, a philosophy of internal relations would insist that there is some codetermining relation between the two. Three, acknowledging a difference between the methods of Hegel and Marx and their subsequent analyses, it is possible (although not necessary) to adopt their methods without their analyses. In other words, using a Hegelian-Marxist dialectic as a research method neither necessitates nor precludes the researcher being a Hegelian or a Marxist.

The dialectical method of inquiry is but one phase of a dialectical process that also includes a distinctive world view, particular methods of exposition and intellectual reconstruction, and dialectical relationships among these phases and between each part and the whole.[9(pp52,271)] The assumptions of this process and of each of its phases are derived from a world view that has been identified as one common to certain nursing perspectives: (a) the basic unit of life is a totality; (b) this totality is characterized by an infinite number of infinitely varied self-transformations; (c) these transformations are incessantly generated by and developed through the interrelationships among the totality's parts; and (d) the interrelationships are themselves dynam-

ic.[6(p73),10(p224)] Any dialectical method, therefore, can be expected to share these identical assumptions.

A dialectic that is specifically identified as Hegelian or Marxist distinguishes itself from other methods in several ways. One of the most significant is an argument common to both Hegel and Marx, ie, that it is impossible to ever know the whole or the totality because of the difference between reality and appearances. Both are equally clear that there is *always* a difference between the way things "seem" to be and the way that they "really" are. For example, even in the simplest act of talking about reality, which, according to Hegel, is the whole,[10(p55)] one must do the impossible of separating from what is assumed to be an indivisible totality. The distortions that are necessary when such a supposedly indivisible reality is even further divided into particulate processes (for example, in order to study, understand, and explain phenomena) result in appearances that parallel the distortions and that in turn are progressively removed from reality or the basic processes of becoming.[9(pp131–135)] Within a Hegelian-Marxist framework, this necessary, albeit distorting, division of reality is studied with the help of two constructs—individuation and abstraction—which have been identified as promising a similar utility for holistic nursing models and their parallel theortical paradox.[5(pp76–78)]

Individuation has been described as "simply a matter of mentally carving up the whole in a different manner for a particular purpose."[9(p19)] Once the act of division is acknowledged, one must face the question of why certain sets of internal relations are grouped together and distinguished from others. Such reasons or purposes are themselves open to considerable discussion, as some dialectical philosophers explain them as a function of an individual's experiences and needs coupled with real similarities found in nature; Marx and others see the individuations to be a function of the particular characteristics of the problem under study; and others have raised the question of whether the divisions are established for simple contrast, to manifest social conditions, or as a natural result of the "human condition."[9(pp267,62,241)] Whatever its reasons or purposes, the act of individuation produces an *abstraction* that has been described as "a part of the whole whose ties with the rest are not apparent: it is a part which *appears* (in original) to be a whole in itself."[9(p61)]

For Hegel and Marx, what appears to be reality, at any moment and from any vantage point, is only one of a series of phases in the system's ongoing process of self-development; each phase is mediated by another, and thereby each is further removed, or abstracted, from the truth. Such a reality is significant in at least two ways for the nurse researcher who works from a Hegelian-Marxist dialectic. One, given the "forces of abstraction," all understanding and knowledge is assumed to be appearance rather than reality; because these appearances are constantly changing, the nurse

researcher is relieved of the burden of discovering the one "true" explanation. Instead, the goals of dialectical study are to identify abstractions, uncovering obscure or covert relationships that in turn will uncover more relationships. Two, the identification, understanding, and explanation of the connections between these individuations add in some way to an understanding of the totality. Dialectics, therefore, allows a value to partial knowledge that is otherwise denied in holistic models.[11]

Dialectics is further refined as Hegel and Marx differ from each other in ways that potentially concern nurse researchers. While not directly significant to the process of inquiry, such differences are obvious factors in the questions chosen for investigation and in the analyses and discussions of the research findings. Hegel, for example, assumes an idealistic stance: "reality" is a series of necessarily distorted "moments," "phases," or "phenomena." These distortions are the projections of an Absolute Truth that resides in an immaterial Mind. This mind is the *only* reality.[10(p224)] Marx, on the other hand, is indisputedly materialistic: reality is a multidimensional network constructed by people interacting with a set of social conditions that influence the ideas and behavior more than disembodied ideas influence the social conditions.[12]

LAWS OF THE DIALECTIC

Several laws in a dialectical universe are already familiar in varying degrees to most professional nurses, although the terminology may differ and they may not necessarily be identified as dialectical. Nonetheless, they are useful. In addition, the laws of the dialectic are significant to the nurse researcher planning a study that is specifically dialectical. First, they help focus, select, structure, and organize the individuations and abstractions under study. Second, they help to explain and analyze the network of internal relations. And three, they help to reformulate our understandings of phenomena and to identify relationships for future research.

The law of transformation of quantity into quality, for example, explains that a change in the number of internal relations constituting any entity produces a new entity that is qualitatively different from the original.[9(p54)] Nurses already base their practice on such an understanding when they recognize that working with a new family is qualitatively different than working individually with a man, a woman, and a baby; or that a group of adolescents will exhibit different behavior than each of the teenagers will alone; or that caring for 32 patients on a unit during eight hours is qualitatively different than seeing 32 individual cases.

The law of polar opposites connects what appear to be distinctly different and opposing entities (or sets of relations) by tracing the internal relations and recognizing, instead, that each is a codetermining factor in the other's

development and both, therefore, share an identity.[9(p54)] The popular examples of good and bad, or masculine and feminine, are translated into nursing practice in particular ways that demonstrate that entities are not either/or, but both this and that: the nurse-patient or student-teacher relationship, for example, in which each is necessarily defined by her or his relationship to the other and in which each grows or learns through the other; or the family of an abusive man that is tied together and defined by his abuse; or the prison guard whose behavior is a function of the people being guarded.

Describing this interaction between polar opposites as one that occurs through the "negation of the negation," a third law of the dialectic has been popularized—some would say vulgarized—into the familiar thesis-antithesis-synthesis formula. Marx follows closely in the Hegelian understanding that reality proceeds in its development when a particular phase of the dialectic (thesis) interacts with one that would seem to contradict the first (antithesis) and incorporates both into the next phase of the dialectic (synthesis).[9(p56)] Similar to the first two laws' inferred relevance to nursing theory and practice, this "development through contradiction," although not explicitly identified, can be seen in common nursing mores, such as the conceptual shift away from a health-illness dichotomy (thesis-antithesis) toward the health continuum (synthesis), or the recognition of illness and crisis as opportunities for growth and the realization of new strengths, or the understanding that "the terrible twos" are a necessary developmental stage in children differentiating their selves from the parent figures.

The fourth law of the dialectic, which holds that reality manifests itself in a "spiral form of development" rather than in a linear fashion[9(p57)] is not as common to or as well developed in nursing's understandings as are the first three. Nonetheless, it does appear to have some parallel in those generally accepted laws which hold that growth and development always proceed from the simple to the complex. In addition, identical terminology is found in Rogers's conceptual system when the principle of helicy is described as a "function of continuous innovative change growing out of the mutual interaction of man and environment along a *spiralling* [emphasis added] longitudinal axis bound in space time."[13(p101)]

THE DIALECTIC AS METHOD

In the most general of terms, "the dialectic method," according to Marxist Ollman, "is best described as research into the manifold ways that entities are internally related."[9(p61)] With the dialectic's focus on internal relations, relationships are the obvious unit of analysis. But with the infinite number of relationships from which to choose, researchers are in obvious need of some direction as they (a) search for and analyze significant relationships and (b)

trace the connections between the originally identified relationships and those uncovered in the research process.

The question of where to begin to study any phenomena is one that has stymied many beginning researchers as they struggle with identifying their problem. The question of where to begin has also presented difficulties for dialecticians who have differentiated themselves as either Hegelian or Marxist by their answer. For example, whereas Marx sees people's consciousness as a product of social act, the idealist Hegel sees the product of a larger whole reproducing itself. But, although Marx clearly states his own preference—"It seems correct to begin with the real and the concrete . . . because it is the concentration of many determinations, hence unity of the diverse"[14(pp100–101)]—he is equally clear that dialectics allows either approach, as he charges those who get caught up in such debates as incorrectly approaching study "as if the task were the dialectical balancing of concepts, and not the grasping of real relations."[14(p90)]

The philosopher Marx worked from a Hegelian framework and adapted a Hegelian dialectic to study people and their relationship to a capitalist society, specifically individuating their relationship to the means of production in such a society as the significant factor in understanding and explaining human behavior.[15(pp283–301)] His theories about the nature of such a relationship are developed from his questions: "How do the ways in which people earn their livings affect their bodies, minds and daily lives?"[16(pxii)] Marx's particular interest as a social scientist further focused his studies to theories derived from such questions as "What is the effect of the workers' alienated labor on its products, both on what they can do and what can be done with them?" and "How did capitalism originate and where is it leading?[16(ppxiii,xiv)] The first question and its resultant theories are of obvious concern to nursing research and practice; the latter two are of less immediate or direct importance to nursing knowledge.

It is important here to respect the distinction between (a) Marx's philosophy and method and (b) his theories and analyses. Given a dialectical universe, we must assume that people continue to enjoy a codetermining relationship with their environment; that both people and their environment have changed since Marx; and that the nature of the relationship has, therefore, also changed since Marx. Although it falls within the domain of Marxist and non-Marxist social scientists and economists to identify the changing and changed nature of the environment since Marx and whether or not his analyses continue to have relevance for today's society, nursing continues to be appropriately concerned with people's relationships to their environment and the most productive ways to study such interactions. Therefore, in addition to the historical interest of 19th-century Marxist theory, Marxist philosophy and method are still significant for nursing research.

The laws of the dialectic help individuate (delimit) the relationships for study as they direct researchers to what appear to be inverse connections or polar opposites in a search for specific contradictions. As with any research, the study begins where there seems to be a problem; with dialectical research, the study most efficiently begins where the problem seems to be a contradiction. Dialectical nursing scholarship, for example, could begin by studying a problem that has been called a "myth" but which could also be identified as a contradiction, ie, how to approach nursing's concerns—which are focused on traditionally feminine values of caring, nurturing, and interaction—with a scientific method that acknowledges masculine values and perpetuates traditionally male standards. The community health nurse might dialectically study the apparent contradiction between the number of homeless people and the number of exorbitantly priced apartments in the same urban area; the occupational health nurse could research connections between a decrease in employee health benefits and an increase in executive exercise programs. Or, nursing's professional organizations might dialectically research the apparent contradiction between (a) the resistance to the nursing baccalaureate as a minimal criterion for entry into practice and (b) the societal value of upward mobility through advanced education.

In addition to helping focus research, the laws of the dialectic are useful in analyzing the findings. Whatever the particular problem, a dialectical study is expected to further clarify the studied relationship by uncovering relationships previously obscured by the forces of abstraction, which in turn indicate future work. Furthermore, given the dialectic, the researcher is expected to account for the original distortion and identify the changes in understanding that have developed through the research process.

A POSSIBLE CASE STUDY: NURSES' WORK DISSATISFACTION

Until the recent emphasis on the relationships among nurses, quality care, and cost containment measures, a prevailing theme of nursing research had been on the factors contributing to nurses' work satisfaction or dissatisfaction. For the purpose of discussion, these studies can be divided into two kinds: those that focus on biopsychosocial variables of the nurse and those that are primarily concerned with factors in the environment. Studies on burnout are an example of the first[17]; the study on magnet hospitals is an example of the second.[18] Although both approaches do acknowledge, or at least assume, a relationship between the nurse and the environment, there has yet to be a detailed dialectical study on *the relationship* in the nursing literature.

From his idealist stance, Hegel would question what aspect of the totality or the Absolute Spirit was manifesting itself in the conflicts between nurses

and their environment; or what could the apparent differences between nurses who are satisfied in their work and those who aren't tell about Reality; or what could be learned about the developmental stage of Reality through an analysis of how the concerns for nurses' satisfaction were replaced by cost containment issues. As a dialectical materialist, Marx would attempt to identify the predominate social system, its institutions and values, and their relationships to what nurses do all day. So, for a simplified example, Marx might study the relationship between nurses' dissatisfaction/satisfaction and the profit/loss figures of the hospital or the larger corporation to which it belongs. A dialectical researcher may choose to do either, both, or neither.

Using the laws of the dialectic as guidelines, a researcher would begin with the assumption that a study of significant relationships for nurses would discover that the "real" problem or contradiction is different from what originally "seemed" to be the problem or contradiction. The nurse-physician relationship has been an obvious place to begin studies about nurses' satisfaction/dissatisfaction. But judging by the on-going conflict despite the number of studies with statistically significant findings, the "apparent" contradiction between nursing and medicine is not the "real" problem. A next step for a dialectical researcher would be to analyze findings from these studies either to re-formulate the original inter-relationship studied or to identify additional, previously unrealized inter-relationships.

There are several obvious possibilities. Perhaps the contradiction in nurses' worklives is one between the polar opposites of masculine and feminine values, or between professional and non-professional workers, or between the workforce (both professional and non-professional) and administration. A dialectical investigation of any of these apparent contradictions would produce its own understandings but then would go on to uncover still other, currently less obvious relationships for study. To re-iterate and emphasize Marx's caveat: the issue is not whether or not the starting point or original individuation is correct but whether or not the dialectical nature of the individuated relationships is acknowledged, respected, accounted for, and studied.

PROMISES AND EMERGING QUESTIONS

Whether the goal of any particular study is to describe, explain, and understand human phenomena or to control, predict, and manipulate it, the increased awareness of contingent relationships available through dialectical analyses is generally helpful as it expands nursing's knowledge base. This increased awareness and sensitivity to the relational nature of reality are potentially the most productive contributions of the dialectic method. To the degree that researchers' use of the method promotes questions about the

predominating world view, *the dialectic is itself an agent of change and an enhancer of the life process.*

Several questions emerging from this discussion need to be addressed as nurse researchers consider the dialectic as a method. Some are shared with other dialectical researchers, eg, if there is some inherent truth in any analysis, how is one determined to be more correct than another? Is it necessary to do so? Or, given the infinite number of analyses and theories to attend to, how is reliability, validity, or significance determined? Others are particular to a professional discipline, eg, how is the public assured that nursing practice is developed from sound theoretical bases if all theories are possible?

CONCLUSIONS

It is understandably unsettling to have change and contradiction as a research goal rather than the definite resolution of a presenting problem. However, given the characteristics of human phenomena, the first is more natural and less contrived, and therefore potentially more productive than the latter. For those same reasons, it is also more complex and potentially more cumbersome, and therefore possibly less attractive for researchers facing constraints on human and material resources.

A Hegelian-Marxist dialectic holds surprising promise for nurse researchers, as its laws and assumptions seem to parallel some of nursing's own. Its logical categories provide possible ways of studying the relationship between parts and the totality that account for the distortions necessary to do so at the same time that they respect and preserve the integrity of the whole. The similarities among nursing philosophies, a Hegelian-Marxist dialectic, and certain nursing practices, as well as the method's special flexibility, argue for further discussion by nursing scholars of the as-yet-unresolved questions and an even more detailed study of the dialectic. If nurses are able to work with the anxieties of the dialectic's incessant changes, to separate (when necessary) a Hegelian-Marxist method from previous political analyses, to identify and manipulate significant dialectical relationships, and to incorporate it all into their research, nursing's knowledge base can be expanded and enriched in ways previously unexplored.

REFERENCES

1. Leininger MM: *Qualitative Research Methods in Nursing.* Orlando, Fla, Grune & Stratton, 1985.

2. Chinn PL: Debunking myths in nursing theory and research. *Image* 1985;17(2):45-49.

3. Allen DG: Nursing research and social control: Alternative models of science that emphasize understanding and emancipation. *Image* 1985;17(2):59-64.

4. Wilson LM, Fitzpatrick JJ: Dialectical thinking as a means of understanding systems-in-development: Relevance to Rogers's principles. *Adv Nurs Sci* 1984;6(2):24-41.

5. Moccia P: A further investigation of "dialectical thinking as a means of understanding systems-in-development: Relevance to Rogers's principles." *Adv Nurs Sci* 1985;7(4):33-38.

6. Moccia P ed.: Dialectics of theory development, in *Patterns in Education: The Unfolding of Nursing.* New York, National League for Nursing, 1985, pp 71-78.

7. Runes DD (ed): *Dictionary of Philosophy.* Totawa, NJ, Littlefield, Adams, 1975.

8. Ricoeur P: What is dialectical? in Birche J (ed): *Freedom and Morality: The Lindley Lectures.* Lawrence, University of Kansas, 1976, pp 173-189.

9. Ollman B: *Alienation. Marx's Conception of Man in Capitalist Society,* ed 2. Cambridge, Cambridge University Press, 1976.

10. Hegel GW: *The Phenomenology of Mind,* Baillie JB (trans). London, Allen & Unwin, 1964.

11. Munhall P: Nursing philosophy and nursing research: In apposition or opposition. *Nurs Res* 1982;31(3):176-177, 181.

12. Marx K: Theses on Feuerbach, in *Karl Marx and Frederick Engels. Selected Works.* New York, International Publishers, 1974, pp 28-31.

13. Rogers ME: *An Introduction to the Theoretical Basis of Nursing.* Philadelphia, FA Davis, 1970.

14. Marx K: *Grundrisse. Foundations of the Critique of Political Economy,* Nicolaus M (trans). New York, Vintage Books, 1973.

15. Marx K: Economic and philosophic manuscripts, in *Writings of the Young Marx on Philosophy and Society,* Easton LD, Guddat KH (ed and trans). New York, Doubleday, Anchor Books, 1967, pp 283-301.

16. Ollman B, Vernoff E: *The Left Academy. Marxist Scholarship on American Campuses,* vol 2. New York, Praeger, 1984.

17. Dailey AL: The burnout test. *Am J Nurs* 1985;85:270-272.

18. American Academy of Nursing: *Magnet Hospitals: Attraction and Retention of Professional Nurses.* Kansas City, MO, American Nurses' Association, 1983.

Chapter 13

Using Philosophical and Historical Methodologies To Understand the Concept of Health

David G. Allen

Nursing research is becoming methodologically more sophisticated and more pluralistic.[1–3] Experimental and quasi-experimental studies use ingenious designs and complex statistical analysis, while at the same time nursing research textbooks, and journals are recognizing diverse approaches to knowledge development. This chapter contributes to the encouragement of methodological pluralism by suggesting how the understanding of a concept central to the nursing profession—health—can be amplified through the intersection of philosophy and history.[4] More specifically, it tries to demonstrate the fruitfulness of combining two methodologies that are often considered distinct—philosophical analysis and critical social theory—for studying the idea of health.

This chapter demonstrates how philosophy and history help us to develop knowledge about health. More precisely, it addresses how certain traditions in philosophy and history help us to understand what it means to develop knowledge about health, what it means to ask the question "What is health?"

It is impossible to represent all branches of philosophy *or* history, much less both. Consequently, it might help to clarify what philosophical and historical approaches have been selected and why. In Ellis's paper[5] from the 1984 Forum on Doctoral Education in Nursing, value clarification and ethics were cited as the chief domain of philosophical knowledge development. Although this paper certainly raises ethical issues, medical ethics will not be the focus for two reasons. First, it is the branch of philosophy with which nurse educators and researchers are already fairly familiar. Second, many

---

Note: An earlier version of this chapter was delivered as a paper at the 1985 Forum on Doctoral Education in Nursing, Birmingham, Alabama, June 1985.

people would agree that ethics is not one of the major philosophical advances of recent history.[6] There is some general agreement that three of the most important areas in contemporary philosophy include (1) Anglo-American analytic philosophy, (2) European hermeneutics, and (3) critical theory.[7] Hermeneutics—in the forms of phenomenological Grounded Theory[8] or Benner's investigations of skill[9]—has begun to appear in nursing publications.[10] Consequently, this chapter focuses on the other two: analytic philosophy and critical theory. Further, these traditions allow the integration of philosophy *and* history[11] and, it is hoped, offer a convincing demonstration of their potential contribution to methodological development in nursing.

The chapter is divided into two major sections. The first focuses on analytic philosophy and tries to demonstrate its benefits for an inquiry into health by discussing what is called the critique of essentialism. The second major section is devoted to critical social theory (CST). In the context of this chapter, CST is used as a generic term for a number of traditions in historical social theory, including Marxism, structuralism, discourse theory, and feminism.[12] Most of the examples are drawn from feminist theory both because feminism is appearing in nursing journals with more regularity than any of the other competing traditions and because feminist scholarship has devoted considerable attention to health.[2,13,14]

The goal of this chapter is not to answer the question "What is health?" Rather, it is to expand our understanding of what we are and are not doing when we ask the question and to suggest that an integration of philosophy and history is requisite to both framing the question "What is health?" and to developing strategies for answering it.

ANALYTIC PHILOSOPHY

When one asks what characterizes contemporary philosophy, the almost universal response is "an emphasis on language."[7] Indeed, it would be difficult to exaggerate either the centrality of language in philosophical analysis or the significance of the philosophical understanding of language for other fields like sociology, psychology, or nursing. Some of the radical possibilities of this field of inquiry may be suggested by briefly describing the critique of essentialism and discussing some of its implications for studying health.

Essentialism

A fundamental movement that has shaped contemporary philosophy and that has profound implications for this project is Wittgenstein's *Philosophical Investigations*[15] and the generation of scholarship it spawned. One pivotal analysis can be called the critique of essentialism. This critique helps to

clarify what it means to ask for a definition of a concept like health and can alert us to some of the conceptual confusions and misdirected efforts that often plague the pursuit of such definitions. Essentialism is the pursuit of essences and is often based on an incorrect understanding of words and how they come to have meaning. Essentialism assumes that words refer to or name things and, when several things are referred to or named by the same word, that they must have certain shared characteristics, a core set of traits, or an *essence* that justifies using the same word to refer to those various objects. One needn't search far for examples of essentialism in nursing, but before turning to health or nursing, the critique of essentialism may become clearer through a more concrete example. We use the word chair to refer to a class of objects, and when we ask for a definition of the word, we often believe that we are asking for a list of the essential features that permit proper use of the word. These features can include functions (something to sit on) or a set of characteristics (four legs, horizontal platform, and a back) or relationships (a chair is *like* a stool only shorter, *like* a bench only it has a back). Yet it is difficult to elaborate a set of features shared by a rocking chair, a beanbag chair, a dining room chair, and a reclining chair. Further, it is unnecessary and probably misleading. It is unnecessary because the meaning of a word is not a function of the physical object it may refer to. Some words don't refer to any object—justice or unicorn, for example—and even if all the chairs in the world disappeared, we would still have a meaningful word chair in our vocabulary. To understand how a word has meaning, it is perhaps easier to think of the world around us as a semantic space, a jigsaw puzzle of meaning.[16] Words are used to carve up that space in useful ways. Eskimos find it helpful to carve the concept of snow into numerous pieces. Most of us only use two: its presence and its absence. The meaning of a word, then, lies in its *use*, in how it is used by native speakers, who may or may not be able to give a *definition*. A dictionary definition provides guidelines as to where a given word fits into other words—the semantic space it occupies—but could never be an adequate guide to its use in everyday life. This is because words like chair do not have an essence, a core of shared features, but rather the objects referred to by the word chair share what Wittgenstein called a "family resemblance." Imagine a photograph of your family reunion. There's no single set of features that everyone shares (brown hair, green eyes, dimpled chin, and so forth). Rather, one brother may have his mother's eyes and his father's chin, while another has his father's eyes and his mother's cheekbones. Similarly with chairs: some have legs, some have platforms or rockers, some have straight backs, some are curved, and so forth. The point is, native speakers know how to use the word chair correctly, even if they can't provide an essential definition, and further, the test of a definition lies in how well *it* fits the word used, *not* vice versa.[16]

Now, admittedly, this seems abstract and somewhat removed from a discussion of methodological approaches to health, but in fact it has profound implications for what we are about. These implications for the notion of health can be suggested by using two more examples. First, consider the concept of the emotion fear. When one asks for a definition of fear, the immediate tendency is to look for a single set of characteristics common to, say, fear of needles and fear of failure.[17] For various historical reasons, we either look in people's experience for a sensation—dry mouth, pit in one's stomach—or in their behavior—trembling, sweaty palms, or catecholamines.[18] But if we look at how the word "fear" is *used*, such a search becomes misleading, for again it implies the meaning of the word is what the word refers to or names. For reasons that cannot be pursued here, the search is not only difficult, but also futile.[19] Fear of needles is a different emotion than fear of failure, although both instances may or may not share some features with each other or with other emotions like fear of bears or fear of nuclear holocaust. These emotions *resemble* one another, they are not identical—they share no essence.[20,21] An essentialist definition will inevitably distort their meaning.

It may help to use one more example that is near and dear to most of our hearts—nursing. Countless hours and thousands of pages have been consumed in the pursuit of the essence of nursing. This is not meant to suggest that this effort is useless; on the contrary, it serves a vital, historical function. The critique of essentialism clarifies the nature of this undertaking, however. On the one hand, it helps us to realize that nursing is a concept, the meaning of which lies in its use, not in what it may or may not refer to. Certainly it is not the case that everyone was using the concept of nursing incorrectly and was merely awaiting the "proper" definition. A definition, remember, is appraised by how well it accords with how the word is used, not vice versa. Nor should we assume that "underneath" the plethora of uses of the concept "nursing" there is a single set of common characteristics. Among its many uses is a complex web of relationships, including the notions of practice, education, and inquiry.[5,22]

The example of nursing has the advantage of highlighting another feature of definitions: they are an exercise in power, struggle, resistance. No one who is familiar with the history of nursing and its struggle for self-determination needs to be reminded of the intimate connection between self-determination and self-definition. The women's movement—in health and elsewhere—has continued to demonstrate the effects of allowing one group—men—to define another—women. Definition is no mere academic enterprise.[23]

Definition is a doubly dimensioned process. First, it is a process of differentiation, defining a semantic space for nursing that is different from the space claimed by medicine. Second, it is a process of unification or cohesion, a gathering together of those people who shall occupy the semantic space of

"nurse." It is worth noting some points that are discussed later in the chapter. First, the unifying process of definition can also mask important differences; labeling a set of concerns as "human" may lead to ignoring critical differences between the positions of men and women relative to those concerns. Second, definitions are always purposeful.[24] At one moment, the purpose of defining nurses is to create separation from physicians; at another, it is to distinguish ourselves from institutionally accredited health aides. Consequently, definitions are inherently historical; they are not a typology of natural kinds, such as Scotch pine or white pine. Just as what it is to be masculine is different now than it was 50 years ago, so the definitions of nursing need to shift from period to period—something we are witnessing in the struggle to define entry into practice.[25]

This discussion of essentialism is clearly relevant to the question "What is health?" The focus here has been less on filling in the content of the semantic space of health than on the process of creating the space itself. First, it should be clear from the discussion of chairs, emotions, and nurses that philosophy helps us to understand what we're *not* doing in trying to answer the question. We are not searching for a hidden essence, an obscured set of features to justify using the word "health" correctly. Second, we need to attend to the *purposes* of the definition. For example, the World Health Organization's definition of health was a political intervention aimed at blocking an attempt to define health in a way that privileged either Western medicine's disease orientation or capitalism's view of choice.[26] Different purposes lead to different definitions.

The critique of essentialism and its accompanying view of language helps us to understand that defining health is a process of delineating differences: in what ways is health *like* the absence of disease or illness or *different* than the presence of prosperity or happiness? Further, we need to specify the purposes or perspectives behind a definition. In a developmental perspective, for example, the absence of illness might be a characteristic of both healthy children and middle-class adults but not of healthy octogenerians. Having income-producing employment may only be relevant to the health of the middle-aged adult. Similarly, there are very real historical and political differences between the idea of "women's health" and that of "men's health."[27] The critique of essentialism demonstrates that different purposes and contexts result in different definitions and that there is no "real" definition to compare them to. Rather, one must study the similarities and differences among the conceptual "space" or family resemblances mapped out by the alternative uses.[28]

CRITICAL SOCIAL THEORY

The concept of definition is also important to CST. CST integrates many of the insights of contemporary analytic and hermeneutic philosophy into a historically grounded social theory. Because many nurse researchers may not

be familiar with CST, this introductory section will relate it to several key issues in the philosophy of science. These issues will then be related to the themes of philosophy and health. The demands of brevity necessitate simply stating positions, not defending them. The issues raised here are widely but by no means universally held. At times, I try to clarify CST by contrasting its position to those of hermeneutics and empiricism, but I would like to add a caveat. I am suggesting the need to *supplement* empiricist and hermeneutic research with CST, not to *replace* them.

CST is part of a tradition of scientific theory that includes such diverse figures as Kuhn,[29] Habermas,[30,31] Wittgenstein,[15] Polanyi,[32] and Ricoeur.[33] This tradition stands in sharp contrast to the foundationist tradition of empiricism, which asserts that there is a "foundation" of pure fact, ie, theory-free observation, that can be appealed to for questions of truth. Instead, critical theory and hermeneutics maintain that standards of truth or evidence are always social. In other words, the criteria that scientists (or anyone) use to separate knowledge from fiction or mere belief are always based on social conventions, on a negotiated agreement, not on some transcendental appeal to neutral "facts" or observation.[34] These conventions or agreements change historically (forming what some call "paradigms").

If standards of truth for a given community of scientists are based on consenting to a negotiated agreement about what will be accepted as evidence or knowledge, it is of the utmost importance that the agreement be as rational, as uncoerced, as possible. Rationality in turn entails two central values: autonomy *and* responsibility. One must be autonomous in the sense of free of any conscious or unconscious constraints because the whole community must base its decisions on the best possible argument. If I am afraid to say what I believe because of an unconscious fear of authority or a conscious fear of retribution, then the interests of truth and rationality are not served. But I am also *responsible* for creating social conditions in which others can speak their minds as freely as I can. If I personally intimidate or socially threaten, then again the community (and therefore I) will suffer from not having heard all possible positions before deciding on the best one.[30]

Critical theory labels its interest in creating conditions of autonomy and responsibility an emancipatory interest. That is, its central interest as a theory is in emancipating speakers from conscious or unconscious constraints in the hopes of making community life more rational. Often the various traditions under the umbrella I am calling CST focus on one or more groups in a society whose autonomy is systematically restricted. Marxists, for example, focus on social class as a mechanism for constraining participation, whereas feminists identify how patriarchal institutions limit the autonomy of women.[35]

Another central assertion of critical theory—and here it is in agreement with the hermeneutic perspective—is that social life is patterned or structured by meanings, rules, conventions, or habits adhered to by individuals as social

beings. In other words, one of the central reasons that social life displays regularities or patterns is that its participants share a language that shapes their interpretation of experience and both facilitates and constrains how they act on the basis of that interpretation.[36] When members of a social group see a certain event in a particular context, they tend to ascribe certain meanings to it. This meaning—eg, whether the event is harmless or threatening—shapes their response.[37] In the latter case, some may flee, some may freeze in terror, and some may bravely stand their ground.

What CST emphasizes is that some of these meanings are adhered to by consent, that is, under conditions of autonomy and responsibility. Others, however, are not, and in fact, their dominance or widespread acceptance actually constrains or limits the autonomy and responsibility of groups within a society. For example, a definition of women's health that suggests that women are too hormonally imbalanced to assume managerial responsibility can be held by both men, as part of their definition of women, *and* women, as part of their self-concept. In either case, autonomy and responsibility are constricted.

Under the ideal conditions of autonomy and responsibility, definitions would be generated by the groups to which they apply and in such a way that they did not limit the autonomy of others. This does not imply an absence of conflict, but rather open negotiation around areas of conflict. Meaning is always social, and one is literally born into a language world. Meaning is produced, reproduced, and altered through social institutions and practices.[11,16,25] The reason that education and media are the constant focus of criticism is that they are highly centralized and pervasive producers and reproducers of meaning.[38]

These meanings are not simply ideas that one chooses to adopt or not to adopt. In the first place, they are an inescapable part of our identity. We act and understand our actions on the basis of these incorporated meanings.[39] This is what feminists mean by "the personal is political"—the development of a healthy sense of self is a social process.[40] In the second place, meanings are incorporated into the way our social world is organized. The tendency to have only women mother, for example, has been linked to boys and girls emerging with very different definitions of intimacy.[41,42] These can hardly be considered "voluntary" self-definitions, and yet we use these internalized meanings to construct our "personal" world.

Where CST and hermeneutics part company is that the latter tends to assume that description and explanation of human action are limited to the account given by the actors involved. CST points to the unconscious and to instances of "false consciousness" to argue that the hermeneutic understanding needs to be supplemented by a theoretical-historical analysis.[7,25,43]

To give a semifictional example, when asked to explain why there should be an autonomous field of nursing, late 19-century nurses might draw on then

current explanatory models and say that the biologically inherent ethical and intuitive superiority of women meant that their health practices should not be supervised by men. The hermeneutist would have to accept this at face value, since it was given by the actors involved. CST would insist that a historical perspective is necessary to understand *why* the model of biological superiority was the dominant model on which these nurses drew for their understanding and its impact on autonomy and responsibility.

Knowledge of social activity, then, is cognizance of the meaning that social actors use to structure their world and of the forces that shape that meaning. This knowledge is always contextual, not universal, because how one acts depends on how one interprets the context in which one is acting. Interpretation is grounded in the last instance on language. Language is socially and historically limited, so knowledge of human action cannot be universal.

To summarize, CST has as its central interest emancipation from conscious and unconscious constraints. An actor's understanding of a situation is based on currently available explanatory paradigms. These paradigms are at times distortive and constraining, as when women or blacks internalize biological explanations of their inferior social status and then act on the basis of those biologistic models. CST argues that a historical framework is necessary to critique and transcend constraining social definitions.

CRITICAL SOCIAL THEORY, HISTORY, AND HEALTH

Thus far some general features of CST have been discussed. These features will next be linked to the three central themes of philosophy, history, and health. The critique of essentialism introduced history through the back door. If there is no "essence" justifying the use of the word nurse, then one cannot assume that contemporary speakers are using it in the same sense that late 19-century speakers did. In fact, when one considers the purposes of definitions to establish differences or boundaries, then as nursing's context changes, one would expect that speakers would need to emphasize different distinctions. Consider, for example, Melosh's discussion[44] of the contested history of the notion of professionalism among nurses, or the extent to which a scientific identity has had to be incorporated into nursing.[3] Less obviously, the concept of emotion also changes across time as different models of the person gain and lose dominance.[19]

But, one might object, all this demonstrates is that one *can* study changes in terminology. The more pressing concern is whether we *should* devote time within nursing research for this endeavor. What would be gained from its inclusion?

To understand why it is a priority, consider two points already raised: (1) definitions are purposeful, an exercise in power, and (2) knowing what a

person believes he or she is doing and why is requisite to both describing and explaining that action. To these add a third concept from CST: ideology. CST is concerned with emancipation, that is, release from conscious and unconscious constraints. One process form of social constraint is ideology. Ideology consists of two moments: first, placing a subject in a certain social space, assigning a definition of white, middle-class man, for example, *and*—this is crucial—obscuring the *act* of placement by making it appear natural or inevitable rather than social or conventional. An example may help: one's definition as a white, middle-class man carries with it all sorts of attributes: desiring dominance, valuing rationality over emotionality, being competitive, and so forth. This social placement has been attributed to a number of nonsocial factors—God, evolution, hormones, brain size, etc—to make it seem "natural" rather than conventional. It might be helpful to emphasize that ideology in the sense that it is used here does not refer to either a set of values, ideas, or beliefs that one carries around in one's head or to the notion of replacing some biased values with neutral beliefs or positive values. Ideology refers to a *process*, a process that tries to obscure the fact that there are values operating at all. This is one sense in which critical social theory is *critical*: it critiques or uncovers processes that, in the very fact of being hidden, limit autonomy and responsibility. Thus a set of practices or beliefs is ideological only when it denies that it *is* a social practice, an assertion of values. It is important to emphasize two points here: (1) these ideological definitions are internalized, part of one's conscious and unconscious identity (and a part we are all aware is difficult to change), and (2) these definitions both *enable and constrain* (in the sense that a grammar both enables one to communicate and constrains what can be said). One's definition as a man enables one to know how to act and constrains the range of possible actions.

Health models have repeatedly served ideological purposes.[27] Definitions of health have been used to enforce social values by making them look "natural." The women's movement has traced countless examples of how masculinist models of health and disease have been used to reinforce the subordination of women to men. Voda's article on menopause in *Cassandra*[45] demonstrates that this is a continuing struggle. Ehrenreich has shown how the discussion around cardiovascular disease in men has been oriented to what she calls a "flight from commitment," the commitment being to share what developed historically as a *family wage* with the women and children for whom it was intended.[46] Similarly, adopting or not adopting the breadwinner role have both been used to classify men as latent or repressed homosexuals. The class, race, and gender biases of many developmental models, like Erickson and Kohlberg, have been analyzed in studies such as those by Poster[47] and Gilligan.[48] There has recently been an upsurge in the pseudoscience of sociobiology in an attempt to root the social dominance of white males in genetic soil.[49] People act on these ideological constructs and use

them to design and strengthen social institutions in ways that undermine autonomy and responsibility.

These social meanings, including health meanings, constitute our present reality. History provides a perspective from which we can displace the present. This displacement is essential for three reasons. First, it unfreezes our understanding, allows us to recognize possibilities that our contemporary language blocks. Second, because definition is an exercise in power, historical analysis helps us to understand whose interests have been served in the development of our current semantic realities. Third, historical understanding is a form of meta-analysis that is necessary for social change. For example, a historical understanding of professionalism is necessary to understand that while a professionalist self-definition has enabled nurses to resist certain attempts to control their practice, it can also be destructive and self-defeating.[50] The reconstruction of the history of the gender identity of women has been pivotal in revealing how values of femininity—which women use to both describe and explain their behavior—carry sedimented within them the seeds of male dominance.[40]

What CST helps us to understand, then, is that history and philosophy converge to highlight the extent to which an enterprise such as asking and answering the question "What is health?" is no technical or apolitical undertaking. It carries considerable potential for both emancipation from previously constraining visions and future enslavement. This is doubly important, since as educators of health professionals, we wield considerable power to install new definitions in the hearts and minds of students and clients.

Further, CST makes manifest the double-sided nature of definitions to exclude and unify in the same moment. We must be cautious not to adopt definitions that help others to constrain our choices or that divide us against ourselves, as witnessed in the recent struggle over "technical" *v* "professional" nurses.

The debate over "professional" and "technical" definitions of nurses pulls together the central themes of this chapter. The critique of essentialism reveals that there need be no essence or shared characteristics among healthy nurses, healthy clients, and healthy research programs. The distinction between behavior and action stresses the necessity of incorporating context and meaning into our inquiry. It is important to most contemporary nurses to think of themselves as professional in their performance, regardless of their academic preparation, just as earlier in the century, many nurses resisted the label of professionalism because it connoted the dominance of commercialism over the credo of caring.[44] Similarly, there are definitional decisions of DNSc *v* PhD or of a content/domain focus *v* a process/method focus need in the doctoral education of nurses to attend to both national debates and the political meanings carried by these issues in the local or state systems in

which the doctoral programs struggle to survive. The meanings vary from context to context and demand different strategies.

CST makes this political dimension of definition visible. Its historical focus highlights the difficulty that nursing has had in acquiring the *autonomy* of self-definition. To this must be coupled the demand for *responsibility*, for creating a unity that can be powerful enough to define differences, defend boundaries, and yet be facilitative of pluralistic voices.

This study has sought to contribute to the increasing diversity of nursing research methodology by demonstrating how the intersection of two research domains—philosophical analysis and critical social theory—can help us to understand what is involved in inquiring into the nature of health. Such an inquiry makes the field of nursing research conceptually richer and adds to the armament of methodologies useful in developing nursing knowledge.

REFERENCES

1. Gortner S: The history and philosophy of nursing science and research. *Adv Nurs Sci* 1983;5(2):1-8.

2. MacPherson K: Feminist methods: A new paradigm for nursing research. *Adv Nurs Sci* 1983;5(2):17-26.

3. Ashley J: Foundations for scholarship: Historical research in nursing. *Adv Nurs Sci* 1978;1(1):25-36.

4. Tinkle M, Beaton J: Toward a new view of science: Implications for nursing research. *Adv Nurs Sci* 1983;5(2):27-36.

5. Ellis R: Nursing knowledge development. Paper delivered at Forum on Doctoral Education in Nursing, University of Colorado, Denver, 1984.

6. Miller R: Marx in analytic philosophy: The story of a rebirth. *Soc Sci Q*:846-861.

7. Thompson J: *Critical Hermeneutics*. Cambridge, Cambridge University Press, 1981.

8. Glaser B, Strauss A: *The Discovery of Grounded Theory: Strategies for Qualitative Research*. Chicago, Aldine, 1967.

9. Benner P: *From Novice to Expert*. Menlo Park, Calif, Addison-Wesley, 1984.

10. Omery A: Phenomenolgy: A method for nursing research. *Adv Nurs Sci* 1983;5(2):49-64.

11. Eagleton T: Wittgenstein's friends. *New Left Review*, September/October 1982, pp 64-90.

12. Giddens A: On the relation of sociology to philosophy, in Secord P (ed): *Explaining Human Behavior*. Beverly Hills, Calif, Sage, 1982, pp 175-187.

13. Chinn P: Debunking myths in nursing theory and research. *Image* 1985;17(2):45-49.

14. Lewin E, Olesen V: *Women, Health and Healing*. New York, Tavistock, 1984.

15. Wittgenstein L: *Philosophical Investigations*, Anscombe GEM (trans). Oxford, Basil Blackwell, 1953.

16. Eco U: *A Theory of Semiotics*. Bloomington, Indiana University Press, 1976.

17. Bedford E: Emotions. *Proc Aristotelian Soc* 1957;57:281-304.

18. Kenny A: *Action, Emotion and Will*. New York, Humanities Press, 1963.

19. Allen D, Bowers B: Nursing education and the concepts of "person" and "emotion." Paper presented at Meeting of Society for Research in Nursing Education, San Francisco, 1985.

20. Rorty E: *Explaining Emotions*. Berkeley, University of California Press, 1980.

21. Solomon R: *The Passions.* New York, Doubleday, Anchor Books, 1976.

22. Allen D: *A Critical Re-examination of the* Social Policy Statement *and Its Implications for Nursing Education.* Society for Research in Nursing Education, San Francisco, 1986.

23. Marks E, de Courtivron J: *New French Feminisms.* New York, Shocken, 1981.

24. Laclau E, Mouffe C: Recasting Marxism: Hegemony and new political movements. *Socialist Review,* November-December 1982, p 66.

25. Ryan M: *Marxism and Deconstruction: A Critical Articulation.* Baltimore, Johns Hopkins University Press, 1982.

26. Sidel V, Sidel R: *A Healthy State,* ed 2. New York, Pantheon, 1983.

27. Allen D, Whatley M: Nursing and men's health: Some critical considerations. *Nurs Clin North Am* 1986;21(1):3-13.

28. Allen A: Feminist analysis of representations of "the family" in nursing textbooks. *Feminist Teacher* 2(2) (in press).

29. Kuhn T: *The Structure of Scientific Revolution,* ed 2. Chicago, University of Chicago Press, 1975.

30. Habermas J: *Legitimation Crisis,* McCarthy T (trans). Boston, Beacon Press, 1975.

31. Habermas J: *Communication and the Evolution of Society,* McCarthy T (trans). Boston, Beacon Press, 1979.

32. Polanyi M: *The Study of Man.* Chicago, University of Chicago Press, 1958.

33. Ricoeur P: *Hermeneutics and the Human Sciences,* Thompson J (trans). New York, Cambridge University Press, 1981.

34. Ravetz J: Ideology in the philosophy of science. *Rad Phil* 1984;37:5-11.

35. Barrett M: *Women's Oppression Today.* London, Verso, 1980.

36. Manicas P, Secord P: Implications for psychology of the new philosophy of science. *Am Psychol* 1983;34(4):399-413.

37. Bologh R: Grounding the alienation of self and body. *Soc Health Illness* 1981;3(2):188-206.

38. Jansen S: Power and knowledge: Toward a new critical synthesis. *J Commun* 1983.

39. Henriques J et al: *Changing the Subject: Psychology, Social Regulation and Subjectivity.* London, Methuen, 1984.

40. MacKinnon C: Feminism, Marxism, method and the state: An agenda for theory. *Signs* 1982;7(3):515-43.

41. Chodorow N: *The Reproduction of Mothering.* Berkeley, University of California Press, 1978.

42. Philison I: Heterosexual antagonisms and the politics of mothering. *Socialist Rev* 1982;66:55-77.

43. Allen D: Nursing research and social control: Alternative models of science that emphasize understanding and emancipation. *Image* 1985;17:2:59-64.

44. Melosh B: *The Physician's Hand.* Philadelphia, Temple University Press, 1982.

45. Voda A: Menopause: An update. *Cassandra* 1985;3:2:18-19.

46. Ehrenreich B: *The Hearts of Men.* New York, Doubleday, Anchor Books, 1983.

47. Poster M: *Critical Theory of the Family.* New York, Seabury Press, 1978.

48. Gilligan C: *In a Different Voice.* Cambridge, Mass, Harvard University Press, 1982.

49. Bleier R: *Science and Gender.* New York, Pergamon Press, 1984.

50. Allen D: Professionalism, division of labor by gender and the control of nursing practice. *Women and Politics* 6:4 (in press). In Geiger S (ed): *Sex/Gender Division of Labor: Feminist Perspectives.* Minneapolis, Center for Advanced Feminist Studies.

Chapter 14

Therapeutic Touch: A Healing Modality or a Caring Strategy?

Harriett J. Lionberger

Therapeutic touch, as developed by Krieger,[1] is traditionally presented as a healing modality based on energy exchange. Although proponents insist that it enhances nursing care, controversy surrounds its use. The notion of healing as a nursing goal has been questioned, and reference to assumed interpersonal energy exchange associated with the practice arouses accusations of pseudoscience.[2] Arguments on both sides involve the very nature and definition of nursing. In this study, caring, an acknowledged nursing concept, was identified as a core feature of therapeutic touch.

THERAPEUTIC TOUCH AS A NURSING INTERVENTION

Therapeutic touch was first described in the literature by Krieger in 1975[3] and has since been incorporated into the practice of growing numbers of nurses nationwide. Consequently, it is gaining in use as a nursing intervention. According to Krieger,[1(pp35–36)] it involves (a) centering oneself physically and psychologically (that is, finding within oneself an inner calm focus of attention), (b) using the tactile sensitivity of the hands to assess the energy field of the client, (c) mobilizing areas in the client's energy field that the nurse may perceive as lacking in effective energy flow, and (d) consciously influencing body energy through use of the hands.

This description involves certain theoretical and practical components that are unfamiliar to most nurses. Although the emphasis on energy is firmly based in Rogers's nursing theory,[4] that theory itself is not well understood or used, even in academic circles, and is as yet unknown to large numbers of practicing nurses. In addition, use of the hands to perceive qualities of energy fields is uncommon to nursing practice. Although touch is ordinarily understood to involve body contact, in therapeutic touch, the hands are used—and perceptions attained—within an area that is a few inches from the

body. For the newcomer to the intervention, this represents a substantial shift, particularly if the theoretical explanation is unfamiliar. Also, the act of centering as one component of therapeutic touch represents a focus of attention that is different from that usually practiced in nursing. Nevertheless, most therapeutic touch research has involved nurses as providers of the treatment.

DISCUSSION OF THE LITERATURE

The first therapeutic touch studies, based on similar earlier research of laying on of hands by a gifted healer, had changes in hemoglobin levels as the outcome measure.[3] Despite findings of statistically significant hemoglobin increases in these early studies, replications of the research have not been reported. The direction of study has turned instead toward measures of anxiety.

Two research studies carried out at New York University under the guidance of Krieger found greater reductions in anxiety levels, as measured by the Spielberger State Anxiety Scale, in hospitalized cardiovascular patients receiving therapeutic touch than in control groups receiving casual touch (pulse taking), no touch, or mock therapeutic touch.[5,6] Fedoruk[7] found therapeutic touch to be associated with reduction of behavioral stress in premature infants. Her measure was the Assessment of Premature Infants Behavior Scale. On the other hand, she found no statistical difference in physiological stress in the infants, as measured by a fall in transcutaneous oxygen pressure.

Physiological indications of anxiety reduction or relaxation effects have been consistently more difficult to detect than have self-reported or behavioral effects. Krieger, Peper, and Ancoli[8,9] found no changes in physiological measures of relaxation during treatment, although the three patients in the study reported pleasurable feelings of relaxation. Similarly, Randolph[10] found no effects on skin conductance levels, muscle tension, or skin temperature among healthy persons who were treated while they watched a stressful film.

A further difficulty associated with therapeutic touch studies involves the operationalization of the intervention. In general, studies have used a close approximation of Krieger's definition, as described earlier. Consequently, certain aspects of the intervention remain unclear to persons who are unfamiliar with the treatment. For example, the therapists' method of mobilizing the energy is not explained, and such crucial aspects of the intervention as intentionality and meanings associated with the practice are not addressed. Additional studies using the same methods are unlikely to increase understanding of underlying phenomena that are taken as axiomatic.

PHENOMENOLOGICAL AND INTERPRETIVE FRAMEWORK

In order to add to existing knowledge regarding the practice, an interpretive study was undertaken.[11] This research sought to discover the interpretations of therapeutic touch offered by nurses practicing the technique, rather than to test a theoretical stance in relation to the findings. In the cultural anthropological tradition of Geertz,[12] a "thick description" of therapeutic touch as it is practiced and experienced was undertaken. That is, an effort was made to look beyond the more evident behaviors associated with the practice, to identify underlying meanings and intents.

Phenomenological Foundations

The study took a Heideggerian phenomenological approach to investigation as described by Taylor[13] and Rabinow and Sullivan.[14] Based on the works of Heidegger,[15,16] phenomenology posits that human beings both constitute and are constituted by their interpretations, with background meanings handed down in language and cultural practices. Heidegger developed the thesis that interpretation is based on a "background" of skills, practices, assumptions, and interpretations that cannot be made completely explicit and cannot be completely rationalized.[17] Because the background practices are interpretation-laden and can never be completely spelled out, the model of study is systematic textual analysis (hermeneutics) and the goal is to provide commentary and interpretation of practices and commonly held meanings associated with the practices being studied.[18–20]

According to Taylor,[13] meanings cannot be separated from the context in which they arise. The importance of this idea to a study of therapeutic touch is that in borrowing portions of the practice and its explanation from other sources, nursing may have altered the meanings involved in unanticipated ways. Understanding may then depend on recognizing the influence of nursing itself on the emerging practice of therapeutic touch. Information about this influence can only come from practitioners. In turn, multiple individual accounts must be examined to find recurring themes. These themes will reveal interpretations common to the culture in which the practice resides and can be expected to provide greater clarity than is found in the understanding of individual practitioners.

It follows, then, that a nursing practice such as therapeutic touch, which in part relies for its explanation on Eastern philosophical thought, will be reinterpreted by its Western users in language and nuance with which they are familiar. In order to arrive at a consensus regarding the underlying explanation of a practice, it is then necessary to go to the practitioners for

descriptions of their individual experiences.[12] With this information in hand, an interpretation of the varied meanings of therapeutic touch can be made.

Interpretive Science

Taylor described interpretive science as an attempt to bring to light an underlying coherence that resides in a cloudy, seemingly contradictory object of study. He delineated three criteria necessary for such interpretation.[13] First, there must be a practice, event, or transaction about which one attempts to make sense. For this study, the practice was therapeutic touch. Second, the meaning in the practice must be capable of more than one expression. Initial cloudiness or confusion about inherent meaning arises from the presence of different and perhaps conflicting expressions. Clarity can be approached only by distinguishing between expressions of the practice and its meaning. The expressions of therapeutic touch are individual modes of practice. Its meaning arises from its practice in a given cultural milieu. Third, there must be a cultural language group for whom the practice has meaning. Meaning as it is used here is for nursing as a discipline. In this study, the interpretive task was to describe the expression of therapeutic touch as it is practiced and interpreted by individual practitioners and recipients of therapeutic touch and to make sense of this information in terms of nursing.

METHODOLOGY

Practice descriptions and interpretations obtained through interviews were the basis for analysis. The main focus was on interviews obtained from nurses, although patient interviews were used to supplement nurse data.

Population and Sampling

A sample of 51 nurses and 20 patients was used. The nurse population included registered nurses who had attended at least one full-day workshop on therapeutic touch, or the equivalent, and had practiced the intervention for at least six months. Most of the nurses in the sample had used therapeutic touch for longer than two years, and more than a third had used it for longer than five years. Two thirds of the sample had used therapeutic touch with more than 50 patients. Findings from the study, therefore, are based on descriptions of therapeutic touch by nurses with moderate to extensive experience.

The patient population included persons who were over 18 years of age, were able to speak English, and had experienced therapeutic touch treatment. Seventeen of the 20 patients, who were primarily recruited by nurse participants, had attended therapeutic touch workshops, and thus most were

exposed to practitioner as well as patient views of the practice. The view of the naive patient was, therefore, underrepresented.

Data-Collection Methods

Data were collected by an audio tape record of face-to-face interviews. An interview protocol was used to guide the questioning and to assure that specific categories of data were systematically obtained from each subject. Interview questions were loosely constructed, giving respondents opportunity to describe their perceptions in their own words. Descriptions of participants' experiences with therapeutic touch, as well as their ideas about what helps or hinders effectiveness of the intervention and how it is similar or dissimilar to usual nursing practice were elicited.

Interview items were devised to assure that the investigator understood the intent of each study participant's responses. To that end, similar information was elicited by two or more questions, addressing the content from somewhat different perspectives.

Procedure

The investigator conducted all of the interviews. Interviews took place in a variety of settings, for the convenience of participants. The protocol was used as a general guide for the questions. Some data were obtained out of order because of the open-ended nature of the questions. Protection of human subjects was assured by adherence to guidelines set down by the Committee on Human Research of a major university.

Data Analysis

The transcribed interviews were treated as text. Interpretation was involved at three levels. The first level was descriptive and captured the nurses' stated practices and interpretations of therapeutic touch. The second level was based on a comparison of the interviews in order to identify common meanings across interviews. Finally, interpretive commentary was developed, based on issues raised in the first two levels of interpretation.

In treating the transcribed interviews as text, the investigator attended to four ways in which Ricoeur describes text as differing from spoken language.[21(pp75–80)] First, the transcriptions fix in time what is said, preserving it for analysis. Second, they dissociate the verbal meaning of the interview from the mental intention of the interviewee, so that meaning can be examined in the larger context of statements from a number of nurses. Third, the transcription extracts meaning from the specific incident so that the description can be seen as part of a larger situation. Fourth, the transcriptions

enable the investigator to excerpt relevant content to share with readers. This increases the breadth of understanding by requiring that the interpretations make sense to a larger audience.

CARING AS THE EPITOME OF THERAPEUTIC TOUCH

Nurse participants saw caring as a feature of usual nursing care that was made visible and operationalized in therapeutic touch. Patients described caring as that part of the therapist-patient interaction that set therapeutic touch interventions apart from other health care practices. Both defined caring in terms of the quality of time spent in the interaction.

Caring was seen in the nurses' efforts to be perceptive to patients' needs, in their intent to help patients use their inherent potential for equilibrium, and in their acknowledgment of the validity of meanings held by patients regarding their illnesses. These elements of caring are not always acknowledged as substantive nursing skills, but have been described as the core of nursing by some.[18,22] They were illustrated most vividly in relation to the two components of therapeutic touch that emerged as essential to effective practice. These were healing intent and focused attention.

Healing Intent

Healing intent was the impetus for the nurse participants' use of therapeutic touch. On the surface, it appeared to consist of an altruistic desire to help. More specific characteristics of intent were identified, however, and these characteristics set the tone for the practice itself.

The nature of intent in therapeutic touch was seen, for example, in the helping goals acknowledged by nurses. These goals were consistently concerned with relieving discomfort, pain, and anxiety and with assisting patients to cope with the contingencies of illness and side effects of medical treatment. Cure of medically diagnosed disease was not part of the healing intent.

Instead, therapeutic touch was undertaken with intent to promote wholeness or wellness in the patient. Intent for wholeness involved awareness of the complexity of being, acknowledging the mental and spiritual aspects of the patient, as well as the physical. Also, the intention for wellness persisted, even when there might not be an expectation of cure of the presenting problem. The following excerpt illustrates this finding:

> You are involved in a compassionate way to try to promote in the person the optimum of wellness. With chronic [problems, the patients] are obviously not going to be totally well again, but you are trying to promote the highest sense of living—experiencing life.

> I don't just think of the physical body being symmetrical. I think . . . emotionally, that they will heal their hurts; mentally, they will be able to have positive thoughts; spiritually, that they will have peace and a sense of greater hope.

Desire to mobilize the patients' natural healing tendencies was a further underlying motive characteristic of the practice of therapeutic touch. Two nurse participants articulated this intent as follows:

> My intentionality was to explore the energy process with this particular individual, and to explore where his level, and his willingness was, to allow the healing process to take place within him.

> I think it's the person healing themselves . . . . I'm the helper, and the other person is the healer. They heal themselves.

The precise nature of expected patient self-help was not detailed by study participants. However, the tone of the explanations was that, given the therapeutic intervention, patients' normal healing capabilities, whether physiological, emotional, or other, were expected to be activated. That is, it appeared less that the nurses expected to teach patients how to improve their health than that they expected natural recuperative tendencies to be enhanced.

Focused Attention

The second component of therapeutic touch identified as conveying caring was the nurses' focused attention, achieved during a process that participants called centering. In contrast with intentionality, which seemed to occur spontaneously, this requisite mental set was described as the most difficult part of therapeutic touch to achieve, although experienced practitioners reported that once learned, it was subsequently accomplished in just a moment. Four distinct characteristics of focused attention were evident in the descriptions: (1) disciplining attention, (2) achieving a calm, relaxed state, (3) establishing receptivity, and (4) becoming a channel.

Disciplining Attention

Disciplining attention involved clearing one's mind of extraneous thoughts in preparation for the therapeutic touch intervention and focusing on the situation, on the nurse's readiness for the intervention, and on the patient. One nurse said that it involved "not allowing other thoughts to interfere with the work I was going to do at the moment." Another example emphasized

clarity of thought: "I clear my mind of external thoughts. I imagine my feet connected to the ground, so that I'm feeling stable in myself. I'm feeling integrated. I'm not distracted thinking about other things that I need to do."

Attention was also focused on the patient: "It triggers something in me so that I can be quiet. So that even if I am still talking, I know that there is a part of me that is quiet and tuning in to the person."

In short, centering brought to bear increased commitment to the nurse-patient interaction.

Achieving Calm

Achieving calm was identified by some nurses as the purpose of centering, by others as their way of knowing that they had attained the desired state. It was related to the nurse's ability to practice the discipline of selectively attending to certain stimuli to the exclusion of others. One nurse described in these words how she felt when the appropriate focus of attention was achieved: "It feels very peaceful, very calming, very relaxed. I feel a sense of peace, and also a sense of control . . . a sense of, like I'm going to deliberate exactly what I plan to do, without anything interfering with that."

This calm state appeared to signal a kind of involved awareness, enhancing the nurse's ability to focus on the emergent situation, to the exclusion of personal or environmental distractions. Coupled with the ability to sort out and choose from aspects of the interaction on which to focus, this awareness may well be important in terms of that age-old question of how involved with the patient a nurse should become. It suggests that a deep relationship can be based on therapeutic as compared with personal concerns.

Establishing Receptivity

Establishment of receptivity appeared to grow out of involved awareness and represented a shift from analytical thinking to perceptual awareness. When asked what they thought about during the various phases of therapeutic touch, nurses gave answers such as: "It isn't an issue of thinking . . . . I take in the information, and I keep my mind clear and receptive . . . . My hands pick up clues, and I'm just going to be receptive to register that information."

One less experienced participant described a continuing struggle to achieve this receptivity. On the other hand, the most experienced practitioners described using this receptivity in their nursing practice, even when not using therapeutic touch per se. It was seen as a way of improving their nursing skills, through acknowledging perceptions arising from interpersonal situations, but previously out of awareness.

Becoming a Channel

What was described as becoming a channel involved considering oneself an instrument for, rather than a provider of, healing. It consisted of a dynamic sense of connection between the nurse, the patient, and the universe, with natural forces viewed as the source of therapeutic effect. Much symbolism was expressed in explanations of this aspect of focusing. One nurse said:

> I think of trees. I think of the tree needing sunshine, but also being grounded into the ground, to get nutrients from the earth. It's just sort of more of a universal feeling.... You just feel like you are... a part of the universe. Because, I really think that you have to be a channel for the energy. It's not that you are really giving it. You are just being a channel. It's making a conscious connection.

This final focus of attention introduced the concept of energy as an explanation of the phenomenon of therapeutic touch. Yet the notion of energy exchange depended on the nurses' awareness and use of compassionate feelings and intents. Visual imagery was frequently used in the interest of maintaining a sense of caring interaction.

The various components of focused attention formed the basis for the assessment and treatment phases of therapeutic touch. Many nurses described directing feelings of good will and caring through the patient's field, as in this example: "I just think a lot of loving things that represent love to me. And, moving through my heart and hands, and into her body.... I visualize the loving force moving from my body to hers. It's not love from me. It's love from the universe." This excerpt illustrates another crucial aspect of channeling; release of any sense of personal attachment, in favor of nonjudgmental acknowledgment of a natural process.

Patient Perceptions

Patient participants indicated that the nurses' attitude, reflected in their intent and focused attention on the patient and the situation, was an important aspect of therapeutic touch for them. One patient said that during therapeutic touch, her impression was that "someone is taking time out to be with you, and try to help. And you know they are working for you, and they care."

Another patient compared the nurse-patient relationship in therapeutic touch with what he had experienced with other nurses. He made the point that, while the therapeutic touch interaction was different from what he expected in usual nursing care, the difference was in the quality of the caring interaction rather than in its presence or absence.

> With [therapeutic touch], there was something about the attitude that brings about a closeness that, say, I wouldn't feel if I were just in a hospital being treated . . . in ordinary circumstances. Or, it would be an unusual nurse if I did feel that . . . . There is definitely a strong, supportive feeling even from people I have not known [previously].

DISCUSSION

This study found strong evidence for the primacy of intentional and freeing aspects of the practice of therapeutic touch. This finding presents an explanation complementary to energy exchange for understanding the interpersonal dynamics of the practice. Descriptions of the use of caring and compassion in manipulation of energy flow testify to the interdependence of these two explanations.

Any single theoretical base is unlikely to capture the complexity of the intervention. An integrated approach is more apt to provide understanding. For example, while Quinn's[6] call for further efforts to validate the reality of energy exchange or derive theorems to support or refute the theory are well taken, other paths of research are suggested by these findings.

The caring component of therapeutic touch can be viewed as a social phenomenon. Several social science theories have dealt with concepts related to caring and may lend themselves to study of that dimension of the practice. The concern of interpersonal attraction theories for the development of positive regard, and its place in the therapeutic relationship,[23,24] offers one such opportunity.

Similarly, a framework of stress and coping could contribute to knowledge concerning the importance of meanings associated with the intervention. The reformulation of views about the possibility of healing at some level, even in the event of terminal disease, might be examined from the perspective of cognitive appraisal as an aspect of coping.[25]

In addition, a person's ability to respond appropriately to stress such as illness has been linked with "emotional and task oriented assistance provided by the social network within which that individual grapples with the crisis event."[26(p4)] Although social networks are usually considered to be constituted of ongoing interpersonal relationships, health care providers are sometimes seen as temporarily providing social support related to specific needs.[26(p5)] In the case of descriptions provided by participants in this study, therapeutic touch provided emotional assistance by conveying caring.

Identification of the importance of feelings of compassion and caring to the therapeutic touch process extends understanding and provides further directions for research. Thus it may ultimately serve nursing by increasing

understanding of caring—a phenomenon traditionally associated with nursing.

REFERENCES

1. Krieger D: *The Therapeutic Touch: How to Use Your Hands to Help or Heal.* Englewood Cliffs, NJ, Prentice-Hall, 1979.

2. Curtin LL: Editorial, nurse quackery. *Supervisor Nurse* 1980;11(3):9.

3. Krieger D: Therapeutic touch: The imprimature of nursing. *Am J Nurs* 1975;75:784-787.

4. Rogers ME: *An Introduction to the Theoretical Basis of Nursing.* Philadelphia, FA Davis, 1970.

5. Heidt PR: Effect of therapeutic touch on anxiety level in hospitalized patients. *Nurs Res* 1984;30:32-37.

6. Quinn JF: Therapeutic touch as energy exchange: Testing the theory. *Adv Nurs Sci* 1984;6:42-49.

7. Fedoruk RB: *Transfer of the Relaxation Response: Therapeutic Touch as a Method for Reduction of Stress in Premature Neonates,* doctoral dissertation. Department of Human Development, University of Maryland, College Park, 1984.

8. Krieger D, Peper E, Ancoli S: Therapeutic touch: Searching for evidence of physiological change. *Am J Nurs* 1979;79:660-662.

9. Peper E, Ancoli S: Physiologic parameters of healing meditation. Unpublished paper, undated.

10. Randolph GL: Therapeutic and physical touch: Physiological response to stressful stimuli. *Nurs Res* 1984;33:33-36.

11. Lionberger HJ: *An Interpretive Study of Nurses' Practice of Therapeutic Touch,* doctoral dissertation. School of Nursing, University of California, San Francisco, 1985.

12. Geertz C: Thick description: Toward an interpretive theory of culture, in *The Interpretation of Cultures.* New York, Basic Books, 1973, pp 3-30.

13. Taylor C: Interpretation and the sciences of man, in Rabinow P, Sullivan WM (eds): *Interpretive Social Science—A Reader.* Berkeley, University of California Press, 1979, pp 25-71.

14. Rabinow P, Sullivan WM (eds): *Interpretive Social Science—A Reader.* Berkeley, University of California Press, 1979.

15. Heidegger M: *Being and Time,* Macquarrie J, Robinson E, (trans). 1927. Reprint. New York, Harper & Row, 1962.

16. Dreyfus HL, Rabinow P: *Michael Foucault: Beyond Structuralism and Hermeneutics.* Chicago, University of Chicago Press, 1982.

17. Dreyfus HL: *Being-in-the-World: A Commentary on Heidegger's Being and Time,* Division I. Berkeley, Philosophy Department, University of California (in preparation).

18. Benner P: *From Novice to Expert: Excellence and Power in Clinical Nursing Practice.* Menlo Park, Calif, Addison-Wesley, 1984.

19. Benner P: *Stress and Satisfaction on the Job: Work Meanings and Coping of Mid-Career Men.* New York, Praeger, 1984.

20. Benner P: *Explanation and Prediction in Nursing Science: A Hermeneutical Perspective.* Paper presented at a meeting of the Western Interstate Council for Higher Education in Nursing, San Francisco, May 3, 1984.

21. Ricoeur P: The model of the text: Meaningful action considered as text, in Rabinow P, Sullivan WM (eds): *Interpretive Social Science—A Reader.* Berkeley, University of California Press, 1979, pp 73-101.

22. Watson J: *Nursing: The Philosophy and Science of Caring*. Boston, Little, Brown, 1979.

23. Hall BA: The effect of interpersonal attraction in a therapeutic relationship: A review and suggestions for further study. *J Psychiatr Nurs Ment Health Serv* 1977;15(9):18-23.

24. Hall BA, Mitsunaga BK: Interpersonal attraction in nursing: An investigation into professional sentiments, in Flynn B (ed): *Current Perspectives in Nursing: Social Issues and Trends*. St Louis, CV Mosby, 1979, vol 2, pp 239-251.

25. Lazarus RS: Cognitive and coping processes in emotion, in Monat A, Lazarus RS (eds): *Stress and Coping: An Anthology*. New York, Columbia University Press, 1977, pp 145-158.

26. Caplan G: *Support Systems and Community Mental Health*. New York, Behavioral Publications, 1974.

Chapter 15

Quantitative and Qualitative Research: Issues in Sampling

Janice M. Morse

As early as 1953, Mead noted that nonprobability sampling is "not a poor and inadequate version" of probability sampling where "n equals too few cases." Rather, *it is simply a different kind of sampling*."[1(p654)] In spite of this, many recent research texts continue to criticize the use of nonprobability sampling because of sampling error,[2,3] bias,[4] nonrepresentativeness,[2,4,5] and the lack of generalizability,[2,3,5] instead of discussing the conditions under which a nonprobability sample would ensure optimal reliability and validity for the research.

This problem may be attributable, in part, to the recent interest in qualitative research methods that has outpaced the availability of adequate instructional manuals and to the frequent omission of a description of qualitative methods from nursing research texts. Because sampling is one of the areas least understood in qualitative research, this chapter explores the differences in the assumptions, purposes, and limitations of nonprobability sampling (used in inductive, qualitative research) and compares these with probability sampling (used in deductive, quantitative research). Next, the criteria of *adequacy* and *appropriateness* as a means for evaluating both types of sampling methods are suggested, and in the final section, the effects of an adequate and appropriate sample on the results of three types of research is discussed.

Note: This research was supported in part by the National Health Research and Development Program by a Research Scholar Award to Dr. J. Morse.

PROBABILITY SAMPLES

Assumptions

The selection of a probability sample is based on the laws of chance and the application of the theory of probability.[6(p2)] In probability samples, every member of the population has an equal chance of being included in the study, and the results of the study should be the same as the results if the total population had been surveyed. Thus, from probability samples, it is possible to estimate population totals, averages, or proportions,[6] while minimizing the research task by reducing the number of cases, costs, and the time needed to conduct the research.[7]

Various techniques ease the task of probability sampling. The major ones are *stratified sampling*, in which the population is divided and sampled according to certain characteristics (eg, demographic characteristics); *cluster sampling*, in which the population is divided into units, sets, or subsets that are subsequently sampled; and *systematic sampling*, in which the first case is randomly selected and subsequent cases are chosen every kth interval.[8] In order to draw a probability sample, the investigator must have considerable knowledge about the characteristics and size of the population and clearly delimit the sampling frame.[7]

Utility

The most common uses of probability samples are *to determine the distribution* (such as attributes or attitudes) in a population and *to test the relationships between variables*. Thus, in Dier's terminology, they are used for association-testing studies and for causal hypothesis-testing studies.[9] The researcher usually has a great deal of information regarding the field of inquiry from previous research and is able to identify the significant variables and construct a conceptual framework to guide inquiry. Ideally, sample size is determined a priori to ensure that it is large enough to detect expected group differences and represent the population.[10]

Limitations

A primary limitation of probability sampling is that it cannot be used to obtain information about the *meaning* of a construct.[11–13] In quantitative research, this must be derived from the literature, observations, and the previous research of others. The large sample size used in probability sampling dictates that the same questions must be asked of each respondent so that data may be compared, and for this reason, the data are considered superficial.[14,15]

A second limitation is that the nurse researcher may not know enough about the characteristics of the population, and this may interfere with the process of identifying the sampling frame and drawing the sample. For example, a researcher may wish to study the siblings of children with cancer. Information pertaining to this population may not be compiled, but listed on the sick children's charts and inaccessible to the nurse researcher.

The third limitation comes from confusing concepts with demographic characteristics.[16,17] For example, with crosscultural studies, it may be convenient to use age grouping for comparison, but cultural differences in roles that occur at certain ages may not be comparable across cultures.[16]

Finally, the demands of a probability sample may not be feasible in the "real" world of nursing research. The holistic nature of nursing research indicates that multiple methods of data collection be used; this is time-consuming, and often the size of the population available to nurse researchers is limited. Furthermore, reduced funding and the "lone ranger approach" (rather than the team method) necessitate the use of small, convenience samples. Although a probability sample may be the correct method for deductive, quantitative research, if it cannot be used, this does not mean that the study should not be carried out. If it is a compromise between doing or not doing the research with a small sample, the costs and benefits should be weighed.[18] Methods to make this evaluation are presented later.

NONPROBABILITY SAMPLES

Assumptions

The assumption underlying nonprobability sampling is that all actors in a setting are not equally informed about the knowledge sought by the researcher. Some members of the group or culture are privy to more information than others, owing to differences in roles, status, age, past experiences, ability to recall, and so forth.[19] Some have better observational skills and are more interested in the research topic than others. Furthermore, some members are more receptive to being interviewed and are more likely to disclose information to the researcher.[20]

Because the researcher is interested in *meaning, understanding a concept,* and *making sense* of the setting, and the object is to obtain data that are comprehensive, relevant, and detailed, the voluminous verbatim notes, in bulk alone, limits the sample size. Thus, because of the small sample size and the time and effort required to collect data, it is essential that the researcher maximize opportunities to obtain the most insightful data possible, ideally selecting informants according to their knowledge base and receptivity.[16]

Data collection and analysis occur simultaneously, and the need to further explore, confirm, or refute the emerging theory determines the selection of

the sample. Sampling (and data collection) ceases when the theory is complete, does not have gaps, makes sense, and has been confirmed. Therefore, the number of subjects cannot be determined in the proposal—a problem that complicates predetermining research costs and time when applying for funding.[16]

The most common types of sampling techniques are volunteer, snowball, and purposeful. The *volunteer, opportunistic,*[16] or *convenience*[9] samples consist of individuals who are available and want to participate in the study. Because these participants may be volunteering for reasons other than specialized knowledge and receptivity (for example, for the prestige of participating in a research project or to get time off work), this method may not optimize the researcher's opportunity to obtain significant data.

The *snowball,*[11,21] or *nominated,*[9] method of sampling is to initially select informants who are receptive and knowledgeable; after the selected informants are interviewed, they are requested to introduce the researcher to other informed persons for subsequent interviews. In this sampling design, receptivity problems are partially overcome, as some trust is established through introductions by a mutual acquaintance, and the researcher is using the first informant's judgment that the next informant has some knowledge of the topic.

The third (and most preferable) type is the *theoretical,*[22,23] or *purposive,*[9] *purposeful,*[11] or *judgment,*[16] method of sampling. With this method, after the researcher has become familiar with the setting and the actors, all informants are deliberately selected by the researcher according to the theoretical needs and direction of the research. This method is "stronger" than snowball sampling because the researcher, rather than the initial informants, is selecting the informants according to research needs. Reliability is ensured by checking information with secondary informants and validity by selecting exceptions or negative cases[22,23] and by comparing interview data with other sources, such as observations, patient records, and so forth.[24]

Utility

The purpose of selecting nonprobability samples is to facilitate understanding, for description, and to elicit meaning. The purpose of the research is to develop, rather than to test, theory. According to Diers's categories, nonprobability samples are used for factor-searching studies.[9]

Limitations

When using nonprobability sampling techniques, the researcher cannot generalize the findings to the population. The researcher knows nothing about the distribution of the phenomena and cannot answer the "How

much . . . " or "How many . . . " questions. However, because this is not the purpose of the research, it should not be a concern to the investigator.[9]

CRITERIA FOR EVALUATING SAMPLES

From this discussion, it is clear that to use the criteria of probability and sample size for evaluating samples is not always legitimate. Rather, I suggest that the criteria of *appropriateness* and *adequacy* are more useful (see Table 15–1). *Appropriateness* refers to the *degree in which the method of sampling "fits" the purpose of the study as determined by the research question.* If a quantitative question is asked, then a probability sampling method should be used and an appropriate criterion is the representativeness of the sample. But if a qualitative research question is asked, then a probability method is inappropriate and a nonprobability method should be used. In this case, an appropriate sample will provide understanding and insight.

Adequacy refers to the sufficiency and quality of the data. In quantitative research, adequacy is evaluated in sample size. This is usually determined a priori by means of a power test and, in an experimental study, should be large enough to detect group differences.[10] In qualitative research, adequacy is evaluated by the quality,[9(p110)] completeness, and amount of information contributed by informants *rather than by the number of cases.* Thus informational adequacy includes the meaning, accuracy, precision, and completeness of the data.[25] Whereas the quantitative research proposal clearly delineates the sampling frame and sample size, this cannot be predetermined in qualitative research. In the latter case, adequacy is attained

Table 15–1 Evaluating Samples for Qualitative and Quantitative Research

Type of Research	*Criteria*	*Evaluation Question*
Appropriateness		
Quantitative	Representativeness of sample	Has the researcher used a probability sample?
Qualitative	Representativeness of information; amount of understanding/insight	Do the methods used to select the sample facilitate understanding?
Adequacy		
Quantitative	Adequacy of sample size	Is the error minor?
Qualitative	Quality/amount of information	Is the theory complete?

and sampling ceases when the researcher gains understanding of the situation or setting, obtains coherence,[26] does not collect any new information, and cannot locate negative cases. When this occurs, the categories are considered "filled."[22,23]

Evaluation of Samples

The procedure for evaluating sampling by using the criteria of appropriateness and adequacy is shown in Table 15–1. First, evaluate the sampling procedure by comparing the research question with the sampling design. As stated, if the research question is attempting to describe attributes of the population, seeking to test relationships or theory, then a probability sample should be used. The most critical issue is that the sample is representative of the population, that the sampling frame be identified and the sample be randomly drawn, so that every member of the study population has an equal chance of being included in the study.

For the qualitative question, when the researcher is seeking to understand meaning, to describe or understand a setting or a concept, then a nonprobability sample should be used. In this case, the appropriate type of nonprobability sample must maximize the researcher's access to data that is representative and contributes to understanding and insight. Thus, for most qualitative research, theoretical sampling is most appropriate.

For adequacy, the number of subjects is critical only for quantitative designs. This is determined a priori by using a power test[10] and, after data collection, by the examination of nonrespondents to assess for possible bias. In qualitative research, adequacy is determined by the quality and amount of information, which includes verification of data with secondary informants and seeking for negative cases.[22,23] When the theory is complete, adequacy is reached and the researcher may stop sampling (and collecting data.)

Outcome

The outcome of evaluating the sampling type for both qualitative and quantitative research is also shown in Figure 15–1. The ideal situation is when the criteria of appropriateness and adequacy are both met. However, as Cochran et al[18] noted, if this cannot be attained, then researchers must consider these risks and, if possible, compensate for these problems. It does not mean that the research should not be carried out or should be discarded. For example, the research may be satisfactory if the sample was inappropriate but adequate. This occurs frequently in nursing research when a convenience rather than a probability sample has been used, and as Figure 15–1 shows, adequacy is the more important criterion of the two.

		APPROPRIATE	
		YES	NO
ADEQUATE	YES	Optimal	Satisfactory
	NO	Serious (Possibly Invalid)	Unacceptable (Invalid)

Figure 15–1. Outcome of Test of Adequacy and Appropriateness for Probability and Nonprobability Samples

If the sample is appropriate but inadequate, the research may still be valid, but this is a serious error. The final possibility is that the sample is neither appropriate nor adequate. In this case, the research is invalid and should not have been conducted.[7]

Quantitative researchers may use some tricks to ensure adequacy when the sample is inappropriate. The most common is triangulation,[27–30] in which multiple methods are used to measure the same concept. Thus error resulting from one measure is reduced with the other measures. For instance, anxiety may be measured with several physiological measures and a standardized anxiety scale. Qualitative researchers are accustomed to using this technique in ethnography, when observations and other types of data are used to confirm or verify interview data.[24,31]

RAMIFICATIONS OF SAMPLING

To consider research as either qualitative or quantitative is simplistic.[32] In reality, research methods may be considered on a continuum from the most

extreme inductive approach (ie, phenomenological) to the most extreme deductive approach (ie, experimental). For the purposes of this illustration, the most common qualitative method (ie, the unstructured interview) will be compared with a common quantitative method (ie, the standardized, structured questionnaire) and an intermediate method that may be used either with induction or deduction (ie, the semistructured questionnaire).

The steps in the research process and the outcomes are shown in Table 15–2. Most important, the purpose of each type of research is different. This should be evident in the research question, and it is the question that determines the method (including the method of sampling) to be used.[11,16,24] As qualitative researchers work inductively, seeking information from the informants, samples are selected purposefully, according to what the researcher needs to know, verify, or attempt to contradict. Voluminous pages of typed notes from data collected using open-ended interviews must be coded and analyzed, thus limiting the number of informants. Sample sizes are usually small, ranging from a single subject case study to less than 30 primary informants. Because the researcher *selects* the informants according to their knowledge, receptiveness, and other characteristics,[19] and as researchers do not waste time interviewing an informant who is reluctant to disclose information, the response rate is 100%. Selecting informants, actively seeking for "negative cases," and verifying data with secondary informants and observations minimize threats to validity.

Limitations arise in the areas of generalizability and replicability. Because the sample was selected according to the knowledge base and personality characteristics of the informants, these informants were not representative of the population. Rather, it has been shown that the best informants are those who are marginal to the group, who have selected roles in the group.[19] But as the purpose of the study was to understand and describe the setting in order to develop theory, this limitation should not concern the researcher.[9] Qualitative reports on a setting pertain only to that point in time. As actors and norms in a setting change over time, the research may not be replicable. As long as the researcher recognizes these limitations, and if questions pertaining to the representativeness or the verification of theory are important, then the researcher must continue the investigation, using quantitative methods.

Structured Questionnaires

As mentioned earlier, the purpose of using a structured questionnaire is to describe relationships, to test theory, and for prediction. As there usually has been considerable research previously conducted on the concepts involved, there is adequate information available to construct a theoretical rationale

Table 15–2 Comparison of Sampling Design on Components of Three Research Methods

	Research Method		
Components	*Unstructured Interview*	*Semistructured Questionnaire*	*Structured, Standardized Questionnaire*
Purpose	Understand, describe, develop theory	Understand, describe, develop theory	Describe, test theory, predict
Development of concept	Little known	Some parameters known	Conceptual framework
Method	Inductive	Inductive or deductive	Deductive
Sample type	Nonprobability	Nonprobability or probability	Probability
Sample size	Small	Medium	Large
Response	100%	Low-high	Medium-high
Sample selection	According to characteristics	Characteristics or by chance	Chance
Validity	Least risk	Medium risk	Greatest risk
Reliabilty	Secondary informants	Consistency with responses	Verify statistically
Replicability	Perhaps	Possible	Probable
Generalizability	None	Limited	Generalizable (within limits)

with a conceptual framework to explicate predicted relationships between variables.

In this type of research, it is usually essential that a large probability sample be used. Ideally, the sample size is predetermined, but bias may be introduced if the nonresponse rate is high. Note that both qualitative and quantitative research share the problem of uncooperative subjects but handle the problem differently. In qualitative research, the reluctant informant is not invited to participate in the research and, therefore, not included in the sample; in quantitative research, in which the selection is based on chance

dictated by demographic or some other characteristic of theoretical importance, the role of the researcher is to try to analyze the nonresponse rate as a check against bias.

The nature of the sample selection, with adequate size and response rate, should ensure that the research is both generalizable to the population and replicable. However, the concerns with this type of research pertain to issues of validity and reliability. Quantitative researchers rely heavily on the work of previous researchers, complete with its biases, assumptions, and methodological limitations, which may not be recognized even with a careful critique during the literature review stage. Threats to validity may not be apparent until there has been adequate challenge to the status quo, so that these problems may be most evident historically. Englehardt's paper on the diseases caused by masturbation is an excellent illustration of such hindsight;[33] perhaps a more current example are the recent challenges to the concept of bonding.[34] Reliability, on the other hand, can be determined by using statistical techniques such as Pearson r and split half reliability or by procedures such as test-retest reliability.[8]

Semistructured Questionnaires

It is in the gray area in the merging of the quantitative and qualitative methods that most of the disagreements occur. Researchers generally use semistructured questionnaires when some aspects of the concepts are known but not enough is known to be able to predetermine all the possible responses to a question or all the areas of the domain. Occasionally, semistructured questionnaires are used when cultural norms prevent open discussion of the topic in an interview format, such as with adolescents' response to menarche.[35]

Semistructured questionnaires may be used inductively or deductively, according to how much is known about the concept. The approach of the researcher will then determine whether a nonprobability or a probability sample should be used. A nonprobability sample is appropriate if the researcher is examining the meaning of a concept, while a probability sample is applicable if the researcher is examining the distribution in a population.

With semistructured interviews, as with structured interviews, the sample size is limited by the amount of data obtained and the methods of analysis. In this case, however, because all the respondents are asked the same questions, the sorting and coding of the data becomes an easier task and sample size is usually between 100 and 200 cases. When coded, if a nonprobability sample was used, nonparametric statistics may be used, or if a probability sample was used, then parametric statistics may be used to test relationships with this form of data.

Validity is a medium risk, as respondents have the freedom to "create" their own answers with minimal prompting from the investigator. Pretesting the questionnaire will ensure that the questions are appropriate and relevant to the respondents, and comments frequently written on the questionnaire provide additional insights for the researcher.

Reliability of the questionnaire is more difficult to establish. The greatest risk is that the respondents may be prohibited from writing their responses because of limited illiteracy or may lead the researcher by providing socially desirable answers. If possible, answers should be checked with other measures or data sets.

The method of sample selection and size will determine the replicability and generalizability of the results. This may be done with more confidence when a probability sample has been used.

DISCUSSION

One type of sampling that has been deliberately omitted from discussion thus far is quota sampling. This method was originally developed for use in quantitative research for designs involving matched pairs. Samples are typically smaller in size than randomly selected samples, and to strengthen the sampling design, subjects are selected according to such characteristics as age, sex, and medical diagnosis.[2] Quota sampling is inappropriately used in qualitative research when the researcher predetermines that a certain number of subjects (for example, five) should be selected according to characteristics to fill a sampling frame. The main source of invalidity is that quota sampling involves using deductive assumptions about the population. If the researcher knows enough about the population to make these types of assumptions, then qualitative methods are probably inappropriate and a quantitative method should be used.

Another weakness with quota sampling is that the researcher may become more involved with finding subjects that fit criteria to fill cells than with the quality of the interviews. Excellent informants may be ignored as these cells have already been filled. Thus the basis of selecting informants is not determined according to the developing theory, but on demographic characteristics of the subjects, which may or may not be pertinent to the research question. A similar problem may occur when using a random or stratified random sample with qualitative methods. Agar notes that, for example, if one third of a sample is giving poor information, sticking to a sampling frame is "pointless ritual adherence to procedure without concern for the intended goals."[16(p121)] Thus the use of probability sampling methods in a qualitative proposal should raise questions by the reviewer with regard to the appropriateness of the methods and the understanding of the problem and methods by

the investigator. It should be clear that the use of nonprobability sampling in quantitative research is a source of invalidity and vice versa.

From this discussion, it is apparent that the most important aspect of selecting a sampling method is the constant awareness of inductive or deductive processes. Induction, for the purpose of theory generation, seeks meanings from the data; deduction, in testing theory, seeks data to confirm or refute theory. This awareness is particularly important when using semistructured interviews or working sequentially with induction or deduction, as in the case of grounded theory. Finally, rather than seeking an ideal method of sampling, researchers and reviewers must accept the restrictions and limitations of the real world and achieve a balance between the ideal and the feasible that demonstrates methodological sensitivity, tolerance, and understanding.

REFERENCES

1. Mead M: National character, in Kroeber AL (ed): *Anthropology Today.* Chicago, University of Chicago Press, 1953.

2. Giovanetti P: Sampling Techniques, in Williamson YM: *Research Methodology and Its Application to Nursing.* New York, John Wiley, 1981, pp 169-190.

3. Reiff-Ross E: Sampling techniques, in Shelley SI: *Research Methods in Nursing and Health.* Boston, Little, Brown, 1984, pp 237-248.

4. Polit D, Hungler B: *Nursing Research: Principles and Methods.* Philadelphia, JB Lippincott, 1978.

5. Bush CT: *Nursing Research.* Reston, Va, Reston Publishing, 1985.

6. Sukhatme PV, Sukhatme BV: *Sampling Theory of Surveys with Applications,* ed 2. Ames, Iowa, Iowa State University Press, 1970.

7. Cochran WG: *Sampling Techniques,* ed 2. New York, John Wiley, 1963.

8. Kerlinger FN: *Foundations of Behavioral Research,* ed 2. New York, Holt, Rinehart & Winston, 1973.

9. Diers D: *Research in Nursing Practice.* Philadelphia, JB Lippincott, 1979.

10. Cohen J: *Statistical Power Analysis for the Behavioral Sciences.* New York, Academic Press, 1977.

11. Bogdan RC, Biklen SK: *Qualitative Research for Education: An Introduction to Theory and Methods.* Boston, Allyn & Bacon, 1982.

12. Filstead WJ: *Qualitative Methodology: Firsthand Involvement with the Social World.* Chicago, Rand McNally, 1970.

13. Leininger MM: *Qualitative Research Methods in Nursing.* Orlando, Fla, Grune & Stratton, 1985.

14. Geertz C: *The Interpretation of Cultures.* New York, Basic Books, 1973.

15. McClintock CC, Brannon D, Maynard-Moody S: Applying the logic of sample surveys to qualitative case studies: The case cluster method, in Van Maanen J (ed): *Qualitative Methodology.* Beverly Hills, Calif, Sage, 1983, pp 149-178.

16. Agar M: *The Professional Stranger: An Informal Introduction to Ethnography.* New York, Academic Press, 1980.

17. Sechrest L: Experiments in the field, in Naroll R, Cohen R (eds): *A Handbook of Method in Cultural Anthropology.* New York, Columbia University Press, 1970, pp 169-209.

18. Cochran WG, Masteller F, Tukey JW: Principles of sampling, in Forcese DP, Richer S (eds): *Stages of Social Research: Contemporary Perspectives.* Englewood Cliffs, NJ, Prentice-Hall, 1970, pp 168-186.

19. Douglas, JD: *Investigative Social Research: Individual and Team Field Research.* Beverly Hills, Calif, Sage, 1976.

20. Spradley JP: *The Ethnographic Interview.* New York, Holt, Rinehart & Winston, 1979.

21. Taylor SJ, Bogdan R: *Introduction to Qualitative Methods: The Search for Meaning,* ed 2. New York, John Wiley, 1984.

22. Glaser BG, Strauss AL: *The Discovery of Grounded Theory: Strategies for Qualitative Research.* New York, Aldine, 1967.

23. Glaser BG: *Theoretical Sensitivity.* San Francisco, Sociology Press, 1978.

24. Field PA, Morse JM: *Nursing Research: The Application of Qualitative Approaches.* Rockville, Md: Aspen Publishers, Inc., 1985.

25. Zelditch M: Some methodological problems of field studies, in Fildstead WJ: *Qualitative Methodology: Firsthand Involvement with the Social World.* Chicago, Rand McNally, 1970, pp 217-231.

26. Churchill SD: The question of verification in phenomenological research: Hermeneutic criteria for reliability and validity. Paper presented at the International Human Science Conference, Edmonton, Canada, May 1985.

27. Denzin NK: *The Research Act: A Theoretical Introduction to Sociological Methods.* Chicago, Aldine, 1973.

28. Jick TD: Mixing qualitative and quantitative methods: Triangulation in action. *Admin Sci Q* 1979;24:602-611.

29. Miles MB, Huberman AM: *Qualitative Data Analysis: A Sourcebook for New Methods.* Beverly Hills, Calif, Sage, 1984.

30. Pelto PJ, Pelto GH: *Anthropological Research: The Structure of Inquiry,* ed 2. Cambridge, Cambridge University Press, 1978.

31. Diesing P: *Patterns of Discovery in the Social Sciences.* New York, Aldine, 1971.

32. Goodwin LD, Goodwin WL: Qualitative vs. quantitative research or qualitative and quantitative research? *Nurs Res* 1984;33(6):378-380.

33. Englehardt HT: The diseases of masturbation: Values and the concept of disease, in Levitt JW, Nunber RL (eds): *Sickness and Health in America: Readings in the History of Medicine and Public Health.* Madison, University of Wisconsin Press, 1978, pp 15-23.

34. Elliot MR: Maternal infant bonding. *Can Nurs* 1983;79(8):28-31.

35. Doan HM, Morse JM: Roadblocks to researching menarche. *Womens Health International.* (in press).

Chapter 16

Comparative Case Study As a Strategy for Nursing Research

Phyllis R. Schultz and Barbara J. Kerr

Several nursing authors have recently called attention to the difficulties associated with designing and conducting research that is consistent with the profession's orientation to holism.[1–7] Two examples of a holistic approach to understanding the world are examining a complex behavioral or social human phenomenon in its context and studying the meaning of an event or experience in a person's life. Unfortunately, many research designs in frequent use will not accommodate such study. The case study is an exception, but concerns about its status as "scientific" may have hampered its development as a potentially useful design and research strategy for advancing nursing science from a holistic perspective. We believe that the case study, especially comparative case study, is worth reexamination in this regard.

PHILOSOPHICAL ISSUES

The single-case study has long been viewed as having little or no value in social science research,[8–12] although it has been widely used as an educational method in business[13] and in the health disciplines such as nursing.[14] In the field of health, following the medical model,[15] it has been used for investigating clinical problems in which generalizations are made from the

Note: Case studies A and B were supported in part by funds from a National Research Service Award, Division of Nursing, DHHS, and a Kellog Fellowship from the Hospital Research and Educational Trust, both to Dr. Schultz. The Research Fund, American Academy of Family Practice and the Southeast Colorado Area Health Education Center supported the study of case C. The Western Colorado Area Health Education Center and the SEARCH (Statewide Education Activities for Rural Colorado's Health) Program provided funds to Suzanne Regan Morris for the study of case D. The authors gratefully acknowledge these sources of research support.

single case.[16] Despite the generally negative reaction by the scientific community, investigators continue to invest in and draw lawlike generalizations and causal inferences from such studies.[12,17,18] The situation invites a reexamination of definitional, methodological, and practical issues associated with this research approach in an effort to identify the specific conditions under which case study research can yield valid and reliable knowledge. In this chapter, inquiry is made into how this form of scientific investigation can be strengthened in order to further theory development and the goals of science and some principles for conducting this type of research are enumerated.

Two Approaches to Doing Science

Basic to scientific evidence are (a) the process of comparison[17,19–21] and (b) control of unwanted variance.[20,22,23–27] Historically, these two basic requirements have evolved into two fundamentally different and controversial approaches: the idiographic, for the comparative requirement, and the nomothetic, for the control of variance.[20] In nearly every discipline within the social sciences, there are those who advocate one or the other of these two approaches,[20] each group equally vehement about the merits of their choice for understanding human behavior and social phenomena and for generating lawlike generalizations—the two principal goals of science. Philosophically, these two approaches have their roots in phenomenology, in the case of the idiographic approach, and in positivism, in the case of the nomothetic. The type of data to be collected tends to be qualitative in the idiographic and quantitative in the nomothetic. Although it is beyond the scope of this chapter to fully examine the historical and philosophical bases for these debates, it is useful to review the case study from each of the two perspectives to help explain why it has not been developed more fully as a research strategy.[18]

The definition of a case study is generally agreed on by investigators from both nomothetic and idiographic perspectives as an in-depth descriptive investigation of the background, current status, environmental characteristics, and interactions of an individual, group, institution, or other social unit.[20,22–24,26,27] Despite some agreement about the definition, the differences between the two perspectives are that those within the idiographic tradition see the case study, with its rich and comprehensive data set and potential for analysis of sequential, especially developmental, events over time, as providing the basis for understanding human behavior in all its complexity (ie, as a "whole").[21] On the other side, those within the nomothetic tradition view the case study as a "first step" in the research process, an opportunity to provide background information for planning research studies, to gain insight into problems that deserve more extensive attention, and to generate the basis for

formulating hypotheses to be tested more rigorously in subsequent research.[26,27] These differences give rise to the tongue-in-cheek charges that the nomothetic scientists know more and more about less and less and that the idiographic scientists know a lot about the whole but little about the parts that make up the whole or about the causal pathways that predict the phenomenon of interest.

These two traditions are reflected in the health science disciplines but in a distinctive way. First of all, as noted earlier, the single case study is a well-accepted approach for the investigation of clinical problems[28] and for teaching students.[14] But the clearly dominant and most prestigious way of doing science in the health field exists within a research context dominated by the nomothetic tradition—(a) the experimental method characteristic of studies in the basic biological and medical sciences and (b) multivariate and quasi-experimental studies characteristic of research conducted by social and behavioral scientists working in the health field.[29] The result is that clinicians, who are working with individual clients, may apply research findings to their case, but how such individual cases are consistent or at variance with the norms or generalizations learned from research is seldom reported in the literature or used as a basis for validating or refuting research-based findings, suggesting new theory, or generating new research studies. Stevens[30(p261)] has specifically identified one unique function of the nurse "as a clinician" to be that of bridging between the particular patient in his or her particular circumstance and statistical norms and generalizations of morbidity and mortality. Thus, if one agrees with Stevens's view, the clinician is uniquely caught between the two opposing views of "doing science," and this dilemma may well account for some of the lack of connection between clinicians and scientists in the health care field.[31]

How nursing and social or health scientists might use the study of single cases for theory development or how they might strengthen case study research is either absent from texts on research[32] or scattered and fragmented in the literature. Campbell recently reexamined his criticism of the single case study and acknowledged that he had "perhaps overlooked a major source of discipline" (ie, control): degrees of freedom within the case itself that come from the multiple implications of any one theory and that can be operationalized as a kind of " 'pattern-matching' . . . in which there are many aspects of the pattern demanded by theory that are available for matching with his [the investigator's] observations."[17] He described three questions to raise in the analysis of the case based on the statistical concept of "degrees of freedom": (1) Is pattern A true? If so, then patterns B, C, and D ought to be logically consistent with pattern A[(p186)]; (2) Is pattern A due to chance?[(pp186–187)]; and (3) Are "multiple comparisons looking for significance" or "data dredging" used?[(p187)] In all of these examples, Campbell seems to be substituting multiple observations as the n's for use with statistical tests.

Polit and Hungler suggest that one way to introduce rigor into clinical case studies that involve therapeutic interventions is by making predictions about the future behavior of an individual based on past patterns of behavior and then making observations to assess the support for the hypotheses.[27] Herson and Barlow have offered a whole set of single case experimental designs[28] for use with individual persons as single cases, and Holm[33] presents arguments for single subject studies in nursing research and suggests designs for both descriptive and experimental study as a way to further nursing theory.

In the December 1979 *Administrative Science Quarterly,* the value of qualitative research on organizations was presented in several articles. The case study was found to be the focus of renewed attention as a research approach and the object of some controversy as to its merits and procedures. For example, in an article by Miles,[34] the case study is described as synonymous with qualitative research, and Miles claims that the methods for analyzing such studies are "not well formulated."[(p590)] In response to Miles, Yin[32] argues that Miles has confused case study as a type of design with the type of data collected in a study. He states that the case study is poorly understood and that it is not a specific method so much as an entire research strategy that may involve both qualitative and quantitative types of data and various types of data-collection procedures, eg, participant observation, ethnography, survey.[(p59)] He goes on to state that "the need to use case studies arises whenever 1) an empirical inquiry must examine a contemporary phenomenon in its real-life context, especially when 2) the boundaries between phenomenon and context are not clearly evident."[(p59)] He further argues that case studies can be *both* exploratory or descriptive *and/or* explanatory,[(p59)] suggesting that they are useful for researchers oriented to either the idiographic or nomothetic perspectives.

With respect to the use of case study for explanatory purposes, Yin defines an explanation as "a complex rendition of causal links far beyond the scope of a single hypothesis."[35] The ultimate goal of analysis, then, is "to treat the evidence fairly, to produce compelling analytic conclusions, and to rule out alternative interpretations."[36(p100)] He describes two basic designs for explanatory case studies: the single case and the multiple case.

In single-case design, the comparisons are made "within-case" by the use of several strategies: (a) pattern-matching, a procedure similar to the one described by Campbell[17] and noted earlier; (b) triangulation, a procedure described by Jick,[37] in which different types of data, eg, qualitative and quantitative, are used to provide a "convergence of evidence" in support of the explanation; and (c) validation of the facts by the major informants.[35] The first two strategies would be consistent with nomothetic research, although the basic logic is similar to the method of analytic induction described by Denzin[21] and Diesing,[38] two idiographically oriented social scientists. The

third strategy is not really a research strategy so much as it is a method for obtaining a validity estimate.

In summary, one strategem for using the single-case study for meeting the goals of advancing nursing as a scientific discipline oriented to holism is to conduct within-case comparisons based on the systematic examination of patterns of relationships from multiple observations.[33,35] For example, the observation from a telephone survey that residents of a small rural community regularly go elsewhere for health care may be corroborated by concerns of providers and local leaders that there is insufficient use of local services to make it economically feasible to maintain them. Another is to formulate hypotheses about future behavior and observe the "case" over time to determine whether the hypotheses are supported.[27,28] For example, an investigator might predict that providing local screening and health education programs in a small rural community might have the effect of increasing the use of local services and decreasing the extent to which residents go elsewhere for health care, which could be tested by collecting utilization data over time.

What remains unattended to in these suggestions is how single-case studies might be systematically compared with one another. Such comparisons of cases would be an especially useful way for clinicians, who treat individuals, groups, or whole communities (such as community health nurses), to accumulate evidence to develop or test theory in the normal course of that treatment, thus bridging the gap between the clinician and the researcher.[31] Case study comparison strategies would also be useful in which the study of the "whole" involves multiple levels of interaction and causation within the case, as is frequently the situation in studies of health in complex social phenomena such as nursing care delivery systems or communities. In such situations, more than one case is needed for analysis in order to estimate whether the explanations are due to some peculiarity of the particular multilevel case.

DEVELOPMENT OF THE COMPARATIVE CASE AS A RESEARCH STRATEGY

All types of case studies, by definition, must cope with the intrinsic problem that "because the context *is* part of the study, there will always be too many 'variables' for the number of 'observations' to be made."[32] If exploration or description of relationships is the focus of the research, the problem is somewhat minimized. But if explanation of the observed relationships is the goal, some form of comparison is required.[20] This problem has given rise to the multiple-case comparison design.

In the multiple-case design, two or more case studies are systematically compared to determine whether a hypothesized explanation holds across the

cases. Several procedures are suggested for conducting the initial studies and the comparisons. Yin[35] suggested selecting or conducting comparable cases by replicating the design at the outset (three to four cases will suffice) and developing an explanation that holds across all cases[(p107)]; *or* completing the first case, developing an explanation, and conducting a modified replication in subsequent, sequential cases that "builds upon" the findings from the previous case.[(p107)] Lipjhart,[39] building on the work of Smelser[40] and Przeworski and Teune,[19] described two strategies: the "most-similar-cases" and the "most-different-systems." The logic of the "most-similar-cases" is akin to Yin's comparable cases design, to select cases on the basis of some comparable characteristic and systematically analyze whether or not they are similar.[39] The logic of the "most-different-systems" design is different.[39] The starting point of this method is the analysis of behavior "at a level lower than that of a social system, often at the level of individual actors."[39] Systemic level factors are considered only if individual level or intermediary level analysis fails to explain the variance or reveal significant relationships among key variables. It is important to note that Przeworski and Teune also urged that a conceptual framework guide the design of each case so that the analysis across levels is consistent with the framework, thus avoiding testing an explanation on the basis of "multiple comparisons."[19] This is a nomothetic prescription. It is logical, however, to suggest that idiographic researchers might "discover"[38] an explanation in a single case and then describe that explanation as the "framework" for subsequent cases for the purposes of comparisons, thus leading to the formulation of generalizations for theory generation.

Lipjhart offered several suggestions for strengthening case studies that are planned for comparisons: (a) selection of "key" variables out of the many for conducting the comparisons; (b) selecting "comparable cases" as a way of reducing the amount of uncontrolled variance; (c) reducing the property-space of the constructs that describe the phenomenon; and (d) maximizing the N.[39] The last recommendation, if followed, approaches the nomothetic research design of classic survey research so that multivariate, correlational techniques can be used to estimate the variance on which the explanation rests.[39] If the last strategy were feasible (economically or as an illuminating way to study the phenomenon in context), it probably would have been chosen instead of the case study in the first place. Herein lies the essence of the scientific problem presented in this chapter.

To summarize this section, comparative case designs of the types identified have been described in some detail because of the promise that they hold for theory generation or development in which (a) experiments, quasi-experiments, or large-scale surveys are not feasible or appropriate for the question; (b) the context of the phenomenon of interest must be examined in its real life attributes; (c) the boundaries between the phenomenon and its context are

obscure—a condition frequently found in the nursing, health care, and social sciences; or (d) there is a need to bridge the gap between clinicians and reseachers in applied disciplines, such as in the nursing and health sciences. To illustrate this "promise," we offer in the second half of this chapter an example of a comparative analysis of four community case studies of rural primary health care services, their organization, and effects.

AN EXAMPLE OF COMPARATIVE CASE STUDY RESEARCH IN COMMUNITY HEALTH

The Problem

Since the mid-1960s, the health and human services sector of American society has been characterized by concern about coordination to prevent fragmentation. This concern prompted research on the study of interorganizational relationships and large-scale funding by the federal government of service delivery programs in mental health, primary health care, and long-term care. There were two primary assumptions underlying these research and service projects: (1) access to and use of health and social services positively affects the health status of a population; (2) interorganizational relationships between providers facilitate access.[41]

In the study of rural primary health care services described below, the two assumptions were made "problematic" in the research sense of formulating them into several research questions that guided the four case studies. Three of the studies were of rural communities designated as "underserved" for primary medical services by the Office of Community Health Services, US Department of Health and Human Services, and the fourth was of a rural community not so designated. Examples of the research questions were:

- What is the health status of the populations in those areas designated as underserved?
- Do certain types of interorganizational relationships facilitate access to appropriate care?
- What is the organizational context of such relationships?
- What is the community context of such relationships?

Conceptual Framework

Conceptually, the research was inspired by the epidemiologic model for health as developed by Blum,[42,43] Dever,[44,45] and LaLonde.[46] In their model, there are five components—health and its four determinants: health care systems (ie, preventive, curative, and restorative), human biology (ie, genetic

inheritance, maturation and aging, complex internal systems), life style (ie, employment, consumption patterns, leisure activity), and environment (ie, social, psychological, and physical).

In the case studies, the health care systems part of the epidemiologic model for health was elaborated and operationalized to include interorganizational and organizational factors as suggested by the recent literature in the sociology of complex organizations.[47] The human biology component was operationalized with such variables as age and sex. The life style component was measured with such variables as education and income, and the community—medically underserved or not—was the descriptor for environment. The community as environment was considered especially important, since distance to care in a rural community is a critical component of access to available care. The health status component of the model was operationalized by using Rutstein's "sentinel events" approach ("desirable and undesirable health events").[48] Variables were constructed to measure unnecessary disease, death, and disability; prevalence of early diagnostic screening tests (blood pressure screening; cholesterol and triglycerides checked; breast, Pap, and rectal exams); preventive measures; the practice of health-promoting health habits (don't smoke, exercise regularly, drink alcohol in moderation, keep right for height and weight, sleep 7 to 9 hours, eat breakfast); and general mental attitude (pleased with accomplishments, not bored, seldom depressed). This approach focused on preventive disease and health promotion aspects of health services systems, rather than on curative or restorative. The rationale for this focus was that with respect to morbidity and mortality, these four communities were typical of the country as a whole, ie, the four leading causes of death were heart disease, stroke, cancer, and accidents. Figure 16–1 illustrates the theoretical relationships among these various components.

The general proposition of the model is: "Factors in communities constrain both organizational characteristics and patterns of interorganizational relationships among community primary health care providers which, in turn, through the health services provided and utilized, are related to the health status of community residents."[41(p33)] The idea here is that residents of rural communities may well choose to live there, but with respect to their choices for seeking health help, they are constrained by the presence or absence of health care provider organizations and by organizational form, ie, how simple or complex the organizations are, whether they are locally owned and operated, how innovative they are.[49,50] This impediment to choice is in turn constrained by the working relationships (or lack thereof)[51,52] among providers. Relationships among health care providers are important because of the very nature of primary health care services (ie, no one provider can provide the full complement of services that may be required by those seeking care). The most general concept is one of circles within circles of constraint

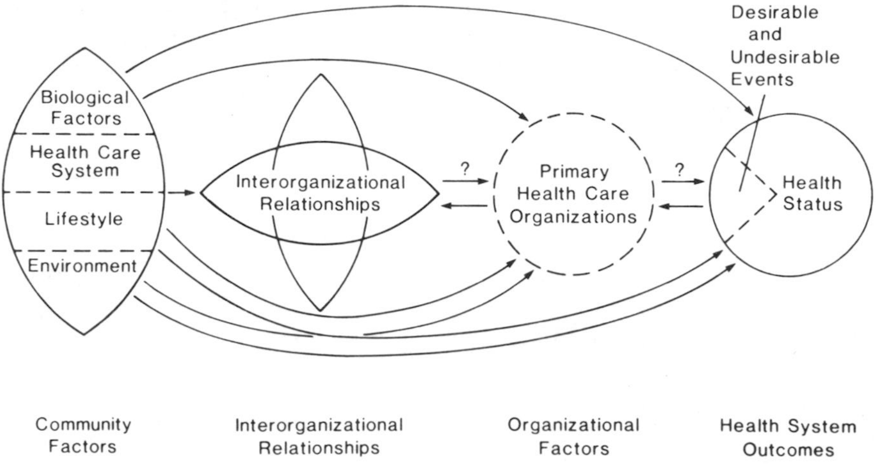

Figure 16–1. An Integrated Model for the Study of Rural Primary Health Care Services

Source: *Field Study of Rural Primary Health Care Services: Their Organization and Effects*, unpublished doctoral dissertation by PR Schultz, University of Denver, 1981.

---

on individual choice. The first circle of constraint is whether the individual will or will not choose to seek health help. The next is the constraint of whether or not a health service provider is available locally or outside the community. The next circle of constraint is whether the provider from whom the individual seeks help is able to provide the help (eg, early diagnostic screening tests) or is connected to another provider so that a referral can be made. The environmental feature of distance to health care is the fourth circle of constraint on individual choice as described in this model.

Rather than constraint, the obverse may be the case. Availability of health care providers, their working relationships with one another, and factors in the community may serve as opportunity structures for residents when they choose to seek health help.

Methodology

A number of the prescriptions for conducting comparative case research of the explanatory or theory development type were incorporated into this study: using a theoretical or conceptual model (see Figure 16–1 and explanation above), systematically replicating the first case in subsequent cases, completing four cases, selecting three cases for their comparability and one case for its "differentness" related to the research questions, selecting

"key variables" for the comparisons, reducing the property space of constructs that describe the phenomenon of interest (ie, creating composite measures of the dependent variables measuring health status), using both quantitative and qualitative data-collection methods, following the logic of the "most different systems" approach described by Przeworski and Teune.[19]

The case studies of Communities A and B were conducted during the summer of 1980. Community C was studied during the fall of 1981, and the field work for data collection in Community D was done in the summer of 1982. Data were collected at four levels of a social system as shown in Table 16–1 and analyzed according to the logic of the "most different system." The case comparisons were begun at the level of the individual household, with quantitative data gathered through a random telephone survey from a 5% sample of the population of each community. The random sample of respondents at this level of the cases justified the use of appropriate inferential statistics to assist in identifying patterns across cases (see Lipjhart[39] and Przeworski and Teune[19] for in-depth treatment of these procedures). The data consisted of information pertaining to residents' access to available health services in their community, whether they went "elsewhere" for their primary care, and information about their disease prevention and health promotion activities within the past one to five years. Measures of interorganizational contacts and organizational dimensions were not taken into account at this level of analysis.

Data analysis questions were formulated to guide the analytic procedures used to discover patterns within and between cases. They were consistent with the conceptual framework. Thus the data analysis questions guiding research procedures at the lowest level of the case studies were:

- Can the variance in health outcomes measured at the individual (household) level be explained owing to factors operating at this level?
- Specifically, does access to a local health care services system contribute more to health outcomes (status) than do personal attributes such as biological endowment, or life style, or the environment?
- Do patterns of relationships among the variables as assessed in analyzing the "most different case" hold across the other cases?

Key variables were selected from the large data set to improve the N-K ratio. The selection of "key variables" for the case comparisons was made on the basis of the conceptual framework. For example, people who live in small rural "health services underserved" communities are in an environment that may influence their health but over which they have little control. Therefore, the community of residence (COM) and time to a regular primary medical care source (TIMEREG) were selected from multiple measures to be the key

Table 16–1 Strategy for Multilevel Comparative Analysis of Communities As Social Systems Using the Integrated General Model

	Community Factors	*IOR Factors*	*Organizational Factors*	*Health Services Outcomes*
Level of Analysis	Type of units	Type of units	Type of units	Type of units
Community	D Comm	Comm	Comm	Comm
Interorganizational	IOR	D IOR	IOR	IOR
Organizational	ORG	ORG	D ORG	ORG
Individual	D IND	D IND	D IND	D IND

Code: D, direct measures are available from the field research.

Source: Field Study of Rural Primary Health Care Services: Their Organization and Effects, unpublished doctoral dissertation by PR Schultz, University of Denver, 1981.

variables for operationalizing the environment part of the model. In the case of TIMEREG, the selection was based on the conceptual model and multivariate factor analysis of several variables to determine the one with the strongest variance and homogeneity.[53] Key variables for operationalizing the other parts of the model were selected similarly. For example, the composite variables of screening measures (SM), health habits (HHS), and mental attitude (MAS) were assessed to be reasonably reliable, thus were used for the criterion variables for comparisons. All variables used in the analysis are shown in Table 16–2. Of the variables on this list, eight are independent variables—community (COM), time to regular medical care source (TIMEREG), number of local health services used (NUMBER), frequency of going elsewhere to a primary medical care source (ELSEWHR), number of years known to regular primary medical care source (TIMEKWN), age (AGE), education (GRADE), and income (INCOME)—and three are dependent variables—screening measures (SM), health habits score (HHS), and mental attitude score (MAS). They are arranged in Table 16–2 according to the components of the epidemiologic model.

Analysis and Findings

The case comparison was begun by using one-way analysis of variance to examine the influence of community on each of the other variables. This procedure assisted in answering the question of whether the first three communities that had been selected as "comparable" because of their status as medically underserved communities were in fact similar to one another and different from the fourth community that had been selected for its "differentness" because it was not designated as "underserved."

Of the eight independent variables, three were revealed by the analysis to exhibit no differences across communities: NUMBER, GRADE, and INCOME. See Table 16–3 for a summary of the statistical analysis. This outcome means that these variables do not distinguish between communities (cases).

Of the remaining independent variables, analysis of the variable TIMEREG reveals that Community D is different from A, B, and C, and residents in this fourth community take the longest to reach their primary medical care. Community A is also different from B in this regard, with residents of B taking longer than A to travel to their primary medical care provider. This outcome is complemented by the results of analyzing the variable ELSEWHR. On ELSEWHR, residents from Community D go "regularly" to care outside their community, residents from Community C go "frequently," and both of these outcomes are statistically different from Communities A

Table 16–2 Key Variables Used in Comparative Case Analysis

Environment	COM	=	rural community of residence of the respondents (physical environment)
	TIMEREG	=	time to regular primary medical care (physical environment)
Health care systems	NUMBER	=	average number of local health services used (systems component)
	ELSEWHR	=	frequency of going elsewhere to care (systems component)
	TIMEKWN	=	time known to primary care source (systems component)
Biological factor	AGE	=	age (human biology component)
Life style	GRADE	=	education (life style component)
	INCOME	=	combined household income in 1979 (life style component)
Health status	SM	=	composite score of screening measures for early detection of life-threatening and chronic diseases (health status component)
	HHS	=	number of health habits practiced out of seven possible (health status component)
	MAS	=	general mental attitude (health status component)

and B (although residents of Community B go elsewhere to care more frequently than those in A). With respect to the variable TIMEKWN, Community D is different from the other three. Residents have known their primary medical care source from 1 to 5 years, whereas residents of Communities A and C have known their source more than five years and residents of Community B have known their source more than ten years. On balance, then, Community D, the community selected because it was not designated as "underserved," was indeed different from the other three communities.

On the variable AGE, in which differences between communities were revealed by the analysis, Community C was shown to have residents considerably older than those in the other three communities. So it emerged as the "most different system" on this key independent variable.

Table 16–3 Comparison of Communities on Key Variables Using One-Way Analysis of Variance

Community	*TIMEREG* 6 = 10 min, 1 = > 3 hrs					*NUMBER*(mean)†					*ELSEWHR* 1 = never, 5 = always					*TIMEKWN* 1 = 1 yr, 6 = 20 yr					*AGE* (yr)					*GRADE* (yr completed)				
	$\bar{X}$	A	B	C	D	$\bar{X}$	A	B	C	D	$\bar{X}$	A	B	C	D	$\bar{X}$	A	B	C	D	$\bar{X}$	A	B	C	D	$\bar{X}$	A	B	C	D
A	4.68					.43					2.69					3.85					42.7					13.00				
B	4.04	*				.42					3.22	*				4.40	*		*	*	45.5					12.10				
C	4.35					.44					3.96	*	*			3.35					54.5	*	*		*	11.20				
D	3.56	*		*		.44					4.52	*	*	*		2.74	*	*	*		39.0					14.70				
	N = 248					N = 226					N = 251					N = 247					N = 201					N = 199				

Community	*INCOME* 1 = don't know, 5 = $10,000–15,000					*SM* 1 = few, 3 = most					*HHS* 1 = poor, 3 = good					*MAS* 1 = mostly negative, 3 = mostly positive				
	$\bar{X}$	A	B	C	D	$\bar{X}$	A	B	C	D	$\bar{X}$	A	B	C	D	$\bar{X}$	A	B	C	D
A	4.08					2.48					2.36					2.43				
B	3.44					2.26					2.41					2.47				
C	4.28					1.97	*	*		*	2.37					2.48				
D	4.16					2.39					2.51	*	*	*		2.40				
	N = 251					N = 205					N = 211									

* Most different communities
† The numbers are the means of the average (or mean) number of services used of those that were available.

Analysis of the criterion composite scores revealed that Community C was different from the other three communities on the number of early diagnostic screening tests reported (SM). Resident scores were considerably lower in this community. On HHS, Community D was different from the other three, specifically the mean score was higher, indicating that residents of this community practice more daily health habits than do residents in the other three communities. There were no differences in the means of the four communities with respect to general mental attitude (MAS). Thus communities C and D have been shown to be the "most different systems": C with a negative and poor health status and it is one of the "underserved" communities, and D with a positive or good health status and it is the case that was selected because it was not designated as underserved.

Analysis of relationships between the independent variables with one another and with the criterion scores revealed that TIMEREG and ELSEWHR were slightly negatively correlated at –.43 (P = .01), meaning that the more often residents go elsewhere to care, the longer their time to regular care, a logical outcome. The reason this is a negative correlation is because the TIMEREG variable was coded as 6 = less than ten minutes to care through 1 = more than three hours to care. Also, when the aggregated means were correlated, the coefficient increased to –.79 (see Table 16–5). None of the independent variables were correlated with the criterion variables at the individual household level despite the fact that there were differences in the means when analyzed by community.

The outcome led to analysis of key variables, using aggregated scores rather than individual respondent scores; that is, the unit of analysis was shifted from individual scores to community scores. The mean scores can be understood as community attributes as measured by the key variables. This is an example of an "analytic property" of a collective, as described by Lazarsfeld and Menzel.[54] The analytical question was whether patterns among the variables can be discerned from which hypotheses can be generated as explanations of the health status of populations in small rural communities. Thus this part of the analysis begins with the criterion variables. Only key variables that were revealed by the one-way ANOVA to have differences across communities were used in this stage of the analysis. The variables, their aggregated means, and correlation coefficients are shown in Tables 16–4 and 16–5.

As shown in Table 16–5, SM was negatively correlated with age at –.92, meaning that the older the aggregated age of a community, the lower the aggregated score on SM. Examination of the aggregated means (refer to Table 16–4) confirms this pattern; that is, the SM mean of residents in Community C is 1.97, the lowest of the four means, and their mean age was 54.5 years, the oldest mean of the four cases. This pattern is supported by the one shown in Table 16–3, in which Community C is significantly different from A, B and D on each of these

Table 16–4 Aggregated Means by Community

Community	*TIMEREG*	*ELSEWHR*	*TIMEKWN*	*AGE*	*SM*	*HHS*
A	4.68	2.69	3.85	42.7	2.48	2.36
B	4.04	3.22	4.40	45.5	2.26	2.41
C	4.35	3.96	3.35	54.5	1.97	2.37
D	3.56	4.52	2.74	39.0	2.39	2.51

The variable means are those that were shown to be significantly different by community using one-way analysis of variance (ANOVA).

Table 16–5 Correlation Coefficients Using Aggregated Means

	TIMEREG	*ELSEWHR*	*TIMEKWN*	*AGE*	*SM*	*HHS*
TIMEREG	1.000	−.7911	.4965	.4396	−.0583	−.9559
ELSEWHR		1.000	−.8254	−.0121	−.3436	.7435
TIMEKWN		−.8254	1.000	.1877	.0351	−.6073
AGE		−.0121	.1877	1.000	−.9217	−.6400
SM		−.3436	.0351	−.9217	1.000	.2942
HHS		.7435	−.6073	−.6400	.2942	1.000
N = 4						

Correlation coefficients of .60 or higher were considered high enough, given the small n of cases, to be indicative of a pattern.

Table 16–6 Mortality Rates in Counties of Communities Studied

County of the Community		*Causes of Death*							
		Heart Disease		Cancer		Stroke		Arteriosclerosis	
		No. of Residents	Rate	No. of Residents	Rate	No. of Residents	Rate	No. of Residents	Rate
Community	A	39	402.8	10	103.3	2	**	4	**
	B	28	600.5	8	171.6	5	107.2	1	**
	C	14	468.5	5	167.3	4	**	3	**
	D	12	112.3	12	112.3	1	**	1	**
State rate		6,411	221.8	3,633	125.7	1,386	48.0	334	11.6

Rates are for 100,000 population. The names of the counties are not used in order to protect confidentiality. ** = Numbers too few to produce reliable rates.

Source: Annual Report of Vital Statistics (p A-13), Health Statistics and Vital Records Division, Colorado Department of Health, 1980.

two variables. The other three communities are not different from one another on these two variables as analyzed by the one-way ANOVA. The hypothesis that can be generated from this pattern is: In small, rural, underserved communities, the older the population, the fewer the early diagnostic screening tests.

Note that residents of Community C "frequently" went elsewhere to obtain their primary medical care, and even this attempt to gain access did not seem to contribute to their screening measures scores. If the hypothesis is true (ie, not owing to chance, and the comparative analysis suggests that it is not), it is especially unfortunate from a practical health care delivery standpoint because three of the four leading causes of death in these communities and throughout the nation—heart disease, cancer, stroke, and arteriosclerosis—can be treated and life prolonged if they are diagnosed early.

Evidence from secondary data sources lends credibility to this hypothesis, specifically the mortality rates for the counties in which these communities are located for the calendar year of 1980, in which deaths were registered by April 1981.[55] Table 16–6 shows the mortality rates for the four counties as compared with the state rates. The rates for Community C are well above the state rate for both heart disease and cancer. There were too few deaths from stroke and arteriosclerosis in these counties to calculate reliable rates. This evidence also points out the implications of the failure to acquire early diagnostic screening for these diseases. Clearly, communities with these characteristics are at greater health risk.

Before explanations for this outcome are explored with other evidence from the cases, a presentation of the analysis of the second significant criterion variable is in order—the correlates of HHS. HHS was negatively correlated with TIMEREG (–.96), TIMEKWN (–.61), and AGE (–.64) and positively correlated with ELSEWHR (.74). Examination of the aggregated means for Community D is instructive: residents of this community (a) regularly go elsewhere for care (4.52 on a scale range of 1 = never, 5 = always); (b) take longer to get to care (3.56 = 30″ or longer on a scale range of 6 = less than ten minutes, 1 = more than three hours); (c) have known their caregiver the shortest time (2.74 = less than 5 years on a scale of 1 = less than 1 year, 6 = more than 20 years); and (d) are younger (mean age is 39 years as contrasted with 54 years for Community C). The hypothesis that can be generated from this pattern is: In a small, rural community that is not medically underserved, where residents are younger, regularly go elsewhere to care, but have known their primary care source five years or less, their health habits are better than in rural communities that are underserved.

Again, referring to Table 16–3 as a check of this hypothesis, the HHS mean of Community D is significantly different from the other three communities. On TIMEREG, D is different from A and C but not B. On ELSEWHR, D is different from A, B, and C; C is different from A and B; and B is different

from A. On TIMEKWN, D is different from A, B, and C, and B is different from A, C, and D. On AGE, only Community C is different from the other three. Thus, on three of the four independent variables related to health habits, Community B is "different" also and the HHS mean is the next highest (2.41) to that of Community D, although it is not statistically different from the means of A and C. The patterns revealed by this analysis suggest that characteristics of the environment (TIMEREG, COMMUNITY) and the "system" of care (ELSEWHR and TIMEKWN) contribute to the practice of health-promoting daily habits.

Discussion

These findings provide some answers to the analytic questions listed earlier. When health outcomes were defined in terms of prevention and health promotion, the variance observed in screening measures (SM) and health habits (HHS) could not be explained at the individual household level, but differences were found across communities. General mental attitude (MAS) did not distinguish between communities (cases), nor was it significantly explained at the individual household level.

Because none of the independent variables was correlated with the criterion variables at the individual household level, neither access to a local health care services system nor personal attributes such as biological endowment nor life style contributed to the health outcome dependent variables. Environment, however, as measured by the community in which respondents lived, appeared to contribute substantially to the health outcomes.

When analysis was moved to the level of the community, two conclusions could be drawn from the analysis: older residents of a medically underserved community had inadequate access to early diagnostic screening measures, with correspondingly high mortality rates for heart disease and cancer. Even going elsewhere for their primary medical care did not seem to improve their access to these important health services. By contrast, the younger residents of Community D (which was not an underserved community), who went regularly to a primary medical care source outside their community, achieved higher health habits scores—habits that contribute to health promotion. The screening measures scores (SM) for the residents of Community D were the second best of the four means, and mortality rates for heart disease and cancer were below the state rate for the county in which Community D is located.

These conclusions emerge from the lowest level of analysis of the cases and the highest or community level. Something about these communities is accounting for the health outcomes. But what? Clues to the explanation may be found at the intermediate levels of the social system examined in these case studies—the organizational level or the interorganizational level (refer to

Table 16–1). A more detailed analysis of these levels has been reported elsewhere.[40,56,57] A summary is provided here to complete the example of the logic of the "most different system." The data collected about these levels of the social system were qualitative and descriptive.

Findings from the Organization and Interorganization Levels

No differences across communities were found with respect to the characteristics of the provider organizations located in these communities, with the exception that the hospitals and nursing homes located within Communities A and B were the largest, employed the greatest number of persons, had the largest budgets, and were administratively somewhat more complex, that is, they had more than one or two administrative levels or departments. The last feature was true for the nursing home in Community C as well. The county health departments that were the provider agency for the public health nurses were similar to the hospitals and nursing homes but were not different across the communities.

Several organizational variables were measured in the case studies. They are characteristics reported in the organizational literature as contributing to client outcomes and to be the context for the level and type of interorganizational relationships that are likely to exist in a given functional domain or geographical locale. They were corporate type (eg, sole proprietary, private or community not-for-profit, private for-profit), dependence on local economy, governing mode (eg, board of directors), size (eg, number of employees, number of clients served, annual budget), locus of decision making for daily or long-range decisions (eg, owner, administrator, board), complexity (eg, number of departments, committees), innovativeness.

Health care services in these communities were provided by one or two private for-profit organizations (eg, the physician, the pharmacy), private not-for-profit or community-owned corporations (eg, nursing homes), or county level governmental agencies, such as mental health clinics or health departments. Most were dependent on the local economy, administratively simple (fewer than five departments and no more than three administrative levels), and governed by the owners or boards of directors. With the exception of the hospitals, nursing homes, and health departments described earlier, most were small, with fewer than 50 employees, served fewer than 1,500 clients per month, and operated with annual budgets of less than $75,000 per year. These characteristics describe part of the organizational context of the interorganizational relationships among providers in these case studies.

Regardless of size or corporate type, few of these organizations had introduced innovations in the past year, and of those that had, the numbers of new services or programs were fewer than five. Innovativeness has been

shown to be an especially important organizational variable related to the number and type of interorganizational relationships.[49] This finding was particularly important in light of the interorganizational interactions (or lack thereof) described in the next section.

With respect to the interorganizational level of analysis of these cases, 12 questions pertaining to interorganizational relationships were asked of the respondents from the provider organizations. Examples of these included frequency of contact, reason for contacts (eg, to request information, to refer clients, to receive clients), common basis of contacts (required by law, formal agreement, common practice, no respond to a need or problem), mode of contact (eg, telephone, person to person). The number of possible contacts in Communities A and B was 90; in Communities C and D, 30. Of these, the reports of "no contacts at all" were from 20% in Communities A and B to more than 50% in Communities C and D. The network of contacts in Communities A, B, and C accounted for all the providers, whereas the public health nurse and the chiropractor providers seldom had contact with the other providers in Community D. Figure 16–2 shows the sociometric patterns of frequency of contacts among all the providers in each of the four cases. There were some differences here, primarily according to which providers were located in the second or third tier of interaction. For example, the public health nurse was more closely connected to the physician, hospital, and nursing home in Community B and the pharmacist there was infrequently connected. In Community D, the ambulance provider was among the three in most constant contact, a different pattern than that of Communities A, B, and C. In three of the four communities, the physician and pharmacist are in the group of providers with the most frequent contact. This is not surprising, since pharmacists are required by law to have a physician's order for prescriptions and physicians often seek information about pharmaceuticals from pharmacists.

Particularly instructive, however, was the answer to the question about the "reason for the contacts." Almost without exception, the reason for the contacts was "to refer or receive clients." Seldom were the contacts for the purpose of coordinating services or to plan to work together to meet community health care needs.

The answer to the question "Do certain types of interorganizational relationships facilitate access to appropriate care?" would seem to be the following: With respect to the early detection of life-threatening and debilitating disease, the types of interorganizational relationships available in these four communities do not facilitate access to appropriate care. The findings suggest that contacts between providers were based on specific client problems—episodic response to presenting complaints or disease entities—rather than on the basis of working together to reduce the incidence of such diseases. There was little recognition of the mortality and morbidity of the

A = Community A
B = Community B
C = Community C
D = Community D

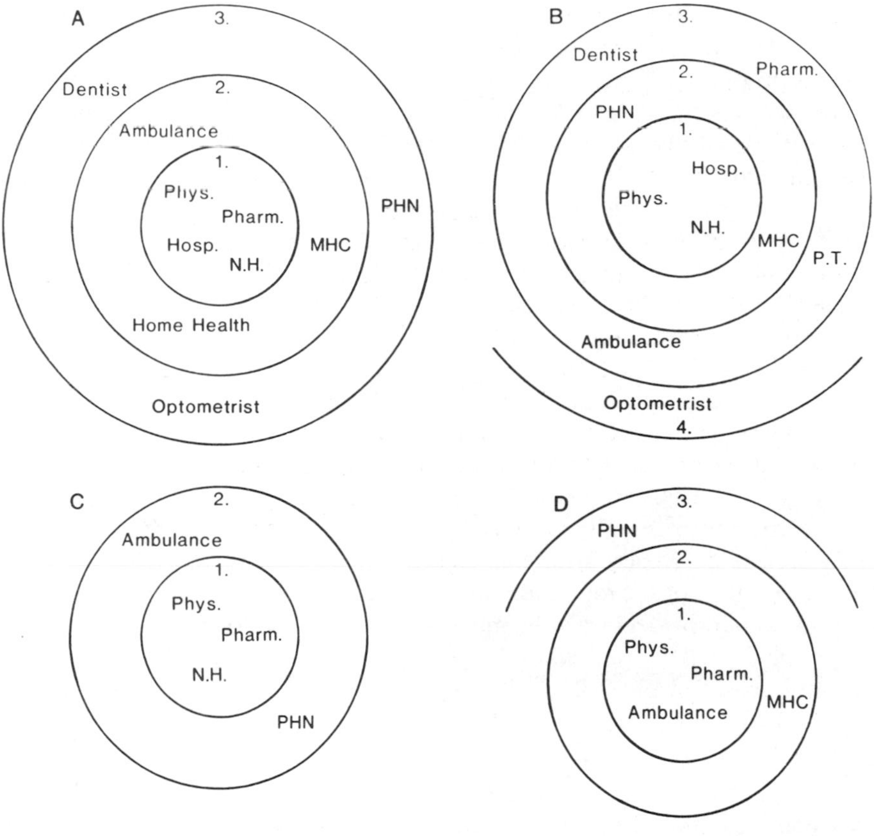

Figure 16–2. Sociometric Illustration of the Frequency of Contacts between Primary Health Care Providers

Source: *Field Study of Rural Primary Health Care Services: Their Organization and Effects*, unpublished doctoral dissertation by PR Schultz, University of Denver, 1981.

---

populations, which might have stimulated the design of cooperative programs to reduce them. The providers did not seem to view themselves as a "health care system" to which the residents had access and that, as such, they were responsible for the health of the populations in these communities. Rather, providers attended to the clients that presented themselves for their particular

type of health service and interacted with only those other providers with whom they were required by law, such as the physician and the pharmacist, or with whom a referral was appropriate. A corollary conclusion can be drawn about health promotion on the basis of the finding that the higher health habits scores among residents of Community D were related to their going elsewhere for their primary medical care, the length of travel time to their primary medical care source, the length of time known to their primary care source, and their age. There may be other reasons, but these are ones based on evidence from the data. In future case studies, it would be valuable, for example, to explore health values and beliefs related to health practices. Such content would enhance this holistic approach.

Conclusions

In conclusion, the number and types of interorganizational relationships do seem to make a difference—a negative one—in health outcomes of a population as defined in this study. Specifically, the evidence suggests that contacts between providers may facilitate the meeting of individual needs for already existing disease, but they do not seem to facilitate health protective, disease preventive, or health promotive care.

Taken altogether, then, the answers to the four research questions that guided these case study investigations suggest that (a) underserved communities, as a type of environment in which people make choices related to health, are not supportive of health protective or health promotive health status outcomes and (b) the lack of interorganizational contacts among the few providers focused on the health protective and health promotive aspects of health services unnecessarily constrains the choices of the population. Put more simply, much opportunity is lost by the failure of providers to view themselves as a "system" of health care for the good of their local populations.

IMPLICATIONS FOR NURSING

The example of comparative case analysis in community health presented here has several implications for nursing research. First, it is an indication that the several prescriptions for conducting comparative case study can be operationalized in the health field with meaningful results. Second, the epidemiological model for health[42] can be operationalized and the merits of the four determinants examined for their relative contribution to health outcomes in a population. Because the epidemiologic model for health was specifically identified as a holistic model,[45] the study reported here gives evidence in support of the thesis that research can be designed to examine human responses in health and illness from a holistic orientation, a third

implication. Fourth, the specific prescription for designing and analyzing comparative case studies from the "most different systems" strategy has been demonstrated in the study reported. The selection of Community D as a small rural community, *not* underserved for health services, that "should be" different from the first three communities studied (because of their underserved status) was sound. Community D was shown by the evidence to be different and yielded the generation of a different hypothesis. Last, having demonstrated the operationalization of a comparative case study for examining the health of a population in its community, interorganizational, and organizational contexts, it seems reasonable to project that the holistic study of individual persons, groups or families, or organizations for delivering nursing services can be similarly operationalized. Specifically, the prescriptions for designing and operationalizing cases to accommodate several levels of analysis and more than one type of data, and following logical analytical procedures, seem to hold promise for nursing research.

REFERENCES

1. Winston-Fry P: The scientific method and its impact on holistic health. *Adv Nurs Sci* 1980;2(4):1-7.

2. Munhall PL: Nursing philosophy and nursing research: In apposition or opposition? *Nurs Res* 1982;31(3):176-177, 181.

3. Oiler C: The phenomenological approach in nursing research. *Nurs Res* 1982;31(3):178-181.

4. Gortner SR: The history and philosophy of nursing science and research. *Adv Nurs Sci* 1983;5(2):1-8.

5. Munhall PL: Methodological fallacies: A critical self-appraisal. *Adv Nurs Sci* 1983;5(4):41-49.

6. Omery A: Phenomenology: A method for nursing research. *Adv Nurs Sci* 1983;5(2):49-63.

7. Tinkle MB, Beaton JL: Toward a new view of science: Implications for nursing research. *Adv Nurs Sci* 1983;5(2):27-36.

8. Lundberg GA: Case work and the statistical method. *Social Forces* 1926;5:60-63.

9. Stouffer SA: Notes on the case-study and the unique case. *Sociometry* 1941;4:349-357.

10. Boring EG: The nature and the history of experimental control *Am J Psychol* 1954;67:573-589.

11. Campbell D, Stanley JC: *Experimental and Quasi-experimental Designs for Research.* Chicago, Rand McNally, 1966.

12. Lipjhart A: Comparative politics and the comparative method. *Am Polit Sci Rev* 1971;65:682-693.

13. Henning M, Jardim A: *The Managerial Woman.* Garden City, NJ, Doubleday/Anchor Press, 1977.

14. Stevens BJ: *Educating the Nurse Manager: Case Studies and Group Work*, Rockville, Md, Aspen Systems, 1982.

15. Breuer J, Freud S: *Studies on Hysteria.* New York, Basic Books, 1957.

16. Farquhar JW: Baby of a phenylketonuric mother: Inferences drawn from a single case. *Arch Dis Child* 1974;49:205-208.

17. Campbell DT: "Degrees of freedom" and the case study. *Comp Polit Stud* 1975;8(July):178-193.

18. Yin RK: *The Case Study Method: An Annotated Bibliography,* 1983-84 ed. Washington, DC, COSMOS, 1983.

19. Przeworski A, Teune H: *The Logic of Comparative Social Inquiry.* New York, Wiley Interscience, 1970.

20. Smelser NJ: *Comparative Methods in the Social Sciences.* Englewood Cliffs, NJ, Prentice-Hall, 1976.

21. Denzin NK: Sociological Methods: A Sourcebook, ed 2. New York, McGraw-Hill, 1978.

22. Miller DC: *Handbook of Research Design and Social Measurement,* ed 2. New York, David McKay, 1970.

23. Nachmias D., Nachmias C: *Research Methods in the Social Sciences.* New York, St. Martin's Press, 1976.

24. Selltiz C: *Research Methods in Social Relations,* ed 3. New York, Holt, Rinehart & Winston, 1976.

25. Kerlinger FN: *Foundations of Behavioral Research,* ed 2. New York, Holt, Rinehart & Winston, 1973.

26. Waltz C, Bausell RB: *Nursing Research: Design, Statistics and Computer Analysis.* Philadelphia, FA Davis, 1981.

27. Polit D. Hungler B: *Nursing Research: Principles and Methods,* ed 2. Philadelphia, JB Lippincott, 1983.

28. Herson M, Barlow DH: *Single-Case Experimental Designs: Strategies for Studying Behavior.* New York, Pergamon, 1976.

29. Klenbaum DG, Kupper LL, Morgenstern H: *Epidemiologic Research: Principles and Quantitative Methods.* London, Lifetime Learning Publications, 1982.

30. Stevens BJ: *Nursing Theory: Analysis Application, Evaluation.* Boston, Little, Brown, 1979.

31. Fletcher RH, Fletcher SW, Wagner EW: *Clinical Epidemiology, the Essentials.* Baltimore, Williams & Wilkins, 1982.

32. Yin RK: The case study crisis: Some answers. *Admin Sci Q* 1981;198a;26(March):58-66.

33. Holm K: Single subject research. *Nurs Res* 1983;32(4):253-255.

34. Miles MB: Qualitative data as an attractive nuisance. *Admin Sci Q* 1979;24:590-601.

35. Yin RK: The case study as a serious research strategy. *Knowledge: Creation, Diffusion, Utilization* 1981;3(September):97-114.

36. Yin RK: *Case Study Research: Design and Methods.* Beverly Hills, Calif, Sage, 1984.

37. Jick TD: Mixing qualitative and quantitative methods: Triangulation in action. *Admin Sci Q* 1979;24:602-611.

38. Diesing P: *Patterns of Discovery in the Social Sciences.* Chicago, Aldine-Atherton, 1971.

39. Lipjhart A: The comparable-cases strategy in comparative research. *Comp Polit Stud* 1975;8(July):158-177.

40. Smelser NJ: Notes on the methodology of comparative analysis of economic activity, in Transactions of the Sixth World Congress of Sociology, vol 2. Evian: International Sociological Association, 1967, pp 101-117.

41. Schultz PR: *Field Study of Rural Primary Health Care Services: Their Organization and Effects,* doctoral dissertation. University of Denver, 1981.

42. Blum HL: *Expanding Health Care Horizons,* ed 1. Oakland, Calif, Third Party Press, 1974.

43. Blum HL: *Expanding Health Care Horizons,* ed 2. Oakland, Calif, Third Party Press, 1983.

44. Dever GEA: An epidemiological model for health policy analysis. *Social Indicators Research* 1976;2:453-456.

45. Dever GEA: *Community Health Analysis.* New York, Aspen Press, 1980.

46. LaLonde M: *A New Perspective on the Health of Canadians.* Ottawa, Office of the Canadian Minister of National Health and Welfare, 1974.

47. Galaskiewicz J: The structure of community organizational networks. *Social Forces* 1979;57:1346-1364.

48. Rutstein DD: Measuring the quality of medical care. *N Engl J Med* 1976;294(11):582-588.

49. Hage J, Aiken M, Marrett C: Organization structure and communication. *Am Sociol Rev* 1968;36:860-871.

50. Rogers D, Whetten D: *Research Needs on Interagency Coordination.* North Central Regional Center for Rural Development. Ames, Iowa, Iowa State University Press, 1979.

51. White H: Social Structure from multiple networks: I. Blockmodels of roles and positions. *Am J Sociol* 1976;81(January):730-780.

52. Kilijanek TS, Drabek TE, Adams CR, et al: The emergence of a post-disaster communication network. Paper presented at the Annual Meeting of the American Sociological Association, Boston, August 1979.

53. Kerr BJ: *Factor Analysis on Seven Variables,* unpublished manuscript. University of Colorado Health Sciences Center, Denver, 1983.

54. Lazarsfeld PF, Menzel H: On the relation between individual and collective properties, in Lazarsfeld P, Pasanella A, Rosenberg M (eds): *Continuities in the Language of Social Research.* New York, Free Press, 1972, pp 225-237.

55. *Annual Report of Vital Statistics (Colorado) 1980,* Health Statistics and Vital Records Division. Colorado, 1980.

56. Schultz PR: *Report to Community C,* unpublished manuscript. University of Colorado Health Sciences Center, Denver, 1982.

57. Morris SR: *Rural Primary Health Care Services,* masters thesis. University of Colorado Health Sciences Center, Denver, 1983.

Chapter 17

Confirmation-Disconfirmation: A Framework for the Study of Interpersonal Relationships

Carol W. Kennedy and Bonnie J. Garvin

The purpose of this chapter is, first, to explain a method of communication analysis that explicates the constructs of confirmation and disconfirmation and, second, to illustrate these communication behaviors as they occurred in actual conversation between nurses and physicians. This method of analysis can be used to understand communication that promotes health in a wide variety of interpersonal relationships, such as those found in family interactions and nurse-client interactions.

Emerging theories and models of nursing have not adequately conceptualized communication and have thereby not furnished a heuristic framework for the systematic study of the individual's interaction with the environment.[1] The constructs of confirmation and disconfirmation have promise in understanding this process in nursing and are the focus of this chapter.

The ability to confirm the existence and experience of another is a uniquely human capacity. Confirmation is a communication quality that contributes to the other's more positive self-evaluation and is one of the most important components in the healthy development of persons involved in interaction.[2] Disconfirmation, on the other hand, is a characteristic of communication that denies the worth of the other and contributes to the other person's diminished valuing of self.

Note: This research project was supported by the Division of Nursing, Bureau of Health Professions Health Resources and Services Administration, U.S. Public Health Service, under grant No. 1 R01 NU00974.

Confirmation was first described by Buber.[3] He saw individuals striving for confirmation from others and deemed a society humane in relation to its ability to confirm people within the society. Confirmation has been described as the single most common factor that influences outcomes in family and organizational settings.[4] Dysfunctional families were described by Laing[5] as having higher levels of disconfirmation. From the work of Buber[3] and Laing,[5] Sieburg[6] developed clusters of communication behaviors related to confirmation and disconfirmation. Over the past 15 years, confirmation and disconfirmation have been studied in many types of dyads and in many contexts.

Confirmation is a relational quality of communication that carries the message that the other exists, that the individuals are relating, and that the other has an experience different from but equally as valid and worthwhile as one's own view or experience.[6] The theoretical basis for the constructs of confirmation and disconfirmation arises from symbolic interactionism and the interactional approach to understanding human adaptive interaction with the environment.[7] Individual development involves a process whereby the individual constructs meaning about self and others through communication.

Communication occurs at many levels. Two primary levels are content and relationship.[2] The content level is what the message is about. The relationship level defines one person in relation to the other and is called metacommunication. It is a process whereby persons in the relationship create the ongoing relationship through mutual role taking.[1] For example, the utterance "Shut the door" carries the content level message that one person has said to the other to close the door. The relationship level message is that the requester has the right to request that the other close the door, and if the request is accepted or unquestioned, the respondent has the responsibility to close the door. If the respondent closes the door, then the relationship is further defined. Both persons in the relationship use relationship messages to give meaning and context to the communication.

Sieburg[6] was the first to operationalize and measure confirmation and disconfirmation. Her original category system contained two functional categories and five dysfunctional categories. This system was refined and revised for use in several communication contexts,[8–13] and the terms confirmation and disconfirmation eventually replaced functional and dysfunctional. There has been a gradual shift from large numbers of disconfirming categories (up to six in one study) to an equal focus on both confirmation and disconfirmation. It is in keeping with the current trend in nursing science to better conceptualize and measure the confirming aspects of communication in order to determine positive effects of communication on healthy development. A review of the literature on confirmation and disconfirmation will provide a broader understanding of the characteristics of these constructs.

STUDIES ON CONFIRMATION AND DISCONFIRMATION

Sieburg[6] found that effective groups (determined by objective performance criteria) used significantly fewer dysfunctional responses and significantly more functional responses than did ineffective groups. Later she wrote that these two types of responses were the two major factors found to describe most and least preferred communication partners.[8] Responses in the functional factor were direct verbal acknowledgment, agreement about content, supporting, clarification of content, and expression of positive feelings. The dysfunctional factor was characterized as impervious, interrupting, irrelevant, tangential, impersonal, unclear, and incongruous. Heineken[14] compared groups of psychiatric clients with a control group of normal people. Three out of four psychiatric client groups scored significantly higher in disconfirming communication than the control group. Further, these psychiatric clients disconfirmed more than twice as much as the control group. Jacobs[10] found that subjects exposed experimentally to disconfirming communication were significantly less satisfied with their relationships than were subjects exposed to confirming communication.

Sundell[9] studied confirmation-disconfirmation in teacher-pupil interaction in the classroom, using the response category system developed by Sieburg and Larson.[8] She found that most teachers (89%) used primarily confirming communication patterns. In addition, she found that confirmation-disconfirmation tended to be reciprocal: when teachers were confirming, students tended to be confirming, and when teachers were disconfirming, students tended to be disconfirming. In another study, hearing officers were more disconfirming in face-to-face interactions than in two teleconferencing conditions. Subtle nonverbal behaviors available in the face-to-face interactions were suggested as the reason for the higher disconfirming findings.[4] Kennedy[15] examined the interruption behavior of highly educated women and men in groups and found no significant differences between the sexes in the production of confirming and disconfirming utterances.

Confirmation has been further studied by measuring the extent to which individuals feel accepted or confirmed by others. Ross[16] found that the only common communication pattern exhibited in four contexts (counselors-juvenile delinquents, spouses, fathers-sons, and supervisors-subordinates) was the dimension of acceptance-rejection of the individual as a person. The characteristics of acceptance and rejection are similar to those of confirmation and disconfirmation, respectively.

In marital dyads, Clarke[17] found that perceived confirmation accounted for 53%, 43%, and 50% of the variance in satisfaction and attraction in couples whose relationships existed for one to three years, four to six years, and more than seven years, respectively. Perceived confirmation accounted for a greater part of the variance than self-disclosure and accuracy of interpersonal

perception. The last two variables accounted for additional but nonsignificant amounts of variation in reported marital satisfaction. Cissna[18] and Cissna and Keating[19] found a moderate relationship between facilitative communication (demonstration of empathy, respect, and genuineness) of one person and the extent to which the other person felt confirmed. Other studies have examined the relationship between confirmation-disconfirmation and agreement and self-disclosure,[20] cultural variation,[21] self-acceptance,[12] self-concept, coorientation and friendship,[22,23] sex of persons in the relationship,[24] communication apprehension,[11] and communication "openness."[25]

Although the methods for categorizing confirmation and disconfirmation have varied slightly in the research on this topic, general levels of confirmation in relationships can be reported. In student-teacher interactions, the majority of teachers confirmed students 89% of the time.[9] Hearing officers were confirming in 95% of their communications with clients.[4] In groups of mentally ill clients, confirmation ranged from 75% to 83% compared with 90% for normal subjects in group interaction.

Garvin and Kennedy[26] examined the communication of four groups of nurses and physicians (ten female nurses and ten male physicians, ten female nurses and ten female physicians, ten male nurses and ten male physicians, and ten male nurses and ten female physicians). Staff nurses and resident physicians volunteered to be videotaped for 30 minutes in a decision-making situation with another health professional. The subjects were asked to jointly decide how they would spend a $35,000 gift to their hospital. They were given a list of hospital needs but were told that they were free to decide how the money should be spent. Garvin and Kennedy found that 87% of the communication was confirming. They discovered no significant differences among the groups in the proportion of confirmation. In addition, no significant differences were found between women and men or between nurses and physicians.

CATEGORY SYSTEM

As stated previously, most of the development in the study of confirmation and disconfirmation has been done on disconfirmation behaviors. Because we wanted to increase the understanding of healthy behavior, we attempted to further develop the construct of confirmation. To do this, we built on the work of Laing[5] and Cissna and Sieburg[7] and categorized confirmation behaviors into three clusters: recognition, acknowledgment, and endorsement. We condensed the six categories of disconfirmation used by Heineken[14] into three categories proposed by Cissna and Sieburg[7]: indifference, disqualification, and impervious. A final category called "other," which included any utterance that could not be scored as confirming or disconfirming, completed the category system.

Confirmation Behaviors

Recognition

Recognition refers to recognizing the presence of the other person. It conveys respect and acknowledges the other's attempt to relate[7] It includes looking at the other, frequent eye contact, a brief vocal show of interest that encourages or facilitates the other to continue talking, eg, "uh huh," interspersed at a pause or after the other person's talk. It also includes appropriate nonverbal responses, such as nodding, smiling, or touching.

The excerpt below from an interaction between a male nurse (MRN) and a male physician (MMD) contains a series of recognition responses. The nurse begins to analyze the situation and the physician encourages the nurse's idea development through a series of "uh huh" responses.

> MRN: You kinda wonder if this is a one-time gift . . .
>
> MMD: Uh huh.
>
> MRN: And even if you have X amount of money to spend, once that's gone, it's gone, so . . .
>
> MMD: Uh huh.
>
> MRN: If you put it in something a little bit less tangible, down the line you know it doesn't do you any good to hire two extra nurses for one year if you're not gonna have them when the money's gone.

The periodic "uh huhs" interspersed at appropriate pauses were accompanied by eye contact and conveyed that the physician was listening and encouraged the nurse to continue. Facilitating behaviors like "uh huhs" and head nods are common recognition behaviors that demonstrate attending to the communication of the other. These facilitation behaviors add to the smooth flow of daily conversations. They are the unobtrusive indicators that the speaker has the listener's permission to continue talking, to retain the speaking turn.

In general, recognition behaviors allow the speaker to develop and complete one or two thoughts. There are times, however, when the overuse of these facilitative behaviors has the effect of encouraging the speaker to talk for an unusually long time, almost in a monologue, except that he or she is being encouraged to do so by his or her partner. In order for this to occur, one partner must be willing to keep talking and express ideas while the other

partner must be willing to take the support role in the conversation and not contribute much to the development of the conversation content.

Acknowledgment

Communication behaviors that demonstrate a relevant and direct response are called acknowledgments. Acknowledgment conveys that one is in a relationship with another. It does not require agreement, but does need to acknowledge the other's perceptions, statements, or questions.[7] Examples of acknowledgment behaviors include such responses as a "yes" or a "no" in response to a question, expansion or elaboration of content, a request for an opinion, clarification of content, laughter with the other person, or the introduction of a different but relevant topic as long as the content of the previous speaker's speech is verbally acknowledged. A simple example of agreeing with the other is seen in the following exchange between a male physician and a female nurse (FRN).

> MMD: If I were donating the money, I'd like it to be used for something specific.
>
> FRN: Right.

Acknowledgment is further demonstrated in the following exchange, in which the physician provides a direct answer to the nurse's question.

> FRN: I wonder how much updating they're talking about?
>
> MMD: Probably 35,000 dollars worth!
>
> FRN: (Laughs with the physician)

Another example of a direct, relevant response is illustrated between a female physician (FMD) and a female nurse:

> FMD: Is there one conference room in each nursing station or are we talking about one big one?
>
> FRN: A big one.
>
> FMD: OK

Acknowledgment behaviors go beyond recognition behaviors to demonstrate that one is responding relevantly to the communication of the other.

Although recognition behaviors facilitate the other's continued talk, acknowledgment furthers the idea, content, or topic being discussed. In the Garvin and Kennedy study,[26] the majority of the confirmation utterances were coded in the acknowledgment category. Conversations characterized by acknowledgments reveal a mutual give and take and conversational equality between the interactants. It is through acknowledgment that ideas are validated, critiqued, and extended.

Endorsement

These confirmation behaviors acknowledge the other's way of experiencing the world, especially the other's feelings. This category includes expressing one's own feelings, clarifying the other's feelings, acknowledging the other's feelings, or communicating that the other is interesting or important. Endorsement communication generally does not focus on the content of the interaction, but on the process occurring between the interactants.

Because the subjects in the Garvin and Kennedy study[26] were strangers and asked to focus on a task, few endorsement speeches occurred (8 out of 10,865 speeches); however, 5 of those exchanges occurred in an interaction between two women. In one example, a female physician shared her feelings with a female nurse:

FRN: OK. I think we're done.

FMD: It has been nice talking to you.

In the second example, a nurse responded in a similar fashion:

FRN: It sounds like we're done. Are we done?

FMD: Yeah.

FRN: Well, I've enjoyed deciding how to spend this money with you. Thanks for your time.

FMD: Thanks for your time too.

Although these examples may sound like superficial responses, they do focus on the process of the communication. This category would be especially appropriate in coding communication between intimate persons, such as family members.

Sieburg,[28] in her most recent work, stated that endorsement is "true confirmation" and occurs only rarely. This is perhaps attributed to the fact

that using endorsement is riskier than using acknowledgment or recognition. When an individual departs from a discussion of content to a sharing of feelings, that person is daring to expose more of himself or herself. When a person attempts to clarify another's feelings, he or she is communicating a broader range of interest and concern for the other. The use of endorsement speeches allows the interactants to explore more of the unique nature of each person.

A review of the confirmation categories reveals that confirmation is a manner of interacting that involves both participants. It involves a give and take and genuine listening to the other such that one's responses are related and relevant to the message of the other. Confirmation is not something that one does, but is a process in which one shares.[7]

Disconfirmation Behaviors

More work has been done on disconfirming behaviors, and thus they have been described in more detail. Taken as a whole, disconfirmation is any communication behavior that is damaging to some aspect of another's self-view.[6] The categories presented below illustrate how this is accomplished.

Indifference

Indifference includes any communication behavior that denies the other's existence.[7] This can be accomplished through the denial of presence or of involvement or through the rejection of the other's attempt to communicate. Indifference conveys the message that the other does not matter or does not exist.

Denial of presence can be seen when one is silent when a reply is expected or through inattentive behaviors, like playing with a pen or reading while another is speaking. Extreme forms of this behavior include turning one's back on the other or physically leaving the interaction. Even in this laboratory study, a female physician physically left the videotaping room without excusing herself to answer a telephone page.

In the interactions between the nurses and physicians in the Garvin and Kennedy study,[26] a common form of denial of presence occurred through silence, ie, no response when one would be expected. A typical example of not responding occurred in an interaction between a female physician and a male nurse:

> FMD: How should we proceed?
>
> MRN: (No response. Appeared to be reading. Did not look up from reading materials.)

FMD: Well, it might be a good idea for each of us to make separate lists of what we think is important.

In this example, the physician went on to suggest an answer to her own question when the nurse did not respond, thus the physician kept the conversation going. In other instances, speakers who did not get a response from their partner were noted to change the entire topic of conversation (almost as if they were searching for a topic to which the partner would respond). Sometimes the first speaker did not try to repair the nonresponse. This resulted in long, awkward silences that left both interactants appearing uncomfortable. Studies have demonstrated that persons who take longer than three seconds to respond to their partner's remark tend to be less socially skilled.[27]

Without at least minimal recognition from the listener, the speaker is left wondering what the listener thinks about the content being presented. The lack of response provides a metacommunication about the relationship that suggests "You do not exist." One is readily reminded of the young child repeatedly trying to get his mother's attention when she is talking to someone else, or the wife who attempts to talk to her husband who continues to read the newspaper. Nurses have described a similar phenomenon when they tell physicians that they need orders for medication (or whatever) and the physician leaves the floor without writing the orders.

Denial of involvement, the second form of indifference, includes behaviors like avoiding eye contact and distancing behaviors, such as crossed arms or moving one's chair back. It also includes using impersonal language, as seen in the earlier example presented under Recognition. The MRN repeatedly used the pronoun you in place of the pronoun I when making a personal statement. Displays of indifference through denial of involvement create feelings of alienation and distance. There is a feeling of aloofness and separateness between the interactants.

The final form of indifference occurs through rejection of communication, which is seen when two speakers talk at once, when one talks at length in a monologue, interrupts the other, introduces three or more ideas in one turn at talk, or introduces a different topic without acknowledging the previous speaker's content. The following is an example of an interruption:

FRN: Ya gotta keep in mind this is donated money.

FMD: That's right and I . . .

FRN: This is from a family, and that's a lot of money to be donated by one family.

In this example the nurse clearly began speaking before the physician finished her thought. The nurse left the impression that the physician had not spoken as she went on with her own idea, disregarding the communication of the physician and violating the physician's right to take a turn at talk. The person who is repeatedly interrupted or whose topics are ignored will not feel heard, attended to, or significant and may soon come to doubt her or his very existence.[7]

Disqualification

This form of disconfirmation may occur in several ways. Messages may disqualify the other person, the message, or self. Other persons are disqualified through direct disparagement, as in name calling, criticism, blame, and hostile attack, but also through such indirect means as sarcasm or laughing at the other person.[7] The net result is for the other to appear or feel too incompetent or unreliable for his or her message to have validity. The other person feels worthless and unimportant.

Message disqualification may occur when the respondent goes off on a tangent and responds to an incidental part of a prior communication, thus missing the intent of the first speaker's message, or when the respondent is reminded of an episode in his or her own experience, making only a token connection with the preceding remark, eg, "That reminds me of a story . . . " Message disqualification may also take the form of a psuedo-response, when the speaker uses a quick "yes" in mock agreement only because the new speaker wants to introduce his or her own topic. This is illustrated in the following excerpt, when a nurse gives token acknowledgment that she heard the physician's statement but then quickly focuses on an irrelevant issue.

> FMD: Even though I am sure they mean for us to spend it however we think it is best, that has to be a key consideration.

> FRN: Yeah. UGH—Grubby pencils (picks up a pencil from the table).

The "yeah" functioned as a superficial acknowledgment, but by being distracted by pencils lying on the table, the nurse in this example conveys a lack of interest in what the physician was saying. The physician was "communicatively" left talking to herself. In another example of message disqualification, a male physician indicates his discomfort with a compliment being paid to him by a female nurse.

> FRN: We'd be great at spending money, you and I.

MMD: Yeah.

FRN: Because we can reason with each other.

MMD: Uh huh. Well, going through this list, we need to decide what we will tell the administrator.

The physician obviously heard the nurse's remarks but quickly moved the conversation to a less emotional, content-oriented topic. This example perhaps provides us with a clue as to what happens in a relationship when one person indicates a willingness to explore a deeper (or more meaningful) aspect of the relationship before their partner is ready to do so.

Self-disqualification occurs when the speaker indicates that "I am not communicating," hence "We are not relating," through sentences that are incomplete, rambling, difficult to follow, qualified, repetitious, incongruent, or heavily laden with euphemisms or cliches. An extreme example of an incomplete utterance on the part of a male physician is responded to by a male nurse.

MMD: Well, yeah . . . I mean . . . outside of that . . . you know . . . those, those . . . see that . . . we don't know.

MRN: We don't know how much lab equipment is going to cost.

Clearly, persons who speak is such an inarticulate manner are not presenting themselves in a favorable light and are disqualifying their own utterances as they speak. The respondent to this type of communication is almost forced to change the topic or guess at the meaning of the speaker's intent. Under these circumstances, the respondent may also be using disqualification by changing the topic in an attempt to repair the conversation.[29]

The literature suggests that women use incomplete and qualified speech more often than do men,[30] particularly when they are interacting with men. Although the results of the Garvin and Kennedy[26] study revealed no significant difference in the types of speech used by males and females, it seems useful to remind speakers (male or female, nurse or physician) that the manner in which they present themselves may have a great deal to do with the way others respond to them. If, for example, female nurses present themselves in an unconfident manner to male physicians, then this behavior may account for the frequently heard complaint that physicians ignore nurses' communication.

Impervious

Impervious refers to a lack of accurate awareness of another's experience.[6] Imperviousness is disconfirming because it distorts the other's experience. This can occur through denial of another's feelings or thoughts, as in a response like "That's silly, you can't possibly think that," or in the case of false reassurance, as in a remark like "Everything will be all right."

Imperviousness can occur through the process of mystification, in which one person implies that he or she knows what is going on inside the other speaker or is in a position to judge the "correctness" of the other's feelings, eg, "What you really mean is . . . " Impervious remarks are sometimes difficult to detect, particularly when they involve a socially acceptable reassurance; for example, in response to a remark like "I'm really dumb," another might say, "No you're not." Although this remark at first appears reassuring, at a deeper level it questions the ability of the speaker to define his or her experience.

Imperviousness is also demonstrated through selective responses, which are responses limited to those topics initiated by self or those that ignore any topic introduced by the other person. This is illustrated in the following exchange between a male physician and a female nurse:

MMD: Laboratory equipment can cost a lot of money.

FRN: Yes it can. I think we'd have to tour the facility and look at equipment, space, etc, to put our priorities in place.

MMD: Thirty-five thousand dollars isn't a lot of money if you're talking about buying laboratory equipment or any other piece of machinery.

FRN: (Silence)

The nurse responded to the physician's comment about laboratory equipment and extended the topic. The MD returned to the topic of the lab equipment without responding to the nurse's suggestion. This impervious response was then met with silence on the part of the nurse. One could infer that the nurse did not respond because she was cognizant of the fact that the physician was not listening anyway.

The disconfirmation categories represent clusters of communication behaviors that deny the existence or relationship, significance, or experience of another. These utterances cannot be judged in isolation and, like the confirmation utterances, must be evaluated in response to some other behavior.

IMPLICATIONS AND RECOMMENDATIONS

The Garvin and Kennedy[26] study described confirmation and disconfirmation occurring between nurses and physicians in order to better understand the quality of the relationships between the two professions. This was a laboratory study in which subjects were strangers to one another. It is recommended that further study of nurse-physician communication be undertaken in the clinical or work setting. A highly stressful environment, like the operating room or emergency room, would probably influence the way nurses and physicians communicate with one another. Routine conversations on any unit of the hospital would also be worthy of study. These conversations might be influenced by the differing goals of the two professions, the perceived time frame for completing work, and differing levels of clinical knowledge and expertise. In a busy hospital or clinic environment, a nonparticipant observer could unobtrusively rate the quality of communication between nurses and physicians, and thereby provide additional insights into how each sees self in relation to the other.

The confirmation-disconfirmation category system used to examine the communication between nurses and physicians in the Garvin and Kennedy[26] study can be used to examine any type of dyadic or group interaction. It is recommended that other interactions of special interest to nurses also be studied, for example, nurse-client interactions. Questions that might be asked of these important relationships are, are there differences in the way nurses communicate with clients of differing age, sex, race, or diagnosis? What are the physiological correlates to confirming and disconfirming communication? A nonparticipant observer in a client room would undoubtedly produce considerable experimenter effects. A less obtrusive data-collection procedure would be to install an electronic recording device in the client's room that could be remotely activated whenever a nurse entered the room. The interactions could then be either coded immediately from the remote site or saved and coded at a later time. Using monitoring equipment, researchers could obtain reliable physiological measures that could then be correlated with receiving and sending confirming and disconfirming messages.

Family interactions are also of interest to nurses. How does parental communication influence the health of children? Are there differences in the communication behaviors of mothers as compared with fathers in interaction with their female *v.* male children of differing ages? If there are differences, what are the longitudinal effects of these differences on the personality and health of the children? Data from these studies would provide important information about the quality of these relationships and could provide important insights in ways of contributing to the health of the interactants.

The confirmation-disconfirmation framework has proved useful in the systematic study of interactions. The category system developed from this

framework has been applied to both dyadic and group interactions. Thus it is a particularly attractive system for nurses to use in their analyses of relationships. Interactions can be analyzed by a nonparticipant observer, or this system can be used by individuals as participant observers to examine their own communication behaviors. It is important for nurses to first be aware of their communication behaviors with others and then, when necessary, this awareness can serve as a basis for enacting more confirming responses.

In addition to describing the quality of nurses' communication with others, it is important to know how the other perceives that communication. Despite the fact that nurses may be communicating what are thought by them to be confirming messages, it is important to know how these messages are interpreted by those with whom they are interacting. Nurses have long known that the helping relationship is best facilitated when the helper understands the experience from the other's point of view. Therefore, identifying the extent to which a person feels confirmed is suggested in addition to the observation of confirmation in interaction.

The purpose of this chapter is to describe a framework for analyzing interpersonal relationships. This framework provides a system for categorizing confirming and disconfirming communication. Further development of this framework will contribute to nursing's body of knowledge related to the individual's interaction with others in the environment.

REFERENCES

1. Kasch CR: Interpersonal competence and communication in the delivery of nursing care. *Adv Nurs Sci* 1984;1:71-88.

2. Watzlawick P, Beavin JH, Jackson DD: *Pragmatics of Human Communication.* New York, WW Norton, 1976.

3. Buber M: Distance and relation. *Psychiatry* 1957;20:97-104.

4. Larson CE, Goldberg A, Rosenfeld LB, Ledesma A: *Confirming and Disconfirming Communication Behaviors in Administrative Fair Hearings,* unpublished manuscript. University of Denver, 1983.

5. Laing D: *The Self and Others.* New York, Pantheon, 1961.

6. Sieburg E: Dysfunctional communication and interpersonal responsiveness in small groups. *Dissertation Abstracts International* 1969;30:2622A. University Microfilms No. 69-21, 156.

7. Cissna KN, Sieburg E: Patterns of interactional confirmation and disconfirmation, in Wilder-Mott C, Weakland JH (eds): *Rigor and Imagination: Essays from the Legacy of Gregory Bateson.* New York, Praeger, 1981, pp 253-282.

8. Sieburg E, Larson CE: *Dimensions of Interpersonal Response.* Paper presented at the International Communication Association Convention, Phoenix, Arizona, April 1971.

9. Sundell W: The operation of confirming and disconfirming verbal behavior in selected teacher-student interactions. *Dissertation Abstracts International* 1972;33:1838A. University Microfilms No. 72-25, 030.

10. Jacobs M: Levels of confirmation and disconfirmation in interpersonal communication. *Dissertation Abstracts International* 1973;34:3593A. University Microfilms No. 73-30, 214.

11. Aveyard BC: *The Relationships Between Communication Apprehension, Self-acceptance of Others, the FIRO-B Scales and Disconfirming Responses*, unpublished bachelor of letters dissertation. University of New England, Australia, 1977.

12. Mathews AJ: Confirming and disconfirming behaviors, self acceptance, and personal values: A descriptive study of librarian-user interactions. *Dissertation Abstracts International* 1977;38:2415A-2416A. University Microfilms No. 77-22, 776.

13. Lifshitz P: *An Experimental Study of the Effects of Cooperation/Competition and Similarity/Dissimilarity on Reciprocity and Compensation*, doctoral dissertation. Wayne State University, Detroit. University Microfilms No. 801 0154.

14. Heineken J: Disconfirmation in dysfunctional communication. *Nurs Res* 1982;31(4):211-213.

15. Kennedy CW: Patterns of verbal interruption among women and men in groups. *Dissertation Abstracts International* 1980;40(10):5425A. University Microfilms No. 80-90, 300.

16. Ross RF: Perceived communication patterns and predictive accuracy of supervisor-subordinate dyads. *Dissertation Abstracts International* 1973;34:3598A. University Microfilms No. 73-28, 534.

17. Clarke FP: Interpersonal communication variables as predictors of marital satisfaction-attraction. *Dissertation Abstracts International* 1973;34:4458A. University Microfilms No. 73-30, 188.

18. Cissna KN: Facilitative communication and interpersonal relationships: An empirical test of a theory of interpersonal communication. *Dissertation Abstracts International* 1975;36:4103A. University Microfilms No. 76-1233.

19. Cissna KN, Keating S: Speech communication antecedents of perceived confirmation. *West J Speech Commun* 1979;43:48-60.

20. Hutchinson JA: *Trust, Attraction, Self-disclosure, Confirmation, and Perceived Variables Between Most Preferred and Least Preferred Relationships.* Paper presented at the Colorado-Wyoming Academy of Science Convention, Pueblo, Colorado, April 1978.

21. Waxwood VA: Intercultural and intracultural communication: A study of relationship areas in the interpersonal setting. *Dissertation Abstracts International* 1976;37:2501A. University Microfilms No. 76-25, 470.

22. Leth SA: Interpersonal response: Confirmation, rejection, and disconfirmation in established friendships. *Dissertation Abstracts International* 1977. University Microfilms No. 77-7482.

23. Leth P: Self-concept and interpersonal response in a classroom: An exploratory study. *Dissertation Abstracts International* 1978. University Microfilms No. 78-13, 080.

24. Keating S: *The Effects of Agreement, Disagreement, Facilitative Communication, and Self-disclosure on the Perceived Confirmation of Males and Females*, master's final research project. Saint Louis University, St Louis, 1977.

25. Jablin FM: An experimental study of message-response in superior-subordinate communication. *Dissertation Abstracts International* 1977. University Microfilms No. 78-03, 241.

26. Garvin BJ, Kennedy CW: Confirmation and disconfirmation in nurse/physician communication. *J Appl Commun* (in press).

27. McLaughlin ML, Cody MJ: Awkward silences: Behavioral antecedents and consequences of the conversational topic. *Hum Commun Res* 1984;8(4):299-316.

28. Sieburg E. *The Family Communication System: An Integrated Approach.* New York, Gardner Press, 1985.

29. Bavelas JB: Situations that lead to disqualification. *Hum Commun Res* 1983;9(2):130-145.

30. Eakins BW, Eakins RG: *Sex Differences in Human Communication.* Boston, Houghton Mifflin, 1978.

Chapter 18

Transitions: A Nursing Concern

Norma Chick and Afaf Ibrahim Meleis

Analysis is a methodological option in the development of knowledge in nursing. It is defined as a process of identifying parts and components, examining them against a number of identified criteria. Analysis includes both concept and theory analysis.

Concept analysis is a useful process in the cycle of theory development and testing and may occur at many points in the process. A number of structures have been provided in the literature as guidelines for concept analysis.[1–4] Strategies for analysis depend on levels of knowledge development within disciplines. As the boundaries of nursing domain develop and are sharpened, analysis takes on new dimensions. The use of multidimensional components of analyses that are more congruent with level of development in nursing would help in further developing nursing knowledge. The components used in analysis of transition are presented below. These may be used sequentially or nonsequentially.

1. Definition, identification, and description of the different dimensions and components of the concept. In defining different dimensions, a description of some of the antecedents to the concept and some of the consequences is essential, matching some of these descriptions with what occurs in nursing practice.

2. Examination and analysis of concept congruency with existing nursing theories and other domain concepts.

Note: The authors collaborated on this paper while Norma Chick was on sabbatical leave as a Visiting Lecturer in the Department of Mental Health and Community Nursing, University of California, San Francisco.

The authors wish to acknowledge their appreciation to Ramona Mercer and Jeanne Qunit-Benoliel for their review of an earlier draft of this manuscript.

3. Development, description, and analysis of exemplars of model cases. This step may include clinical or empirical results that are related to the concept.
4. Comparison with other concepts with similar properties and dimensions to establish its boundaries.
5. Development, description, and analysis of contrary cases to the normative cases. Situations in which the concept appears sometimes or under a new set of conditions are called borderline cases and are also useful in analyzing concepts.
6. Analysis of the research potential related to the concept by consideration of its properties as dependent and independent variable. This component is completed when measurement issues are considered.

Each of these processes has a methodology of its own and could be used as a test of the occurrence of a concept. These tests are both conceptual and clinical. When these processes are complemented by testing through empirically valid and reliable research instruments, the cycle of theory-research-theory is complete.

The purpose of this chapter is twofold: to articulate an argument for the centrality of transitions as a concept within the domain of nursing by using the guidelines of concept analysis identified earlier and to provide an analysis of transition as an exemplar for concept analysis.

DEFINITION, DIMENSIONS, AND COMPONENTS OF TRANSITION

Transition is a familiar concept in developmental theories and in stress and adaptation theories. It accommodates both the continuities and discontinuities in the life processes of human beings. Transitions are invariably related to change and development, both of which are highly pertinent themes for nursing. Superimposed on developmental transitions are other forms of transition that are linked more directly to situational and health-illness events. One example of the latter is hospitalization for acute illness or injury, which automatically precipitates the person into contact with nurses and nursing. In some instances, transition is initiated by events beyond the individual's control; in other cases, it may be sought deliberately through events such as marriage, migration, career change, or cosmetic surgery.

Transitions are those periods in between fairly stable states. Transitions fall within the domain of nursing when they pertain to health or illness or when responses to the transition are manifested in health-related behaviors. It is conceivable that in the first instance, the health-illness condition is the independent variable and the transition, the dependent variable. An acutely

ill patient who is hospitalized, a patient who is discharged from a health care institution, and a patient undergoing surgery are all examples of conditions or situations with an impending state of transition. In the second instance, exemplified by immigration, transition is the independent variable that may predispose human beings to health problems. The transition may also influence responses to health problems and types of action taken because of potential or actual health problems.

A number of writers have argued that there is now sufficient consensus about the discipline's central concerns—human beings, environment, and health—for these concepts to be accepted as summarizing nursing's domain.[5] While each of these, singly or in various combinations, is the concern of scholars and researchers from many disciplines, nursing's concern lies in their interrelatedness as the irreducible minimum from which knowledge for nursing practice can evolve. Given that this triad forms the basic structure for nursing knowledge, it is conceivable that additional concepts will be required before we can identify all the intricate patterns that make up the whole of nursing. Transition is one such concept. It offers a key to interpreting person-environment interactions in terms of their actual and potential effects on health. In the wake of sound empirically based descriptions of transition, both as process and as outcome, more prescriptive theory can be generated to impact on practice. Nursing practice stands to gain from careful conceptualization of transition and its consequences in all the biopsychosociocultural variations.

Definition

The noun transition is derived from the Latin verb *transire*, meaning to go across. That sense is reflected in the first meaning given in *Webster's Third International Dictionary*[6]: "a passage or movement from one state, condition, or place to another." Because there are connotations of both time and movement, transition can be thought of as linking change with experienced time.

As conceptualized in this chapter, transition, as passage from one life phase, condition, or status to another, is a multiple concept embracing the elements of process, time span, and perception. Process suggests phases and sequence; time span indicates an ongoing but bounded phenomenon; and perception has to do with the meaning of the transition to the person experiencing it. The process involves both the disruption that the transition occasions and the person's responses to this interference. The time span extends from the first anticipation of transition until stability in the new status has been achieved. Perception of the transition will reflect how the associated role ambiguity and threat to self-concept are experienced. In summary, transition refers to both the process and the outcome of complex

person-environment interactions. It may involve more than one person and is imbedded in the context and the situation. (J. Benoliel, personal communication, 1985).

One important characteristic of transition is that it is essentially positive. The completion of a transition implies that the person has reached a period of greater stability relative to what has gone before. Even if overall, by comparison with a pretransition state, the changes seem more decremental than incremental, this does not mean that the transition outcome cannot be positive. The completed transition would then signify that the potential for disruption and disorganization associated with the precipitating circumstances had been countered. As Hall noted, "A theory focused on transition could deal with decreases as well as increases."[7(p3)]

Defining characteristics of transition include process, disconnectedness, perception, and patterns of response.

Process

Whether the event that causes the transition is anticipated or not, and whether the event is short or long term, transition is a process. Its beginning and end do not occur simultaneously; there is a sense of movement, a development, a flow associated with it. The distance between the beginning and the end may be short or long, and its end may or may not have the same characteristics as its beginning. Certain boundaries imply limits to the process. Although Bridges conceptualized the structure of life transitions a little differently, referring to "(1) an ending, followed by (2) a period of confusion and distress, leading to (3) a new beginning,"[8(p9)] there is still the same sense of transition being an ongoing and bounded phenomenon.

Although certain aspects of an individual's life will be affected more than others by the transition that he or she is currently experiencing, the extent and intensity of this influence may vary over time. Further, the boundaries of transition-related behavior are not fixed, but may expand and recede in accordance with other happenings in the total context of the person's life. Events and circumstances that are likely to be precursors to the process of transition are listed in Table 18–1.

Disconnectedness

Perhaps the most pervasive characteristic of transition is disconnectedness associated with disruption of the linkages on which the person's feelings of security depend. It is interesting in this regard to note that the authors of an extensive review of factors related to health commented that all the findings they described have "as a common element the importance to health of being 'connected.' . . . These connections are not passive, but require that people actively relate to one another and with the environment."[11(p354)] Other

Table 18–1 Events Leading to a Process of Transition

Illness	Loss	Pregnancy
Recovery	Immigration	Retirement
Birthing	Migration	Maturation
Death	Hospitalization	

characteristics allied to disconnectedness are loss of familiar reference points, incongruity between expectations based on the past and perceptions dictated by the present, and discrepancy between needs and the availability of, as well as access to, means for their satisfaction.

Perception

Meanings attributed to transition events vary between persons, communities, and societies, and thus influence the outcome. Hospitalization is considered necessary for healing by some and as a step toward dying by those from another culture.[11] A patient describing her hemiparesis after a stroke—"I feel like I have a dead body in bed with me" (N. Doolittler, personal communication, February 1985)—aptly illustrates the individuality of perception. This characteristic suggests that differences in perception of transition events may influence reactions and responses to such events, so making them less predictable.

Awareness

Transition is a personal phenomenon, not a structured one. Processes and outcomes of transitions are related to definitions and redefinitions of self and situation. Such defining and redefining may be done by the person experiencing the transition or by others in the environment. However, it is contended here that to be in transition, a person must have some awareness of the changes that are occurring. In the event that the changes have not yet reached the level of awareness, or are being denied either totally or in terms of their implications (irrespective of whether the denial is conscious or unconscious), then that person is not yet in transition. He or she is still in a pretransition phase. In such cases, it would be necessary to resolve barriers to awareness of transition before attempting to facilitate the transition itself.

Patterns of Response

Patterns of response arise out of the observable and nonobservable behaviors during the process of transition that, however disturbed or

dysfunctional they may appear, are not random occurrences. The behaviors embody patterns that reflect both intrapsychic structure and processes as well as those of the wider sociocultural context.[11] Pattern recognition would be an important part of developing a taxonomy of transitions. Table 18–2 shows the labels commonly applied to some of these patterns. Examples are disorientation, distress, and perhaps elation and happiness.

Dimensions

Transitions are not experienced uniformly by different people even when the circumstances, such as first-time parenting, are similar. However, there are some commonalities. First of all, there is a general structure consisting of at least three phases: entry, passage, and exit. It may be, too, that research will reveal some general dimensions that can be used to categorize transitions across different types of events: life cycle, situational, and health-illness.

The sequence is invariant, but the duration of each phase and associated degree of disruption are not. Impediments to the passage can occur at any point. Phases are more likely to merge into one another than to be discrete. Research would yield information on which to base a typology of transitions. This knowledge in turn would open up the possibility of prediction about general forms and specific phases most likely to generate stress. Such understanding would provide a useful background against which to interpret an individual's perception of a particular transition. Some of the possible dimensions by which transitions can be described are duration, scope, magnitude, reversibility, effect, and the extent to which the transition is anticipated and voluntary and has clear boundaries. Some of the dimensions along which it is proposed that transitions may vary are listed in Table 18–3 as a set of polar opposites.

Knowledge of general patterns would be useful for guiding nursing assessment, but planning and implementation, to be effective, must take account of how the transition and associated events are perceived by the

Table 18–2 Patterns of Response to Transition Events

Disorientation	Changes in self-concept
Distress	Changes in role performance
Irritability	Changes in self-esteem
Anxiety	(And others)
Depression	

Table 18–3 Dimensions of Transitions

Single transition *v* multiple transitions
Clear entry and exit *v* ambiguous entry and exit
Impeded passage *v* unimpeded passage
Minor disruption *v* major disruption
Particular disruption *v* pervasive disruption
Brief duration *v* extended duration
Temporary *v* permanent
Positive value *v* negative value
Pleasant *v* unpleasant
Desired *v* undesired
Planned/predicted *v* unplanned/unpredicted

person experiencing them. In recognition of the likely degree of individual variation, one aspect of theory development in this area would concern instrument construction. The dimensions described earlier could provide the starting point for an instrument that would allow the nurse to generate a profile of how the individual perceives the transition of which he or she is the center. Its further development would depend on feedback from research and conceptual analysis. Cues from such a profile would help the nurse to more accurately infer the meaning that the situation has for the patient, this latter being the only valid data base from which to plan intervention. The transition event, the meaning and the consequences, are depicted in Figure 18–1.

Congruence with Nursing Theories and Relationship to Domain Concepts

There are strong threads of congruence among the many current theories in nursing. Each theorist appears to be working with different parts of the whole rather than with entirely different entities. The concept of transition has the potential for both accommodating and being accommodated by these various theoretical schemes.

Nursing theories, almost by definition, must address change in one form or another. The rationale for that assertion is that nursing's focus—responses to health-illness events—usually entails change and instability for the person concerned, and the achievement of nursing's health-related goals generally

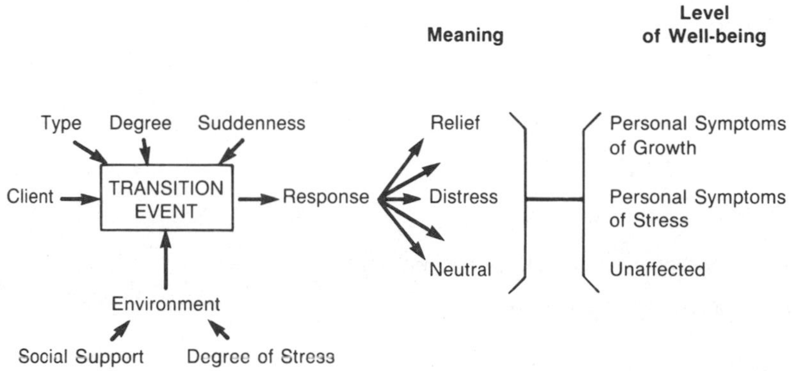

Figure 18–1. Factors Related to Response to a Transition Event

---

depends on initiation of changes in interaction between person and environment.

An early nursing theory such as that of Peplau,[12] with its emphasis on illness as an opportunity for personal growth and development, could be restated in terms of transition, as could the later work of Travelbee,[13] which focuses on the evolution of a therapeutic relationship between nurse and patient and on the need for the patient to find meaning in the illness experience. Transition is also compatible with those theories that emphasize adaptation, such as the Roy Adaptation Model.[14,15]

Transition involves patterns as well. Both Rogers[16,17] and Newman[18,19] see patterning as crucial to their theories. In Rogers's formulation, transitions would mark phases in the person's evolving unitary organization. In Orem's theory, self-care is the key concept,[20,21] and transitions are inextricably linked to shifts in self-care capability.

Transition and Nursing Therapeutics

The most important raison d'être for nursing is the care of patients. This is based on knowledge related to care strategies, ie, the nursing therapeutics that would enable nurses to select the most fruitful kinds of action and optimal intervention points for achieving the desired health maintenance or health promotion goals. Nursing therapeutics could be conceptually considered in relationship to transitions, antecedents, and consequences. To develop knowledge related to nursing therapeutics, the dimensions of time, pattern,

type of transition, and timing of intervention should be considered. These dimensions will lead to the effective development of theoretical and researchable questions. Specifying other components of therapeutic or preventive clinical therapeutics may be useful to further the development of transition specific clinical therapeutics. For example, therapeutic intervention is conceptualized as occurring after the transition consequences have been experienced, and preventive intervention, as occurring before the transition or before the consequences.[22]

Examples of existing studies that can be viewed from this perspective are numerous in the nursing literature. Lindeman's[23,24] work on preoperative teaching exemplifies preventive clinical therapeutics. Other examples are work related to patient compliance-adherence with treatment regimens[25], that of Johnson,[26] which is geared toward strategies for reducing the stress associated with certain treatment procedures; and a study of role supplementation in the postnatal transition and in a cardiac rehabilitation program.[27,28] These are all instances in which nurses have been concerned with facilitating, either preventively or therapeutically, the transition processes that clients experience. Some of the domain concepts and their relationship to the transition process are depicted in Figure 18–2.

Transition and Environment

Transition and environment are related in two main ways. On the one hand, changes in the environment may constitute, or be part of, the events that make the process of transition necessary. Adjustment to slowly occurring change may be so gradual as to be almost imperceptible. There is little, if any, sense of transition. More rapidly occurring environmental changes, whether they be natural, as in the case of an earthquake, or man-made, in the form of urban redevelopment, call for a larger response. Such events not only require adjustment to a new environment, but at the same time severely disrupt the usual sources of support that the individual draws from the environment. This leads to a second way in which transition and environment are linked. Irrespective of the source of the initiating conditions for the transition, its course may be mediated by what the environment offers in the way of support. The particular nature of the environment in which it occurs may either impede or facilitate a transition. In the transition from disabled person to able person, an example of a facilitating environment would be one that gives high priority to ensuring wheelchair access for the physically handicapped.

Another factor that may influence how smoothly a transition is experienced is the extent to which the environment in which the transition is occurring is itself stable or in flux. Concurrently occurring transitions compound one another. For instance, it has been commonly observed,

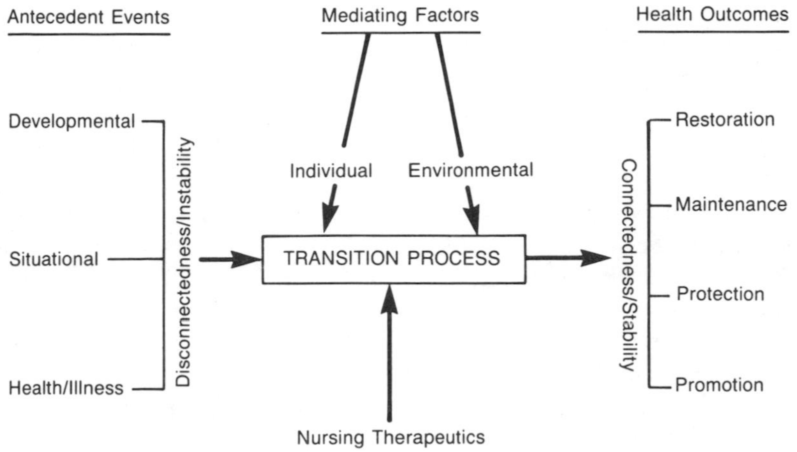

Figure 18–2. Relationships of Transitions to Other Domain Concepts

although perhaps not so well documented, that in clinical units in which staff are rotated and a large proportion change at one time, the ensuing unsettled period is reflected in patient states. Implications of this observation offer a source of pertinent questions for nursing research.

Transition and the Nursing Client

As with all person-environment interactions, neither processes nor outcomes are ever determined entirely by individual or environmental variables. Different sets of factors may be dominant at various points in time, but mostly what eventuates results from complex interplay between individual and environmental characteristics.

Unfortunately, the concept of transition is not immune to stereotyped thinking, so a note of caution has to be sounded. There is a danger that we will impose explanation rather than allow understanding of the concept to emerge from evidence of how transitions are actually experienced by those undergoing them. There may be a tendency to use one's own experience or feelings as a frame of reference rather than elicit meanings from the client. Thus, on the basis of personal experience and societal values, the transition to

motherhood may be assumed always to be experienced positively. Negative connotations are simply not perceived. To take a further example, for most of us, colostomy poses a threat to autonomy over a natural bodily function, and hence is viewed negatively. Such a conclusion ignores the possibility that, for a particular individual, the colostomy and associated transition may be experienced as a positive resolution to a prolonged distressing and anxiety-provoking condition.

Technological advances in medicine are now subjecting people to transitions not dreamed of a few decades ago. At the moment, it is the associated ethical dilemmas that are attracting attention. In the meantime, nurses, by their very "thereness" (compared with the intermittent contacts of other care givers), are ideally placed to be in the vanguard to help patients and their families with these unprecedented situations.

EXEMPLARS

The critical question for the proposed conceptualization linking transitions with health is what utility it would have for nursing practice. Most currently used assessment guides and other documentation associated with the nursing process model are intended to alert nurses to life context variables relevant to the person's current health-illness status. Therefore, it is germane to ask if the concept of transition adds anything. We suggest that it does. For instance, as a focus for nursing intervention, it helps us to incorporate the "at-risk" status that accompanies many forms of transition not directly related to health-illness events. However, even when it is too late for preventive measures, nursing assessment done with the aim of highlighting the kinds of personal and social transitions in which the client is involved has much to offer. It will help to ensure that interventions are maximally relevant, and therefore genuinely therapeutic rather than merely being palliative.

Viewing transition as both process and outcome means that focus can be readily shifted between end result and process. Either can be the subject of assessment. In the first instance, comparisons would be made between present characteristics and those exhibited (or reported to have been present) at a pretransition phase. Some may have been lost, others modified, and some entirely new ones may have emerged. The values (both social and personal) placed on these characteristics will influence the degree of stress associated with such losses and gains. So the notion of transition is likely to be useful in formulating goals for nursing practice. It can also be applied retrospectively to help the nurse understand how a person feels about the outcome of a transition and the process that has led to it.

The concept of transition is consistent with the philosophy of holistic health, which is central to nursing practice. It is unavoidable that at a given point in time, attention will be focused on some aspects of the person more

than on others. In practice, there is no way that we can attend to the whole person simultaneously, but we can recognize the coextensiveness of the many dimensions of the person. Thinking in terms of transition promotes continuity not only across time, but also across dimensions of the person.

With transition viewed as a process, the aim would be to anticipate points at which the person is most likely to reach peaks of vulnerability with respect to health. Efforts could then be directed toward establishing and reinforcing defenses as well as modifying hazards. As knowledge accumulates concerning the likely course or trajectory of different types of transition, it will become increasingly possible to plan interventions according to the optimum moment and manner.

Nursing practice based on a transition model would run counter to therapeutic interventions aimed only at cure. Return to a disease-free state may not be possible, and even the premorbid level of health may be unattainable. A goal for nursing is that the client emerge from any nursing encounter not only more comfortable and better able to deal with the present health problem, but also better equipped to protect and promote health for the future.

Sometimes in the drama of a life-threatening event such as might be associated with admission to an intensive care unit or a cardiac care unit, the important point is lost, which is that for the ill person and significant others, the episode is part (perhaps just the beginning) of transition. By definition, crisis care is present-oriented. Yet the questions going through the minds of patient and family are likely to be future-oriented. First of all, "Is there a future? Is this the end?" Then, "If I do recover, what will I be like?" Even the questions themselves indicate a transition, from a time when such doubts and anxieties were nonexistent or peripheral to the moment of their present compelling impact. In other instances, the tendency may be for the person to be fixed in the past as a defense against both present and future. Here the nurse has to work at starting the transition process. The earlier these doubts and uncertainties are recognized and worked through, the sooner the transition to recovery will be achieved. Once the person perceives himself or herself as an invalid (ie, as being invalidated as a normal person), it may be difficult to eradicate this perception, even in the presence of seemingly good physical recovery. The difficulty will increase the longer the perception persists.

For some time now, acute care hospitals have been examining their admission procedures in terms of how this transition to inpatient might be facilitated. Currently, too, discharge planning is receiving much attention. Generally, these processes have not been explicitly conceptualized as transition, but there could well be gain in doing so. Tornberg, McGrath, and Benoliel[31] are quite specific in describing their transition services as "a model of nursing practice designed to offer personalized services and continuity of

care to patients and families living with changing demands of progressive, deteriorating illness."[29(p131)]

We know of another facility that, without labeling itself as a transition service, functions as one for people who have undergone plastic surgery. Such patients, especially in the case of cosmetic surgery, are often elderly. After the immediate postoperative period, they do not require the complex services of an acute care hospital (in fact, such an atmosphere may not be inducive to their recovery). Nor are they always ready for the full independence of returning home, particularly if they live alone. A short stay in an intermediate facility helps to smooth the multiple facets of this kind of transition.

ANALYSIS OF TRANSITION IN RELATION TO OTHER CONCEPTS

Transition, Change, and Other Change-related Concepts

Part of the process of concept analysis is to compare the concept to others with comparable properties and dimensions in order to establish its boundaries.[30,31] Although Hall[7] saw certain risks in nursing's present emphasis on change concepts (principally, that we may come to equate understanding change with understanding people), it can still be argued that, for nursing, change is both a raison d 'être and a means of goal achievement. Just as it is change in health status that brings about the need for health care, so the goal of intervention usually is to facilitate changes that will restore health to a premorbid level or better. Yet to say that nursing is about managing change is little more than a truism.

A broad concept such as change contains too much ambiguity for it to be effective in guiding either nursing conceptualizations or therapeutics. That is why Becker[32] suggested that nursing might gain more from the exploration of microconcepts. Transition, although not quite micro in the sense intended by Becker, has similar advantages. It can be differentiated from the general concept of change sufficiently to make it useful in alerting nurses to relevant aspects of the life context of clients. In this instance, transition is seen as a special case of the general phenomenon of change.

When looking at the wider social science literature, one cannot but be struck by similarities between our thinking about transitions and other change-related phenomena being discussed by psychologists and sociologists. For instance, *Uprooting and Development* is a volume of essays described in the foreword as having to do with "one of the fundamental properties of human life—the need to change—and with the personal and social mechanisms for dealing with the need."[33(pxi)] The author of the foreword goes on to emphasize dislocation as a distinguishing feature of uprooting events that range from self-imposed relocations and migrations to natural and man-made

disasters. Another contributor to the volume offers the following metaphorical description of what the experience of being uprooted is.

> The closest human counterpart to the root structure by which a plant nourishes itself is, I suggest, the structure of meaning by which each of us sustains the relationships to people, work, and the physical and social circumstances on which our lives depend. Like roots, these structures of meaning are at once generic and sensitively adapted to the particular setting in which they are embedded; like roots, too, they transplant from this established setting only at the risk of wilting and stunting.[34(p101)]

The concern with meaning is germane to our approach, which lends itself well to interpretive research methodologies. Preserving continuity of meaning, either by reestablishing disrupted connections or by substituting new ones, is an essential part of the transition process, and hence the ways of doing these things are of vital concern to nurses. Our sense of transition makes the latter concept complementary to notions such as uprooting. Transition is a response to the disrupting events. It takes up the developmental theme of the book title just cited.

As well as the focus on transition as a response, another difference from these other writings is provided by the health emphasis that emanates from our nurse-scientist perspective. Admittedly, the difference is largely one of emphasis. Writers in other disciplines are sensitive to the health hazards associated with change. Since the research of the 1960s and 1970s, we have been aware of the deleterious effects of accumulated stress from sequential and contiguous life changes.[35,36] Some, such as Coelho and Stein,[37] refer specifically to health risks associated with rural to urban migrations. In all these instances, however, health risks are seen as consequents or dependent variables, that is, they are effects of the change phenomena. Perhaps subtler relationships emerge when, as from our health-centered focus, illness and injury are viewed as antecedent or independent variables that initiate the need for transition and, by their characteristics, help to determine the trajectory that the transition will follow. In this sense, the illness, injury, or "at-risk" status becomes analogous to the uprooting events described earlier.

RESEARCH POTENTIAL

Transition may enter the formulation of a research question as either an independent or a dependent variable, as indicated in Figures 18–3 and 18–4.

Transition as an Independent Variable

A transition resulting from such events as immigration, migration, relocation, pregnancy, birthing, and loss may lead to health-related consequences in the form of biophysical symptoms or psychosocial symptoms and may lead to ineffective health-seeking or help-seeking behavior. It may also lead to overutilization of health care services. Studies of transition as an independent variable may consider several relationships. These relationships are discussed and demonstrated in Figure 18–3.

Transitions and Health

Some transitions reflect movement along the health-illness continuum more directly than others. For instance, catastrophic illness, a diagnosis of chronic or degenerative disease, and discharge from hospital after a severe illness are all clearly related to health status. Certain developmental transitions, such as childbirth, aging, and dying also come within the orbit of health-illness services because of the way in which they have been institutionalized in Western societies.

In other circumstances, the relationships are less clear-cut. Instead of figuring directly in the situation, the transition provides the ground against which the health-illness episode or period of increased vulnerability to risk occur. McKinlay[38] supports the view that ethnographic studies, historical epidemiology, and observations in societies where rapid increase of technology has occurred indicate that people who are in a state of physical and cultural transition have higher risk of illness. All too often the contribution of a concurrent transition is recognized only after a crisis, for example, acute depression, has occurred.

Although the foregoing discussion has emphasized the tendency for transition to increase vulnerability to health hazards, transitions can also be viewed as opportunities. Transition can mean gain or loss. The perturbations associated with the beginning of the transition process may create fertile

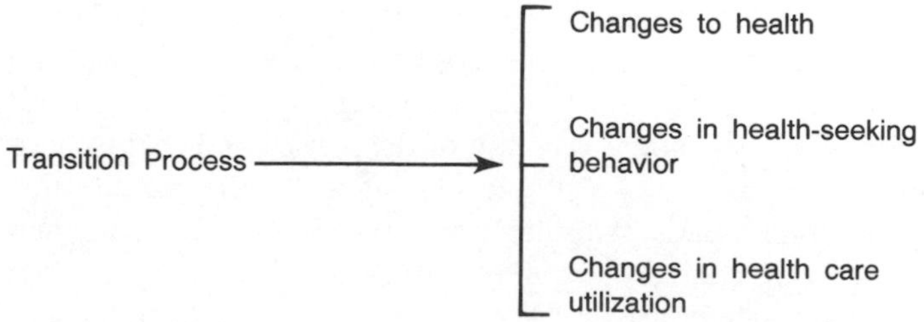

Figure 18–3. Transition as an Independent Variable

ground for new learning. In this sense, the concept of transition is consistent with eudaimonistic and self-actualizing views of health.[39]

Transitions and Health-Seeking Behaviors

For someone in transition, health-seeking behavior may be inhibited simply because the appropriate course of action is no longer obvious. For instance, a new immigrant still operating within the norms of the culture of origin may not perceive the physician as a satisfactory substitute for the traditional healer and, in the absence of the latter, may delay taking any action until forced to do so by a crisis. Not knowing the available options, or even how to initiate entry into the health care system, is a further cause of inaction. Choosing a new physician in a strange city can be a daunting task for anyone. For a person unfamiliar with the customs and perhaps not fluent in the language, it may seem an insurmountable obstacle. One can only conjecture how often people in this situation are labeled by health care providers as irresponsible with respect to their children's health.

Retirement is another event that launches people into a period of transition. Particularly when involuntary, it is an outward sign of growing old. One effect of this transition on older persons is that, because of prevailing confusion between the effects of aging and symptoms of illness, they tend to accept distressing symptoms such as decreased sensory acuity and urinary incontinence as inevitable aspects of aging, and therefore are reluctant to seek advice or treatment. Thus to fully understand a person's response to being in transition, it is important to understand how they perceive the transition process and what expectations they have for the outcome.

Transitions and Health Care Utilization

Even if the transition does not prevent the person from seeking health care, it may result in changes in utilization of health services.[38] A familiar example is the new immigrant's utilization of the hospital emergency department when what is needed is a regular office visit. There are at least two possible reasons for this behavior. One is the visibility of the service and relative ease of access as compared with visiting a physician's office or other facility that operates on an appointment basis. Another is that the strangeness of the new environment and lack of familiar resources may result in a high level of uncertainty and anxiety, which leaves the person unable to make judgments about the severity and seriousness of symptoms. Consequently, there may be a tendency to overrely on professionals for reassurance.

Transition as a Dependent Variable

In this case, transition occurs as a result of illness and changes in health status as is presented in Figure 18–4. People who experience life-threatening illnesses pass through a transition. Although we have some insightful descriptive accounts,[40,41] there is still much that is unknown about the meanings that are constructed out of these events and why—irrespective of the actual amount of pathology involved—they are more devastating for some people than for others. Rehabilitation and reablement programs assume a transition. The effectiveness of such programs depends on congruence between the goals of the client and those of the therapist. This in turn presumes knowledge about the transition process and the client's perception of it.

In approaching measurement issues associated with developing the concept of transition, it is likely that we will be able, in part, to build on existing work. The conclusion of a recent review paper was that "there are currently at least 27 published scales that measure various aspects of social functioning and that have been reasonably well developed and tested."[42(p1257)] No doubt some of these overlap with the dimensions that we deem especially pertinent to the transition process. The growing literature on coping strategies is another likely source of material.

SUMMARY AND CONCLUSIONS

This chapter illustrates one of the options for theory development—concept analysis and clarification. The broad concept of transition, a period of change between two relatively stable states that comes to be associated with some degree of self-redefinition, has been explored specifically within a nursing context, a context in which the central domains are person-client, health, and environment. Ramifications of the definition were traced. It was argued that a theory with transition as its central concept would provide continuity with directions evident from historical analysis of the work of other nurse theorists, meet nursing's present needs, and at the same time be

---

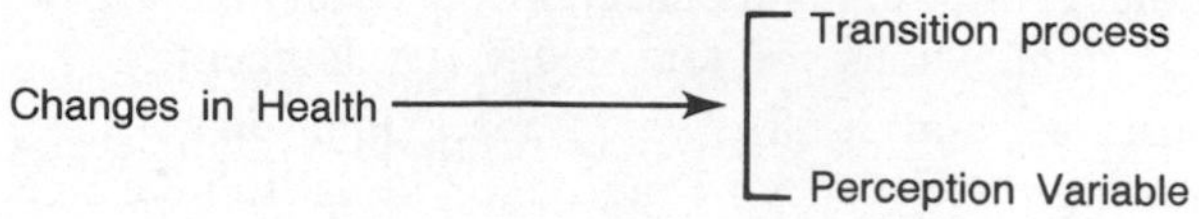

Figure 18–4. Transition as a Dependent Variable

congruent with trends in knowledge development in related fields. We see such a framework as conducive to more integrated and effective theoretical and research programs for nursing.

It is contended that the kind of theoretical development proposed would have at least the following three advantages that will have implications for further knowledge development.

1. Nurses sometimes tend to view clients historically, and therefore, they fail to recognize or meet the client's needs at the point where the client presently is in his or her perception of the situation. Conceptualizations that encompass flexible time orientation incorporating past, present, and future, as does transition, promote greater synchrony between the time orientations of nurse and client, and therefore provide a basis from which to more accurately define client needs.

2. Although the trend toward adopting "models of nursing practice" may be useful in alerting nurses to sets of problems associated with particular diagnostic categories, there is much that we still need to learn about how to set priorities in individual cases. There is a commonly held view that inadequacies in nursing care are due less to paucity of data than they are to failure by nurses to appreciate the relevance of data that are available. A transition framework would have the heuristic value of prompting researchers to pose questions pertinent to cue recognition and utilization.

3. An integrating and organizing conceptual framework makes it easier for a nurse to capitalize on what he or she knows already and to use existing knowledge more insightfully. This is not to deny the need for nurses to continually update their knowledge, which is a basic requirement in any practice discipline. But most nurses—through both education and experience—have already acquired a good deal of knowledge about human development and person-environment interactions. Unfortunately, such knowledge is not always well articulated and so made maximally available to benefit practice. Transition theory could be the key to changing this situation. This, broadly, has been the intent of this chapter: to analyze the concept of transition for the purpose of knowledge development in nursing.

We are aware that, in suggesting transition as a focus for theory development and research in nursing, the concept is not an entirely new one. Other disciplines are already working with it. However, analysis from a nursing perspective with the further development of theoretical and empirical linkages with nursing's other central domain concepts does signify an original approach with significant implications for knowledge development.

A theory linking transitions and health would meet Johnson's[43] three criteria for evaluating nursing theory: social congruence, social significance, and social utility. The ubiquity of the term transition in the recent nursing literature is evidence of its congruence with current orientations to change held by health care users and providers. That transition is a concept relevant

to many of nursing's immediate concerns is evident from the frequency with which the term has appeared in recent nursing literature in the context of transition and nursing practice,[29,44,45] transition, education, and service,[46] research in transition,[47] and theory development.[48]

Significance must be judged, finally, on empirical evidence. That the concept of transition already pervades much of the current thinking about nurses and nursing suggests that it is not a trivial notion or passing fad. In the body of this chapter, we have endeavored to show how the concept has potential application in a wide spectrum of nursing practice settings. It follows that the utility value of the concept is expected to be high. We see applications transculturally, for all age groups, and independent of clinical speciality. Yet, having micro aspects, it avoids the limitations of grand theory. Some general concepts that appear insightful in the broad scene have little to say in the individual case. So utility may in fact be this concept's major strength. Certainly nursing needs new knowledge, but it also needs tools and strategies that assist nurses to make best use of existing knowledge and to use it in a uniquely nursing way. Part of the work of theories is to generate new knowledge. They also serve to organize extant knowledge and make it more accessible. It may be that the concept of transitions will be a catalyst in the task of uncovering the knowledge embedded in clinical practice.[49,50]

Finally, in order to meet the challenge of the American Nurses' Association policy statement that defines nursing as the "diagnosis and treatment of human responses to actual and potential health problems,"[51(p9)] a plurality of theories is needed. A theory linking health, illness, and nursing with transition would not supercede the variety of theoretical formulations that now inform nursing research and practice. Certainly there would be some overlap (this speaks to the issue of validity), but transition theory offers a framework and a perspective for organization of knowledge related to events and responses to transitions. The realization of such a theory would depend on a program of inquiry aimed at clarifying theoretical and operational linkages between transition and a broad spectrum of health-illness states. The next stage would be the empirical testing of several kinds of propositions, such as those linking the transition process with health-illness states and those linking it with nursing therapeutics.

REFERENCES

1. Wilson J: *Thinking with Concepts.* London, Cambridge University Press, 1983.

2. Chinn PL, Jacob M: *Theory and Nursing: A Systematic Approach.* St Louis, CV Mosby, 1983.

3. Walker LO, Avant KC: *Strategies for Theory Construction in Nursing.* Norwalk, Conn, Appleton-Century-Crofts, 1983.

4. Norris CM: *Concept Classification in Nursing.* Rockville, Md, Aspen Systems, 1982.

5. Stevens B: *Nursing Theory: Analysis, Application and Evaluation*, ed 2. Boston, Little, Brown, 1984.

6. *Webster's Third International Dictionary.* Springfield, Mass, G & C Merriam, 1971.

7. Hall B: The change paradigm in nursing: Growth versus persistence. *Adv Nurs Sci* 1981;3:1-6.

8. Bridges W: *Transitions.* Reading, Mass, Addison-Wesley, 1980.

9. Lyndheim R, Syme L: Environment, people and health. *Ann Rev Public Health* 1983;4:335-359.

10. Lipson JG, Meleis AI: Issues in health care of middle eastern patients. *West J Med* 1983;139:854-861.

11. Newman MA: The Newman model: Overview. Paper presented at the Nurse Theorist Conference, Edmonton, Alberta, Canada, 1984.

12. Peplau H: *Interpersonal Relations in Nursing.* New York, GP Putnam's Sons, 1952.

13. Travelbee J: *Interpersonal Aspects of Nursing*, ed 2. Philadelphia, FA Davis, 1971.

14. Roy C: *Introduction to Nursing: An Adaptation Model.* Englewood Cliffs, NJ, Prentice-Hall, 1984.

15. Roy C, Roberts S: *Theory Construction in Nursing.* Englewood Cliffs, NJ, Prentice-Hall, 1981.

16. Rogers M: *An Introduction to a Theoretical Basis of Nursing.* Philadelphia, FA Davis, 1970.

17. Rogers M: Nursing: A science of unitary man, in Riehl JP, Roy C (eds): *Conceptual Models for Nursing Practice*, ed 2. New York, Appleton-Century-Crofts, 1980.

18. Newman MA: *Theory Development in Nursing.* Philadelphia, FA Davis, 1979.

19. Newman MA: Newman's health theory, in Clements I, Roberts F (eds): *Family Health: A Theoretical Approach to Nursing Care.* New York, John Wiley, 1983.

20. Orem D: *Nursing: Concepts of Practice.* New York, McGraw-Hill, 1971.

21. Orem D: *Nursing: Concepts of Practice*, ed 3. New York, McGraw-Hill, 1985.

22. Meleis AI: Role insufficiency and role supplementation: A conceptual framework. *Nurs Res* 24:264-271.

23. Lindeman CA: The challenge of nursing research in the 1980s, in *Communicating Nursing Research: Directions for the 1980s.* Boulder Col, Western Interstate Commission for Higher Education, 1980.

24. Lindeman CA, Van Aernam B: Nursing intervention with the presurgical patient: The effects of structured and unstructured preoperative teaching, in Downs F, Newman M (eds): *A Source Book in Nursing Research.* Philadelphia, FA Davis, 1973.

25. Dracup KA, Meleis AI: Compliance: An interactionist approach. *Nurs Res* 1982;31:31-36.

26. Johnson JE: Effects of structuring patients' expectations on their reactions to threatening events. *Nurs Res* 1972;21:499-504.

27. Dracup K, Meleis AI, Baker C, Edlefsen P: Family focused cardiac rehabilitation: A role supplementation program for cardiac patients and spouses. *Nurs Clin North Am* 1984;19:112-124.

28. Meleis AI, Swendsen L: Role supplementation: An empirical test of a nursing intervention. *Nurs Res* 1978;27:11-18.

29. Tornberg M., McGrath B, Benoliel J: Oncology transition services. *Cancer Nurs* April 1984, pp 131-137.

30. Norris C: *Concept Clarification in Nursing.* Rockville, Md, Aspen Publishers, 1982.

31. Walker LD, Avant KC: *Strategies for Theory Construction in Nursing.* Norwalk, Conn, Appleton-Century-Crofts, 1983.

32. Becker C: A conceptualization of a concept. *Nursing Papers: Perspectives on Nursing* 1983;15:51-57.

33. Bryant JH: Foreword, in Coelho CV, Ahmed PI (eds): *Uprooting and Development.* New York, Plenum Press, 1980.

34. Marris P: The uprooting of meaning, in Coelho CV, Ahmed PI (eds): *Uprooting and Development.* New York, Plenum Press, 1980.

35. Holmes TH, Rahe RH: The social readjustment rating scale. *J Psychosom Med* 1967;11:213-218.

36. Holmes TH, Masuda M: Life change and illness susceptibility, in Dohrendwend BP (ed): *Stressful Life Events: Their Nature and Effect.* New York, John Wiley, 1974.

37. Coelho CV, Stein JJ: Change, vulnerability, and coping: Stresses of uprooting and overcrowding, in Coelho CV, Ahmed PI (eds): *Uprooting and Development.* New York, Plenum Press, 1980.

38. McKinlay J: Some issues associated with migration, health status, and use of human services. *J Chronic Dis* 1975;28:579-592.

39. Smith JA: The idea of health: A philosophical inquiry. *Adv in Nurs Sci* 1981;3:43-50.

40. Smith DW: *Survival of Illness: Implications for Nursing.* New York, Springer, 1981.

41. Schwartz D: Catastrophic illness: How it feels. *Geriatr Nurs* 1982;3:303-306.

42. Weissman M, Sholomskas D, John K: The assessment of social adjustment. *Arch Gen Psychiatry* 1981;38:1250-1258.

43. Johnson D: Development of theory. *Nurs Res* 1974;23:372-377.

44. Benoliel JQ: Dying is a family affair, in Prichard ER, Collard J, Starr J, Lockwood JA, Kutscher AH, Beland I (eds): *Home Care: Living with Dying.* New York, Columbia University Press, 1979.

45. Norris C: Restlessness: A nursing phenomenon in search of meaning. *Nurs Outlook* 1975;23:103-107.

46. Weiss S: The effect of transition modules on new graduate adaptation. *Res Nurs Health* 1984;7:51-59.

47. Gortner S: Nursing science in transition. *Nurs Res* 1980;29:180-183.

48. Meleis AI: *Theoretical Nursing: Development and Progress.* Philadelphia, JB Lippincott, 1985.

49. Benner P: Uncovering the knowledge embedded in clinical practice. *Image* 1983;15:36-41.

50. Benner P, Wrubel J: Skilled clinical knowledge: The value of perceptual awareness. *Nurse Educator* 1982;7:11-17.

51. American Nurses' Association: *Nursing: A Social Policy Statement.* Kansas City, Mo, American Nurses' Association, 1980.

Chapter 19

Generating Knowledge for Nursing Practice: Methodological Issues in Studying Immigrant Women

M. Judith Lynam and Joan M. Anderson

Since the 1960s there has been a dramatic change in the ethnic composition of North American society. Canada, for example, has seen a rise in immigration from regions like South Asia, with women (including female children) making up more than 50% of the newcomers. More than half a million women have settled in Canada since the 1970s.[1,2] Yet little systematic research has been done that informs us of the special circumstances of the lives of these women. For the most part, their experiences have been subsumed under those of men. It has become widely recognized, however, that women's experiences are determined by their position in the social structure. Because this position is different from that of men, it stands to reason that women's experiences must also differ from those of men.[3–7]

Many women who immigrate to Canada work out of economic necessity and are employed in the lower echelons of the Canadian labor force.[8] Little is known, however, about the experiences of women from different ethnic groups in the workplace, their social mobility in Canadian society, the quality of their lives in general, including how they cope with the stresses and strains of occupational demands. Arnopoulos[9] brings to our attention the serious side effects of certain occupations, specifically piecework in the garment industry, and the research that is available identifies immigrant women as a population at risk for developing health and social problems.[10] Although a variety of programs and health resources are in place to serve the entire population and some programs have been specifically developed for immigrant groups,[11] the limited amount of data collected indicate that immigrant women do not perceive that there are resources available to meet their

needs.[10,12] So, although immigrant women in the workforce may be at risk for health and social problems, it is not clear what health care resources and social support networks are used by them.

In an attempt to find out more about the experiences of immigrant women in the workforce, we designed a program of research focusing on immigrant women. The research was conducted in three phases and started by examining the health status of immigrant women in the lower echelons of the Canadian labor force.[13] In another study, Lynam[14] examined the social support networks used by immigrant women. In further joint study, we explored the experiences of women in the workforce and examined the ways in which work, health, and social support are related. The latter study provided the opportunity to build on the previous research on the health of immigrant women and the social support networks that they use. As well, it permitted examination of women's perceptions of how their physical appearances (ie, skin color, physical features, dress) influence their subjective experiences within the context of Canadian society. There is some evidence that the experiences of visible minorities are different from the experiences of persons from ethnic minorities whose physical appearance is similar to the mainstream population.[15] The study therefore aimed to identify how ethnicity and "visibility" influence the experiences of women in the workplace. The studies addressed the following questions:

- What are the work experiences of immigrant women located within the lower echelons of the Canadian labor force?
- What are the primary concerns of immigrant women surrounding their health?
- What are the experiences of immigrant women surrounding help seeking?
- What do immigrant women perceive as sources of support in meeting identified needs?
- What discrimination, if any, have these women perceived toward themselves?

This chapter examines the methodological issues that were encountered in conducting this research. Examples have been taken from the studies to elucidate the points that are addressed. Although women from a variety of ethnic groups were included in one of the studies,[14] the discussion focuses on two groups of women—Indo-Canadian and Greek—since, because of language barriers, several issues had to be dealt with in the studies with these women. But before embarking on this discussion, we will make explicit how we see this area of research in relation to the domain of nursing.

THE RELATIONSHIP OF THE RESEARCH QUESTIONS TO NURSING

It might be argued that life events such as work and immigration are concerns that are outside nursing's domain. In a recent article, however, Fawcett[16] recognizes the importance of life events to the individual and identifies that one type of knowledge nursing needs to develop pertains to the "patterning of human behavior in interaction with the environment in normal life events and critical life situations."[16(p2)]

The need for nursing to develop an understanding of the meaning that individuals assign to life events has also been identified in the nursing literature. Davis[17] argues that the effectiveness of nursing interventions is enhanced when the practitioner is able to understand and take direction from clients' perspectives. Nursing research must seek to understand the individual's perspective if research is intended to provide guidance to clinical practice. Furthermore, Tinkle and Beaton[18] have stated: "If research studies regarding patient behavior fail to ascertain the patients' perception of the rationale for their own actions, interpretation of research results will reflect only a one-sided bias in favor of what the nurse thinks the patient thinks."[p31] Describing the meaning assigned to events within the context of individual experiences is necessary because it can provide an understanding of how people develop their ideas about what is important in relation to an event and how their ideas influence their behavior.

Many conceptual models for nursing include in their foci the individual's responses to situational or life events. Although the dynamics of an individual's response to life events and the relationship between an individual's perception and behavior have been conceptualized differently from one nursing model to another, there are some common elements.

Johnson's[19] systems model conceptualizes events that influence behaviors within the client system as "variables." Variables may be external or internal influences on the system. A life event could be conceptualized as an external variable, and how the event is perceived by the individual, an internal variable.

In relation to the development of nursing knowledge, Johnson has argued that nursing research should aim at the "elucidation of the determinants of behavior, from either the biological, psychological, or social perspective, or of the interrelationships of these factors as they regulate and control behavior."[20(p7)]

In the Travelbee developmental model,[21] the illness experience is described as having objective and subjective dimensions that must be understood. The problem that is the focus of nursing includes the individual's perception of the illness experience. The model conceptualizes how perceptions of the illness experience influence the individual's response to illness and suffering.

Neuman's[22] open system adaptation model conceptualizes the individual in interaction with his or her total interface with the environment. Individuals are subject to the impact of stressors. Stressors are conditions arising from the environment and are capable of causing instability. They may be interpersonal, intrapersonal, or extrapersonal. Many are universal but others are unique because of their meaning to the individual.

From this brief review of selected conceptual models for nursing, three points may be made: (1) the nurse must explore the impact of the environment on the client; (2) life events have the potential to interfere with optimal functioning as it is conceptualized in different nursing models; and (3) individuals' perceptions of life events influence their behavioral responses to these events.

The conceptual model for nursing developed by the University of British Columbia (UBC) School of Nursing reflects the common elements described in the preceding models. It characterizes the individual as a behavioral system composed of nine subsystems. The structure of each subsystem consists of two parts: (1) an innerpersonal region representing a basic human need and abilities to meet that need and (2) a psychological environment representing the need-satisfying goal and the forces influencing its attainment.[23(p6)] Each subsystem is responsible for the satisfaction of one basic human need. To meet the need of a subsystem, an individual uses coping behaviors, which are defined as "responses which indicate the way in which a subsystem is attempting to satisfy a basic need for the system."[24(p7)]

Forces influence goal achievement in each subsystem by acting on the individual's coping behaviors. They may arise from the needs and abilities of the subsystems (personal, eg, perceptions, values, physiological states), from other behavioral systems (sociocultural, eg, actions of other individuals), or from the impersonal aspects of a situation (impersonal, eg, availability of resources).[24] According to the UBC model for nursing, a nurse may intervene during critical periods, which can be a "maturational event or an unpredictable event in the life cycle requiring the development and use of suitable coping behaviors to satisfy basic human needs, achieve [system] stability and reach optimal health."[24(p7)]

This model is compatible with different philosophies of science and guides the researcher in the formulation of a variety of research questions, including those questions that explore individuals' perceptions of events and the meaning of these events for them. By addressing such questions, the researcher is able to generate nursing theories that can guide nursing practice. Such theories, as Chinn and Jacobs point out, "represent the individual and collective efforts of nurses to define and direct the profession, and as such provide the basis for continued theoretical development."[25(p5)]

The conceptualizations of nursing reflected in the preceding models locate questions related to life events within nursing's domain, since responding to

such questions will help nurses to understand how a particular life event affects the individual. By eliciting clients' perspectives, nurses can identify groups at risk for developing health problems and obtain knowledge that can guide nursing interventions with immigrant women. As well, such knowledge might also facilitate the development of more effective and economical health care services to women. It could provide the basis for evaluating the effectiveness of the existing services and for identifying the need for further services.

METHODOLOGICAL PERSPECTIVE

The nature of the research questions concerning the lives of immigrant women in the workforce warranted the use of the phenomenological method of inquiry. Omery states that "the goal of the method is to describe the total systematic structure of lived experience, including the meanings that these experiences had for the individuals who participated in them."[26(p50)] She adds: "The concern of the phenomenological researcher is to understand both the cognitive subjective perspective of the person who has the experience and the effect that perspective has on the lived experience or behavior of that individual."[26(p50)]

This approach permits the researcher to develop theories relevant to nursing practice that are grounded in the experiences of the individual. Munhall points out:

> Theories must evolve from the world we are seeking to understand. We need to dwell in the world of nursing, to live, to listen, and to communicate in this world. We need a vision of ourselves, and of those we care for—a vision that is derived from intimate association with ourselves and others, not from a detached, objective perspective, instrumentalized from theories derived from other perspectives.[5(p44)]

The phenomenological method directs the researcher to collect data about events of concern and to explore the meaning and importance assigned to events by individuals.

METHODS AND PROCEDURES

Twenty-seven Indo-Canadian and 19 Greek women participated in the studies described earlier. Indo-Canadian women were selected because of the dramatic increase in the number of immigrants from South Asia since the 1970s. These women were compared with Greek women, who more closely

resemble the mainstream population yet have some similar attributes to Indo-Canadian women. Both groups of women usually experience a rural-to-urban transition on their arrival in Canada; both groups have similarities in terms of their education and their ability to communicate in English.

Many immigrant women from these two ethnic groups are employed within the lower echelons of the Canadian labor force. Therefore, the women who were selected for the studies worked primarily as janitresses. With the exception of a few, the majority of the women spoke little or no English.

Access to the two ethnic communities was obtained through interviewers hired for the studies. A purposive sampling technique was used to recruit informants. That is, women were selected on the basis of their ability to address the issues of concern in the studies. No claims to statistical representation were made. As discussed by Conrad,[27] sampling techniques enable a researcher to gain theoretical insights and a conceptual understanding of the phenomenon under investigation.

Two Indo-Canadian women conducted the interviews with the Indo-Canadian women. One interviewer had immigrated to Canada from India and the other had immigrated from Southeast Asia. Both women worked for different community agencies whose clientele included Indo-Canadian women. Informants for the study, however, were recruited through the interviewers' other personal contacts as well.

Four women interviewed the Greek women who participated in the study. Three of the interviewers were Greek: one had immigrated directly from Greece and the other two had immigrated to Canada by way of other countries. One of the interviewers was of Italian descent. She interviewed women who were able to communicate in English. All of the interviewers worked independently of one another. As well as interviewing, they translated research materials, recruited study participants, and discussed the interviews with the researchers.

Before commencing the interviews, training sessions in the techniques of interviewing were conducted with the interviewers. A variety of strategies were used to ensure their competence in interviewing. For example, extensive use was made of simulated situations, which were videotaped. As well, regular meetings were held with each interviewer to review not just the data, but also to clarify questions about the interviewing process. The researchers also accompanied the interviewers on some of the visits to women's homes. Even when the researchers did not understand the language, the visits helped to develop rapport with the women, and to get some sense of the process of the interviews. The visits also provided an opportunity for the women to "put a face" on the researchers and ask them direct questions concerning the studies, even though these questions had to be clarified through an interpreter.

The studies were carried out over a period of two years. Up to six data-collection interviews were conducted with each woman. "Trigger" questions, developed primarily from the literature, guided the initial interviews. Interviewers were trained, however, to follow cues from the informants and took direction from them in subsequent interviews. The number of interviews depended on the depth of data obtained in a given interview and a woman's willingness to participate in future interviews.

Data collection and analysis were carried out concurrently. As the informants were interviewed, data were reviewed by the members of the research team and analytic themes identified from the data. In further data-collection interviews, the interviewers sought to validate and develop the emerging themes. In this way, concepts and categories were systematically worked out in relation to the data during the course of the research.

METHODOLOGICAL ISSUES

If nurses are to provide effective care, there is the need to generate nursing knowledge based on research with nursing's diverse client population. Researchers, therefore, have a moral obligation to find ways and means for conducting research with people whose language and culture are different from their own. Although researchers in disciplines like anthropology and sociology have long confronted the problem of conducting phenomenological research with people from different sociocultural groups, it is only recently that nurse researchers have embarked on this kind of research. As the nursing profession has sought to develop a body of nursing knowledge, so nurse researchers have shifted their foci to study new topics and client groups and to use methodologies appropriate to the topic of study. It is crucial, however, that nurse researchers come to terms with the methodological issues they are likely to face.

In this chapter, three sets of issues inherent in phenomenological research with persons whose language is different from that of the researcher are examined. The first set of issues pertains to the collection and analysis of study data. The second set of issues are ethical and pertain to recruiting participants and obtaining informed consent. The third issue relates to confidentiality. These issues are interrelated but, for purposes of clarity, are addressed separately. As well, the discussion includes an examination of how other researchers have dealt with similar issues.

Data Collection and Analysis

The essence of the phenomenological method is the intersubjective construction of meaning within the context of an interpersonal encounter. It is acknowledged that both researcher and participant bring interpretive

competencies to the situation through which events are made sense of. As such, the researcher is part of the process in the construction of what becomes "data."[28–30] A problem arises when a common language is not shared by researcher and study participants and when an interviewer becomes an intermediary between the researcher and the participants. One might ask, "Under these circumstances, what becomes data?"

Yet other researchers have found ways of interviewing people from different sociocultural groups and of "working through" interviewers. For example, Berreman,[31] in his efforts to understand all aspects of everyday life in a Himalayan village community, displayed how this can be managed. He argues that the type of data collected is determined in part by who collects the data, the texture of the interpersonal encounter between interviewer and interviewee, and how data are recorded. He discusses the merits of having a variety of interviewers with a basic understanding of the culture and its language but also having backgrounds different from those of the informants. In Berreman's case, the interviewers were of different religions. He observed that the topics individual villagers chose to discuss with the interviewers varied somewhat according to their perceptions of the interviewer's interests and values. Berreman's experience demonstrated that validity of the data was enhanced when several interviewers were used—major themes could be verified when different interviewers collected similar data. In addition, when data from each interview were analyzed, different dimensions of village life were revealed. The different perspectives of the interviewers enriched the interpretations of the data collected. In Berreman's research, interviewers' backgrounds and experiences and their interpretations of village life became part of the study data.

In order to understand the everyday lives of the villagers, observations of everyday activities formed another data base. Berreman emphasized, however, the importance of not showing undue interest in any specific practices, thereby giving the villagers the message that such practices, to the exclusion of others, were perhaps of greater importance or interest to him. Therefore, data were often recorded in private, after an event.

Many similarities exist between the processes of data collection and analysis used by Berreman and those used in the studies being discussed here. Several interviewers from a variety of backgrounds collected the data. In this study, three types of data were collected. Hand-recorded notes and transcriptions of interviews with the participants formed one type; observations of the surroundings and the affect of participants during the interviews formed another type; and transcriptions of discussions between the interviewers and the researchers formed the third type.

The discussions between the researchers and the interviewers provided opportunities to study the responses to the interview questions, to discuss emerging themes, and to explore the interviewers' interpretations of the data.

As the researchers "interviewed the interviewers," they were able to identify how the interviewers' own experiences and interpretations were reflected in the data.

The following account illustrates the processes involved in the critical examination of the data. On one occasion, an interviewer provided an interpretation of the data that was unlike the interpretation of the other interviewers and was inconsistent with the participants' responses to study questions. The example is drawn from a discussion about the differential value attached to janitorial work within the Greek community. The interviewer described her own situation and declared emphatically that she would not do janitorial work. She tied her explanation to the evolution of women's roles in society:

> See, in Greece, 10 years ago among most couples, the male is dominant and the wife is just the housewife. Now they change a lot because they are trying to get into the American system that women are equal. As a woman, I work first for myself because I develop self worth and independence, and second, I contribute to society.

This perspective provided her with a way of making sense of the data from women. In the discussions, it was pointed out that her viewpoint was not consistent with the data collected during the interviews with women. All the study participants had emphasized repeatedly that the family was the priority, and they worked to contribute to the family. The interviewer explained:

> If a woman has a career she has to choose a career versus a family. A Greek woman cannot choose both. It might be a part of the Greek culture that the husband doesn't like the woman to have a career . . . . As a result, women who want to have a family don't go along with a career, or they will destroy their marriage.

She went on to explain that the women in the study "don't have a career, their work is not extremely important, it is just work, a job. They have the belief the family is first and their job is second, because the job is not a career." She was asked about the priorities of professional women—how would a lawyer, for example, view her career? According to the interviewer, "she will say her career comes first."

In the previous account, the interviewer provided one way of making sense of women's views about their work and led the researchers to question the circumstances surrounding women's lives that influenced the ways in which work was perceived in relation to the family. This interviewer's interpretation of the data also prompted a systematic exploration of a variety of topics with

the women. For example, the researchers began to explore the similarities and differences between the working experiences of women who had undergone a downward mobility since coming to Canada and women who had never worked before their present job, or who had worked in unskilled positions before immigrating. The discussions added another dimension to such analytic categories as life goals and career planning and the relationship between work and self-confidence. But more than this, it helped the researchers to bring an analytic perspective to the data. Instead of simply describing the women's experiences, they started to examine the ways in which these experiences were located within the social organization of the family and society, which provide the framework for women's expectations of themselves. In fact, this enabled them to make the link between the women's subjective experiences (micro level of analysis) and the objective organization of society (macro level of analysis).

The interviewers functioned independently of one another and explored the topics identified in the interview guides. All interviews were reviewed at intervals to examine how completely the topics had been addressed. If data were scant, the participant was reinterviewed. During data analysis, analytic themes that were consistent through all of the interviews were identified, as well as other subthemes that recurred within sets of interviews. Furthermore, when all data-collection interviews were completed, both researchers reviewed the interview data and the transcribed discussions with the interviewers to verify the major themes that had been identified during the course of the research as well as to identify new themes. Then, each researcher reviewed all the materials independently and identified data relating to each theme. Working with the data in this way ensured that all conceptualizations were grounded in the data. Although the researchers did not conduct the interviews and relied on others' translations of the interview materials, through the processes described, they were able to assign meaning to the data.

Ethical Considerations

In a phenomenological study, identification of eligible participants is determined by their ability to address the topic of concern. As Anderson has pointed out:

> In using this method, subjects are selected on the basis of their experience with the phenomenon being studied—that is, subjects should be "experts" in the area under investigation. Data are gathered through lengthy interviews, in which subjects are encouraged to describe experiences from their own perspective.[13]

Frequently, individuals are recruited as participants in research studies through a formal process, by agency contact. When this is not desirable because of the sensitivity of the study question, researchers might contact participants informally through members of the group being studied, through associations, by word of mouth, or through community agencies. When studying the organization of family violence, for example, Epstein, Ng, and Trebble[32] used the informal approach.

In this study, the procedure used to make initial contact with potential participants was determined in part by the desire to ensure that the women's rights were protected. The question that arose was, how could the sample be obtained without violating the women's rights?

To ensure that the women's decisions regarding participation in the study were not influenced by their perceptions of the researchers' relationship to their employers, it was decided not to recruit potential study participants through their place of employment. The women were instead recruited by the interviewers through informal contacts in both ethnic communities. Once the interviews began, it became clear that the decision to use an informal approach was well founded. Many women indicated that they were afraid that if their employers were aware of their participation in the study, they might lose their jobs.

Recruiting participants in this manner was time-consuming for the interviewers because they relied on a networking approach. Furthermore, some women who were contacted, particularly those from the Greek community, chose not to participate. Besides fearing a loss of their jobs, they decided not to participate in the study because of some women's perception of the low status of janitorial work within their ethnic community. Many women did not want others to know what type of work they did. This created difficulties for the interviewers. One interviewer explained that even though she was sometimes aware of a woman's occupation from another source, this knowledge could not be used in her attempts to recruit women. Therefore, the interviewers could only approach women who indicated that they were employed in janitorial work.

Other issues had to be dealt with over the course of the research. The studies were originally designed to comply with the ethical guidelines established by the UBC for research involving human subjects. These guidelines include obtaining written consent from informants. The interviewers were expected to explain the purposes of the study to the women, inform them of their rights, and, if they decided to participate, request that they sign a consent form that had been translated into their own language. None of the women agreed to sign the consent form, and although they indicated that they would participate in interviews, most of them did not want the interviews to be audiotaped. As a result, several methodological issues arose.

In considering how written consent would be obtained, alternatives were explored with the interviewers. It was emphasized to the interviewers that it was essential for potential participants to be made aware of their rights in relation to participating in the study, that participation was voluntary, that materials would be kept confidential, and that names of the women and their employers would not be recorded. The interviewers explored the women's hesitancy to sign consents and explained that this behavior was consistent with their behavior in other situations. Generally, immigrant women choose not to sign anything, for fear of the legal implications. Audiotaped interviews were also unacceptable to the women, out of concern that their voices might be recognized on tape. Explanations about confidentiality did not allay this anxiety.

The UBC Behavioral Sciences Screening Committee for Research and Other Studies Involving Human Subjects was approached and, on receiving an explanation of the situation, waived the criterion for written consent, with the understanding that the women's rights would be explained to them. Ideally, the transactions between the women and the interviewers would have occurred verbally and be audiotaped, but because most women did not want the interviews to be audiotaped, this was not possible. Instead of audiotaping, the interviewers recorded the women's consent and their responses to the interview questions by hand.

Recruiting participants and obtaining consent were two methodological issues that were primarily ethical, so were considered together. A third issue also related to ethics is confidentiality. However, because its implications extend beyond ethical concerns, the topic of confidentiality is considered separately.

Confidentiality

It is a usual and necessary practice of researchers to ensure study participants of confidentiality; this is one reason ethical guidelines for research have been established. It was mentioned that in embarking on the research studies, the researchers adhered to established ethical guidelines, but in conducting the research, they identified that women had concerns regarding confidentiality for which there were no guidelines.

Although confidentiality has been discussed in earlier work,[13,14] the importance of the concept warrants further discussion here. Ensuring confidentiality is an issue with both ethical and methodological dimensions. It is an ethical issue because, in conducting research, participants' rights must be respected. It is a methodological issue because if women do not feel that the interviewers or researchers can be trusted to keep information confidential, they may choose not to participate in the study, or when being

interviewed, they may choose not to discuss important aspects of their experiences.

In order to protect the women's rights, the participants were provided with a detailed explanation of how confidentiality would be maintained, ie, by not using names, by restricting access to the data to the one interviewer and the two researchers, and by not discussing interviews with other participants or with members of the respective ethnic communities. The researchers also made it clear that they were conducting the research because of their interest in the needs of immigrant women, and that they had no social ties to the women's ethnic communities. Further requests from the women during the course of the studies to ensure confidentiality were responded to. One example of a request regarding confidentiality pertained to where the interviews were conducted. It was originally anticipated that it would be most convenient for the women if the interviews were carried out in their homes. However, the interviewers identified that some women wanted to participate in the study but preferred the interviews be conducted outside their homes. Some women did not want other family members to know they were participating in the studies, and others did not want family members to hear their responses to the questions.

In studying people from different cultures, the researcher is made aware of cultural rules and values that influence an individual's behaviors. In the case of these studies, if the researchers had relied on their own definitions of confidentiality, they would not have been able to adequately respond to the women's concerns regarding the topic. As the research questions were being explored in interviews, the initial view of confidentiality was expanded, thereby contributing to the generation of further data.

For these women, confidentiality was a concern that extended beyond participating in a study; it was a concern that dominated their everyday lives. In the interviews, the women identified topics that they felt were best kept confidential and the reasons confidentiality was so important to them. All of the women were concerned about maintaining confidentiality with members of their social circle. As one woman put it, "It is safe to talk to someone only when you know them. Otherwise, there can be a lot of gossip in the community. It is safer to talk to Canadians if there are no communication problems."

There are many indications that researchers who would respect confidentiality and who were outside of the women's social circles would be able to access information that would not have been shared with others. The following account from one of the Greek interviewers provides an example of how confidentiality and janitorial work were related: "The women were afraid they would lose their job, that the interviewer would betray an established trust. Also, even if the women like their job they are hesitant to

say they have one . . . they are cleaning ladies, so they don't want me to know they are cleaners."

In designing the study, the researchers had anticipated women's fears regarding the loss of employment. However, the account above identifies another aspect of the concerns regarding confidentiality. It is implied that the women would rather not have others know what kind of work they were performing. One of the Indo-Canadian interviewers provides one explanation for this behavior:

> Her spouse is presently not working. In fact, after he left his previous job he has not worked at all because he wants an executive job which he is unable to get. This lady is educated in the national language and has worked as a junior teacher back home for years. Presently, she is doing a clean up job which she does not feel good about at all. Back home, clean up and many other labor jobs are considered undignified and low to be precise, and looked down upon. As the work she is doing becomes a prestige point in the community both husband and wife feel upset and pressured about it.

The woman being described here was able to share personal aspects of her experience with the interviewer, thereby providing insight into how she perceived janitorial work. The interviewer was also able to identify that for this woman, performing janitorial work affected how she viewed herself and her relationship with other community members.

Further interviews with this woman and other participants emphasized the importance of maintaining family honor. Not discussing family-related issues with others was one way of ensuring the integrity of the family unit. However, in order to address the research questions, it was necessary to access information that was seen as confidential, but women were free to refuse to discuss topics that made them uncomfortable.

Additional information regarding topics that were perceived as confidential came as a result of comparing data collected by each of the interviewers. For example, some interviewers were able to access more data regarding family relationships than others. Other interviewers gained access to detailed information regarding roles and expectations of spouses when women were employed in the paid labor force. When such topics were raised in one interview, they were then explored in discussions with the other interviewers and their perceptions of the topics were elicited. In this way, all topics introduced during any of the interviews were explored for all of the participants.

SUMMARY

In order to develop knowledge to guide the practice of nursing, it is necessary to conduct research aimed at understanding nursing's diverse client population. It has been argued that, to provide effective care, nurses should have an understanding of how a particular life event affects individuals. The studies discussed here examined women's responses to migration, and the relationship between migration, health, and social support networks. To respond to the research questions, the phenomenological method of inquiry was used. Three types of methodological issues resulting from the use of the method with groups that did not share the researchers' language were discussed. As well as illustrating how methodological issues were resolved, the examples demonstrated the relationship that exists between conducting research and generating research data. As the researchers worked to resolve the methodological issues, information regarding the study population and women's perceptions of events was generated. The patterns that emerged and the questions that were raised expanded the concepts that were being developed.

Although it was anticipated that there would be difficulties associated with conducting research with non-English-speaking immigrant women, this was not seen as an adequate reason to abandon research with this group. By working with the basic tenets of the research method chosen, and by taking direction from work done by others, the methodological issues that presented themselves were resolved. It is hoped that the experiences of these researchers and the information shared in this chapter will provide guidance to others conducting similar studies with immigrant women.

REFERENCES

1. *Employment and Immigration. 1980 Immigration Statistics.* Ottawa, Ministry of Supply and Services, 1982.
2. *Manpower and Immigration. 1970 Immigration Statistics.* Ottawa, Information Canada, 1971.
3. Chinn PL: Women's health, *Adv Nurs Sci* 1981;1(1):1-125.
4. Gilligan C: In a different voice: Women's conceptions of self and morality. *Harvard Educ Rev* 1978;47;481-517.
5. Munhall PL: Methodologic fallacies: A critical self-appraisal. *Adv Nurs Sci* 1983;5(4):1-6.
6. Pinch W: Feminine attributes in a masculine world. *Nurs Outlook* 1981;12:29-36.
7. Smith D: A sociology for women, in Sherman JA, Beck ET (eds): *The Prism of Sex: Essays in the Sociology of Knowledge.* Madison, University of Wisconsin Press, 1979, pp 135-187.
8. Department of Manpower and Immigration: A report of the Canadian Immigration and Population Study No. 4. *Three Years in Canada.* Ottawa, Information Canada, 1974.
9. Arnopoulos S: *Problems of Immigrant Women in the Canadian Labour Force.* Ottawa, Canadian Advisory Council on the Status of Women, 1979.

10. Ng R, Ramirez J: *Immigrant Housewives in Canada.* A report available from the Immigrant Women's Centre, Toronto, 1981.

11. Nann B: Settlement programme for immigrant women and families, in Nann R (ed): *Uprooting and Surviving Adaptation and Resettlement of Migrant Families and Children.* Boston, D. Reidel, 1982.

12. Nagata JA: Adaptation and integration of Greek working class immigrants in the city of Toronto, Canada: A situational approach. *International Migration Review* 1969;4(1):44-70.

13. Anderson JM: Perspectives on the health of immigrant women: A feminist analysis. *Adv Nurs Sci* 1985;8(1):61-76.

14. Lynam MJ: Support networks developed by immigrant women. *Social Science and Medicine* 1985;21(3):327-333.

15. McCurdy GF: Human rights and racism, in D'Oyley V (ed): *Black Presence in Multi-Ethnic Canada.* Vancouver/Toronto, Centre for the Study of Curriculum and Instruction, Faculty of Education, University of British Columbia, and the Ontario Institute for Studies in Education, 1978, pp 453-456.

16. Fawcett J: Hallmarks of success in nursing research. *Adv Nurs Sci* 1984;7(1):1-11.

17. Davis A: The phenomenological approach in nursing research, in Chaska N (ed): *The Nursing Profession: Views Through the Mist.* New York, McGraw-Hill, 1978, pp 186-196.

18. Tinkle MB, Beaton JL: Toward a new view of science: Implications for nursing research. *Adv Nurs Sci* 1983;5(2);27-36.

19. Johnson DE: The behavioral system model for nursing, in Riehl JP, Roy C (eds): *Conceptual Models for Nursing Practice,* ed 2. New York, Appleton-Century-Crofts, 1980, pp 207-216.

20. Johnson DE: One conceptual model of nursing. Paper presented at Vanderbilt University, Nashville, April 25, 1968.

21. Travelbee J: *Interpersonal Aspects of Nursing,* ed 2. Philadelphia, FA Davis, 1971.

22. Neuman B: The Betty Neuman health-care systems model: A total person approach to patient problems, in Riehl JP, Roy C: *Conceptual Models for Nursing Practice,* ed 2. New York, Appleton-Century-Crofts, 1980, pp 207-216.

23. Campbell MA, Cruise MJ, Murakami TR: A model for nursing: University of British Columbia School of Nursing. *Nursing Papers/Perspectives on Nursing,* 1976;8(2):5-9.

24. The U.B.C. Model for Nursing, unpublished document. University of British Columbia School of Nursing, April 1980.

24. Chinn PL, Jacobs MK: *Theory and Nursing: A Systematic Approach.* Toronto, CV Mosby, 1983.

26. Omery A: Phenomenology: A method for nursing research. *Adv Nurs Sci* 1983;6(2):49-63.

27. Conrad P: The meaning of medications: Another look at compliance. *Social Sci Med* 1985;20(1):29-37.

28. Anderson JA: An Interpretive Approach to Clinical Nursing Research: *Nursing Papers/ Perspectives on Nursing* 1981;13(4):6-12.

29. Cicourel A: *Method and Measurement in Sociology.* New York, The Free Press, 1964.

30. Wilson T: Normative and interpretive paradigms in sociology, in Douglas J (ed): *Understanding Everyday Life.* Chicago, Aldine, 1970; pp 57-79.

31. Berreman GD: *Behind Many Masks: Ethnography and Impression Management in a Himalayan Village.* Monograph 4. New York: Society for Applied Anthropology, 1962.

32. Epstein R, Ng R, Trebble M: *The Social Organization of Family Violence: An Ethnography of Immigrant Experience in Vancouver.* A report to the Non-Medical Use of Drugs. Ottawa: Directorate, Health and Welfare Canada, 1978.

Chapter 20

Conceptual and Technical Issues in Using Time-Series Methodology in Clinical Nursing Research

Jacqueline F. Clinton

To date, the use of time-series designs in both experimental and descriptive research in nursing is uncommon, yet nursing practice involves periodic monitoring of multiple parameters in the same client or aggregate over time. Evaluation of nursing actions are based on the nurse's judgment about the magnitude and direction of change observed in the same parameters. At a purely descriptive level, it is critical that, as the domains of clinical nursing are labeled, described, and measured, there is also the generation of systematic knowledge about whether and how such phenomena naturally fluctuate over time in different populations. There is a need for nurse scientists to investigate clinical processes, and time-series designs are particularly well suited for research in nursing practice.

PURPOSE

There is currently a dearth of literature on the problems, decision rules, and resulting trade-offs related to the use of time-series methods in field research. Major previous works, although excellent, focused almost exclusively on issues of design validity or statistical procedures and technologies.[1–7] The purpose of this chapter is to explore other conceptual and technical issues in using time-series designs for nursing research and to identify solutions to common problems that discourage their use.

Note: This research was supported by a grant from the United States Department of Health and Human Services, Division of Nursing (No. R01NU00977). The author also gratefully acknowledges the help of Harriet Werley in reviewing early drafts of the manuscript.

ISSUES AND ALTERNATIVES

Issues particularly germane to conducting time-series research in clinical nursing can be classified into two categories: human issues and conceptual-technical issues. Included in the first category are problems of subject retention, confidentiality and privacy, investigator burnout, and clinician-researcher role conflict, which have been reported elsewhere.[8] The second category of conceptual-technical issues includes problems in the conceptualization and measurement of time as the independent variable, desensitization of subjects to repeated measurement, control of seasonal influences, budget planning, data management, tracking the illusive *N*, and comparability of constructs over time. In the following discussion, these generic problems are described and decision rules and protocols related to each are explored.

Conceptualization and Measurement of Time

Time is the cardinal independent variable in any time-series study. Therefore, considerable effort should be devoted to its conceptualization and measurement. Each study is unique and requires a definition of time that is uniquely suited to its research aims and the nature of phenomena under investigation. There are three major decision to be made: (1) determination of what amount of time constitutes a standardized interval in the data-collection series; (2) determination of a time reference point that can be used as a basis for labeling and coding all time points in the research design; and (3) determination of the acceptable parameters or grace period around the standardized time interval.

To illustrate, consider a study designed to evaluate the effects of a specific nursing protocol on the range of motion in patients with serious burns on their extremities. The standard interval for measurement of dependent variable (range of motion in extremities) might be every 48 hours. The time reference point might be hospital admission date. The acceptable grace period for measurement of range of motion might be plus or minus two hours for each standardized data-collection time point. Or, another example would be a study monitoring pregnant women's health and self-care practices over the course of pregnancy. The standard interval for measurement of dependent variables might be every lunar month. The time reference point would be expected date of confinement. The grace period for data collection could be plus or minus four days.

Desensitization

A major threat to the internal validity of any time-series design is the possibility that exposure to repeated testing might increase or decrease a

subject's sensitivity or responsiveness over time.[3] In research with only a single group of subjects, this is particularly problematic, since there is no control group with comparable data that can be observed for similar trends not attributable to the independent variables under study. The best solution to the problem of desensitization is to use alternate, analogous measurement items that can be administered at different times for the same subject. This solution, however, is costly, and budget planning should include appropriate time and personnel effort devoted to the construction, testing, and printing of instruments. Although the problem of desensitization is amenable to investigator control, it is difficult to test directly the effectiveness of controls. One way is to statistically compare variances in the same variable over time in the same study group. If the variances follow a pattern of decreasing at subsequent time periods, desensitization should be suspected.

Seasonal Variations

Seasonal variations and their possible influence on health factors are potential confounding influences in any time-series study in nursing that extends over the course of a year. This may be particularly problematic in geographic regions with dramatic climate changes over a typical year. To control for the potential confounding effects of seasonal changes, the actual calendar date of each data-collection episode should be coded and entered into all computerized data sets. Then, before final analyses, seasonal effects on any dependent health measure can be tested using regression analysis. If a study has more than one group, as in a comparative descriptive design or an experimental design, data should be collected concurrently for all groups in an effort to equalize seasonal factors.

Budget Planning

The monetary cost of repeated measures research is substantial and of special concern in nursing research, which has a long history of scarce funding in both the public and the private sector. The greatest hazard is to underestimate costs in a grant application with the hope that reviewers will be impressed that the investigator commits to rigorous protocols that cost so little to carry out. Should such a proposal be funded at the level requested, the investigator will have great difficulty, even nightmares, trying to maintain the integrity of the research as the money runs out far too soon, and chances of "supplemental funding" in the middle of the grant year are slim.

Successful budget planning for time-series studies can be done, and there are several cardinal factors that should be considered to assist in estimating costs. The most crucial cost estimate in prospective time-series research involving human subjects is the personnel effort required for data collection. First,

consider the amount of personnel time (calculated in minutes) required for a single data-collection episode. It is advisable to overestimate this time by one third to allow for the inevitable problems that arise with human subjects, such as no-shows, those who show up late or are not immediately available to research staff, and some who require additional time because of health or other reasons.

Next, calculate the total number of data-collection episodes required to complete the study. Consider a hypothetical study designed to monitor 400 expectant fathers' stress levels and physical and emotional health status at monthly intervals over the ten lunar months of pregnancy. The total number of expected data-collection episodes is 4,000, or an average of 166 episodes per month on a study funded for 24 months. Because the investigator plans to devote the last three months of the study to analyses and findings, the average of 166 per month is an underestimate, for there will be only 21 months devoted to data collection. Hence the estimate is readjusted to 190 data-collection episodes per month for the first 21 months of the study.

Then multiply the average number of data-collection episodes per month by the estimated average number of personnel minutes required to complete one. In the example of the expectant father study, let's say it takes 45 minutes to complete one episode. The total amount of personnel time per month devoted exclusively to data collection would be 142.50 clock hours. This latter figure can then be translated into full-time personnel equivalents (FTE); in this case, it is .89 FTE solely devoted each month to data collection. This FTE figure is a minimal estimate of personnel effort needed for data collection and should serve only as a beginning estimate. Additional FTEs would be needed to account for personnel time spent in travel, subject recruitment, securing informed consent, rescheduling missed appointments, training, and staff meetings.

It also should be kept in mind during the budget planning process that any estimated average data-collection episodes per month make mathematical sense, but in reality, it is not likely that the calculated average number of subjects would be enrolled in a study every month. That is, subjects are enrolled in a study as they become available. It is unlikely that 190 subjects in the hypothetical example would be recruited the first month of the study. It is more accurate to anticipate that the number of actual data-collection episodes completed every month over the course of the study would be distributed in a bell-shaped curve and might range from 40 to 220. For budget planning, overall personnel costs should be based on peak data-collection periods, which can be estimated by plotting the expected number of new and continuing subjects over the entire course of the study. During uncommon slacks in data collection, project personnel can be assigned to other tasks, such as subject recruitment, coding, data management, and dissemination activities.

Personnel and computer costs for data management and analyses also are crucial considerations in planning a budget for a time-series study. In the

hypothetical study, for example, if data were to be collected on 200 variables at each data-collection episode, there would be an anticipated total of 800,000 data points to manage. Personnel time for coding this large volume of data can be calculated by timing how long it takes to code a single episode, multiplying that time by anticipated total episodes, and translating this into FTEs. These costs should be built into the first-year budget, as data management, similar to data collection, is nearly continuous over the course of any time-series project. Consultation from computer experts also is useful for projecting the expenses for computer space, time, programming, and additional features needed for managing time-series data.

Data Management

Data accumulate rapidly in time-series research, and keeping track of overall progress is considerably more complex compared with one-time data-collection studies. Especially noteworthy are concerns such as (a) What data have been collected for which standardized time points? (b) Has the appropriate time sequence been assigned to each data-collection episode? (c) How many more additional data-collection times are required for each subject? (d) Which data have been coded and entered on the computer? (e) Which subjects have dropped and are there sufficient time points to retain their data? (f) On any given day, how many subjects have completed the study and how many remain in the study?

A structured data-collection worksheet can be used to document progress on the numerous tasks previously mentioned over the duration of a study. Table 20–1 shows how an investigator can keep track of overall study progress for the proposed study on expectant fathers described in the budget section. Its format and use are easily adaptable to any repeated measures study. The first column contains subject identification numbers, which are listed in order to accommodate easy reference. When subjects enter the study, EDC (expected date of confinement) can be recorded in the second column, as it is the point of reference for calculating standardized time points (lunar month of partner's pregnancy). As repeated measures data are collected, the calendar date for each episode can be logged sequentially on the progress sheet before raw data are filed away. The circled number below each calendar date signifies the standardized time point assigned to the data collected on the calendar data above. This sheet also can be used to keep track of coding and computerization progress. As data for a given time point are coded and entered on the computer, the cell on the sheet pertaining to those particular data can be marked with color-coded slash marks. The progress sheet should be accessible to all project staff and updated on a daily basis. Used in this way, it can be invaluable for assessing weekly progress and priority setting throughout the course of a study.

Table 20–1 Repeated Measures Data-Collection Progress Sheet

Subject ID	*EDC*	*Repeated Measures Interview Record by Calendar Date and Lunar Month*									
001	4/15/84	9/20/83	10/25/83	11/29/83	12/27/83	1/30/84	2/29/84	3/29/84	4/24/84	6/13/84	
		②	③	④	⑤	⑥	⑦	⑨	⑩	⑪	
002	5/14/84	9/19/83	10/24/83	11/21/83	12/20/83	1/17/84	2/13/84	3/14/84	4/18/84	5/12/84	6/26/84
		①	②	③	④	⑤	⑥	⑦	⑧	⑨	⑪
003	8/16/84	2/14/84	3/14/84	4/11/84	5/21/84	6/25/84	7/26/84	8/13/84	9/11/84		
		③	④	⑤	⑦	⑧	⑨	⑩	⑪		

Note: ID = identification
EDC = expected date of confinement

Tracking the Illusive *N*

Unlike one-time data-collection studies, in which it is relatively simple to keep track of sample size, time-series research requires continuous monitoring of both the total number of participants and, more important, the current sample size for each standardized time point in the repeated measures sequence. In other words, the fact that 250 subjects are participating in a time-series study does not guarantee automatically an *N* of 250 for every time point designated in the design. This is because human beings, both subjects and data collectors, do not always show up at the right place at the right time owing to numerous crises, other priorities, and various daily hassles that plague our species. It is unreasonable, indeed a mental health hazard, for investigators to expect the same level of commitment to a project as they have themselves. When dealing with human subjects in a time-series study, missing data are inevitable, and investigators should anticipate it, continuously monitor it, and minimize the effects on the scientific integrity of the study.

The monitoring of sample size for standardized time points is accomplished easily by use of a data-collection progress sheet, such as the one shown in Table 20–1. Tallies for sample size at each time point should be done routinely, preferably every two weeks, but at least once a month. It becomes even easier to tally if each standardized time point is color coded. It is ideal if the data-collection progress sheet is programmed into a computer. In the absence of such a monitoring device, the principal investigator may reach the end of the study period and suddenly discover that sample size at certain time points is insufficient for inferential testing purposes. With proper planning, this should not happen.

Another way to minimize the damage done by missing data is to overrecruit subjects intentionally. If 250 subjects is the goal, enroll 300 subjects in the study and be sure to calculate the extra costs for additional subjects in the budget of funding proposals.

Then there also is a last, to repeat *last*, resort. Even after careful monitoring and overrecruitment, it is likely that there still will be some missing data (not much it is hoped) at the end of any time-series project that involves human subjects. If the missing cases are minimal and sprinkled throughout the entire data set, the investigator can estimate scores for missing cases, but a word of caution is warranted. The wrong way to do this is to take the group mean for a given item and assign it to any subject with missing data on the same item at a given time point. This procedure plays havoc in getting an accurate picture of variance. A better alternative is to use regression procedures to estimate a given subject's missing value, using the same subject's data on the item at other time points.

Comparability of Constructs over Time

Nursing and nursing phenomena are complex, and most studies in the field include the measurement of multiple variables. To minimize the potential for Type I errors resulting from repeated use of univariate procedures, it is common for investigators to reduce data before final analyses. Usually, conceptually related measurement items are submitted to factor analyses, with the intent of reducing large volumes of data to a few theoretically meaningful, parsimonious constructs that then are used in final analyses of the major research questions. In a one-time data-collection study, such procedures are commonly used and reported in the literature.

In time-series research that involves multiple, conceptually linked variables, data reduction is far more complex. First, the data from each time point must be reduced. Second, the constructs produced by these procedures should be examined to determine if the factor loadings generated from the same items are comparable at different time points. It is possible that the underlying structure of the phenomena being studied changes over time in the same groups of individuals. If the factor loadings on constructs are markedly different in the same sample at different time points, the factors should not be used for repeated measures analyses. Such analyses would be meaningless because they would not constitute examination of the magnitude and direction of change over time in *the same phenomena*. The third step is to make a decision about which empirical constructs produced by factor analyses are comparable, and thereby suitable for inclusion in time-series analyses. For those data that are not, alternative but less sophisticated procedures for data reduction can be used to ensure comparability of constructs over time. For example, in an investigation of nursing interventions designed to reduce various types of disabilities, a simple linear summation of total disability days for each kind of disability at each time point would be logical and meets the criteria for comparable measurement over time. However, this alternative is totally dependent on decisions made early in a study about how variables are conceptualized, measured, and scaled before any data collection.

SUMMARY

Based on previous experience in conducting time-series studies in nursing, I have explored major conceptual and technical issues unique to time-series methodology applied to clinical nursing research. The decision rules and protocols related to these issues are described in sufficient detail to assist other nurse scientists in conducting time-series research despite its many deterrents.

REFERENCES

1. Box GEP, Jenkins GM: *Time Series Analysis: Forcasting and Control.* San Francisco, Holden Day, 1976.
2. Box GEP, Tiao GC: Intervention analysis with applications to economic and environmental problems *J Am Stat Assoc* 1975;5:70-92.
3. Cook T, Compbell DT: *Quasi-experimental Design and Analysis Issues for Field Settings.* Chicago, Rand-McNally, 1979.
4. Hay RA: *Interactive Analysis of Interrupted Time Series Models Using SCRUNCH.* Evanston, Ill, Northwestern University, Department of Sociology, and Vogelback Computing Center, 1979.
5. McCleary R, Hay RA: *Applied Time Series Analysis for the Social Sciences.* Beverly Hills, Calif, Sage, 1980.
6. Pindyck RS, Rubinfield DL: *Econometric Models and Economic Forecasts.* New York, McGraw-Hill, 1976.
7. Metzger BL, Schultz S: Time-series analysis: An alternative for nursing. *Nurs Res* 1982;31(6):375-378.
8. Clinton J, Beck R, Radjenovic D, Taylor L, Westlake S, Wilson S: Time-series designs and clinical nursing research: Human issues. *Nurs Res* 1985 (in press).

Chapter 21

Cantril Self-Anchoring Ladders: Methodological Considerations for Nursing Science

Kathleen M. McKeehan, W. Richard Cowling III, and May L. Wykle

Cantril self-anchoring ladders appear to be surfacing more frequently in nursing research.[1–3] It is one of the few instruments that measures client's perceptions of their own worlds of reality. One criteria for assessing the appropriateness of an instrument for a research study is to evaluate the congruence between the assumptions of the instrument and the phenomenon being investigated. McKeehan used Cantril self-anchoring ladders in her study of *Decision Making by Clients Planning for Continuing Health Care* and found some surprising results.[1] The purpose of this chapter is fourfold: (1) to present an historical profile of the development of the Cantril ladders; (2) to discuss constitutive assumptions of the self-anchoring approach; (3) to point out some psychological reactions that occurred in subjects during the administration of the instrument; and (4) to show how the results of the Cantril ladders were handled statistically.

HISTORICAL DEVELOPMENT OF CANTRIL LADDERS

The basic notions of self-anchoring scaling was developed by Kilpatrick and O'Donnell;[4] however, the person who is most famous for the use and refinement of this measurement is Hadley Cantril. The seminal article by Kilpatrick and Cantril[4] and the book by Cantril[5] set forth for the research world a renewed way of viewing human behavior: measuring the perceptions of subjects based on their own unique worlds of reality.

Note: A special acknowledgment is made to the patients, nurses, and social workers at Lakewood Hospital in Lakewood, Ohio for their participation in the McKeehan[1] study.

Cantril, a social psychologist, had been involved in studying human perceptions most of his professional life. His early work centered around perception as a "transactional" approach in research. Perceiving was seen by Cantril as a total person-environment transaction. Transaction meant the active participation of the "organism-in-the-environment-as-a-whole."[6(p20)] According to Cantril,[5(p340)] "from the vast array of happenings going on around us, we select for *attention* those related to our *intention*."

Cantril strongly believed that a researcher could not accurately appraise a subject's world of reality if the subject was "forced to make choices between categories, alternatives, symbols, or situations posed to them."[5(p21)] Therefore, Cantril and his colleagues designed a self-anchoring Likert-type scale, which later became known as the Cantril self-anchoring ladder. The ladder has two major visual characteristics that set it apart from other Likert-type instruments: (1) it is a vertical continuum as opposed to the usual horizontal continuum and (2) the divisions on the ladder are not verbally anchored. Figure 21–1 shows the traditional Cantril ladder.

Cantril[5(p25)] has emphasized that because of the subjectivity in self-ratings, "a given rating cannot have a precise and universal connotation like an intelligence test." However, according to Kilpatrick and Cantril,[4(p161)] the data is psychologically directly comparable, meaning "the scale level selected by one person or group (average of selections) can be specifically and

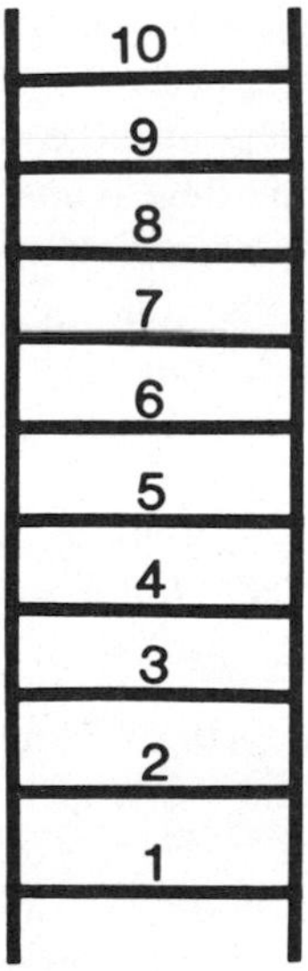

Figure 21–1. Traditional Cantril Ladder

Source: Reprinted with permission from *Journal of Individual Psychology* (1960;16:159), Copyright © 1960, University of Texas Press.

meaningfully said to be higher, lower, or equal to the scale level of some other individual or group (when) the frames of reference of the replies are in fact similar psychologically."

The general format of the Cantril ladder is to have subjects define their own anchoring points of a continuum that represent poles, such as "best and worst" extremes, and then, based on their own perceptions, goals, values, and assumptions, they are asked to give an estimate of their current situation by locating themselves along a vertical scale.[4] Most studies that have used the Cantril ladders report ten divisions in the ladder; however, according to Kilpatrick and Cantril,[4] there is no set number of divisions. Cantril's purpose for developing the self-anchoring scale was to encourage researchers to see the world as it exists from the perceptions of subjects instead of imposing their own worlds on subjects. Cantril had a major interest in the substantive information given by clients that defined their anchoring ends. It is unfortunate that reported research using Cantril ladders seldom describes any information regarding the anchoring ends of the scales.

CONSTITUTIVE ASSUMPTIONS OF THE SELF-ANCHORING APPROACH

Results of a review of the literature outside of nursing indicates that self-anchoring ladders have been widely used to measure client perceptions.[4,5,7–15] Although the predominant variable measured by the Cantril ladder is life satisfaction, it is generally agreed that the scale could be used to measure a variety of other variables.[4,8,9] In nursing research, the variable frequently measured by the Cantril ladder is health.[2,3]

One way to evaluate the appropriateness of the Cantril ladder for nursing research is to examine the constitutive assumptions that underlie the self-anchoring approach. Morgan[16] has argued that the rationale for a specific research strategy is grounded in assumptions regarding ontology and human nature described as constitutive assumptions. Such a network of assumptions provides a foundation for research practice that includes the researcher seeing and interpreting the world from one perspective rather than from another.[16(p21)] Choice of research approaches involve relationships between theory and method, concept and object, and researcher and researched. Four major assumptions of the self-anchoring process are presented to help nurse scientists to decide if the self-anchoring approach best fits the design of their research.

The first assumption of the self-anchoring process is that the reality world of each individual is always, to some degree, unique.[4] One implication of this assumption is that the unique reality world of the individual may be useful for morphongenic or clinical prediction, as differentiated from actuarial prediction.[17] Actuarial predictions are based on statistical generalizations that hold

with small error for large populations but not for any given individual. An individual within the large population is a unique being with a genetic inheritance and life experiences all her or his own, as well as influences unknown to the statistician. These factors may offset average probabilities for this particular individual. As practitioners, we are often concerned with prediction for such an individual that has been labeled morphongenic.[17] Self-anchoring allows for prediction of an intensive vertical order (within the person) rather than merely of a dimensional or horizontal order (extending across people).

The second assumption of the self-anchoring process is that self-knowledge evidenced by one's own perception is central to the design of the research study. The centrality of human perception implies a first-person point of view rather than a third-person point of view that emphasizes an objectively definable reality that, except for error, is the same for all.[4(p158)] The first-person point of view emphasizes the perceptions of individual subjects, providing for subjective validation.

The third assumption of the self-anchoring process is that certain goal-related variables (ie, striving, self-evaluation, expectations) have significant meaning, and that "it makes sense to compare people in these regards, but only if the unique perceptions, goals, and values of each individual are taken into account."[4(p159)] An individual assigns significance to what he or she perceives in terms of his or her life's purpose.[5] The individual's expression of concerns, values, goals, and perceptions is incorporated into the establishment of a self-defined measurement continuum.

Finally, a major assumption of the self-anchoring process is Cantril's particular use of perception as *transaction*. Perceiving is viewed as contextual, never existing independent of the total life situation of which both perception and object are a part.[18] Thus perception represents a manifestation of human environmental transaction rather than as consequence of interaction—one acting on the other. Active participation of the human and environment with each other (organism-in-environment-as-a-whole) is implied.

These constitutive assumptions are worthy of consideration for the purposes of research in nursing. As Morgan[16(p377)] has noted: "One route to a reflective understanding of research practice lies in exploring the nature and consequences of the assumptions that frame different modes of inquiry." Rather than choosing a method blindly, examination of the assumptions that underlie a particular research approach allows for consideration of the congruence between the theoretical perspectives of the researcher and a selected method.

The self-anchoring approach has some obvious relevance to emerging theoretical perspectives embraced by nursing researchers. For example, the uniqueness of individuals has been valued as a perspective in nursing historically and is expressed conceptually in Rogers'[19] unitary framework.

The centrality of perception and self-knowledge of clients is evidenced in the practice literature, particularly in relation to therapeutic change and patient education. The assumption of the significance of goal-related variables assigned meaning by the individual is congruent with the scope of nursing science as encompassing processes by which changes in health status are brought about.[20] Last, the assumption of perception as transaction emphasizes the human-environmental process relevant to many of nursing's conceptual models. More specifically, the notion of transaction is congruent with a methodological perspective that is context-dependent rather than context-stripping, which Newman[21] has advocated for nursing science.

PSYCHOLOGICAL REACTIONS ASSOCIATED WITH THE CANTRIL LADDERS

Based on a pretest of clients in the study of McKeehan,[1] it appears that the self-anchoring process of the Cantril ladders acts as a stimulus to evoke strong emotions. McKeehan[1] conducted a study that investigated the decision-making capabilities of clients planning for continuing health care posthospitalization. Her subjects consisted of elderly clients with skilled needs on discharge who had planned to have home care or go to a nursing care facility. She designed six Cantril ladders to measure the variables of freedom of choice, risk, hope, time, decision-making readiness, and decision-making action. The shape of the ladders were modified to resemble a slope because all subjects had some degree of functional limitation, and it was assumed that a gradual incline would be more meaningful than climbing a ladder. Figure 21–2 shows the modified Cantril ladder used by McKeehan in her study.

Based on research by Simonton et al,[22] it was important to McKeehan not to magnify the negative; therefore, "extremes" were not used to label the poles of the ladders. For example, the poles on the hope Cantril ladder were set at a lot of hope and little hope, as opposed to great hope and no hope. When the six Cantril ladders were pretested on 20 subjects, approximately 90% of the subjects cried and shared meaningful feelings about their decision for continuing health care. Even though the subjects cried, they repeatedly placed themselves on the upper portion of the scale, indicating that they felt more positive regarding their perception of the variable. This consistent placement on the upper end of the continuum led McKeehan to believe that a skewed distribution of data would result on the pretest; therefore, she also designed and pretested a scaled questionnaire to measure the variables. Both instruments were used in her actual study consisting of 85 subjects. The questionnaire was administered first, followed immediately by administration of the Cantril ladders. When the questionnaire and Cantril ladder were administered in this sequence, only about 14% of the subjects cried and

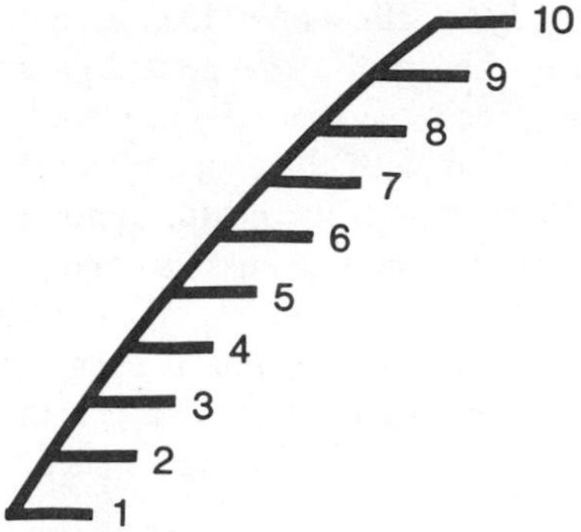

Figure 21–2. Modified Cantril Ladder

Source: Adapted with permission from *Journal of Individual Psychology* (1960;16:159), Copyright © 1960, University of Texas Press.

shared meaningful feelings. Intuitively, it appeared to the investigator that the objectivity of the questionnaire prevented the subjects from sharing their unique perceptions. It was as if the subjects were pulled into the researcher's perspective, which is implicit in the design of any questionnaire. McKeehan believes that if the Cantril ladders had been used alone or administered first, the percentage of subjects showing strong emotions would have been much higher, as evidenced in the pretest. It is suggested that if Cantril ladders are used as a second measure of variables, that their sequence of administration might be alternated with the other instrument.

Although the n was small (20) in the pretest by McKeehan in which the Cantril ladders were used alone, the instrument evoked strong emotions in approximately 90% of the subjects. This finding warrants the concern that the Cantril ladders be administered by interviewers who are trained to be sensitive to the emotions of subjects and clinically astute enough to refer clients for follow-up if they encounter difficulties. Researchers have an ethical responsibility to support clients when testing certain phenomena that evoke strong emotional feelings.

Adequate amounts of time need to be spent with clients after the administration of the instrument to ensure that subjects return to relatively normal emotional states. There are some questions as to what made the 20 subjects in the pretest respond to the Cantril ladders so quickly. Perhaps the Cantril ladders have the power to strip away the subjects' denial prematurely through the use of self-disclosure around a sensitive issue. Stripping away an individual's denial without recognizing the consequences could be a major risk factor in using Cantril ladders. Loss of the denial defense can be

frightening to a subject; therefore, it is imperative that the investigator and the interviewer administering the Cantril ladders understand human behavior and the emotional reactions that occur with self-disclosure. It is also important that interviewers be aware of their own feelings evoked by subjects' responses to the Cantril ladders so that they can remain objective in their support. Assessment of signs of anxiety or other intense emotional reactions would be helpful to determine how much support a subject may need as he or she participates in a study.

It is recognized that the size of the samples in the McKeehan study was small and nonrandom; therefore, no generalizations can be made. As scholars, however, it is important that the psychological reactions of subjects to the Cantril ladders be reported so further exploration can be conducted. There is no indication in the literature that the Cantril ladders have this "evoking" power. Researchers who use this instrument need to document client reactions. If reactions to the instrument are a psychological risk, procedures need to be developed to minimize the risk. The methodological challenge is to decrease the psychological risk but not the reliability and validity of the instrument. Important questions need to be asked. **Are psychological reactions to the Cantril ladders variable-specific?** In other words, would subjects react in the same way to a ladder measuring the variable of hope as they would to a ladder measuring the variable of health? **Are psychological reactions to the Cantril ladders population-specific?** In the McKeehan[3] study, the subjects were elderly individuals who had recently made meaningful decisions regarding their impending health care. All the subjects were planning to be discharged from the hospital within a few days of the interview. **Are the strong psychological reactions to the Cantril ladders interviewer-specific?** The personality of the interviewer may add to the evoking power of the Cantril ladders. *It is important to ask whether all psychological reactions to the Cantril ladders are necessarily negative.* McKeehan found that in most instances, the psychological reactions of subjects led to a therapeutic release of feelings when appropriate support was given during and after the interview.

STATISTICAL TREATMENT OF RESULTS

Research studies that have either used or discussed the Cantril ladders treat the scaling at interval levels and use parametric statistics when statistical tests are indicated.[4,5,7–15] McKeehan[1] found that all the distributions of the Cantril ladders used in her actual study of 85 individuals were negatively skewed. Figure 21–3 is one example of the six histograms that show the negatively skewed distributions. All six histograms looked about the same. Three types of variable transformations were used in an effort to normalize the distributions: natural logarithm, a base 10 logarithm, and

```
Code
     :
  4. *** (      2)
     :
     :
  5. *** (      2)
     :
     :
  6. ******* (      6)
     :
     :
  7. ***** (      4)
     :
     :
  8. ************ (     11)
     :
     :
  9. *********** (     10)
     :
     :
 10. ***************************************************** (      50)
     :
     :
     :.........:.........:.........:.........:.........:
     0        10        20        30        40        50
     Frequency
```

Figure 21–3. Histogram of Cantril Ladder Results (n=85)

square root. All three transformations failed to normalize any of the distributions. Because the assumptions of normality for parametric statistics could not be met, the data from the Cantril ladders in the McKeehan study were treated as ordinal level data and the nonparametric statistic of Kendall Tau Correlations coefficients were used to interpret the results. Kendall Tau Coefficients were favored over Spearman Rho because of all the ties. When the Kendall Tau Coefficients were compared with the Pearson R Coefficients that measured the results of the questionnaire in her study, there was considerable convergence on many of the variables.

Most published research using Cantril ladders has treated the data at an interval level and applied parametric statistics; therefore, the following questions need to be asked: Are all distributions of variables measured by Cantril ladders skewed? If so, are we justified in applying parametric statistics to the results? Future research may answer this question.

SUMMARY

Cantril self-anchoring ladders have valuable potential for measuring subject perception relevant to key variables of interest to nursing. An analysis

of the development of the self-anchoring approach and of the constituted assumptions underlying them suggest a high degree of congruence between the ontological and epistemological perspectives of the self-anchoring strategy and some of the philosophical and theoretical perspectives espoused in nursing science. Issues related to administration of the self-anchoring ladder and to statistical analysis of data generated from this approach warrant considerations and further investigation by nurse researchers.

REFERENCES

1. McKeehan KM: *Decision Making by Clients Planning for Continuing Health Care*, doctoral dissertation. Case Western Reserve University, Frances Payne Bolton School of Nursing, Cleveland, 1985.

2. Engle, V: *A Study of the Relationship Between Self-assessment of Health, Function, Personal Tempo, and Time Perception in Elderly Women*, doctoral dissertation. Wayne State University, Detroit, 1981.

3. Gass, KA: *Appraisal of Bereavement, Coping, Counterharm Resources, and Health Status of Conjugally Bereaved Aged Widows*, doctoral dissertation. Case Western Reserve University, Frances Payne Bolton School of Nursing, Cleveland, 1984.

4. Kilpatrick FP, Cantril H: Self-anchoring scaling: A measure of individuals' unique reality worlds. *J. Individ Psychol* 1960;16:158-173.

5. Cantril H: *The Pattern of Human Concerns*. New Brunswick, NJ, Rutgers University Press, 1965.

6. Cantril H, Bumstead CH: *Reflections on the Human Venture*. New York, New York University Press, 1960.

7. Bortner RW, Hultach DF: A multivariate analysis of correlates of life satisfaction in adulthood. *J Gerontol* 1970;25(1):41-48.

8. Campbell A, Converse PE, Rodgers WL: *The Quality of American Life: Perceptions, Evaluations and Satisfactions*. New York, Russell Sage Foundation, 1976.

9. George LK, Bearon LB: *Quality of Life in Older Persons: Meaning and Measurement*. New York, Human Sciences Press, 1980.

10. Goldberg EI, Comstock GW, Hornstra RK: Depressed mood and subsequent physical illness. *Am J Psychiatry* 1979;136(4-B):530-534.

11. Mangen DJ, Peterson WA: *Research Instruments in Social Gerontology: Clinical and Social Psychology*. Minneapolis, University of Minnesota Press, 1982.

12. Monk A, Cryns AG, Milbroth K: Personal and social value concerns of Scandinavian elderly: A multivariate study. *Int J Aging Hum Dev* 1976;7(3):221-230.

13. Naditch MP, Gargan MA, Michael LB: Denial, anxiety, loss of control, and discrepancy between aspirations and achievements as components of depression. *J Abnorm Psychol* 1975;84(1):1-9.

14. Palmer E, Luikart C: Health and social factors related to life satisfaction. *J Health Soc Behav* 1972;13:68-80.

15. Palmer E, Kinett V: Change in life satisfaction: A longitudinal study of persons. *J Gerontol* 1977;32(3):311-316.

16. Morgan G: *Beyond Method: Strategies for Social Research*. Beverly Hills, Calif, Sage, 1983.

17. Allport GW: The general and unique in psychological science, in Reason P, Rowan J (eds): *Human Inquiry: A Sourcebook for New Paradigm Research*. New York: John Wiley & Sons, 1981, pp 63-76.

18. Ittelson WH, Cantril H: *Perception: A Transactional Approach*. New York, Doubleday, 1954.

19. Rogers ME: *An Introduction to the Theoretical Basis of Nursing*. Philadelphia, FA Davis, 1970.

20. Gortner SR: Nursing science is transition. *Nurs Res* 1980;29:180-183.

21. Newman MA: Editorial. *Adv Nurs Sci* 1983;5(2):x-xi.

22. Simonton OC, Matthews-Simonton S, Creighton JL: *Getting Well Again*. New York, Bantam Books, 1980.

Chapter 22

Secondary Analysis As a Strategy for Nursing Research

Marie L. Lobo

Nurses collect or generate an immense amount of data during research and in clinical practice. Many times these data have not been analyzed during the initial evaluation of the data. These data may or may not have been organized in a systematic manner when they were initially collected. Clinical data available to nurses for research include nursing notes, vital sign sheets, and input and output sheets. The documents created as a result of nursing research and nursing practice can provide an immense amount of information about the diagnosis and treatment of human responses to actual or potential health problems. These documents can be used as resources and can provide information about what kinds of actions nurses take and the impact of those actions on their individual clients. The research strategy used to analyze material for purposes other than that for which it was originally collected is termed secondary analysis. Although this strategy is usually considered when data collected specifically for research purposes are available, as nurses, we also have access to a large amount of data that are naturally generated as a result of our practice. The issues surrounding secondary analysis have only recently been mentioned in the nursing literature.[1]

There are several definitions of secondary analysis. Glaser[2] gives the most pragmatic definition: "the study of specific problems through analysis of

---

Note: This paper is adapted from a presentation made at Marquette University, Milwaukee, Wisconsin, Sigma Theta Tau, Dalta Gramma Chapter, Research Day, February 11, 1982. The author would like to acknowledge the support of Dr. Kathryn E. Barnard and Dr. Nancy Fugate Woods, both of the University of Washington School of Nursing, for their assistance and guidance during the research projects discussed in this paper.

Funding for the Nursing Child Assessment Project, Kathryn E. Barnard, Principle Investigator was provided by the Division of Nursing Doctoral Program Development Grant.

Funding for the Women's Roles, Mental Ill Health and Illness Experience, Nancy Fugate Woods, Principal Investigator was funded by a grant from the American Nurses Foundation.

Support was also provided by a NRSA, PHS Individual Tuloneship, Division of Nursing.

existing data which were originally collected for other purposes."[(p11)] It is unusual for the primary investigator to use all of the data collected in a research project. Often, variables are not analyzed at all, or different relationships may be examined. In the clinical environment, much of the data collected are not systematically analyzed on all patients with a given problem.

Polit and Hungler[3(p212)] identify five rationale for proposing secondary analysis as a nursing research strategy.

1. Significant variables can be identified that were not analyzed in the original study. For example, one research project with which I was involved needed a sample of primaparas couples with vaginal delivery.[4] Because initial data were gathered prenatally, there were a number of subjects who had had unplanned cesarean deliveries. The couples with cesarean deliveries provided a subsample of data to analyze the answer to a different question.[5]
2. Different relationships among variables can be explored. Data that were collected and analyzed as aggregate data relating to characteristics of parent-child interaction when the parent was at risk for being abusive were reanalyzed to look for sex differences in parent-infant interaction during a structured teaching interaction.[6,7]
3. Changes in the unit of analysis can be made. As an example, a study that focused on women's health within the context of her family and employment[8] was reanalyzed with the family as the unit of analysis.[9]
4. Subsample analysis specific to one segment of the sample can be done. For instance, in a study of professional women's decision to parent, subsamples of nurses with graduate education, physicians, lawyers, and social workers were available for further analysis.[10]
5. The statistical method of analyzing the data can be changed.

In the past, nominal and ordinal data have been analyzed with a variety of interval statistical procedures. The rationale given for use of inappropriate statistics was that appropriate statistics did not exist. With the development of nonparametric analysis strategies and further statistical developments this is no longer true. As nurses become more sophisticated in statistical analysis, "old data" needs to be reanalyzed to discover if the findings continue to hold when more appropriate statistics are used for analysis. At the point of reanalysis there may be an exploration for potentially new relationships. Some proponents of secondary analysis believe this is the only reason which justifies secondary analysis.[11]

The primary reason most investigators use secondary analysis as a research strategy is economics. The economics of time, money, and personnel[12] are some of the most frequent arguments used to support the need for secondary

analysis. There is a need to understand both the costs and benefits of using secondary analysis as a research strategy.

TIME

Individuals proposing to use secondary analysis believe that it saves time. The belief is that time will be saved by not having to perform such tasks as recruiting a sample; creating, disseminating, and collecting instruments; and conducting interviews or observations. Additional time may be saved when there is no need to code data or enter it into the computer or create a record-keeping system. When the research is initiated, there may be a belief that the research question can be answered in a shorter period of time than if the project were begun anew.

However, many and varied unforeseen problems may occur to hinder the pace of a secondary analysis of data. A subsample from the original sample may need to be identified before the question being asked can be answered through secondary analysis. It may take sorting through data or charts by hand to assist in identification of certain patterns or characteristics of the subsample needed to answer the question. This sorting may take a considerable amount of time because of the manner in which the data were originally collected or subsequently coded and organized. The data may be incomplete in the variable of interest because the original investigator was not interested in that variable. Or data may be missing because of careless charting or record keeping on the clinical record. The identification of patterns of missing information may not be found until an investigator using secondary analysis is well into a study, causing a great amount of frustration as well as loss of time.

Additional problems creating time delays may be encountered when it is discovered that the primary investigator had not corrected coding errors in a particular part of the data set. It may take an investigator doing secondary analysis much more time than anticipated to learn how to work with someone else's code book. Extensive recoding and manipulation of the data may be needed to collapse the data into usable categories or a meaningful quantification of the variable or variables of interest.

MONEY

A second belief about secondary analysis is that a great deal of money can be saved by secondary analysis. Some of the beliefs parallel those about time. There is no need to recruit and remunerate subjects. There is no need to print and distribute instruments. It may be cheaper to buy data from an existing data base than to collect new data. There may be a belief that the bottom line

in research costs will be lower if fewer persons are paid less money to find the same answer from previously collected data than if they were doing the project from the beginning.

As with time, there are also unforeseen problems that increase the financial costs of secondary analysis. The data being used may not contain the necessary variables, so a great amount of personnel time may be spent attempting to manipulate the variables so the research question can be answered. When the amount of personnel time is increased, the cost of the project increases. If a large data set is used, a great amount of money can be spent on transferring card or computer file data and editing that data to make it usable to answer a new question. High computer costs may be incurred until data are in a usable form. If the original data were on videotape, expensive equipment, copying of tapes, and personnel costs for becoming reliable in observing the phenomena of concern must be considered. Diary or narrative data also include hidden costs in the duplication of data and in training reliable research assistants to abstract the appropriate data.

PERSONNEL

There is a common belief that secondary analysis can be done by fewer persons and that a savings is made because data collectors or coders are not needed. There is also a belief that there is less of the busy work that consumes so much of the personnel time during an original data collection.

The most significant unfavorable aspect about the "economy" of personnel is the disadvantage that the lone researcher may experience in not having colleagues who understand the project readily available to discuss questions, concerns, and ideas. The final aspect is that the researcher using secondary analysis must rely totally on the generosity of the primary investigator of the original project for information about the project and the data that were generated. It may take an incredible amount of personnel time to examine and understand the original analysis as well as other aspects of the project, such as the code book and the choice of instruments.

To prevent getting caught in the negative aspects of secondary analysis, it is important not to assume that a principal investigator who designed a study, collected the data, coded and analyzed the data, did so accurately, even if the researcher is highly regarded by peers or the sponsoring agency has credibility in the scientific community. "Begin by assuming the worst and seek out the same kinds of information about sample selection procedures, sample size, response rates, field procedures, and coding conventions that you would insist on if you were collecting your own data."[11(p722)] It is also wise for an investigator who is planning to do secondary analysis to familiarize herself or himself with the new data set by attempting to replicate some of the previously published tables or other data configurations. Finally, if the

investigator performing secondary analysis believes that she or he has found a "better" interpretation of the data set than the original author, or an error is identified, it is appropriate to share those findings with the original author. There may have been inconsistencies in the analysis strategies used by the two individuals.[11(p723)]

Now that some of both the positive and the negative aspects of secondary analysis as a research strategy have been presented, two research projects that specifically used secondary analysis of data as all or part of the data for the projects will be discussed. The first study is that of infants with failure to thrive (FTT). Control subjects for this prospective study of infants with FTT were obtained from a sample of infants on whom data had been previously collected for the Nursing Child Assessment Project at the University of Washington.[13] Because previous data were available on the control infants, this influenced the research design and data-collection techniques on the subjects with FTT. The second study was a report of family health, for which the original data were collected for a Women's Health Study.[8] In the secondary analysis in the latter case, the unit of analysis was changed from the individual woman to the family.

The first study was of infants under 1 year of age with a diagnosis or partial diagnosis of FTT admitted to a major children's hospital in the Pacific Northwest between December 1978 and June 1979.* Nurse researchers contributed information on variables concerning the quality of the parent-infant interaction. This variable was measured using the Nursing Child Assessment Feeding Scale (NCAFS) and the Nursing Child Assessment Teaching Scale (NCATS). These tools were developed as part of a longitudinal study, the Nursing Child Assessment Project. Subjects who had been videotaped during a feeding situation and during a teaching situation as part of their participation in this longitudinal project served as controls for the sample with FTT.

The purpose of the FTT study was threefold. The first aspect of the study was to prospectively study patients entering a major child health facility fitting a predetermined criteria for FTT. These infants, in the first year of life, would be compared with a group of healthy infants used as controls. Each subject was to have both social and medical aspects of their lives recorded in a systematic manner to facilitate a comparison of the sample. The final aspect of the study was to observe the behaviors of the child and the parent in a structured situation that was part of their usual pattern of interaction. The scores from the structured interaction situation would be compared between the infants with FTT and the healthy control infants.

---

*John Coombs MD, Principal Investigator, Kathryn Barnard Ph.D., R.N., Co-investigator, Marie L. Lobo R.N. Research Associate. Funded in part by Children's Orthopedic Hospital, Seattle, WA and Division of Nursing Doctoral Study Program Development Grant.

The physician member of the research team had identified specific physiological information that he wanted included as variables. The classic definition of FTT of weight below the third percentile was used to initially identify potential subjects for the study. The physician investigator was chief resident at the time of the investigation, and in that role, he reviewed all admissions to the institution on a daily basis. The research team had the ability to identify all of the potential sample because of this review. The social variables were identified during discussions among the research team members and through an extensive literature review. The choice of the social variables measured in the study were also profoundly affected by those variables previously identified as most important in predicting healthy children at 4 years of age in the Nursing Child Assessment Project.

Because the NCAP project began during the seventh month of prenatal care, a decision had to be made about which of the "prenatal" variables should or could be included in a prospective study of FTT. Besides collecting information on the characteristics of the mother, several of the measures identified as most predictive of healthy outcomes at 4 years of age in the control sample were identified for inclusion in the prospective FTT study. In some cases, this meant modifying tools so questions could be asked retrospectively of the parents of the FTT infants instead of prospectively. Twelve of 24 infants with FTT completed all data collection; 17 control families were identified.

The tools from the NCAP used for the FTT study included Holmes and Rahe's Schedule of Recent Life Events, questions on expectations about infant development, questions on perceived partner support and involvement in infant care, and questions on social support from friends and family.

The control infants were selected from NCAP subjects who had videotaped feeding and teaching interactions at 4 months of age, and these videotapes were available to the investigators. Four months of age was chosen because this was the mean age of the subjects with FTT. Control subjects were above the 25th percentile for weight. All other social data were complete for these infants. These infants had no major physical impairments, so all of their physiological variables were considered negative or absent for the purposes of this study. Seventeen mother-infant dyads met the criteria for inclusion into the control subject group. An interesting comment was made by the statistician during the identification of the control group. Initially, the individuals identifying the significant variables in the longitudinal study were unsure if the percentile for weight should be included as a variable. Until the current study, the variable had not been used. In the case of this secondary analysis study, the inclusion of this variable in the initial data made identification of the control group much easier. If the percentile information had not been available, then the weights of all of the children who were

videotaped would have been examined and percentile weights would have been computed.

When the data were analyzed, the fact that part of the data were collected prenatally and part of the data were collected during the postpartum period needed to be considered in the interpretation of all of the data. The findings were significantly different in several areas. The parents of FTT babies reported more problems and had higher stress scores, fewer psychosocial assets, less father involvement, and less support from friends than did the members of the control group. One of the most intriguing findings of the study was that the parents of babies with FTT expected their infants to develop an awareness of their environment much later than did the parents of the control infants. This is particularly significant given that the data on developmental expectations were obtained prenatally in the control group and during hospitalization for FTT sometime during the first year of life for the identified group. The patterns of parent-infant interaction occurring during the feeding and teaching situations were quite different for the healthy controls, children with organic FTT, and children with parent-infant interaction-problem FTT. To have collected original data on all of the control subjects would have greatly increased the amount of time to complete the study. The increase in time would have cost more money. Although one person could have performed the interaction assessments and the physical and social data collection of a control sample, this would have also greatly increased the length of time that person was employed.

The study generated many more questions than expected. There are now thousands of scores on healthy parent-infant interactions during the feeding and teaching situation with which to compare this sample. In addition, other investigators have collected data on infants with FTT. However, the major problem in doing a secondary meta analysis of children with FTT is the lack of consistent information about the physical and social characteristics of the samples.

The second study is a family health study[8] generated from data collected for the study Women's Roles, Mental Ill Health and Illness Experiences.[7] In the initial analysis of the data, only the women's data were used, although part of the data-collection method used a health diary format, which generated data on the women's partner and her children.

The purpose of the secondary analysis of the data was to examine the contribution of the individual family members to an overall rating of family health and to examine the data for potential recorder bias. In designing the secondary analysis strategies to be used, an extensive review of the literature and many discussions on the family as the unit of analysis were explored. The raw data, in the form of the 21-day health diaries, were examined, and attempts were made to identify patterns within the family as reported by the wife-mother. This form of exploratory data analysis is proposed by Tukey.[14]

Attempts were made to display the data with graphs, using different colors for each family member and the overall rating of family health. Patterns seemed to emerge in some of the families. This finding led to the decision that a more comprehensive computer analysis would be done.

The sample included 97 women with health diaries. Of those 97 women, 83 reported on their two-, three-, or four-person family. Thirty women reported on themselves and their spouses, 28 women reported on a husband and one child, and 25 women reported on a husband and two children.

The information from the health diaries was already coded and on the computer. The pertinent variables were identified and a new data file was created with the desired variables in the new file. The assistance of the principal investigator in the primary study was critical in developing the correct input format statement to create the new file. Access to the complete code book for the initial study was also critical. The need for the original code book was particularly critical when variables had been recoded, either at the time of initial data entry or during computer manipulation of the files. Because neither the father's nor the children's data had been previously analyzed, it needed to be carefully examined for coding errors.

An unanticipated problem may occur in understanding the logic of labeling variables. An individual who did not collect the original data may find the labeling of the variables particularly challenging to understand. Each investigator is likely to conceptualize the titling of variables differently. For instance, in this study, the family health variables were labeled FHA, FHB, FHC, and so forth, whereas the father's variables were labeled FF, FSX, or FCO. It may take time for the investigator doing secondary analysis to become accustomed to the labeling conventions of the primary investigator.

Previous analysis on these diary data had focused on the presence of physical or mental problems of the woman keeping the diary. These data were reconceptualized to examine absence of data about physical or mental health problems to indicate a "healthy day" as a positive finding. Thus, rather than the number of illness symptoms being a positive finding, the absence of physical symptoms became a positive finding.

One of the major scales in the study was coded so that good was rated as one and poor was rated as six. This was the opposite of other scales in the study, so that strong negative correlations became positive findings. Thus an investigator doing secondary analysis needs to be aware of the coding conventions and how they can affect the output from the data analysis. If an investigator were not sensitive to the positive nature of a negative finding, the results might have been misinterpreted. The feeling, function, and symptom data were all recorded by the mother, in her home. A major disadvantage of using this data set for family-level analysis was that the mother was the only individual providing input about the family. However, it must be noted that family health information is traditionally obtained from the mother.

In this secondary analysis, a particular problem was discovered concerning the family-level data. The major question in the health diary that focused on family-level information was "Please check what kind of a day it was for you" with responses of six blocks to check with anchor points ranging from Happy-Relaxed to Tiring-Tense. It was impossible to know if the mothers were thinking of all of the family members or only themselves. This tool has been extensively used for approximately ten years, and no modification or clarification of this issue had been attempted. This problem was addressed in a subsequent family study, with modification in language made.[15]

In this study, attempts were made to generate family models. However, in the set of data used for this secondary analysis, there was much less information about the characteristics of the father and the children than about the characteristics of the mother. This was a direct result of the original purpose of the research. Again, this study generated many questions. The initial study use in secondary analysis resulted in a second study, which proved that recorder bias is present in family health reports as reported by father, mother, and an older school-aged child.[15]

SUMMARY

Secondary analysis can facilitate the growth of nursing knowledge. Expensive, time-consuming data collection and coding can be avoided during a secondary analysis of data. Expensive and time-consuming control or normative data may be present from other studies, providing matched samples at a great savings of time and money.

There have been a number of large nursing research studies that have generated massive data. These projects can provide data banks for secondary analysis. Investigators are often willing to share their data, providing a rich source of data to researchers.

The various positive aspects as well as concerns of secondary analysis need to be carefully considered before an investigator opts for secondary analysis as a strategy to answer a research question of interest. However, particularly for students and new researchers, it may be an optimal method of entering the research arena. With the increasing availability of data generated through nursing research, the use of secondary analysis to assist us in finding the answers to nursing problems must be considered as a strategy.

REFERENCES

1. McArt EW, McDougal LW: Secondary data analysis—A new approach to nursing research. *Image* 1985;17(2):54-57.

2. Glaser BG: Retreading research materials: The use of secondary analysis by the independent researcher. *Am Behav Scientist* 1963;6:11-14.

3. Polit D, Hungler B: *Nursing Research: Principles and Methods,* ed 2. Philadelphia, JB Lippincott, 1983.

4. Lobo ML: *Mother's and Father's Perceptions of Family Resources and Marital Adjustment and Their Adaptation to Parenthood,* dissertation. University of Washington, Seattle, 1982.

5. Lobo ML: Adaptation to parenthood when delivery is by cesarean section. Paper presented at meeting of Western Society for Research in Nursing, Portland, May 1983.

6. Park Fast GA: Father's differential socialization of male and female infants (abstract) *Communicating Nursing Research* 1980;13:43-44.

7. Gruis M: Mother's differential socialization of male and female infants (abstract). *Communicating Nursing Research* 1980;13:44.

8. Woods NF: *Women's Roles, Mental Ill Health and Illness Experiences,* dissertation. University of North Carolina, Chapel Hill, 1978.

9. Lobo ML: Influence of the mother on family health reports (abstract). *Communicating Nursing Research* 1982;15:90.

10. Killien MG: Birth Planning Values and Intentions of Professional Couples, dissertation. University of Washington, Seattle, 1982.

11. Miller JD: Secondary analysis and science education research. *J Res Sci Teach* 1982;19:719-725.

12. Hyman HH: *Secondary Analysis of Sample Surveys: Principles, Procedures, and Potentialities.* New York, John Wiley, 1971.

13. Barnard KE, Eyres SJ (eds): *Child Health Assessment: Part II.* Hyattsville, Md, US Department of Health, Education and Welfare, 1979.

14. Tukey JW: *Exploratory Data Analysis.* Reading, Mass, Addison-Wesley, 1977.

15. Lobo ML: Mother, father and school aged child reports of family health. Paper presented at meeting of Western Society for Research in Nursing, May 1984, San Francisco.

Index

D

E

F

G

H

P

Q

R

S

T

U

V

W

Z